International Business

4e

Les R. Dlabay
James Calvert Scott

SOUTH-WESTERN
CENGAGE Learning™

Australia • Brazil • Japan • Korea • Mexico • Singapore • Spain • United Kingdom • United States

International Business: 4th Edition
Les R. Dlabay, James Calvert Scott

Editorial Director: Jack W. Calhoun

Vice President/Editor-in-Chief:
Karen Schmohe

Executive Editor: Eve Lewis

Senior Developmental Editor: Dr. Inell Bolls

Editorial Assistant: Anne Kelly

Marketing Manager: Diane Morgan

Content Project Management: Pre-Press PMG

Senior Media Editor: Sally Nieman

Senior Manufacturing Buyer: Kevin Kluck

Production Service: Pre-Press PMG

Senior Art Director: Tippy McIntosh

Internal Design: Pre-Press PMG

Cover Designer: Lou Ann Thesing

Cover Image: ©Stock Connection/Alamy

Permissions Acquisition Manager/Text:
Roberta Broyer

Permissions Acquisitions Manager/Photo:
John Hill

For product information and technology assistance, contact us at
Cengage Learning Customer & Sales Support, 1-800-354-9706

For permission to use material from this text or product,
submit all requests online at **www.cengage.com/permissions**
Further permissions questions can be emailed to
permissionrequest@cengage.com

Exam *View*® is a registered trademark of eInstruction Corp. Windows is a registered trademark of the Microsoft Corporation used herein under license. Macintosh and Power Macintosh are registered trademarks of Apple Computer, Inc. used herein under license.

© 2008 Cengage Learning. All Rights Reserved.

Library of Congress Control Number: 2009942535

Student Edition ISBN 13: 978-0-538-45042-3

Student Edition ISBN 10: 0-538-45042-8

Annotated Instructor's Edition ISBN 13: 978-0-538-45051-5

Annotated Instructor's Edition ISBN 10: 0-538-45051-7

South-Western Cengage Learning
5191 Natorp Boulevard
Mason, OH 45040
USA

Cengage Learning products are represented in Canada by Nelson Education, Ltd.

For your course and learning solutions, visit **school.cengage.com**

Printed in the United States of America
1 2 3 4 5 6 7 13 12 11 10

ABOUT THE AUTHORS

Les R. Dlabay, Ed.D., Professor of Business at Lake Forest College in Illinois, has taught more than 30 courses including Cultural Perspectives of International Business, Global Marketing, African Cultures and Business Development, Latin American Global Business, and Asia Business Culture and Trade Relations. Professor Dlabay has presented more than 300 teacher workshops and seminars, and has taught in high school, community college, university, teacher preparation, and adult education programs. He is author of Business Finance and Intro to Business, also published by South-Western Cengage Learning. His interests include a cereal package collection from over 100 countries and banknotes from 200 countries, which are used to teach economic, cultural, and political influences on global business.

James Calvert Scott, Ph.D., recently retired as a professor in the Department of Business Information Systems at Utah State University. He three times served as a visiting professor at the Bristol Business School, University of the West of England, Bristol. He earned his B.A. from Boise State University and his Ed.M. and Ph.D. from Oregon State University. He completed postdoctoral work in international business at the University of South Carolina at Columbia. An award-winning researcher, he has authored more than 200 publications. Active in business education-related organizations, he has served as editor for The Delta Pi Epsilon Journal and for two National Business Education Association yearbooks. In 2007 he received the John Robert Gregg Award for excellence in business education.

REVIEWERS

Raushanah Butler
Business Education Teacher
North Cobb High School
Kennesaw, Georgia

Lisa Hearon
Business Teacher
Wilton High School
Wilton, Connecticut

Kathy Holdge
Business Teacher
Newman Smith High School
Carrollton, Texas

Karen Kummerlen, MBA
Global Business and
  Entrepreneurship Magnet
  Teacher
Palm Beach Gardens
  High School
Palm Beach Gardens, Florida

Stephanie McCall
Career and Technical
  Education Department
  Chair
Business Teacher
Northview High School
Duluth, Georgia

Charlotte Mitchell
Business Teacher
McClarin High School
College Park, Georgia

Shannon Molloy
Business Education Teacher
Washington Township High
  School
Sewell, New Jersey

Michelle Venable-Foster
Computer Science & Mathematics
  Teacher
South Gwinnett High School
Snellville, Georgia

Dr. Michael Wayne
Business Instructor
Peachtree Ridge High School
Suwanee, Georgia

Lisa Williams
Business Education Teacher
Paul D. West Middle School
East Point, Georgia

HOW TO USE THIS BOOK

Engage Student Interest

GLOBAL FOCUS Introduces real-world examples of companies engaged in international business activities.

GLOBAL FOCUS

Disney Theme Parks Adjust to Local Culture

Bridging cultures was a major goal when the Walt Disney Company developed Euro Disneyland in France. While planning the theme park, which is now called Disneyland Paris, Disney learned that not everyone was happy about the project. Some people thought that having an icon of American culture in their country would threaten French culture. Disney had not experienced this kind of opposition when it developed a theme park in Japan.

In an attempt to calm fears, Walt Disney Company pointed out that its founder was of French descent and the family name was originally D'Isigny. The company chose to use French as the primary language for signs and designed new attractions with French and European themes. The dress code for employees, also known as cast members, was tailored to reflect the local culture. After initially suffering poor attendance, the theme park adopted the widespread European custom of selling alcoholic beverages at entertainment venues.

In Hong Kong, Disney tried to be sensitive to local culture in everything from the design of the park to souvenirs in the gift shops and menus in restaurants. Hong Kong Disneyland was built observing principles of feng shui, the traditional Chinese art of having elements in harmony with each other and nature to maximize good luck. Clocks are not sold at the theme park stores because the phrase for giving a clock sounds similar to a phrase used when paying last respects to the dead. In one instance, Disney stumbled by being too local. Shark fin soup, a Hong Kong favorite, was pulled from the menu when environmentalists objected.

Think Critically

1. What barriers did the The Walt Disney Company face when planning and operating Disneyland Paris?
2. Why do you think Disney emphasized the original form of the Disney family name?
3. Go to the web sites for the The Walt Disney Company and the theme parks to obtain additional information about the international operations of the company. Prepare a report of your findings.

WORK AS A TEAM Stimulates group discussion and cooperative learning.

Work as a Team

Discuss the personal beliefs, values, and assumptions that make up your cultural baggage.

GLOBAL TECHNOLOGY TRENDS

Online Exporting Assistance

What are the best countries for exporting electronics components? How can I contact distributors in Asia to sell packaged food products? These and many other questions can be easily answered online. Various government agencies and other organizations offer extensive information related to international business activities, including exporting.

- The International Trade Administration of the U.S. Department of Commerce offers information on exporting, trade missions, and trade statistics.
- Export.Gov offers information about exporting, foreign markets, and trade shows.
- U.S. Customs and Border Protection offers importing and exporting information.

- The U.S. Small Business Administration provides assistance in starting an export business.
- The Foreign Agricultural Service offers information about exporting food products.
- The Federation of International Trade Associations offers access to many global business resources.

Think Critically

1. Using one of the resources mentioned above, obtain specific information that would be useful to a company involved in exporting.
2. How do these web sites benefit businesses, consumers, and society?

GLOBAL TECHNOLOGY TRENDS Analyzes the technological needs and concerns of businesses in a global context.

Real-World Perspective

A Question of Ethics

PAYING FOR SPECIAL FAVORS

Aggressive companies in some regions of the world commonly use payoffs to gain access to new markets. Some countries consider bribes to be tax-deductible business expenses. However, U.S. companies can face hefty fines and prison sentences when U.S. laws are violated. The Foreign Corrupt Practices Act (FCPA)

prohibits bribery of foreign government officials by U.S. businesspeople. FCPA is designed to prevent obtaining favorable business decisions using methods that would be illegal in the United States. Companies may be fined up to $2 million for violations. In recent years, the United Nations has adopted similar anti-bribery rules.

Sometimes companies cave in to local customs. A U.S. computer

company offered Chinese journalists the equivalent of $12 to attend its news conferences. The company said the money was for taxi fares; however, the amount was equal to a week's pay for some journalists.

Think Critically

According to the guidelines for ethical analysis, are the payments to Chinese journalists ethical?

A QUESTION OF ETHICS Challenges students to analyze the ethical implications of certain global business scenarios.

COMMUNICATION ACROSS BORDERS

COMMUNICATION ACROSS BORDERS Explains the importance of communication as a tool for conducting international business.

DISAPPEARING LANGUAGES

Language experts predict that in the next 50 years, almost half of the world's 6,000 languages will disappear. The native languages of people are becoming extinct twice as fast as endangered mammals. This trend could mean a world

in the future dominated by only a dozen languages.

Of the 250 languages once spoken in Australia, 150 are extinct and 70 are endangered. Some language loss is natural and predictable. For a language to remain healthy, it must be passed on to the next generation.

Fewer languages may seem better for business. However, fewer languages may also mean fewer diverse thoughts. Language diversity reflects the music, history, literature, and culture of a society.

Think Critically

1. What causes languages to become extinct?
2. Why is language diversity important?

INTERNATIONAL BUSINESS PERSPECTIVE

History

INTERNATIONAL BUSINESS PERSPECTIVE Provides analysis of cultural, social, or historical conditions in the various regions around the world.

TEOTIHUACAN

Imagine a city of 200,000 people with a well-planned road system, production facilities, beautiful art, and ball courts for sports. This sounds like a modern city of today. However, the city of Teotihuacan, located about 40 kilometers (25 miles) northeast of Mexico City, declined into ruins more than 1,300 years ago.

The civilization of Teotihuacan began around 200 B.C. and flourished until about 650 A.D. During this period, the city was an influential commercial and religious center. The people of Teotihuacan developed many art forms into a high degree of elegance, including sculpture, ceramics, stone masks, and murals. In addition, major monuments were constructed, including the Pyramid of the Moon and the Pyramid of the Sun.

The people of Teotihuacan had close contact with the Mayan culture in the Yucatan area of Mexico and Guatemala. They were also a strong influence on later Mexican cultures, such as the Aztecs.

Today Teotihuacan is an archaeological site. This location contains the remains of the largest pre-Columbian city in the Western Hemisphere. The Avenue of the Dead, the city's main roadway, can still be seen passing through the ruins of temples and other structures.

Think Critically

1. Conduct an Internet search for Teotihuacan to obtain information about the commercial activities in this ancient city. Prepare a one-page report of your findings.
2. In what ways did the Teotihuacan society influence current international business activities?

Photodisc/Getty Images

Hands-On Projects & Research Suggestions

GLOBAL BUSINESS SPOTLIGHT Provides case studies related to international business concepts as they are presented in the lessons.

NET BOOKMARK Provides online activities for students on the website.

GLOBAL BUSINESS SPOTLIGHT

CONSUMER PROTECTION LAWS AROUND THE WORLD

Many countries have laws to protect people who buy and use products. Here are a few examples.

- In Canada, packages and labels must be printed in both French and English.
- In Venezuela, the price of every retail product must be clearly marked, together with the date on which the price was marked.
- In Belgium, laws limit how loud a lawn mower engine can be.
- In Greece, advertising toys on television is not allowed.

Think Critically

1. How might consumer protection laws affect international business activities?
2. Conduct an Internet search to locate examples of laws in various countries that are designed to protect consumers. Present your findings to the class.

Every country, no matter how developed, has a class system. Access the web site shown below and click on the link for Chapter 3. Read the web article describing the caste system in modern India. After reading the article, write a brief paragraph describing how the caste system differs from the class system of the United Kingdom as described on page 65.

www.cengage.com/school/genbus/intlbiz

THE GLOBAL ENTREPRENEUR Presents students with an ongoing project that emphasizes data collection and analysis in the creation of an international business plan.

The GLOBAL Entrepreneur

CREATING AN INTERNATIONAL BUSINESS PLAN

Assessing Political Risk and Legal Restrictions

As a company considers doing business in another country, the political and legal environment must be assessed. To help evaluate the advantages and disadvantages, as well as the risks, of making such an expensive investment, companies collect specific information about the "investment climate" of the country. The more favorable the climate, the more likely the company will profit from the investment.

Using your international business file and research skills, gather information on the investment climate for a country. Prepare a written or short oral report with information on the following topics.

1. Political stability of the country and possible civil disruptions.
2. Labor laws, labor costs, and occupational safety laws.
3. Trade barriers or investment restrictions.
4. Tax and other investment incentives to foreign companies.
5. Laws concerning establishing or restricting investment.
6. Other information you think for important to making an investment decision.

Compare the investment climate of your chosen country with those of other students. Which countries would be the best locations for manufacturing plants? Sources of information to research the country may include the following.

- reference books such as encyclopedias, almanacs, and atlases
- current newspaper articles from the news, business, and travel sections
- current news and business magazine articles, including news stories, company profiles, and advertisements
- Internet search for country information
- interviews with people who have lived in, worked in, or traveled to the country

Photodisc/Getty Images

Development for the Future

GLOBAL CROSS-CULTURAL TEAM PROJECT Provides an opportunity for students to work as a team to better understand cross-cultural business activities.

WINNING EDGE Helps students prepare for DECA, BPA, and FBLA competitive events.

GLOBAL | Cross-Cultural Team Project

Explore International Business Environments

Each day, millions of people work in teams to plan and implement business activities. The activities of these teams range from creating new products for international markets to cross-cultural negotiations for joint venture agreements. While many teams involve people from the same country or similar cultures, other work groups require interaction among people with different backgrounds.

Goal
Explore economic, geographic, political, and cultural influences on a region's business activities.

Activities
Working in teams, select a geographic region you will represent—Africa, Asia, Europe, Latin America, Middle East, or North America.
1. Conduct research about the geography, culture, and business activities of several countries in your region. Obtain information from printed and online resources, and by talking to people who have lived in or visited that area.
2. Identify geographic factors that are unique to your region, such as climate, terrain, and natural resources. Describe how they might affect business activities.
3. Describe how the unique customs, traditions, and culture of your regions affect international business activities. Provide three examples of how these things influence business activities using a different country for each example. Your examples might focus on how business cards are exchanged or what types of gifts are considered appropriate to exchange with business partners.
4. Research the economic systems and conditions in the region. Identify economic influences on business that are unique to this region.
5. Describe political situations and business regulations in your region. How do these things influence international business?
6. **Global Business Decision** An international organization plans to do business in various countries in your region. What can it do to ensure success? What products or services might be most successful in your region?

Team Skill   Benefits of Cross-Cultural Teams
Discuss with your team members the benefits of working on cross-cultural teams for both employees and business organizations. How might the geographic and cultural influences of your regions shape team activities and decision-making?

Present
- Write an individual report summarizing your regional findings and your experiences working on this simulated cross-cultural team.
- Create and present a team summary describing the business environments in your region. Consider using an in-class presentation, video, web site, newsletter, poster, photo display, slide presentation, or display of items (maps, clothing, food, music, packages, money) from your region.

International Business Plan Event

International trade has opened new opportunities for increased business profits. Multinational companies realize the value of locating in more than one country. Some companies complete different phases of their business process in countries that are the most cost effective.

One to three students will write an international business plan for conducting business in a country other than the United States. You will apply marketing skills in an international setting. The body of the business plan cannot be more than 30 pages. This project requires you to research the demographics of the country where you will locate your business. You must also consider customs, political conditions, trade regulations, currency exchange, and other cultural factors that will influence your business in the other country. Your international business plan must follow the guidelines that appear in the DECA Guide. These guidelines are also available online at the DECA web site.

The competition consists of two parts: the written document and the oral presentation. The written document will account for 60 points and the oral presentation will account for 40 points.

Performance Indicators Evaluated
- Define the reasons for locating your business in a foreign country.
- Define the demographics of the country.
- Explain special considerations for locating a business in a foreign country.
- Explain the management function of your business.
- Describe the political, social, and economic factors to consider for your business.
- Develop financial statements that project the financial results of your business.
- Describe how the workforce in the foreign country is suited for your business.
- Explain training, development, and management of your workforce.

For more detailed information about performance indicators, go to the DECA web site.

Think Critically
1. Why do U.S. businesses move to other countries?
2. Why is more research required before deciding to locate a business in another country?
3. Why are demographics so important to consider for international business?
4. How will you handle U.S. workers concerned about outsourcing jobs?

www.deca.org

GOALS Begin each lesson and offer an overview.

4-1 | Political Environment and Global Business

GOALS
- **Discuss various political systems around the world.**
- **Explain the political relations of a company's host and home countries.**

Types of Political Systems

A country's economy usually reflects its political system. A **political system** is the means by which people in a society make the rules that control and influence their lives. Political systems vary around the world, ranging from democracy to totalitarianism.

DEMOCRACY

In a **democracy**, all citizens have the opportunity to take part in making the rules that govern them. A democracy emphasizes the importance of the individual's needs and interests. In this political system, people have equal rights, including the right to vote for political leaders. They also have many freedoms, including freedom of speech and freedom of religion.

A democracy's emphasis on individual rights and freedoms extends to its economy. In a democratic society, people have the freedom to own and operate private businesses. Democratic societies, therefore, usually have a market economy. In a country with a market economy, there is little or no government ownership or central planning of business and industry. Individuals or groups of individuals run most businesses. Companies, therefore, either succeed or fail based on their owners' abilities to compete effectively in a market. The United States is basically a market economy.

Organized for Success

✓ **Check**Point

How does the business subculture of a country affect which countries it is most likely to do business with?

CHECKPOINT Short questions within lesson to assist with reading and to assure students are grasping concepts.

2-3 Assessment

Study Tools
www.cengage.com/school/genbus/intlbiz

REVIEW GLOBAL BUSINESS TERMS
Define each of the following terms.

1. factors of production   4. market economy
2. economic system   5. mixed economy
3. command economy   6. privatization

REVIEW GLOBAL BUSINESS CONCEPTS

7. List examples of the three factors of production.
8. What are the basic economic questions?
9. What are the **three** characteristics of capitalism?

SOLVE GLOBAL BUSINESS PROBLEMS
Indicate whether each of the following situations describes a command economy, market economy, or mixed economy.

10. The **government** tells you what type of job you will have.
11. The government owns the mill that supplies steel to private construction firms.
12. Private investors **own** a mine that supplies gold to a family jewelry maker.
13. You are free to **choose** when and where you will buy a new CD for your friend.
14. A privately owned clothing store buys electricity from a government-owned power company.

THINK CRITICALLY

15. Is one of the three factors of production more important than the others? Explain your answer.
16. If you could choose to live in communism, capitalism, or socialism, which one would you choose? Why?

MAKE ACADEMIC CONNECTIONS

17. **HISTORY** Conduct research to find examples of countries that have changed from a command economy to a market economy. What kind of changes did the country need to make?
18. **SCIENCE** Describe how scientific developments have changed the skills needed for labor.

STUDY TOOLS Provides an interactive review of every lesson with games such as Beat the Clock, First Things First, Labeler, Scenario, Sort it Out, and Test Your Knowledge.

CHAPTER **4** ASSESSMENT

Quiz Prep
www.cengage.com/school/genbus/intlbiz

CHAPTER SUMMARY

4-1 POLITICAL ENVIRONMENT AND GLOBAL BUSINESS

A The main political systems operating in the world are democracies, totalitarian systems, and mixed systems.

B A multinational company must operate within existing economic, social, and legal constraints of a host country. In addition, the company is expected to comply with the social, economic, and legal mandates of its home country.

4-2 HOW GOVERNMENT DISCOURAGES GLOBAL BUSINESS

A A government can discourage international trade with protectionism policies, tariffs, quotas, boycotts, and licensing requirements.

B Political risks can disrupt global business activities through trade sanctions (such as embargoes), expropriation, economic nationalism, and civil unrest or war.

C The main taxes governments impose are customs duties, sales taxes, excise taxes, payroll-related taxes, value-added taxes, and income taxes.

4-3 HOW GOVERNMENT ENCOURAGES GLOBAL BUSINESS

A A government can encourage international business with free-trade zones, most-favored-nation status, and free-trade agreements.

B The Export-Import Bank of the United States (EXIM) provides export loans, export loan guarantees, and export credit insurance. The Overseas Private Investment Corporation (OPIC) provides investment insurance to U.S. companies that establish operations in developing countries.

C A government can encourage international business with tax incentives such as tax credits on foreign income, double-taxation avoidance treaties, and tax holidays.

GLOBAL REFOCUS

Read the Global Focus at the beginning of this chapter, and answer the following questions.

1. You are the manufacturer of Grandma's Original Jams and Jellies. In what ways could the FAS help you develop export markets for your products?

2. FAS also guarantees loan payments to U.S. banks for foreign sales of U.S. agricultural commodities. Why is this necessary and how does it help U.S. banks.

3. The USDA provides export subsidies, or grants, to U.S. farmers who export. How could this be viewed as an obstacle for a foreign farmer who does not receive export subsidies from his or her own government but is trying to export?

CHAPTER ASSESSMENT Contains Chapter Summary, Global Refocus, Review Global Business Terms, Make Global Business Decisions, and Make Academic Connections

Contents

UNIT 1

THE WORLD OF INTERNATIONAL BUSINESS 2

REGIONAL PROFILE NORTH AMERICA 3

GLOBAL CROSS-CULTURAL TEAM PROJECT
Explore International Business
Environments 106

WINNING EDGE DECA
International Business Plan Event 107

CHAPTER 1 We Live in a Global Economy 6

GLOBAL FOCUS TESCO TAKES GLOBAL ACTIONS 7
1.1 THE FOUNDATION OF INTERNATIONAL BUSINESS 8
1.2 INTERNATIONAL BUSINESS BASICS 14

ASSESSMENT AND REVIEW
Checkpoint   9, 10, 12, 15, 18, 19
Global Business Terms   13, 21
Global Business Concepts   13, 21
Global Business Problems   13, 21
Think Critically   13, 21
Make Academic Connections   13, 21
Chapter Review   22–24

SPECIAL FEATURES
Global Business Spotlight   9, 15
Global Technology Trends   12
International Business Perspective   20
Net Bookmark   10
A Question of Ethics   17
The Global Entrepreneur   25

CHAPTER 2 Our Global Economy 26

GLOBAL FOCUS DUAL ECONOMIES 27
2.1 ECONOMICS AND DECISION MAKING 28
2.2 BASICS OF ECONOMICS 32
2.3 ECONOMIC SYSTEMS 36
2.4 ACHIEVING ECONOMIC DEVELOPMENT 41
2.5 RESOURCES SATISFY NEEDS 45

ASSESSMENT AND REVIEW
CheckPoint   28, 30, 33, 34, 37, 39, 41, 43, 45, 49
Global Business Terms   31, 35, 40, 44, 51
Global Business Concepts   31, 35, 40, 44, 51
Global Business Problems   31, 35, 40, 44, 51
Think Critically   31, 35, 40, 44, 51
Make Academic Connections   31, 35, 40, 44, 51
Chapter Review   52–54

SPECIAL FEATURES
Communication Across Borders   34
Global Business Spotlight   37, 39, 42
Global Technology Trends   48
International Business Perspective   50
Net Bookmark   49
The Global Entrepreneur   55

Photodisc/Getty Images

©afotoshop, 2009/ Used under license from Shutterstock.com

<table>
<tr><td>CHAPTER 3</td><td>Cultural Influences on Global Business</td><td>56</td></tr>
</table>

GLOBAL FOCUS DISNEY THEME PARKS ADJUST
TO LOCAL CULTURE 57

3.1 CULTURE AROUND THE WORLD 58

3.2 CULTURE AND SOCIAL ORGANIZATIONS 62

3.3 COMMUNICATION ACROSS CULTURES 67

3.4 VALUES AROUND THE WORLD 74

ASSESSMENT AND REVIEW

CheckPoint	59, 60, 62, 65, 69, 70, 72, 76, 77
Global Business Terms	61, 66, 73, 79
Global Business Concepts	61, 66, 73, 79
Global Business Problems	61, 66, 73, 79
Think Critically	61, 66, 73, 79
Make Academic Connections	61, 66, 73, 79
Chapter Review	80–82

SPECIAL FEATURES

Communication Across Borders	72
Global Business Spotlight	59, 69, 76
International Business Perspective	78
Net Bookmark	65
A Question of Ethics	63
The Global Entrepreneur	83

<table>
<tr><td>CHAPTER 4</td><td>Government and Global Business</td><td>84</td></tr>
</table>

GLOBAL FOCUS FOREIGN AGRICULTURE SERVICE
PROMOTES FOOD EXPORTS 85

4.1 POLITICAL ENVIRONMENT AND
GLOBAL BUSINESS 86

4.2 HOW GOVERNMENT DISCOURAGES
GLOBAL BUSINESS 91

4.3 HOW GOVERNMENT ENCOURAGES
GLOBAL BUSINESS 97

ASSESSMENT AND REVIEW

CheckPoint	87, 88, 93, 94, 95, 98, 99, 100
Global Business Terms	90, 96, 101
Global Business Concepts	90, 96, 101
Global Business Problems	90, 96, 101
Think Critically	90, 96, 101
Make Academic Connections	90, 96, 101
Chapter Review	102–104

SPECIAL FEATURES

Global Business Spotlight	92, 94
Global Technology Trends	100
International Business Perspective	89
Net Bookmark	93
A Question of Ethics	99
The Global Entrepreneur	105

©Alexander Chalkin, 2009/ Used under license from Shutterstock.com

UNIT 2

ORGANIZING FOR INTERNATIONAL BUSINESS 108

REGIONAL PROFILE ASIA-PACIFIC RIM 109

GLOBAL CROSS-CULTURAL TEAM PROJECT
Organize International Business Activities 240

WINNING EDGE BPA
Extemporaneous Speaking 241

CHAPTER 5 Structures of International Business Organizations 112

GLOBAL FOCUS MITSUBISHI: FROM TRADING COMPANY TO MULTINATIONAL CORPORATION 113
5.1 FORMS OF BUSINESS OWNERSHIP 114
5.2 OPERATIONS OF GLOBAL BUSINESSES 121
5.3 STARTING GLOBAL BUSINESS ACTIVITIES 126

ASSESSMENT AND REVIEW
CheckPoint   115, 117, 118, 119, 123, 128, 130
Global Business Terms   120, 125, 131
Global Business Concepts   120, 125, 131
Global Business Problems   120, 125, 131
Think Critically   120, 125, 131
Make Academic Connections   120, 125, 131
Chapter Review   132–134

SPECIAL FEATURES
Communication Across Borders   122
Global Business Spotlight   118, 123, 130
International Business Perspective   124
Net Bookmark   116
A Question of Ethics   128
The Global Entrepreneur   135

CHAPTER 6 Importing, Exporting, and Trade Relations 136

GLOBAL FOCUS THE SCOOP ON ICE CREAM EXPORTS   137
6.1 IMPORTING PROCEDURES   138
6.2 EXPORTING PROCEDURES   143
6.3 IMPORTANCE OF TRADE RELATIONS   150
6.4 THE NATURE OF COMPETITION   156

ASSESSMENT AND REVIEW
CheckPoint   139, 140, 147, 148, 151, 154, 158, 160
Global Business Terms   142, 149, 155, 161
Global Business Concepts   142, 149, 155, 161
Global Business Problems   142, 149, 155, 161
Think Critically   142, 149, 155, 161
Make Academic Connections   142, 149, 155, 161
Chapter Review   162–164

SPECIAL FEATURES
Communication Across Borders   140, 157
Global Business Spotlight   146, 153
Global Technology Trends   144
International Business Perspective   141
Net Bookmark   152
The Global Entrepreneur   165

stask/iStockphoto.com

Contents **xi**

©Voloh 2009/ Used under license from Shutterstock.com

CHAPTER 7 Foreign Exchange and International Finance 166

GLOBAL FOCUS AN UNEXPECTED CURRENCY FOR UKRAINE 167

7.1 MONEY SYSTEMS AROUND THE WORLD 168

7.2 FOREIGN EXCHANGE AND CURRENCY CONTROLS 174

7.3 CURRENCY TRANSACTIONS BETWEEN NATIONS 180

ASSESSMENT AND REVIEW

CheckPoint   170, 172, 177, 178, 182, 183
Global Business Terms   173, 179, 185
Global Business Concepts   173, 179, 185
Global Business Problems   173, 179, 185
Think Critically   173, 179, 185
Make Academic Connections   173, 179, 185
Chapter Review   186–188

SPECIAL FEATURES

Global Business Spotlight   172, 176, 178
Global Technology Trends   181
International Business Perspective   184
Net Bookmark   177
A Question of Ethics   175
The Global Entrepreneur   189

CHAPTER 8 Legal Agreements Around the World 190

GLOBAL FOCUS TRADEMARKS, BRAND NAMES, AND INTERNATIONAL BUSINESS 191

8.1 INTERNATIONAL LEGAL SYSTEMS AND LIABILITY 192

8.2 PROPERTY AND CONTRACTS 198

8.3 RESOLVING LEGAL DIFFERENCES 204

ASSESSMENT AND REVIEW

CheckPoint   194, 195, 201, 202, 205, 207, 208
Global Business Terms   197, 203, 209
Global Business Concepts   197, 203, 209
Global Business Problems   197, 203, 209
Think Critically   197, 203, 209
Make Academic Connections   197, 203, 209
Chapter Review   210–212

SPECIAL FEATURES

Communication Across Borders   202
Global Business Spotlight   193, 205
International Business Perspective   196
Net Bookmark   208
A Question of Ethics   200
The Global Entrepreneur   213

holgs/iStockphoto.com

CHAPTER 9 Global Entrepreneurship and Small Business Management 214

GLOBAL FOCUS SOCIAL ENTREPRENEURSHIP 215
9.1 ENTREPRENEURIAL ENTERPRISES 216
9.2 THE BUSINESS PLAN AND SELF-EMPLOYMENT 223
9.3 OPERATING AN ENTREPRENEURIAL ENTERPRISE 229

ASSESSMENT AND REVIEW
CheckPoint   219, 220, 221, 225, 226, 231, 234
Global Business Terms   222, 228, 235
Global Business Concepts   222, 228, 235
Global Business Problems   222, 228, 235
Think Critically   222, 228, 235
Make Academic Connections   222, 228, 235
Chapter Review   236–238

SPECIAL FEATURES
Communication Across Borders   234
Global Business Spotlight   224, 233
Global Technology Trends   219
International Business Perspective   227
Net Bookmark   221
The Global Entrepreneur   239

Digital Vision/Getty Images

UNIT 3

MANAGING IN A GLOBAL ENVIRONMENT 242

REGIONAL PROFILE EUROPE 243

GLOBAL CROSS-CULTURAL TEAM PROJECT
Manage International Business Operations 354

WINNING EDGE DECA
Marketing Management Role Play 355

CHAPTER 10 Management Principles in Action 246

GLOBAL FOCUS VIRTUAL CORPORATIONS HERE TODAY AND GONE TOMORROW 247
10.1 MANAGERS AND CULTURAL DIFFERENCES 248
10.2 MANAGEMENT PROCESS AND ORGANIZATION 254
10.3 THE CHANGING PROCESS OF MANAGEMENT 261

ASSESSMENT AND REVIEW
CheckPoint   250, 252, 254, 256, 259, 263, 265
Global Business Terms   253, 260, 267
Global Business Concepts   253, 260, 267
Global Business Problems   253, 260, 267
Think Critically   253, 260, 267
Make Academic Connections   253, 260, 267
Chapter Review   268–270

SPECIAL FEATURES
Global Business Spotlight   252, 264
Global Technology Trends   254
International Business Perspective   266
Net Bookmark   251
A Question of Ethics   250
The Global Entrepreneur   271

CHAPTER 11 Human Resources
              Management   272

GLOBAL FOCUS I WANT TO GO HOME—NOW!   273
11.1 FOUNDATIONS OF HUMAN RESOURCES
     MANAGEMENT   274
11.2 SELECTING AND HIRING STAFF   281
11.3 MAXIMIZATION OF HUMAN RESOURCES   286
11.4 RETAINING HUMAN RESOURCES   292

ASSESSMENT AND REVIEW

CheckPoint   275, 279, 281, 282, 283, 287, 288,
                  290, 293, 295, 296
Global Business Terms   280, 285, 291, 297
Global Business Concepts   280, 285, 291, 297
Global Business Problems   280, 285, 291, 297
Think Critically   280, 285, 291, 297
Make Academic Connections   280, 285, 291, 297
Chapter Review   298–300

SPECIAL FEATURES

Global Business Spotlight   287, 289
International Business Perspective   284
Net Bookmark   290
A Question of Ethics   293
The Global Entrepreneur   301

©David P. Lewis, 2009/Used under license from Shutterstock.com

CHAPTER 12 Labor Around
              the World   302

GLOBAL FOCUS SOLIDARITY IN POLAND   303
12.1 MIGRATION OF LABOR   304
12.2 MILESTONES OF THE LABOR MOVEMENT   309
12.3 UNIONS IN THE WORKPLACE TODAY   317

ASSESSMENT AND REVIEW

CheckPoint   305, 306, 307, 310, 312, 314, 319,
                 321, 322
Global Business Terms   308, 316, 323
Global Business Concepts   308, 316, 323
Global Business Problems   308, 316, 323
Think Critically   308, 316, 323
Make Academic Connections   308, 316, 323
Chapter Review   324–236

SPECIAL FEATURES

Global Business Spotlight   307, 310
Global Technology Trends   322
International Business Perspective   315
Net Bookmark   319
A Question of Ethics   321
The Global Entrepreneur   327

echo1/iStockphoto.com

CHAPTER 13 — International Career Planning — 328

GLOBAL FOCUS A GLOBAL BUSINESS CAREER — 329
13.1 SEARCHING FOR YOUR FIRST JOB — 330
13.2 APPLYING FOR A JOB — 338
13.3 OBTAINING FUTURE JOBS — 344

ASSESSMENT AND REVIEW
CheckPoint	332, 333, 335, 339, 341, 342, 345, 348
Global Business Terms	337, 343, 349
Global Business Concepts	337, 343, 349
Global Business Problems	337, 343, 349
Think Critically	337, 343, 349
Make Academic Connections	337, 343, 349
Chapter Review	350–352

SPECIAL FEATURES
Communication Across Borders	347
Global Business Spotlight	340, 348
Global Technology Trends	333
International Business Perspective	336
Net Bookmark	331
The Global Entrepreneur	353

©Daniel Leppens, 2009/ Used under license from Shutterstock.com

UNIT 4

INFORMATION AND PRODUCTION SYSTEMS FOR GLOBAL BUSINESS — 356

REGIONAL PROFILE AFRICA — 357

GLOBAL CROSS-CULTURAL TEAM PROJECT
Implement International Business Operations — 400

WINNING EDGE BPA
Presentation Management—Team Event — 401

CHAPTER 14 — Information Needs for Global Business Activities — 360

GLOBAL FOCUS SOUTH AFRICAN COMPANY PROVIDES TECHNOLOGY SOLUTIONS — 361
14.1 CREATING GLOBAL INFORMATION SYSTEMS — 362
14.2 GLOBAL INFORMATION SYSTEMS CHALLENGES — 369

ASSESSMENT AND REVIEW
CheckPoint	363, 366, 371, 372, 374
Global Business Terms	368, 375
Global Business Concepts	368, 375
Global Business Problems	368, 375
Think Critically	368, 375
Make Academic Connections	368, 375
Chapter Review	376–378

SPECIAL FEATURES
Communication Across Borders	365
Global Business Spotlight	364, 374
International Business Perspective	367
Net Bookmark	370
A Question of Ethics	370
The Global Entrepreneur	379

<table>
<tr><td>CHAPTER 15</td><td>Production Systems for Global Business</td><td>380</td></tr>
</table>

GLOBAL FOCUS MAURITANIA'S RICHES FROM
THE SEA   381
15.1 GLOBAL PRODUCTION METHODS   382
15.2 EXPANDING PRODUCTIVE ACTIVITIES   389

ASSESSMENT AND REVIEW

CheckPoint   383, 385, 387, 391, 392, 393
Global Business Terms   388, 395
Global Business Concepts   388, 395
Global Business Problems   388, 395
Think Critically   388, 395
Make Academic Connections   388, 395
Chapter Review   396–398

SPECIAL FEATURES

Communication Across Borders   387
Global Business Spotlight   384, 390
Global Technology Trends   392
International Business Perspective   394
Net Bookmark   386
The Global Entrepreneur   399

guenterguni/iStockphoto.com

UNIT 5

MARKETING IN A GLOBAL ECONOMY   402

REGIONAL PROFILE CENTRAL AND SOUTH AMERICA 403

GLOBAL CROSS-CULTURAL TEAM PROJECT
Plan International Marketing Activities   506

WINNING EDGE FBLA
Emerging Business Issues Event   507

<table>
<tr><td>CHAPTER 16</td><td>Global Marketing and Consumer Behavior</td><td>406</td></tr>
</table>

GLOBAL FOCUS BREAKFAST AROUND THE WORLD   407
16.1 MARKETING AROUND THE WORLD   408
16.2 THE MARKETING MIX AND THE
MARKETING PLAN   414
16.3 PLANNING GLOBAL MARKETING ACTIVITIES   420

ASSESSMENT AND REVIEW

CheckPoint   409, 411, 416, 418, 421, 422, 424
Global Business Terms   413, 419, 425
Global Business Concepts   413, 419, 425
Global Business Problems   413, 419, 425
Think Critically   413, 419, 425
Make Academic Connections   413, 419, 425
Chapter Review   426–428

SPECIAL FEATURES

Global Business Spotlight   409, 424
Global Technology Trends   417
International Business Perspective   412
Net Bookmark   424
A Question of Ethics   422
The Global Entrepreneur   429

CHAPTER 17 Developing Goods and Services for Global Markets **430**

GLOBAL FOCUS WATER, WATER ... ALMOST EVERYWHERE **431**
17.1 GLOBAL PRODUCT PLANNING **432**
17.2 DEVELOPING AND RESEARCHING PRODUCTS **438**
17.3 AN INTERNATIONAL PRODUCT STRATEGY **446**

ASSESSMENT AND REVIEW

CheckPoint   433, 435, 436, 442, 444, 448, 449
Global Business Terms   437, 445, 451
Global Business Concepts   437, 445, 451
Global Business Problems   437, 445, 451
Think Critically   437, 445, 451
Make Academic Connections   437, 445, 451
Chapter Review   452–454

SPECIAL FEATURES

Communication Across Borders   436
Global Business Spotlight   434, 440
Global Technology Trends   449
International Business Perspective   450
Net Bookmark   447
The Global Entrepreneur   455

©Eric Gavaert, 2009/ Used under license from Shutterstock.com

CHAPTER 18 Global Pricing and Distribution Strategies **456**

GLOBAL FOCUS TOYS "R" US IN JAPAN **457**
18.1 INTERNATIONAL PRICING ACTIVITIES **458**
18.2 GLOBAL DISTRIBUTION ACTIVITIES **465**
18.3 MOVING GOODS AROUND THE WORLD **472**

ASSESSMENT AND REVIEW

CheckPoint   459, 462, 463, 466, 470, 473, 475
Global Business Terms   464, 471, 477
Global Business Concepts   464, 471, 477
Global Business Problems   464, 471, 477
Think Critically   464, 471, 477
Make Academic Connections   464, 471, 477
Chapter Review   478–480

SPECIAL FEATURES

Communication Across Borders   470
Global Business Spotlight   461, 468, 475
International Business Perspective   476
Net Bookmark   474
A Question of Ethics   463
The Global Entrepreneur   481

©RAGMA IMAGES, 2009/ Used under license from Shutterstock.com

CHAPTER 19 Global Promotional Strategies **482**

GLOBAL FOCUS UNILEVER: AN ADVERTISING GIANT 483
19.1 GLOBAL COMMUNICATIONS AND PROMOTIONS 484
19.2 PLANNING GLOBAL ADVERTISING 490
19.3 GLOBAL SELLING AND SALES PROMOTIONS 496

ASSESSMENT AND REVIEW
CheckPoint 485, 487, 494, 499, 500
Global Business Terms 489, 495, 501
Global Business Concepts 489, 495, 501
Global Business Problems 489, 495, 501
Think Critically 489, 495, 501
Make Academic Connections 489, 495, 501
Chapter Review 502–504

SPECIAL FEATURES
Global Business Spotlight 498
Global Technology Trends 493
International Business Perspective 488
Net Bookmark 492
A Question of Ethics 487
The Global Entrepreneur 505

©alexwhite, 2009/ Used under license from Shutterstock.com

UNIT 6

GLOBAL FINANCIAL MANAGEMENT **508**

REGIONAL PROFILE MIDDLE EAST 509

GLOBAL CROSS-CULTURAL TEAM PROJECT
Finance International Business Operations 578

WINNING EDGE FBLA
Entrepreneurship Case Study 579

CHAPTER 20 Global Financial Activities **512**

GLOBAL FOCUS KOOR INDUSTRIES, LTD 513
20.1 FINANCING GLOBAL BUSINESS OPERATIONS 514
20.2 GLOBAL FINANCIAL INSTITUTIONS 519
20.3 GLOBAL BANKING ACTIVITIES 524

ASSESSMENT AND REVIEW
CheckPoint 515, 517, 521, 522 525, 526, 527
Global Business Terms 518, 523, 529
Global Business Concepts 518, 523, 529
Global Business Problems 518, 523, 529
Think Critically 518, 523, 529
Make Academic Connections 518, 523, 529
Chapter Review 530–532

SPECIAL FEATURES
Global Business Spotlight 521, 527
Global Technology Trends 522
International Business Perspective 528
Net Bookmark 526
The Global Entrepreneur 533

©akva, 2009/ Used under license from Shutterstock.com

CHAPTER 21 Global Financial Markets 534

GLOBAL FOCUS STOCK EXCHANGES AROUND THE WORLD 535

21.1 GLOBAL STOCK MARKETS 536
21.2 BOND MARKETS AND OTHER FINANCIAL MARKETS 541
21.3 GLOBAL INVESTMENTS 547

ASSESSMENT AND REVIEW

CheckPoint	537, 538, 539, 542, 543, 544, 548, 549, 550
Global Business Terms	540, 546, 551
Global Business Concepts	540, 546, 551
Global Business Problems	540, 546, 551
Think Critically	540, 546, 551
Make Academic Connections	540, 546, 551
Chapter Review	552–554

SPECIAL FEATURES

Communication Across Borders	538
Global Business Spotlight	550
International Business Perspective	545
Net Bookmark	537
A Question of Ethics	543
The Global Entrepreneur	555

CHAPTER 22 Managing International Business Risk 556

GLOBAL FOCUS LLOYD'S OF LONDON 557

22.1 GLOBAL RISK MANAGEMENT 558
22.2 INTERNATIONAL INSURANCE 563
22.3 REDUCING GLOBAL RISKS 568

ASSESSMENT AND REVIEW

CheckPoint	560, 561, 564, 565, 571, 572
Global Business Terms	562, 567, 573
Global Business Concepts	562, 567, 573
Global Business Problems	562, 567, 573
Think Critically	562, 567, 573
Make Academic Connections	562, 567, 573
Chapter Review	574–576

SPECIAL FEATURES

Communication Across Borders	570
Global Business Spotlight	559, 564, 572
International Business Perspective	566
Net Bookmark	569
A Question of Ethics	561
The Global Entrepreneur	577

©Patricia Marks, 2009/ Used under license from Shutterstock.com

MAPS 580

GLOSSARY 594

INDEX 601

UNIT 1

The World of International Business

Chapter

1 **We Live in a Global Economy**

2 **Our Global Economy**

3 **Cultural Influences on Global Business**

4 **Government and Global Business**

REGIONAL PROFILE

North America

If You Were There

...Aztec Empire at the end of the 14th century

The year is 1385, 100 years before Cortés was born. Friends and family gather to celebrate the wedding of a 16-year-old Aztec woman. The bride lives in a city of 100,000 people that will one day be the site of Mexico City. Her father is a merchant and her mother cares for the house and the younger children. Her older brother recently finished school and is training for a military career.

The homes in the bride's neighborhood are adobe, and each has a courtyard containing a sauna that is surrounded by beautiful flowers. The groom designs streets, canals, and irrigation systems for the city.

This evening, burning pine branches will light the way as an older woman carries the bride on her back to the groom's house. While sitting before the hearth, the groom's tunic will be tied to the bride's blouse as a symbol of their union.

©Holger Mette, 2009/ Used under license from Shutterstock.com

The First North Americans

The vast land that we now call North America was discovered and settled by people who probably migrated to Alaska from Asia. Over a period of 30,000 years, more groups arrived and gradually built a variety of civilizations in this Western Hemisphere. The Aztec example above is just one Native American culture in which you could have been born. You also could have lived among the Leni-Lenape of the eastern woodlands or on the plains with the Arapaho. You might have raised a family in the great complexes built by the Anasazi in cliffs near the Grand Canyon. Hundreds of cultural groups were spread throughout the continent—each with its own unique language, religion, government, and customs.

The Norwegians explored North America in the tenth and eleventh centuries, but they had little effect on the native cultures. Explorers and settlers from Spain, Britain, France, Holland, and Sweden arrived in great numbers during the sixteenth and seventeenth centuries, bringing with them cultures that conflicted with those they met. The native population decreased quickly as a result of battles and the diseases carried by the newcomers. And so began a great cultural transformation—a destructive and creative process that continues today. Soldiers, farmers, trappers, artisans, and merchants came from Europe to help build colonies for their mother countries. Some came to escape religious and political persecution, while others came to share their religion.

Struggles for Independence

Wars were fought to establish control over these valuable lands that held great resources. In 1810, a priest named Miguel Hidalgo y Costilla set off the Mexican War of Independence from Spain. Poor natives and mestizos (of mixed native and European ancestry) fought the war. Although Miguel Hidalgo y Costilla soon died, another priest, José María Morelos y Pavón, continued to lead the movement that led to independence in 1813. Morelos was captured and shot, but Mexico eventually formed a republic in 1824.

The French lost control of Canada to the British in 1763, but the French heritage is still evident throughout Canada and most especially in the province of Quebec. Over the next 100 years under the British Crown, the Canadian assemblies gradually won power without a war. In 1867, the Dominion of Canada was established, and in 1931, Canada became a completely independent nation.

The United States won its independence from Britain through a treaty signed in 1783. Immigrants came to the new country from all over the world. Some stayed in the eastern cities and worked in the textile mills, while many others headed west with wagon trains hoping to build a new life in Kentucky, Ohio, California, and all the territories in between.

©Photodisc/Getty Images

Slavery

The economies of the West Indies and the southern United States depended on labor that was supplied by the violent importation of Africans to be used as slaves.

Olaudah, an Ibo man, describes his trip to North America in 1756: "The shrieks of the women and the groans of the dying rendered it a scene of horror almost inconceivable. . . I began to hope that death would soon put an end to my miseries."

Colonial America thrived on this slave labor. By 1860, the South was producing three-quarters of the world's supply of cotton.

Immigrants Build the Economy

After the Civil War, Chinese, Japanese, Mexican, Irish, German, and Italian immigrants joined former slaves and Union and Confederate veterans to work in factories and fields. Together they created the world's most powerful industrial economy.

Canada's earliest immigrants came from France, England, Ireland, and Scotland. In the twentieth century, Russians, Ukrainians, and Germans were attracted to the western prairies. As in the United States, more recent immigrants to Canada are Asian and Latin American.

North America Today

Canada's 3.8 million square miles of territory is second in size only to Russia. The majority of the country's 33 million people are concentrated near its southern border with the United States. The cold northlands hold exquisite natural environments but few inhabitants. Canada's abundance of natural resources and manufacturing industries have produced a high standard of living for most of its people. Its service industries create most new jobs.

Mexico is the largest and most populous Spanish-speaking country in the world. Its population is growing by about 1.1 percent each year. Since 1950, land reform and a growing manufacturing base have increased incomes for a large number of Mexicans. Many, however, still live in extreme poverty.

Silver, industrial minerals, petroleum, and manufacturing are responsible for much of Mexico's recent economic growth. Also, the country's white beaches, Aztec ruins, and other historic areas attract tourists from all over the world.

All of the nations of continental North America and the West Indies have developed unique cultures that combine the diverse richness of Native Americans, Europeans, Africans, and Asians. Although conflicts still exist, the future of these societies depends upon the mutual appreciation of this diversity.

Think Critically

1. Which Native Americans once had communities where you live?
2. Why do you think Columbus receives most of the credit for "discovering" North America?
3. How do you think the geographic features of the United States influenced the settlement of the West?
4. How do you think Canada has influenced the culture of the United States and vice versa?

COUNTRY PROFILES

The World Factbook, published online by the Central Intelligence Agency, includes country profiles for the nations of North America. Each country's profile includes an overview followed by detailed information about the country's geography, people, government, economy, communications, transportation, military, and transnational issues.

©jeffwang/iStockphoto.com

We Live in a Global Economy

1-1 The Foundation of International Business

1-2 International Business Basics

GLOBAL FOCUS

Tesco Takes Global Actions

With stores in more than 15 countries, Tesco is committed to international business. This British company started selling groceries from a street stall in London's East End in 1919. Today, Tesco is the world's third largest food retailer after Wal-Mart and Carrefour. With more than 1,800 stores outside of Britain, Tesco serves customers around the world by providing a variety of goods and services. Depending on where you are, you might purchase gasoline, do some banking, get lunch, or shop for groceries. In some Tesco stores you could do all these things and more.

Tesco operates different types of stores in different locations. Some of the Tesco stores in Britain are hypermarkets that offer many types of foods and other products. This is a contrast to stores in China where the company makes use of the Tesco Express store format. As the name implies, these are convenience stores with a limited product line.

The company's strategy for entering markets depends on the location. To enter the South Korea market, Tesco partnered with Samsung, the largest electronics company in the world. In addition to selling food in Korea, the company operates Tesco Homeplus where they sell electronics and other items for the home. In the Czech Republic and Hungary, the company purchased former Kmart stores and renamed them Tesco.

After success in Europe and Asia, Tesco decided to enter the U.S. market. The company opened Fresh & Easy Neighborhood Market stores in California, Arizona, and Nevada. These stores are smaller than most American supermarkets but still offer many choices. The grocery product line ranges from basics, including dairy, meat, vegetables, to ready-to-serve meals, along with specialty items and organic foods. In their more than 100 U.S. stores, Tesco sells items using their "Fresh & Easy" label as well as brand name products available in other stores.

Think Critically

1. What are some reasons that companies expand their business operations into other countries?
2. What actions might companies take to be more successful with their international business activities?
3. Conduct a web search for Tesco to find some of the benefits and drawbacks of doing business in other countries. Prepare a brief summary of your findings.

1-1 The Foundation of International Business

GOALS

- Distinguish between domestic business and international business.

- Discuss the reasons why international business is important.

- Understand that international trade is not just a recent event.

©Photodisc/Getty Images

What Is International Business?

In the early days of the United States, most families grew the food they ate and made the clothes they wore. Then the population increased. Production and distribution methods improved. People began to depend on others for goods and services. That dependence grew as more people specialized in the work they did. Today, the United States has a complex business system. The system is based on specialization and makes a wide variety of goods and services available.

In the same way that people within a country are dependent on each other to produce goods and services, countries also are dependent on each other. Nations that have extensive production and distribution facilities—such as the United States, Canada, Japan, and the western European nations—have some level of economic independence. However, they are still dependent on other countries. For example, most of the coffee used in the United States comes from Brazil, and Japan depends on other countries for almost all of its oil.

Most business activities take place inside a country's own borders. Making, buying, and selling goods and services within a country is called **domestic business**. If you purchase a soft drink made in your own country, you are participating in domestic business.

On the other hand, if you buy a shirt made in Thailand while shopping at your favorite store, you are involved in the global economy. The purchase was made in the United States and the garment was made halfway around the globe. **International business** includes all business activities needed to create, ship, and sell goods and services across national borders. International business may also be called *global business, international trade,* and *foreign trade.*

Why Is International Business Important?

International business allows you to purchase popular items made in other countries, such as televisions, shoes, and clothing. Without global business, your life would probably be different. People around the world would not have the opportunity to enjoy goods and services made in other countries.

International business is important for many reasons. It provides a source of raw materials and parts and demand for foreign products. Global business allows for new market and investment opportunities. It can even help improve political relations.

MATERIALS, PARTS, AND DEMAND

Products made in the United States often include materials from around the world. Each year, American companies buy oil and steel from other nations to use in factories. Nearly every U.S.-built car has parts that were manufactured in Japan, Mexico, France, Korea, England, and many other countries.

A **global dependency** exists when items that consumers need and want are created in other countries. For example, drought and other weather conditions in an African country might cause crop failures. As a result, the African country must obtain food from other countries.

GLOBAL OPPORTUNITIES

Companies such as Kellogg sell to customers in other countries to expand business opportunities. Many businesses, large and small, increase sales and profits with foreign trade. These companies are involved in the global economy.

Many people invest in businesses to earn money for themselves. As companies expand into other countries, they create new

GLOBAL BUSINESS SPOTLIGHT

EMERGING MARKETS AND THE GLOBAL ECONOMY

Global business growth is occurring in *emerging markets*, places where consumer incomes and buying power are increasing because of economic expansion. When a country exports products, it results in more income for workers. With some of this income, a nation's workers buy things from other countries. When consumers in a nation have more money to spend, businesses from around the globe want to sell products in that country.

Emerging markets exist in most regions of the world. These include the Czech Republic and Poland in Eastern Europe; Indonesia and Malaysia in Asia; Argentina and Chile in Latin America; Egypt and Turkey in the Middle East; and South Africa and Nigeria in Africa. The improved economic situation in these previously poor countries is based on several factors including stable political systems, improved education, and expanded use of technology. In some countries the availability and use of natural resources is also a factor.

One specific group of emerging markets is very visible. Brazil, Russia, India, and China; known as the BRIC countries, are experiencing economic growth. This growth is a result of producing goods and services and providing raw materials for use in manufacturing. The BRIC countries share two things that make them attractive to foreign companies. All four countries have large and growing populations, and the buying power of consumers in these countries is rising. The BRIC countries are emerging markets.

Think Critically

1. What factors make emerging markets an important element of international business activities?
2. Conduct research to obtain information about economic growth and business activities in one of the emerging markets mentioned.

Work as a Team

Work with other students to come up with a list of five ways your community benefits from international business.

investment opportunities. Investors also provide funds to foreign companies that are either just getting started or are growing enterprises.

IMPROVED POLITICAL RELATIONS

An old saying suggests "countries that trade with one another are less likely to have wars with each other." International business activities can help to improve mutual understanding, communication, and the level of respect among people in different nations.

The impact of international business is far-reaching. Even if business owners do not deal directly with companies in other countries, they are still affected. Every business competes against companies that are either foreign-owned or that sell foreign-made products. As a result, even when you may not realize it, international business is affecting your life.

✓ **Check**Point

List ways that international business is important to companies and countries.

When Did International Business Start?

International business is not a new idea. Evidence suggests that countries such as China, India, and Japan were trading products throughout the world 15,000 years ago. There is also evidence that Africans traded with South Americans several thousand years ago.

The Phoenicians developed trade in the Mediterranean in ancient times. The conquests of Alexander the Great opened up trade with India and China. Later, the Roman Empire dominated trade along the Mediterranean Sea.

The next few centuries had limited foreign trade activity. Following the fall of the Roman Empire, the Vikings

©Photodisc/Getty Images

NETBookmark

Globalization affects almost every aspect of our lives. Many people around the world benefit from globalization while others do not. Access the web site shown below and click on the link for Chapter 1. Next, click on "Issue Briefs" and select one of the topic areas. Read the article for this issue. Prepare a brief written summary of the positive and negative aspects of globalization related to this topic.

www.cengage.com/school/genbus/intlbiz

traveled as far as Iceland, Greenland, and Russia to trade. Islamic empires of the early Middle Ages connected the Iberian Peninsula, North Africa, the Arabian Peninsula, and what is now called Iran. Charlemagne created the Holy Roman Empire out of most of Europe. Viking explorers reached Iceland and Greenland.

The eleventh century saw renewed interest in global commerce. European countries such as England, France, Spain, and Portugal were shipping products by water. By the fifteenth and sixteenth centuries, explorers such as Columbus and Magellan sought a shorter water route to India. Instead of sailing east around Africa, they ventured west.

From about 1500 to 1900, many European countries established colonies in Africa, Asia, and North and South America. These colonies provided European businesses with low-cost raw materials and new markets for selling products. However, these colonies were often created at the expense of the native inhabitants.

Most European countries maintained strong economic and political control over their colonies for years. However, these colonies eventually achieved independence. The United States declared independence from the United Kingdom in 1776. Almost two hundred years later, Mozambique gained independence from Portugal in 1975. For more information about colonial heritage, see Figure 1-1.

Various inventions created between 1769 and 1915 expanded interest in and opportunities for international business. These discoveries included the cotton gin, the steam engine, and the telephone. The inventions from this period improved communication, distribution, and production. They also helped create new global industries.

Recent world events continue to highlight the importance of international business. Expanded trade among companies in different countries increases interdependence. A number of wars in the twentieth century demonstrated the need for political cooperation. These military conflicts limited global business activities. World peace is important if countries want to achieve economic benefits from international trade.

SELECTED COUNTRIES AND THEIR COLONIAL HERITAGE

Country	Colonized By	Date of Independence
Australia	United Kingdom	1901
Brazil	Portugal	1822
Cambodia	France	1953
Canada	France, United Kingdom	1867
Chad	France	1960
Chile	Spain	1818
Cyprus	Turkey, United Kingdom	1960
El Salvador	Spain	1821
Iceland	Norway, Denmark	1944
Mexico	Spain	1821
Mozambique	Portugal	1975
Namibia	Germany, South Africa	1990
South Africa	United Kingdom, Netherlands	1910
United States	United Kingdom, France, Spain, Russia	1776
Vietnam	France	1955

Figure 1-1 Many countries did not achieve independence until the last half of the twentieth century.

GLOBAL TECHNOLOGY TRENDS

Global E-Commerce

"In how many countries does your company do business?" This question is heard often among global managers. Today, the answer is likely to be "Wherever there is Internet access."

Technology allows buying and selling in almost every geographic setting. Grandparents living in Ohio can purchase a book online and have it delivered to their grandchild in France. A Kenyan businesswoman living in Japan might make a similar purchase. But, what if her family needs groceries or airtime for Internet access? She might consider using a company that specializes in global e-commerce in Kenya. Web sites such as MamaMikes and Babawatoto process

payments for school fees, fuel vouchers, electricity, and other necessities of life in Kenya. They can also facilitate the delivery of gifts such as chocolates, flowers, and an mbuzi—a live goat.

Think Critically

1. Identify two types of international business activities that are faster and easier because of technology.
2. Find a web site of a business based outside your home country that buys or sells online. Describe some of the company's products or services.

The creation of the European Union, started in the 1950s, is changing the way most countries do business with one another. Political freedom among former communist countries has created new global business opportunities in these emerging economies. The international business marketplace is expanding daily.

✓ Check Point
What factors have driven the development of international business throughout history?

©Photodisc/Getty Images

REVIEW GLOBAL BUSINESS TERMS

Define each of the following terms.

1. domestic business

2. international business

3. global dependency

REVIEW GLOBAL BUSINESS CONCEPTS

4. How does domestic business differ from international business?

5. Why is international business important?

6. What are some examples of international business activities that occurred before 1800?

SOLVE GLOBAL BUSINESS PROBLEMS

McDonald's has 30,000 restaurants in 120 countries, adapting its menu to various tastes. In Hong Kong burgers are served between two rice patties, while in Norway the *McLaks* is a grilled salmon sandwich. Started in 1955, the company opened its first restaurants outside the United States in 1967. Today, in some countries, such as Brazil and Egypt, McDonald's offers delivery.

7. What factors may have influenced McDonald's to open restaurants outside the United States?

8. How have social and cultural factors affected the company's international business activities?

9. What risks might a company encounter when doing business in other countries?

10. Go to McDonald's web site or other web sites to prepare a map showing the location of the company's international business operations.

THINK CRITICALLY

11. How are you affected by international business?

12. What factors affect a country's decision to trade goods and services with another country?

MAKE ACADEMIC CONNECTIONS

13. TECHNOLOGY How are the Internet and other technologies expanding international trade and global business activities?

14. MATHEMATICS Find information about the main products and services created in your state. Create a graph displaying the top five items in dollar value produced in your state.

15. HISTORY Describe an event from world history. Explain how that event might have influenced trade among countries.

1-2 International Business Basics

GOALS

- Describe basic international business activities.
- Explain the components of the international business environment.
- Name important skills for international business and describe the importance of international business for workers, consumers, and citizens.

©paul prescott, 2009/ Used under license from Shutterstock.com

The Fundamentals of International Trade

What happens when a country has too much of a good thing? Perhaps the country produces more grain than it can consume, mines more coal than it needs, or produces more furniture than it can use. When a country has an abundance of goods or services, businesses look for trade opportunities. That's what happens when companies in different countries trade goods or services.

These foreign trades usually are not an exchange of items for items. Instead, cash payments are usually made for the items bought or sold. For example, a manufacturing company in Korea can sell radios to an electronics store in the United States. Also, a computer company in the United States might sell its products to a retailer in Russia.

These trade activities can be viewed from two sides—the buyer and the seller. For the buyer, products bought from businesses in other countries are called **imports**. In the previous example, the United States is importing radios. Russia is importing computers.

For the seller, **exports** are products sold in other countries. Using the same example, Korea is exporting radios. The United States is exporting computers. Figure 1-2 shows the flow of imports and exports for a country. The figure provides examples of imports coming into the United States and exports being sent out of the country.

Imports and Exports of the United States

IMPORTS   EXPORTS

Figure 1-2 The United States imports many products including agricultural products, cars and car parts, clothing, crude oil, electronics, furniture, and toys. U.S. exports include agricultural products, aircraft, chemicals, computers, and medicines.

Although the process sounds simple, obstacles can arise. These obstacles are called trade barriers. **Trade barriers** are restrictions that reduce free trade among countries. These barriers could appear in several forms.

- Import taxes increase the cost of foreign products.
- Quotas restrict the number of imports.
- Laws prevent certain products from coming into a country.

✓ **Check**Point
How do imports differ from exports?

GLOBAL BUSINESS SPOTLIGHT

U.S. COMPANIES FACE TRADE BARRIERS

Many countries require imported foods to carry nutrition information on the product label. Labeling requirements vary from nation to nation. Several nations impose import taxes on products from other countries. These are examples of trade barriers mentioned in an annual report from the Office of the United States Trade Representative. This government agency encourages other nations to reduce or eliminate trade barriers for U.S. exports. In exchange, restrictions on imports to the United States are lowered or removed. These efforts are aimed at creating a worldwide free trade environment.

Think Critically

1. Why do governments create trade barriers to discourage imports from other countries?
2. What are some examples of trade barriers that are not created by government actions?

The International Business Environment

Buying and selling goods and services is similar in most parts of the world. Consumers try to satisfy their needs and wants at a fair price. Businesses try to sell products at a price that covers costs and provides a fair profit. So, why is international business any different from local business?

INTERNATIONAL BUSINESS ENVIRONMENT FACTORS

In many parts of Iran, the exchange of goods and services takes place in an open-air market. Consumers in Japan buy meals that non-Asians might not enjoy. In Cuba, office workers have been required to work several weeks in the fields to increase the country's food supply. These are some examples of factors that make up the international business operating environment.

Figure 1-3 shows the four major categories of the international business environment. Global business is influenced by geographic conditions, cultural and social factors, political and legal factors, and economic conditions.

Geographic Conditions The climate, terrain, seaports, and natural resources of a country influence business activities. Very hot weather limits the types of crops that can be grown. It also restricts the types of businesses that can operate in that climate. A hot, sunny climate is critical for growing tropical fruit, but not suitable for a ski resort. Mountainous terrain offers opportunities for mining but limits the amount of land available for crops. A nation with many rivers or seaports is able to easily ship products for foreign trade. Countries with few natural resources must depend on imports.

Figure 1-3 Geographic, cultural, political, and economic factors influence business operations, market opportunities, and global risks for international business around the world.

Cultural and Social Factors In some societies, hugging is an appropriate business greeting. In other societies, a handshake is the custom. These differences represent different cultures. **Culture** is the accepted behaviors, customs, and values of a society. A society's culture has a strong influence on business activities. For example, in Spain and parts of Latin America, businesses traditionally were closed for several hours in the middle of the day for a long lunch or a period of rest.

©Photodisc/Getty Images

The main cultural and social factors that affect international business are language, education, religion, values, customs, and social relationships. These relationships include interactions among families, labor unions, and other organizations.

Political and Legal Factors Each day, we encounter examples of government influence on business. Regulation of fair advertising, enforcement of contracts, and safety inspections of foods and medications are a few examples.

A Question of Ethics

In some countries, people expect family members to be given jobs in a company before others. In other countries, payments or gifts are expected before a company does business.

These cultural differences can create ethical problems. Ethics are principles of right and wrong guiding personal and business decisions. When considering the ethics of business situations, you should ask yourself the following questions.

Is the action legal? Laws vary among countries. Most companies base international decisions on the statutes in their home country. When a conflict occurs, managers usually consider such other factors as professional standards and the effect of the action on society.

Does the action violate professional or company standards?
Professional or company standards will frequently exceed the law. This helps to ensure that decisions will be in the best interest of both the company and the country in which it operates.

Who is affected by the action and how? Although an action may be legal and within professional or company standards, decision makers should also consider possible effects on employees, consumers, competitors, and the environment.

Think Critically

1. How do cultural differences create problems when business is done in different countries?
2. What actions can global managers take to avoid ethical problems?

Work as a Team
Prepare a list of examples for the four components of the international business environment.

In general, however, people in the United States have a great deal of freedom when it comes to business activities. However, not all countries are like the United States. In many places, government restricts the activities of consumers and business operators. The most common political and legal factors that affect international business activities include the type of government, the stability of the government, and government policies toward business.

Economic Conditions Everyone faces the problem of limited resources to satisfy numerous needs and wants. This basic economic problem is present for all of us. We continually make decisions about the use of our time, money, and energy. Similarly, every country plans the use of its land, natural resources, workers, and wealth to best serve the needs of its people.

Factors that influence the economic situation of a country include the type of economic system, the availability of natural resources, and the general education level of the country's population. Other economic factors include the types of industries and jobs in the country and the stability of the country's money supply. Available technology for producing and distributing goods and services also influences a nation's economic situation.

✓ CheckPoint
What are the four components of the international business environment?

The Global Business World

International business is an important field of study. Certain basic skills and knowledge are needed in our global economy.

INTERNATIONAL BUSINESS SKILLS

Some skills are needed in every type of job. For example, you must be able to read work manuals, do calculations, and write reports. These skills will continue to be important as business activities among countries increase. In addition, knowledge of specific subjects is important for success in global business.

©Photodisc/Getty Images

- **History** Your awareness of the past can help you better understand today's international business relations.
- **Geography** Geography is more than names on a map. Knowledge of geography will help you understand how the climate and terrain of a country can affect transportation, housing, and other business activities.
- **Foreign language** As countries increasingly participate in foreign trade activities, your ability to communicate effectively with people from other societies increases in importance.
- **Cultural awareness** Understanding that cultures vary from nation to nation allows people to be more sensitive to customs and traditions of all societies.
- **Study skills** Asking questions, taking notes, and doing research are the tools necessary to keep up to date on changes in international business.

THE GLOBAL CITIZEN

As a country becomes more involved in international business, the lives of its citizens change. Consumers have more choices because the selection of goods and services is no longer limited to items produced in their own country. There might be more products, different products, or products that cost less. Career opportunities expand for workers as international business creates demand for additional workers and different kinds of jobs. Some business owners benefit from international trade by expanding an existing business or starting a new one. Other business owners might see new or stronger competition.

As a consumer and worker involved in international business you have an obligation to act responsibly. For example you might want to make sure that companies you buy from and work for follow ethical business practices. The decisions you make are likely to have an impact locally and around the world.

> ✓ **Check**Point
> Other than business skills, what knowledge is important for working in international business? How does international business affect you as a consumer and worker?

INTERNATIONAL BUSINESS PERSPECTIVE
Geography

CANADA'S VAST NATURAL RESOURCES

Canada occupies more than 3.8 million square miles (9.8 million square kilometers), making it the second largest country in the world. With fewer than seven people per square mile, compared to about 80 people per square mile in the United States, Canada is an immense haven of forests, lakes, rivers, and farmland. The country's economy is dependent on these abundant natural resources.

Canada's 1.3 million square miles (3.4 million square kilometers) of forests are a major source of wealth. More than 150 species of trees are native to Canada. Forestry-related products, such as paper, wood pulp, and timber, account for about 15 percent of the country's exports.

Commercial fishing has been a part of Canada's economy for 500 years. The Atlantic and Pacific Oceans and the most extensive bodies of freshwater in the world make fishing an important industry. Common commercial species caught include cod, haddock, herring, salmon, lobster, scallops, and halibut.

Canada's fast-flowing rivers are also an important source of energy. The country is the world's second leading producer of hydroelectricity. Its coasts provide natural seaports in cities such as Vancouver, Halifax, and St. John. Water access through the St. Lawrence River earns Montreal, Toronto, and Quebec City recognition as vital shipping ports.

Wheat—grown in the western prairie provinces of Alberta, Manitoba, and Saskatchewan—is Canada's primary farm product. Other agricultural commodities include barley, potatoes, corn, soybeans, and oats. Livestock such as beef cattle, poultry, dairy cows, hogs, sheep, and egg-laying hens are also major exports.

As a result of its natural beauty, over 40 million tourists visit Canada each year. Many of these travelers go to the cities; however, fishing, hunting, camping, and other outdoor activities are also major tourist attractions. Spending by visitors brings in over $3 billion a year to the Canadian economy.

Think Critically

1. What advantages in the global economy are created by Canada's natural resources?
2. How should Canada use its natural resources to expand its international business activities?
3. Conduct an Internet search for additional information about Canada's economy and international trade activities.

©Photodisc/Getty Images

REVIEW GLOBAL BUSINESS TERMS

Define each of the following terms.

1. imports   2. exports   3. trade barriers   4. culture

REVIEW GLOBAL BUSINESS CONCEPTS

5. What are the four parts of the international business environment?

6. What cultural factors affect international business activities?

7. Name four factors that influence a country's economic conditions.

8. What skills are important for success in an international business?

9. How does international business affect you as
   a. a consumer

   b. a worker

   c. a citizen

SOLVE GLOBAL BUSINESS PROBLEMS

A U.S. company plans to sell farm equipment in a country in Asia. This country traditionally had not conducted business with companies outside of its geographic region. Answer these questions for the U.S. company.

10. What geographic factors might influence the company's international business activities?

11. How might economic conditions affect business decisions?

12. What social and cultural influences could affect this business?

13. How could politics and laws affect the company's exporting activity?

THINK CRITICALLY

14. What actions might a country take to encourage other countries to buy its goods and services?

15. How could geography create international business opportunities?

16. What responsibilities do you believe people have as citizens in our global economy?

MAKE ACADEMIC CONNECTIONS

17. **GEOGRAPHY** Describe how the terrain, climate, and waterways of a country might influence international trade activities.

18. **LAW** Describe some laws in foreign countries that are different from those in the United States.

CHAPTER SUMMARY

1-1 THE FOUNDATION OF INTERNATIONAL BUSINESS

A International business includes all the business activities needed to create, ship, and sell goods and services across national borders. International business is also referred to as *global business, international trade*, and *foreign trade*.

B International business is important as a source of raw material and a supplier of foreign products. It allows for new market and investment opportunities, and paths to improved political relations.

C Trading products throughout the world started more than 15,000 years ago. The Roman Empire dominated international business for more than 600 years. The eleventh century saw renewed interest in global commercialism. From 1500 to 1900, several European countries established colonies in Africa, Asia, North America, and South America.

1-2 INTERNATIONAL BUSINESS BASICS

A Trade activities are viewed from two sides—the buyer and the seller. Products bought from businesses in other countries are called imports. Products sold in other countries are exports.

B The four major categories of the international business environment are geographic conditions, cultural and social factors, political and legal factors, and economic conditions.

C Success in learning about international business requires knowledge of history, geography, foreign language, culture, and study skills.

D As a worker, you have new career opportunities created by international business. As a consumer, you have more buying choices. As a citizen, you must have an increased awareness of the world.

GLOBAL REFOCUS

Reread the Global Focus at the beginning of this chapter, and answer the following questions.

1. Based on what you learned in this chapter, what factors might have prompted Tesco to open stores outside of Britain?

2. Describe some social and cultural factors that could affect the company's international business activities.

3. What risks may occur when opening stores in other countries?

4. What actions might Tesco consider to continue its success in international business?

REVIEW GLOBAL BUSINESS TERMS

Match the terms listed with the definitions.

1. Products sold in other countries.
2. People need and want goods and services produced in other countries.
3. The activities necessary for creating, shipping, and selling goods and services across national borders.
4. Making, buying, and selling goods and services within a country.
5. Products bought from businesses in other countries.
6. The accepted behaviors, customs, and values of a society.
7. Restrictions that reduce free trade among countries.

a. culture
b. domestic business
c. exports
d. global dependency
e. imports
f. international business
g. trade barriers

MAKE GLOBAL BUSINESS DECISIONS

8. Explain how both domestic and international business activities create jobs.
9. What are some examples of our global dependency on other countries?
10. How do investments by a company in a foreign country help the economies of both nations?
11. What actions might a country take to encourage exporting of goods and services?
12. Why might a country use trade barriers?
13. How might religious beliefs affect international business activities?
14. How could a country's type of government affect its business activities?
15. Why would a country with many natural resources have the potential for a strong economy?
16. What actions could you take to improve your history, geography, foreign language, cultural awareness, and study skills?

©Photodisc/Getty Images

MAKE ACADEMIC CONNECTIONS

17. **GEOGRAPHY** Use the library or Internet to prepare a map poster that shows locations of the major trading partners of the United States.

18. **COMMUNICATIONS** Survey students and other people about their knowledge of international business. Prepare a list of eight or ten questions on the geography, culture, and economies of different countries. Ask ten people to answer the questions. Determine the topics on which people are most informed and least informed, and write a one-page summary of your findings.

19. **HISTORY** Write a one- to two-page paper about how a historic event has affected international business. Consider topics such as early Chinese trade with other areas of the world, European colonization, the Industrial Revolution, the creation of the European Community, and the recent political freedom of eastern European countries.

20. **CULTURAL STUDIES** Interview a person who has lived or worked in another country. Ask him or her about the cultural and business differences of that country compared to the United States (or compared to your native country). Prepare a report of your findings.

©Photodisc/Getty Images

21. **SCIENCE** Find a newspaper, magazine, or online article about current scientific or technological developments. Prepare a short written or oral summary of the information in the article. Explain how this information might expand trade among countries.

22. **MATHEMATICS** Select a country other than the United States. Research the major imports and exports of that nation for a recent year. Calculate the difference between the country's total exports and imports and the percentage change in exports and imports from the previous year.

23. **CAREER PLANNING** Based on current articles, advertisements, product packages, and an Internet search, prepare a list of international business job opportunities. Describe some of the skills needed for a successful international business career.

The GLOBAL Entrepreneur

CREATING AN INTERNATIONAL BUSINESS PLAN

Creating an International Business Resource File

To help you learn about international business relationships, you could create an international business plan. This instructional experience will allow you to build your knowledge and skills. The first activity involves creating an international business resource file that you will use for future assignments.

Start a file of articles, information and materials on a country and a company involved in international business. Obtain information related to the geography, history, culture, government, and economy of the country. For the international company file, include a list of products sold in different countries, examples of ways the company adapted to different societies, and other information about its foreign business activities.

Sources of information and materials to create your file may include any of the following.

- reference books such as encyclopedias, almanacs, and atlases
- current articles from newspapers, magazines, and online sources
- current company news and financial information from the company's web site and annual report
- graphs, tables, photos, advertisements, packages, and other visuals from online sources for the country and company
- printed and online materials from companies, airlines, travel bureaus, government agencies, and other organizations involved in international business
- interviews with people who have lived in, work in, or traveled to the country

Prepare a written summary or present a short oral report (two or three minutes) about your country and company. Give an example or situation involving international business. Plan to add things to your file throughout the course, as these materials will be used for other chapter projects.

Our Global Economy

2-1 Economics and Decision Making

2-2 Basics of Economics

2-3 Economic Systems

2-4 Achieving Economic Development

2-5 Resources Satisfy Needs

Joe Raedle/Newsmakers/Getty Images

Dual Economies

In Mexico City, people working for multinational companies are often within a couple of blocks of people selling items on the street. You will see modern buildings with the latest office technology. While just a short drive out of the city, people are conducting business as they did more than 50 years ago. These contrasting situations are examples of a *dual economy*, in which two very different business settings exist in the same country.

Dual economies exist in every region of the world. These diverse settings represent two extreme levels of economic development. The modern economy could be described as an *industrialized economy*. The traditional business activities may be viewed as *less developed*.

These two different levels of economic development are often observed in the difference between urban and rural areas in emerging markets. Cities will often have large companies that are the foundation of a country's economy. The countryside is home to traditional enterprises, such as creating hand-made crafts and operating small farms. The level of participation in international business is a characteristic of this urban-rural dual economy. Companies in cities are more likely to be involved with cross-border commerce and global trade, while traditional businesses in rural areas are usually only involved in local markets.

Another dimension of the dual economy within every country involves street vendors, pushcarts, home-based businesses, and other unregistered enterprises. Commonly called the *informal economy,* these businesses are in contrast to formal enterprises that obtain required permits and pay taxes. Millions of Mexican workers are employed in the informal sector. Economists estimate that nearly half of the jobs in Mexico City involve informal business activities.

Dual economies exist in almost every country including industrialized countries such as Canada and the United States. As some business activities lead to economic growth, others fall behind. Problems of poverty, hunger, and homelessness are symptoms of this economic underdevelopment. Individual countries and global development agencies work to address the gap that results from dual economies in an effort to alleviate poverty and avoid social unrest.

Think Critically

1. What is a dual economy?
2. Talk to a person who has lived in another country. Find out if the person observed any examples of the dual economy. Ask the person to describe the situations.

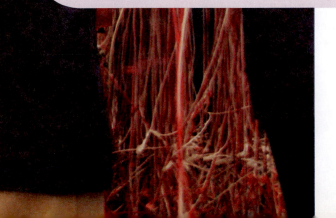

2-1 Economics and Decision Making

GOALS

- Describe the basic economic problem.
- List the steps of the decision-making process.

Photodisc/Getty Images

The Basic Economic Problem

Each day people throughout the world make economic decisions. For example, selecting what groceries to buy is an economic choice. Choosing whether to buy a shirt or download music is an economic choice. As you make choices, you probably are not able to obtain everything you want. These choices are the basis of economics.

You are limited by the amount of time and money you have available to acquire the things you want. Countries and individuals have limited resources. As a result, decisions are necessary to make the best use of resources.

Scarcity refers to the limited resources available to satisfy the unlimited needs and wants of people. All people and all nations face scarcity every day. A country must decide whether to grow its own food or to import agricultural products so its workers can produce other items. Many factors affect the choices made by an individual, a company, or a country. The study of how people choose to use limited resources to satisfy their unlimited needs and wants is called **economics**.

Economics can be an exciting topic to study. Knowledge of economics helps people understand why some earn more than others and why certain items cost more at different times of the year. Economic principles can explain why business managers make one choice over another.

CheckPoint
What is economics?

Making Economic Decisions

People and countries cope with scarcity by making decisions. Every time you decide how to use your time, money, and energy, you are making an economic decision. Companies and nations also have to make choices.

THE DECISION-MAKING PROCESS

One way to help make economic choices is to use the decision-making process. Using the steps shown in Figure 2-1 can help people make wiser decisions and get the best use of resources. This process can help consumers and businesses make faster and better choices. Saving time and money when making a decision is something most people want. There are six steps in the decision-making process.

Step 1 **Define the problem** What do I need or want?

Step 2 **Identify the alternatives** What are the different ways my problem can be solved?

Step 3 **Evaluate the alternatives** What are the advantages and disadvantages of each of the choices available?

Step 4 **Make a choice** Based on the advantages and disadvantages, which would be my best choice? Can I live with the consequences of that choice?

Step 5 **Take action on the choice** What needs to be done to put the decision into action?

Step 6 **Review the decision** Did your decision solve the problem? As time goes by, what different actions might be necessary? Were there consequences you did not predict when you evaluated the alternatives?

Work as a Team
Discuss an important decision that you might have to make in life, such as buying a car or going to college. Work through the six steps of the decision-making process to help you make your decision.

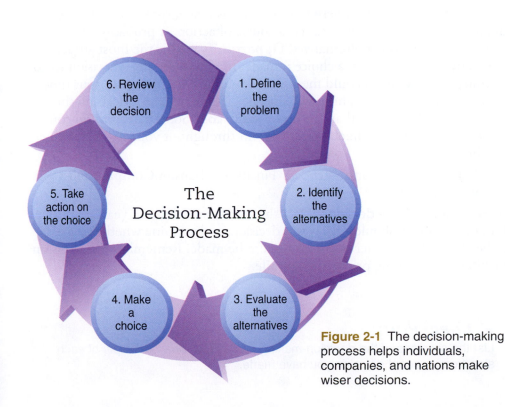

Figure 2-1 The decision-making process helps individuals, companies, and nations make wiser decisions.

DECISION MAKING IN ACTION

How do companies use the decision-making process? An example of economic decision making for international business could involve a company in the United States that wants to increase the sales of its product.

Photodisc/Getty Images

Step 1 Define the problem The problem might be "How can the Benson Electric Company continue to increase its sales over the next five years?" Right now, the company only sells electronic products in the United States.

Step 2 Identify the alternatives Solutions include

- Increasing advertising to attract new customers
- Reducing prices to attract more customers
- Selling products online and e-mailing information to customers in other countries
- Shipping products to sell in other countries
- Producing and selling products in other countries

Step 3 Evaluate the alternatives Each of these choices has costs and benefits. The process of evaluating these options involves comparing the risks and costs of each alternative. Benson Electric must consider the expected increase in sales from each alternative. For example, reducing prices may increase the number of customers but could reduce total dollar sales. The cost of producing products in another country could be greater than the money earned from additional sales.

Step 4 Make a choice Every time a choice is made, something else is given up. So, once Benson Electric selects a course of action, it probably will not be able to choose other alternatives. **Opportunity cost** is the most attractive alternative given up when a choice is made. In your own life, a decision to go to college, for example, could mean you would not be able to use your time to earn money in a job right now. Generally, the benefits of a decision should be more valuable to you than the opportunity cost. So, the decision to continue your education is likely to benefit you throughout your life with higher earnings.

Step 5 Take action on the choice Finally, the Benson Company must put its choice into action.

Step 6 Review the decision Over the weeks, months, and years that follow, the company should review this decision to determine whether it needs to be changed or if other decisions need to be made. Remember that decision making is an ongoing process in your life.

✓ **Check**Point
List the six steps of the decision-making process. Give an example of each step from a recent decision you have made.

2-1 Assessment

Study Tools
www.cengage.com/school/genbus/intlbiz

REVIEW GLOBAL BUSINESS TERMS

Define each of the following terms.

1. scarcity

2. economics

3. opportunity cost

REVIEW GLOBAL BUSINESS CONCEPTS

4. What is the basic economic problem?

5. Describe the six steps of the decision-making model.

6. Why does every decision have an opportunity cost?

SOLVE GLOBAL BUSINESS PROBLEMS

For each of the following international business situations, describe the problem and list two or three alternatives that the company could take to solve the problem.

7. A food company is having trouble selling its frozen products in other countries because it is very expensive to transport frozen foods.

8. A computer store is losing business to a competitor. The competitor is selling imported software at a very low price.

9. Buyers of a tool exported to Bermuda are not following the safety directions, and users are being injured.

THINK CRITICALLY

10. Explain how scarcity affects you and your family, school, and community.

11. What are some examples of situations in which you make decisions without thinking about every step of the decision-making process?

12. Think of three choices you have made recently. What were the opportunity costs of those choices?

MAKE ACADEMIC CONNECTIONS

13. **COMMUNICATION** Talk to a person who works in the business world. Obtain an example of a business decision that the person has made.

14. **TECHNOLOGY** Explain how new computer systems have improved decision making for companies involved in international business.

15. **MATHEMATICS** A cloth manufacturer has the opportunity to purchase new machinery for its factory for $1 million. The machinery will require five equal annual payments while the equipment is being installed. How much will the company have to pay each year for the machinery? During installation, the company can expect profits to rise by $100,000 per year. After that, they can expect profits to rise by $250,000 per year. How long will it be before the increase in profit pays for the machinery entirely?

2-2 Basics of Economics

GOALS

- Describe how the market sets prices.
- Explain the causes of inflation.

Photodisc/Getty Images

Price-Setting Activities

Price is one of the most visible economic factors you encounter every day. The amount paid for goods and services results from economic decisions made by consumers, businesses, and governments. Daily economic decisions affect you in many ways. For example, if people purchase many snowboards, more stores will make snowboards available. In addition, more jobs will be available for people producing and selling snowboards. If consumers no longer want a certain snowboard, the availability or price of that snowboard will decrease.

Have you ever noticed that when something has limited availability and many people want to buy it, the price increases? If many people want to buy tickets for a hockey game or a concert, for example, ticket prices are likely to go up. When freezing temperatures destroy the fruit blossoms and reduce the number of oranges available, prices go up.

The opposite is also true. If a musical group is no longer popular, prices of its posters, music, and T-shirts are likely to go down. The price system is a method of balancing unlimited needs and wants with limited resources.

Determining prices involves two main elements—supply and demand. **Supply** is the relationship between the amount of a good or service that businesses are willing and able to make available and the price. The amount of an item supplied tends to go up when producers see an opportunity to make money. For example, many years ago only a couple of companies made baseball and other sports cards for collecting. As these cards became more popular, other companies got involved in the sports card business.

Supply also works the other way. If companies can no longer make money producing an item, they will get out of that business. As videotape replaced film, companies that made film projectors for schools and libraries went into other types of businesses. The number of film projectors available declined.

On the buyer's side is **demand**, which is the relationship between the amount of a good or service that consumers are willing and able to purchase and the price. In general, as the amount of a good or service that people want increases, the price of that item goes higher. If more people want tickets to a sports event or concert, the price of admission can be set higher for those events. If fewer people want tickets, the price will likely be lower. For example, near the end of the summer, swimsuits are usually at their lowest prices.

The downward sloping line marked *D* in Figure 2-2 shows that as price declines, demand increases. This is called the *law of demand*. For example, at a price of $12, ten videos are demanded, but if the price is $2, sixty videos are demanded. On the supply side (the *S* line), higher prices mean a greater amount supplied because businesses can make a larger profit. At a price of $2, twenty videos are offered for sale, while at $8, fifty videos are available.

The point at which supply and demand cross is called the **market price**. Look at Figure 2-2. At a price of $6 sellers are willing to offer 40 videos and consumers are willing to buy 40 videos. The market price, therefore, is $6. This point is also known as the *equilibrium price*. While supply and demand in the real world do not work as neatly as the graph shows, market forces do cause prices to rise and fall.

Work as a Team

Explain how new technology and bad weather could affect the supply (or demand) for products and how prices might change.

✓ CheckPoint
How do supply and demand determine the market price?

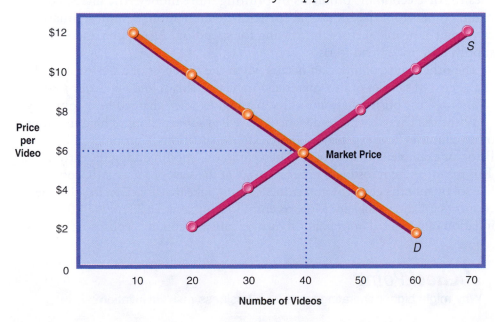

Market Price is Set by Supply and Demand

Price per Video — Number of Videos

Figure 2-2 The point where supply equals demand is known as the market price.

DISAPPEARING LANGUAGES

Language experts predict that in the next 50 years, almost half of the world's 6,000 languages will disappear. The native languages of people are becoming extinct twice as fast as endangered mammals. This trend could mean a world in the future dominated by only a dozen languages.

Of the 250 languages once spoken in Australia, 150 are extinct and 70 are endangered. Some language loss is natural and predictable. For a language to remain healthy, it must be passed on to the next generation.

Fewer languages may seem better for business. However, fewer languages may also mean fewer diverse thoughts. Language diversity reflects the music, history, literature, and culture of a society.

Think Critically

1. What causes languages to become extinct?
2. Why is language diversity important?

Changing Prices

Prices constantly change. The price of the foods we buy can vary during the year and over longer periods of time. For example, prices for fresh fruits and vegetables may rise and fall as weather affects the available supply. Milk also has price variations. When people decide to drink less milk, lower demand is likely to cause the price to decline. Or, when the milk supply is reduced due to fewer farmers raising cows, the price goes up.

A common economic concern is continually rising prices. An increase in the average prices of goods and services in a country is known as **inflation**. Inflation allows people to buy fewer goods and services. Inflation is an indication of the buying power of a country's monetary unit (such as the U.S. dollar, the British pound, or the Japanese yen).

Inflation has two basic causes. First, when demand exceeds supply, prices go up. This is called *demand-pull inflation*. It can occur when a government tries to solve economic problems by printing more money. The increased demand comes from the additional currency in circulation. A similar situation can occur if people increase borrowing for spending. Again, demand exceeds supply, and prices tend to rise.

The other cause of inflation occurs when the expenses of a business (such as the cost of salaries or raw materials) increase. This is known as *cost-push inflation*. Cost-push inflation results in a higher price charged by a company.

While the United States and Canada have had some periods of high inflation, other countries have experienced more extreme situations. Consumer prices in Peru, for example, increased by 400 percent in one month during the early 1990s. This meant an item costing one Peruvian sol at the start of the month, cost five sol by month's end. The government had to take drastic action to solve the country's inflation problem. More recently, in Zimbabwe, a 231,000,000 percent inflation rate resulted from political turmoil and an economic collapse.

✓ CheckPoint

Why might higher operating costs for a business result in inflation?

REVIEW GLOBAL BUSINESS TERMS

Define each of the following terms.

1. supply   2. demand   3. market price   4. inflation

Study Tools

www.cengage.com/school/genbus/intlbiz

REVIEW GLOBAL BUSINESS CONCEPTS

5. What factors affect the supply of a good or service?

6. How does consumer demand create inflation?

7. How can the price of raw materials affect inflation?

SOLVE GLOBAL BUSINESS PROBLEMS

Identify the type of inflation that will result from each of the following situations.

8. The price of silicon used to make computer chips increases.

9. The government prints more money to pay its expenses.

10. Consumers borrow more to buy additional goods and services.

11. Labor unions make employers increase workers' pay.

THINK CRITICALLY

12. Sometimes demand goes up even if prices go up. Describe an example when that might occur.

13. Describe three situations in which inflation has affected you, your family, or your friends. What were the possible causes of that inflation?

MAKE ACADEMIC CONNECTIONS

14. **HISTORY** Research a period in history when a country experienced a period of extremely high inflation. Where and when did this period of inflation occur? What were the causes of the inflation? What measures were taken to end the period of extreme inflation? Did that country later experience another period of extreme inflation?

15. **MATHEMATICS** The graph to the right illustrates supply and demand for sweaters at a local clothing store. Use the graph to identify the market price. How many sweaters will be bought and sold at that price?

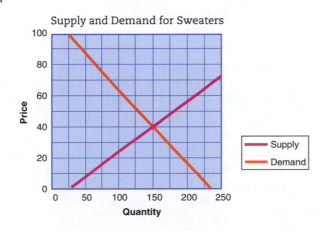

Supply and Demand for Sweaters

2-3 Economic Systems

GOALS

- Name the three main factors of production.
- Understand how different countries make economic decisions.

Photodisc/Getty Images

Economic Resources Satisfy Needs

Every country makes economic decisions. These decisions provide a basis for solving the basic economic problem—satisfying unlimited needs and wants with limited resources. The production of goods and services is a primary activity to satisfy the needs and wants of consumers.

To start a company that makes a product requires several elements. These elements are the **factors of production**, which are the three types of resources used to produce goods and services. These resources are natural, human, and capital, as shown in Figure 2-3.

Natural resources Also known as *land*, these resources are the raw materials that come from the earth, from the water, and from the air. Iron ore, gold, silver agricultural products, rivers, and oxygen are examples of natural resources. These items are used in the production of goods and services consumed by individuals, businesses, and governments.

Human resources Also known as *labor*, these resources are the people who work to create goods and services. While technology has changed or eliminated certain tasks previously performed by people, new types of work are continually being created.

Capital resources Also called *capital*, these resources include buildings, money, equipment, and factories used in the production process. These items are expensive and are used over several years by business organizations.

Factors of Production

Natural Resources

Human Resources

Capital Resources

Figure 2-3 The factors of production are used individually or in combination to produce the goods and services in any economy.

GLOBAL BUSINESS SPOTLIGHT

FACTORS OF PRODUCTION FOR FAST-FOOD COMPANIES

Companies such as Arby's, Burger King, KFC, McDonald's, Subway, and Wendy's sell their products to the consumers of Mexico. Each of the companies combined money, buildings, and equipment (capital resources) with beef, chicken, and wheat (natural resources) and hired local workers (human resources) to provide meals at their restaurants. Some of the most popular locations for the fast-food restaurants are Acapulco, Cancun, Tijuana, and suburban Mexico City.

Think Critically

1. Go to the web site of one of these fast-food companies to obtain additional information about its business operations in different countries. Prepare a one-page summary of your findings.
2. What might cause problems in obtaining factors of production to do business in another country?

✓ CheckPoint
Name the three factors of production, and give an example of each.

Types of Economic Systems

Every nation decides how to use its factors of production to create goods and services for its people. The way in which these resources are used differs from country to country. The economic choices of a country relate to three basic questions.

- What goods and services are to be produced?
- How should the goods and services be produced?
- For whom should the goods and services be produced?

Every country must decide how to use its productive resources to answer these three basic economic questions. An **economic system** is the method a country uses to answer the basic economic questions. Nations organize for production and distribution of goods and services based on customs, political factors, and religious beliefs.

Economic systems can be categorized based on ownership of resources and government involvement in business activities. The three common types of economic systems are command, market, and mixed economies.

COMMAND ECONOMIES

Throughout history, many nations decided to answer the basic economic questions by using *central planning*. In a **command economy**, the government or a central-planning committee regulates the amount, distribution, and price of everything produced. The government also owns the productive resources of the country. Any income from these resources is used to help fund government activities. In the early years of the 21st century, Cuba is one of the few countries using a command system of economic decision making. The political and economic environment where the government owns all of the productive resources of the economy and a single party controls the government is called *communism*.

In some command economies, consumers have very few choices of products to buy. A government agency could even decide what job a person will have.

MARKET ECONOMIES

In contrast to command economies, where all of the decisions are made by the government, market economies are based on the forces of supply and demand. **Market economies** are those in which individual companies and consumers make the decisions about what, how, and for whom items will be produced. The economic and political environment where a market economy exists is called *capitalism*. This system has three main characteristics.

- **Private property** Individuals have the right to buy and sell productive resources and to own business enterprises.

- **Profit motive** Individuals are inspired by the opportunity to be rewarded for taking business risks and for working hard.

Photodisc/Getty Images

- **Free, competitive marketplace** Consumers have the power to use their choices to determine what is to be produced and to influence the prices to be charged.

Because market economies have minimal government involvement with business, they are commonly called *free enterprise systems or private enterprise economies*. Because every country has some governmental regulations affecting business activities, no perfect market economies exist. The United States, although not a pure market economy, is one of the best examples of this type of economic system. Despite strong government involvement in business activities, the Japanese, Australian, and Canadian economies are also usually labeled as market economies.

MIXED ECONOMIES

Many economies are a blend between government involvement in business and private ownership. This is known as a **mixed economy**. For example, some countries have publicly owned transportation companies, communication networks, and major industries. The income from these enterprises is used to help fund government activities.

Socialism refers to a political and economic system with most basic industries owned and operated by government with the government controlled by the people as a whole. In socialism, individuals are usually free to engage in other business opportunities and free to make buying choices. In recent years, examples of socialist countries include Sweden and France.

In changing from a command economy to a market economy, a country may sell government-owned industries to private companies. This process of changing an industry from publicly to privately owned is called **privatization**. In recent years, local governments in the United States have hired private companies to provide services such as trash collection, landscaping, road repairs, and fire protection.

GLOBAL BUSINESS SPOTLIGHT

PUBLIC SERVICES GOING PRIVATE

In recent years, many countries have decided to let private companies buy and operate various government-owned businesses. For example, the Mexican government sold control of the country's telephone company, airlines, and banks to private companies. This action helped to save the country tax dollars. The businesses also became more profitable. Privatization was also very popular in the countries of eastern Europe as they changed from command to market economies.

Think Critically

1. What are some examples of privatization in your school or community?
2. What problems might be associated with privatization?

✓ CheckPoint

What are the three types of economic systems?

2-3 Assessment

REVIEW GLOBAL BUSINESS TERMS

Define each of the following terms.

1. factors of production
2. economic system
3. command economy
4. market economy
5. mixed economy
6. privatization

REVIEW GLOBAL BUSINESS CONCEPTS

7. List examples of the three factors of production.
8. What are the basic economic questions?
9. What are the **three** characteristics of capitalism?

SOLVE GLOBAL BUSINESS PROBLEMS

Indicate whether each of the following situations describes a command economy, market economy, or mixed economy.

10. The **government** tells you what type of job you will have.
11. The government owns the mill that supplies steel to private construction firms.
12. Private investors **own** a mine that supplies gold to a family jewelry maker.
13. You are free to **choose** when and where you will buy a new CD for your friend.
14. A privately owned clothing store buys electricity from a government-owned power company.

THINK CRITICALLY

15. Is one of the three factors of production more important than the others? Explain your answer.
16. If you could choose to live in communism, capitalism, or socialism, which one would you choose? Why?

MAKE ACADEMIC CONNECTIONS

17. **HISTORY** Conduct research to find examples of countries that have changed from a command economy to a market economy. What kind of changes did the country need to make?
18. **SCIENCE** Describe how scientific developments have changed the skills needed for labor.

Achieving Economic Development

Photodisc/Getty Images

GOALS

- **Describe the factors that affect economic development.**
- **Identify the different levels of economic development.**

Development Factors

In some countries, people travel on a high-speed bullet train to manage a computer network in a high-rise building. In other countries, people go by ox cart to a grass hut to operate a hand loom to make cloth for family members and other people in their village. These differences in living and work environments reflect the level of economic development. The main influences on a country's economic development are literacy level, technology, and agricultural dependency.

- **Literacy level** Countries with better education systems usually provide more goods and services that are of higher quality for their citizens.
- **Technology** Automated production, distribution, and communication systems allow companies to create and deliver goods, services, and ideas quickly.
- **Agricultural dependency** An economy that is largely involved in agriculture does not have the manufacturing base to provide citizens with a large number of high quality products.

✓ **CheckPoint**
What factors influence a country's economic development?

Types of Development

The level of economic development of a country can be categorized in three different ways. A country can be industrialized, less developed, or developing. Each of the different levels has unique characteristics.

INDUSTRIALIZED COUNTRIES

The nations with the greatest economic power are usually those with many large companies. An **industrialized country** is a country with strong business activity that is usually the result of advanced technology and a highly educated population. Such countries have attained high levels of industrialization with high standards of living for their residents. Population tends to be centered in large cities and suburbs rather than in rural areas.

Another factor that supports international trade in industrialized countries is infrastructure. **Infrastructure** refers to a nation's transportation, communication, and utility systems. A country such as Germany—with its efficient rail system, high-speed highways, and computers—is better prepared for international business activities than many other nations with weaker infrastructures.

Industrialized countries are actively involved in international business and foreign trade. A portion of the wealth of these nations is the result of successful business activities conducted throughout the world. Countries commonly described as industrialized include Canada, the United Kingdom, France, Germany, Italy, Japan, and the United States.

GLOBAL BUSINESS SPOTLIGHT

TYPES OF INFRASTRUCTURE

The infrastructure of a country usually refers to the transportation, communication, and utility systems that facilitate business activities. These may be referred to as the *physical infrastructure.*

Countries also have a *natural infrastructure.* This includes climate, waterways, farmland, and other natural resources that contribute to a nation's economic development.

Business activities are also affected by a nation's *social infrastructure.* This involves family relationships, labor unions, the church, educational institutions, and other social organizations.

Finally, the *managerial or entrepreneurial infrastructure* involves the ability of people to organize and implement business activities. For example, when McDonald's first opened a restaurant in Russia, company representatives worked with local businesspeople to teach managerial skills. They taught them how to obtain, coordinate, and use the food products, workers, buildings, and equipment necessary to operate a fast-food restaurant.

Think Critically

1. Explain why "infrastructure" refers to more than just the transportation, communication, and utility systems.
2. How do the various types of infrastructure affect the economic development of a country?

LESS-DEVELOPED COUNTRIES

Many countries of the world have a very low standard of living. A **less-developed country** (LDC) is a country with little economic wealth and an emphasis on agriculture or mining. Sometimes these countries have abundant resources but no technology to make use of them. Most LDCs have an average annual income per person of less than $1,000. This compares to the U.S. average annual income per person of more than $30,000.

As a result of low incomes in less-developed countries, citizens often have problems such as inadequate housing, starvation, and poor health care. This situation results in a high death rate among infants, a shorter life expectancy, and the potential for political instability. Examples of LDCs include countries such as Bangladesh, Cambodia, Chad, Haiti, Nepal, Niger, and Sudan.

Future economic development for less-developed countries presents a challenge for all nations. Industrialized countries tend to assist LDCs with the problems of poor health care, limited natural resources, low literacy rates, low levels of employment skills, shortage of investment capital, and uncertain political environments. As these obstacles are overcome, all countries will benefit.

DEVELOPING COUNTRIES

Between the extremes of economic development are the **developing countries** that are evolving from less developed to industrialized. These nations are characterized by improving educational systems, increasing technology, and expanding industries. These factors result in an increasing national income. Examples of developing countries, also referred to as *emerging markets*, include Argentina, Brazil, Ecuador, India, Kenya, Hungary, Poland, South Africa, Turkey, Thailand, and Vietnam. Figure 2-4 summarizes the factors that affect a country's level of economic development.

Levels of Economic Development

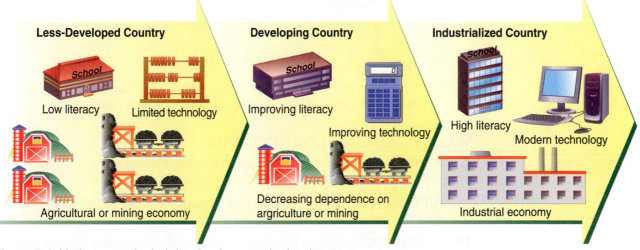

Figure 2-4 Nations vary in their levels of economic development.

**CheckPoint**
Describe each of the different levels of economic development.

2-4 Assessment

REVIEW GLOBAL BUSINESS TERMS

Define each of the following terms.

1. industrialized country
2. infrastructure
3. less-developed country (LDC)
4. developing country

REVIEW GLOBAL BUSINESS CONCEPTS

5. What are the main influences on a country's economic development?
6. Why is infrastructure important to the economic development of a country?
7. What types of business are commonly found in developing countries?

SOLVE GLOBAL BUSINESS PROBLEMS

For each of the following factors, indicate if the item would usually result in an *improving* or *declining* level of economic development for a country.

8. Increased spending on schools and education.
9. Government tax reductions to attract businesses that build new factories.
10. Use of manual labor instead of automated machinery to harvest crops.
11. Reduced government spending for literacy programs.
12. Expanded use of computers for record keeping by business organizations.

THINK CRITICALLY

13. Why would a modern infrastructure give a country an advantage over other countries?
14. What actions can improve a country's education level?
15. Use the Internet to research ways that industrialized countries are working with less-developed and developing countries to create economic growth.

MAKE ACADEMIC CONNECTIONS

16. **SCIENCE** Describe how new scientific discoveries might improve the economic development of a country.
17. **CULTURAL STUDIES** Describe how a country's customs and traditions can influence economic development.
18. **TECHNOLOGY** Use the Internet to research ways a developing country is trying to improve the quality of life for its people.

Photodisc/Getty Images

GOALS

- **Discuss economic principles that explain the need for international trade.**
- **Identify various measures of economic progress and development.**

The Economics of Foreign Trade

In the past, economies were viewed solely in terms of national borders. With continuing expansion of international trade, these boundaries are no longer completely valid in defining economies. Countries are interdependent with each other and so are their economies. Consumers have come to expect goods and services from around the world, not just from suppliers in their own country.

Buying and selling among companies in different countries is based on two economic principles. **Absolute advantage** exists when a country can produce a good or service at a lower cost than other countries. This situation usually occurs as a result of the natural resources or raw materials of a country. For example, South American countries have an absolute advantage in coffee production, Canada in lumber sales, and Saudi Arabia in oil production.

A country may have an absolute advantage in more than one area. If so, it must decide how to maximize its economic wealth. For example, a country may be able to produce both computers and clothing better than other countries. The world market for computers, however, might be stronger. This means the country would better serve its own interests by producing computers and buying clothing from other countries. This is an example of the second economic principle, **comparative advantage**. In this situation, a country specializes in the production of a good or service at which it is relatively more efficient.

✓ CheckPoint

Describe an absolute advantage a country may have as a result of natural resources.

Measuring Economic Progress

The World Cup, the World Series, and the Olympics are sports events that involve scorekeeping. As with sports, international business also keeps score. Various economic measures are used to evaluate and analyze the economic conditions of a country.

MEASURE OF PRODUCTION

Gross domestic product (GDP) measures the output of goods that a country produces within its borders. It includes items produced with foreign resources. For example, the GDP of the United States would include automobiles manufactured in the United States by foreign-owned companies.

Gross national product (GNP) measures the total value of all goods and services produced by the resources of a country. GNP is like GDP but also includes production in other countries using resources of the country whose GNP is being measured.

Because all nations have different populations, comparing total GDP or GNP is not always meaningful. To help compare the economic progress of countries, businesspeople use a *per capita* comparison, which refers to an amount per person. The per capita GDP of the United States is total GDP divided by the number of people in the country. Figure 2-5 shows per capita GDP in U.S. dollars for selected countries.

PER CAPITA GROSS DOMESTIC PRODUCT FOR SELECTED COUNTRIES

Country	Per Capita GDP*	Country	Per Capita GDP*	Country	Per Capita GDP*
Liechtenstein	$118,000	Saudi Arabia	$21,300	India	$2,900
Luxembourg	85,100	Hungary	20,500	Sudan	2,200
Kuwait	60,800	Poland	17,800	Cambodia	2,100
United States	48,000	Argentina	14,500	Kenya	1,800
Canada	40,200	Turkey	12,900	Chad	1,600
Sweden	39,600	Cuba	12,700	Bangladesh	1,500
Australia	39,300	South Africa	10,400	Haiti	1,400
United Kingdom	37,400	Brazil	10,300	Tanzania	1,400
Japan	35,300	Thailand	8,700	Nepal	1,000
Germany	34,800	Peru	8,500	Ethiopia	800
France	32,700	Ecuador	7,700	Niger	700
Italy	31,000	Vietnam	2,900	Liberia	500

*Amounts are stated in U.S. dollars
Source: *The World Factbook*

Figure 2-5 Per capita GDP can be used to compare economic output among nations.

INTERNATIONAL TRADE ACTIVITY

An important measure of a country's international business activity is its balance of trade. **Balance of trade** is the difference between a country's exports and imports. When a country exports (sells) more than it imports (buys), it has a favorable balance of trade. This is also called a *trade surplus*. However, if a country imports more than it exports, the nation has an unfavorable balance of trade, or a *trade deficit*. Figure 2-6 illustrates Canada's favorable balance of trade. Canada has a trade surplus. Figure 2-7 illustrates an unfavorable balance of trade, or trade deficit, for the United Kingdom.

In the process of doing international business, payments must be made among businesses in different countries. Because different nations have different monetary units, a comparison of the value of currencies is required. The **foreign exchange rate** is the value of one country's money in relation to the value of the money of another country. Each day in the business section of newspapers or online at various web sites, you can see the changing value of currencies for different countries.

When you buy more than your current income allows, you go into debt. In the same way, when a country continually has an unfavorable balance of trade, it owes money to others. **Foreign debt** is the amount a country owes to other

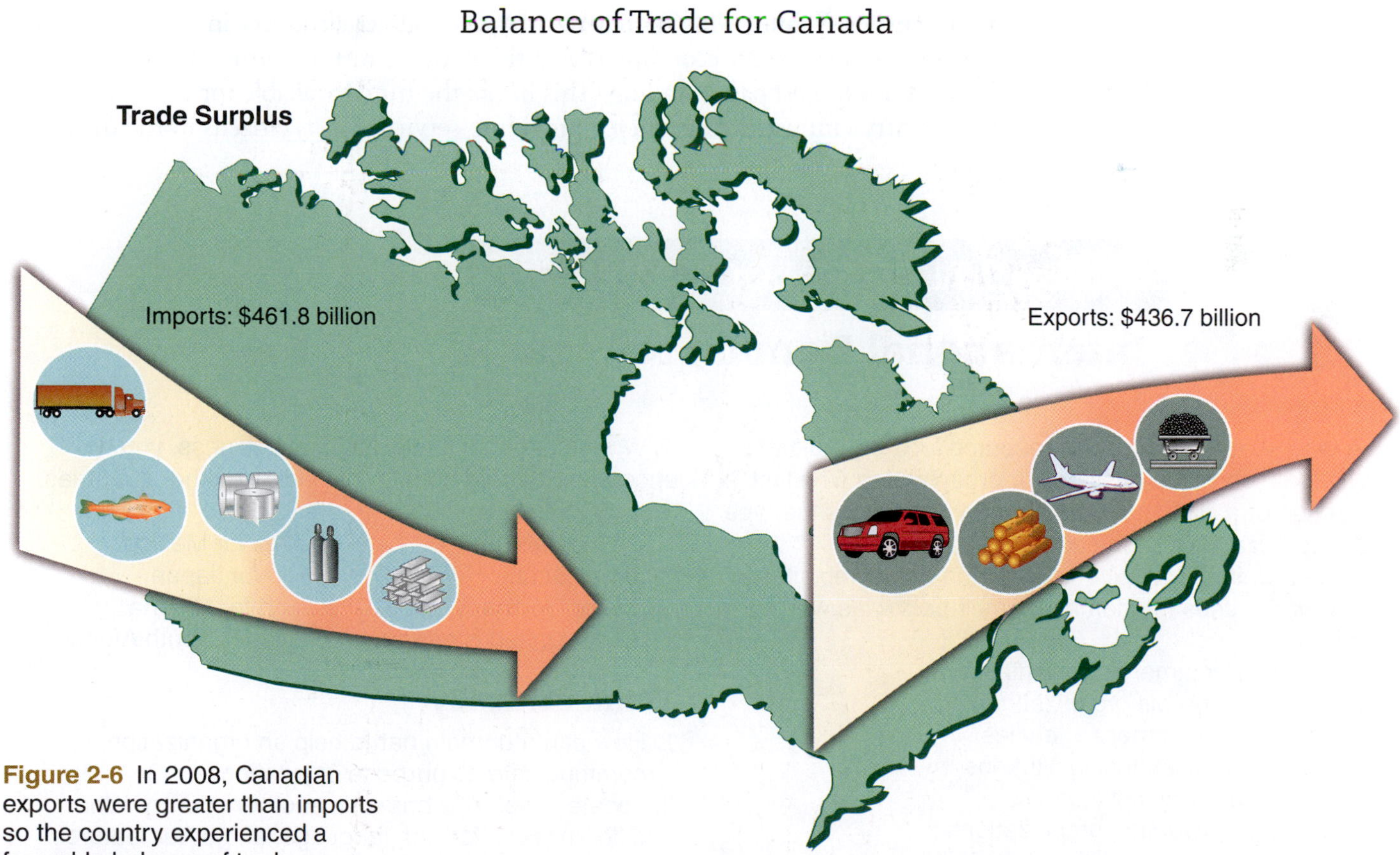

Balance of Trade for Canada

Trade Surplus

Imports: $461.8 billion

Exports: $436.7 billion

Figure 2-6 In 2008, Canadian exports were greater than imports so the country experienced a favorable balance of trade—a trade surplus.

Balance of Trade for the United Kingdom

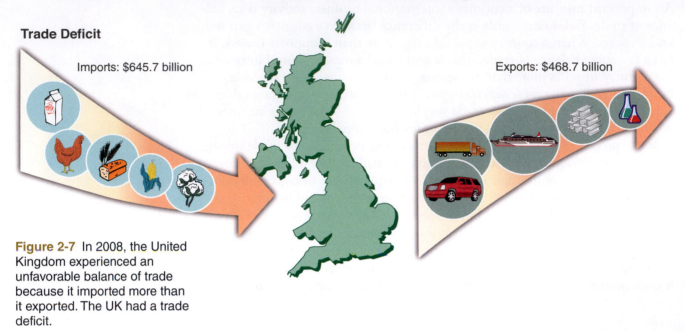

Trade Deficit

Imports: $645.7 billion

Exports: $468.7 billion

Figure 2-7 In 2008, the United Kingdom experienced an unfavorable balance of trade because it imported more than it exported. The UK had a trade deficit.

countries. While owing money to others will affect a country in several ways, the largest effect on the economy is that the nation must use future income to pay for current and past spending. This limits the funds available for improving a country's infrastructure and for providing services for its citizens in the future.

GLOBAL TECHNOLOGY TRENDS

International Domain Names

A web site's URL (uniform resource locator) indicates the location of the business or organization. The last section of a URL, the domain name, indicates the type of organization and the country location.

The United States, which has the most web sites in the world, uses the domain names below, as well as others.

.com for commercial organizations
.org for nonprofit organizations
.gov for government agencies
.edu for educational institutions
.mil for military institutions
.net for networking organizations

In recent years, additional domain names have been added. These include .biz, .info, and .tv.

When conducting international business, you will encounter domain names that indicate other countries. Some examples include:

.ca for Canada   .mx for Mexico
.br for Brazil   .jp for Japan
.de for Germany   .ng for Nigeria
.uk for United Kingdom   .za for South Africa

Think Critically

1. How can a domain name help an organization communicate its purpose or location?
2. Locate a web site based in another country. What differences of format, language, and other features are present?

OTHER ECONOMIC MEASUREMENTS

Inflation refers to general increases in prices in a country. In the United States, inflation is measured by the **consumer price index (CPI)**. The CPI is a federal government report published by the Bureau of Labor Statistics. Each month, data are provided on price levels for various products and services in different regions of the country. This information can help consumers and business managers make buying decisions. Inflation rates for other countries are available on the Internet or in reference books.

A final indicator of a country's economic situation is the *unemployment rate*. When people are not earning an income, they cannot purchase needed goods and services. This causes other people to lose their jobs. The result is a weaker economy. For any country to operate efficiently, a constant flow of money must be in circulation. When this monetary flow slows down, the economic potential of a nation is not realized.

Photodisc/Getty Images

✓ CheckPoint

What are common economic measurements of production and international trade activity?

NETBookmark

The "Big Mac Index" is a light-hearted way to look at the economy. A measurement of prices around the world, the "Big Mac Index" was developed by a London-based magazine, *The Economist*. This calculation reports *purchasing power parity* by comparing the hamburger cost in 120 countries to the price in the United States. Access the web site shown below and click on the link for Chapter 2. Select one of the links that reports the "Big Mac Index" or an article about the index. Study the information presented and write a summary paragraph.

www.cengage.com/school/genbus/intlbiz

Work as a Team

Describe situations in which a person or country would have an absolute or comparative advantage.

INTERNATIONAL BUSINESS PERSPECTIVE
Careers

GLOBAL BUSINESS CAREERS

Are you ready to fly to Istanbul to meet the new joint venture partners? Or, could you prepare a country analysis of Ghana to help us plan our marketing strategy for a new food product? Or, maybe you could negotiate the selling price for delivery trucks to our customers in Brazil? These are just a few of the activities that a person working in international business might encounter. Career titles related to this field can range from international sales manager and customs broker, to foreign investment analyst and cross-cultural training specialist. Some of the main categories of international business careers include international business marketing, global operations and logistics, foreign trade, international finance and accounting, international law, global information systems, and international development.

People who work in international business careers are often required to have specialized skills, for example:

- Language training would be needed by interpreters and translators
- A knowledge of international law is necessary to be an international regulatory lawyer
- Global financial markets education is the foundation for working in international finance
- Cross-cultural communications would be critical for a global marketing career

In addition, there are skills needed by nearly everyone involved in global business work. These competencies include cultural awareness, knowledge of geography, and foreign language. Also vital is training in business courses such as management, marketing, accounting, finance, and information technology.

As international trade continues to expand, so will your career opportunities. While job prospects will vary depending on global economic cycles, the training and experiences you obtain will likely be in demand in various international business settings.

Think Critically

1. What aspects of a career in international business would be of interest to you for a future career?
2. Search the Internet to obtain additional information on a specific type of international business career.

kwanisik/iStockphoto.com

REVIEW GLOBAL BUSINESS TERMS

Define each of the following terms.

1. absolute advantage
2. comparative advantage
3. gross domestic product (GDP)
4. gross national product (GNP)
5. balance of trade
6. foreign exchange rate
7. foreign debt
8. consumer price index (CPI)

Study Tools

www.cengage.com/school/genbus/intlbiz

REVIEW GLOBAL BUSINESS CONCEPTS

9. What is the difference between absolute advantage and comparative advantage?

10. What does gross domestic product (GDP) measure?

11. How does a country's balance of trade affect its foreign debt?

SOLVE GLOBAL BUSINESS PROBLEMS

Using the data from Figures 2-5 and 2-6, answer the following questions.

12. Which country has the highest per capita GDP? Which has the lowest?

13. Despite having extensive economic activity, why does India have relatively low per capita GDP?

14. What is the amount of the trade surplus for Canada?

THINK CRITICALLY

15. How can a nation create an absolute advantage through its investment activities?

16. How would a high inflation rate affect a country's economic image in the world?

MAKE ACADEMIC CONNECTIONS

17. **GEOGRAPHY** Locate examples of natural resources that would give a country an absolute advantage.

18. **MATHEMATICS** A country has exports of $4.2 billion and imports of $4.6 billion. (a) What is the country's balance of trade? (b) Is this amount a trade surplus or a trade deficit?

19. **VISUAL ART** Select one or more economic statistics for several countries. Prepare a graph comparing these data.

20. **TECHNOLOGY** Use the Internet to find current per capita GDP data for ten countries. Choose countries in the same region. For example, you might choose countries in Africa or Southeast Asia. Report your findings in a table similar to Figure 2-5.

CHAPTER SUMMARY

2-1 ECONOMICS AND DECISION MAKING

A The basic economic problem involves scarcity—balancing limited resources with unlimited needs and wants.

B The steps of the decision-making process are (1) define the problem, (2) identify the alternatives, (3) evaluate the alternatives, (4) make a choice, (5) take action, and (6) review the decision.

2-2 BASICS OF ECONOMICS

A The main factors that affect prices are supply and demand.

B Inflation occurs when demand exceeds supply or when business operating costs increase. There are two basic causes for inflation: demand-pull inflation and cost-push inflation.

2-3 ECONOMIC SYSTEMS

A The three main factors of production are natural resources (land), human resources (labor), and capital resources (money and equipment).

B Countries make economic decisions using command economies, market economies, and mixed economies.

2-4 ACHIEVING ECONOMIC DEVELOPMENT

A The main influences on a country's economic development are literacy level, technology, and agricultural dependency.

B The three levels of economic development are industrialized countries, less-developed countries, and developing countries.

2-5 RESOURCES SATISFY NEEDS

A Absolute and comparative advantages are economic principles that explain buying and selling among companies in different countries.

B Measures of economic progress and development include gross domestic product, gross national product, balance of trade, foreign exchange rate, foreign debt, and consumer price index.

GLOBAL **REFOCUS**

Read the Global Focus at the beginning of this chapter, and answer the following questions.

1. What are some actions that Mexico and other countries might take to reduce the concerns associated with the dual economy?

2. How might international trade affect the dual economy of a country?

3. Conduct a web search to obtain additional information about informal economic activities in Mexico.

REVIEW GLOBAL BUSINESS TERMS

Match the terms listed with the definitions. Some terms may not be used.

1. The difference between a country's exports and imports.
2. A situation that exists when a country specializes in the production of a good or service at which it is relatively more efficient.
3. The study of how people choose to use limited resources to satisfy their unlimited needs and wants.
4. The amount of a good or service that businesses are willing and able to make available at a certain price.
5. The process of changing an industry from public to private ownership.
6. The limited resources available to satisfy the unlimited needs and wants of people.
7. The amount of a good or service that consumers are willing and able to purchase at a certain price.
8. The method a country uses to answer the basic questions of what to produce, how to produce it, and for whom to produce it.
9. A measure of the productive output of a country within its borders, including items produced with foreign resources.
10. The monthly United States federal government report on inflation.
11. The amount a country owes to other countries.
12. A measure of the total value of all goods and services produced by the resources of a country.
13. A nation's transportation, communication, and utility systems.
14. The three types of resources used to produce goods and services.

a. absolute advantage
b. balance of trade
c. command economy
d. comparative advantage
e. consumer price index (CPI)
f. demand
g. developing country
h. economics
i. economic system
j. factors of production
k. foreign debt
l. foreign exchange rate
m. gross domestic product (GDP)
n. gross national product (GNP)
o. industrialized country
p. inflation
q. infrastructure
r. less-developed country (LDC)
s. market economy
t. market price
u. mixed economy
v. opportunity cost
w. privatization
x. scarcity
y. supply

15. A country's ability to produce a good or service at a lower cost than other countries.
16. The most attractive alternative given up when a choice is made.
17. An increase in the average prices of goods and services in a country.
18. The method a country uses to answer the basic economic questions.
19. A country with little economic wealth and an emphasis on agriculture or mining.
20. The point at which supply and demand cross.

MAKE GLOBAL BUSINESS DECISIONS

21. Describe situations of people, companies, and nations facing the basic economic problem of scarcity.

22. Explain how a person goes through the decision-making process many times a day, usually without thinking about the specific steps.

23. If the demand for a product in our society is high, what are some things that happen to reduce that demand?

24. Give examples of capital resources that are used by business organizations to produce goods and services.

25. If you were creating an economic system for a country, what traits would you want it to have? Explain your answer.

26. What problems may arise when a government decides to sell government-owned businesses to private companies?

27. How are people in all countries affected by poor economic conditions in less-developed countries?

28. Name a famous person who is able to do something better than anyone else. This is an absolute advantage. Now, for an example of comparative advantage, describe a person who does several things well but selects only one of these talents to make a living.

29. What actions could a country take to improve its balance of trade?

30. What factors could affect the value of a country's currency compared to that of another country?

MAKE ACADEMIC CONNECTIONS

31. **COMMUNICATIONS** Find an article about changes in prices. Prepare a one-minute oral explanation about how supply and demand influence these prices.

32. **SCIENCE** Prepare a poster or display that shows how the factors of production are used to create a specific product.

33. **GEOGRAPHY** Prepare a research report on a less-developed country. Describe ways in which that nation could improve its economic development and the quality of life for its citizens.

34. **HISTORY** Conduct research on the historic factors of production previous to the Industrial Revolution. What types of factories existed in Europe and Asia before 1870?

35. **CAREER PLANNING** Find a recent news article that deals with achange in the economy as a result of international business. Describe how the events in the article could affect the supply and demand for certain international jobs.

The GLOBAL Entrepreneur

CREATING AN INTERNATIONAL BUSINESS PLAN

Economic Conditions around the World

Obtain data on GDP, per capita income, balance of trade, and unemployment for six countries for three recent years. Choose two less-developed countries, two developing countries, and two industrialized countries. (Include the country you chose in Chapter 1.) Use library reference materials, such as an almanac, or on-line sources such as *The World Factbook* to obtain your data.

Find additional information about each country. Locate the countries on a world map or globe. Try to picture their climates, geography, and neighbors. What is it like to live in each of the countries? What natural resources are available? What type of economic system operates in each country: command, market, or mixed? What is the literacy rate in each country? Does most of the population live in an urban or a rural setting?

1. Prepare four graphs: one that compares GDP for the countries over the past three years, one that compares per capita income, one that compares balance of trade, and one that compares unemployment.

2. Prepare a written report that answers the following questions. Include your graphs as part of the report.

   - How has the level of economic development changed in recent years for less-developed countries? for developing countries? for industrialized countries?

   - What do these changes mean for countries involved in international business?

   - Are GDP, per capita income, balance of trade, and unemployment related to each other in any way? If so, how are they related?

   - How could a company involved in international business use this information to make better company decisions?

Photodisc/Getty Images

CHAPTER 3

Cultural Influences on Global Business

3-1 Culture Around the World

3-2 Culture and Social Organizations

3-3 Communication Across Cultures

3-4 Values Around the World

AP Photo/Tsugufumi Matsumoto

GLOBAL FOCUS

Disney Theme Parks Adjust to Local Culture

Bridging cultures was a major goal when the Walt Disney Company developed Euro Disneyland in France. While planning the theme park, which is now called Disneyland Paris, Disney learned that not everyone was happy about the project. Some people thought that having an icon of American culture in their country would threaten French culture. Disney had not experienced this kind of opposition when it developed a theme park in Japan.

In an attempt to calm fears, Walt Disney Company pointed out that its founder was of French descent and the family name was originally D'Isigny. The company chose to use French as the primary language for signs and designed new attractions with French and European themes. The dress code for employees, also known as cast members, was tailored to reflect the local culture. After initially suffering poor attendance, the theme park adopted the widespread European custom of selling alcoholic beverages at entertainment venues.

In Hong Kong, Disney tried to be sensitive to local culture in everything from the design of the park to souvenirs in the gift shops and menus in restaurants. Hong Kong Disneyland was built observing principles of feng shui, the traditional Chinese art of having elements in harmony with each other and nature to maximize good luck. Clocks are not sold at the theme park stores because the phrase for giving a clock sounds similar to a phrase used when paying last respects to the dead. In one instance, Disney stumbled by being too local. Shark fin soup, a Hong Kong favorite, was pulled from the menu when environmentalists objected.

Think Critically

1. What barriers did the The Walt Disney Company face when planning and operating Disneyland Paris?
2. Why do you think Disney emphasized the original form of the Disney family name?
3. Go to the web sites for the The Walt Disney Company and the theme parks to obtain additional information about the international operations of the company. Prepare a report of your findings.

3-1 | Culture Around the World

Photodisc/Getty Images

Cultural Influences

Some people have their evening meal at five o'clock. Others eat at nine or ten. This is a simple but distinct example of differences in culture.

A **culture** is a system of learned, shared, unifying, and interrelated beliefs, values, and assumptions. Beliefs are ideas about the nature of a person, thing, or concept. Values are the positive and negative ideals, customs, and institutions of a group. Assumptions are ideas that are taken for granted as fact. Cultural beliefs, values, and assumptions are directly and indirectly acquired throughout a lifetime. They are accepted and valued by other members of the group. They cause group members to respond in similar and usually predictable ways. Put another way, culture is a mind-set, or a way of thinking that is acquired over time. To members of a particular culture, their ways are logical and reasonable. To outsiders, their ways sometimes seem different or even strange.

A culture is the sum of a group's way of life. Some, but not all, of the parts are discussed and recorded. Different aspects of culture are taught in different arenas including homes, schools, religious institutions, and work. Still other parts are learned indirectly through experiences. Members of cultural groups often are reluctant to share their cultures with outsiders.

A culture can be compared to an iceberg. You can easily see the tip. Most of the beliefs, values, and assumptions of a culture are hidden beneath the surface, just as most of the iceberg is hidden beneath the water. You can easily see such objects of a culture as clothes, foods, and vehicles. You can read a culture's literature and hear its music. You can also observe the behaviors of its members. However, these things alone do not make a culture. Hidden away are unseen but important parts of culture. These include the supporting expectations, attitudes, values, beliefs, and perceptions of its members.

THE SAME OR DIFFERENT?

When a company does business in another country, it must decide whether to use a standardized product or a customized product. While some products can be sold in basically the same form throughout the world (cameras, computers, motor vehicles), others must be adapted to a culture.

Fast-food menus around the world are customized to tastes, customs, and religious beliefs. In some countries, Tide detergent is sold in three forms—powder, liquid, and bar. The detergent bar is used for washing clothes by hand in areas that do not have washing machines.

Think Critically

1. Name some products that might be sold in the same form around the world.
2. What aspects of culture might require a company to adapt its product when selling in another country?

✓ CheckPoint

How do members of a group learn its culture?

The Subcultures Within a Society

A **subculture** is a subset of a larger culture. A subculture may have some values, beliefs, and assumptions that are different than the larger culture of which it is a part. You are a member of many different subcultures. You are a member of the general culture of your country, but you are also a member of some of its component groups. You are a member of the student subculture. You are also a member of a gender subculture. You are a member of an ethnic-based subculture, and you might identify with other subcultures. However, you are not a member of some subcultures because you don't meet the requirements. For example, high school students are not members of the senior-citizen subculture because of their age.

Subcultures often choose from the allowable behaviors within their respective general cultures. For example, music is part of the general U.S. culture. However, not all U.S. subcultures choose to listen to the same music. Young people may prefer heavy metal, alternative, and hip-hop music. In contrast, the adult subculture might prefer contemporary, jazz, or classical music.

INFLUENCES OF CULTURES AND SUBCULTURES

Cultures and subcultures are important because they influence the actions of their members. **Cultural baggage** is the idea that you carry your beliefs, values, and assumptions with you at all times. Your cultural baggage influences how you respond to others. In business settings, your cultural baggage influences what you say and do as you conduct business.

Cultures and subcultures set the standards against which people judge behaviors. Consequently, people behave in ways that are acceptable to other members of their culture and subcultures. You have learned through experience that if you behave in unacceptable ways, members of your

Photodisc/Getty Images

culture will let you know. If you are rude to your parents, for example, they may discipline you. If you insult your friends, they may not ask you to join them in future activities. If you steal a car, you may go to jail. The influences of cultures and subcultures on the behaviors of individuals are quite strong.

SUBCULTURE OF U.S. BUSINESS

The U.S. business subculture is composed of the business-related part of the general U.S. culture. This business subculture has certain beliefs, values, and assumptions that differentiate it from the general U.S. culture. With some exceptions, businesspeople share a core of common beliefs, values, and assumptions that shape their behaviors. These common behaviors allow U.S. business to be conducted in predictable ways.

Many of the important beliefs, values, and assumptions of the U.S. business subculture appear in common sayings. Cultural groups use such sayings to preserve and transmit important guiding principles to others. For example, the saying, *don't count your chickens before they hatch,* suggests that you must not count on predictable outcomes. The value of persistence is reflected in the saying, *if at first you don't succeed, try, try again.*

VARIATIONS IN BUSINESS SUBCULTURES WORLDWIDE

Just as the U.S. business subculture has its own set of beliefs, values, and assumptions, so do other business subcultures. Consequently, no two business subcultures are identical. However, when two general cultures are similar, their business subcultures are apt to be similar.

For example, the United States trades extensively with Canada and the United Kingdom. One reason for these trade links is that the business subcultures of these countries are similar. These similarities cause U.S., Canadian, and British people to conduct business in somewhat similar ways. Less trade may occur between American and Vietnamese or Kenyan businesses because their business subcultures are much different.

People cannot escape the influences of business subcultures. These subcultures are powerful. They shape the personal and professional behaviors of businesspersons everywhere. Your behavior in the business world will be guided by the standards that are deemed permissible in your country's business subculture. Business subcultures in other countries operate with different sets of beliefs, values, and assumptions. Becoming aware of these cultural differences is the first step toward understanding them and their influence.

✓ CheckPoint
How does the business subculture of a country affect which countries it is most likely to do business with?

REVIEW GLOBAL BUSINESS TERMS

Define each of the following terms.

1. culture
2. subculture
3. cultural baggage

REVIEW GLOBAL BUSINESS CONCEPTS

4. How is a subculture different from a culture?
5. Why is it important to understand a country's business subculture?

SOLVE GLOBAL BUSINESS PROBLEMS

Which of the following statements are characteristic and uncharacteristic of the U.S. business subculture? Why?

6. Hard work is valued and rewarded.
7. Leisure is more important than work.
8. Intention is more important than accomplishment.

THINK CRITICALLY

9. Explain why cultural knowledge of a country is necessary for being successful in international business.
10. What actions must a person take when doing business in countries with strong family-work relationships?
11. What are some assumptions of the U.S. business culture?
12. What is one item that makes your culture different from other cultures?

MAKE ACADEMIC CONNECTIONS

13. **TECHNOLOGY** How can the use of technology help to preserve and destroy cultures?
14. **COMMUNICATIONS** Interview a person who has visited or lived in another country. How is the culture of that nation different from that of the United States.?
15. **LAW** Every country has its own culturally sanctioned legal system. What are the fundamental characteristics of the common law system of the United States?
16. **CULTURAL STUDIES** Use the Internet to find examples of businesses that have had to adapt their business practices to local cultural conditions.

3-2 Culture and Social Organizations

GOALS

- Describe how family relationships can affect culture.

- Explain the role of societal influences on culture.

Photodisc/Getty Images

Family Relationships

Cultures and subcultures influence the ways in which societies organize themselves. Social organization includes the relationships between both the family unit and society. These components affect not only the entire culture, but also many other institutions, including the business community.

FAMILY UNITS

Most societies are at least partially organized around family units. A **nuclear family** is a group that consists of a parent or parents and unmarried children living together. Most developed countries have societies organized around nuclear families. An **extended family** is a group that consists of the parents, children, and other relatives living together. Other relatives might include married children, grandchildren, the parents' parents, the brothers and sisters of the parents, and others. Many developing countries have societies organized around extended families.

FAMILY-WORK RELATIONSHIPS

Family ties to business are weak in some cultures and strong in others. In Canada, the United States, and most northern European countries, links between family and business are weak. Fairly often there is no connection at all. However, in most of the remainder of North and South America, much of southern Europe, most of Asia, northern Africa, and the Middle East, family

ties to business are strong. Quite often employees of businesses in these areas are family members. It is difficult to separate family from business.

✓ CheckPoint

How can family relationships affect the culture in a country?

Society's Institutions

The institutions of a society can be just as important to a culture as family relationships. Social institutions such as education, gender roles, mobility, and class system also influence people's lives.

EDUCATION

The family unit provides the early education for its younger members. It instructs the young in the ways of its culture. In economically developed societies, the family often shares responsibilities with other cultural institutions for providing later education. Religious groups often provide moral and spiritual education. Schools provide formal education, which prepares people to function productively as members of society. Businesses sometimes provide specialized work-related education and training. This upgrades the job-related knowledge, skills, and attitudes of employees.

Photodisc/Getty Images

Families and their societies decide what types and amounts of education will be made available to members. In the United States, a person has many opportunities to receive different types and amounts of education. One reason for the global economic success of the United States is that its workers are well educated and trained.

GENDER ROLES

In most cultures, family members are assigned different roles to fulfill. Sometimes these roles are assigned based upon gender. In some cultures, only males or females are allowed to fill certain roles. In some societies, females are the primary workers outside the household. In others, males are the primary workers away from home. In still other societies, both males and females are employed outside the home.

Viewpoints vary worldwide about the roles males and females can fill in business. Some business subcultures may favor males over females in the workplace. In the United States, women increasingly participate in international business activities as equals with men.

In Japan, in the past, native women had very inferior workplace opportunities when compared to men. Japanese women traditionally participated in the international business activities of Japanese companies only as translators and interpreters. In Libya, women have very limited workplace opportunities. They do not typically participate in international business activities.

MOBILITY

Some cultures, such as the dominant one in the United States, have relatively little geographic attachment. In other words, the family members are not usually tied to their current location. They are mobile and willing to relocate for

Work as a Team

Suggest ways in which technology might affect the culture of a nation.

better employment opportunities. In some other cultures, the ties to birthplace or region are much stronger. Members of these cultures would almost never consider moving away.

People who would not consider leaving their region permanently are sometimes willing to move elsewhere temporarily for better work opportunities. For example, guest workers from Turkey are a significant portion of the population of Germany. Guest workers bring their native culture with them. They also maintain strong ties with their home country. Sometimes their culture conflicts with that of the host country. Some host cultures do not make adjustments for guest workers. Other host cultures try to ensure that guest workers are treated similarly to native workers.

CLASS SYSTEM

Cultures also organize their members beyond the family unit. A **class system** is a means of dividing the members of a cultural group into various levels. The levels can be based upon such factors as education, occupation, heritage, conferred or inherited status (nobility), and income. In some cultures, you can move from one class to another. This is true to a great extent in the United States, where the class system is weak.

Sometimes the levels are based upon your lineage. When this occurs, you can become locked into your class. It is very difficult or impossible for you to change classes. In the United Kingdom, to a significant degree, your bloodline still influences your class and occupational choices. If you are born into the British aristocracy, you belong to the highest class. If you work, you might oversee your family's property and fortune. However, you probably would not engage in trade. That would be considered beneath your privileged position. For the remainder of British society, nobility is not a factor. Some people do shift class levels. However, it is more difficult to change class level in the United Kingdom than it is in the United States.

✓ CheckPoint
What types of social organization are commonly found in most cultures?

NETBookmark

Every country, no matter how developed, has a class system. Access the web site shown below and click on the link for Chapter 3. Read the web article describing the caste system in modern India. After reading the article, write a brief paragraph describing how the caste system differs from the class system of the United Kingdom as described on page 65.

www.cengage.com/school/genbus/intlbiz

3-2 Assessment

REVIEW GLOBAL BUSINESS TERMS

Define each of the following terms.

1. nuclear family

2. extended family

3. class system

REVIEW GLOBAL BUSINESS CONCEPTS

4. How does social organization influence general cultures?

SOLVE GLOBAL BUSINESS PROBLEMS

Historically, the United Kingdom has had a rigid class system in which members of the aristocracy have enjoyed special privileges. In contrast, the United States has a flexible class system that allows individuals to shift from one class to another.

5. Why doesn't the United States have a reigning king or queen like the United Kingdom?

6. What fundamental principle in the United States requires that the class system be flexible, at least theoretically?

7. Why do you think there are attempts in the United Kingdom to break down some of the barriers of its class system?

THINK CRITICALLY

8. Why do nuclear families often have a higher living standard than extended families?

9. Why are countries with well-educated and trained citizens likely to be economically successful?

10. How does high geographic attachment handicap workers in a global economy?

MAKE ACADEMIC CONNECTIONS

11. **HISTORY** Name some countries that have monarchs.

12. **CULTURAL STUDIES** What role is traditionally given to women in the Islamic Middle East?

13. **GEOGRAPHY** Why are there more extended families in Mexico than in Canada and the United States?

14. **CULTURAL STUDIES** Use the Internet to research countries or cultures that have rigid class systems.

和平、進歩
迎接新世紀

PEACE PROGRESS FOR A
BETTER WORLD

Photodisc/Getty Images

GOALS

- Understand the importance of knowing another language for global business success.

- Compare direct and indirect communication.

- Describe the influence of nonverbal communication.

Language Differences

All cultures and subcultures use language to communicate with other societies. Language facilitates international business transactions. Without language, conducting business would be very difficult.

Many languages are used for business purposes. However, English is widely considered to be the language of international business. More people use English to conduct international business than any other language. More people speak Mandarin Chinese than any other language. However, English is understood in almost every country around the world. Figure 3-1 shows the numbers of native speakers of major world languages.

As a language for conducting business, English has some advantages over other languages. It contains many words drawn from other languages, and ideas can be expressed in many ways. It also has a large number of business-related words. Further, English can be concise and precise. Often it takes fewer words to send the same message in English than to send it in other major languages. For example, the French version of a message may be 20 percent longer than the English version. The Spanish version may be 30 to 40 percent longer and the Russian version may be 35 to 50 percent longer than the English version.

Learning a Second Language

Being a native speaker of English is both an advantage and a disadvantage. It is an advantage because you already know the major language of international business. It is a disadvantage because you may decide wrongly that there is

Work as a Team

Discuss which language besides English you would choose to learn in order to get ahead in international business.

MAJOR WORLD LANGUAGES

Language	Number of Native Speakers	Where It Is Used
Chinese, Mandarin	873,000,000	China
Spanish	322,000,000	Spain, Mexico, most Central and South American countries
English	309,000,000	United Kingdom, United States, Canada, Ireland, Australia, India, numerous African and Asian countries
Hindi	180,000,000	India
Portuguese	177,000,000	Portugal, Brazil
Bengali	171,000,000	India, Bangladesh
Russian	145,000,000	Russia, former republics of the Soviet Union
Japanese	122,000,000	Japan
German, standard	77,000,000	Germany, Austria, Switzerland, numerous European countries
Chinese, Wu	77,000,000	China
Korean	67,000,000	Korea
French	64,000,000	France, Canada, numerous European and African countries

Source: *The World Almanac and Book of Facts, 2008*

Figure 3-1 Most of the world's citizens are not native speakers of English, which is the generally accepted language of international business.

little need to learn another language. Because people often prefer to transact business in their native language, you could also learn a second language.

You may be wondering which foreign language is most useful for business purposes. The answer is not easy; all languages have use in some business situations. Languages such as Japanese, French, Spanish, German, Chinese, Russian, Arabic, Portuguese, Italian, and Korean often are recommended to native U.S. English speakers for their usefulness for business purposes.

When deciding to learn a second language, you might consider the language of one of the United States' dominant trading partners. This would mean learning Japanese or Chinese, or possibly French, German, or Spanish.

Learning any language, the highest form of a group's culture, will help you to understand the culture of those who speak it. As you learn the language, you learn how things are done where that language is spoken. You learn the beliefs, values, and assumptions of that society.

Over time, you may learn to think and communicate like a native. This helps you conduct business like a member of that society. Being fluent in a second language for business purposes is a competitive advantage. It will help you succeed in the world of international business.

Direct and Indirect Communication

One important feature of communication is that it can be direct or indirect. **Contexting** refers to how direct or indirect communication is. A low-context culture is one that communicates very directly. These cultures value words and interpret them literally. The general and business subcultures of both Germany and the United States are relatively low context. Members of these groups convey information directly and explicitly.

A high-context culture is one that communicates indirectly. These cultures attach

Photodisc/Getty Images

GLOBAL BUSINESS SPOTLIGHT

SAYING "NO" THE JAPANESE WAY

Carla Boyd, a U.S. businessperson, asked her Japanese trading partner, Yasuo Watanabe, for a lower price on the Japanese products she was purchasing. Mr. Watanabe smiled and replied, "I will do my best." Two weeks later Ms. Boyd discovered that the product was invoiced at the original price. Ms. Boyd appealed to Mr. Watanabe, asking that the price be decreased because of the order size. Mr. Watanabe replied, "That will be very difficult." Two weeks

later Ms. Boyd received another invoice, and it showed the original price. Ms. Boyd felt let down by Mr. Watanabe because he had not said "no" directly.

Several weeks later, in an international business seminar, Ms. Boyd learned that the Japanese culture is a high-context culture. Suddenly, things made sense to Ms. Boyd. Mr. Watanabe was not being deceptive after all; he was being very polite and indirect. Both "I will do my best" and "That will be very difficult"

suggest an unlikely outcome. Mr. Watanabe had been consistently saying "no" in the correct Japanese manner, but Ms. Boyd was prepared to understand "no" only in the direct manner of U.S. businesspersons.

Think Critically

1. Why do different cultures have different ways of saying "no"?
2. What are some other countries that say "no" indirectly?

little value to the literal meanings of words and interpret them figuratively. The general and business subcultures of both Japan and Saudi Arabia are relatively high context. Members of these groups convey information indirectly and implicitly.

The concept of *face-saving* or minimizing personal embarrassment is directly related to contexting. In low-context cultures, people are not too concerned about being personally embarrassed. In high-context cultures, however, personal embarrassment must be avoided at all costs. If you cause a Japanese business partner to lose face by singling him or her out from the group, you have blundered badly. You have jeopardized your personal and business relationship with that person.

✓ **Check**Point

How does a high-context culture communicate differently than a low-context culture?

Nonverbal Communication

Not all communication takes place with language. **Nonverbal communication** is communication that does not involve the use of words. You have probably heard the saying that actions speak louder than words. Actions are an example of nonverbal communication.

Body Language One type of nonverbal communication is called body language. **Body language** refers to the meaning conveyed by facial expressions, upper and lower body movements, and gestures. All cultures and subcultures use body language. However, they do not always attach the same meanings to body language. The meaning of body language is not universal. For example, in Japan, you should cross your legs only at the knees and ankles. You should not rest your foot on your knee. The Japanese believe this position is offensive. They believe the bottom of a foot is unclean and should not be exposed to view.

Appearance In the international business world, your appearance counts. Your clothing has no voice, but it can communicate. Although people dress differently in various parts of the world, they dress similarly when conducting international business. For such purposes, you should dress in a conservative manner. You might, for instance, wear dark-colored suits and white shirts or blouses. As a male, you would choose color-coordinated ties that are not too bright. As a female, you might choose simple jewelry to complement your outfit. Of course, your clothing should be clean and well pressed. Your hair should be carefully groomed, too. Your business associates will be favorably impressed if you always dress and behave in a professional manner. If you care about your appearance, you are likely to care about business matters, too.

Eye Contact Eye movements vary from culture to culture. They are another means of nonverbal communication. In the United States, you should have direct eye contact with the person to whom you are speaking. That is

Work as a Team

Convey an idea using only nonverbal communication techniques.

not the case, however, in South Korea. There you traditionally show respect for the person speaking by looking away from the eyes of the speaker. This is also true in many other Asian cultures.

Touching Touching is another part of nonverbal communication. What kind of touches are acceptable varies worldwide. In Arab countries, business associates hug and kiss each other when they meet. They may also hold hands as they discuss business matters. Such behaviors may be considered inappropriate for business in many other regions of the world.

Personal Space Different cultural groups use space differently for communication purposes. Jordanians confer very close to each other with only a few inches separating them. People in the United States require more distance. They often confer with each other at arm's length. Japanese prefer even more distance between speakers than do people in the United States. When businesspersons with different space requirements interact, they must remember to respect the space needs of others. If they don't, they may find themselves dancing around the room because as one person moves forward, the other steps back.

Color Other forms of nonverbal communication exist. Color is one. For example, the U.S. culture values dental products that produce white teeth. However, in Southeast Asia, teeth blackened by chewing betel nuts are valued. This value could pose a problem for a U.S. company trying to sell its toothpaste in that area of the world.

Numbers Numbers also communicate. In the United Kingdom and continental Europe, the first floor is the floor above the ground floor. The first floor in a building in the United States is customarily the ground floor. Numbers can confuse businesspersons because numbers sometimes carry different meanings in different cultures and subcultures. For example, in many Western countries, the number 13 is considered unlucky. In parts of Asia, the number 11 is a favorable sign.

Emblems Emblems or other symbols communicate. A Canadian could wear a cross-shaped necklace in many countries. However, in a country that does not practice Christianity, doing so would be culturally

Photodisc/Getty Images

COMMUNICATION ACROSS BORDERS

THE CANADIAN HANDSHAKING CODE

Canadian businesspersons customarily shake hands when meeting others. For a Canadian not to shake an associate's hand would be considered impolite and rude.

A brief cursory handshake with only one limp pump suggests little warmth in the relationship. A handshake with several pumps suggests a neutral relationship. An extended handshake with a number of firm pumps suggests a warm and friendly relationship. Such a handshake is usually reserved for close colleagues. Thus, Canadian businesspersons send subtle messages about their relationships with others as they shake hands. In many cases, foreigners are not aware of the cultural meanings Canadian businesspersons attach to their handshakes and miss the intended messages.

Think Critically

1. Why do you think that information about the Canadian handshaking code is not widely known outside of Canada?
2. Locate a web site that provides more information about the cultural practices of Canadians. What surprising information did you uncover?

insensitive. In fact, it is illegal to display non-Islamic religious symbols in Saudi Arabia.

Smells Smells are another means of nonverbal communication. Natural body odors are considered unacceptable in the United States. Selling such products as deodorants and colognes, therefore, is big business. In most African and Middle Eastern countries, body odors are accepted as being natural and distinctive. People there do not try to hide them. Consequently, the market for deodorants and colognes in those regions is much smaller.

Photodisc/Getty Images

✓ CheckPoint

What are some common methods of nonverbal communication?

3-3 Assessment

REVIEW GLOBAL BUSINESS TERMS

Define each of the following terms.

1. contexting
2. nonverbal communication
3. body language

Study Tools
www.cengage.com/school/genbus/intlbiz

REVIEW GLOBAL BUSINESS CONCEPTS

4. Which languages are the most useful for international business purposes? Why?
5. How is nonverbal communication different from other forms of communication?

SOLVE GLOBAL BUSINESS PROBLEMS

You and a friend are discussing which foreign language to study for business purposes. You think you might study Spanish. Your friend is leaning towards French. Both languages are highly recommended for business. Both are widely available throughout the United States.

6. Which language will allow you to talk with more potential customers?
7. Which language is useful in more countries?
8. What are some reasons why it might be sensible to learn the other language anyway?

THINK CRITICALLY

9. Describe ways in which knowing a different language could benefit you both personally and professionally.
10. How long do you think it would take you to learn to communicate in a foreign language like a native speaker does?

MAKE ACADEMIC CONNECTIONS

11. **TECHNOLOGY** How might technology help you learn a foreign language?
12. **MATHEMATICS** Using the data in Figure 3-1, what is the approximate ratio of Spanish speakers to Russian speakers?
13. **CULTURE STUDIES** Why do you think that the Korean culture is likely to be a high-context culture?
14. **GEOGRAPHY** Which is a region where many high-context cultures are found?
15. **COMMUNICATION** Use the Internet to research methods of nonverbal communication and their uses in business situations around the world.

3-4 Values Around the World

- Identify and explain five values that vary from culture to culture.

- Describe the two major reactions to cultural differences.

Photodisc/Getty Images

Values Vary Among Cultures

Values are ideas that people cherish and believe to be important. They tend to vary from culture to culture, often creating major differences among cultures. Some of the more important fundamental values involve individualism versus collectivism, technology, leadership, religion, and time.

INDIVIDUALISM AND COLLECTIVISM

Individualism is the belief in the individual and her or his ability to function relatively independently. Self-reliance, independence, and freedom are closely related to individualism in the United States. However, many other cultures see individualism as undesirable. They do not approve of the negative aspects of self-centeredness and selfishness. Instead, they prefer **collectivism**, the belief that the group is more important than the individual.

The Japanese culture has a strong collective orientation. It has a saying that translates "The nail that stands out is soon pounded down." This saying means that individuals should not stand out from the group. If they do, the group will force these individuals to conform to the expectations of the group. Japanese businesspersons tend to function collectively. Consequently, they do not make decisions without getting consensus, or group agreement. Group harmony is more important to them than individual gain. In contrast, U.S. businesspersons tend to function individually. They often make decisions without consulting fellow employees. Individual gain is more important to them than group harmony.

No culture is based entirely on individualism or collectivism. All cultures have both, but most cultures lean toward one or the other. Cultures that lean toward individualism are apt to value the entrepreneurial spirit. That means people are willing to accept some risk for possible personal gain.

TECHNOLOGY

Fundamental beliefs about technology also vary from culture to culture. Some cultures embrace technology as a means of providing more and better material objects. Most developed countries have business subcultures that view improvements positively. Often less-developed countries have business subcultures that resist improvements in technology. Some countries view technology negatively for cultural or religious reasons. For example, attitudes toward technological change are generally positive in France. In India, they are mixed. India tries to balance the use of technology so that it does not intrude on important spiritual beliefs and displace people from menial tasks. Technological change is viewed at best as neutral and often as negative in some countries. For example, in the People's Republic of China, some Internet content is unavailable because the government has deemed the content inappropriate.

LEADERSHIP, POWER, AND AUTHORITY

Different cultures have different values relating to leadership, power, and authority. These three are shared among a number of different people and institutions in democratic societies. For example, in the United States, the power to govern is divided among the legislative, judicial, and executive branches of the government. That way no one individual or group has too much power.

In authoritarian societies, leadership, power, and authority are granted to a few. Much of the power in these societies seems to be in a chosen person and not in the institution. In the People's Republic of China, the leadership, power, and authority are concentrated in the hands of a few older leaders, who govern without question. They make all of the major decisions, which are carried out by middle-aged bureaucrats. The younger generation essentially has no power. Student protests for more freedom are viewed as threatening the time-honored Chinese tradition of respect for the wisdom of age, which is a major cultural value.

RELIGION

Religious beliefs also regulate the behaviors of members of many cultural groups, including business organizations. Such beliefs influence how people view the world. Some cultural groups are dominated by one religion. This is the case in Iran, for example, which is strongly influenced by Islam. Businesspersons there must follow Islamic practices. Some countries, such as the United States, have several major religions. Businesspersons in those countries must respect the value choices of various religious practices. In some countries, such as the United Kingdom, religion is not a major social force. The relationship between religions and business is controversial. Good arguments can be raised that various religions both encourage and discourage business activity.

TIME

Time is another factor to which different cultural groups attach different meanings. In most developed countries, time is seen as a scarce resource that must be carefully spent. Many business activities are driven by appointments, agendas, schedules, and deadlines. It is viewed this way in both Canada and the United States. In most less-developed countries, time is often viewed as unending cycles of day and night and the seasons. Time is viewed this way

GLOBAL BUSINESS SPOTLIGHT

SAUDI ARABIA PROTECTS ITS OWN CULTURAL VALUES

To work in Saudi Arabia, guest workers and their families must agree to respect and adapt to the Saudi culture. They must live a lifestyle that is acceptable to Saudis. This includes wearing modest clothing and abstaining from alcoholic beverages. Women may not drive and must have written permission from their husbands to travel beyond their neighborhoods. In addition, male chaperones must accompany them.

To reduce the influences of foreign cultures on Saudi culture, guest workers and their families typically live in designated neighborhoods or developments known as compounds. Most of the goods and services needed by guest workers are available in or near their compounds. Consequently, they have little need to interact with most Saudis and have little opportunity to influence Saudi culture.

Think Critically

1. Why would a country such as Saudi Arabia want to protect its culture?
2. What are other ways that countries might limit the influence of foreigners on their cultures?

in many underdeveloped parts of the world. Businesses generally are more successful in cultures that view time as a valuable resource carefully allocated to achieve business objectives.

✓ CheckPoint
Name five major types of values that can vary from culture to culture.

Adjusting to Cultural Differences

In order to be successful, individuals and businesses must adjust to cultural differences. In other words, they must adapt to different cultural values. To show respect for other cultural groups, you may need to make adjustments when dealing with them. These changes will help to minimize the differences that separate the cultural groups. Businesses that operate in other countries adapt to the local culture.

ETHNOCENTRISM

Ethnocentrism is the belief that one's culture is better than other cultures. Ethnocentrism is a major obstacle to conducting successful international business. Cultures and subcultures are different worldwide. However, different does not mean that one is better than the other. Different simply means that the cultures are not alike.

When you engage in international business, you will frequently have to deal with other cultures. Interacting with a person from another culture is called a cross-cultural experience. As an international businessperson, you will have many cross-cultural experiences. With patience and practice, you can learn how to adapt to other cultures.

REACTIONS TO CULTURAL DIFFERENCES

When you enter another culture or subculture, you will experience culture shock. **Culture shock** is a normal reaction to all the differences of another culture. When you experience culture shock, you have a sequence of reactions starting with happiness, followed by frustration, then adaptation, and finally acceptance. When you complete the lengthy culture shock adjustment process, you accept the new culture for what it is and enjoy it.

When you return to your native culture after having been gone for a while, you will experience reverse culture shock. *Reverse culture shock* is your reaction to becoming reacquainted with your own culture after having accepted another culture. Reverse culture shock is a normal reaction to the cultural readjustment process. The intensity of reverse culture shock is determined by the length of time spent in another culture and the degree of isolation from your native culture.

If you return to the United States after a long stay in England, you may notice the excesses of the U.S. culture. For example, room temperatures are carefully controlled. Most areas are brightly lit. People speak in harsher and louder tones. You may be initially overwhelmed by all of the choices. For instance, the grocery store has 50 different cereals from which to choose. You may realize that you are homesick for the other culture. As you readjust to life at home, the symptoms of reverse culture shock decrease. Usually they disappear within a year after a long stay abroad.

Photodisc/Getty Images

To be a successful participant in the global economy, you must be culturally sensitive. You must understand the major role that culture plays in shaping human behavior. You must understand not only your own general culture and its business subculture, but also that of your international business partners. You must consider all the various components of culture and how they affect your international business communication. You must be willing to make accommodations because of differences in your own and your international partners' cultures. Developing cultural sensitivity is one key for success in the global economy.

Work as a Team
Prepare a list of ethnocentric statements U.S. citizens make.

✓ CheckPoint
What are two ways people react to different cultures?

INTERNATIONAL BUSINESS PERSPECTIVE
Culture

THE CHANGING FRENCH BUSINESS LUNCH

Which country offers the best business lunch, a staple of international business? Perhaps the most heard answer around the world is France. French cuisine is highly regarded nearly everywhere.

Food plays an important role in French culture. It serves as both a means of sustaining life and as a treasured art form. Food is usually consumed with animated social conversation over a several hour period. French food is valued for its high-quality ingredients, its proven culinary techniques, and the recognition that time is an important factor in the preparation of outstanding food.

At a formal French lunch, which is sometimes the main meal of the day, you might enjoy *hor d'oeuvres* (side dishes or starters) of thinly sliced smoked meats and assorted vegetables marinated in oil, radishes with butter, and crusty bread. This would be followed by a main course of fish, meat, or poultry or even an omelet with a side of potatoes. Next, you might have a separate vegetable course. It could be asparagus with *hollandaise* (a rich sauce made from egg yolks, butter, and lemon juice). The next course, designed to cleanse your palate, would be a salad with a light vinegar-and-oil dressing. For dessert, you could eat fresh fruit and cheese with *crème gateau* (cake).

Over time the elaborate formal French lunch has given way to something simpler. Today traditional sit-down business lunch often features the *plat du jour* (platter of the day or daily special) at a local *brasserie* (unpretentious restaurant). In a land of civilized lunchers, a ban on smoking and tight budgets are creating gastronomic indignity: gourmet dining is increasingly being replaced by the more economical alternative, sandwiches with French flair.

A taste for sandwiches has grown in France in recent years, especially among young professionals, who in a break from tradition, often eat lunch at their desks. Boutique sandwich bars have sprung up across business districts in Paris and other French cities, offering such fillings as *foie gras* (specially fattened goose liver) with onion *confit* (preserves) to long lines of hungry businesspersons. Chains such as Lina's, home of *le beautiful sandwich*, are taking over as providers of lunchtime fare.

Think Critically

1. How are global business values changing the business lunch in France?
2. Conduct an Internet search for additional information about the food culture of France. How are French meals like and unlike the meals you typically eat?

3-4 | Assessment

REVIEW GLOBAL BUSINESS TERMS

Define each of the following terms.

1. individualism
2. collectivism
3. ethnocentrism
4. culture shock

REVIEW GLOBAL BUSINESS CONCEPTS

5. What are five important value categories that differ from culture to culture?

6. Why do people and businesses need to make adjustments for cultural differences?

SOLVE GLOBAL BUSINESS PROBLEMS

A potential business partner from Shanghai, Wang Jian-Jun, will meet with you next Monday to discuss an opportunity for trading clothes for machinery. Mr. Wang has never traveled to the United States before, and you have never traveled to China. Nonetheless, you know that your cultures are much different. How might you bridge the following cultural differences?

7. Mr. Wang may nod politely or bow slightly when he greets you.

8. Mr. Wang understands some spoken English but communicates primarily in the Wu (Shanghai) dialect of Chinese, which you do not understand.

9. Mr. Wang eats with chopsticks; you eat with a knife, fork, and spoon.

THINK CRITICALLY

10. Why do many people think their native culture is best?

11. Why might it take a year or more of living abroad to get to the point where you enjoy the local culture?

MAKE ACADEMIC CONNECTIONS

12. **TECHNOLOGY** Why might advanced technology be negatively viewed in a developing country with a large, uneducated workforce?

13. **HISTORY** Why did the culture of Iran change considerably after the Shah was removed?

14. **GEOGRAPHY** Why might countries near the equator tend to perceive time in a fluid sense?

15. **LAW** In what countries, besides Iran, is Islamic law found?

CHAPTER SUMMARY

3-1 CULTURE AROUND THE WORLD

A Culture influences global business by shaping the personal and professional behaviors of businesspersons around the world.

B Subcultures are parts of larger cultures that may vary in some aspects from the larger cultures from which they developed.

3-2 CULTURE AND SOCIAL ORGANIZATIONS

A Most societies are at least partially organized around family units. There are both nuclear and extended families.

B Societies are comprised of many institutions. Some of these institutions are schools, religious groups, and professional groups. Gender roles and the degree of mobility differ greatly between cultures.

3-3 COMMUNICATION ACROSS CULTURES

A Although many languages can be used for international business purposes, English is often considered the language of international business.

B Knowing another language is important for global business success because it allows you to transact business much like a native speaker of that language does.

C Direct communication attaches considerable value to words and interprets them literally; indirect communication attaches much less value to words and interprets them figuratively.

D Nonverbal communication influences business activities through such non-word means as body language, appearance, eye contact, touching, personal space, color, numbers, emblems, and smells.

3-4 VALUES AROUND THE WORLD

A Five major types of values that vary from culture to culture involve individualism versus collectivism; technology; leadership, power, and authority; religion; and time.

B Two major reactions to cultural differences are culture shock and reverse culture shock.

GLOBAL **REFOCUS**

Read the Global Focus at the beginning of this chapter, and answer the following questions.

1. Name some locations outside the United States where the Walt Disney Company has theme parks.

2. Why did many French people oppose Euro Disneyland?

3. How did Disney adapt to local culture in France and Hong Kong?

4. Why would the locally popular shark fin soup be pulled from the menu in Hong Kong?

REVIEW GLOBAL BUSINESS TERMS

Match the terms listed with the definitions. Some terms may not be used.

1. A system of learned, shared, unifying, and interrelated beliefs, values, and assumptions.

2. A type of nonverbal communication where facial expressions, upper and lower body movements, and gestures convey what is meant.

3. A group that consists of parents, children, and other relatives living together.

4. Communication that does not involve the use of words.

5. The belief that the group is more important than the individual.

6. A group that consists of a parent or parents and unmarried children living together.

7. The belief in the individual and her or his ability to function relatively independently.

8. The belief that one's culture is better than other cultures.

9. A subset or part of a larger culture.

10. A means of dividing the members of a cultural group into various levels.

11. A normal reaction to all the differences of another culture.

12. The idea that you carry your beliefs, values, and assumptions with you at all times.

a. body language
b. class system
c. collectivism
d. contexting
e. cultural baggage
f. culture
g. culture shock
h. ethnocentrism
i. extended family
j. individualism
k. nonverbal communicaton
l. nuclear family
m. subculture

MAKE GLOBAL BUSINESS DECISIONS

13. How is culture like the programming in a computer?

14. What evidence suggests that geographic attachment is weak in the general U.S. culture and in its subcultures?

15. Swahili is the Bantu language of the Swahili people in eastern Africa. It is also a trade and governmental language among speakers of other languages in Tanzania, Kenya, and parts of Zaire. Do you think this language has significant potential for international business purposes? Why or why not?

16. What do you think is the cultural relationship between the personal space business communicators prefer and touching behaviors?

17. What are some other countries besides the People's Republic of China where leadership, power, and authority are concentrated in the hands of a few people?

18. A good friend recently said that she wouldn't even think of living temporarily in another country. Is her statement ethnocentric? How do you know?

19. Make a list of some of the subcultures to which you belong.

20. What are some common sayings that might reflect important beliefs, values, and assumption of the U.S. business subculture?

21. What benefits related to international business might be derived from reading fiction written in a language other than English?

MAKE ACADEMIC CONNECTIONS

22. **GEOGRAPHY** Using library sources and the Web, investigate how the people of the French-speaking province of Quebec are trying to protect their French cultural heritage. What effects are their actions having on the people in other parts of Canada, who are primarily speakers of English? Do you think these differences will eventually lead to the breakup of Canada? Why or why not? Debate this matter with your classmates.

23. **COMMUNICATIONS** After interviewing a local businessperson, create a poster that depicts his or her cultural baggage.

24. **HISTORY** Find out about the caste system in India, which is a highly structured class system, by interviewing a native of the country or by using library resources. Write a paper that explains the caste system and what the Indian government has done in an attempt to eliminate this system.

25. **CULTURAL STUDIES** Select one primary color (red, yellow, or blue) and one secondary color (orange, green, or purple). Find out what these two colors represent in an eastern and western culture of your choice.

26. **CAREER PLANNING** Interview someone who has worked in another country. What similarities and/or differences did he or she find in the job application process in the other country?

27. **TECHNOLOGY** What are some ways in which technology might be used to benefit learners of a culture?

28. **LANGUAGE** Using library sources and the Internet, investigate one of the accents of the English language. How is the researched accent like and unlike the accent you have?

©Getty Images/PhotoDisc

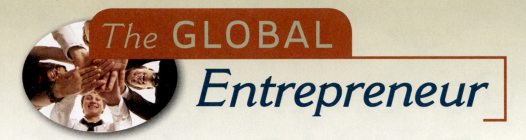

The GLOBAL *Entrepreneur*

CREATING AN INTERNATIONAL BUSINESS PLAN

Cultural Analysis of a Foreign Market

Select a country to research. Prepare a business cultural file with the following information about that nation's culture.

- history that influences current business activities
- languages and verbal and nonverbal communication customs
- education systems and literacy rates
- role of social institutions, such as family, religion, labor unions, and place of employment
- shopping practices and commonly eaten foods unique to the country
- major holidays and customs
- business practices related to place of employment, types of businesses, length of workday, and hiring practices

Sources of information for researching culture include the following.

- printed and online reference materials such as encyclopedias, almanacs, and atlases
- printed and online materials from companies, airlines, travel bureaus, government agencies, and other organizations involved in international business
- interviews with people who have lived in, worked in, or traveled to the country

Prepare a written summary suitable for inclusion in a business plan. Based on the written summary, develop a short oral report. Your report should last about two or three minutes. Present the main findings about the country's culture.

CHAPTER 4

Government and Global Business

4-1 Political Environment and Global Business

4-2 How Government Discourages Global Business

4-3 How Government Encourages Global Business

GLOBAL FOCUS

Foreign Agriculture Service Promotes Food Exports

Each year the United States exports goods worth more than a trillion dollars. About ten percent of these exports are food products such as popcorn, apples, poultry, seafood, and even frozen dinners. The Foreign Agricultural Service (FAS), an agency of the U.S. Department of Agriculture (USDA), helps American farmers and food manufacturers export their products. According to its mission statement, the FAS works to improve foreign market access for U.S. products, build new markets, and improve the competitive position of U.S. agriculture in the global marketplace.

To improve access to existing foreign markets and open new markets, FAS conducts international market research to find the best countries for selling U.S. food products. A database containing information on more than 20,000 foreign buyers of food and agricultural products is used to identify potential customers for U.S. food products. FAS also promotes food and agricultural products at trade shows in Europe, Asia, the Middle East, and Latin America.

Developing agricultural trade policy and negotiating trade agreements are part of the strategy to making U.S. agriculture more completive around the world. FAS is involved in obtaining agreements with other countries to reduce trade barriers in an effort to maintain and expand international sales of U.S. food products.

FAS has trade offices in more than 90 countries—the major foreign markets for U.S. agricultural and food products. This global network includes agricultural economists, marketing specialists, international trade negotiators, and other specialists working devoted to the FAS mission.

Think Critically

1. Why do you think the U.S. government spends tax dollars to promote the export of U.S. agricultural and food products?
2. How might foreign countries benefit by the actions of the Foreign Agricultural Service?
3. Go to the Foreign Agricultural Service web site to obtain additional information about a specific FSA program or career opportunities. Summarize your results in a short oral report.

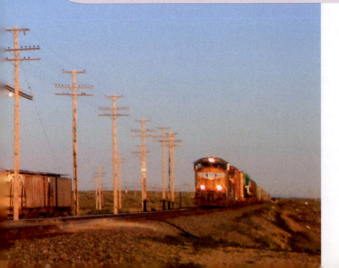

4-1 Political Environment and Global Business

GOALS

- Discuss various political systems around the world.

- Explain the political relations of a company's host and home countries.

Photodisc/Getty Images

Types of Political Systems

A country's economy usually reflects its political system. A **political system** is the means by which people in a society make the rules that control and influence their lives. Political systems vary around the world, ranging from democracy to totalitarianism.

DEMOCRACY

In a **democracy**, all citizens have the opportunity to take part in making the rules that govern them. A democracy emphasizes the importance of the individual's needs and interests. In this political system, people have equal rights, including the right to vote for political leaders. They also have many freedoms, including freedom of speech and freedom of religion.

A democracy's emphasis on individual rights and freedoms extends to its economy. In a democratic society, people have the freedom to own and operate private businesses. Democratic societies, therefore, usually have a market economy. In a country with a market economy, there is little or no government ownership or central planning of business and industry. Individuals or groups of individuals run most businesses. Companies, therefore, either succeed or fail based on their owners' abilities to compete effectively in a market. The United States is basically a market economy.

TOTALITARIANISM

In a **totalitarian system**, most people are excluded from making the rules by which they live. In this system, political control is held by one person, a small group of people, or one political party. Examples of totalitarian systems include monarchy and dictatorship. In a pure monarchy, the right to absolute rule for life is based on heredity. In a military dictatorship, a member of the armed forces makes all the decisions. Although all totalitarian systems are not the same, in a totalitarian system, people's rights and freedoms are restricted. People may not be allowed to express their opinions, to travel freely outside the country, or to practice the religion they choose.

Totalitarian systems usually have command economies. In a command economy, the national government owns and controls almost all businesses. Individuals may be allowed to own a small one-employee business. But the government owns all larger businesses, industries, farms, utilities, transportation, and mining operations. Traditional communist countries, such as Cuba and North Korea, are basically command economies.

MIXED SYSTEMS

In reality, there is no pure form of either a democracy or a totalitarian system. Most political systems are considered mixed. That means they have characteristics of both systems and fall somewhere in between. In the same way, economic systems of most countries are considered mixed systems. In most countries, the majority of businesses are privately owned, and some key industries are owned and run by the government. Key industries include steel production, mining, national airlines, and telephone and public utilities. Many European countries are mixed economies.

✓ CheckPoint
How does a democracy differ from a totalitarian system?

©Alexander Chalkin, 2009/ Used under license from Shutterstock.com

> ## Work as a Team
> Discuss how key industries are owned in your country. Discuss the advantages and disadvantages of this type of ownership for the industries and the citizens.

Political Relations with Host and Home Countries

International business activities can be affected by the political environments in which companies operate. Companies often will have different perceptions of their responsibilities to host and home countries.

GLOBAL COMPANIES OPERATING IN HOST COUNTRIES

A **host country** is the country in which a multinational enterprise is a guest. Multinational enterprises fulfill a number of positive roles in host countries while operating within the existing economic, social, and legal environment.

Multinational enterprises stimulate economic activity. Whenever feasible, they purchase land, goods, and services locally. They provide employment for citizens of the host country. Often they introduce more advanced technologies that help the economic development of the host country.

Host countries expect multinational enterprises to comply with societal expectations and standards. Social responsibility is key to the success or failure of a multinational enterprise. **Social responsibility** is the process whereby people function as good citizens and are sensitive to their surroundings. For example, a multinational enterprise that pollutes the host country's environment is not operating in a socially responsible manner. The company is failing to meet the set standards regarding the environment. The multinational enterprise is harming the environment and its inhabitants.

To have the right to operate within a host country, a multinational enterprise must substantially benefit the host country. The company must be able to document that it operates in full compliance with the local social and legal standards. If a multinational enterprise does not meet these conditions, then the host country may restrict or deny its right to conduct business. In rare cases where the offensive actions are long-standing or serious, the government of the host country might seize the assets of the multinational enterprise.

A GLOBAL COMPANY'S RELATIONSHIP WITH ITS HOME COUNTRY

In addition to being a good guest while conducting business around the globe, a multinational enterprise has responsibilities in its home country. A **home country** is the country where a multinational enterprise is headquartered. A multinational enterprise is expected to comply with the home country's social, economic, and legal mandates.

The home country expects multinational enterprises based within its borders to demonstrate social responsibility. Multinational companies must comply with societal expectations and standards and meet both the spirit and the letter of the laws of their home country.

Improper actions could jeopardize the ongoing operations of the business. Fines, sanctions, and other legal actions are possible. In the most serious cases, the multinational enterprise could be restricted from engaging in business in the home country.

 ✓ **Check**Point
What is social responsibility, and why is it important?

INTERNATIONAL BUSINESS PERSPECTIVE
History

TEOTIHUACAN

Imagine a city of 200,000 people with a well-planned road system, production facilities, beautiful art, and ball courts for sports. This sounds like a modern city of today. However, the city of Teotihuacan, located about 40 kilometers (25 miles) northeast of Mexico City, declined into ruins more than 1,300 years ago.

The civilization of Teotihuacan began around 200 B.C. and flourished until about 650 A.D. During this period, the city was an influential commercial and religious center. The people of Teotihuacan developed many art forms into a high degree of elegance, including sculpture, ceramics, stone masks, and murals. In addition, major monuments were constructed, including the Pyramid of the Moon and the Pyramid of the Sun.

The people of Teotihuacan had close contact with the Mayan culture in the Yucatan area of Mexico and Guatemala. They were also a strong influence on later Mexican cultures, such as the Aztecs.

Today Teotihuacan is an archaeological site. This location contains the remains of the largest pre-Columbian city in the Western Hemisphere. The Avenue of the Dead, the city's main roadway, can still be seen passing through the ruins of temples and other structures.

Think Critically

1. Conduct an Internet search for Teotihuacan to obtain information about the commercial activities in this ancient city. Prepare a one-page report of your findings.
2. In what ways did the Teotihuacan society influence current international business activities?

Photodisc/Getty Images

4-1 Assessment

REVIEW GLOBAL BUSINESS TERMS

Define each of the following terms.

1. political system
2. democracy
3. totalitarian system
4. host country
5. social responsibility
6. home country

REVIEW GLOBAL BUSINESS CONCEPTS

7. How are businesses owned in a democracy?
8. How are businesses owned in a totalitarian system?
9. What relationship does a global company have with a host country and its home country?

SOLVE GLOBAL BUSINESS PROBLEMS

For each of the following descriptions, determine whether the country is a democracy, totalitarian system, or mixed system.

10. Farmers must produce a required quantity of crops to meet government requirements.
11. Citizens are free to start and operate any kind of business.
12. Government owns most businesses.
13. Government regulates some large businesses in the essential industries, but the businesses are mostly privately owned.

THINK CRITICALLY

14. Would a totalitarian system of government encourage or discourage trade with other countries?
15. Explain how a host country might put political pressure on a global company operating within its borders.

MAKE ACADEMIC CONNECTIONS

16. **HISTORY** Obtain information about changes in the past ten years to the political systems operating in various eastern European countries.
17. **CULTURAL STUDIES** Describe the incentives workers have to achieve high standards of production in a totalitarian system.

How Government Discourages Global Business

AP Photo/ Khaled El-fiqi

Government Activities Influence Business

Every day businesses throughout the world must comply with thousands of government laws and regulations. Some of these laws protect workers and consumers while others protect domestic businesses. In both cases the laws have the potential for discouraging international business.

LAWS THAT PROTECT WORKERS AND CONSUMERS

Why do governments regulate businesses? Often it is to protect the health and safety of workers. Many countries establish occupational protection laws to protect workers from dangerous conditions on the job. For example, in many countries, the law requires factory workers to wear safety equipment such as protective eye goggles, hard hats, and earplugs. Other worker protection laws prohibit employing children as farm or factory workers. Today there is growing interest in establishing safety requirements for employees who use computers all day.

   In addition to occupational protection laws, governments establish consumer protection laws to ensure that products are safe to use. For example, most developed countries require that all food ingredients be listed on product labels. And most developed countries have electrical safety standards to protect consumers from purchasing faulty electrical appliances, such as hair dryers and toasters. Laws also exist to protect consumers from deceptive or false advertising practices, such as claiming a particular medicine can cure the common cold.

Complying with worker and consumer protection laws usually increases the cost of doing business for companies. These increased costs may make a product less competitive with products manufactured in countries that do not have such laws. In general, occupational and consumer protection laws are not as strict in poor developing countries as they are in major industrialized countries. A product made in Canada will probably cost more than a similar product made in Mexico, even if both are sold in Ireland.

TRADE BARRIERS

Specific actions by governments can directly discourage or prevent the growth of international business. To protect local businesses from foreign competition, governments may establish trade barriers. *Trade barriers* are government actions or policies that make it difficult to trade across borders. Governments that establish such trade barriers are enforcing protectionism. **Protectionism** is a government policy of protecting local or domestic industries from foreign competition. Governments impose restrictions on foreign competition in several ways.

- Establishing tariffs or customs duties to increase the price of imported products
- Placing quotas on the importing of certain products
- Requiring domestic companies to boycott particular countries
- Enacting restrictive licensing requirements for importers

Tariffs A government can place a tariff, or duty, on imported products. A tariff, or **duty**, is a tax placed on products that are traded internationally. Duties raise the cost of the product to the importer, which discourages consumers from buying the imported product. Duties are a common trade barrier.

Quotas Governments also may place quotas on certain imported products. A **quota** is a limit on the quantity or monetary amount of a product that can be imported from a given country. Once the quota has been

GLOBAL BUSINESS SPOTLIGHT

CONSUMER PROTECTION LAWS AROUND THE WORLD

Many countries have laws to protect people who buy and use products. Here are a few examples.

- In Canada, packages and labels must be printed in both French and English.
- In Venezuela, the price of every retail product must be clearly marked, together with the date on which the price was marked.
- In Belgium, laws limit how loud a lawn mower engine can be.
- In Greece, advertising toys on television is not allowed.

Think Critically

1. How might consumer protection laws affect international business activities?
2. Conduct an Internet search to locate examples of laws in various countries that are designed to protect consumers. Present your findings to the class.

met, no more of that product can be imported for a certain period of time. The quota creates a limited supply of the imported good and increases the price. This action attempts to protect domestic products from too much foreign competition. Import quotas have been used to protect the textile, shoe, automobile, and steel industries in some countries.

Boycotts Sometimes a government issues an absolute restriction on the import of certain products from certain countries. This is called a **boycott**. For example, in India, the importation of many consumer goods is banned. This ban forces foreign companies that want to sell consumer goods in India to invest in India and manufacture the products locally. Norway protects its apple and pear producers by allowing imports only after the domestic crop has been sold.

Licensing requirements Some governments control imports by requiring that companies have a government *import license*. The license grants permission to import a product. This license can be withdrawn at any time.

Eliminating trade barriers can encourage "free trade." However, some smaller and less-developed economies may not be able to compete in the global marketplace. The "fair trade" movement has attempted to create a more equitable international trade environment. Access the web site shown below and click on the link for Chapter 4. Read the article entitled "Free Trade vs. Fair Trade." According to the article, what are some differences between free trade and fair trade? Explain how free trade can hurt disadvantaged workers and business owners?

www.cengage.com/school/genbus/intlbiz

✓ **CheckPoint**

What are four trade barriers governments use to directly discourage international business?

Political Risks in International Business

The possibility of government actions or political policies that could adversely affect foreign companies is called *political risk*. Major political risks to international business include trade sanctions, expropriation, economic nationalism, and civil unrest or war. All of these actions can temporarily or permanently disrupt global business activities.

TRADE SANCTIONS

Governments can impose trade restrictions against another country to protest that country's behavior. This use of trade barriers is usually the direct result of political disputes between countries. For example, in the early 1990s, the United States banned the sale of high-technology equipment to China. The United States was protesting China's apparent sale of missile technology to Pakistan, which violated an international arms-control agreement.

Trade sanctions range from tariffs to boycotts. A country can impose a **trade embargo** against another country and stop all import-export trade with that country. In recent years, the United States issued a trade embargo against several countries due to various political differences, one of those being acts of international terrorism. These embargoes banned the export of any goods, technology, or services from the United States to those countries.

GLOBAL BUSINESS SPOTLIGHT

POLITICAL RISKS AND PERSONAL DANGER

While companies face risk when doing business in other countries, individuals may also be in danger. Workers and travelers may encounter robberies, attacks, and abductions while living in or visiting another nation.

The U.S. State Department issues travel warnings to reduce the chance of danger for people involved in international activities. These public notices list countries to which Americans are advised not to travel.

Think Critically

1. Find examples of current travel warnings. What are some common warnings?
2. What factors create potential dangers for people working and living in other countries?

EXPROPRIATION

Expropriation occurs when a government takes control and ownership of foreign-owned assets and companies. In 2009, the president of Venezuela ordered the expropriation of an American-owned rice processing plant when the company allegedly violated government price controls.

ECONOMIC NATIONALISM

Economic nationalism is a political force that can also create political risk for companies conducting international trade. **Economic nationalism** refers to the trend of some countries to restrict foreign ownership of companies and to establish laws that protect against foreign imports. Economic nationalism is a form of protectionism. Protectionist governments may encourage their people to "buy domestic" instead of purchasing imported products.

CIVIL UNREST OR WAR

Civil unrest interrupts production, sales, and other business activities. Transportation of goods may be hindered, and people may not be able to shop because of a curfew, gunfire, or rioting. When unrest escalates to war, there is often massive destruction of property and goods. A war with another country has the same kind of disruptive effect on business activities.

✓ **Check**Point

Name four political risks that can seriously affect global business.

International Taxes

Governments collect revenues to pay for welfare programs, to build roads and bridges, to provide health care insurance, and to support military forces, among many other things. Revenue to pay for these programs comes from many types of taxes, including taxes on purchases, property, income, and wealth.

CUSTOMS DUTY

A *customs duty*, or import tax, is a tax assessed on imported products. While sometimes used by governments as an import trade barrier, customs duties are also collected to raise revenue to pay for government programs.

SALES TAX

A *sales tax* is a tax on the sale of products. The consumer pays it at the time of purchase. Sales taxes are considered *regressive* taxes because the same rate of tax is charged to all consumers, no matter what their income level. Some countries, such as Singapore and Canada, have taxes similar to sales taxes called consumption taxes or goods and services taxes (GST).

EXCISE TAX

An *excise tax* is a tax levied on the sale or consumption of specific products or commodities—such as alcoholic beverages, tobacco, telephone service, airline tickets, gasoline, and motor vehicles. For example, the United States collects gasoline excise taxes for highway construction and repair. These taxes are often based on the "benefits received" principle, meaning that only drivers, who would receive the most benefit from well-maintained highways, are assessed the tax.

PAYROLL-RELATED TAX

Payroll-related taxes fall into two categories: taxes withheld from employee pay and taxes paid by the employer based on employee pay. Taxes to pay for Social Security and Medicare fall into both categories. The taxes are withheld from employees' pay and the employer makes a matching payment. Income taxes are withheld from employees' pay. Payroll taxes paid by the employer include unemployment taxes and worker's compensation taxes.

VALUE-ADDED TAX (VAT)

A *value-added tax* (VAT) is a tax assessed on the increase in value of goods from each stage of production to final consumption. The tax on each stage is levied on the value that has been added before moving the product to the next stage. Value-added taxes are used in most European countries. VAT is similar to a national sales tax.

INCOME TAXES

A tax on the amount of income a person or corporation earns, minus allowable deductions and credits, is called an *income tax*. Income tax is usually a *progressive* tax because the percentage a person pays increases, or progresses, the more income a person makes. This tax is based on the "ability to pay" principle—the more income a person has, the more tax that person is able to pay.

Corporations also pay income tax, which is based on corporate annual income, minus allowable business deductions and tax credits. Governments may give companies various tax credits to enable them to purchase new equipment, invest in research and development, and employ new people.

A corporate income tax is viewed as an *indirect* business tax on consumers. Corporations pass along the cost of the tax indirectly to the consumer by charging a higher price for the goods or services sold or produced by the company.

Work as a Team
Describe the characteristics of what most people would consider a "fair" tax.

✓ CheckPoint
What are the common types of taxes paid by consumers and businesses?

4-2 Assessment

www.cengage.com/school/genbus/intlbiz

REVIEW GLOBAL BUSINESS TERMS

Define each of the following terms.

1. protectionism
2. duty
3. quota
4. boycott
5. trade embargo
6. expropriation
7. economic nationalism

REVIEW GLOBAL BUSINESS CONCEPTS

8. Why do governments establish trade barriers to discourage international business?
9. What political risks could companies encounter when doing business in other countries?
10. What is the "ability to pay" principle of taxation?

SOLVE GLOBAL BUSINESS PROBLEMS

Decide if the following situations would increase or decrease the political risk faced by companies involved in international business.

11. A country reduces custom duties on imports.
12. A trade embargo has been created by a nation against several of its major trading partners.
13. The ruling party in a country has changed three times in the past five years.
14. A host country expands its use of expropriation.
15. The government of a country eliminates import quotas.

THINK CRITICALLY

16. What problems might an international company have when trying to do business in a country that is fighting a civil war?
17. How can taxes be used by the government to encourage or discourage the use of a certain good or service?

MAKE ACADEMIC CONNECTIONS

18. **HISTORY** Find examples of war or civil unrest that resulted in a company having buildings taken away or destroyed.
19. **CULTURAL STUDIES** Go to the web site for Transparency International and Transparency USA to obtain information about the political risks in other countries.
20. **LAW** Go to the web site of the Internal Revenue Service to obtain information about current tax rates for U.S. taxpayers.

How Government Encourages Global Business

Photodisc/Getty Images

GOALS

- **Explain government actions that can encourage global business activities.**

- **Discuss U.S. government agencies that can help reduce international risk.**

- **Describe how tax incentives encourage global business.**

Encouraging International Business

Specific actions by governments encourage and promote international business. Governments around the world encourage domestic industries to export by providing export counseling and training, export insurance, and export subsidies and tax credits. Governments view exporting as an effective way to create jobs and expand economic prosperity. Governments encourage business through a number of techniques.

- Establishing free-trade zones
- Granting most-favored-nation status
- Establishing free-trade agreements
- Providing export insurance to exporters to guarantee against commercial and political risks
- Providing free or subsidized export marketing assistance to exporters to help research foreign markets and promote their products in other countries
- Providing tax incentives for foreign companies to invest and to locate manufacturing plants in their countries
- Reducing or eliminating trade barriers such as tariffs and quotas

Free-trade zones To promote international business, governments often create free-trade zones in their countries. A **free-trade zone** is a designated area, usually around a seaport or airport, where products can be imported duty-free and then stored, assembled, and used in manufacturing. Only when the product leaves the zone does the importer pay duty.

Most Favored Nation A government can also encourage international trade by granting most-favored-nation status to other countries.

Latin American Integration
Association Members

Figure 4-1 The Latin American
Integration Association took over
from the Latin American Free
Trade Association in 1981.

Most-favored-nation (MFN) status
allows a country to export into the
granting country under the most favorable trade conditions that the importing
country offers to any of its trading partners. Products from countries with MFN
status are subject to the lowest duty rate.
In some cases the lowest rate is zero.

Free-trade Agreements A growing
trend throughout the world is for countries to establish free-trade agreements
with each other. Under a **free-trade
agreement**, member countries agree
to eliminate duties and trade barriers
on products traded among members.
This results in increased trade between
the members. For example, the United
States, Canada, and Mexico signed the
North American Free Trade Agreement
(NAFTA) in 1993. NAFTA eliminated
duties on many goods traded among the
three countries. This action also eased
transportation restrictions for movement
of goods among the countries. In addition to NAFTA, the United States has
free trade arrangements with more than
30 other countries through various regional and bilateral trade agreements.

Another example of a free-trade agreement is the Latin American Integration
Association (LAIA). Its members
include Argentina, Bolivia, Brazil, Chile,
Colombia, Cuba, Ecuador, Mexico,
Paraguay, Peru, Uruguay, and Venezuela.
The goal of LAIA is to further trade
between member states and promote regional economic integration. The
member countries of LAIA are shown in Figure 4-1.

Common markets Some countries join together in a common market
to promote more trade among members. In a **common market**, members
eliminate duties and other trade barriers, allow companies to invest freely
in each member's country, and allow workers to move freely across borders.
Common-market members also have a common external duty on products
being imported from nonmember countries. Examples of common markets
include the European Union (EU) and the Southern Cone Common Market
(Mercosur) originally formed by Argentina, Brazil, Paraguay, and Uruguay, with
Bolivia, Chile, Colombia, Ecuador, Peru, and Venezuela also participating.

✓ **Check**Point
What are four ways governments can encourage global business?

Government Protection from International Risk

How can a company protect itself from international political risk? U.S. companies can protect their international sales and assets by using the services of two U.S. government agencies—the Export-Import Bank of the United States (EXIM) and the Overseas Private Investment Corporation (OPIC).

EXIM is the U.S. government agency that helps to finance the export sales of U.S. products. It provides export loans, export loan guarantees, and export credit insurance. An exporting company can purchase an export credit insurance policy from EXIM that will provide 100 percent protection from political risk for international sales. This includes protection from foreign governments that refuse to convert local currency to dollars. It also covers damage or destruction of a shipment caused by wars, revolutions, and civil disorders. If these political actions occur, the exporter can then file a claim with EXIM for 100 percent reimbursement of all export sales losses.

The Overseas Private Investment Corporation (OPIC) provides investment insurance to U.S. companies that establish operations in developing countries. A U.S. company can protect its overseas investment by purchasing OPIC insurance. This shields the company from several types of political risk—including expropriation and damage or destruction caused by war, revolution, terrorism, and sabotage. If any of these political actions occur, the U.S. company can file a claim with OPIC to recover financial losses.

 **CheckPoint**

For what types of political risks does the Overseas Private Investment Corporation provide protection?

A Question of Ethics

PAYING FOR SPECIAL FAVORS

Aggressive companies in some regions of the world commonly use payoffs to gain access to new markets. Some countries consider bribes to be tax-deductible business expenses. However, U.S. companies can face hefty fines and prison sentences when U.S. laws are violated. The Foreign Corrupt Practices Act (FCPA) prohibits bribery of foreign government officials by U.S. businesspeople. FCPA is designed to prevent obtaining favorable business decisions using methods that would be illegal in the United States. Companies may be fined up to $2 million for violations. In recent years, the United Nations has adopted similar anti-bribery rules.

Sometimes companies cave in to local customs. A U.S. computer company offered Chinese journalists the equivalent of $12 to attend its news conferences. The company said the money was for taxi fares; however, the amount was equal to a week's pay for some journalists.

Think Critically

According to the guidelines for ethical analysis, are the payments to Chinese journalists ethical?

GLOBAL TECHNOLOGY TRENDS

Online Exporting Assistance

What are the best countries for exporting electronics components? How can I contact distributors in Asia to sell packaged food products? These and many other questions can be easily answered online. Various government agencies and other organizations offer extensive information related to international business activities, including exporting.

- The International Trade Administration of the U.S. Department of Commerce offers information on exporting, trade missions, and trade statistics.
- Export.Gov offers information about exporting, foreign markets, and trade shows.
- U.S. Customs and Border Protection offers importing and exporting information.

- The U.S. Small Business Administration provides assistance in starting an export business.
- The Foreign Agricultural Service offers information about exporting food products.
- The Federation of International Trade Associations offers access to many global business resources.

Think Critically

1. Using one of the resources mentioned above, obtain specific information that would be useful to a company involved in exporting.
2. How do these web sites benefit businesses, consumers, and society?

Tax Incentives

A basic practice of companies is to treat all business taxes as regular business costs. Companies recover those costs by increasing the price of the products they sell. The actual burden of tax payment, therefore, is usually shifted to consumers in the form of higher prices.

In conducting international business, U.S. companies want to avoid being taxed twice on income they earn from their foreign operations. The U.S. government allows companies a corporate tax deduction on income earned by their foreign subsidiaries.

The U.S. government has double-taxation avoidance treaties with some countries. This provides relief from double taxation of U.S. multinational corporations. This is a *tax incentive* that foreign governments use to attract U.S. companies to invest in their countries and create local jobs. U.S. companies are more likely to invest in countries with a favorable tax environment.

As a further tax incentive, many foreign governments provide a foreign company with a tax holiday. A **tax holiday** means the corporation does not pay corporate income taxes if it invests in their country. These tax holidays may last for as long as ten years.

✓ **Check**Point
How does the U.S. government protect U.S. companies from double taxation?

4-3 Assessment

REVIEW GLOBAL BUSINESS TERMS

Define each of the following terms.

1. free-trade zone
2. most-favored-nation (MFN) status
3. free-trade agreement
4. common market
5. tax holiday

Study Tools

www.cengage.com/school/genbus/intlbiz

REVIEW GLOBAL BUSINESS CONCEPTS

6. Why do countries join in free-trade agreements?

7. How do U.S. government agencies help reduce political risks for companies involved in international business?

8. Why do governments give tax incentives to foreign companies to invest in their countries?

SOLVE GLOBAL BUSINESS PROBLEMS

For the following situations, name the type of action being taken to encourage international business among countries.

9. Countries in Africa decide to join together to eliminate tariffs and other trade barriers.

10. A country in eastern Europe attempts to attract foreign investors by eliminating their taxes for the next seven years.

11. The U.S. agrees to allow imports from selected countries at the lowest customs duty rates.

12. Mexico and Israel agree to eliminate certain tariffs and trade barriers on products sold between the two countries.

13. A Middle Eastern country designates an area for manufacturing with no import duties.

THINK CRITICALLY

14. What actions might a government take to attract foreign companies to do business in its country?

15. How does a common-market agreement benefit citizens of a member country?

MAKE ACADEMIC CONNECTIONS

16. **GEOGRAPHY** How might the natural resources in a region encourage countries to join together to create a common market?

17. **TECHNOLOGY** Locate a web site for your state department of commerce or other state government agency that promotes international trade by companies in your state. Find out what tax and financial incentives are available to attract foreign companies to invest in your state.

CHAPTER SUMMARY

4-1 POLITICAL ENVIRONMENT AND GLOBAL BUSINESS

A The main political systems operating in the world are democracies, totalitarian systems, and mixed systems.

B A multinational company must operate within existing economic, social, and legal constraints of a host country. In addition, the company is expected to comply with the social, economic, and legal mandates of its home country.

4-2 HOW GOVERNMENT DISCOURAGES GLOBAL BUSINESS

A A government can discourage international trade with protectionism policies, tariffs, quotas, boycotts, and licensing requirements.

B Political risks can disrupt global business activities through trade sanctions (such as embargoes), expropriation, economic nationalism, and civil unrest or war.

C The main taxes governments impose are customs duties, sales taxes, excise taxes, payroll-related taxes, value-added taxes, and income taxes.

4-3 HOW GOVERNMENT ENCOURAGES GLOBAL BUSINESS

A A government can encourage international business with free-trade zones, most-favored-nation status, and free-trade agreements.

B The Export-Import Bank of the United States (EXIM) provides export loans, export loan guarantees, and export credit insurance. The Overseas Private Investment Corporation (OPIC) provides investment insurance to U.S. companies that establish operations in developing countries.

C A government can encourage international business with tax incentives such as tax credits on foreign income, double-taxation avoidance treaties, and tax holidays.

GLOBAL **REFOCUS**

Read the Global Focus at the beginning of this chapter, and answer the following questions.

1. You are the manufacturer of Grandma's Original Jams and Jellies. In what ways could the FAS help you develop export markets for your products?

2. FAS also guarantees loan payments to U.S. banks for foreign sales of U.S. agricultural commodities. Why is this necessary and how does it help U.S. banks.

3. The USDA provides export subsidies, or grants, to U.S. farmers who export. How could this be viewed as an obstacle for a foreign farmer who does not receive export subsidies from his or her own government but is trying to export?

REVIEW GLOBAL BUSINESS TERMS

Match the terms listed with the definitions that follow.

1. A government system in which political control is held by one person, a small group of people, or one political party.

2. A tax on imported products.

3. A limit on the amount of a product that can be imported from a given country.

4. Government policy used to protect local, or domestic, industries from foreign competition.

5. The country in which a multinational enterprise is headquartered.

6. Designated area where products can be imported duty-free.

7. Designation given to certain countries that allows their products to be imported into the granting country under the most favorable trade conditions that the importing country offers to any of its trading partners.

8. An arrangement between countries that eliminates duties and trade barriers on products traded among members.

9. A policy of restricting foreign ownership of local companies and hindering foreign imports.

a. boycott
b. common market
c. democracy
d. duty
e. economic nationalism
f. expropriation
g. free-trade agreement
h. free-trade zone
i. home country
j. host country
k. most-favored-nation (MFN) status
l. political system
m. protectionism
n. quota
o. social responsibility
p. tax holiday
q. totalitarian system
r. trade embargo

10. The process whereby people function as good citizens and are sensitive to their surroundings.

11. Complete ban on any trade with a particular country.

12. A political system in which all people have the opportunity to take part in making the rules that govern them.

13. A country in which a multinational enterprise is a guest.

14. Member countries eliminate trade barriers, encourage investment, and allow workers to move freely across borders.

15. Means by which people in a society make the rules that control and influence their lives.

16. Government takeover of a foreign-owned business.

17. Absolute restriction on the import of certain products from certain countries.

18. Tax incentive used by governments to attract foreign investment where a corporation does not pay income taxes for a time after investing.

MAKE GLOBAL BUSINESS DECISIONS

19. As a consumer, why might you object to your government creating import trade barriers, such as high customs duties or restrictive import quotas?

20. How could the study of international affairs and world current events help a company anticipate and evaluate potential political risks around the world?

21. How effective do you think trade embargoes are as a method of "punishing" another country for its actions?

22. What factors, other than tax incentives, should companies evaluate before deciding to invest in a particular country?

23. What services are provided by the U.S. government to help promote the export of nonagricultural products, such as manufactured products and consumer goods?

MAKE ACADEMIC CONNECTIONS

24. **TECHNOLOGY** What types of laws might be needed to protect workers and consumers as a result of the expanded use of computers?

25. **GEOGRAPHY** Conduct research to obtain information about various free-trade agreements, such as the European Union, MERCOSUR, and ASEAN. Prepare a map that shows the countries involved in these organizations.

26. **COMMUNICATIONS** Interview a small business owner about the actions of government (local, state, and federal) that influence business activities. What ways has government made it more difficult to do business? What ways has government helped business?

27. **CULTURAL STUDIES** Talk to people who have lived in or visited other countries. How do political freedoms differ in those countries compared to the freedoms in the United States?

28. **LAW** Prepare arguments in favor of and in opposition to legislative actions for the creation of trade barriers, such as higher tariffs and import quotas.

29. **MATHEMATICS** One household has an annual income of $40,000 while another has an annual income of $80,000. Each household spends $10,000 a year on food. If the sales tax on food is 5 percent, show how this would be an example of a regressive tax.

30. **CAREER PLANNING** Conduct library research about another country's government regulations of wages, employment opportunities, and occupational safety.

31. **TECHNOLOGY** Use the Internet to find examples of trade barriers in use around the world today.

32. **TECHNOLOGY** Use the Internet to find a list of all the current members of a free-trade zone or a common market.

33. **POLITICAL SCIENCE** Create a list of ten countries. Using information collected on the Internet, classify each country's government as a democracy, totalitarian system, or mixed.

The GLOBAL

Entrepreneur

CREATING AN INTERNATIONAL BUSINESS PLAN

Assessing Political Risk and Legal Restrictions

As a company considers doing business in another country, the political and legal environment must be assessed. To help evaluate the advantages and disadvantages, as well as the risks, of making such an expensive investment, companies collect specific information about the "investment climate" of the country. The more favorable the climate, the more likely the company will profit from the investment.

Using your international business file and research skills, gather information on the investment climate for a country. Prepare a written or short oral report with information on the following topics.

1. Political stability of the country and possible civil disruptions.

2. Labor laws, labor costs, and occupational safety laws.

3. Trade barriers or investment restrictions.

4. Tax and other investment incentives to foreign companies.

5. Laws concerning establishing or restricting investment.

6. Other information you think for important to making an investment decision.

Compare the investment climate of your chosen country with those of other students. Which countries would be the best locations for manufacturing plants? Sources of information to research the country may include the following.

- reference books such as encyclopedias, almanacs, and atlases

- current newspaper articles from the news, business, and travel sections

- current news and business magazine articles, including news stories, company profiles, and advertisements

- Internet search for country information

- interviews with people who have lived in, worked in, or traveled to the country

Photodisc/Getty Images

GLOBAL Cross-Cultural Team Project

Explore International Business Environments

Each day, millions of people work in teams to plan and implement business activities. The activities of these teams range from creating new products for international markets to cross-cultural negotiations for joint venture agreements. While many teams involve people from the same country or similar cultures, other work groups require interaction among people with different backgrounds.

Goal

Explore economic, geographic, political, and cultural influences on a region's business activities.

Activities

Working in teams, select a geographic region you will represent—Africa, Asia, Europe, Latin America, Middle East, or North America.

1. Conduct research about the geography, culture, and business activities of several countries in your region. Obtain information from printed and online resources, and by talking to people who have lived in or visited that area.
2. Identify geographic factors that are unique to your region, such as climate, terrain, and natural resources. Describe how they might affect business activities.
3. Describe how the unique customs, traditions, and culture of your regions affect international business activities. Provide three examples of how these things influence business activities using a different country for each example. Your examples might focus on how business cards are exchanged or what types of gifts are considered appropriate to exchange with business partners.
4. Research the economic systems and conditions in the region. Identify economic influences on business that are unique to this region.
5. Describe political situations and business regulations in your region. How do these things influence international business?
6. **Global Business Decision** An international organization plans to do business in various countries in your region. What can it do to ensure success? What products or services might be most successful in your region?

Team Skill   Benefits of Cross-Cultural Teams

Discuss with your team members the benefits of working on cross-cultural teams for both employees and business organizations. How might the geographic and cultural influences of your regions shape team activities and decision-making?

Present

- Write an individual report summarizing your regional findings and your experiences working on this simulated cross-cultural team.
- Create and present a team summary describing the business environments in your region. Consider using an in-class presentation, video, web site, newsletter, poster, photo display, slide presentation, or display of items (maps, clothing, food, music, packages, money) from your region.

International Business Plan Event

International trade has opened new opportunities for increased business profits. Multinational companies realize the value of locating in more than one country. Some companies complete different phases of their business process in countries that are the most cost effective.

One to three students will write an international business plan for conducting business in a country other than the United States. You will apply marketing skills in an international setting. The body of the business plan cannot be more than 30 pages. This project requires you to research the demographics of the country where you will locate your business. You must also consider customs, political conditions, trade regulations, currency exchange, and other cultural factors that will influence your business in the other country. Your international business plan must follow the guidelines that appear in the DECA Guide. These guidelines are also available online at the DECA web site.

The competition consists of two parts: the written document and the oral presentation. The written document will account for 60 points and the oral presentation will account for 40 points.

Performance Indicators Evaluated

- Define the reasons for locating your business in a foreign country.
- Define the demographics of the country.
- Explain special considerations for locating a business in a foreign country.
- Explain the management function of your business.
- Describe the political, social, and economic factors to consider for your business.
- Develop financial statements that project the financial results of your business.
- Describe how the workforce in the foreign country is suited for your business.
- Explain training, development, and management of your workforce.

For more detailed information about performance indicators, go to the DECA web site.

Think Critically

1. Why do U.S. businesses move to other countries?
2. Why is more research required before deciding to locate a business in another country?
3. Why are demographics so important to consider for international business?
4. How will you handle U.S. workers concerned about outsourcing jobs?

www.deca.org

UNIT 2

Organizing for International Business

Chapter

5 Structures of International Business Organizations

6 Importing, Exporting, and Trade Relations

7 Foreign Exchange and International Finance

8 Legal Agreements Around the World

9 Global Entrepreneurship and Small Business Management

Asia-Pacific Rim

If You Were There

...Present-day Java

Rahayu was born in the city of Jakarta on the island of Java in Indonesia. Once known as the Dutch East Indies, Indonesia is an archipelago, made up of thousands of islands, located south of the Asian mainland. The teen speaks Bahasa Indonesian, the official language, but he often hears Dutch, English, and local languages such as Javanese in the capital city where more than 8 million people live. Rahayu sells food to tourists and thinks about moving west to Sumatra where relatives work on offshore oil rigs.

...Present-day Japan

Taro was born in Toyota City, in Aichi Prefecture on Japan's largest island. Toyota City is the ultimate company town. Taro attends a Toyota-owned school, lives in a Toyota-built home, and plans to work in a Toyota facility. He looks forward to making an excellent salary and continuing to enjoy the natural beauty, rich heritage, and culture of his community.

©CHEN WEI SENG, 2009/ Used under license from Shutterstock.com

Early Asian Civilizations

Archaeologists believe that one of the earliest Asian civilizations flourished from about 2500 to 1600 B.C. Its ruins lie in present-day Pakistan and India in the Indus River Valley. These ancient Asian cities included well-planned streets, large public buildings, and multistory houses with indoor bathrooms.

Our knowledge of early Chinese civilization comes from the discovery of oracle bones that were used instead of paper. Priests in the Shang Dynasty (1700 to 1000 B.C.) would scratch a question to their ancestors on an animal bone before firing the bone, forcing it to crack. The priest would interpret the pattern of cracks as an answer to the question.

China, Oldest Civilization in the World

China has the oldest continuous civilization in the world. Mountain barriers, the Gobi Desert, and large bodies of water have protected it from invasion and cultural influences for centuries. For added protection, the Great Wall in northern China was completed in about 200 B.C. By the 19th century A.D., a weak Chinese dynasty gave in to European demands for trading privileges, causing large sections of China to be claimed by Great Britain, France, Germany, Russia, and Japan. This control was the result of a series of unequal treaties that established the basic pattern for China's relations with the West for the next century. The communist government of the People's Republic of China (the ruling party since 1949) reacted to this western influence by isolating China. However, recent economic reforms have led to a more open policy.

Japan, From Isolation to a Global Economy

The Japanese archipelago consists of four main islands and thousands of smaller ones. Together these islands make up the modern nation of Japan. Japan's history is rather brief when compared to that of India or China. By 500 A.D., it was ruled by emperors and powerful clans (noble families). The shoguns (great generals) took power in the twelfth century and created the shogunate (military government) that lasted until 1867.

Photodisc/Getty Images

Japan's cultural development had some influence from the Chinese. In the sixth century, Prince Shotoku encouraged the Japanese to accept the Chinese political philosophy that stressed the importance of an orderly society with obedience to authority. The Chinese also brought Buddhism to Japan. Siddhartha Gautama (563-483 B.C.), known as Buddha, or "enlightened one," founded Buddhism. The tradition teaches that you let go of desire by meditating and that, through this process of intense striving, you attain enlightenment.

Like the Chinese, the Japanese wanted to protect the purity of their culture by preventing trade with the West. However, in 1853, the United States sent Commodore Matthew Perry and four warships to Japan to force an end to Japan's isolation. Instead of war, the shogun signed trade treaties with Britain, France, the Netherlands, Russia, and the United States.

By the twentieth century, Japan was competing actively in the global economy. With an expanding economy and population, Japan fought wars with Russia and China over control of Korea and Manchuria. By 1940, Japanese troops had taken the northern and eastern parts of China and Southeast Asia, where they gained access to rich deposits of oil, rubber, and other essential natural resources. The United States then cut off exports to Japan in response to its occupation of China. The Japanese navy attacked the U.S. naval base at Pearl Harbor in Hawaii on December 7, 1941. This pushed the United States into World War II.

The atomic bombs dropped on Hiroshima and Nagasaki in August of 1945 killed about 100,000 people. Many thousands more were injured, and Japan surrendered on September 2, 1945. Economic recovery began after the war, and the manufacture of products for export has helped to drive an economy that provides one of the highest standards of living in the world.

Southeast Asian Peninsula

The Southeast Asian peninsula juts out of the Asian continent south of China. Ten countries make up Southeast Asia: Brunei, Cambodia, Indonesia, Laos, Malaysia, Myanmar, the Philippines, Singapore, Thailand, and Vietnam.

Vietnam, a long narrow country, runs along the peninsula's east coast. Like other countries in the area, Vietnam contains lush tropical rain forests and fertile river valleys. Stronger countries have dominated Vietnam throughout history. China ruled Vietnam for about 1,000 years, and it was a French colony from the 1880s until it was lost to the Japanese in World War II.

The French returned when the Japanese were forced out. After the Vietnamese defeated the French in 1954, negotiations divided the country into North and South Vietnam. About 500,000 U.S. soldiers were sent to Vietnam during the Cold War to prevent the communist-ruled North from taking over the South. However, the U.S. troops were forced out in 1973, and a unified Communist Vietnam was formed in 1975. For the next twenty-five years, Vietnam struggled to recover from the war, the loss of support from the Soviet Union, and the effects of a centrally planned economy. By the turn of the century, Vietnam embraced more liberal economic policies. In 2001, it entered into trade agreements with the United States. As a result, between 2001 and 2007, trade with the United States increased 900 percent. Vietnam joined the World Trade Organization in 2007 and continues its efforts to expand its economy and reduce poverty.

Down Under

Australia and New Zealand constitute the continent of Australia in the Southern Hemisphere. Australia, about the size of the United States, was originally settled by the Aborigines who are thought to have migrated there from southeast Asia about 40,000 years ago. Great Britain used Australia as a penal colony from 1788 to 1839 and settled about 161,000 prisoners there. Many remained after completing their sentences. Other European settlers, attracted by gold mining and farming opportunities, settled in Australia and gave the country its western traditions. Australia has vast deserts and mountain ranges, and its Great Barrier Reef extends over 1,200 miles on the northeast coast.

Photodisc/Getty Images

New Zealand lies about 1,200 miles southeast of Australia. Maori people from other Polynesian islands first settled on New Zealand. Europeans, primarily from Great Britain, settled there in the eighteenth and nineteenth centuries. New Zealand is mountainous with fertile plains.

Both New Zealand and Australia are noted for liberal social policies. New Zealand was the first country in the world to allow women to vote.

A Region of Contrasts

The Asia-Pacific Rim is a region of contrasts. People living in Australia, Japan, and New Zealand enjoy a stable economy, while political and economic instability has occurred in Pakistan, Bangladesh, and Laos. Food shortages and human suffering have been common for millions of people in these countries. The region is faced with various challenges. Indians seek relief from religious and ethnic violence. Young reformers battle political repression in China. Koreans struggle with reunification. Efforts to build modern industrial states compete with attempts to maintain cultural traditions and social customs.

Think Critically

1. Why do you think so many of the Asian countries resisted ties with Western countries?
2. How do the mountainous regions of Asia and Australia affect trade?
3. Research the history of China, and discover what inventions are attributed to it.

COUNTRY PROFILE

The World Factbook, published online by the Central Intelligence Agency, includes country profiles for the nations of Asia and the Pacific Rim. Each country's profile includes an overview followed by detailed information about the country's geography, people, government, economy, communications, transportation, military, and transnational issues.

CHAPTER 5

Structures of International Business Organizations

5-1 Forms of Business Ownership

5-2 Operations of Global Businesses

5-3 Starting Global Business Activities

Digital Images/Getty Images

GLOBAL FOCUS

Mitsubishi: From Trading Company to Multinational Corporation

Founded by Yataro Iwasaki as a trading company in 1870, Mitsubishi soon became involved in mining, banking, shipbuilding, railroads. The family-run conglomerate continued to grow and expanded into other business activities. In 1946, the organization divided into over 100 separate entities.

Twelve years later, Mitsubishi Trading established a division in the United States to export U.S. goods and to import raw materials to Japan. As a result of growth and foreign investments, Mitsubishi has expanded into 30 different manufacturing and service areas including financial services, information technology, chemicals, food products, motor vehicles, paper mills, steel, glass production, energy plants, and textiles and clothing.

The company describes itself as a "community with a multitude of independent companies," with approximately 200 member companies. In addition, an informal group of associated companies also exists. In total, more than 400 separate enterprises worldwide use the Mitsubishi name, while hundreds of other divisions of the organization operate under different names. Despite what appears to be a loose business operation, the organization is unified by three guiding principles: corporate responsibility to society, integrity and fairness, and international understanding through trade.

In addition to its many divisions, the Tokyo-based company has business partners around the world. For example, Mitsubishi is part owner of the world's highest-producing copper mine in Chile. QDM, a joint venture of Mitsubishi Heavy Industries, China Shipbuilding Industry, and Wartsila Corporation of Finland, manufactures marine diesel engines. Caterpillar and Mitsubishi have a joint venture agreement to manufacture and market forklifts around the world. Mitsubishi is truly a global company.

Think Critically

1. What economic and social factors may have contributed to Mitsubishi actions to being involved in a wide variety of goods and services?
2. How might Mitsubishi expand its international business activities in the future?
3. Go to the Mitsubishi web site to obtain additional information about the company's structure and main business divisions. Prepare a brief written or oral summary.

5-1 Forms of Business Ownership

GOALS

- Describe the advantages and disadvantages of a sole proprietorship.

- Describe the advantages and disadvantages of a partnership.

- Explain the characteristics of a corporation.

- Name other forms of business ownership.

Photodisc/Getty Images

The Sole Proprietorship

Have you ever wondered how a business gets organized? Almost every company you can think of started small with the efforts of one or two people. Both Microsoft and Apple Computer were started by people who had ideas for a new business opportunity. As a business grows in size, the company is likely to expand its operations and increase the number of owners. Every business organizes as one of three types: sole proprietorship, partnership, or corporation.

Most companies in the world are started and owned by one person. In the United States, more 70 percent of all businesses are sole proprietorships. A **sole proprietorship** is a business owned by one person. Many of the stores, companies, and other businesses you see each day have a single owner, even though they employ many people.

For a person to start a sole proprietorship, three major elements are needed. First, the new business owner must have a product or service to sell. Second, money for a building, equipment, and other start-up expenses will be required. Third, the owner must know how to manage the business activities of the company or hire someone else who knows how.

ADVANTAGES OF A SOLE PROPRIETORSHIP

Before you decide to organize your business as a sole proprietorship, you need to consider the advantages and disadvantages of this form of business organization.

Percentage of U.S. Businesses by Method of Organization

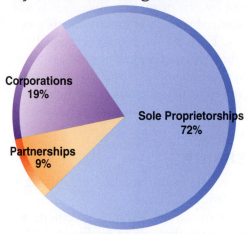

Corporations
19%

Partnerships
9%

Sole Proprietorships
72%

Figure 5-1 Most businesses in the United States are organized as sole proprietorships.

Ease of Starting Obtaining a business license and meeting other minor legal requirements are usually the only steps needed to start a sole proprietorship. Your idea, funds, and willingness to accept the risk associated with running a business are all you need to get started. Throughout the world each day, thousands of people start companies that serve their customers and create employment opportunities.

Freedom to Make Business Decisions As a sole proprietor, all company decisions are your own. As the single owner, you can run things yourself or hire others.

Owner Keeps All Profits The difference between money taken in and payments for expenses is called **net income** or **profit**. Because you are taking all of the risk, you receive all of the financial rewards.

Pride of Ownership As your own boss, you have the chance to see the results of your efforts. Many people like to have their own company so they do not have to work for someone else.

DISADVANTAGES OF A SOLE PROPRIETORSHIP

Even though there are advantages to running a business as a sole proprietorship, there are also disadvantages to this form of business organization.

Limited Sources of Funds The ability to raise money for a sole proprietorship is limited to the owner's contribution plus loans. As a new business owner, lenders may see you as a risky borrower. Even if you get a loan, it is likely to have a high interest rate, which will add to the cost of operating the business.

Long Hours and Hard Work Because many new and small companies find it difficult to compete against established businesses, you will probably put in many long hours. When you own your own business, you cannot call in sick or take a vacation unless you have dedicated employees you trust.

Unlimited Risks In other forms of business organizations, several owners share the risks. As the sole owner, you are responsible for all aspects of the enterprise. The owner has unlimited liability. **Unlimited liability** means that the owner's personal assets can be used to pay for any debts of the business.

Limited Life of the Business If the owner dies or is unable to run the business, the enterprise will either cease to exist or be sold to someone else. When the business is sold, it becomes a different company with a new owner.

✓ *Check*Point
What is unlimited liability?

Partnership

A **partnership** is a business that is owned by two or more people, but is not incorporated. A partnership may be organized when a company needs more money or the talents of additional people. Each owner, or partner, usually shares in both the decision making for the company and the profits.

Partnerships can be formed for any type of business. Stores, manufacturing companies, and restaurants can be organized as partnerships. Law firms and many professional sports teams use this type of ownership format.

ADVANTAGES OF A PARTNERSHIP

Although partnership is not as common as sole proprietorship, organizing a business as a partnership has three important advantages.

Ease of Creation A partnership is easy to start. A written agreement is created to communicate responsibilities and the division of profits.

Additional Sources of Funds With several owners, a partnership can raise more capital, expand business activities, and earn larger profits.

Availability of Different Talents Many partnerships can take advantage of the different skills of people. One partner may be responsible for selling, another takes care of company records, while a third supervises employees.

DISADVANTAGES OF A PARTNERSHIP

Even though there are advantages to running a business as a partnership, there are also disadvantages to this form of business organization.

Partners Are Liable As with the sole proprietorship, a partnership has *unlimited liability*. Any or all of the partners may be held personally responsible for the debts of the business.

Profits Are Shared among Several Owners The written partnership agreement determines the division of profits. Even if an uneven workload occurs, the net income is divided based on the agreement.

Potential for Disagreement among Owners Differences in opinions are likely to occur in every work situation. Two or more people who work closely together may have disagreements. Some people suggest that you avoid going into business with friends or relatives to prevent possible personal conflicts.

Business Can Dissolve Suddenly When one partner dies or cannot continue in the partnership, the business must stop. At this point, a new company and partnership agreement must be created. This may not be easy because some of the company assets may have to be sold to buy the departing partner's share of the business.

NETBookmark

Starting your own business can be a rewarding experience but it can be risky. Taking time to examine your motivation for starting a business can reduce the risk of failure. It also helps to examine your current financial picture and your financial goals. Access the web site shown below and click on the link for Chapter 5. Take the "Business Start-Up Quiz." How ready are you to start a business? How do your think taking this quiz might help people who are thinking about starting a business?

www.cengage.com/school/genbus/intlbiz

Corporation

While sole proprietorships are the most common type of business in the United States, corporations account for more than 80 percent of the sales, as shown in Figure 5-2. A **corporation** is a business that operates as a legal entity separate from any of the owners.

Percentage of Sales by Method of Businesses Organization

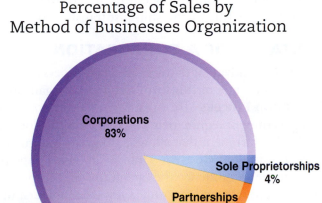

Figure 5-2
Corporations account for the major portion of sales in the U.S. economy.

A corporation raises money for business activities through the sale of stock to individuals and organizations that wish to be part owners of the corporation. The owners of a corporation are called **stockholders**, or **shareholders**. Stockholders usually have two main rights. The first is to earn dividends, and the second is to vote on company policies. Many people buy stock in corporations to earn **dividends**, which are a share of company profits.

Stockholders also indirectly control the management of the company. A stockholder typically has one vote for each share of stock owned. The stockholders vote to elect the board of directors of the company. The board of directors hires managers to run the company.

Unlike sole proprietorships and partnerships, in which individual owners are responsible for any actions of the business, corporations act as a legal entity on behalf of the owners.

ADVANTAGES OF A CORPORATION

A corporation has several advantages when compared to partnerships and sole proprietorships.

More Sources of Funds As a result of having many people interested in being part owners, corporations have an easier time raising funds than a sole proprietorship or partnership. A company can use this capital to start or expand the business. It might be used to operate the business, to purchase equipment or to build factories.

Work as a Team
Suggest ways a person could obtain funds to start a new business.

Fixed Financial Liability of Owners The business risk of a corporation is spread among many owners. A company such as General Electric or Wal-Mart has thousands of stockholders. Each person who buys a share of stock has **limited liability**, which means stockholders are only responsible for the debts of the corporation up to the amount they invested. Unlike sole proprietors and partners, people who become part owners of a corporation can only lose the amount of money paid for the stock.

Specialized Management Most corporations can afford to hire the most skilled people to run the company. The board of directors of the corporation hires the president and other administrative employees.

Unlimited Life of the Company Unlike a sole proprietorship or partnership, a corporation is a continuing entity. When stockholders die or sell out, the company still exists. Ownership just transfers to other people.

DISADVANTAGES OF A CORPORATION

Even though there are advantages to running a business as a corporation, there are also disadvantages of this form of business organization.

Difficult Creation Process The organizers of a corporation must usually meet complex government requirements. A **charter** is the document granted by the state or federal government that allows a company to form a corporation.

Owners Have Limited Control Unless you own a large portion of the stock, you are unable to influence the operations of a corporation. Small or family-held corporations may have only a few stockholders, but most large corporations are owned by thousands of people.

Double Taxation Sole proprietors and partners pay individual income tax on their companies' earnings. However, a corporation pays corporate income taxes as a separate entity. Then stockholders pay personal income tax on the dividends they receive. Therefore, corporate earnings are taxed twice.

 **Check**Point
What are the rights of the owners of a corporation?

GLOBAL BUSINESS SPOTLIGHT

CORPORATE NOTATIONS

In the United States, you can tell that a business is a corporation if the word *corporation* is in the company name or the abbreviation *Inc*. (incorporated) follows the company name. In Canada, Japan, and the United Kingdom, *Ltd*. (limited) is used, referring to the limited liability of the owners. The notation used in other countries varies depending on the words, phrases, and symbols that represent the concept of incorporation in various languages. Examples of some other common corporate notations are listed below.

France, Belgium	Sarl
Germany, Switzerland	GmbH
Italy	Srl
Denmark	A/S
Spain, Mexico, Brazil	S.A.
Netherlands	N.V.

Think Critically

1. Conduct an Internet search to find some corporations based in other countries.
2. What cultural factors might influence corporate notations?

Other Forms of Business Organization

Most businesses are organized as sole proprietorships, partnerships, or corporations. However, other types of business organization exist for special situations. Increasingly, many of them also engage in international business activities.

A **municipal corporation** is an incorporated town or city organized to provide services for citizens rather than to make a profit. You might think that a city would only engage in local activities. However, many cities have partnerships with cities in other countries, import goods and services, and engage in cultural exchanges.

Nonprofit corporations are created to provide a service and are not concerned with making a profit. Included in this category are churches, synagogues, and mosques, some hospitals, private colleges and universities, many charities, the American Red Cross, Boy Scouts of America, and The Salvation Army. Nonprofits provide a significant portion of the jobs in the labor force in some countries. These organizations employ more than 6 percent of the total workforce in the Netherlands, Ireland, Belgium, Israel, United States, Australia, and Britain. Many local nonprofit organizations are affiliated with international organizations.

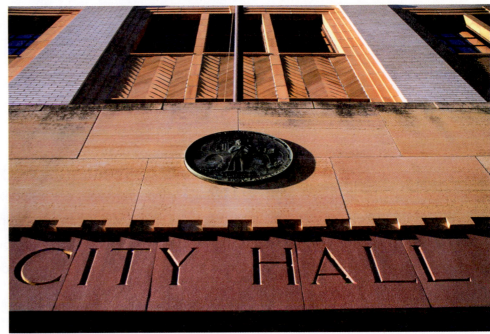

Photodisc/Getty Images

Nonprofit organizations are also referred to as nongovernmental organizations, or NGOs. In recent years, NGOs such as labor unions, environmental groups, and public interest organizations have taken action on various social and economic issues. Labor groups are concerned about lost jobs and safe working conditions, while environmental organizations work to protect clean air and water.

A **cooperative** is a business owned by its members and operated for their benefit. Consumer cooperatives may be formed by a group of people in a community or at a place of worship. The group is organized to purchase food or other goods and services at a lower cost than usual. Any profits are returned to the cooperative members. A credit union is a cooperative created to provide savings and loan services to its members.

✓ **Check**Point

Discuss situations when municipal corporations, nonprofit corporations, and cooperatives would be the best business organization to implement.

5-1 Assessment

REVIEW GLOBAL BUSINESS TERMS
Define each of the following terms.

1. sole proprietorship
2. net income, or profit
3. unlimited liability
4. partnership
5. corporation
6. stockholders, or shareholders
7. dividends
8. limited liability
9. charter
10. municipal corporation
11. nonprofit corporation
12. cooperative

REVIEW GLOBAL BUSINESS CONCEPTS
13. What are the advantages of a proprietorship?
14. What are the disadvantages of a partnership?
15. What are the disadvantages of a corporation?
16. Give an example of a municipal corporation, a nonprofit corporation, and a cooperative.

SOLVE GLOBAL BUSINESS PROBLEMS
For each of the following situations, what type of business organization would you recommend?

17. A group of programmers in India plan to start a software company and sell stock to other investors.
18. A person in Italy wants to turn a jewelry-making hobby into a business.
19. Three doctors in Bali wish to share office space, staff, and equipment.
20. Three friends in Finland are opening a small store to sell sports equipment.

THINK CRITICALLY
21. "Because of the advantage of limited liability, every business should be organized as a corporation." Do you agree? Explain.
22. Is buying stock in a corporation a good investment?
23. How do nonprofit organizations benefit society?

MAKE ACADEMIC CONNECTIONS
24. **BUSINESS** Name a sole proprietorship, a partnership, and a corporation in your community. Speculate about why each of these businesses chose its form of organization.
25. **CULTURAL STUDIES** Why are nonprofit organizations more popular in some countries than others?

Operations of Global Businesses

©Alexandr Makarov, 2009/ Used under license from Shutterstock.com

GOALS

- **Describe the activities and characteristics of multinational companies.**

- **Identify concerns related to multinational companies.**

Multinational Companies

In 1670, King Charles II of Britain granted a business charter to create a trading company named after English explorer Henry Hudson. The Hudson's Bay Company started as an international fur trading enterprise and today operates nearly 500 stores throughout Canada.

Just as the Hudson's Bay Company started as a global business, many firms today operate in several countries. A **multinational company or corporation (MNC)** is an organization that conducts business in several countries. MNCs are also called global companies, transnational companies, and worldwide companies. Figure 5-3 shows an example of the global business operations that a multinational company might have.

MNCs usually consist of a parent company in a *home country* and divisions or separate companies in one or more *host countries*. For example, Mitsubishi of Japan (home country) consists of more than 200 companies doing business in more than 70 countries (host countries). Whirlpool has manufacturing facilities in North America, South America, Europe, and Asia with products sold in more than 170 countries. Coca-Cola sells its products in about 200 countries.

Multinational Companies Cross Borders

Figure 5-3 A multinational company has business operations in different countries.

COMMUNICATION ACROSS BORDERS

KOMATSU ABANDONS JAPANESE FOR ENGLISH

When industrial giant Komatsu was founded in Japan, it marketed its products within the country. The Japanese language served Komatsu well.

As Komatsu expanded and began to market its heavy equipment elsewhere in the region, it continued to rely primarily on Japanese. However, as Komatsu developed worldwide markets in direct competition with the likes of Caterpillar, the Japanese language proved to be a handicap. Its employees and customers increasingly were not fluent in Japanese, which created major communication problems. To better compete in the global marketplace, Komatsu decided that it needed to switch from Japanese to English.

The transition is in process—even at the home office in Japan. To facilitate the conversion to English, Komatsu is providing its employees with English language lessons. Over time, Komatsu will reach its goal of being an English-speaking multinational organization.

Think Critically

1. Why did Japanese serve Komatsu reasonably well when it expanded into nearby countries?
2. What do you think would be some of the challenges for a business that abandons the language of the home country?

Today, as a result of widespread international business activities, thousands of multinational corporations exist. Many of these companies are very large. Royal Dutch/Shell, Exxon, Wal-Mart, General Electric, IBM, and Toyota each have annual sales that exceed the GDP of many countries in the world.

MULTINATIONAL COMPANIES IN OPERATION

Multinational companies get involved in global activities to take advantage of business opportunities in other geographic areas. The potential for MNCs to sell goods or services in other countries is the result of a competitive advantage held by a company. This edge can be the result of technology, lower costs, location, or availability of natural resources.

Another major activity of MNCs is adapting to different societies. Social and cultural influences along with political and legal concerns must be continually monitored. For example, if a company is not aware of changes in a country's tax law, the result could mean lower profits.

CHARACTERISTICS OF MULTINATIONAL COMPANIES

Multinational companies commonly have the following characteristics:

- **Worldwide Market View** They view the entire world as their potential market. Companies seek product ideas through foreign subsidiaries and obtain raw materials on a worldwide basis.
- **Standardized Product** Companies look for similarities among markets to offer a standardized product whenever possible.
- **Culturally-Sensitive Hiring** They use consistent hiring policies throughout the world but are also culturally sensitive to host countries. The companies recruit managers internationally rather than just from the organization's countries of operation.
- **International and Local Perspective** Businesses distribute, produce, price, and promote both with an international outlook and a local perspective.

Concerns about Multinational Companies

Work as a Team
Debate the benefits and potential problems of multinational companies.

The presence of a multinational company can have many benefits for a host country. Benefits include more jobs, products, services, and even improved infrastructure, such as roads, built by the MNC. However, there are two main concerns about MNCs—economic dependence and political interference.

As a foreign company becomes a major business, the MNC's economic power can make a host country dependent. Workers will depend on the MNC for jobs. Consumers will depend on the company for needed goods and services. The MNC could become a country's main economic entity.

When this occurs, the MNC could start to influence and even control the country's politics. The company may require certain tax laws or regulations that only benefit the powerful MNC. The regulation and control of global companies is likely to be an issue in years to come.

CheckPoint
What are two concerns host countries have about multinational companies?

GLOBAL BUSINESS SPOTLIGHT

SWOT ANALYSIS

Before a company introduces a new product or goes into another country, managers may conduct a SWOT analysis to determine the strengths, weaknesses, opportunities, and threats of the situation.

- Strengths involve company advantages not possessed by competitors, such as new technology or a well-known brand.
- Weaknesses are internal concerns of the organization, and may include limited production capacity.
- Opportunities result from social and economic trends, such as an aging population or lower interest rates.

- Threats are external limitations based on government regulations and actions by competitors.

A SWOT analysis can be used in a variety of international business situations.

Think Critically

1. Describe various international business situations in which a SWOT may be used.
2. Select an international business situation. Prepare a SWOT analysis.

INTERNATIONAL BUSINESS PERSPECTIVE
Geography

LANDLOCKED COUNTRIES

A country's ability to ship goods to customers around the world is vital for international business success. However, 44 nations are landlocked, meaning they do not have a coastline on the ocean or a major sea.

Because of their location, landlocked countries need to transport goods by land through another country to gain access to a seaport. The time and expense involved in moving raw materials, parts, and finished goods have economic consequences. The economic impact varies among countries.

Although Austria and Switzerland are landlocked, they are among the world's wealthiest nations. Both countries have per capita GDP near $40,000, considerably higher than the world average of $10,500. On the other end of the spectrum, landlocked Afghanistan and Zimbabwe are two of the poorest countries with per capita GDPs of $800 and $200 respectively.

Thirty-one landlocked countries are developing economies, with a poor infrastructure, weak productive capacities, and limited access to world markets. In 2003, the United Nations held a conference in Almaty, Kazakhstan to address some of the issues landlocked developing countries face. The resulting action plan focuses on improving access to seaports, increasing safety and efficiency of transportation systems, and reducing shipping costs of exports and delivery costs of imports.

Think Critically

1. How does being landlocked affect a developing country's business potential and economic development?
2. Use library and Internet resources to learn more about a landlocked developing country. Prepare a short summary of your findings including ideas for economic development.

Landlocked Countries

AFRICA		ASIA		EUROPE		SOUTH AMERICA
• **Botswana**	• **Malawi**	• **Afghanistan**	• **Laos**	• Andorra	• **Macedonia**	• **Bolivia**
• **Burkina Faso**	• **Mali**	• **Armenia**	• **Mongolia**	• Austria	• **Moldova**	• **Paraguay**
• **Burundi**	• **Niger**	• **Azerbaijan**	• **Nepal**	• Belarus	• San Marino	
• **Central African Republic**	• **Rwanda**	• **Bhutan**	• **Tajikistan**	• Czech Republic	• Serbia	
	• **Swaziland**	• **Kazakhstan**	• **Turkmenistan**	• Hungary	• Slovakia	
• **Chad**	• **Uganda**	• **Kyrgyzstan**	• **Uzbekistan**	• Kosovo	• Switzerland	
• **Ethiopia**	• **Zambia**			• Liechtenstein	• Vatican City	
• **Lesotho**	• **Zimbabwe**			• Luxembourg		

Figure 5-4 Forty-four countries are landlocked. The 31 countries shown in bold are considered landlocked developing countries.

5-2 Assessment

REVIEW GLOBAL BUSINESS TERMS

Define the following term.

1. multinational company or corporation (MNC)

REVIEW GLOBAL BUSINESS CONCEPTS

2. What is the relationship between a home country and a host country?

3. What kinds of competitive advantages can a multinational company have?

SOLVE GLOBAL BUSINESS PROBLEMS

For each of the following situations, decide whether the situation reflects a characteristic of a multinational company.

4. A product is designed to meet the strictest consumer protection laws so that it will be marketable in any country.

5. Advertising themes are the same in all countries, but the language is changed.

6. A company hires host country citizens as managers as often as possible.

7. Each country is considered a separate market, and a product is formulated to be sold in a single country.

8. Products are shipped to other countries only by mail.

THINK CRITICALLY

9. Is it likely that a well-managed multinational company could be successful in every country in the world? Explain.

10. Describe ways a global company could provide social and economic benefits to a host country.

MAKE ACADEMIC CONNECTIONS

11. **MATHEMATICS** Go to the web site of a multinational company. Determine the percentages of the company's sales for different regions of the world, such as Africa, the Middle East, and Asia.

12. **CULTURAL STUDIES** Talk to a person who has worked or lived in another country. Ask how cultural differences can benefit and create problems within a multinational company.

13. **HISTORY** Locate information about the history of a multinational company including where and when it was started. In addition, find out when the company expanded to become a multinational company. Create a time line showing at least five significant dates in the company's history.

5-3 Starting Global Business Activities

GOALS

- Identify five low-risk methods for getting involved in international business.

- Discuss higher-risk methods for getting involved in international business.

Photodisc/Getty Images

Low-Risk Methods for Getting Involved in International Business

Companies use nine main ways to get involved in international business, as shown in Figure 5-5. As you move up the steps, the firm has more control over its foreign business activities as well as more risk. For example, indirect exporting has less risk

Methods for Getting Involved in International Business

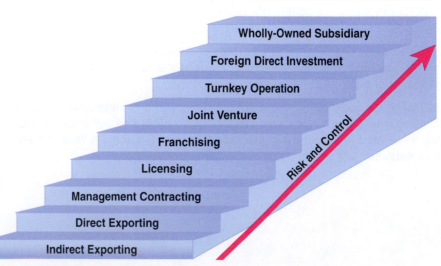

- Wholly-Owned Subsidiary
- Foreign Direct Investment
- Turnkey Operation
- Joint Venture
- Franchising
- Licensing
- Management Contracting
- Direct Exporting
- Indirect Exporting

Risk and Control

Figure 5-5 A company may choose from a variety of methods to get involved in international business.

associated with it than a joint venture. However, a company has more direct control over its business dealings with a joint venture than with indirect exporting.

INDIRECT EXPORTING

At first, a business organization may get involved with international business by finding a demand for its service or product without really trying. **Indirect exporting** occurs when a company sells its products in a foreign market without any special activity for that purpose.

During a sales meeting or another business encounter, for example, someone in a foreign company may show interest in your product. A buyer who represents several companies may tell a small manufacturing company about the need for its product in Southeast Asia. Because the company was not looking for foreign business opportunities, indirect exporting is sometimes called *casual* or *accidental* exporting. Indirect exporting makes use of agents and brokers who bring together sellers and buyers of products in different countries. This method of international business has minimum costs and risks. Many companies have started their international business activities using this method.

DIRECT EXPORTING

Direct exporting occurs when a company actively seeks and conducts exporting. Direct exporting might be the first international business activity for a company or it may be a natural outgrowth of indirect exporting. When sales increase and a company decides to get more involved in international business, the organization probably will create its own exporting department. The company may still use agents or brokers from outside of the organization. However, a manager within the company plans, implements, and controls the exporting activities.

While direct exporting involves higher costs than indirect exporting, the company has more control over its foreign business activities. The risk is still relatively low because the firm does not have an extensive investment in other countries. The exporting process is discussed in greater detail in the next chapter.

MANAGEMENT CONTRACTING

Knowledge is a powerful tool in business. An ability to find business opportunities, coordinate resources, solve problems, and make productive decisions is a skill that will be in demand throughout your life. It is also a skill that can be exported.

A **management contract** is an agreement under which a company sells only its management skills. This has a fairly low risk for a company because the agreement spells out the relationship between the parties and provides safeguards to protect against risks.

An example of management contracting may involve a European-based hotel management company agreeing to operate a hotel chain in Southeast Asia. In exchange, the owners of the hotel chain would pay the management company for its services.

A variation of this type of agreement is *contract manufacturing*. This arrangement involves a company in one country producing an item for a company located in another country. This relationship allows a business to enter a foreign market without investing in production facilities. Contract manufacturing is usually considered as having low to moderate risk.

Digital Images/Getty Images

Photodisc/Getty Images

LICENSING

To produce items in other countries without being actively involved, a company can allow a foreign company to use a procedure it owns. **Licensing** is selling the right to use some intangible property (production process, trademark, or brand name) for a fee or royalty. The Gerber Company started selling its baby food products in Japan using licensing. The use of television and movie characters or sports team emblems on hats, shirts, jackets, notebooks, luggage, and other products is also the result of licensing agreements.

A licensing agreement provides a fee or royalty to the company granting the license. This payment is in return for the right to use the process, brand name, or trademark. The Disney Company, for example, receives a royalty from the amusement park it licensed in Japan. Licensing has a low monetary investment, so the potential financial return is frequently low. However, the risk for the company is also low.

FRANCHISING

Another method commonly used to expand into other countries is the **franchise**, which is the right to use a company name or business process in a specific way. Organizations contract with people in other countries to set up a business that must meet certain requirements, which often includes a look and operations similar to the parent company. The company obtaining the franchise will usually adapt various business elements. Marketing elements such as the taste of food products, packaging, and advertising messages must meet cultural sensitivities and meet legal requirements.

Franchising and licensing are similar. Both involve a royalty payment for the right to use a process or famous company name. Licensing, however, usually involves a manufacturing process, while franchising involves selling a product or service.

Franchise agreements are popular with fast-food companies. McDonald's, Burger King, Wendy's, KFC, Domino's Pizza, and Pizza Hut all have used franchising to expand into foreign markets.

✓ CheckPoint
What are five relatively low-risk methods of getting involved in international business?

A Question of Ethics

STEALING SECRETS BY FOREIGN PARTNERS

Working relationships between foreign enterprises and companies in host countries can be strained by the loss of technology secrets. In a closed society (one with a centralized government), outside companies may be required to provide their local partners with computer hardware, software, and knowledge to operate these systems. However, often the technology is then borrowed and duplicated by the local company to start a new business.

Think Critically
According to the guidelines for ethical analysis, how will the actions of the government and companies in the host country affect the business and economy of the other partner?

Higher-Risk Methods for Getting Involved in International Business

It is often true that business activities with higher risks return greater profits. The profit potential is used to justify taking those risks.

JOINT VENTURES

A partnership can provide benefits to all owners. One type of international partnership is the **joint venture**, an agreement between two or more companies from different countries to share a business project. A joint venture is illustrated in Figure 5-6.

The main benefits of a joint venture are sharing raw materials, shipping facilities, management activities, production facilities, distribution channels, and other business resources. Some drawbacks are sharing profits and limited control.

Joint venture arrangements can share costs, risks, and profits in any combination. One company may have only 10 percent ownership and the other 90 percent. It depends on the joint venture agreement.

Joint ventures, often called *strategic partnerships*, can be used for any type of business activity. This arrangement is especially popular for manufacturing. These joint ventures may include home appliances manufactured in Korea based on technology developed in Germany, and sold as a store brand name in the United States. Or, an agreement between two food-processing companies in different countries to create a new product line sold in many other nations.

TURNKEY PROJECT

A *turnkey project* allows a company to enter a foreign market by creating a ready-to-use business facility. For example, a European-based energy company may create a power plant in Africa. Once the installation is ready to generate power, a local company takes over. In the turnkey process, a project manager is in charge of construction activities, which may include training local workers to operate the facility.

The turnkey process may be used to export technology or a production plant that will be used by a company buying the project. The facility

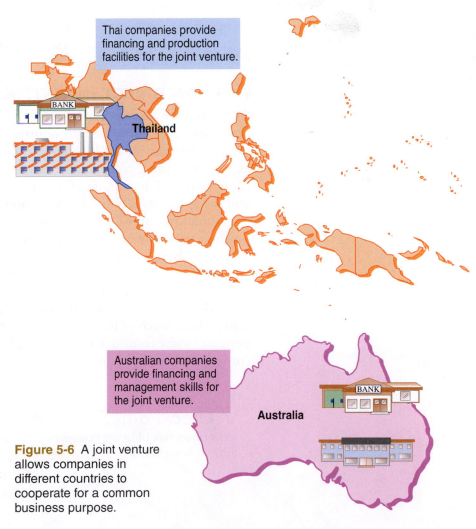

A Joint Venture in Action

Thai companies provide financing and production facilities for the joint venture.

Thailand

Australian companies provide financing and management skills for the joint venture.

Australia

Figure 5-6 A joint venture allows companies in different countries to cooperate for a common business purpose.

GLOBAL BUSINESS SPOTLIGHT

CEREAL PARTNERS WORLDWIDE

Cheerios with Nestlé on the box instead of General Mills would seem strange to most consumers in the United States. However, in Latin America, Europe, the Middle East, and other areas of the world, this is a common sight. Cereal Partners Worldwide (CPW) is a joint venture between these two companies.

General Mills brought popular brands, such as Trix and Golden Grahams, into the partnership. Nestlé, well known throughout the world, has an extensive distribution system and strong brand

presence in grocery stores and supermarkets.

Created in 1990, Cereal Partners Worldwide is now the second-largest cereal company outside of North America. CPW operates in more than 130 countries. In addition to the well-known General Mills brands, CPW has created some cereal products for specific markets. The joint venture company has sold Zucosos in Chile, Chocapic in Spain, and Snow Flakes in the Czech Republic. CPW makes it possible to buy Trix or

Cheerios at a rural store in Chile as well as in a supermarket in Israel.

Think Critically

1. What factors influenced the creation of CPW?
2. What are some examples of products you use each day that might need to be adapted to other cultures?
3. Go to the web site of General Mills to obtain current information about the activities of CPW and other joint ventures of the company.

is turned over to the new owners once it is completed and ready to go into operation. A turnkey project may be planned by the selling company or it may be built to specifications provided by the buyer.

FOREIGN DIRECT INVESTMENT

As a company gets more involved in international business, it may make a direct investment in a foreign country. **A foreign direct investment (FDI)** occurs when a company buys land or other resources in another country. Real estate and existing companies are common purchases under this method. Many British, Japanese, and German companies own office buildings, hotels, and shopping malls in the United States.

Another type of FDI is the **wholly-owned subsidiary**, which is an independent company owned by a parent company. Multinational companies frequently have wholly-owned subsidiaries in various countries that are the result of foreign direct investment. In the past, foreign companies have owned U.S.-based businesses such as Burger King, Pillsbury, and Green Giant.

To prevent economic control of one country by another, a nation may restrict how much of its land or factories may be sold to foreign owners. For example, some countries allow a foreign investor to own only 49 percent of companies in those countries.

✓ CheckPoint

How does risk of doing business internationally differ for exporting and direct foreign investment?

REVIEW GLOBAL BUSINESS TERMS

Define each of the following terms.

1. indirect exporting
2. direct exporting
3. management contract
4. licensing
5. franchise
6. joint venture
7. foreign direct investment (FDI)
8. wholly-owned subsidiary

Study Tools

www.cengage.com/school/genbus/intlbiz

REVIEW GLOBAL BUSINESS CONCEPTS

9. Why is management contracting a safe method for getting involved in international business?

10. What is the difference between licensing and franchising?

SOLVE GLOBAL BUSINESS PROBLEMS

For each of the following situations, indicate what method the company is using for its global business activities.

11. A Vietnamese company shares production costs and profits of a chemical manufacturing enterprise with an Israeli company.

12. A British toy company allows a Japanese company to create clothing and school supplies with one of the British company's doll characters on the products.

13. A company in Egypt has purchased 51 percent of the stock of a company in Peru.

14. A small food-packaging firm cannot afford to sell in other countries, so it asks an export agent to obtain orders for the company.

THINK CRITICALLY

15. What factors would affect how the parties in a joint venture divide future profits?

16. In what ways does a company making a direct foreign investment in a new factory have more control than a company engaged in direct exporting?

MAKE ACADEMIC CONNECTIONS

17. **CULTURAL STUDIES** Visit a toy store, sporting goods store, or another kind of store that sells merchandise printed with logos or images belonging to other companies. List the items you see and any information on the tags or packaging that indicates a licensing agreement.

18. **TECHNOLOGY** Do an Internet search for "joint venture." Select a site that describes a joint venture involving two countries. Write a report on the companies and countries involved, the products, and other major details about the joint venture.

CHAPTER SUMMARY

5-1 FORMS OF BUSINESS OWNERSHIP

A The advantages of a sole proprietorship are ease of starting, individual business freedom, owner gets all profits, and pride of ownership. The disadvantages are limited funds, potential long hours, unlimited liability, and limited life of the business.

B The benefits of a partnership are ease of creation, additional sources of funds, and availability of different talents. The possible drawbacks are partners are each liable, profits are shared, potential for disagreement, and business can dissolve suddenly.

C Advantages of a corporation are more sources of funds, limited liability, management availability, and unlimited life. Disadvantages include difficult creation process, owners' limited control, and double taxation.

D Other forms of business ownership include municipal corporations, nonprofit corporations, and cooperatives.

5-2 OPERATIONS OF GLOBAL BUSINESSES

A Multinational companies take advantage of business opportunities in several geographic areas by adapting to cultural and economic influences in different societies. Multinational companies with a global perspective consider the entire world as their potential market. They look for similarities among markets in order to offer a standardized product whenever possible.

B The main concerns related to MNCs are economic dependence and political interference.

5-3 STARTING GLOBAL BUSINESS ACTIVITIES

A Low-risk methods used for getting involved in international business include indirect exporting, direct exporting, management contracting, licensing, and franchising.

B Higher-risk methods used for getting involved in international business are joint ventures, turnkey operations, foreign direct investment, and wholly-owned subsidiaries.

GLOBAL **REFOCUS**

Read the case at the beginning of this chapter, and answer the following questions.

1. What are the benefits and potential problems of a company being involved in many types of products and services?

2. Describe a joint venture that might be appropriate for Mitsubishi in the future.

REVIEW GLOBAL BUSINESS TERMS

Match the terms listed with the definitions. Some terms may not be used.

1. A business owned by its members and operated for their benefit.
2. The difference between money taken in and expenses.
3. The owners of a corporation.
4. Selling the right to use some intangible property for a fee or royalty.
5. The situation in which a business owner is only responsible for the debts of the business up to the amount invested.
6. The document granted by government allowing a company to organize as a corporation.
7. The selling of a company's products in a foreign market without any special activity for that purpose.
8. An independent foreign company owned by a parent company.
9. The situation in which a business owner's personal assets can be used to pay any debts of the business.
10. A business that operates as a legal entity separate from any of the owners.
11. An agreement under which a company sells only its management skills.
12. A share of corporate earnings paid to stockholders.
13. The right to use a company name or business process in a specific way.
14. An agreement between two or more companies from different countries to share a business project.
15. A company actively seeking and conducting exporting.
16. The purchase of land or other resources in a foreign country.
17. An organization that conducts business in several countries.

a. charter
b. cooperative
c. corporation
d. direct exporting
e. dividends
f. foreign direct investment (FDI)
g. franchise
h. indirect exporting
i. joint venture
j. licensing
k. limited liability
l. management contract
m. multinational company or corporation (MNC)
n. municipal corporation
o. net income, or profit
p. nonprofit corporations
q. partnership
r. sole proprietorship
s. stockholders, or shareholders
t. unlimited liability
u. wholly-owned subsidiary

MAKE GLOBAL BUSINESS DECISIONS

18. List reasons why most companies in the world start out and remain sole proprietorships. How does being a sole proprietorship benefit or limit a company's ability to become involved in international business?
19. Describe a situation in which a partnership or sole proprietorship could raise capital to expand business activities more easily than a corporation.

20. Why do you think the government makes the creation of a corporation more difficult than the creation of other forms of business ownership?

21. Name goods and services that could be the basis for creating a consumer cooperative.

22. What are some ways a multinational company can have a competitive advantage over local businesses?

23. What types of restrictions might a foreign government put on a multinational corporation doing business in its country?

24. Describe actions a manager might take when (a) planning, (b) implementing, and (c) controlling a company's exporting activities.

25. What are some services companies could sell to other countries using management contracts?

26. How would a business that sells licenses and franchises control the image of the company name?

27. What are some concerns people might have about a company making many foreign investments in their country?

MAKE ACADEMIC CONNECTIONS

28. **GEOGRAPHY** Locate examples of multinational companies in different countries. Create a map showing where the companies are based and the other nations in which the companies operate.

29. **COMMUNICATIONS** Interview a local business owner about the form of business organization used by his or her company. Ask the owner how the company got started, and ask for suggestions he or she could give to others who want to start a business.

30. **HISTORY** Conduct library research about a major foreign company and its home country. Obtain information on how the country's history may have influenced the development of the company.

31. **CULTURAL STUDIES** Describe how a multinational company might need to adapt its products to meet the traditions, customs, and cultural norms of various societies.

32. **SCIENCE** Collect advertisements, articles, and other information about multinational companies. Describe what natural resources and production processes would be necessary to create the products of these companies.

33. **MATHEMATICS** Conduct an opinion survey of students and others to determine their attitudes toward products and companies from other countries. Survey questions could include: (a) Which countries make the best products? (b) Do consumers benefits from being able to buy products from other countries? (c) Should our government restrict products from other countries? (d) Should foreign governments restrict U.S. products from entering their markets? Prepare a chart showing your results.

34. **CAREER PLANNING** Talk to someone who owns a business. Obtain information about the types of jobs the person had before becoming an entrepreneur.

The GLOBAL

Entrepreneur

CREATING AN INTERNATIONAL BUSINESS PLAN

Planning and Organizing Global Business Operations

Select a company that you might consider as a strategic partner for business. Make use of previously collected materials, or do additional research to obtain the information you need.

1. Describe how your company might have started as a sole proprietorship or a partnership. Explain the factors that may have influenced the owners' decision to select this form of business organization.

2. If the company becomes a multinational corporation, what benefits and problems could result?

3. Describe appropriate international business opportunities for the company. What products and services would be most appropriate for different geographic regions? What economic, cultural, legal, or political influences must the company consider?

4. Which of the methods described in the final section of this chapter (see Figure 5-5) would be appropriate for the company to use for international business activities?

5. Explain the possible use of two or more of these methods for getting involved in international business.

6. Prepare a written report or present a short oral report (two or three minutes) that answers these questions. Or if instructed by your teacher, create a poster, display, or computer presentation with visuals and information that answer these questions.

Importing, Exporting, and Trade Relations

6-1 Importing Procedures

6-2 Exporting Procedures

6-3 Importance of Trade Relations

6-4 The Nature of Competition

PhotoDisc/Getty Images

GLOBAL FOCUS

The Scoop on Ice Cream Exports

What's your favorite ice cream flavor? Popular flavors in Japan include octopus, seaweed, corn, and sweet potato. In Venezuela, people eat tuna and carrot ice cream. While these are not the most common flavors in these countries, local preferences need to be considered when exporting ice cream.

In addition to figuring out what flavors to offer, U.S. producers of ice cream face other concerns as they seek new international customers. Refrigeration, or rather the lack of it, can greatly influence market potential. In many areas of China, for example, few homes have freezers. As a result, most Chinese prefer their ice cream in the form of small snacks and consume at the point of purchase.

During the late 1980s, annual exports of U.S. ice cream to Japan were only $200,000. This was due to a Japanese import quota for ice cream and frozen yogurt. With the elimination of that trade barrier, Japanese customers bought more ice cream from U.S. companies. After ice cream sales in Asian countries dropped in the late 1990s due to poor economic conditions, demand started to increase when the economy improved.

In Costa Rica and other Central American countries, there was little or no market for ice cream in the mid 1990s. The market improved when Costa Rica honored its commitment to the World Trade Organization by reducing a 44 percent tariff and increasing the 500-ton import quota.

Another strong growth area for ice cream exports is the Caribbean market. The hot climate attracts many tourists to the region where they create a strong demand for frozen snacks and desserts.

Think Critically

1. What factors have increased the demand for U.S. ice cream in other countries?
2. What obstacles might an ice cream exporter encounter when doing business in other countries?
3. Go to the web site of the Foreign Agricultural Service of the U.S. Department of Agriculture to obtain current information about ice cream exports.

6-1 Importing Procedures

GOALS

- Explain the importance of importing.
- Identify the four steps for importing.

PhotoDisc/Getty Images

The Importance of Importing

Imagine how life in the United States would be without international business. Most television sets, athletic shoes, and coffee bought in the United States come from other countries. And these products are only a few of the imported products in use each day. Importing provides a wide variety of products and services for U.S. consumers. Exporting creates jobs and expands business opportunities. Importing and exporting are primary international business activities.

Imports are services or products bought by a company or government from businesses in other countries. Businesses can get involved in international trade by importing goods and services and selling them in their own country. The importing business can create new sales or expand sales with existing customers. Companies get involved in importing for one of three reasons: (1) consumer demand for products unique to foreign countries, (2) lower costs of foreign-made products, or (3) sources of parts needed for domestic manufacturing.

Product Demand Customers who want a unique item or a certain quality may purchase a foreign-made product. Some goods and services may be available only from other countries. Almost all bananas, cocoa, and coffee consumed in the United States are imported.

Lower Costs The prices of goods and services are constantly changing. An item from one country may be less expensive than the same item from another country. Electronic products manufactured in Asian countries are frequently less expensive than similar items produced elsewhere.

Production Inputs Companies regularly purchase raw materials and components for processing or assembly from other countries. These production inputs may not be easily available in the company's home country. For example, the radios, engines, transmissions, and windshield washer systems for many cars assembled in the United States come from companies in Canada, Mexico, Brazil, Japan, Korea, and other countries.

✓ **Check**Point
What are the three main reasons companies import?

Work as a Team
Work with your team to identify 20 items that you own or use regularly that were imported. Examine labels and other marks on clothing and other items to determine the country of origin.

Importing Activities

What does a company have to do to become an importer? Importing usually involves four main activities or steps, as shown in Figure 6-1 on the next page.

STEP 1 DETERMINE DEMAND

The first activity is to determine potential consumer demand for imports. Companies must conduct market research to find out if people will buy certain imported products. As with any business venture, there are risks. Sometimes companies import goods, only to have these items remain in a warehouse because no one wants them due to differences in buying habits.

STEP 2 CONTACT SUPPLIERS

The second importing activity is to contact foreign suppliers. It takes time and energy to locate foreign companies that are able to provide what you want when you want. By using information sources, such as government agencies and foreign business contacts, importers can identify the companies that will best serve their needs.

STEP 3 FINALIZE PURCHASE

The third importing activity is to finalize the *purchase agreement*. The importing company must come to an agreement with the supplier on specific terms for the purchase. The agreement must include the price the importer will pay for the goods, but there are other things that need to be agreed upon. Who will pay for shipping? When will items be delivered? How will payment

Importing Activities

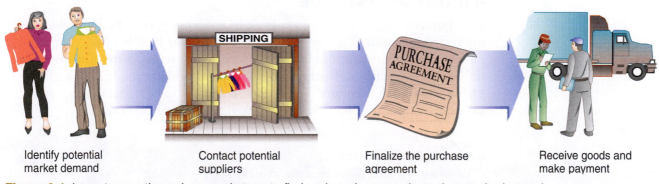

Identify potential market demand   Contact potential suppliers   Finalize the purchase agreement   Receive goods and make payment

Figure 6-1 Importers go through several steps to find and purchase products that are in demand.

GLOBAL BUSINESS SPOTLIGHT

AN IMPORTING ERROR

Clear and complete communication for foreign suppliers is vital. Misunderstandings or lack of oversight can result in costly mistakes as demonstrated by the following example.

A U.S. retailer contracted with a foreign company to manufacture cashmere sweaters. The contract stated that the sweaters must be made of 100 percent cashmere. The manufacturer provided shirt labels to that effect. The manufacturer produced sweaters that were 20 percent cashmere and 80 percent wool.

Without verifying the material content, the U.S. company accepted the shirts and sold them with the incorrect information on the label. The Federal Trade Commission fined the company for deceptive labeling.

Think Critically

How might this situation have been avoided?

---

be made? Will payment be made in advance, during shipping, or after the receipt of the goods? These are just some of the details that need to be described in the purchase agreement.

STEP 4 RECEIVE GOODS

The fourth activity is to receive the goods and make payment. This includes checking the order for accuracy and damage, paying for the order, and paying any import duties. This tax can be based on either the value of goods or other factors, such as quantity or weight.

Import duties are paid to customs officials. A **customs official** is a government employee authorized to collect the duties levied on imports. The term *customs* also refers to the procedures involved in the collection of duties. You may have heard a person traveling to another country say "I have to go through customs." This means travelers must report to customs officials the value of anything bought in the country they are leaving or anything they plan to sell in the country they are entering.

IMPORT ASSISTANCE

U.S. government agencies are available to assist companies and individuals interested in importing. For example, Customs and Border Protection (CBP), part of the Department of Homeland Security, provides current information on import regulations. The Food and Drug Administration (FDA) and the Department of Agriculture (USDA) are resources for companies importing agriculture products, food, drugs, cosmetics and medical devices.

✓ CheckPoint

What are the four steps involved in importing?

IMPORT-EXPORT OPPORTUNITIES

"Will the shipment arrive by the 23rd of the month?" "Do we have the proper paperwork to clear customs in Cambodia?" "Are the shirts properly labeled for sale in this country?"

People who work in import and export careers face these kinds of concerns each day. Businesses involved in importing and exporting offer a wide variety of career opportunities. Some positions that deal with regulations, transportation, and finance are unique to international business.

Businesses involved in importing or exporting need professionals who understand the rules and regulations related to cross-border transactions. For example, an export document control specialist creates and maintains databases of required licenses and agreements. These documents are required for both sides of the transactions. They allow products to be shipped out of the exporting country and they permit products to enter the receiving nation. In addition to knowing and understanding import and export regulations, this position requires strong communication skills for interacting with colleagues, suppliers, and customers around the world. Adaptability to change and willingness to learn are required because import-export regulations change frequently.

Working for a freight forwarder as a logistics coordinator is an example of a career in the transportation aspect of importing and exporting. A freight clerk plans travel routes and prepares necessary shipping documents. In some cases, a freight clerk may also be involved in negotiating cargo space and pricing. This position requires strong math and computer skills, along with a working knowledge of geography. Time management skills and the ability to work under pressure are important.

With over 300,000 U.S. import companies bringing goods worth more than $600 billion into the country each year, financing activities create other career opportunities. The Export-Import Bank, for example, employs loan specialists, accountants, financial analysts, and economists. Preparation for these careers usually requires a college degree in business. Some positions require graduate degrees.

In addition to the skills required for a specific position, interpersonal skills and the ability to work well with people from different cultural backgrounds are critical in the international business environment. The ability to speak more than one language is an asset for any career related to importing and exporting.

Think Critically

1. What skills required for import-export careers are you interested in developing?
2. Conduct an Internet search to obtain additional information about career opportunities in importing and exporting.

stask/iStockphoto.com

6-1 Assessment

REVIEW GLOBAL BUSINESS TERMS

Define the following term.

1. customs official

REVIEW GLOBAL BUSINESS CONCEPTS

2. What are the main reasons companies import goods?

3. What is the purpose of the customs department of a country's government?

SOLVE GLOBAL BUSINESS PROBLEMS

For each of the following situations, predict whether the imports will be successful in your country. Explain your reasons.

4. Imported ice skates that are more expensive than those already on the market but that have the reputation of being the best in the world.

5. Ten thousand cases of shampoo in bottles with foreign-language labels that can be sold for a price matching the lowest-price shampoo on the market.

6. An imported soy-based dessert called *Zenzip*.

7. Imported clothing sized in an inconsistent manner compared with other brands.

8. An imported packaged dinner entrée that contains blue pasta.

THINK CRITICALLY

9. What types of imports should not be allowed to enter the United States?

10. Do imports threaten the jobs of people in the importing country?

MAKE ACADEMIC CONNECTIONS

11. **STATISTICS** If South Korea has exports of $419 billion, Singapore $235 billion, and Taiwan $255 billion, what is the average value of exports for the three countries?

12. **TECHNOLOGY** Find a web site for one of the larger countries in the Asia-Pacific Rim Country Regional Profile. List the country and its five largest imports.

13. **VISUAL ARTS** Prepare a flow chart or other visual representation of the importing process.

14. **CULTURAL STUDIES** Collect examples of unusual food products imported from other countries.

6-2 Exporting Procedures

PhotoDisc/Getty Images

GOALS

- Identify the steps of the exporting process.
- Describe the exporting of services.

The Exporting Process

Companies commonly export goods or services to companies in other countries. *Indirect exporting* occurs when a company sells its products in a foreign market without actively seeking out those opportunities. More often, however, a business will conduct *direct exporting* by actively seeking export opportunities.

Exporting activities are the other side of the importing transaction. As exporters, however, businesses face different decisions. The process of exporting involves five steps, as shown in Figure 6-2.

The Exporting Process

STEP 1	STEP 2	STEP 3	STEP 4	STEP 5
Find Potential Customers	Meet the Needs of Customers	Agree on Sales Terms	Deliver Products or Services	Complete the Transaction

Figure 6-2 Successful exporting can help a nation expand its economic activities and create additional jobs.

GLOBAL TECHNOLOGY TRENDS

Online Retailing and Lower Barriers to Entry

Buying books, music, videos, software, clothing, and even groceries without leaving home is nothing new. People have been able to do this for years with mail-order buying and television shopping channels. Today this buying process is even easier.

The Internet has reduced some barriers to entry for new companies. In the past, an entrepreneur had to rent a store, hire employees, obtain inventory, and advertise when starting a business. Now a person can begin operations with a computer. Contacting suppliers, promoting the company, and filling orders are all done online.

This ease of start-up for an online retailer (sometimes called an *e-tailer*) has resulted in lower barriers to entry and increased competition. No longer must a company have a store, an office, or a factory. Instead, a book or clothing seller can serve customers with an online transaction, with the shipping company representative being the only one who has to leave home.

Think Critically

1. What types of enterprises are best suited for doing business online?
2. How will expanded online buying affect job opportunities and economic development in local communities?
3. Locate a web site that offers customers a variety of products online. How does the company attempt to attract customers?

STEP 1 FIND POTENTIAL CUSTOMERS

Before you sell anything, you have to find buyers. Who are the people who want to buy your goods and services? Where are these people located? Are the potential customers willing and able to purchase your products?

Answers to these questions may be found through an Internet search and library research. Businesses use many sources to find out about the buying habits of people in different countries. Also, businesspeople familiar with foreign markets have experience helping companies that want to sell in other countries.

The U.S. Department of Commerce and other agencies and organizations provide *trade leads* listing export opportunities for companies planning to do business overseas. For example, a recent listing identified an opportunity to sell cosmetics manufacturing machinery in Chennai, India. The U.S. Commercial Service, the Foreign Agricultural Service, and the Federation of International Trade Associations are sources for information on potential customers in other countries.

STEP 2 MEET THE NEEDS OF CUSTOMERS

Next, determine if people in other countries can use your product or service. Sending company representatives to possible markets around the world is one way to make sure your product can be sold there. If visits are not possible, companies can obtain reliable information from other sources.

Will your product be accepted by foreign customers exactly as it is, or will it be necessary to adapt it? Product adaptation may need to be in the form of smaller packages, different ingredients, or revised label information to meet geographic, social, cultural, and legal requirements.

Some products are *standardized* or sold the same around the world. Popular soft drinks, some clothing, and many technical products (such as cameras, computers, and home entertainment systems) are frequently sold in various geographic areas with only minor changes. However, food products, personal care items, and laundry detergent usually need to be *adapted* to the tastes, customs, and culture of a society.

STEP 3 AGREE ON SALES TERMS

Every business transaction involves shipping and payment terms. These terms require businesses to answer a number of important questions. What is the price of the items? How will the products be shipped? Who will pay for shipping costs, the buyer or the seller? In what currency will the payment be made? What foreign exchange rate will be used? When is the payment due?

Shipping costs vary for different types of transportation. Airfreight is more costly than water transportation. However, it is much quicker. Items in high demand or perishable products might require the quickest available method of delivery.

Transportation costs can be a major portion of the cost of exporting. It is important to consider which party will pay transportation costs. Sometimes the seller pays for shipping. In other situations, the buyer pays. Certain terms are used to describe the shipping and payment methods. **Free on board (FOB)** means the selling price of the product includes the cost of loading the exported goods onto transport vessels at the specified place. **Cost, insurance, and freight (CIF)** means that the cost of the goods, insurance, and freight are included in the price quoted. **Cost and freight (C&F)** indicates that the price includes the cost of the goods and freight, but the buyer must pay for insurance separately.

Banks and other financial institutions are likely to be involved in the payment phase of export transactions. A company may have to borrow funds to finance the cost of manufacturing and shipping a product for which payment will not be received until a later date. Besides loans, international financial institutions may also offer other exporting services.

Work as a Team
Suggest ways to encourage companies to get involved in exporting.

choicegraphx/iStockphoto.com

STEP 4 DELIVER PRODUCTS OR SERVICES

After agreement is reached on selling terms, the products or services must be delivered. This means raw materials, parts, or finished goods are shipped. If the exchange involves a service, the company must now perform the required tasks for its foreign customers.

Some exporters make arrangements for shipping their own products, but others prefer to rely on experts for help with shipping. A **freight forwarder** is a company that arranges to ship goods to customers. Like a travel agent for cargo, these companies take care of the reservations needed to get an exporter's merchandise to the required destination.

GLOBAL BUSINESS SPOTLIGHT

EXPORTING CULTURE

The demand for U.S. clothing, soft drinks, fast food, candy, movies, music, television programs, and other entertainment is very strong in many parts of the world. Jeans, T-shirts, sports team hats, and athletic shoes are top sellers around the globe. People in some nations will wait in line for hours to pay for Coca-Cola or for a McDonald's hamburger.

Television programs such as *The Simpsons, Grey's Anatomy, Survivor, and Lost* are seen by hundreds of millions of television viewers each day. CNN, ESPN, and MTV have created international channels for worldwide viewing. Movie characters such as Batman, Spiderman, Indiana Jones, Lara Croft, James Bond, and Harry Potter earn film studios millions of dollars in profits outside the United States. The music of Miley Cyrus, Beyonce, Usher, and the Jonas Brothers is played on radio stations, in stores, and in homes in more than 150 countries.

While soccer (called football in most countries) remains the world's most popular sport, others are attempting to gain ground. National Basketball Association (NBA) teams have held games in 10 countries outside of North America. In recent years, the World Baseball Classic has included teams representing 16 nations. And, the National Football League (NFL) has a European league, while NFL games have been played in England, Japan, Germany, and Mexico.

Think Critically

1. What effect could exporting of U.S. culture have on the cultural environment of other countries?
2. What are the benefits associated with exporting culture?
3. Locate a web site with information about country's cultural exports. What are the country's largest cultural exports? How does the volume of cultural exports compare with other exported goods and services?

Photodisc/Getty Images

Often a freight forwarder will accumulate several small export shipments and combine them into one large shipment to get lower freight rates. Because these companies are actively involved in international trade, freight forwarders are excellent sources of information about export regulations, shipping costs, and foreign import regulations.

Companies must prepare export documents for shipping merchandise to other countries. Customers, insurers, government agencies and others involved in the process have specific documentation requirements. Two common shipping documents are a bill of lading and a certificate of origin. A **bill of lading** is a document stating the agreement between the exporter and the transportation company. This document serves as a receipt for the exported items. A **certificate of origin** is a document that states the name of the country in which the shipped goods were produced. This document may be used to determine the amount of any import tax.

STEP 5 COMPLETE THE TRANSACTION

If payment has not already been received, it would be due when the products are received by the purchaser. Often, payment involves exchanging one country's currency for another's. Financial institutions convert currency and are usually involved in the payment step. Electronic payments are common.

✓ CheckPoint
What are the five steps of the exporting process?

Other Exporting Issues

In addition to the five steps of exporting described above, companies face a variety of obstacles. Also, the exporting of services must be addressed in a slightly different manner than the global selling of a tangible product.

OBSTACLES TO EXPORTING

The United States Department of Commerce estimates that thousands of small and medium-sized businesses could easily get involved in international business, but they don't. There are several reasons companies may not export.

- No company representatives in foreign countries
- Products not appropriate for foreign consumers
- Insufficient production facilities to manufacture enough goods for exporting
- High costs of doing business in other countries
- Difficulty understanding foreign business procedures
- Difficulty obtaining payment from foreign customers

Many of these obstacles could be overcome if companies obtained assistance from agencies

Photodisc/Getty Images

such as the U.S. Department of Commerce, the U.S. Small Business Administration, and the USA Trade Center.

EXPORTING SERVICES

Most people can relate to selling, packing, and shipping a tangible item. However, a major portion of U.S. exports involves the sale of *intangible* items—services. Service industries account for about 70 percent of GDP in the United States. International trade by service industries is significant. Services provided by U.S. companies are more than 20 percent of the world's total cross-border sales of services.

Companies export services with some of the same techniques they use to export products. These techniques include international consulting, direct exporting, licensing, franchising, and joint venture.

The most commonly exported services include hospitality (hotels and food service), entertainment (movies, music, television production, and amusement parks), and financial services (insurance and real estate). Other areas of expanding service exports involve health care, information processing, distribution services, and education and training services. Exporting of services, such as health care, occurs when a company provides on-site training, technical assistance, or medical treatment services in another country.

✓ **Check**Point

What services are most commonly exported by U.S. companies?

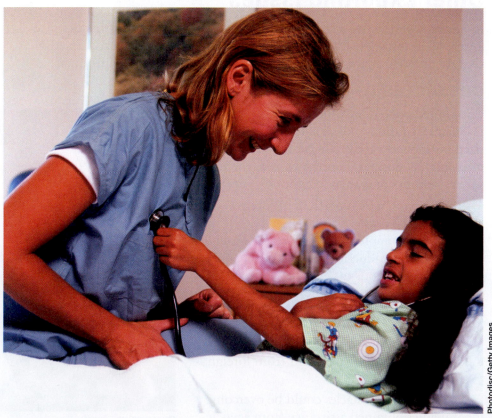

Photodisc/Getty Images

6-2 Assessment

REVIEW GLOBAL BUSINESS TERMS

Define each of the following terms.

1. free on board (FOB)
2. cost, insurance, and freight (CIF)
3. cost and freight (C&F)
4. freight forwarder
5. bill of lading
6. certificate of origin

Study Tools

www.cengage.com/school/genbus/intlbiz

REVIEW GLOBAL BUSINESS CONCEPTS

7. How can exporting companies determine if their products can be sold in other countries?

8. Why are banks often involved in export transactions?

9. What determines whether an exporter ships by air or water?

SOLVE GLOBAL BUSINESS PROBLEMS

For each of the following exporting situations, decide whether the company should sell the same product (standardize) as in other countries or adapt the product (customize) to local tastes, customs, and culture. Explain your reasons.

10. Exporting World Cup championship shirts and hats.

11. Exporting digital cameras for sale in major cities across Europe and North America.

12. Exporting electrical appliances to a country with a different voltage system.

13. Exporting plain, unflavored yogurt to a country in which the people do not usually eat yogurt.

14. Exporting forklift trucks for use in warehouses in Asia.

THINK CRITICALLY

15. How does the exporting of services differ from exporting goods?

16. Why are governments frequently interested in encouraging exports?

MAKE ACADEMIC CONNECTIONS

17. **TECHNOLOGY** Visit the web site of the Bureau of Industry and Security to learn more about exporting regulations faced by U.S. companies.

18. **SCIENCE** Describe recent scientific developments that have improved the speed and efficiency of exporting.

19. **HISTORY** Research the effect of various inventions on the major exports of a country.

20. **TECHNOLOGY** Use the Internet to research local rules and regulations for exporting from various countries around the world.

6-3 Importance of Trade Relations

- Identify the economic effects of foreign trade.
- Describe the types of trade agreements between countries.

Photodisc/Getty Images

The Economic Effect of Foreign Trade

Every importing and exporting transaction has economic effects. The difference between a country's exports and imports is called its *balance of trade*. Some countries continually buy more foreign goods than they sell. The result is a **trade deficit**, which is the result of importing more goods and services than the country is exporting. In contrast, a **trade surplus** occurs when a country exports more than it imports.

The United States, despite being the largest exporter in the world, has had a trade deficit for many years. This situation can result in a country borrowing from other countries. Borrowing means the country must pay back money in the future, reducing the amount available for other spending. Balance of trade does not include all international business transactions, just imports and exports. Another economic measure is needed to summarize the total economic effect of foreign trade. **Balance of payments**, illustrated in Figure 6-3, measures the total flow of money coming into a country minus the total flow going out. Included in this economic measurement are exports, imports, investments, tourist spending, and financial assistance. For example, tourism can help a country's balance of payments as a result of an increase in the flow of money entering the nation.

A country's balance of payments can be either positive or negative. A *positive*, or *favorable*, balance of payments occurs when a nation receives more money in a year than it pays out. A *negative* balance of payments is *unfavorable*. It is the result when a country sends more money out than it brings in.

Balance of Payments

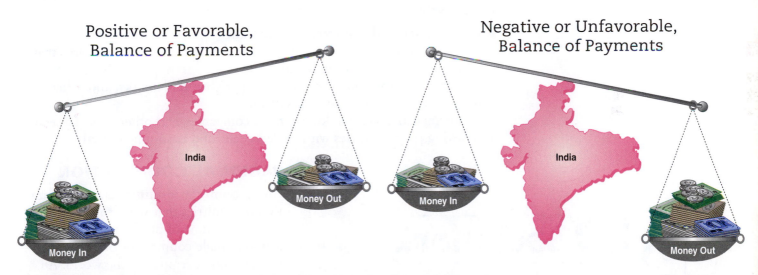

Figure 6-3 Balance of payments is the total flow of money coming into a country minus the total flow of money going out of a country. A country may have a favorable balance of payments some years, as shown on the left. In other years the balance of payments may be unfavorable, as shown on the right.

 **CheckPoint**
What action results in a country having a trade deficit?

Trade Agreements

How can a country improve its international trade situation? One answer is by negotiating trade agreements. Trade agreements between countries promote economic development on a worldwide basis or in a geographic region. In some cases individual nations and companies enter agreements that encourage international business activities.

THE WORLD TRADE ORGANIZATION

After World War II, world leaders who wanted to promote peaceful international trade developed a set of ground rules to guide the conduct of international trade. The General Agreement on Tariffs and Trade (GATT) was negotiated in 1947 and began operating in January 1948 when 23 countries signed the treaty agreement.

This multicountry agreement intended to reduce trade barriers and to promote trade. The goals of GATT were to promote world trade through negotiation and to make world trade secure. Working toward these goals helped increase global economic growth and development.

In 1995, GATT was replaced by a new organization—the World Trade Organization (WTO). With over 150 member countries, WTO has many of the same goals as GATT. But in addition, WTO has the power to settle trade disputes and enforce the free-trade agreements between its members.

Based in Geneva, Switzerland, the WTO deals with the rules of trade between nations. Its goal is to help producers of goods and services, exporters, and importers conduct their business. The WTO encourages international trade in several ways.

- Lowering tariffs that discourage free trade
- Eliminating import quotas, subsidies, and unfair technical standards that reduce competition in the world market
- Recognizing protection for patents, copyrights, trademarks, and other intellectual properties, such as software
- Reducing barriers for banks, insurance companies, and other financial services
- Assisting poor countries with trade policies and economic growth

REGIONAL COOPERATION

An **economic community** is an organization of countries that work together to allow a free flow of products. The group acts as a single country for business activities with other regions of the world. An economic community is also called a *common market*. Membership in an economic community has several main benefits.

- Expanded trade with other regions of the world
- Reduced tariffs for the member countries
- Lower prices for consumers within the group
- Expanded employment and investment opportunities

Work as a Team

Prepare a list of benefits and concerns associated with economic communities and countertrade.

NETBookmark

The World Trade Organization (WTO) is a major international organization that helps assure that trade flows smoothly and freely. WTO focuses on the global rules of trade between nations. To learn more about the history and functions of this organization, access the web site shown below and click on the link for Chapter 6. After navigating this web site and reading the information, discuss one benefit of and one misunderstanding about the WTO trading system.

www.cengage.com/school/genbus/intlbiz

EUROPEAN UNION

The European Union (EU) is an economic and political organization with member nations across Europe. This relationship allows over 500 million consumers to purchase products from any of the countries without paying import or export taxes.

The European Union is headquartered in Brussels, Belgium. The EU Commission has 20 commissioners who are responsible for areas such as labor, health, the environment, education, transportation, and trade. The policy-setting body is the Council of the European Union consisting of the heads of state or government from the member countries. Voters in each member country elect the European Parliament. The parliament, with more than 700 representatives, is in Strasbourg, France.

This economic community works toward several goals.

- Eliminating tariffs and other trade barriers
- Creating a uniform tariff schedule
- Forming a common market for free movement of labor, capital, and business enterprises
- Establishing common agricultural and food safety policies
- Channeling capital from more advanced to less developed regions

In 1999, the EU introduced a common currency—the *euro*. During the transition to full use of this new monetary unit, prices in the stores of EU countries were stated in both euros and the previous national currencies such as the franc, lira, and deutsche mark.

After starting with six countries, today the EU has 27 members. Bulgaria and Romania are the most recent additions.

Think Critically

1. What are some concerns with a highly integrated economic community such as the European Union?
2. Go to the web site of the European Union to obtain current information about the activities of this economic community. Which countries, if any, are currently members of the EU? Which countries, if any, are seeking to gain membership to the EU?

Examples of this type of regional economic cooperation among countries include the European Union (EU), Latin American Free Trade Association (LAFTA), the Association of Southeast Asian Nations (ASEAN), the Economic Community of West African States (ECOWAS), and the North American Free Trade Agreement (NAFTA).

BARTER AGREEMENTS

Most people have traded one item for another at some time. The exchange of goods and services between two parties with no money involved is **direct barter**. A company may use this method for international business transactions.

Because trading items of equal value is difficult, a different barter method is used. **Countertrade** is the exchange of products or services between companies in different countries with the possibility of some currency exchange. For example, when PepsiCo owned Pizza Hut, it sold soft drinks in China in exchange for mushrooms used on pizzas. Countertrade can involve companies in several countries, as shown in Figure 6-4 on the next page.

Because countertrades are quite complex, they usually involve large companies. Smaller companies, however, can get involved in countertrade by working with large trading agents who bring together many buyers and sellers.

Companies use countertrade to avoid the risk of receiving payment in a monetary unit with limited value. Currencies from some nations are not in demand due to the weakness of those countries' economies. Countertrade

Countertrade in Action

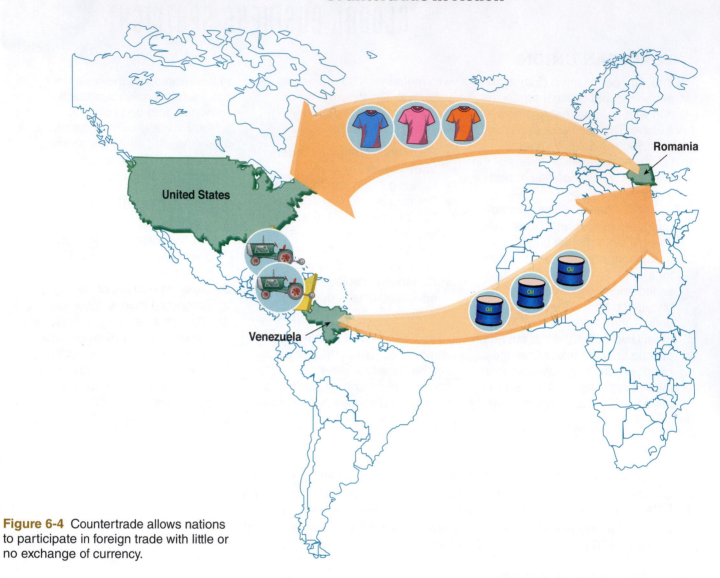

Figure 6-4 Countertrade allows nations to participate in foreign trade with little or no exchange of currency.

also occurs when the government of an importing country requires the selling company to purchase products in return. This helps the importing country to avoid a trade deficit while stimulating economic growth.

FREE-TRADE ZONES

A *free-trade zone* is an area designated by a government for duty-free entry of nonprohibited goods. Free-trade zones are commonly located at a point of entry into a nation, such as a harbor or an airport. Merchandise may be stored, displayed, or used without duties being paid. Duties (import taxes) are imposed on the goods only when the items pass from the free-trade zone into an area of the country subject to customs.

✓ **Check**Point
What are examples of trade agreements among countries?

REVIEW GLOBAL BUSINESS TERMS

Define each of the following terms.

1. trade deficit
2. trade surplus
3. balance of payments
4. economic community
5. direct barter
6. countertrade

REVIEW GLOBAL BUSINESS CONCEPTS

6. How can a trade deficit affect a country's economy?

7. Why is countertrade used in international business?

SOLVE GLOBAL BUSINESS PROBLEMS

For the company or country mentioned in each of the following situations, decide whether the balance of payments or the trade balance is affected and whether the effect would be favorable or unfavorable.

8. A country in Europe receives foreign aid from the government of another country.

9. A six-month long World's Fair is held in the United States and attracts over a million tourists from other countries.

10. An Asian country imports oil that it will pay for later.

11. A multinational company in England pays cash for a factory in India.

12. A new advance in genetic testing is made in Argentina, and the technology is exported all over the world.

THINK CRITICALLY

13. What can a government do to improve a trade deficit?

14. What are some possible concerns of labor unions, environmental groups, and public interest organizations regarding actions of the World Trade Organization?

MAKE ACADEMIC CONNECTIONS

15. **MATHEMATICS** If a country has inflows of $376 billion and outflows of $402 billion, what is the amount of the favorable (or unfavorable) balance of payments?

16. **HISTORY** Research the start of the European Economic Community in the 1950s. What factors influenced the start of this common market?

17. **COMMUNICATIONS** Without using words, demonstrate a barter transaction between people from different cultures.

6-4 The Nature of Competition

GOALS

- List factors that affect international business competition.
- Explain the types of competitive market situations.

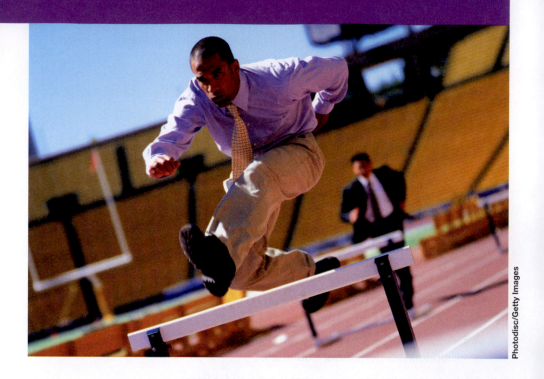

Photodisc/Getty Images

International Business Competition

Most likely you have participated in a sport or an activity in which you attempted to do better than others or better than you had done previously. While winning may not always be the main goal, competition is an on-going activity for people, companies, and nations. In an effort to improve a country's economic situation, a strong competitive effort may be beneficial.

Companies compete in both domestic and international markets. The *domestic market* is made up of all the companies that sell similar products within the same country. In contrast, the *international market* is made up of companies that compete against companies in several countries. For example, major soft drink companies have competition in other countries with Crazy Cola in Russia and Thums Up Cola in India.

For companies or countries to gain a competitive advantage they need to do something better, faster, or cheaper than others do. While many people believe the best product is always successful, sometimes a company can also succeed through an effective delivery system. For example, candy products from Nestlé are available around the world. This distribution program creates a *competitive advantage* and makes it difficult for other candy manufacturers to gain sales.

Companies can also compete by successfully doing one thing and doing it well. For example, the demand for airplanes made in Japan is not as high as the demand for planes made in the United States. Japanese companies, however, have specialized in producing components used by U.S. aircraft manufacturers, such as fuselage parts, landing-gear doors, and on-board computers. In addition to direct exporting, the airline parts companies are involved in hundreds of joint ventures and licensing agreements. These efforts have resulted in a significant increase in Japanese aerospace exports.

FACTORS AFFECTING COMPETITION

Three major factors affect the degree of competition among businesses. These factors are the number of companies, business costs, and product differences.

Number of Companies When many companies are selling the same product, there may appear to be a high degree of competition. However, if just a few large firms control the major portion of sales, then competition is limited.

Business Costs The cost of doing business often affects competition. Expensive equipment or having to compete against well-known brands might prevent new companies from starting. Conditions that make it extremely difficult to enter a business are called *barriers to entry*. For example, if a business needs large amounts of capital and equipment to start operations, only a few companies are likely to enter the market. Or, if an existing company has an established brand name, it will be very costly for new companies to make their name known.

Product Differences The third factor that creates competition is product differences. Companies use advertising, brand names, packages, and ingredients to convince consumers that their products are different and better. The addition of flavoring to toothpaste and packaging that can be reused for other purposes are examples of attempts by companies to gain a competitive advantage. Companies use advertising messages to inform consumers about the benefits of their products and to persuade them to buy.

COMMUNICATION ACROSS BORDERS

UNDERSTANDING ASIAN NAMES

When communicating with Asians about trading opportunities, it is important to realize that their naming practices may be different from yours.

A surname, also known as a family name, is the name that links family members. Many surnames have their origins in occupations and locations. In the United States, a surname often is called a last name.

In many Asian countries, the family name comes first, followed by the given name. In Korea, Kim Yun is Mr. Kim, not Mr. Yun.

In the People's Republic of China, more than 100 million people, about 10 percent of the population, have the same surname—Zhang. Fewer than 20 surnames account for more than 60 percent of the population. In Korea, four surnames account for more than 50 percent of the population. Thus, the surnames in some Asian countries are not as distinctive an identifier as they are in the United States. Therefore, it is necessary to learn full names, titles, and divisions within a business in order to communicate with the desired Asian business associates.

Think Critically

1. What kind of an impression will you create if you reverse the order of the names of a potential Asian business partner?
2. What question should you ask to find out about the naming customs in another country?

Work as a Team

Discuss the way you compete with other students in academics, athletics, and social relationships. Then discuss the advantages and disadvantages of such competition.

BENEFITS AND CONCERNS OF COMPETITION

Competition can improve the economic situation and living conditions of a nation. Individual and company efforts to create better goods and services in less time have been a benefit for many nations. Some business competition, however, can result in major concerns. If a company becomes so large that it controls a geographic area or a portion of an economy, many people may suffer. Consumers will have to pay whatever the business charges. Workers will have to work for the amount the company wants to pay because other jobs may not be available. For these reasons, most countries have laws that limit the power of companies.

✓ **CheckPoint**

What are common barriers to entry for new competitors in an industry?

Types of Competitive Situations

Have you ever wondered why there are so many breakfast cereals or why only a few stores sell a certain brand of shoes? These questions can be answered with an understanding of the competitive situations in an industry. An **industry** refers to companies in the same type of business. For example, Kellogg, General Mills, Kraft General Foods, and Quaker are the major companies in the breakfast cereal industry. Nike, Reebok, and Adidas are in the athletic shoe industry. The competitive situation among companies is also called the *market structure* of an industry. Four main competitive situations may be present in a country's economy, as shown in Figure 6-5.

©Osa, 2009/ Used under license from Shutterstock.com

PURE COMPETITION

Pure competition is a market situation with many sellers, each offering the same product. For example, when farmers sell their wheat or corn, there is little difference from one bushel to another. Supply and demand determines the price. Rivalry among businesses is most free when many companies offer identical or very similar products to buyers. Various factors in our economy and society, however, limit pure competition.

Competitive Market Situations

Pure Competition
- Many sellers
- Same product

Monopolistic Competition
- Many sellers
- Slightly different product

Oligopoly
- Few sellers
- Slightly different product

Monopoly
- One seller
- Usually government regulated

Figure 6-5 The number of businesses and differences in products affect the amount of competition in a market.

MONOPOLISTIC COMPETITION

In order for companies to attract customers, they make their products slightly different. One fast-food hamburger restaurant offers a special sauce, another adds bacon and cheese, while another gives away a game or toy with the sandwich. **Monopolistic competition** refers to a market situation with many sellers, each with a slightly different product. The difference in products can be actual (such as ingredients) or implied (such as different advertisements, a brand name, or a package design).

OLIGOPOLY

When a few large companies control an industry, an **oligopoly** exists. In this market situation, the few sellers usually offer products that are slightly different. However, competition is mainly the result of large companies being able to advertise and sell their goods in many geographic areas. For example,

Photodisc/Getty Images

only a few large companies make automobile tires. Therefore, these large manufacturers are able to control the market. Another example is that with only a few countries having oil as a natural resource, companies in these nations can influence the availability and price of oil.

MONOPOLY

When one company controls the total supply of a product or service, there is no competition. A **monopoly** is a situation in which one seller controls the entire market for a product or service. It is very unusual for this to happen without actions by government or other businesses. Like pure competition, few examples of true monopolies exist. Situations that are near monopolies include South Africa's diamond mines and a small village or town served by only one store. Monopolies that exist in the United States, such as cable television, local water service, and first-class mail delivery service, are government regulated.

✓ CheckPoint
What are the four types of competitive situations?

6-4 Assessment

REVIEW GLOBAL BUSINESS TERMS

Define each of the following terms.

1. industry
2. pure competition
3. monopolistic competition
4. oligopoly
5. monopoly

REVIEW GLOBAL BUSINESS CONCEPTS

6. What are the main factors that affect the amount of business competition?

7. What are the advantages of competition?

8. What is the difference between actual and implied differences in monopolistic competition?

SOLVE GLOBAL BUSINESS PROBLEMS

For each of the follow situations, decide which competitive situation is present: pure competition, monopolistic competition, oligopoly, or monopoly.

9. A country in Asia allows only one company to manufacture a product.

10. In a European country, four companies control over 85 percent of sales in the supermarket industry.

11. In a region of western Africa, minerals are mined and sold by many extracting companies.

12. In an area of the Middle East, many small shops offer a variety of clothing styles.

THINK CRITICALLY

13. What types of actions could consumers and government take to promote competition?

14. What kind of competition exists in the microcomputer operating systems market today?

MAKE ACADEMIC CONNECTIONS

15. **CULTURAL STUDIES** Select a product that you use frequently. Determine what appeals to you about the product, including how it is advertised. Consider whether the elements you have determined would appeal to people in other countries. Write a summary of your findings.

16. **LAW** Research the start of antitrust legislation in the United States. What applications of those laws are in the news today?

CHAPTER SUMMARY

6-1 IMPORTING PROCEDURES

A Importing is important to business for meeting consumer demand, lowering operating costs, and obtaining production inputs.

B The four steps of importing are (1) determine demand, (2) contact suppliers, (3) finalize purchases, and (4) receive goods.

6-2 EXPORTING PROCEDURES

A The five steps of the exporting process are (1) find potential customers, (2) meet the needs of customers, (3) agree on sales terms, (4) provide products or services, and (5) complete the transaction.

B The exporting of services can be a significant percentage of a country's export activities.

6-3 IMPORTANCE OF TRADE RELATIONS

A A country's balance of payments measures the total flow of money coming into a country minus the total flow going out and may be positive or negative. A trade deficit is the total amount a country owes to other countries as a result of importing more goods and services than are exported.

B The main types of trade agreements are the World Trade Organization, economic communities, barter agreements, and free-trade zones.

6-4 THE NATURE OF COMPETITION

A The competitive situation in a country is affected by (1) the number of companies, (2) business costs, and (3) product differences.

B The four main types of competitive markets are pure competition, monopolistic competition, oligopoly, and monopoly.

GLOBAL REFOCUS

Read the Global Focus at the beginning of this chapter, and answer the following questions.

1. What actions might an ice cream company take to expand export activities?

2. How could foreign companies become more competitive in the global ice cream industry?

REVIEW GLOBAL BUSINESS TERMS

Match the terms listed with the definitions. Some terms may not be used.

1. Government employee who is authorized to collect the dutites levied on imports.
2. A company that arranges to ship goods to customers.
3. The exchange of products or services between companies in different countries with the possibility of some currency exchange.
4. Control of an industry by a few large companies.
5. A document that states the agreement between the exporter and the transportation company.
6. The total flow of money coming into a country minus the total flow going out.
7. A market situation with many sellers, each with a slightly different product.
8. An organization of countries that bond together to allow a free flow of products.
9. Terms of sale that mean the selling price of the product includes the cost of loading the exported goods onto transport vessels at the specified place.
10. A situation in which one seller controls the entire market for a product or service.

a. balance of payments
b. bill of lading
c. certificate of origin
d. cost and freight (C&F)
e. cost, insurance, and freight (CIF)
f. countertrade
g. customs official
h. direct barter
i. economic community
j. free on board (FOB)
k. freight forwarder
l. industry
m. monopolistic competition
n. monopoly
o. oligopoly
p. pure competition
q. trade deficit
r. trade surplus

11. The cost of the goods, insurance, and freight are included in the price quoted.
12. The exchange of goods and services between two parties with no money involved.
13. A group of companies in the same type of business.
14. A document that states the name of the country in which the shipped goods were produced.
15. A market situation with many sellers, each offering the same product.
16. The result of a country importing more goods and services than the country is exporting.
17. The price includes the cost of the goods and freight, but the buyer must pay for insurance separately.

MAKE GLOBAL BUSINESS DECISIONS

18. Name some examples of imported products that the people in the United States need and want.
19. Why are taxes imposed on products imported into various countries?
20. List some resources you could use to determine the buying habits in different countries.
21. What factors would affect whether the buyer or the seller pays for the shipping costs in an international business transaction?

22. Why might a country's balance of payments be a better measurement of its international business activities than its balance of trade?

23. What problems might arise when nations create an economic community for international trade?

24. Describe some examples of countertrade involving products from different countries with which you are familiar.

MAKE ACADEMIC CONNECTIONS

25. TECHNOLOGY Go to the web site of the World Trade Organization to obtain additional information about the current activities of this global trade association.

26. LAW Investigate the duties and customs procedures of one of the following countries: Malaysia, Australia, Taiwan, China, India, South Korea, Singapore, or New Zealand.

27. GEOGRAPHY Find the location of the free-trade zone closest to your city. Draw a map that includes your state, the location of the free-trade zone, and all states in between. Then draw a line between your city and the free-trade zone. Mark the distance above the line. If the free-trade zone is in your city, draw a map of your city, and identify the location of the free-trade zone.

28. COMMUNICATIONS Talk to someone who has shipped goods to another country. Prepare a short oral report about the procedures for transporting merchandise to a foreign country.

29. CULTURAL STUDIES Collect advertisements, packages, and other information about products made in another country and sold in the United States. Ask five friends or relatives to identify the country of origin for the product.

30. SCIENCE Many products in our society compete on the basis of very minor differences. Collect information on five different brands of soap, toothpaste, breakfast cereal, or shampoo from advertisements, packages, and periodicals. Based on your analysis and comments from others, list the similarities and differences of the brands selected. *Consumer Reports* is a good source of information for this activity.

31. CAREER PLANNING Obtain information about the imports and exports of a country of your choice. What types of job opportunities would be created by these foreign business activities?

32. TECHNOLOGY Use the Internet to find examples of businesses that are involved in pure competition, monopolistic competition, oligopolies, and monopolies.

33. ECONOMICS Go to the web site of an economic community. Make a list of the members of that community and some of the activities in which it engages.

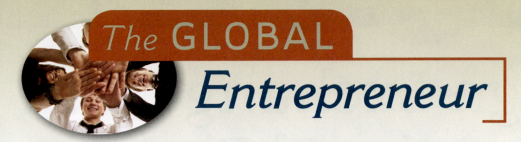

The GLOBAL *Entrepreneur*

CREATING AN INTERNATIONAL BUSINESS PLAN

Developing an Exporting Plan

Use a product or service that your chosen company is actively exporting or that you believe has potential for sales in other countries. Then select a country that would provide a market opportunity for that product or service. Use information collected for Chapters 1–5 and additional research to prepare an exporting plan. Include the following components.

1. Product description
   - Describe the product or service in detail, including specific features.
   - Describe any changes in the product or service that may be necessary before exporting.

2. Foreign business environment
   - List cultural and social factors that may affect the sale of the product.
   - Discuss the geography of the country to which you have chosen to export this product or service.
   - Describe economic conditions that may affect exporting this product.
   - Report any political or legal factors that could affect exporting activities.

3. Market potential
   - Describe the type of customer who is best suited for this product or service in the country you have chosen.
   - Identify methods that could be used to contact potential buyers in the country you have chosen.
   - Estimate sales for the product or service based on country size, market demand, and competition.

4. Export transaction details
   - Describe import taxes or other restrictions that may affect exporting costs.
   - Discuss the shipping and documentation requirements for the country you have selected.
   - Identify the amount of time the exporting plan will take to execute.

Sources of information for researching your exporting plan are listed below.

   - reference books such as encyclopedias, almanacs, and atlases
   - current news, business, and travel articles, including news stories, company profiles, and advertisements
   - web sites for exporting information
   - materials from companies, airlines, travel bureaus, government agencies, and other organizations involved in international business
   - interviews with people who have been to the country

Foreign Exchange and International Finance

7-1 Money Systems Around the World

7-2 Foreign Exchange and Currency Controls

7-3 Currency Transactions Between Nations

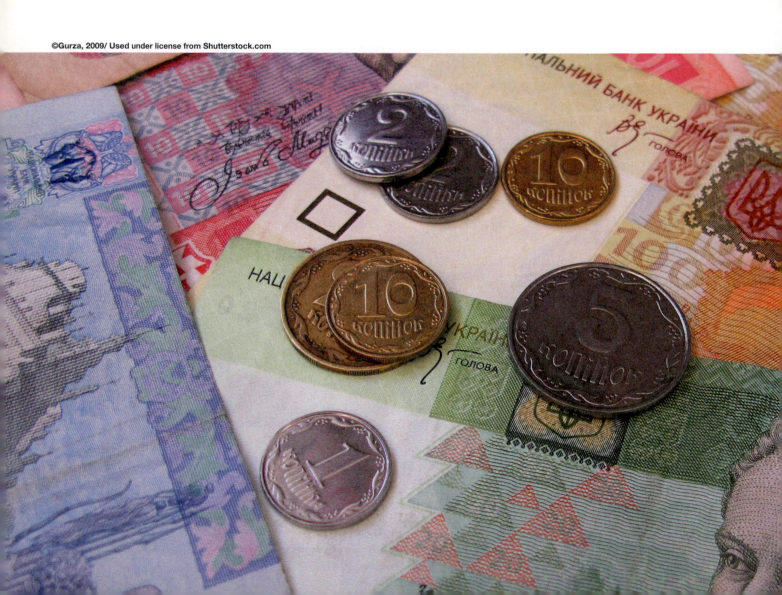

GLOBAL FOCUS

An Unexpected Currency for Ukraine

In the early 1990s, the formerly united Soviet Union divided into separate countries. When this occurred, the Russian ruble was no longer the monetary unit for some of the newly independent nations.

While the people of Ukraine were waiting to convert to a new currency, the need to have money in circulation was critical. To prevent a financial crisis, the Ukrainian government issued coupons for use in buying the country's limited supplies of food and other products. These coupons, called *Karbovanets*, were not originally intended to be the new Ukrainian currency. However, as Ukraine's economy developed, these coupons became widely accepted as money. At first, Ukrainians were using both the coupons and the Russian ruble. As the new monetary system replaced the old one, rubles became less acceptable for making purchases. The acceptance of the ration coupons made them the unofficial currency of Ukraine.

The use of these coupons as legal tender eventually ended. Today Ukraine's currency is the *hryvnia*. This word, used since the eleventh century, comes from a word that originally referred to the valuable things worn around the neck. Introduced in 1996, the hryvnia has been one of the most stable currencies in this region of the world.

To build on the stable monetary value and expand the country's economic development, the World Bank has provided Ukraine with several loans. These funds helped to improve the country's agricultural productivity and to expand food product exports especially grains, sugar beets, and vegetables.

Think Critically

1. What problems can occur in an economy that does not have enough money in circulation?
2. What made the ration coupons valuable in the Ukrainian economy?
3. What made the Russian ruble less acceptable among Ukrainians?

7-1 Money Systems Around the World

GOALS

- Explain the role of money and currency systems in international business.

- Identify factors that affect the value of currency.

Photodisc/Getty Images

Money and Currency Systems

Each day billions of people buy goods and services using something called *money*. Have you ever thought about what makes money valuable? The metal and paper that make up coins and currency have very little actual value. So why can you use these items to buy goods and services?

Most people take money for granted. If they have money and can buy what they need, they usually don't care how it works. However, an understanding of how money works can help you better understand international business transactions.

WHAT IS MONEY?

Money is anything people will accept for the exchange of goods and services. Throughout history, many different things have served as money, including corn, cattle, tobacco, shells, and salt. There are almost 200 slang terms for money in English. Many are related to food, such as bread, cabbage, clams, and dough. Colors are also commonly associated with money in slang terms—gold, green, greenbacks, greenies, and lean green. Other money descriptors include do-re-mi, folding stuff, scratch, mint sauce, and palm soap (especially when referring to a bribe). No matter what it's called, money has five main characteristics, as shown in Figure 7-1.

Acceptability The most important characteristic of money is that it is *acceptable*. In other words, people must be willing to take an item in exchange for what they are selling.

Scarcity For something to be used as money, it also must be *scarce*. If the item being used as money is very plentiful, it will not maintain its value. As items used for money become common, they lose their buying power.

Durability A problem with some items used as money in the past, such as farm products, was that they spoiled or got damaged easily. Items used as money should be *durable*. Gold and silver, commonly used as money because of durability, were first made into coins in the seventh century B.C. in Greece.

Divisibility For money to be useful, it should also be *divisible*. What would happen if someone wanted to buy an item using a cow as payment? The item to be purchased would have to be of equal value to the cow since livestock is not easy to divide into smaller monetary units. Most nations have different units of money. In the United States, for example, we have the five dollar bill, the ten dollar bill, quarters, dimes, nickels, and pennies. In Mexico, the peso is divided into 100 centavos. In India, the rupee is divided into 100 paise. And in Thailand, the baht is divided into 100 satang.

Portability Some objects used as money in the past could not be moved easily from one place to another. As people became more mobile, they demanded a money form that was *portable*. The earliest known paper currency was issued by banks in China in the eleventh century.

WHY IS MONEY USED?

Money serves three main purposes. It acts as a medium of exchange, a measure of value, and a store of value. Before the widespread acceptance of money, people would make exchanges through barter. *Barter* is the direct exchange of goods and services for other goods and services. However, you may not want what someone else is offering. Money allows you to put a value on something you have to sell and to use the money received to buy something else.

Medium of Exchange Money is useful only if people are willing to accept it in exchange for goods and services. As a medium of exchange, money makes business transactions easier. At a store, you know you can use coins, currency, or checks rather than having to trade a good or service.

Measure of Value If you work for four hours, is your time worth dinner at a restaurant or a pair of jeans? Without money, it would be difficult to put a value on such things as food and clothing. As a measure of value, money allows us to put a value on various goods and services. Money makes it possible to compare prices for different items so you can make the wisest spending decisions.

Store of Value You may not want to spend all of your money at the same time. As a store of value, money can be saved for future spending. However, the amount you can buy with your money in the future may be reduced because prices increase.

Characteristics of Money

ACCEPTABLE

SCARCE

DURABLE

DIVISIBLE

PORTABLE

Figure 7-1 For something to be used as money, it must have these five characteristics.

Foreign Exchange

Would you be willing to pay 40 pesos for a hamburger? Or is 4,200,000 yen a good price for an automobile? Business transactions between companies in different countries create money problems. Japanese companies want to receive payment in yen, while Mexican businesses expect to pay in pesos.

Since countries have different currency systems, a method of determining the value of one nation's money in terms of another's is needed. As companies in different countries exchange goods and services, payment must be made. A company usually wants its payment in the currency of its home country. As a result, the money of one country must be changed into the currency of another country. **Foreign exchange** is the process of converting the currency of one country into the currency of another country.

The **exchange rate** is the amount of currency of one country that can be traded for one unit of the currency of another country. Each day these values change slightly depending on changing conditions and perceptions. Figure 7-2 shows the value of various currencies in relation to the U.S. dollar in mid 2009. For example, one peso was worth 6.95 cents in U.S. money, and you could exchange 14.37 pesos for one U.S. dollar.

The value of a currency, like most things, is affected by supply and demand. If a country's money is believed to be a solid store of value, people will accept it as payment and its value will increase. However, if a country is having financial difficulties, its currency is likely to lose value compared to the money of other countries.

EXCHANGE RATES FOR SELECTED CURRENCIES

Currency	Country	Symbol	Code	Value in U.S. Dollars	Units per U.S. Dollar
pound	Britain	£	GBP	$1.47	0.68 pound
dollar	Canada	$	CAD	1.23	0.81 Canadian dollars
euro	European Union	€	EUR	1.35	0.74 euro
rupee	India	Rs	INR	0.0198	50.40 rupees
yen	Japan	¥	JPY	0.0102	98.04 yen
peso	Mexico	Mex$	MXN	0.0695	14.39 pesos
riyal	Saudi Arabia	SRls	SAR	0.267	3.75 riyals
rand	South Africa	R	ZAR	0.105	9.52 rand
real	Brazil	R$	BRL	0.445	2.25 real
bolívar	Venezuela	Bs	VEB	0.0005	2,000.00 bolívars
yuan	China	Y	CNY	0.1464	6.83 yuan

Figure 7-2 Currencies have different values compared to the U.S. dollar.

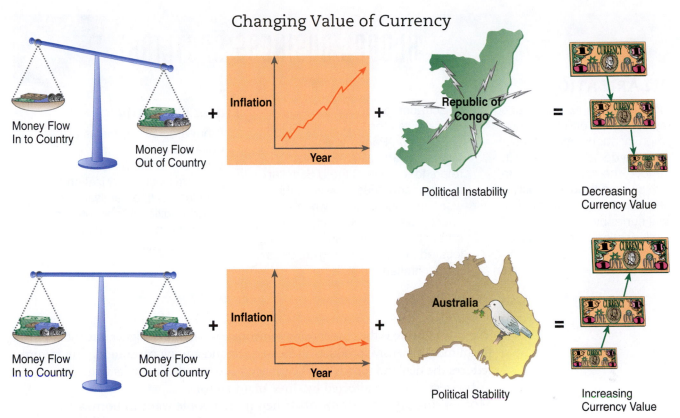

Changing Value of Currency

Figure 7-3 Currency exchange rates are affected by a nation's balance of payments, economic conditions, and political stability.

Currency exchange rates between countries are affected by three main factors. These factors are the country's balance of payments, its economic conditions, and its political stability, as shown in Figure 7-3.

BALANCE OF PAYMENTS

The *balance of payments* is a measure of the total flow of money coming into a country minus the total flow going out. When a country has a favorable balance of payments, the value of its currency is usually constant or rising. This situation arises when there is an increased demand for both the nation's products and for its currency.

However, when a nation has an unfavorable balance of payments, its currency usually declines in value. This decline results from lower demand for the monetary unit since fewer companies need to obtain the currency to make payments for goods and services purchased.

ECONOMIC CONDITIONS

Every nation faces the economic conditions of potential inflation and changing interest rates. When prices increase and the buying power of the country's money declines, its currency will not be as attractive. Inflation reduces the buying power of a currency. High inflation in Brazil, for example, would reduce the demand for the *real*.

The cost of borrowing money also has an impact on the value of a currency. When individuals, businesses, and countries borrow money, they incur a cost.

GLOBAL BUSINESS SPOTLIGHT

DOLLARIZATION

In the late 1990s, Ecuador faced many economic difficulties including high inflation, increased poverty, and a declining value of its currency—the *sucre*. Actions to address these problems included adoption of the U.S. dollar as official currency.

Dollarization is the official use of a currency by a country other than its own currency. In addition to Ecuador, other countries that officially use the U.S. dollar include El Salvador, Panama, and East Timor. Dollarization most often refers to the use of the U.S. dollar by other countries. However, this word can also indicate when any country uses the currency of another country. For example, Tuvalu, located in the Pacific region, uses the Australian dollar.

Think Critically

1. What are some benefits of dollarization?
2. What are some possible problems with dollarization?
3. Conduct an Internet search to obtain additional information on dollarization. Prepare a summary of your research results.

The **interest rate** is the cost of using someone else's money. Higher interest rates mean more expensive products and lower demand among consumers. This in turn reduces the demand for a nation's currency, causing a decline in its value.

Interest rates are affected by three main factors.

Money supply and demand When more people want to borrow than to save money, interest rates increase. In contrast, if money is available but few are borrowing, interest rates decline.

Risk The higher the risk associated with a loan, the higher the interest rate charged. The higher rates cover the business costs incurred when lenders try to collect on loans and when loans are not repaid.

Inflation As prices rise, the buying power of money declines, so lenders charge higher interest rates on loans. Lenders need to collect more money for a loan when inflation is present so they can cover the lost buying power of the currency they receive in later payments from the borrowers.

To address concerns of an unstable currency and poor economic conditions, some countries use the currency of a more stable economy. For example, the U.S. dollar is the official currency of Ecuador, El Salvador, and Panama. This process is referred to as *dollarization*.

POLITICAL STABILITY

Companies and individuals want to avoid risk when doing business in different nations. If a government changes unexpectedly to create an unfriendly business environment, a company may lose its building, equipment, or money on deposit in banks. Political instability may also occur when new laws and regulations are enacted. These rules may not allow foreign businesses to operate as freely. Uncertainty in a country reduces the confidence businesspeople have in its currency.

Work as a Team

Suggest actions that could be taken to lower interest rates in a country.

✓ **Check**Point

What three factors influence the value of a country's currency?

7-1 Assessment

REVIEW GLOBAL BUSINESS TERMS

Define each of the following terms.

1. money
2. foreign exchange
3. exchange rate
4. interest rate

Study Tools
www.cengage.com/school/genbus/intlbiz

REVIEW GLOBAL BUSINESS CONCEPTS

5. What are the five characteristics of money?
6. How does a country's balance of payments affect the value of its currency?
7. How does risk affect interest rates?
8. How does political instability affect the value of a country's currency?

SOLVE GLOBAL BUSINESS PROBLEMS

Which of the characteristics of money would make each of the following items not practical to use as money, even if some people found them acceptable?

9. Shells
10. Works of art
11. Produce (fruit, vegetables, herbs, etc.)
12. Diamonds

THINK CRITICALLY

13. If a country had to create a money system other than coins and currency, what items might be used?
14. How would printing additional money affect the value of a country's currency?

MAKE ACADEMIC CONNECTIONS

15. **TECHNOLOGY** What are the potential advantages and disadvantages with an electronic money system that uses plastic cards similar to credit cards?
16. **LAW** What problems would be created in a country if every business were allowed to create its own money system?
17. **CULTURAL STUDIES** Describe the types of events commonly portrayed on a country's coins and currency.
18. **ECONOMICS** Based on the data in the Country Profile, describe what influences the value of a country's currency.
19. **ECONOMICS** Use the Internet to find the current exchange rates for all the currencies in Figure 7-2 on page 170.

7-2 Foreign Exchange and Currency Controls

GOALS

- Discuss foreign exchange activities.

- Describe the main activities of the World Bank and the International Monetary Fund.

Photodisc/Getty Images

Foreign Exchange Activities

The value of a country's currency is important for success in international business. If trading partners do not accept a country's currency, the country may have to make payment in another currency. A currency that is not easy to exchange for other currencies is called **soft currency**. While the currency is a medium of exchange in its home country, the monetary units have limited acceptance value in the world marketplace. These *weak* currencies, usually from developing economies, tend to fall in value due to economic and political uncertainty.

In contrast, currencies such as the Japanese yen, the Canadian dollar, the euro, the Swiss franc, and the U.S. dollar are accepted for most global transactions. Companies in most nations accept these monetary units. **Hard currency** is a monetary unit that is freely converted into other currencies. Also referred to as a *strong currency,* these highly acceptable funds are usually from an industrialized country. The steady value in the world market is a result of political and economic stability.

CHANGING EXCHANGE RATES

In the past, the value of a country's currency was set in most countries by its government in relation to the value of gold. Today, most countries use a system of floating exchange rates. **Floating exchange rate** is a system in which currency values are based on supply and demand. When a country exports large amounts of goods and services, companies in that nation want payment in their own currency. To make these payments, buyers must purchase this monetary unit. As the demand for the currency increases, the value of that monetary unit also increases.

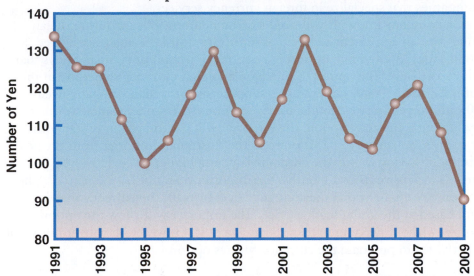

Japanese Yen Per U.S. Dollar

Figure 7-4 The value of the U.S. dollar compared to the Japanese yen has changed repeatedly in recent years.

For most of the 1980s, Japan had a very favorable balance of payments as a result of high foreign demand for its automobiles, electronic products, and other goods. Because Japanese companies wanted payment in yen, importers in other countries had to buy yen in order to make their payments. This demand for Japanese currency resulted in its increased value. In recent years, the yen has varied in value compared to the U.S. dollar as a result of changing economic conditions in Japan, as shown in Figure 7-4.

THE FOREIGN EXCHANGE MARKET

The process of exchanging one currency for another occurs in the foreign exchange market. The **foreign exchange market** is the network of banks and other financial institutions that buy and sell different currencies. Most large banks are part of the foreign exchange market and may provide currency services for businesses and consumers. Before citizens travel outside of the United States, they can exchange dollars for the currencies of the countries

A Question of Ethics

PRINTING MORE MONEY

In difficult economic times, a country might try to solve its problems by printing more money. As unemployment increases, the government would issue additional currency so people could buy needed goods and services. However, fewer items are being produced. Therefore, the increased demand would cause prices to rise, while the value of the currency declines. This higher inflation usually results in greater suffering among the people. In addition, the lower value of the currency hurts the country in the international trade marketplace.

Think Critically

According to the guidelines for ethical analysis in Chapter 1, how will the printing of additional money affect various groups in an economy?

they will visit. This exchange can be completed at most large banks or companies that specialize in foreign currency services.

If a company knows it will need a certain currency in the future, it can enter into an agreement to buy that monetary unit later at a price agreed upon today. A **currency option** is a contract a person or company buys that allows the buyer the option to purchase a foreign currency sometime in the future at today's rate. For example, suppose an Australian company needs 20 million yen in two months to pay for imports from a Japanese company. By buying a currency option, the importer will get the yen in two months at today's exchange rate. This protects the Australian importer from the possibility of having to buy the currency later at a higher price. However, if yen are less expensive in two months, the importer does not have to exercise the option to buy the yen at the contract price. Instead, the currency may be purchased at the going market price. The importer will allow the option to expire, without needing to take advantage of it. However, the buyer must still pay the fee to purchase the currency futures option.

FOREIGN EXCHANGE CONTROLS

To maintain the value of its currency, a nation may limit the flow of money out of the country. **Exchange controls** are government restrictions to regulate the amount and value of a nation's currency. These controls can be either a fixed exchange rate or a limit on the amount and cost of currency. A common exchange control limits the amount of local currency a person can take out of a country. In recent years, some of the countries that have made use of exchange controls are Argentina, China, Cuba, Egypt, India, Malaysia, South Africa, and Venezuela.

GLOBAL BUSINESS SPOTLIGHT

CALCULATING FOREIGN EXCHANGE

Calculating foreign exchange can be a confusing process. However, there are some steps you can take to make the process less confusing.

First, foreign exchange rates are usually quoted as a certain amount of one currency per unit of another currency. For example, a recent exchange rate was listed as 1.27 U.S. dollars per euro. An exchange rate is considered a price for foreign currency. In the example, the price of one euro is $1.27.

To buy five notepads that are $1.27 per notepad, multiply the price by 5. The notepads would cost $6.35.

5 × 1.27 = 6.35

So to buy 5 euros at 1.27 dollars per euro, it would cost $6.35.

Foreign exchange rates can work the other way as well. You can use an exchange rate to figure out how much of a foreign currency you can buy. For example, a recent exchange rate was listed as 1.88 U.S. dollars per British pound. For $1.88 you can buy £1. But how many pounds can you get for $1?

If gasoline is $1.88 per gallon and you have $10, to find out how many gallons you can buy, divide the amount you have by the price per gallon. You can buy 5.32 gallons of gasoline. (10 × 1.88 = 5.32 to the nearest hundredth.)

So if you want to buy $10 worth of British pounds at 1.88 dollars per pound, you could buy £5.32.

Think Critically

1. How much would seven Brazilian reals cost you if the exchange rate is 0.34 U.S. dollars per real?

2. How many Saudi Arabian riyals could you buy with $25 if the exchange rate is 3.75 U.S. dollars per riyal?

3. Locate a web site that lists current exchange rates. Recalculate questions 1 and 2 with the current exchange rates.

✓ CheckPoint

What is the purpose of the foreign exchange market?

International Financial Agencies

Exchange controls can help maintain the value of a nation's money by limiting the amount in the foreign exchange market. Two international agencies, the International Bank for Reconstruction and Development and the International Monetary Fund, work to maintain a stable system of foreign exchange.

THE WORLD BANK

The International Bank for Reconstruction and Development, commonly called the World Bank, was created in 1944 to provide loans for rebuilding after World War II. Today the **World Bank** is a bank whose major function is to provide economic assistance to less developed countries. Its funds build communications systems, transportation networks, and energy plants.

The World Bank, with over 180 member countries, has two main divisions. The International Development Association (IDA) makes funds available to help developing countries. These loans can be paid back over many years (up to 50) and have very low interest rates. The International Finance Corporation (IFC) provides capital and technical assistance to businesses in nations with limited resources. The IFC encourages joint ventures between foreign and local companies to encourage capital investment within the developing nation.

INTERNATIONAL MONETARY FUND (IMF)

The **International Monetary Fund (IMF)** is an agency that helps to promote economic cooperation by maintaining an orderly system of world trade and exchange rates. The IMF was established in 1946, when the economic interdependence among nations was escalating at a greater pace than ever before in history.

Before the International Monetary Fund, a country could frequently change the value of its currency to attract more foreign customers. Then as other countries lost business, they would impose trade restrictions or lower the value

Photodisc/Getty Images

GLOBAL BUSINESS SPOTLIGHT

FOREIGN EXCHANGE AND TOURISM

Travelers visiting other countries usually have a choice of making payments with cash, traveler's checks, debit cards, or credit cards. You would think the payment method would not affect the cost of a purchase. However, due to changing exchange rates and other factors, one payment method can be more costly than another. The foreign exchange on credit card purchases is not calculated until the charges reach the credit card office. If a foreign currency is declining in value, you would be charged less than if you had paid cash.

As the value of the dollar increases in relation to other currencies, the cost of traveling to other countries decreases. For example, at one point in time, a hotel room in London that cost £100 required about $200. Two weeks later the hotel room still cost £100. However, the exchange rate had changed, and it cost $179.

Increased availability of cash machines makes it easier to obtain cash when traveling. But transaction fees and the exchange rate at ATMs in another country may be much higher than expected.

Think Critically

1. Conduct an Internet search to locate information about travel costs in other countries.
2. What factors influence the cost of different payment methods used when traveling to other countries?

of their currency. As one nation tried to outdo another, a trade war could have resulted. Today cooperation among IMF nations makes trade wars less likely.

The IMF, also with over 180 member nations, is a cooperative deposit bank that provides assistance to countries experiencing balance of payment difficulties. When a nation's debt continues to increase, its currency declines in value, resulting in more debt. High debt payments mean less money is available for the country to improve its economic development. To prevent this situation, the International Monetary Fund has three main duties.

- **Analyze economic situations** In an attempt to help countries avoid economic problems, the IMF will monitor a country's trade, borrowing, and government spending.

- **Suggest economic policies** After analyzing the economic factors of a nation, the IMF will suggest actions to improve the situation. If a country imposes restrictions that limit foreign trade, for example, the IMF may recommend changes to encourage global business.

- **Provide loans** When a country has a high foreign debt, the IMF lends money to help avoid major economic difficulties. These low-interest loans can keep a country from experiencing an escalating trade deficit and a declining currency value.

✓ CheckPoint
How does the International Monetary Fund encourage economic development?

7-2 Assessment

REVIEW GLOBAL BUSINESS TERMS

Define each of the following terms.

1. soft currency
2. hard currency
3. floating exchange rate
4. foreign exchange market

5. currency option
6. exchange controls
7. World Bank
8. International Monetary Fund (IMF)

REVIEW GLOBAL BUSINESS CONCEPTS

9. What purpose do exchange controls serve?

10. What is the World Bank?

11. What are the main activities of the International Monetary Fund?

SOLVE GLOBAL BUSINESS PROBLEMS

Calculate the following.

12. A hamburger at a restaurant in Tokyo costs 400 yen. If the exchange rate is 0.008 U.S. dollars per yen, how much would the hamburger cost in U.S. dollars?

13. A Thai company is buying a computer from a company in the United Kingdom. The computer costs 1,700 British pounds. If the exchange rate is 0.025 pounds per Thai baht, how much does the computer cost in baht?

14. A Philippine company has 83,000 pesos to purchase grain from a Canadian farmer. If the exchange rate is 40 pesos per Canadian dollar, how many dollars' worth of grain can the Philippine company purchase?

THINK CRITICALLY

15. How might currency exchange controls affect the trade situation of a country?

16. Suggest ways in which the World Bank and the International Monetary Fund might reduce economic difficulties in developing nations.

MAKE ACADEMIC CONNECTIONS

17. **TECHNOLOGY** Go to the web site of the International Monetary Fund, and determine the source of funds for money loaned to member countries.

18. **MATHEMATICS** Select a country other than the United States. Using newspapers that report exchange rates, find the exchange rate for the country's currency on the first day of the month for the last six months. Prepare a line graph of the rate.

7-3 Currency Transactions Between Nations

GOALS

- Discuss payment methods and financing sources for international business transactions.

- Explain other payment methods and financial documents used in international trade.

Photodisc/Getty Images

International Financial Transactions

When you buy something, you must decide how to pay for it. You might use cash, write a check, or swipe a credit card. In a similar manner, global buyers must decide how to pay for an import purchase.

FOREIGN TRADE PAYMENT METHODS

Three types of payment methods are commonly used for international business transactions—cash in advance, letter of credit, and sale on account.

Cash in Advance Making payment before receiving goods can be risky for the buyer. After paying in advance, you might not receive the items, or you might have difficulty obtaining a refund. Cash in advance is not often used. This method, however, is usually required for first-time customers, small orders, or customers in high-risk countries. Because the payment was made before shipping, goods will usually be sent without delay.

Letter of Credit A **letter of credit** is a financial document issued by a bank for an importer in which the bank guarantees payment. A letter of credit is a method of payment in which the importer pays for goods before they are received but after the goods are shipped. This agreement, issued by the importer's bank, promises to pay the exporter a set amount when certain documents are presented. The letter of credit indicates that the exporter will receive payment once the goods are shipped. Prior payment, certain documents—usually including a *bill of lading*—must be presented as proof that the goods have been shipped.

Sale on Account Almost every business buys or sells on credit at one time or another. A common practice in the United States is to sell *on account*. This means regular customers have a certain time period to make payment, usually 30 or 60 days. **Credit terms** describe the time required for payment and other conditions of a sale on account.

When selling on account, a company can encourage fast payment by offering a discount. In the United States, companies can sell on account with credit terms of 2/10, n/30. This means that customers can take a 2 percent discount if they pay within 10 days or pay the net (full) amount in 30 days. Another example is 1/15, n/EOM. This means a 1 percent discount may be taken if paid in 15 days. The net amount is due by the end of the month (EOM).

SOURCES OF INTERNATIONAL FINANCING

Buying and selling on credit means that one party (an individual or a company) uses the money of another party (an individual, a company, or a financial institution). This is commonly called *financing*. Financing can be either short-term (one year or less) or long-term (more than one year).

Short-term Financing Most business transactions involve credit. A company may allow customers 30 days to make their payments. The same company probably buys store supplies, raw materials, and other items from suppliers on credit. Buying or selling on account is called **trade credit**. Trade credit comes in two forms, accounts receivable and accounts payable.

An **account receivable** is an amount due from a customer to a company that sells on credit. Accounts receivable are the result of sales on account. A company that sells on credit allows its customers a certain time period to pay for purchases. An **account payable** is an amount owed to a supplier. Accounts payable are the result of purchases on account.

Accounts receivable and accounts payable may seem confusing. A helpful way to distinguish between them is that receivables are amounts to be received and payables are amounts to be paid.

Business loans, also called commercial loans, are another source of short-term financing. Business loans are commonly obtained from banks and other financial institutions.

Work as a Team
Create a list of reasons a company might present when attempting to borrow money to expand its global business operations.

GLOBAL TECHNOLOGY TRENDS

Mobile Phone Banking

In India, many African countries, and elsewhere, cell phones are changing the economic lives of people. In rural areas, where banks are rare, mobile payment systems allow a person to manage a checking account and obtain a microloan.

Microloan funds are often used to start a small business as well as pay for household expenses. In Bangladesh, for example, the Grameen Bank leases phones that help people start businesses such as a grocery shop, village kiosk, or café. This allows people to earn a small income and improve their lives.

Think Critically

1. How does access to financial services help a person start and operate a business?
2. Conduct an Internet search to obtain additional information about cell phone banking in developing economies.

Photodisc/Getty Images

Long-term Financing Some business activities require financing for more than one year. Companies commonly need large sums of money for expensive business projects that will occur over several years. For example, a Japanese company need funds to build a manufacturing plant in Canada, or a German company wants to buy a food company in Mexico. An expensive, long-term financial activity is a **capital project**. Examples of capital projects introducing a new product, buying an existing company, building a factory, buying new equipment, and opening a new office.

Capital projects often require millions of dollars. To pay for capital projects, companies can do one of two things, borrow the necessary funds from a bank or another financial institution or issue bonds. A **bond** is a certificate representing money borrowed by a company over a long period of time, usually between 5 and 30 years. This document represents the company's promise to repay the money by a certain date with interest. Bonds are a type of financing commonly used by large companies.

✓ **Check**Point

Describe three common payment methods for international business transactions.

Other Payment Methods and Financial Documents

With hundreds of nations and millions of companies in the world, there are many ways of doing business. Besides the import-export documents and payment methods already mentioned, several other methods of payment are commonly used for global business.

Promissory Note A **promissory note** is a document that states a promise to pay a set amount by a certain date. Promissory notes are signed by buyers to confirm their intention to make payment. These documents communicate to both the buyer and the seller the amount of a purchase, the date by which payment must be paid, and any interest charges.

Bill of Exchange A **bill of exchange** is a written order by an exporter to an importer to make payment. The instructions to the importer include the amount, the due date, and the location of where to make the payment, usually a bank or another financial institution.

Electronic Funds Transfer Moving payments through banking computer systems is known as **electronic funds transfer (EFT)**. After an importer receives the ordered goods, a bank can be instructed to transfer the payment for the merchandise to the exporter's bank. The main advantage of EFT is prompt payment. Electronic funds transfer systems are commonly used by consumers to obtain cash, deposit money, and make payments.

A variation of EFT common for international business transactions is the *wire transfer*. This payment method moves money between a buyer's bank account and a seller's bank account in different countries. The wire transfer process, which occurs over a secure financial network system, is not immediate and may take several hours or even days for the funds to

A Commercial Invoice

ExIm EXPRESS   10155 Columbia Pkwy   Spring Hill TN 37174   (931) 555-0835

SOLD TO:	Serendipity, Sarl	SHIPPED TO: Order of Shipper
	14 Surin Road	
	Bangkok, Thailand	

ORDER DATE	: Jan. 03, 20--	ORDER NUMBER	:	IMP 12
INVOICE DATE	: Jan. 11, 20--	INVOICE NUMBER	:	EI/SS/06/10
DATE SHIPPED	: Jan. 16, 20--	SHIPPED VIA	:	Ocean freight on CU WINGED SOUL

TERMS: **Sale :** CIF Bangkok   **Payment :** Sight Draft

PACKAGE NO	QUANTITY	OUR NO.	DESCRIPTION	PRICE PER UNIT	AMOUNT
1-40	100	10	Fire Extinguishers	US$ 40	US$ 4000
			Total shipment EX WORKS MADEIRA		US$ 4000
			Plus: Inland Freight to Port		US$ 200
			Total Boston Port		US$ 4200
			Plus: Ocean Freight		US$ 75
			Plus: Insurance		US$ 23
			Total CIF Bangkok Thailand		US$ 4298

We certify that this invoice is true and correct and that the origin of these goods is the United States of America.
These goods licensed by the United States for ultimate destination Thailand.
Diversion contrary to U.S. law prohibited. LIC. G-DEST.

Jennifer Hamm, Export Manager
ExIm Express

Figure 7-5 A commercial invoice gives the details of an international business transaction.

be received. Wire transfers are the most common payment method among countries in Europe.

Commercial Invoice A **commercial invoice**, prepared by the exporter, provides a description of the merchandise and the terms of the sale. This document includes details about the buyer, seller, merchandise, amounts, prices, shipping method, date of shipment, and terms of payment. A sample commercial invoice is shown in Figure 7-5.

Insurance Certificate Proof of insurance is usually a part of import-export transactions. An **insurance certificate** explains the amount of insurance coverage for fire, theft, water, or other damage that may occur to goods in shipment. This document also lists the name of the insurance company and the exporter.

✓ CheckPoint
Name five different payment methods and financial documents.

INTERNATIONAL BUSINESS PERSPECTIVE
Culture

CURRENCY NAMES AROUND THE WORLD

Most people have heard of the dollar, the peso, and the euro. How about the baht, the kwacha, and the rand? More than 90 currency names, including the afghani and the zloty, are used in more than 200 countries around the world.

Some currency names are used in more than one country. For example, the peso is the currency of Mexico, the Philippines, and several Latin American countries. The word *peso* means "weight." The original peso was a Spanish coin with a standard weight and silver content.

The *franc* is the currency name in more than 25 countries in Africa and other nations that were influenced by France through colonization and trade. Similarly, the *shilling* is used in Kenya, Somalia, Tanzania, and Uganda, which were previously British colonies.

The *pound sterling* has been the currency of the United Kingdom for over 900 years. It was originally an old English silver coin. *Pound* comes from "pund," which is from the Latin word "pondus," meaning "weight." *Sterling* is most likely from an old English word "steorra," meaning "star"—a small star appeared on early pennies. However, another explanation also exists. At one point, the English referred to their coins as Easterlings, a region with skilled metal refiners. "Easterling silver" may have become "sterling silver."

Some monetary unit names have unusual origins. The *quetzal* in Guatemala is the name for a Latin American bird with a long, feathered tail. In Malawi and Zambia, the *kwacha* is based on the slogan "New dawn of freedom."

How about the *dollar*? This word is from the 16th century German word "thaler." This was short for "Joahimsthaler," which was a coin made from metal mined in Joahimsthal, a town in what is now the Czech Republic. Over time, the dollar became associated with the money of the United States and over 30 other countries.

Think Critically

1. What factors influence the names of the currency used in different countries?
2. Conduct an Internet search to locate additional information about the name origins and current values of various world currencies.

©Voloh 2009/ Used under license from Shutterstock.com

7-3 | Assessment

REVIEW GLOBAL BUSINESS TERMS

Define each of the following terms.

1. letter of credit
2. credit terms
3. trade credit
4. account receivable
5. account payable
6. capital project
7. bond
8. promissory note
9. bill of exchange
10. electronic funds transfer (EFT)
11. commercial invoice
12. insurance certificate

Study Tools
www.cengage.com/school/genbus/intlbiz

REVIEW GLOBAL BUSINESS CONCEPTS

13. Why is cash not usually paid in advance of shipping?

14. Why do capital projects usually require a company to borrow money?

SOLVE GLOBAL BUSINESS PROBLEMS

Which type of financial document or payment method would be appropriate for the following situations?

15. A business in India needs to borrow money to build a factory that produces computers.

16. A company wants to delay payment for 60 days but is willing to pay interest on the amount owed during that time period.

17. A business in Costa Rica needs to make payment to a supplier in Thailand today.

18. A supplier in Canada requires that its customer in Singapore have a bank guarantee payment for a shipment of machine parts.

THINK CRITICALLY

19. Why do you think the letter of credit is the most popular payment method used for international business transactions?

20. What are the benefits for a company that offers a discount to customers who pay within 30 days?

MAKE ACADEMIC CONNECTIONS

21. **TECHNOLOGY** How does technology result in new capital projects for companies expanding their business operations to other countries?

22. **MATHEMATICS** You receive an invoice from a company in India for 100,000 rupee with payment terms as 2/20, n/60. What would be the amount of the discount you could take if you pay within 20 days?

CHAPTER SUMMARY

7-1 MONEY SYSTEMS AROUND THE WORLD

A Money has five characteristics: acceptability, scarcity, durability, divisibility, and portability. The purpose of money is that it serves as a medium of exchange, a measure of value, and a store of value.

B A country's balance of payments, economic conditions, and political stability influence the value of money. Money supply and demand, inflation, and risk affect interest rates.

7-2 FOREIGN EXCHANGE AND CURRENCY CONTROLS

A Foreign exchange involves the process of exchanging one currency for another in the foreign exchange market. This market consists of banks and other financial institutions that buy and sell different currencies.

B The main activity of the World Bank is to provide economic assistance to less developed countries. The International Monetary Fund helps to promote economic cooperation among countries by maintaining an orderly system of world trade and exchange rates.

7-3 CURRENCY TRANSACTIONS BETWEEN NATIONS

A Cash in advance, a letter of credit, and sale on account are the main payment methods for international business. The main financing sources for international business transactions are trade credit, bank loans, and bonds.

B Common payment methods and financial documents used in international trade include the promissory note, bill of exchange, electronic funds transfer (EFT), commercial invoice, and insurance certificate.

GLOBAL **REFOCUS**

Read the Global Focus at the beginning of this chapter, and answer the following questions.

1. What actions can a government take to create and maintain an appropriate currency system?

2. Go to the web site of the World Bank or the web site of the International Monetary Fund to obtain current information about Ukraine and other developing economies in Eastern Europe.

REVIEW GLOBAL BUSINESS TERMS

Match the terms listed with the definitions. Some terms may not be used.

1. The network of banks and other financial institutions that buy and sell different currencies.
2. The amount of currency of one country that can be traded for one unit of the currency of another country.
3. The cost of using someone else's money.
4. Anything people will accept for the exchange of goods and services.
5. A currency that is not easy to exchange for other currencies.
6. A certificate representing money borrowed by a company over a long period of time.
7. Buying or selling on account.
8. An expensive, long-term financial activity.
9. A contract a person or company buys that allows the buyer the option to purchase a foreign currency sometime in the future at today's rate.
10. A financial document issued by a bank for an importer in which the bank guarantees payment.
11. Government restrictions to regulate the amount and value of a nation's currency.
12. A monetary unit that is freely converted into other currencies.
13. A method of moving payments through banking computer systems.
14. A system in which currency values are based on supply and demand.

a. account payable
b. account receivable
c. bill of exchange
d. bond
e. capital project
f. commercial invoice
g. credit terms
h. currency option
i. electronic funds transfer (EFT)
j. exchange controls
k. exchange rate
l. floating exchange rate
m. foreign exchange
n. foreign exchange market
o. hard currency
p. insurance certificate
q. interest rate
r. International Monetary Fund (IMF)
s. letter of credit
t. money
u. promissory note
v. soft currency
w. trade credit
x. World Bank

MAKE GLOBAL BUSINESS DECISIONS

15. What actions could a country take to make its currency more widely accepted around the world?
16. Some people believe that interest rates are one of the most important economic indicators. How are people and businesses affected by interest rates?
17. Give some examples of capital projects in your community. How do capital projects benefit the people of a community?
18. What are some concerns people might have about electronic banking?

MAKE ACADEMIC CONNECTIONS

19. GEOGRAPHY Research travel costs for three different countries in various regions of the world. Obtain information on the costs of hotels, meals, rental cars, and other travel expenses.

20. COMMUNICATIONS Interview a local business owner about buying and selling on credit. Ask the owner about the benefits and problems encountered when doing business on account.

21. VISUAL ARTS
Prepare a poster, bulletin board, newsletter, web site, or another visual that displays the changing value of the dollar in relation to other major currencies of the world.

22. HISTORY Conduct research on the history of money systems that have been used in other countries.

23. CULTURAL STUDIES
Interview a person who has traveled to another country. Obtain information about how purchases were made and the exchange rate that was paid.

Photodisc/Getty Images

24. MATHEMATICS Calculate the following foreign exchange transactions.
   a. A U.S. citizen is renting a hotel room in Paris for $184.92 a night. If one euro equals $1.20 in U.S. funds, how many francs will the tourist need for each night's stay?

   b. A U.S. tourist receives a $5AUS traffic ticket in Australia. If each Australian dollar is equal to $0.74 in U.S. money, what is the cost of this driving violation in U.S. dollars?

   c. A videotape made in the United States costs 115 kroner in Norway. If each krone is worth $0.15 in U.S. funds, what is the cost of the videotape in U.S. dollars?

25. CAREER PLANNING Obtain information about the value of a nation's currency. Explain how changes in a country's exchange rate might affect the jobs in that nation.

The GLOBAL Entrepreneur

CREATING AN INTERNATIONAL BUSINESS PLAN

The Changing Value Of Currencies

Select a country, and research its currency. Obtain information to answer the following questions.

1. What is the main monetary unit used in the country? How is it divided into other units?

2. Over the past couple of years, what have been the economic conditions of the country (inflation, interest rates, unemployment)? How have these affected the value of the currency?

3. How has the country's balance of payments affected the value of its currency?

4. How have political factors affected the value of the currency?

Photodisc/Getty Images

5. Describe any exchange controls used by the country.

6. What factors might affect changes for this currency over the next few months?

7. Graph the recent value of the currency in relation to two other major currencies (e.g., U.S. dollar, Japanese yen, British pound, the euro, Swiss franc).

Prepare a written report with a summary of this information and your graphs. Indicate on the graph any events that have caused a major increase or decrease in the value of the currency.

Sources of information include the following.

- reference books such as encyclopedias and almanacs
- current newspaper articles from the news, business, and travel sections
- web sites that provide current information on foreign currency values.

CHAPTER 8

Legal Agreements Around the World

8-1 International Legal Systems and Liability

8-2 Property and Contracts

8-3 Resolving Legal Differences

GLOBAL FOCUS

Trademarks, Brand Names, and International Business

Apple. Dove. Windows.

To some people, these are a fruit, a bird, and a part of a house. To others, these are a computer, a soap, and computer software.

Trademarks and brand names are an important part of a company's identity. These emblems and words allow customers to quickly know what they are buying and from whom. The process of registering a trademark or brand name requires an application with the U.S. Patent and Trademark Office.

In 1999, the Trademark Law Treaty and Implementation Act (TLTIA) took effect. This law simplifies the process for obtaining a trademark. TLTIA also coordinates U.S. trademark laws with those of other countries participating in this agreement.

When doing business in other countries, trademarks may not be protected due to lack of enforcement. A local company may use a well-known name to attract customers. In South America, Asia, and other regions, small business owners often use this practice. Some have used names such as "Macdonalds" instead of "McDonald's". Or, in Ethiopia, the name "Olive's Garden" was adapted by a local company from a restaurant chain in the United States.

The translation of brand names may also cause problems. When Kellogg's used *Bran Buds* as a cereal name in Sweden, it was roughly translated as "burned farmer." Companies need to be aware of potential translation problems and take steps to avoid using names with inappropriate meaning.

Think Critically

1. Name some other examples of common words that have become trademarks or registered brand names.
2. What problems might be encountered when a company uses a brand name while doing business in other countries?
3. Conduct an Internet search to obtain information on trademarks and brand names used in different countries.

8-1 International Legal Systems and Liability

GOALS

- Identify and describe the legal systems upon which international law is based.

- Explain product liability.

Photodisc/Getty Images

Legal Systems

Businesspeople of all nations must be familiar with the laws of their own countries. They must obey all laws affecting the ownership and operation of their companies. If they do not, they are subject to legal action, which could result in large losses to the companies.

When people conduct business in a country other than their own, they must observe the laws of the host country as well as the laws of their own country. International managers must assess the internal political situation of the host country. Then they must decide whether profits will outweigh any risks. These risks include political instability, war, or hostilities between the business' native country and the host country. Once a country enters into business in or with a foreign country, business relationships are often guided by treaties and trade agreements.

People involved in international business are guided by the principles of international law as well as by trade agreements. Unlike the domestic laws of individual countries, there are few effective ways of enforcing international law. Nevertheless, there is a growing body of international law that many countries respect.

International law is largely based on the legal principles of western civilization. This is a result of the continuous dominance by the West in world affairs since the time of the Roman Empire. The main legal systems around the world are civil law, common law, and statutory law.

CIVIL LAW

Civil law, also called *code law*, is a complete set of rules enacted as a single written system or code. When a government enacts a civil code, it attempts to write down all of the laws and rights that govern every aspect of its society.

Hammurabi, a Babylonian king, enacted the first civil laws in the seventeenth century B.C. Modern civil law is based on the Justinian Code and the Napoleonic Code. Justinian was the leader of the Byzantine Empire, which had conquered almost the entire world known to the West. To maintain an orderly administration of this empire, in 529 A.D. Justinian codified the law in a complete system of rules to govern the empire's citizens. The Justinian Code was based on the traditions of the Roman Empire that had preceded the Byzantine Empire and described in detail the rights of Byzantine citizens, including rights to private property.

In 1804, Napoleon Bonaparte became emperor of France and established a civil code, also based on the Roman model. The Napoleonic Code established as law many of the changes that occurred in the aftermath of the French Revolution, including rights to a jury trial and civil equality. Currently, the majority of countries are governed by civil law, including many that were once a part of the Roman Empire, such as Italy, Spain, Germany, and France.

COMMON LAW

England is the only western European country that did not develop a comprehensive set of rules at one time. Instead, England approached the establishment of law on a case-by-case basis. This approach came to be known as **common law**, which is a legal system that relies on the accumulation of decisions made in prior cases.

English common laws grew out of the deterioration of the feudal system. In medieval times, feudal lords were the supreme rulers of their castles, lands, and the serfs who lived within their territory. Disputes between lords were settled mainly in battle, and serfs had very few rights. Thus, there were few laws.

As serfs began to attain some rights as tenant farmers, disputes between them needed to be resolved. At first, the feudal lords and later judges or magistrates would simply listen to both sides of the dispute and then make a judgment. Because there were no laws to guide these early magistrates in their decisions, they began

GLOBAL BUSINESS SPOTLIGHT

DIPLOMATIC IMMUNITY

Imagine receiving hundreds of parking tickets but not being required to pay any fines. Or what if you accidentally drove into another car, causing several thousand dollars' damage, were not held liable for the damage?

These are examples of *diplomatic immunity*, which is an exemption from taxation and ordinary legal processes given to diplomatic personnel in a foreign country. Diplomatic personnel include ambassadors, consulate members, and others serving in an official capacity. Some family members of diplomatic personnel may also be given this immunity.

Diplomacy refers to the practices and institutions by which nations conduct their relations with one another. The privilege of diplomatic immunity, with some freedom from arrest or legal action, is intended to help speed the legal process and to avoid causing political disputes between countries.

Think Critically

1. Why do countries with normal political relations provide immunity for diplomats?
2. When might diplomatic immunity not be appropriate?
3. Conduct an Internet search to obtain additional information about diplomatic immunity.

to write down their decisions so they and others had something to refer to when similar cases arose.

After the conquest of England in 1066 by William the Conqueror, who was also the Duke of Normandy, English kings established a legal system alongside the developing common law. In this system, the king was the highest legal authority. Because most kings were not knowledgeable about common law, they based their decisions on common sense and the principle of fairness, or equity. The king's courts were, therefore, referred to as the *equity courts*. Equity courts had exclusive jurisdiction over contracts. Gradually, the equity courts merged into the common law system.

England is still governed by common law, as is the United States. In modern common law, also referred to as *case law*, judges make their decisions guided by rulings in previous cases. The principle of equity, or fairness, is often cited. It retains particular influence in business law, where the concept of fairness is very important.

STATUTORY LAW

Statutes are those laws that have been enacted by a body of lawmakers. The German Reichstag, the British Parliament, the Chinese National People's Congress, and the United States Congress, for example, were all formed to pass laws to govern their citizens. Statutes are most often enacted to add to or change existing laws and to define laws for new situations that arise. Figure 8-1 identifies the legislative bodies of the world's ten most populous countries.

✓ **Check**Point
What are the main types of legal systems in operation around the world?

LAWMAKING BODIES OF THE TEN MOST POPULOUS COUNTRIES

Rank	Country	Lawmaking Body
1	China	National People's Congress (*Quanguo Renmin Daibiao Dahui*)
2	India	Parliament (*Sansad*)
3	United States	Congress
4	Indonesia	House of Representatives (*Dewan Perwakilan Rakyat*)
5	Brazil	National Congress (*Congresso Nacional*)
6	Pakistan	Parliament (*Majlis-e-Shoora*)
7	Bangladesh	National Parliament (*Jatiya Sangsad*)
8	Nigeria	National Assembly
9	Russia	Federal Assembly (*Federalnoye Sobraniye*)
10	Japan	Diet (*Kokkai*)

Source: *CIA World Factbook*

Figure 8-1 Laws are made by a set of decision makers whose specific purpose is to make laws. The name and structure of law-making bodies varies by country.

Liability

Liability is a broad legal term referring to almost every kind of responsibility, duty, or obligation. In business law, these responsibilities can relate to debt, loss, or burden.

Liability for Debt, Loss, and Injury Liability for debt generally includes such claims against a company as wages owed to employees, dividends owed to stockholders, taxes owed to government, and loans owed to banks. Business owners are also responsible for the condition and contents of their facilities and must ensure that their work procedures are safe. Thus, if an employee experiences any loss or burden as a result of unsafe conditions, the company could be declared negligent and, therefore, liable for that loss or injury.

Product Liability The specific responsibility that both manufacturers and sellers have for the safety of their products is called **product liability**. A person can hold a company and its officers responsible for product defects that cause injury, damage, or death to buyers, users, or even bystanders. If a manufacturer does not use "due care" in designing and making a product, it may be guilty of either intentional or negligent harmful action.

Intent to cause harm by a manufacturer or seller is rarely proven. **Negligence**, which is the failure of a responsible party to follow standards of due care, can also be difficult to prove. Thus, modern law has developed the concept of strict liability to help consumers who have suffered a loss due to a defective product to prove the manufacturer's liability.

Strict liability imposes responsibility on a manufacturer or seller for intentionally or unintentionally causing injury to another. For a manufacturer to be held liable for damages under strict liability laws, all of the following six conditions must be met.

- The product was sold in a defective condition.
- The seller is in the business of routinely selling the product.
- The product reached the user without having been substantially changed.
- The product was unreasonably dangerous to the user.
- The user of the product or a bystander suffered harm or injury by using the product.
- The defect was the primary cause of the injury.

Product liability laws vary from country to country. Many countries, such as the United States and members of the European Union, enforce strict liability on manufacturers, sellers, and importers of defective products. International law recognizes the general principle that a responsible party owes just compensation to the injured party.

Work as a Team

Select a product that has been in the news recently because of a claim that it harmed someone. Discuss how the product meets the six conditions for strict liability.

✓ CheckPoint

How are manufacturers and sellers legally responsible for the safety of their products?

INTERNATIONAL BUSINESS PERSPECTIVE
History

TAIWAN

Taiwan, officially called the Republic of China, is an island nation off the southeast coast of mainland China between the East and South China Seas. Mountains form the backbone of the country, but the western slopes are fertile and well cultivated. Most of Taiwan's people live in the lowlands on the western side of the island.

Chinese immigrants came to the island in the seventeenth century. After a brief period of Dutch rule (1620–1662), Taiwan experienced about 160 years of Chinese control. Japan ruled from 1895–1945, using the island for farming and military operations. After World War II, civil war between the Nationalist and Communist factions broke out in China. The leader of the Chinese Nationalist party, Chiang Kai-shek, fled to Taiwan. He proclaimed Taipei the provisional capital of China, renamed Taiwan the Republic of China, and took control of the island. Both the People's Republic of China on the mainland and the Nationalist Chinese government in Taiwan continued to claim sovereignty over Taiwan.

The conflict regarding whether the Communist government, which was based on mainland China, or the Nationalist government, which was based in Taiwan, was the legitimate government of China was the source of bitterness, international tension, and military action throughout the 1950s and 1960s. By the late 1980s, however, hostilities had decreased. In 1986, the mainland Chinese government announced that the principle of "one country, two systems" would be applied to Taiwan. This policy retains Taiwan's economic independence and army but submits it to China in matters of foreign policy.

After World War II, Taiwan enjoyed rapid industrial growth and now has one of the strongest economies in Asia. The country's strong educational system is one of the main influences on Taiwan's economic success. Taiwan is one of the most literate countries in the world, with a literacy rate above 95 percent. Most of the countries people are employed in industry or service jobs; only about 10 percent work in agriculture. Taiwan particularly promotes high-tech industries, such as those that produce electronics, chemicals, and pharmaceuticals. Taiwan's economy is largely based on exports, which account for more than half of its gross domestic product.

Think Critically

1. What factors contributed to the economic development of Taiwan?
2. Conduct a Internet search for additional information about the current cultural, political, and economic situation of Taiwan.

holgs/iStockphoto.com

REVIEW GLOBAL BUSINESS TERMS

Define each of the following terms.

1. civil law
2. common law
3. statutes
4. liability
5. product liability
6. negligence
7. strict liability

Study Tools

www.cengage.com/school/genbus/intlbiz

REVIEW GLOBAL BUSINESS CONCEPTS

8. The justice systems for most countries in the world are based on what kind of law?

9. How did common law develop?

10. Does negligence have to be proven in a successful strict liability case? Why or why not?

SOLVE GLOBAL BUSINESS PROBLEMS

For each of the following situations, explain why the manufacturer of the product can be held liable for damages under strict liability laws.

11. A driver is injured after the car's transmission fails on the highway; the driver had used motor oil instead of transmission fluid.

12. A baby chokes on a small piece of metal that broke off of a toy.

13. You are injured pushing a lawnmower up and down a steep hill.

14. You are hospitalized after eating a salad dressing that contains an ingredient, not listed on the label, to which you are allergic.

THINK CRITICALLY

15. Why might a country prefer code law to a common law system?

16. In the United States, new drugs require FDA (Food and Drug Administration) approval before they can be released. Do you think FDA approval should relieve the manufacturer of product liability?

MAKE ACADEMIC CONNECTIONS

17. **COMMUNICATIONS** Select a consumer product that has extensive instructions and other text on or in the package. List the sentences you think attempt to protect the manufacturer from product liability lawsuits.

18. **LAW** Use the Internet or library to research a product liability case. Write a summary of the case, and give your opinion on the verdict.

19. **CULTURAL STUDIES** Use the Internet to research the legal system of a country.

8-2 Property and Contracts

GOALS

- Explain laws and international trade agreements that protect property rights.

- Describe when an agreement has all of the components of a contract.

Photodisc/Getty Images

Property Rights and Responsibilities

Property includes everything that can be owned. Property includes land, money, stocks and bonds, buildings, factories, and other goods. There are three main categories of property. Land and whatever is built on or attached to that land is *real property*. Property that is tangible but does not have a permanent location is *personal property*. Property based on ideas (such as patented inventions, trademarks, and copyrights for literary, musical, and artistic works) is *intellectual property*.

PROPERTY LAW

All democratic countries recognize the individual's right to private property. The law protects these rights. **Property rights** are the exclusive rights to possess and use property and its profits, to exclude everyone else from interfering with it, and to dispose of it in any legal way.

A number of international agreements protect the rights of individuals and businesses to own property. These agreements were designed to ensure that individuals and corporations living or located in foreign countries were not deprived of their property except under due process of law or when just compensation had been made. For example, the 1883 Paris Convention of Industrial Property, to which more than 95 countries are members, provides international protection for copyrights, patents, and trademarks.

At different times in history, some countries have rejected individuals' rights to own private property. For example, Communist countries, especially when they were newly formed, subjected both domestic- and foreign-owned property to controls that amounted to a complete loss of property.

Developing countries, particularly those that are former colonies, sometimes expropriate, or confiscate, the property of foreigners. Often this expropriation is made in the name of nationalism or for the developing countries' best interests. As these countries enter into the mainstream of international relations, however, they tend to submit to international laws that recognize the rights of both individuals and businesses to private property. For example, the People's Republic of China, a Communist country, adopted a new constitution in 1982 that included assurances to foreigners engaged in business relationships with China that agreements and contracts will be honored and that violations by Chinese businesses will not be allowed. This new constitution was a direct result of leader Deng Xiaoping's far-reaching changes to move China into the international marketplace.

INTELLECTUAL PROPERTY

Often the greatest asset of a business is its intellectual property. **Intellectual property** is the technical knowledge or creative work that an individual or company has developed. This type of situation is especially true for computer software companies, clothing designers, film companies, writers, inventors, and many others. When intellectual property rights are not protected, dishonest competitors can steal knowledge to make products similar to the original product and deceive consumers into buying them.

The World Intellectual Property Organization (WIPO) is part of the United Nations. This agency, with over 170 nations as members, coordinates various international treaties designed to protect patents, trademarks, copyrights, and other intellectual property. *Piracy*, the illegal use of intellectual property, is a great concern for the companies that first developed these products. As trade becomes more global, the protection of intellectual rights will be a major focus of international law.

Patents The grant of an exclusive right of an inventor to make, sell, and use a product or process is called a **patent**. To be protected, a product or process must be new and useful. Once a patent expires in the United States, it cannot be renewed unless a new improvement or design is incorporated into the idea or product.

Patent rights are only available for a limited time, ranging from five to twenty years in different countries. Patent rights granted in one country do not necessarily extend to other countries. To be protected, a company must apply for patent rights in each country in which it plans to do business. There are, however, international agreements that coordinate and streamline this process.

The Patent Cooperation Treaty also makes the international patent process simpler and more efficient. More than 40 countries—including the United States, Japan, Russia, and members of the European Union—are parties to this treaty. A company can file a single patent application in which it names the countries in which it seeks patent coverage. The application will then be filed in each of those countries.

Work as a Team

Suggest ways that international trade agencies could protect the intellectual properties of businesses.

Other regional treaties provide similar coordination of patent rights. The Inter-American Convention serves the United States and Latin American countries, and the European Patent Organization coordinates protection among European Union members. The United Nations also works to coordinate intellectual property agreements among countries.

Trademarks A distinctive name, symbol, word, picture, or combination of these that is used by a business to identify its services or products is called a **trademark**. Trademark protection was designed to protect the good reputation of businesses' services and goods. It prevents competitors from representing their products as being those of another business. Such misrepresentation deceives the public and unfairly takes business away from reputable companies.

The symbol ® indicates that a name is a registered trademark in the United States. Most labels of brand-name products include the symbol identifying the name as a registered trademark. To remain protected, a trademark must be in continual use and must continue to be identified with the original business. Once a term becomes accepted to mean all things of that kind, it is no longer protected. For example, T-shirt and aspirin were once trademarks, but they are no longer protected by trademark because they have become everyday terms.

Trademark protection is covered by several international agreements. The Paris Convention of Industrial Property covers trademarks as well as patents. The Madrid Agreement of 1891 concerning the International Registration of Marks enables member countries to submit a single application for protection in all of its member countries. The European Union has a trademark office that is responsible for the recognition and protection of trademarks used in all EU countries, including those belonging to companies based in countries outside of Europe.

Copyrights A legal right that protects the original works of authors, music composers, playwrights, artists, and publishers is called a **copyright**.

A Question of Ethics

COUNTERFEIT PRODUCTS

Have you ever seen "Mickey" and "Minnie" characters at a local park and wondered if they are authorized by the Disney Company? Have you seen street vendors selling "Rolex" watches that don't look quite right or DVDs for a movie that just opened in theaters?

These are just a few of the many examples of counterfeit products and piracy occurring around the world. Each year it is estimated that financial losses from counterfeiting amount to 5 to 7 percent of world trade—over $300 billion.

Violations of trademarks and copyrights are very common in some countries, including Turkey, China, and Thailand. In Italy, vendors selling pirated products control 25 percent of the music CD market. At the same time, unlicensed software in the country accounts for over 40 percent of that market.

While these pirated products give consumers lower prices, sales income is taken away from lawful companies. Efforts to prevent production, distribution, and sales of counterfeit products must involve local and international agencies as well as consumers.

Think Critically

1. Use the guidelines for ethical analysis presented in Chapter 1 to examine the above situations.
2. How do counterfeit products affect businesses and consumers?

A copyright gives the originator exclusive rights to publish, sell, and exhibit his or her creative work for his or her lifetime plus 70 years. For a copyright to be valid, the copyrighted item must be an original and fixed expression. For an item to be fixed, it must be set down in a permanent fashion in a way that others can understand—written words, standard computer codes, or blueprints. The copyright is only extended to the fixed original expression, not to the ideas behind it. The copyright notice © followed by the name of the copyright owner and the date of publication must be prominently displayed on the publication. Anyone who uses work protected by copyright without the creator's permission can be subject to legal action.

The Berne Convention of 1886 established the International Union for the Protection of Literary and Artistic Works. Today, more than 90 countries, including all members of the European Union, participate in this agreement. The Berne Union extends copyright protection in all member countries to its members as long as the first publication takes place in one of those countries. The International Copyright Convention of 1955 also provides international copyright protection based on the agreement that each member country will offer the same protection to foreign works that it does to domestic works.

✓ **Check**Point

What do the Patent Cooperation Treaty, the Paris Convention of Industrial Property, and the International Copyright Convention protect?

Contract Law

A contract is a legally enforceable agreement between two or more persons either to do or not to do a certain thing or things. A contract encourages competent parties to abide by an agreed-upon set of items. Contracts are the basis for almost all business arrangements.

Contracts can be either implied or express. An *implied contract* is one that is not explicitly agreed to by the parties but is inferred either from the parties' conduct or from the law. An *express contract* is one whose terms are openly declared, either orally or in writing. Businesses nearly always enter into express contracts because it is wise for parties to agree to and set forth very clearly what is expected of everyone. However, both implied and express contracts are binding on both parties, and neither party can withdraw without the agreement of the other party.

COMPONENTS OF A CONTRACT

For a contract to be considered valid, it must contain the following essential components: capacity, mutual agreement, consideration, and legal purpose.

Capacity All parties must be competent, of legal age, and mentally capable.

Mutual agreement One party offers valid terms and the other party accepts.

COMMUNICATION ACROSS BORDERS

WHEN IS A CONTRACT NOT A CONTRACT?

When doing business in Japan, it is important to realize that the communication known as a contract may not have the same meaning to Japanese businesspersons as it does to U.S. businesspersons. The Japanese often aren't eager to sign contracts, although they will do so because they know most Western businesspersons require them. Because Japanese businesspersons consider agreements based on personal promises to be binding, they discount the importance of contracts, which are agreements based on written words that are flexible in meaning. As a result, Japanese businesspersons view signed contracts as a point from which to begin negotiations when circumstances change or disputes arise, not as the absolute rules for business transactions, as U.S. businesspersons view them.

Think Critically

1. Why do you think Japanese businesspersons consider written words and contracts to be flexible in meaning?
2. How do Japanese businesspersons benefit by valuing personal promises over written contracts?

Consideration Something of value must be given by both parties.

Legal purpose The terms of the contract must be in agreement with the law.

For a contract to be enforceable, the contract must be valid—that is, it must meet all four of the conditions. Either party can enforce a valid contract.

Businesspeople in the international arena frequently enter into contracts with representatives of companies from other countries and with the governments of other countries. Such agreements are most often made according to the rules of international law. Cultural factors also may influence contractual situations. In many *high-context* societies, the trust achieved through verbal agreements are often considered as valid as the written contract.

TREATIES AND TRADE AGREEMENTS

Treaties and trade agreements between countries are examples of contracts that have a tremendous effect on global business activities. These agreements impose a degree of stability and uniformity for trade relations where members have different cultures and customs. Because contracts are the basis of business relationships, many trade agreements provide guidelines for the enforcement of contracts.

Some of the most far-reaching international trade agreements in force today include the following.

- The World Trade Organization with more than 150 member countries
- The European Union which allows the free flow of goods, services, labor, and capital between the member countries of the EU
- The North American Free Trade Agreement, designed to ensure open markets and fair competition between companies in Canada, Mexico, and the United States

✓ CheckPoint

What is necessary for a trade agreement to be an enforceable contract?

REVIEW GLOBAL BUSINESS TERMS
Define each of the following terms.

1. property
2. property rights
3. intellectual property
4. patent
5. trademark
6. copyright
7. contract

Study Tools

www.cengage.com/school/genbus/intlbiz

REVIEW GLOBAL BUSINESS CONCEPTS

8. What are the three types of property?
9. What four elements must be present for a contract to be valid?

SOLVE GLOBAL BUSINESS PROBLEMS
For each of the following intellectual properties, decide if the item would be protected by a patent, trademark, or copyright.

10. The brand name of a packaged food product
11. A musical composition
12. A process for sending photos over the Internet
13. A logo for a sports team
14. This book

THINK CRITICALLY

15. What actions could be taken to protect intellectual property in a country?
16. Why are persons of a certain age not allowed to enter into a legally binding contract?

MAKE ACADEMIC CONNECTIONS

17. **TECHNOLOGY** How do the Internet and other technology make protection of patents, trademarks, and copyrights more difficult?
18. **GEOGRAPHY** How might the climate and terrain of a country affect contracts?
19. **LAW** Find an article about a recent lawsuit involving intellectual property. Write a brief summary of the article and offer your opinion about how the lawsuit might affect international business.
20. **VISUAL ARTS** Create a poster or tabletop display that compare and contrast the three main forms of intellectual property. Include examples of each.
21. **COMMUNICATION** Research the impact of property rights infringement and create a plan a public service campaign including print, radio, and television to inform the public about the issue.

8-3 Resolving Legal Differences

GOALS

- Identify several different ways to resolve international legal disputes.

- Explain the litigation process.

- Describe the role of the International Court of Justice in International Business.

Photodisc/Getty Images

Resolving Legal Differences Without Court Action

Throughout the world, most legal disputes are resolved without the parties ever going to court. This is true of disputes between individuals, businesses, and nations.

There are many reasons why businesses, particularly those in the international arena, are willing to settle conflicts out of court. The time and expense involved in lawsuits, the need for a quick resolution, the concern about bad publicity, the uncertainty of outcomes, and the desire to maintain a good relationship with the other party all must be considered. Businesses also may fear that they will receive discriminatory treatment in a foreign court. Moreover, the complexity involved in determining which country's laws to use and the location of the trial contributes to companies' preference for dispute resolution outside of the courtroom. The two major means of alternate dispute settlement used by businesses in the international arena are mediation and arbitration.

MEDIATION

Mediation is a dispute resolution method that makes use of a neutral third party, or *mediator*. A mediator attempts to reconcile the viewpoints of the disputing parties. A mediator is involved with the substance of the dispute and makes suggestions and proposals. Therefore, the mediator is often an attorney or expert in the disputed matter. Mediators cannot make binding decisions. Only when the disputing parties voluntarily agree to a mediator's decision is a settlement reached. Thus, mediation is most successful when both parties are willing to compromise.

Some cultures have a strong tradition of using mediation to settle disputes. In Japan, for example, it is a point of honor to settle disputes without having to go to court. In the People's Republic of China, approximately 90 percent of all civil disputes are settled by mediation. More than 800,000 Mediation Committees exist throughout China, each composed of a group of knowledgeable people on various topics.

ARBITRATION

Arbitration is a method of conflict resolution that uses a neutral third party to make a binding decision. Unlike a mediator, an *arbitrator's* decision is legal and binding on both parties. An arbitrator acts as a private judge at a location of the disputing parties' choice and establishes procedures and rules of evidence. The parties specify the issues to be decided by the arbitrator. In this way, they avoid receiving a decision based on legal technicalities or other reasons that are not central to the issue being decided.

Arbitration is particularly well suited to settling disputes involving international business. Such disputes normally do not involve serious or complicated legal issues. So most businesses prefer to resolve disputes in a speedy, economical, and private way. Most often a dispute comes to arbitration because a contract either requires it or allows a party to demand it. Such provisions are common in union contracts.

In the international business arena, a contract will frequently include a requirement of arbitration. An intermediary, a person both parties agree is impartial, also may be provided for in the original contract. A representative from the international business community is often chosen to be an arbitrator. A typical choice is an officer in a chamber of commerce or a trade association from a third country.

Work as a Team

Describe a trade difference that might occur between countries. Present both sides of the situation. Have a group member serve as a mediator or an arbitrator for the situation.

✓ CheckPoint

Why would a company want to avoid court action to settle a dispute?

Resolving Legal Differences Using Court Action

Two parties may decide on litigation when they are unable or unwilling to resolve their differences through mediation or arbitration or through their own agreements or compromises.

LITIGATION

Litigation is a lawsuit brought about to enforce the rights of a person or an organization or to seek a remedy to the violation of their rights. Litigation involves many complex procedural rules. These rules vary widely from country to country and even among courts within a given country. Most countries have a federal or national court. Many also have state or provincial courts, as well as even more localized courts. Nearly all legal systems have separate rules for criminal and civil cases.

People living in or doing business in a foreign country are usually subject to the laws of that country. Thus, if a dispute arises between a business and someone in the host country, the matter must be settled in the host country's courts. When a conflict arises between two companies of different countries, the conflict may be settled either in the courts of the country in which the agreement was made or in the courts of the country in which the contract will be fulfilled. Figure 8-2 provides a brief outline of dispute settlement methods and options.

If a government violates the terms of a contract with a foreign company, the company is expected to pursue a remedy within that host country. If the company is unable to obtain a resolution, it may present its claim to its own government, which may then press an international claim against the foreign country on behalf of the company. However, many governments are unwilling to press such claims for two reasons. First, the company is presumed to have had a clear conception of the risks involved in entering into such an agreement. Second, pressing such a claim may interfere with the delicate political balance that might exist between the two countries.

Another type of litigation is the *class-action suit,* in which several parties (individuals or organizations) take legal action as a group. In this type of lawsuit, a few bring a suit on behalf of many, the *class,* who have all suffered the same alleged injustice. Class action suits may result from many people buying the same defective vehicle or thousands of utility customers being overcharged on their electric bill. This legal action is especially useful when the amount for one person is small, but the total could be significant. In an international setting, a class action suit may involve a miscalculation for foreign shipping which results in overcharging many export companies.

Photodisc/Getty Images

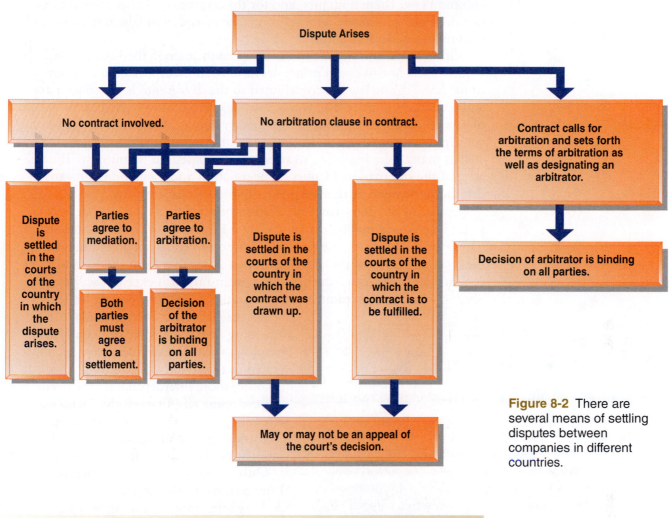

Dispute Resolution Across Borders

Figure 8-2 There are several means of settling disputes between companies in different countries.

✓ Check Point
When might litigation be appropriate?

The International Court of Justice

The International Court of Justice was established in 1946 by the Charter of the United Nations. It is located in The Hague in the Netherlands. The **International Court of Justice** is a court that settles disputes between nations when both nations request that it do so and also advises the United Nations on matters of international law. The decisions of the Court are binding for all parties.

Many of the procedures of the International Court of Justice are derived from Western civil law systems. For example, the International Court primarily uses documentary evidence to decide a case. This court also has the power to request additional evidence.

The International Court does not use procedures that are routine under common law. There is no jury, and for that reason, oral testimony is rarely heard. Evidence is rarely removed from the record, and false testimony and documents are simply ignored.

While Western principles of law are predominate in the International Court, some non-Western principles have been incorporated into international law. Islamic law has contributed to the division of law into primary and secondary sources. The *primary source* corresponds to the Islamic concept of certain, or definite, proof. The *secondary source* corresponds to the Islamic concept of reasoned proof. The great majority of international rules of war, as well as many rules regarding treaties, are also based on Islamic law. The reliance of the International Court on negotiation and mediation as means of dispute settlement are derived primarily from Asian customs.

Because of the dominance of Western principles, some newly developed states have found that international law is in conflict with their interests. Communist and developing nations, for example, do not accept many of the legal principles of the older developed states that form the basis of international law. Because of the past and continuing influence of the West, the effect of these newer countries on international law has been slight.

Because law must change to adapt to emerging situations, some principles not in harmony with Western ideas have been integrated into international law. As the world becomes more interdependent, the needs of developing countries receive increased attention. As a result, these developing countries become more willing to abide by international law and offer new concepts to it.

Only nations can be parties before the International Court of Justice. Individuals and organizations, including businesses, are specifically excluded. Thus, very few commercial cases are heard by the Court. Such cases are heard only when a government presses an international claim on behalf of a company.

What then is the importance of the International Court of Justice to the world of international business? The answer is that it provides guidelines for acceptable ways of doing business around the world.

The continuation and expansion of world trade requires that businesses in foreign environments be treated in a consistent manner. Businesspeople in all countries want to engage in profitable relationships. As long as international principles of law are observed—particularly property rights and responsibilities and enforcement of contracts—international business can result in better relations among nations.

NETBookmark

The International Chamber of Commerce (ICC) is a global business organization that promotes global economic activity. The ICC promotes economic growth, job creation, prosperity and understanding between national economies. To visit the ICC web site, access the web site shown below and click on the link for Chapter 8. Read the information in the section "What is the ICC?" Then write two paragraphs outlining the functions of the ICC.

www.cengage.com/school/genbus/intlbiz

Photodisc/Getty Images

✓ CheckPoint

What is the purpose of the International Court of Justice?

REVIEW GLOBAL BUSINESS TERMS

Define each of the following terms.

1. mediation
2. arbitration
3. litigation
4. International Court of Justice

REVIEW GLOBAL BUSINESS CONCEPTS

5. What is the difference between mediation and arbitration?

6. What are some of the reasons why two businesses from different countries might prefer to resolve a dispute through mediation or arbitration rather than litigation?

7. What is the importance of international law to businesses engaged in international trade?

SOLVE GLOBAL BUSINESS PROBLEMS

For each of the following situations, decide if the dispute should be resolved using mediation, arbitration, or litigation.

8. After years of negotiation, a company is unable to collect for the value of property lost by a shipping company.

9. A company and a supplier in another country have slight differences about a recent business transaction.

10. Mediation between two companies has not been successful. The businesses want a third party to decide a legally binding settlement.

11. A labor union and management want a third party to recommend a possible settlement for the differences in their contract negotiations.

THINK CRITICALLY

12. Why is the International Court of Justice important to international business?

13. While not legally binding, why is the mediation process sometimes effective for settling disputes?

MAKE ACADEMIC CONNECTIONS

14. **TECHNOLOGY** What are some international legal concerns that could result from increased use of technology in business?

15. **LAW** Write a contract to use when doing a job for a neighbor, such as taking care of pets, mowing a lawn, installing a computer, or babysitting.

16. **LAW** Use the Internet to research the International Court of Justice and some of its recent cases and decisions.

CHAPTER SUMMARY

8-1 INTERNATIONAL LEGAL SYSTEMS AND LIABILITY

A The main legal systems of the world are civil law, common law, and statutory law.

B Manufacturers and sellers are responsible for the safety of their products. Intent to cause harm and negligence are difficult to prove, so the principles of strict liability apply in product negligence in many countries.

8-2 PROPERTY AND CONTRACTS

A Property rights are protected through government actions such as patents, trademarks, and copyrights.

B Contracts are the basis for almost all business arrangements. A valid contract must have four components: capacity, mutual agreement, consideration, and legal purpose.

8-3 RESOLVING LEGAL DIFFERENCES

A International legal disputes may be resolved without court action through mediation or arbitration.

B Litigation is court action used to resolve global business disputes.

C The International Court of Justice settles legal disputes between nations when both nations request that it do so. This court also advises the United Nations on matters of international law.

GLOBAL **REFOCUS**

Read the Global Focus at the beginning of this chapter, and answer the following questions.

1. What actions might a company take to plan, implement, and protect its international brand names and trademarks?

2. How might a joint venture help a company protect its trademarks?

3. Go to the web site of the World Intellectual Property Organization to obtain current information related to trademarks and brand names.

REVIEW GLOBAL BUSINESS TERMS

Match the terms listed with the definitions. Some terms may not be used.

1. A legal system that relies on the accumulation of decisions made in prior cases.
2. A legal right that protects the original works of authors, music composers, playwrights, artists, and publishers.
3. A legally enforceable agreement between two or more persons either to do or not to do a certain thing or things.
4. Everything that can be owned.
5. A court that settles disputes between nations when both nations request that it do so and also advises the United Nations on matters of international law.
6. The specific responsibility that both manufacturers and sellers have for the safety of their products.
7. Those laws that have been enacted by a body of lawmakers.
8. The failure of a responsible party to follow standards of due care.
9. A distinctive name, symbol, word, picture, or combination of these that is used by a business to identify its services or products.
10. A dispute resolution method that makes use of a neutral third party.
11. The exclusive right of an inventor to make, sell, and use a product or process.
12. A method of conflict resolution that uses a neutral third party to make a binding decision.

a. arbitration
b. civil law
c. common law
d. contract
e. copyright
f. intellectual property
g. International Court of Justice
h. liability
i. litigation
j. mediation
k. negligence
l. patent
m. product liability
n. property
o. property rights
p. statutes
q. strict liability
r. trademark

MAKE GLOBAL BUSINESS DECISIONS

13. If you were creating the laws for a country, what would some examples of those laws be?
14. Describe a situation in which a person or an organization might be held negligent for injury or property damage.
15. Some people believe patents, copyrights, and trademarks create monopolies. Describe the advantages and disadvantages of protecting intellectual property.
16. List examples of contracts commonly entered into by individuals and companies.
17. Describe a situation in which a company might use mediation or arbitration in an international business situation.

18. Jean Claude Nallet, an eight-year-old French boy, received a model fire engine as a present. While playing with the toy, a sharp tip on the toy ladder punctured Jean Claude's finger, and he required medical treatment. Later the family found out that the fire engine was defective and had been recalled by the manufacturer.

a. In your opinion, do Jean Claude's parents have a legitimate reason to file a product liability claim?

b. Under the guidelines of strict liability, which elements apply to Jean Claude's case?

MAKE ACADEMIC CONNECTIONS

19. COMMUNICATIONS Write a letter to a publishing company or a music video production company requesting permission to copy an artist's work. Save a copy of your letter, and summarize the response you receive in a short written report.

20. VISUAL ART Look for examples of trademarks on products sold around the world. Based on these examples, create a picture for a trademark and brand that might be used for international business.

Photodisc/Getty Images

21. COMMUNICATIONS Create a logo or package design for a product that could be used in many countries around the world.

22. LAW Create a legal system for a new country that just became independent from another country that had controlled its political and legal activities in the past.

23. CULTURAL STUDIES How might the culture of a country affect the format and conditions of a contract?

24. SCIENCE Research a patent on a product. Identify the inventor, the year the patent was granted, and the product's function. Prepare a summary report of your findings.

25. CAREER PLANNING Find out what types of legal agreements a person would encounter when applying for a job with and working for a multinational company.

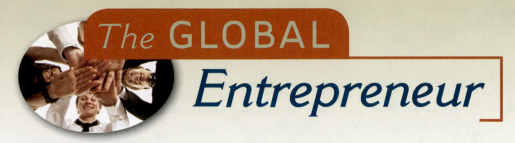

The GLOBAL Entrepreneur

CREATING AN INTERNATIONAL BUSINESS PLAN

Laws Around the World

Research the legal system of a foreign country. Focus your research on cultural issues and political influences on legal agreements and business regulations in that country. Obtain information for the following questions.

1. What are the basic components of the country's legal system?

2. How does the culture of the country affect its legal system?

3. What are the issues that affect legal agreements in the country?

4. What legal restrictions affect international trade with the country?

5. What sort of out-of-court resolution process might be used in the country to settle legal differences?

Sources of information for your research may include the following.

- reference books such as encyclopedia, almanacs, and atlases

- current newspaper and magazine articles

- web sites for the CIA Factbook and other country information

- materials from companies, airlines, travel bureaus, government agencies, and other organizations involved in international business

- interviews with people who have lived in, worked in, or traveled to the country

Prepare a written summary or present a short oral report (two or three minutes) of your findings.

Photodisc/Getty Images

Global Entrepreneurship and Small Business Management

9-1 Entrepreneurial Enterprises

9-2 The Business Plan and Self-Employment

9-3 Operating an Entrepreneurial Enterprise

Sipa via AP Images

GLOBAL FOCUS

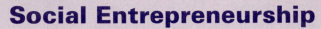

Social Entrepreneurship

How might business activities eliminate hunger, disease, and poverty? Today, social entrepreneurs around the world are helping to solve these problems and address other concerns. They mix traditional business practices with innovation and commitment to drive social change. A desire to improve society rather than making a profit motivates them.

Plenty of problems need attention. Poverty, food shortages, insufficient health care, pollution, illiteracy, and inadequate housing are all potential targets. Most social entrepreneurs focus their attention on a specific issue, often something with a personal connection. They look for the underlying issues and seek innovated sustainable solutions. Social entrepreneurs use their own skills and collaborate with experts in other fields. Social entrepreneurship requires traditional business skills and knowledge along with expertise related to the initiative. For example, a social entrepreneur might seek help from an engineer or hydrologist when developing a clean water project.

Social entrepreneurs operate around the globe. Many initiatives focus on improving society in developing countries while other programs target social problems that persist in the wealthiest countries. Examples of social entrepreneurship include homes for AIDS orphans in Africa and preschools for children in the Middle East, programs to end forced labor in South Asia and to create sewing cooperatives in South America, the manufacture and marketing of agricultural tools in Africa, and a solar energy project in Brazil.

Social entrepreneurs are passionate about their visions and their enthusiasm can be contagious. Successful programs often grow and expand their impact locally or globally. For example, the success of the Grameen Bank, which Muhammad Yunus started in Bangladesh with $27, triggered microfinance programs in more than 100 countries.

Think Critically

1. Describe *social entrepreneurship* in your own words.
2. What motivates social entrepreneurs?
3. Conduct an Internet search to obtain additional information about social entrepreneurship.

9-1 Entrepreneurial Enterprises

GOALS

- Explain the importance of entrepreneurs in the development of an economy.

- Differentiate between the types of entrepreneurial businesses.

- Describe telecommuting and the effect of technology on home-based businesses.

Photodisc/Getty Images

The Economic Importance of Entrepreneurs

Nations do not start out highly industrialized with international airports, superhighways, and computer networks. In every country, people get ideas and take action to make products better, faster, and more available. This entrepreneurial spirit plays a significant role in economic development and improved quality of life around the world.

World events such as the end of the cold war and advances in technology, including the Internet and cell phones, have opened up opportunities for small businesses all over the globe. In most Eastern European countries, the shift from a Soviet-style command economy to a market economy has resulted in an increase in the number of new businesses. Access to news and technology has increased opportunities for entrepreneurs in Africa, the Middle East, and Central and South America, giving men and women the chance to own and operate small businesses. Small businesses are booming in emerging markets in Asia such as Thailand, Indonesia, and the Philippines.

Just as entrepreneurship is growing in emerging economies, small businesses also are thriving throughout North America, Western Europe, and parts of Asia including Japan, Singapore, and South Korea. Small businesses help countries remain competitive and ready to take advantage of new opportunities in the global economy.

INNOVATION AND THE ENTREPRENEURIAL SPIRIT

An **entrepreneur** is a risk taker who operates a business. Every business combines land, labor, and capital to sell a product or service. An entrepreneur is the person who brings together these resources for a company to get started and operate successfully.

Entrepreneurs are often people with a creative vision, such as David Filo and Jerry Wang, who founded Yahoo!, or Lydia Moss Bradley, who made millions in real estate development and went on to found Bradley University. A common trait of entrepreneurs is that they don't listen to people who say "It can't be done!" These business innovators have an idea they believe in and dedicate their time, money, and effort to its success.

ECONOMIC AND SOCIAL BENEFITS OF SMALL BUSINESS

Most entrepreneurs start small. Some have started in a basement or garage. Small companies are an important part of every economy. A **small business** is an independently owned and operated business that does not dominate an industry.

Small businesses are commonly categorized by number of employees. The U.S. Small Business Administration defines a small business as one with fewer than 100 employees. About 95 percent of all businesses in the United States have fewer than 50 employees. Of the more than 20 million businesses in the European Union, more than 90 percent of these organizations have fewer than ten employees.

Entrepreneurial efforts provide a nation with three main economic and social benefits.

1. **Small businesses are major creators of new products.** Entrepreneurs are willing to take risks and try ideas that may be rejected by larger companies. Entrepreneurs have invented products such as personal computers, ballpoint pens, video games, and fiberglass snow skis.

2. **Small businesses are the major source of jobs.** In recent years, the largest companies in the United States reduced their work forces, while small businesses hired millions of employees. Business organizations with fewer than 500 employees employ more than half of all U.S. workers and create about three out of four new jobs in the economy.

3. **Small businesses often provide personal service.** In that way, they compete successfully against larger companies to meet the individual needs of customers. A local bank, for example, can grant loans to people in its community who may be denied funding by larger financial institutions. Small manufacturing companies can produce custom-made parts for foreign companies, an activity that large businesses might not find profitable.

Photodsic/Getty Images

Common Entrepreneurial Businesses in Europe and Asia

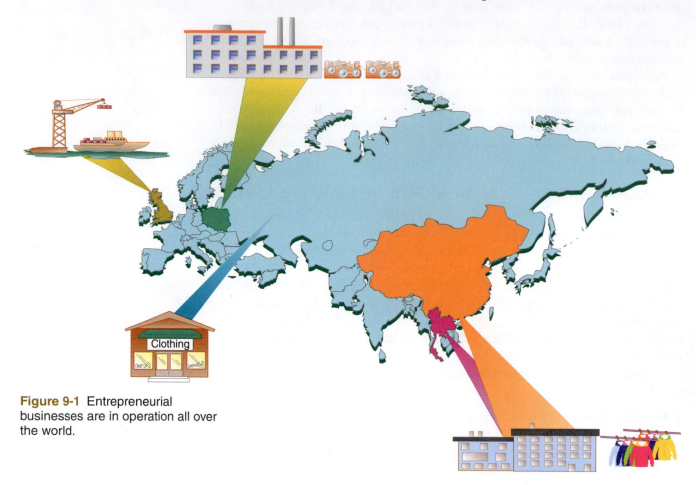

Figure 9-1 Entrepreneurial businesses are in operation all over the world.

ENTREPRENEURS AND EXPORTING

Entrepreneurs often turn to international business to expand their markets. Exporting is promoted by the U.S. Department of Commerce, Small Business Administration, World Trade Centers, and state departments of economic development. Similar actions are taken by the Small Business Commissioner for the Australian Capital Territory in Australia. The Canadian Ministry of Small Business and Consumer Services and the Malaysian Entrepreneurship Development Centre exist for a similar purpose. These agencies and organizations help entrepreneurs plan and execute international business activities.

Entrepreneurs may invent ways to adapt products and services to meet the economic, cultural, and legal needs of customers in other countries. The activities of small businesses in Europe and Asia have energized economic development. Thailand started as an agricultural society with a system of landlords and peasants. Chinese influence in the late 1800s helped change the economic emphasis of Thailand. By the 1970s, over 30 major companies were based in the country. Entrepreneurial activities stimulated economic development. Today Thailand is one of the largest and fastest-growing economies in the world.

✓ **Check**Point

What are the three main economic and social benefits small businesses provide?

Types of Entrepreneurial Businesses

Types of entrepreneurial enterprises are as varied as types of large corporations. Entrepreneurial businesses can be grouped into five major categories: extracting companies, manufacturing companies, wholesalers, retailers, and service companies.

Agricultural, Mining, and Extracting Companies Diamond-mining companies in South Africa, oil companies in Saudi Arabia, and flower growers in California are all examples of extractors. These enterprises grow products or take raw materials from nature. Extracting companies include businesses involved in agriculture, fishing, forestry, and mining.

Manufacturing Companies Manufacturing involves changing raw materials and parts into usable products. Entrepreneurs in this category range from computer manufacturers with many employees to basket weavers with just a few workers.

Wholesalers Products must get from producers to consumers. If clothing manufactured in Taiwan is not shipped to appropriate selling locations, the garments have little value. A wholesaler is a business that buys from a manufacturer and sells to other businesses. Wholesalers are commonly called *intermediaries* because they are links between producers and sellers of products.

Retailers A retailer is a business that sells directly to consumers. In a typical week, you probably go to several stores. You may also buy from mail-order companies or vending machines. These are examples of retailing businesses. Online retailers are retailers that operate over the Internet.

GLOBAL TECHNOLOGY TRENDS

An Internet Entrepreneur Expands

All you need is a computer, an Internet connection, a printer, a scanner, a credit card business account, and a delivery service. Then what do you have? You have an online business capable of competing with major companies.

Online, it is hard to distinguish a large company from a small business. Take away the big buildings, fancy offices, and well-dressed employees, and what do you have left? A company image that is judged on the content and services provided on the Internet.

When Amazon.com started, it began selling books without any experience in that industry. It started with technology and the idea to provide bestsellers online. Next, the cyber-retailer expanded into CDs, videos, software, toys, video games, and home improvement products. More recently, the company started selling clothing, food, furniture, appliances, personal care products, jewelry, magazines, sports equipment, and electronics. Today they have sales that exceed most traditional stores.

The company's international sales also continue to expand. Separate web sites have been created for Canada, the United Kingdom, Germany, France, Japan, and China.

Think Critically

1. What are the benefits of online businesses for employees and consumers?
2. What actions might be taken for Amazon.com to expand its international operations?
3. Locate a web site for an online business that is probably a small operation but is able to compete against larger companies.

Work as a Team
Discuss the advantages and disadvantages of working from home.

Service Companies How often does someone in your household have clothes cleaned, get the car washed, use a phone, get a haircut, or obtain medical care? These are all examples of services. Consumer services include businesses such as law offices, doctors' offices, dentists' offices, hair salons, daycare centers, Internet service providers, repair shops, travel agencies, and music schools.

Service companies also sell business services to other companies. Business services include advertising, information systems, custodial, security, and equipment rental. These companies are commonly called *business-to-business (B2B)* enterprises because they sell to other companies rather than to individual consumers.

FUTURE GROWTH FOR SMALL BUSINESS

In addition to more than 12 million self-employed workers in the United States, there are several million others who operate part-time businesses while working for someone else. Government agencies and business experts project that in the coming years, entrepreneurs involved in the following types of enterprises have the greatest potential for success.

- Health-care services
- Retailing and food service companies, especially those using the Internet and other technology to interact with customers
- Environmental businesses that recycle and offer environment-friendly goods and services
- Training and education enterprises to help workers adapt to a changing workplace
- Personal services such as childcare, financial planning, entertainment, and recreation
- Commercial services such as marketing, financial consultants, delivery, transportation, and information systems

These business opportunities will be available in both the United States and other countries.

✓ **Check**Point
How does a wholesaler differ from a retailer?

Home-Based Businesses

Years ago most people worked from their homes as farmers, weavers, and toolmakers. These home-based businesses are still present in many countries, including the Philippines, Pakistan, Chad, Liberia, Kenya, and Peru.

In major population areas of industrialized countries, however, most work moved to factories, stores, and offices during the industrialization process. However, technology is currently providing the opportunity for many workers to return to their homes to work. Today over 5 million people in the United States and more than 2 million in Canada operate businesses from their homes.

Other types of common home businesses include real estate brokers, insurance agents, construction contractors, repair shops, hair stylists, pet groomers, childcare providers, accountants, and tax preparers. Also, home-based

Internet businesses have expanded to include almost any type of business, such as retailers, auto parts suppliers, online greeting cards, grocery stores, and flower delivery services.

Telecommuting In addition to running their own businesses from home, many people also are working for another company by telecommuting. **Telecommuting** involves using a computer and other technology to work at home instead of in a company office or factory. Telecommuting is best suited to jobs that do not require regular in-person contact with others and may be done through computer networks and other telecommunications equipment. This employment arrangement is common for writers, editors, researchers, economists, accounting clerks, information processing workers, database supervisors, and computer programmers.

Employers who use telecommuting report several benefits.

PhotoDisc/Getty Images

- Businesses save money because they do not need as much office space.
- Companies are able to keep talented employees who may not want to work in a structured environment.
- Workers save time and energy since they do not travel to a place of employment.

Many home-based entrepreneurs and telecommuters select working at home so they can have more control over their schedules. For most people this means a better balance between work, family, and other obligations.

People planning to work at home must consider the government regulations for these types of businesses. For example, in recent years in Toronto, operating a mail-order company from your home was considered illegal.

✓ CheckPoint
What are the advantages of telecommuting to a company?

NETBookmark

Entrepreneurial activities exist in every country of the world. Access the web site shown below and click on the link for Chapter 9. Read the introduction on the InternationalEntrepreneurship.com home page, and then select a country. Write a brief that describes the business and entrepreneurial environment in that country. What are the main factors that might need to be considered when starting a business in the country you selected?

www.cengage.com/school/genbus/intlbiz

9-1 Assessment

REVIEW GLOBAL BUSINESS TERMS
Define each of the following terms.

1. entrepreneur
2. small business
3. telecommuting

REVIEW GLOBAL BUSINESS CONCEPTS
4. Why do entrepreneurial businesses frequently turn to international business?
5. What are five common types of entrepreneurial businesses?
6. What kinds of jobs are best suited to telecommuting?

SOLVE GLOBAL BUSINESS PROBLEMS
Determine whether each of the following companies is primarily engaged in extracting, manufacturing, wholesaling, retailing, or providing a service.

7. Company that acquires kitchen appliances and sells them to construction companies.
8. Toy store.
9. Employment agency.
10. Airline.
11. Company that printed this textbook for the publishing company.
12. Person who traps lobsters and sells them to seafood stores and restaurants.

THINK CRITICALLY
13. What actions could a government take to encourage the start up of new businesses?
14. How would differences in cultures affect the operation of a small business in various countries?
15. When you work from home, you need to be especially well disciplined. You also may miss interacting with other people. How could you overcome these disadvantages of working at home?

MAKE ACADEMIC CONNECTIONS
16. **GEOGRAPHY** Describe how a country's natural resources could encourage entrepreneurial activities.
17. **LAW** What legal restrictions might a person face when starting a new business?

The Business Plan and Self-Employment

Digital Vision/Getty Images

GOALS

- Evaluate self-employment as a career option.
- Describe the first three sections of a business plan.

Self-Employment as a Career

When you own your own business, the good news is that you don't have to listen to a boss anymore—because you are the boss. The bad news is that you can't call in sick unless someone else can be trusted to keep things going.

ADVANTAGES OF SELF-EMPLOYMENT

The two main advantages of owning a business are independence and pride of ownership. A small business owner makes the company decisions and is at the center of action. Because of political and legal restrictions, however, this same independence may not be available to entrepreneurs in all countries.

As entrepreneurs achieve success, they usually gain a feeling of accomplishment. They gain confidence in their ability to organize resources, make decisions, and manage business activities. Serving customers, employing workers, and contributing to the economic growth of a community or nation can also provide a sense of satisfaction for entrepreneurs.

DISADVANTAGES OF SELF-EMPLOYMENT

Being an owner-operator of a company also has disadvantages. The drawbacks of self-employment are the time commitment, uncertain income, and possible loss of investment. Every small business owner can tell you about the time involved. More than half of all small business owners who sell their companies do so because of boredom or burnout.

GLOBAL BUSINESS SPOTLIGHT

STREET ENTREPRENEURS IN LATIN AMERICA

Photodisc/Getty Images

In Brazil, *feiras*, or street fairs, provide a wide variety of healthy, fresh produce within walking distance of home. *Tianguis*, or open air markets, sell a variety of products to meet the daily needs of consumers in Mexico. Vendors selling herbs and spices often can be seen on the streets of Bolivia. These local entrepreneurs have the flexibility to locate their operations where their customers live, work, and play. This mobility gives these informal retailers a competitive advantage over traditional stores.

Informal businesses and retailers are common in Latin America. These businesses include pushcarts, temporary street stands, and peddlers on foot, as well as unregistered offices, shops, and factories in homes and other locations. In Mexico, the number of street-vendor stalls is estimated at over 450,000. In Peru, an estimated 40 percent of the GDP occurs in the informal market. Throughout Latin America, this informal economy can represent between 40 and 60 percent of business activities.

While street vendors may post prices in writing, these informal retailers commonly "deal" with both regular customers and tourists. These negotiated prices can benefit the needs of low-income community members.

Think Critically

1. What economic and social factors cause a person to become a street entrepreneur?
2. What are the benefits and drawbacks of street entrepreneurs for a country?

As a business owner, income is uncertain. In the first few years of owning a business, it is possible that the owner will not earn enough to get a salary. Business experts recommend that money be set aside for personal living expenses before starting a new business. Even after the business has been operating for awhile, poor economic conditions can reduce sales and profits.

Each year, more than 50,000 businesses fail in the United States, with owners and investors losing millions of dollars. The most common causes of business failure are limited cash, poor management decisions, and a weak economy. Despite these difficulties, more than half a million new businesses start each year in the United States. After three years, three out of four of these new companies are still operating.

QUALITIES OF SUCCESSFUL ENTREPRENEURS

What are successful entrepreneurs like? Most entrepreneurs have a desire for adventure. They are risk takers who are willing to give up a secure job in exchange for the chance to own and operate a business. Global entrepreneurs must consider the added risk of potential cultural, social, political, and legal barriers.

Being self-confident is another quality of successful entrepreneurs. Successful entrepreneurs believe in themselves and believe they can get others to get things done. Remember that it may mean getting things done in different ways in foreign markets. People in different cultures have different attitudes and behaviors regarding work and business relationships.

Entrepreneurs spend almost all their time either on the job or thinking about their business. Hard-working people have the potential for being the most successful. Are you someone who is willing to put in extra time and effort for your business?

Someone once said that if you don't know where you are going, you might end up somewhere else and not even know it. A goal-oriented person has a clear direction for the company, stated in the business plan. Goals should be clear and realistic. Goals also should have a time limit for achievement and should be measurable in some numeric way. For example, a business goal may be to have ten new customers in Greece within the next three months.

Is there some activity you participate in and perform well? Your knowledge, experience, and enjoyment of a skill or topic can be the foundation for a business idea.

A new product idea or an old idea presented in a new way can both be paths for entrepreneurial success. Creativity is a key to entrepreneurial success. Think about ways that existing products can be improved, or create a business that can make the lives of busy people a little easier.

Finally, knowing about the world of business is important for success as an entrepreneur. Business knowledge involves having an understanding of economics, organizational structure, decision making, advertising, finance, and technology. Business knowledge for the global entrepreneur should include information about foreign cultures, exchange rates, shipping methods, product labeling, and more.

✓ **Check**Point
What are the main characteristics of a successful entrepreneur?

Creating a Business Plan

Before you start any business, you should first develop a business plan. This document will guide you through the complex process of establishing, financing, and running a business.

THE BUSINESS PLAN

Every driver planning a trip, every team, and every company needs a plan to achieve its goal. A **business plan** is a guide used to start and operate a business. Every small business needs a plan to guide it to success. A business plan has two main uses. First, this document may be used to attract new investors or to convince a bank to lend money to the company. Second, the business plan provides a blueprint for company activities.

A business plan includes the seven main sections shown in Figure 9-2. The first three sections—the business description, the organizational structure, and the marketing activities—are all related to setting up a business.

PARTS OF A BUSINESS PLAN
1. Business description
2. Organizational structure
3. Marketing activities
4. Financial planning
5. Production activities
6. Human resource activities
7. Information needs

Figure 9-2 A business plan is designed to help a manager organize business activities. The first three sections of the plan are all related to setting up a business.

Image Source Black/Jupiter Images

Business Description The introductory section of a business plan covers three topics. First, the legal name and location of the company is identified. Second, a brief description of the background and experience of the owners and main employees is provided. Third, an overview of the company's product or service, potential customers, and competition is presented.

Organizational Structure Most businesses are organized as sole proprietorships, partnerships, or corporations. A company's organizational structure, covered in the second section of the business plan, will be based on its size, number of owners, and method of financing. Companies involved in international trade and exporting would explain about their foreign business partners. This section would include an explanation of any joint ventures, licensing agreements, distributor contracts, and supplier relationships.

Marketing Activities Two vital activities for every business, communicating with and serving customers, are discussed in the third section of the business plan. **Marketing** includes the business activities necessary to move goods and services from the producer to the consumer. Marketing activities include product or service planning, risk management, marketing information management, promotion, pricing, financing, distribution, purchasing, and selling.

Many companies organize this phase of their business with a marketing plan. A **marketing plan** is a document that details the marketing activities of an organization. A marketing plan includes information about customer needs, social factors, competition, target markets, economic trends, the political environment, and the marketing mix. Global marketing for companies involved in exporting and other business activities will also take into account the geography, history, culture, and trade barriers of other countries.

✓ **Check**Point

What are the first three sections of a business plan?

Geography

AN UNCERTAIN FUTURE FOR THE WILDLIFE OF INDIA

Their neighbors include crocodiles, leopards, rhinoceroses, tigers, and musk deer. The people in India share their land with more varieties of wildlife than any other nation. The country has over 400 national parks and sanctuaries to preserve these natural wonders. Despite protected areas, however, many species still face extinction.

Hunting and killing for food, animal skins, horns, and tusks result in vanishing breeds. Cutting down trees for firewood and using natural vegetation to feed livestock also threaten these endangered animals. Many species of wildlife no longer have the habitat necessary for survival. In recent years, the country had more than 120 animals on its list of endangered species.

As the second most populous nation in the world, India's diminishing resources are already stretched to an extreme. Tree planting and other conservation activities may help. Only time will tell if these efforts will allow for the survival of such animals as the jackal, the Asiatic lion, the Golden Leaf monkey, and the Bengal tiger.

Think Critically

1. How could the extinction of various animal species affect the economic environment of a country?
2. Conduct an Internet search for current information about the wildlife of India.

Photodisc/Getty Images

9-2 Assessment

Study Tools

www.cengage.com/school/genbus/intlbiz

REVIEW GLOBAL BUSINESS TERMS

Define each of the following terms.

1. business plan
2. marketing
3. marketing plan

REVIEW GLOBAL BUSINESS CONCEPTS

4. What are the advantages of owning your own business? What are the disadvantages?

5. What are the two main uses of a business plan?

6. What kinds of marketing activities should be included in a marketing plan?

SOLVE GLOBAL BUSINESS PROBLEMS

Answer the following questions. If you answer "yes" to most of the questions, you probably would enjoy being a small business owner.

7. Are you comfortable making decisions even when others might not agree?

8. Do you have leadership ability? Are you respected as a leader?

9. Do you complete tasks without becoming discouraged?

10. Are you able to assess situations from different viewpoints?

11. Can you clearly communicate your ideas both orally and in writing?

12. Are you able to start a project without encouragement from others?

13. Are there situations in which a failure helped you to learn and improve?

14. Are you willing to do tasks that are necessary but unpleasant?

THINK CRITICALLY

15. Describe hobbies and activities that might be useful when preparing to be an entrepreneur.

16. In what ways would an entrepreneur use a business plan?

MAKE ACADEMIC CONNECTIONS

17. TECHNOLOGY Use the outline feature of a word processing software package to outline the first three sections of a business plan.

18. STATISTICS Use the *U.S. Statistical Abstract* or a similar publication from the library or an Internet search to explore data about the number of companies, their size, number of employees, form or organization, percentage of small businesses in particular industries, and other statistical data. Create a bar graph or pie chart for one type of data.

Operating an Entrepreneurial Enterprise

Photodisc/Getty Images

GOALS

- Outline the process of financing a small business.

- Identify the major business activities of a small business manager.

Financing a Small Business

The most important part of the business plan may be the financial planning section. This is the fourth part of the business plan as illustrated in Figure 9-3. Money is needed for many purposes when starting and running a business. Funds are needed to buy advertising, to pay employees, to purchase supplies, and to acquire equipment. A **budget** is a financial tool that estimates a company's funds and its plan for spending those funds. One of the most common causes of business failure is lack of money to pay company expenses. Constantly changing exchange rates are an additional problem for small companies involved in international business. The process of financing a business starts with calculating operating costs and determining how to acquire the funds to pay those costs.

ANALYZING COSTS

One of the most difficult tasks when starting a new business is determining how much money will be needed to get started and continue operations. *Start-up* costs are those expenses that occur when a company is new. Start-up costs include equipment purchases, remodeling costs, legal fees, utility company deposits, and beginning inventory expenses.

PARTS OF A BUSINESS PLAN

1. Business description
2. Organizational structure
3. Marketing activities
4. Financial planning
5. Production activities
6. Human resource activities
7. Information needs

Figure 9-3 The most important part of the business plan may be the financial planning section.

Work as a Team
Select a type of business. Prepare a list of variable and fixed costs that would be necessary for this business to operate.

Continuing expenses are business operating costs that occur on an on-going basis. Continuing expenses include rent, utilities, insurance, salaries, advertising costs, employee training costs, taxes, and interest on loans.

Variable costs are business expenses that change in proportion to the level of production. For example, the cost of materials and parts to make radios depends on the number of radios that are produced. If parts and materials cost $8 per radio, the variable costs for making 100 radios would be $800. The variable costs for making 10 radios would be $80.

Fixed costs are expenses that do not change as the level of production changes. For example, rent of $1,000 a month and a manager's salary of $3,200 a month will be the same whether the company makes 10 or 100 radios.

BREAKEVEN POINT

A comparison of variable and fixed costs with sales revenue will tell a company the amount of profit or loss. The **breakeven point** is the number of units a business must sell to make a profit of zero. Sales below the breakeven point will result in a loss for a business. Sales above the breakeven point will result in a profit for a business.

Calculating the breakeven point involves two steps. First, you must find the **gross profit** on each item you sell. The gross profit, or gross margin, is the difference between the cost of an item for a business and the price for which the business can sell that item. For example, a company can make a radio for $8 and then sell it for $12. So the gross profit on one radio is $4.

$$\text{Cost} - \text{Selling price} = \text{Gross profit per unit}$$
$$\$12 - \$8 = \$4$$

Next, you must calculate how many items you must sell to cover all the fixed costs for a business, the breakeven point. To do this, you divide the total fixed costs for a business by the gross profit per unit. In the example above, the manufacturer has fixed costs of $44,000. That company must then sell 11,000 units to cover all its fixed costs.

$$\text{Total fixed costs} \div \text{Profit per unit} = \text{Breakeven units}$$
$$\$44,000 \div \$4 \text{ per unit} = 11,000 \text{ units}$$

At the breakeven point of 11,000 units, costs are covered but no profit is earned.

SOURCES OF FUNDS

Where do companies get the money to finance the start-up costs and continuing expenses? This funding can be secured in one of two ways, either through equity or through debt. **Equity funds** are business funds obtained from the owners of the business. Equity is the money the owners of a business have invested from their personal accounts.

Debt funds are business funds obtained by borrowing. The amounts owed by a business are called the debts of the company. Loans from financial institutions also help to finance companies and are debt funds. Many less-developed economies have weak banking systems. As a result, small businesses often depend on *microfinance*. These small loans, sometimes as little as $35 or $50, can have a significant impact on economic development.

FINANCIAL RECORDS OF SMALL BUSINESSES

The financial records of a company are like the scoreboard for a sporting event. Financial record keeping helps a business keep track of its financial status, just like a scoreboard helps fans keep track of how the teams on the field are doing. A **balance sheet** is the document that reports a company's *assets* (items of value), *liabilities* (amounts owed to others), and *owner's equity* (net worth). Assets include cash and anything that could be sold for cash, such as equipment, land, and inventory. The relationship among the items on a balance sheet can be expressed as an equation.

$$\text{Assets} - \text{Liabilities} = \text{Owner's equity}$$

For example, if a company has $4 million of assets and $1.5 million in liabilities, the owner's equity is $2.5 million.

$$\$4 \text{ million} - \$1.5 \text{ million} = \$2.5 \text{ million}$$

An **income statement** is a document that summarizes a company's revenue from sales and its expenses over a period of time, usually one year. On the income statement, a business will total all of the revenues it brings in as well as all of its expenses. It will then subtract the expenses from the revenues to find its profit or loss. For example, a company had sales revenue of $670,000 and $430,000 in operating expenses. Its profit would be $240,000.

$$\begin{array}{ccccc} \text{Sales revenue} & - & \text{Operating expenses} & = & \text{Profit} \\ \$670,000 & - & \$430,000 & = & \$240,000 \end{array}$$

The continuing costs of a business are usually paid for with current cash flows. **Cash flow** is the inflow and outflow of cash. The major sources of *cash*

inflows are cash sales and money collected from customers that is owed on account. Occasionally, a company will require additional cash inflows due to slow sales or a need to buy expensive equipment. When this happens, the business will need to borrow or get additional investments from owners.

The main *cash outflows* of a business are for current operating expenses, new equipment, debt payments, and taxes. A *cash flow statement* reports the current sources and amounts of cash inflows and outflows. Weak cash inflows are a major cause of small business failure.

Photodisc/Getty Images

✓ CheckPoint

How does a balance sheet differ from an income statement?

Major Activities of Every Business

MARKETING

FINANCE

PRODUCTION

HUMAN RESOURCES

INFORMATION SYSTEMS

PHOTO CREDITS
Top row:
gvictoria/iStockphoto.com
webking/iStockphoto.com
gmnicholas/iStockphoto.com
Bottom row:
RBFried/iStockphoto.com
gbrundin/iStockphoto.com

Figure 9-4 Every company has five major management areas.

Managing the Small Business

In a large company, a manager is usually responsible for only one area of the business, such as marketing or finance. In a small business, however, the owner may be responsible for several or all areas of management. The five major management areas of every business are shown in Figure 9-4 above. These areas, along with a description of the business and the organization of the business, are all covered in the business plan as shown in Figure 9-5.

PRODUCTION MANAGEMENT

The factors of production are combined to create goods and services. Every business must produce something to sell. That something may not always be too obvious. For example, what does a school produce? Or what does a retail store produce?

The production department of a company may involve a factory with machinery or an office with computers. In both situations, production takes place. Production methods are influenced by the cultural and economic situation of a nation. A country with few machines will use more manual activities than automated methods.

PARTS OF A BUSINESS PLAN

1. Business description
2. Organizational structure
3. Marketing activities
4. Financial planning
5. Production activities
6. Human resource activities
7. Information needs

Figure 9-5 The management areas of a business are all covered in the business plan.

HUMAN RESOURCES MANAGEMENT

Labor is probably the most important factor of production. Without people, highly automated equipment could not be built, operated, or repaired. Every business owner and manager must recognize this fact. Human resources are one of the most important components of every organization. Human resources management involves activities needed to obtain, train, and retain qualified employees.

First, a human resources manager must hire needed employees. A description that lists the qualifications for a job is advertised to prospective employees. Hiring involves screening applicants, interviewing candidates, and selecting the most qualified people for available positions.

A second major duty of human resources managers is training employees. Training does not occur only when a person starts a job. It is a continuous process. Technology, the economy, and legal rulings often have an effect on the job skills employees need in order to be productive. Ongoing training is important for all workers.

Photodisc/Getty Images

GLOBAL BUSINESS SPOTLIGHT

FINANCING WOMEN ENTREPRENEURS IN NIGER

Guy Roget, a mother of nine, is a Muslim living in Niger. According to religious and cultural tradition, she should not work outside the home. However, her family has very little income.

Guy is not alone. About 13 million people live in Niger. Two thirds of the country, which is located in Central Africa, is covered by desert. By any standard it is a poor country—the per capita GDP is about $700. In recent years, Niger faced economic difficulties because of a decline in the world price for the country's main export, uranium. Political unrest also contributed to the economic instability.

Guy Roget worked to improve economic conditions in her community. She helped start a women's organization. The group's members contribute to a fund from which they borrow to start small businesses.

Guy started her enterprise by selling seasonings on the street and eventually was able to save enough to acquire a tiny grocery store. Other women in the capital city of Niamey are involved in raising cattle, growing vegetables, collecting firewood, making pottery, and weaving brightly patterned traditional fabrics.

Think Critically

1. How do geographic and political factors influence business opportunities?
2. In what ways can community organizations encourage new business enterprises?

The final duty of human resources managers is to maintain employee satisfaction. Workers must be paid adequately so they do not become discouraged or leave the company. Most businesses also provide employee benefits such as paid holidays and vacations, medical insurance, retirement plans, and discounts for company products. Human resources managers also motivate employees with awards, bonuses, and prizes for productivity, customer service, safety, and ideas that save the company money.

INFORMATION MANAGEMENT

Managing information has always been important to running a successful business. In recent years, computers and other technology have made information easier, faster, and less expensive to obtain, organize, and share. The main areas of information needed by every business include data about finances, production and inventory, marketing, and human resources.

A *management information system (MIS)* is an organized method of processing and reporting data for business decisions. An MIS involves a plan for all of the following:

1. identifying a company's information needs
2. obtaining the information
3. organizing the information in a useful manner
4. distributing reports to those who make decisions
5. updating data files as needed

Management information systems have created many career opportunities including software engineers, systems analysts, network administrators, computer support specialists, and information systems managers.

✓ **Check**Point
What activities does human resources management involve?

COMMUNICATION ACROSS BORDERS

CHOOSING A COMPANY LANGUAGE

Sooner or later every business must choose one or more designated company languages to facilitate communication among its employees, suppliers, customers, owners, and regulatory agencies. As the business grows domestically and internationally, the language choice becomes more critical.

A very small business in India could use any one of more than 700 local languages. If it operates within one region of India, it might choose one of 15 governmentally recognized regional languages. If it operates throughout India, it might choose one of the official languages of the country, Hindi or English, which are spoken by less than one-third of the population. As the business spreads beyond India, it will probably choose English as the designated company language if it hasn't already done so. Choosing English will allow international businesses to communicate in many countries around the world since most international businesspersons speak English as either a first or second language.

Think Critically

1. Why might choosing an official company language be more challenging for a very small business in rural India than for a very small business in rural United States?
2. Why would a business have two or more official languages?

REVIEW GLOBAL BUSINESS TERMS

Define each of the following terms.

1. budget
2. variable costs
3. fixed costs
4. breakeven point
5. gross profit
6. equity funds
7. debt funds
8. balance sheet
9. income statement
10. cash flow

REVIEW GLOBAL BUSINESS CONCEPTS

11. How do variable costs differ from fixed costs?

12. What are the three major activities of human resources management?

13. What is a management information system?

SOLVE GLOBAL BUSINESS PROBLEMS

Indicate whether each of the following business activities would be the responsibility of a marketing, finance, production, human resources, or information systems manager.

14. Checking quality control of finished goods.

15. Monitoring information records on salaries and vacation time.

16. Creating a system to provide data for decision making.

17. Recommending advertising activities for the company.

18. Coordinating parts and supplies for the assembly line.

19. Projecting the organization's cash inflows and outflows.

THINK CRITICALLY

20. When expanding into another country, should a business use equity funds or debt funds? Explain your choice.

21. How could the culture of a country affect the duties of a human resources manager?

MAKE ACADEMIC CONNECTIONS

22. **TECHNOLOGY** Find the web site of a major corporation that presents career opportunities in the organization. Find a job that appeals to you, and write a brief description of the job responsibilities.

23. **MATHEMATICS** Calculate the net income (or loss) of a company with $168,000 of sales revenue and $145,000 of operating expenses.

24. **MATHEMATICS** Calculate the breakeven point for a product selling for $5 with variable costs per unit of $3. Fixed costs are $38,000.

CHAPTER SUMMARY

9-1 ENTREPRENEURIAL ENTERPRISES

A Entrepreneurs are important in the development of an economy because they create new products and services, create new jobs, and provide personal service.

B The main types of entrepreneurial businesses are extracting companies, manufacturing companies, wholesalers, retailers, and service companies.

C Telecommuting involves using a computer and other technology to work at home instead of in a company office or factory.

9-2 THE BUSINESS PLAN AND SELF-EMPLOYMENT

A The advantages of self-employment as a career option are independence and pride of ownership. The disadvantages are the time commitment, uncertain income, and possible loss of investment.

B The first three sections of a business plan are the business description, organizational structure, and marketing activities.

9-3 OPERATING AN ENTREPRENEURIAL ENTERPRISE

A Financing a small business involves determining variable and fixed costs while obtaining the use of equity and debt funds.

B The major business activities of a small business manager involve marketing, finance, production, human resources, and information systems.

GLOBAL REFOCUS

Read the Global Focus at the beginning of this chapter, and answer the following questions.

1. Why should social entrepreneurs develop a detailed business plan for their programs?

2. Describe an opportunity for social entrepreneurship in your community or around the world.

REVIEW GLOBAL BUSINESS TERMS

Match the terms listed with the definitions.

1. Business funds obtained by borrowing.

2. Business expenses that change in proportion to the level of production.

3. Business funds obtained from the owners of the business.

4. An independently owned and operated business that does not dominate an industry.

5. The business activities necessary to get goods and services from the producer to the consumer.

6. A financial tool that estimates a company's funds and its plan for spending those funds.

7. A guide used to start and operate a business.

8. The document that reports a company's assets, liabilities, and owner's equity.

9. Expenses that do not change as the level of production changes.

a. balance sheet
b. breakeven point
c. budget
d. business plan
e. cash flow
f. debt funds
g. entrepreneur
h. equity funds
i. fixed costs
j. gross profit
k. income statement
l. marketing
m. marketing plan
n. small business
o. telecommuting
p. variable costs

10. A risk taker who operates a business.

11. The production level at which profit is zero.

12. The inflow and outflow of cash in a business.

13. Using a computer and other technology to work at home instead of in a company office or factory.

14. A document that details the marketing activities of an organization.

15. The document that summarizes a company's revenue from sales and its expenses over a period of time.

16. The difference between the cost of an item for a business and the price for which the business can sell that item.

MAKE GLOBAL BUSINESS DECISIONS

17. What are some problems in the world that might be solved by new products or services created by entrepreneurs?

18. Name some ways small businesses can provide personal service better than larger companies.

19. Why are wholesaling companies important to the business environment of a country?

20. Why do people give up secure jobs and start their own businesses?

21. Explain how a budget helps a business.

22. As a manager, how would you decide if you should let some employees work from their homes?

MAKE ACADEMIC CONNECTIONS

23. GEOGRAPHY Conduct library and Internet research about entrepreneurial activities in other countries. Locate articles and other information about new businesses, the types of products and services they offer, and the problems they encounter. Prepare a short written or oral report about the influence of geographic factors on the success of entrepreneurs in various countries.

24. COMMUNICATIONS Interview the owner of a small local company about the influences of international business on the firm's activities. How has the company's competition changed due to global business? Are any local companies owned or controlled by foreign corporations?

25. VISUAL ART Create a poster or computer presentation with variable and fixed costs for

Photodisc/Getty Images

different types of businesses. Use photos and other visuals to show examples of these two types of business operating expenses.

26. CULTURAL STUDIES Talk to someone who has lived in or worked in another country. Obtain information about the types of small businesses operated by entrepreneurs in that nation. Ask about differences in the hiring process used by companies and the benefits provided to employees.

27. SCIENCE Research recent technology to obtain information about a scientific development that could create new opportunities for home-based businesses.

28. MATHEMATICS A company sells shirts for $15. Each shirt has a variable cost of $9. The company has fixed costs of $7,200. What is the breakeven point for this business?

29. CAREER PLANNING Interview the owner of a small business who exports or sells imported products. Ask the entrepreneur about the skills needed to be successful in that type of business. What should a person learn in school to prepare for a career as an entrepreneur?

The GLOBAL Entrepreneur

CREATING AN INTERNATIONAL BUSINESS PLAN

Starting Your Own Business

Develop a plan for starting your international business based on the company you have been using in this continuing project, or create a new idea for your business. Make use of previously collected information, and do additional research. This phase of your business plan should include the following components.

1. General description of the company—list the name, location, and major international business activities of the company.

2. Organizational structure—(a) explain what type of organization (sole proprietorship, partnership, or corporation) the company uses; and (b) list foreign business partners (joint ventures, licensing agreements, distributor contracts, and supplier relationships).

3. Marketing activities—describe the company's customers, distribution systems, and advertising methods.

4. Financing activities—(a) estimate start-up costs, and (b) estimate sources of cash inflows and operating expenses for the company's global business activities.

5. Production activities—explain how the company obtains the products or services it sells.

6. Human resources activities—list the main types of jobs in the company and the general qualifications needed for these positions.

7. Information needs—describe financial, production and inventory, marketing, and human resources information needed by managers to make appropriate international business decisions.

Photodisc/Getty Images

UNIT 2

GLOBAL Cross-Cultural Team Project

Organize International Business Activities

When international enterprises begin operations in other countries, decisions related to organizing their business activities are needed. To gain a wider perspective for these decisions, companies frequently use cross-cultural teams.

Goal

To organize international business activities using information from various regions of the world.

Activities

Working in teams, select a geographic region you will represent—Africa, Asia, Europe, Latin America, Middle East, or North America.

1. Obtain information related to the major imports, exports, regional trade agreements, currencies, and common legal systems in your region. Library materials, web research, and personal interviews are recommended.
2. List major imports and exports of several countries in your region. Explain why these items are commonly bought and sold by people in the region.
3. Identify the major currencies in the region. Research factors that might affect the value of these currencies. If possible, conduct an interview with a person who has visited this region to obtain information about the monetary system and shopping activities. What economic and political factors influence currency values in the region? How do these differ from factors in other regions?
4. Locate examples of laws that affect business activities and international business trade in your region. How do these compare with business regulations in other areas of the world?
5. Small businesses are important for jobs and economic growth in every country. List the common types of businesses of small organizations (less than 10 employees) in your region. What difficulties are commonly faced when starting or operating a small business in your region?
6. **Global Business Decision** Your team is planning to start a new business. What type of business might have the greatest success in your region? Explain your answer. Choose a country within the region and explain why it would be a good place to start the business.

Team Skill   Characteristics of Productive Teams

Discuss with your team members the characteristics of productive cross-cultural teams and how productivity might be measured. How might the geographic and cultural influences of your region influence team productivity?

Present

- Write a summary report of your regional information.
- Make a 1-2 minute presentation to report a couple of key findings from your research and your simulated cross-cultural team experience.

240

Extemporaneous Speaking

Success in the business world depends on strong communication skills and the ability to make decisions within a limited time frame. Extemporaneous speaking provides you with the opportunity to analyze a situation or topic for a short period of time and then present a speech to actual business leaders who determine the effectiveness of the communication.

Public speaking is enhanced by the confidence gained from experience. International business has numerous issues for possible speech topics. Some examples of international topics include, illegal immigrants working in the United States, trade barriers, free trade agreements, stealing secrets by foreign business partners, international business opportunities, and outsourcing U.S. jobs to other countries.

When participating in extemporaneous speaking, you will improve your chance for success by reading current international events and watching the news. Taking an international topic from the news and outlining the main points to highlight in a speech can help you gain valuable experience.

Tips to prepare for extemporaneous speaking include:

- Watch the news and read newspapers to keep up-to-date on the latest international events.
- Outline news items and identify strategies to solve different problems.
- Record personal experiences involving customer service and how businesses could handle situations more effectively.
- Network with business leaders who provide practice extemporaneous speeches.
- Enter competitions on the local, district, state, and national levels to increase confidence.
- Dress professionally to feel confident.

Performance Indicators Evaluated

- Explain how international business can jeopardize trade secrets.
- Understand the reason for copyright laws and patents.
- Describe the risks associated with international business agreements.
- Explain different value systems (codes of ethics) throughout the world.
- Explain strategies for reducing global risks.

For more detailed information about performance indicators, go to the BPA web site.

Think Critically

1. How can international business jeopardize a trade secret?
2. What is one strategy to reduce theft of trade secrets by an international business partner?
3. Why should a business seek international trade opportunities, considering the related risk?
4. How can technology be protected from potential international theft?

www.bpa.org

Managing in a Global Environment

Chapter

10 **Management Principles in Action**

11 **Human Resources Management**

12 **Labor Around the World**

13 **International Career Planning**

Europe

If You Were There

...Berlin, November 9, 1989

A journalist thinks back to 1962 when Peter Fechter bled to death after being shot by East German border guards when he tried to climb the Berlin Wall. He was one of the first to die trying to escape to the West. Between 1961 and 1989, thousands were successful but more than 100, and perhaps as many as 200, people lost their lives while seeking freedom.

Tonight is very different. At midnight the border guards and their weapons are silent as thousands of East Germans rush over and around the Berlin Wall. Some guards are seen lifting children and helping people as they move to the West. The Wall stood for 28 years as a symbol of the Cold War that divided Europe and imprisoned eastern Europe under the rule of the Soviet Union.

Berliners from both sides are overwhelmed and the journalist records their joy. In a few days, she will be watching as the Wall is all but destroyed and people scoop up souvenirs—pieces of concrete, pieces of history.

©Carsten Medom Madsen, 2009/ Used under license from Shutterstock.com

The Roman Empire

The nearly half century of Soviet dominance over eastern Europe was relatively brief when compared to that of Romans, who controlled western and southern Europe for more than five centuries. They subdued their neighbors with superior military power and forced people of different cultures to live together. The Roman Empire established local governments and created an economy that depended on roads, bridges, and public buildings.

The Roman Emperor Constantine gave Christians freedom of religion in the year A.D. 313. By 392, Christianity had become the official religion of the Roman Empire, and it continued to strengthen its influence in Europe by making alliances between popes and various kings who ruled the continent. On December 25, 800, Charlemagne—a Frankish king who had conquered nearly all the Germanic

tupungato/iStockphoto.com

lands—was attending church services at St. Peter's Cathedral in Rome when Pope Leo III placed a gold crown upon his head. The Pope proclaimed him Charles Augustus, "Emperor of the Romans."

The newly crowned emperor expanded his empire until it stretched from the Danube River to the Atlantic, from Rome to the Baltic Sea. Those living within the empire who were not already Christians or Jews were forced to accept Christianity. They were also forced to accept all laws made at Charlemagne's capital at Aix-la-Chapelle (present day Aachen, Germany). These were diverse people who lived great distances from one another and spoke many different languages.

The task of controlling the empire was too great for Charlemagne's successors. After his death, the empire began to dissolve as local nobles regained power. This set the stage for a return to the political and economic system known as feudalism, which had preceded Charlemagne's empire.

The Byzantine Empire

At the same time that Charlemagne was building his empire, the Byzantines in southeastern Europe were fighting to control land on both sides of the Mediterranean Sea. The Byzantine Empire was the eastern portion of the Roman Empire, which survived after the western provinces and Italy were lost to the Germans. The empire was centered in Constantinople (present day Istanbul, Turkey), which was built on a point of land above the Bosporus Straits that separates Europe and Asia.

Throughout history, Persians, Arabs, Russians, Europeans, and Turks have fought over this strategic location because it links the trade routes between Europe, the Middle East, Asia, and Africa.

Other Attempts to Control Europe

Later attempts to control the European continent were short-lived. Napoleon I, like Charlemagne, wanted to be crowned emperor by the Pope. Unlike Charlemagne, however, the French Emperor called the Pope to Paris, where he took the crown from the Pope and crowned himself. By 1812, Napoleon controlled most of Europe. Nevertheless, his dreams were soon destroyed when most of his empire rebelled against him after his disastrous invasion of Russia.

Hitler's attempt to control Europe started World War II. By 1941, Hitler's armies occupied most of Europe, threatened England, and marched into Russia. Hitler committed the same mistake as Napoleon: He stranded his troops in the harsh Russian winter, and Soviet counterthrusts stopped the German advance.

Conflicts between Ethnic Groups

The many ethnic groups of eastern and southeastern Europe have lived side by side within empires for centuries. Many conflicts have resulted from their nationalistic interests in self-determination. Bulgaria, Greece, Montenegro, and Serbia declared war on Turkey in 1912 to free members of their nationalities from Turkish rule. In 1914, a Serb assassinated the Austrian Archduke Franz Ferdinand in support of Bosnian nationalism. This event helped begin World War I. When they sought greater freedom, the Hungarians (in 1956) and the Czechs (in 1968) were violently crushed by the Soviets, who dominated the region after World War II.

As the might of the Communist systems in the Soviet Union and eastern Europe crumbled in the late 1980s and early 1990s, some nationalist forces peacefully formed new governments. Others, such as those in the former Yugoslavia, began killing each other over historical hatred or current jealousy.

Europe's Contributions to Civilization

Although the history of this continent is heavily marked by wars and political repression, its writers, explorers, philosophers, scientists, and artists have created a world that is known as Western Civilization. The entire planet has been enriched by the likes of Homer and Plato, Chaucer and Shakespeare, Michelangelo and Renoir, Pasteur and Einstein, and Bach and the Beatles.

Europeans have contributed many things to the world, including self-government; the abolition of slavery; the first microscopes and telescopes; vital antiseptics and vaccines; theories of evolution and psychoanalysis; and initial discoveries in molecular physics, electricity, radioactivity, relativity, and rocketry.

The European Union

While strong nationalistic values continue to separate Europeans, another attempt to unify the region is in progress. The key players this time are not emperors and dictators with swords and tanks. Rather, they are economists armed with arguments about competition from the United States, China, India, and Japan. The European Union has eliminated trade barriers among the member countries with a European Central Bank and a common European currency adopted by most members. The Treaty of Maastricht provides for a common European citizenship and European passports.

Photodisc/Getty Images

Think Critically

1. Use library and Internet resources to identify countries that currently base their authority on a particular religion. Do they have anything in common?
2. Do you think that a powerful nation should force people of different cultures to live together peacefully as one nation?
3. How do ocean ports, inland waterways, railroads, and highways affect trade among nations in Europe? How does it affect different cultures in Europe?
4. What effect do you think the European Union will have on the individual cultures within the member nations?

COUNTRY PROFILES

The World Factbook, published online by the Central Intelligence Agency, includes country profiles for the nations of Europe. Each country's profile includes an overview followed by detailed information about the country's geography, people, government, economy, communications, transportation, military, and transnational issues.

CHAPTER 10

Management Principles in Action

10-1 Managers and Cultural Differences

10-2 Management Process and Organization

10-3 The Changing Process of Management

Photodisc/Getty Images

GLOBAL FOCUS

Virtual Corporations Here Today and Gone Tomorrow

The virtual corporation offers promising approaches to the tough facts of life in the global marketplace. A virtual corporation is a temporary network of individuals or companies that come together to produce a product or service. Flexibility and efficiency are hallmarks of a successful virtual corporation.

Most large companies cannot react fast enough to take advantage of changing opportunities. By the time managers of giant companies get the necessary people and other resources ready, those opportunities have vanished. The managers of smaller companies often lack the influence and resources to respond to opportunities that are here today and gone tomorrow.

Managers who want to form virtual corporations must first identify what their company does best. Then they must form ties with other companies that represent "the best of the best." These fast-reacting, sharply focused, world-class competitors have the muscle and cutting-edge technology to pounce on short-term opportunities.

The U.S. film industry already functions in this way. Virtual corporations have replaced the old Hollywood studio system. Various industry talents temporarily link up for specific film projects before going their separate ways. Perhaps it's no small coincidence that the U.S. film industry has been very successful in the global marketplace. It is one of the biggest export successes for the country. Maybe Hollywood managers could teach other managers worldwide a lesson or two!

Think Critically

1. Why do virtual corporations exist?
2. What characteristic describes each component of a virtual corporation?
3. Go to the web site of MGM Motion Pictures, Paramount Motion Pictures, or Sony Pictures Entertainment to learn about the structure and management of the film company.

10-1 Managers and Cultural Differences

GOALS

- Explain the characteristics of successful managers and how management styles vary.

- Understand the effects of cultural differences on a global workforce.

Managers in Organizations

Managers are people in charge of organizations and their resources. They are men and women who assume responsibility for the administration of an organization. Managers work with and oversee employees to meet organizational goals in an ever-changing environment. They try to use the available resources for maximum gain, just as you try to use your time and money to derive the most desirable benefits.

Whether you realize it or not, you already have some managerial experience. You are in charge of and responsible for yourself. You are responsible for other people and things. You are also responsible for your textbooks, school supplies, and assigned homework. You may even be responsible for cleaning your own room or for maintaining your own car. Consequently, managing is not a totally foreign concept to you.

CHARACTERISTICS OF MANAGERS

Successful managers possess a wide variety of conceptual, technical, and interpersonal abilities. Supporting these abilities are certain skills and personal characteristics. One characteristic of managerial ability is leadership. Leadership is the ability to get others to follow. Another characteristic is the ability to communicate effectively. Managers must have strong writing, reading, listening, speaking, and presenting skills to be successful.

The ability to plan and organize is important. Managers must be able to use resources to achieve goals. They must be able to gather and analyze information to solve problems. The ability to make decisions is also important.

Managers must be able to take reasoned positions based on relevant information and to live with the consequences of the decisions.

Managers must be able to judge when they should be in charge and when they should delegate and allow others to be in charge. The ability to be objective is also useful. Managers need to know their strengths and weaknesses, as well as the strengths and weaknesses of others. Managers must be willing to lead others in new, untried directions and must be able to adapt to change. You might already possess a number of these important skills that influence managerial success.

Photodisc/Getty Images

STYLES OF MANAGERS

One way to examine managers is to look at how they use power or authority. There are three distinct types of management styles. These styles are *autocratic, participative,* and *free-rein.* These three styles can be placed along a continuum that represents managerial power or authority, as Figure 10-1 shows. Autocratic managers maximize their personal power or authority to control others. Free-rein managers minimize their personal power or authority to control others. Participative managers balance their personal power or authority to control others against the power people assume for themselves.

Autocratic Management Style Managers who centralize power and tell employees what to do are **autocratic managers**. They are authoritarian and rule with a heavy hand. The autocrat takes full authority and assumes full responsibility. If an autocratic manager uses power negatively, then the employees feel uninformed, insecure, and afraid. If an autocratic manager uses power positively, then rewards are distributed to those who comply. Sometimes the term "benevolent autocrat" is used to refer to an autocratic manager who uses power positively.

Most people do not work well under autocratic managers, especially negative ones. Autocratic management is considered an old-fashioned style of management and should be replaced by a more participative management style.

Use of Power or Authority by Managers

Maximize → Power or Authority to Control Others → Minimize

| Autocratic Managers | Participative Managers | Free-Rein Managers |

Figure 10-1 Autocratic, participative, and free-rein managers use power or authority differently.

Work as a Team

Discuss how widespread beliefs, values, and assumptions within the culture of the United States influence the actions of managers in this country.

Participative Management Style Managers who decentralize power and share it with employees are **participative managers**. The manager and employees work together to achieve goals. Participative managers keep employees informed and encourage them to share ideas and suggestions. The participative manager uses group forces rather than power or authority to keep the unit operating effectively. For most managerial situations, the participative style is recommended.

Free-Rein Management Style Managers who avoid the use of power are **free-rein managers**. They let employees establish their own goals and monitor their own progress. Employees learn on their own and supply their own motivation. Managers exist primarily as contact persons for outsiders. Because free-rein management can lead to chaos in many situations, experts recommend that managers use it in circumstances where employees are self-disciplined and self-motivated and can make wise choices for themselves.

A Question of Ethics

SHARING CONFIDENTIAL INFORMATION

Geir Alver works for a Norwegian multinational corporation as a senior manager. His sister Gerd Grieg works for a competing company in a similar position. Because they work for rival organizations, they have mutually agreed never to discuss corporate business with each other. The two siblings enjoy a close personal relationship and see each other every two or three weeks.

Yesterday when Geir and his family were visiting Gerd and her family, their visit was interrupted by a long-distance telephone call from the New York headquarters of Gerd's employer. Although Gerd took the call in another room and closed the door behind her, the animated conversation spilled into the hallway and the nearby room where the others were finishing their desserts and beverages. As Geir walked down the hall to the kitchen with a stack of dishes a few minutes later, he overheard Gerd confirming privileged strategic information that would be very useful to his organization. Having that information could give his organization a competitive advantage over its American rival. Best of all, because his sister was not aware that he had overheard the information, she would never realize that she had inadvertently been the source of the leaked information. If he relayed the strategic information to top-level managers, Geir was certain that he would be rewarded with either money or a promotion—or maybe even both.

Think Critically

1. Since Geir and Gerd did not discuss the privileged information from the New York headquarters, did either of them engage in unethical behavior?
2. If you were Geir, what would you do with information you overheard from a rival corporation? Explain.

✓ **Check**Point

How do the styles of managers vary along a continuum?

Influences of Cultural Differences

Managers must remember that people's behaviors are shaped by their cultural backgrounds. Every culture and subculture has norms or standards for its members. However, certain members of cultural groups will deviate from those norms. People from different cultural backgrounds may not be alike even though they may appear to be similar on the surface. They may actually have very different beliefs, values, and assumptions. Consequently, managers must be very careful when managing people. Managers must be very sensitive to and respectful of cultural differences. They also must be aware that certain culturally based patterns of behavior exist and need to be considered.

Participation in Making Decisions For example, some cultural groups want subordinates to be actively involved in decision making. This is generally true for natives of the United States. In contrast, natives of Venezuela may prefer little or no role in decision making. They typically prefer to have managers tell them what to do.

Hiring Preferences Different cultural groups value different selection criteria for hiring employees. For example, natives of the United States tend to value job-related qualifications. Natives of Greece tend to value family membership or friendship above other qualifications.

Permanence of Employment Attitudes about the permanence of employment vary among members of different cultural groups. Natives of the United States generally accept less employment security than natives of Japan. U.S. workers are frequently laid off during economic downturns and receive minimal company compensation. They also freely look for new opportunities with other companies. The Japanese are less mobile and until recently, expected lifetime employment from a company.

Labor-Management Relationships U.S. laborers tend to have confrontational attitudes towards managers. They believe that confrontation brings about more equitable work and more satisfying relationships. By contrast, in Sweden many workers help to determine their work and rewarding relationships by serving on managerial boards. In general, U.S. managers are shaped by a culture and subcultures that value personal freedom, independence, and self-respect. Employees from other cultural groups—especially European and Asian—tend to view these values as selfish and insensitive. Such opposing

NETBookmark

For a firsthand account of some of the issues facing cross-cultural workers, access the Indonesian Expatriate web site through the web site shown below. Click on the link for Chapter 10. Read the article entitled "Business Across Cultures" by George Whitfield. How can a multinational company avoid misunderstandings about what is acceptable behavior on the job? How could you, as a cross-cultural worker, avoid making an embarrassing mistake?

www.cengage.com/school/genbus/intlbiz

cultural perspectives can lead to conflicts between managers and employees in the culturally diverse business world unless those differences are sensitively addressed.

While it is useful for managers to be aware of prevailing cultural preferences, they must realize that not all individuals fit their cultural molds. Consequently, managers must temper their understandings about cultural preferences. They must also consider the values, beliefs, and assumptions of the individuals involved. Managers who fail to consider individual differences and cultural norms will be less successful in the culturally diverse global business environment.

GLOBAL BUSINESS SPOTLIGHT

THE BALKING STORE MANAGERS

As the new store manager, Nina Smith, a U.S. citizen, was shocked during her first encounters with her local Panamanian managers, Guillermo, Maria, and Diego. They refused to participate in decision making, politely deferring to Nina's judgments instead. When Nina finally made decisions on her own for the managers, she noticed that they made good-faith efforts to implement those decisions. Nina was puzzled by their reactions involving decision making. Was there something wrong with her managerial style? Did the Panamanian managers resent being supervised by a foreigner?

When Nina mentioned her uncooperative decision makers to another Panamanian store manager, she was surprised by the explanation she received. Most Panamanians, like many Latin Americans, come from cultural backgrounds that place little value on acting independently or as a consultant. Rather than feeling empowered when a superior seeks their opinion, these employees question the superior's decision-making abilities. When faced with the culturally unacceptable task of making

decisions that they believed the store manager should make, the Panamanian managers did not co-operate. To them, their participation in decision making undermined the role of the new store manager.

Nina learned her lesson quickly. She tried to manage in a more culturally sensitive way. Rather than relying on participative U.S.-style management, she started making the decisions for her Panamanian supervisors. The employees were quite comfortable being told what to do. They carefully carried out Nina's decisions, and soon their working relationships with Nina became "muy simpático"—very congenial.

Think Critically

1. Why was Nina Smith unaware of Panamanian perspectives about the roles of managers?
2. Why did Guillermo, Maria, and Diego fail to make managerial decisions on their own?
3. Which managerial style did Nina use that was effective with the Panamanian managers?
4. How could you find out more about Panamanian attitudes toward managerial styles?

✓ CheckPoint

How do cultural differences affect managers of a global workforce?

Study Tools
www.cengage.com/school/genbus/intlbiz

REVIEW GLOBAL BUSINESS TERMS

Define each of the following terms.
1. managers
2. autocratic managers
3. participative managers
4. free-rein managers

REVIEW GLOBAL BUSINESS CONCEPTS

5. Which personal characteristic distinguishes among autocratic, participative, and free-rein managers?

6. What are four culturally influenced dimensions of behavior to which managers should be sensitive?

SOLVE GLOBAL BUSINESS PROBLEMS

"I have been managing the Bristol office of a global corporation for seven years. The office has an international workforce drawn from 18 countries on four continents. Every employee is highly competent in his or her specialty. Consequently, I have learned that I can rely on their judgments to a significant degree. I spend much of my time conferring with employees. Most decisions can be worked out by sharing our viewpoints, discussing the merits of those viewpoints, and selecting the best mutually agreeable viewpoints for implementation. It has been years since I have had to dictate the solutions to my employees."

7. Using a detailed map of the United Kingdom as a guide, describe the location of Bristol, the city in which the British manager works.

8. What is the British manager's prevailing management style?

9. What facts from the narrative support your conclusion about the management style?

THINK CRITICALLY

10. Why do managers often use a combination of autocratic, participative, and free-rein management styles?

11. How can managers increase their sensitivity to cultural differences?

MAKE ACADEMIC CONNECTIONS

12. **TECHNOLOGY** How can technology help a manager monitor the work of subordinates?

13. **COMMUNICATIONS** Why is effective business communication considered to be the lifeblood of management?

14. **HISTORY** Why was autocratic management the dominant managerial style in the United States until well into the twentieth century?

15. **CULTURAL STUDIES** Use the Internet to find online cultural resources for international managers.

10-2 Management Process and Organization

GOALS

- Describe the basic components of the process of managing.
- Differentiate between organizational structures based on function, product, and geography.

Photodisc/Getty Images

Process of Managing

The process of managing includes the following major components.

- Planning and decision making
- Organizing, staffing, and communicating
- Motivating and leading
- Controlling

These components are illustrated in Figure 10-2. The exact mix of these components varies depending on the type of managerial job and the people and other resources involved. However, sooner or later managers will be involved with all four broad managerial components.

PLANNING AND DECISION MAKING

Planning and decision making are important components of managing. Planning relates to setting goals or objectives to be attained. Planning is similar to deciding where you want to go. You have to know your destination before you can get there.

Once you decide the goal, you can explore different options or routes that lead to the goal. At various points along the way, you have choices to make. You should weigh the advantages and disadvantages of each alternative and select the best alternative overall. In other words, you should make thoughtful decisions.

ORGANIZING, STAFFING, AND COMMUNICATING

Organizing, staffing, and communicating are also important components of managing. Organizing involves structuring business operations in logical and meaningful ways. Sometimes organizing relates to how business activities or functions are put together. Sometimes organizing involves assembling the necessary resources in a manner that facilitates the accomplishment of goals.

Staffing is the process of acquiring employees with the necessary knowledge, skills, and attitudes to fill the various positions in the organization. Communicating is interacting with people through verbal and nonverbal means. Communicating is a vital managerial task. An organization cannot function cohesively and reach its goals unless all employees give, receive, and share information in a timely and effective manner.

The Managerial Process in Action

Planning and Decision Making

Organizing, Staffing, and Communicating

Controlling

Motivating and Leading

Photodisc/Getty Images

Figure 10-2 The managerial process includes four major components: planning and decision making; organizing, staffing, and communicating; motivating and leading; and controlling.

GLOBAL TECHNOLOGY TRENDS

Virtual Business Plans

Although BizPlanIt markets its online business planning services through its web site, it also provides a variety of free services. One particularly useful free service for managers is the detailed information about creating a virtual business plan.

The BizPlanIt web site has a link to Virtual BizPlan, which provides practical guidance for managers as they develop business plans. It identifies the different sections and what kinds of topics to address in each. It also identifies common errors to avoid when developing business plan sections. By following the guidance that is provided, even managers with limited experience can create sound business plans that will help their organizations prosper in the competitive world of global business.

Think Critically

1. Why is it good business strategy for the managers of BizPlanIt to include free information about business plans at the web site that promotes its services?
2. Why is developing a business plan the BizPlanIt way almost foolproof?
3. After viewing the Virtual BizPlan link would you feel comfortable writing a business plan? Why or why not?

MOTIVATING AND LEADING

Motivating is creating the desire to achieve. Managers realize that motivation comes from internal and external sources. Internal motivation comes from within the employee. The desire to perform work more efficiently is an example of internal motivation. External motivation comes from outside the employee. A salary increase is an example of external motivation.

Leading is getting employees to voluntarily pursue the goals of the organization. Managers who are effective leaders create a desire within employees to want to achieve what the organization sets out to achieve.

CONTROLLING

Controlling is regulating the operations of a business. It involves taking both preventive and corrective actions to keep business activities on track. Controlling helps to ensure that business operations are both efficient and productive. Activities such as verifying, adjusting, and testing help a firm to operate efficiently. For example, businesses have the accounting records audited by outsiders periodically as a preventive measure. This verifies the accuracy and truthfulness of the financial records. Manufacturers regularly examine production, adjust inputs and equipment, and inspect output to achieve quality control. Companies compare actual and recorded inventory, note differences and reasons why, and correct their records and methods to control inventory.

Many companies look for innovative ways to control costs. For example, some delivery services plan their routes to eliminate or avoid left tuns. This increases efficiency by cutting down on the time drivers spend waiting to make left turns. It also saves gasoline and reduces accidents.

What are the four major components of managing?

Structures of Organizations

Businesses use various organizational structures to achieve their goals. An **organizational chart** is a drawing that shows the structure of an organization. Line and staff are two types of positions. *Line positions* are managerial. Individuals with line positions have authority and responsibility over people and resources. *Staff positions* are nonmanagerial. Individuals with staff positions assist or advise those in line positions.

An organization can be either tall or flat. A tall organization is one that has many levels of management. One manager generally supervises a small number of employees. This results in more levels of managers. A flat organization is one that has few levels of management. Organizations are increasingly becoming flatter with fewer levels of management.

Businesses are commonly organized in one of three ways: by function, by product, or by geography. Each of these organizational structures have advantages.

Work as a Team

Identify the ways employees communicate within an organization.

ORGANIZATION BY FUNCTION

When a business is organized by function, the departments are determined by what people do. For example, in a sportswear manufacturing company, the function of the manufacturing department is to produce sportswear, the function of the sales department is to sell sportswear, and the function of the accounting department is to keep accurate financial records. Other functional groups might be linked together and given relevant departmental names, too. Figure 10-3 shows part of the organizational chart of a business organized by function.

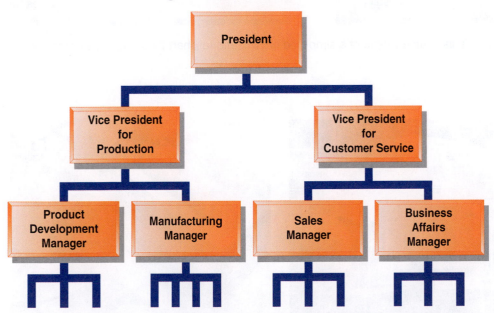

Organization by Function

Figure 10-3 A simplified organizational chart for a business organized by function might look something like this.

ORGANIZATION BY PRODUCT

Another way to organize a business is by product. When a business organizes itself in this way, related products are grouped together to form departments. This type of organization is helpful when the product lines are very different. For example, a large manufacturing company that makes airplane parts and consumer appliances may form two divisions. One division could be for the airplane parts, and it might be called the aviation parts division. Another division could be for the consumer appliances, and it might be called the consumer appliance division. Figure 10-4 shows part of the organizational chart of a business organized by product.

Organization by Product

President

Vice President

Aviation Parts Division

Consumer Appliance Division

Engines

Navigation Systems

Kitchen

Laundry

Small Appliances

Figure 10-4 This is an example of a simplified organizational chart for a business organized by product.

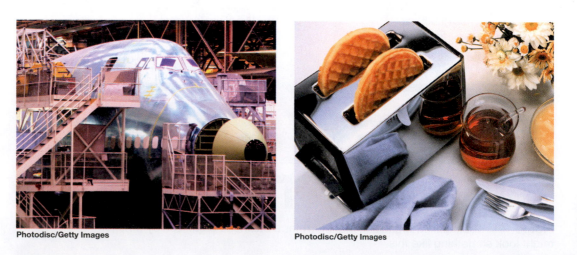

Photodisc/Getty Images

Photodisc/Getty Images

ORGANIZATION BY GEOGRAPHY

Still another way to organize a business is by geography. When a business chooses this option, it organizes itself on some geographic basis. The geographic basis might be by city, county, state, region, country, or continent. Companies that operate beyond the borders of one country often use geographic organization, as do some domestic companies. For example, a global corporation may have a single division for Asia and Australia along with separate divisions for Africa, Europe, North America, and South America. Each division would specialize in business operations in its designated territory. Figure 10-5 shows part of the organizational chart of a business organized by geography.

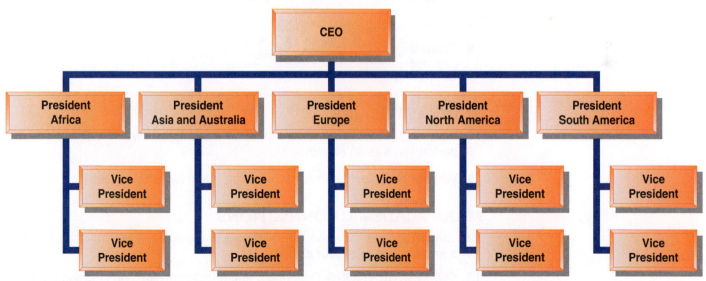

Figure 10-5 This is an example of a simplified organizational chart for a business organized by geography.

What are three common business organizational structures?

10-2 Assessment

REVIEW GLOBAL BUSINESS TERMS

Define the following term.

1. organizational chart

REVIEW GLOBAL BUSINESS CONCEPTS

2. How do good managers decide how to achieve goals?

3. What is the difference between a line position and a staff position?

4. What is a tall organization?

SOLVE GLOBAL BUSINESS PROBLEMS

ChemVision Corporation is a research company that develops chemicals, processes, and medicines for various industries. Clients come to ChemVision with a problem to be solved, and ChemVision assembles a team to work on the problem. The company's central management personnel administer the human relations, sales, and accounting functions. Each team is headed by a research scientist. Scientists are recruited to a team based on their reputation, experience, and expertise; and the best-known is usually appointed to head the team. The scientists are personally motivated to make new discoveries to enhance their professional reputations. As a result, however, the scientists all have their own agendas and they jealously guard their research. How well is ChemVision succeeding in the following processes of managing?

5. Planning

6. Staffing

7. Communicating

8. Motivating

9. Controlling

THINK CRITICALLY

10. What factors motivate you as a student? What factors would motivate you to perform well as an employee?

11. Why is no single organizational structure ideal for all businesses?

MAKE ACADEMIC CONNECTIONS

12. **TECHNOLOGY** Use available software to create an organizational chart for a small business of your choice.

13. **COMMUNICATIONS** Describe a real or fictional situation in which poor communications could prevent an organization from achieving its goals.

14. **TECHNOLOGY** Use the Internet to find the organizational structure for an international business.

10-3 The Changing Process of Management

Photodisc/Getty Images

Levels of Management

All businesses have managers in charge of operations. The number of managers a business needs, the lines of authority that are established, and the delegation of responsibility all depend on the size of the business and the complexity of its operations.

SPAN OF CONTROL

The **span of control** is the number of employees a manager supervises. A small business with limited operations is likely to have an owner-manager. The owner-manager oversees and supervises all employees and business activities.

When the volume of business, the complexity of business, or the number of employees grows, one person may no longer be able to manage the business. The owner could hire someone to manage part of the operations. This would reduce the span of control of the original owner.

As a business continues to expand, more managers are needed. **Front-line managers** are needed to oversee the day-to-day operations in specific departments. The front-line managers may report to a middle manager. **Middle managers** oversee the work and departments of a number of front-line managers. A number of middle managers may report to a senior manager. **Senior managers** oversee the work and departments of a number of middle managers. In a large corporation, senior managers report to the chief executive officer. The **chief executive officer (CEO)** is the highest manager within a company. Figure 10-6 shows the span of control of various levels of managers within a large organization.

LINES OF AUTHORITY

Regardless of the organizational structure and the number of levels of management, a business must establish clear lines of authority. **Lines of authority** indicate who is responsible to whom and for what. The need for having clear lines of authority grows as the business expands. When a business starts, there may be one owner-manager who is clearly in charge. The owner-manager has the authority or right to make all decisions. As the business expands and other managers are added, lines of authority must be clearly established. Clear lines of authority allow an organization to run smoothly and efficiently. Managers need to be aware of the specific area for which they are responsible. They also need to have a clear understanding of their relationship to other managers.

DELEGATION OF AUTHORITY AND RESPONSIBILITY

One important decision that managers must make relates to how much authority and responsibility they delegate or transfer to others. If managers retain too much authority and responsibility, they become autocratic. This may cause some employees to feel powerless which can lead to discontent. If managers

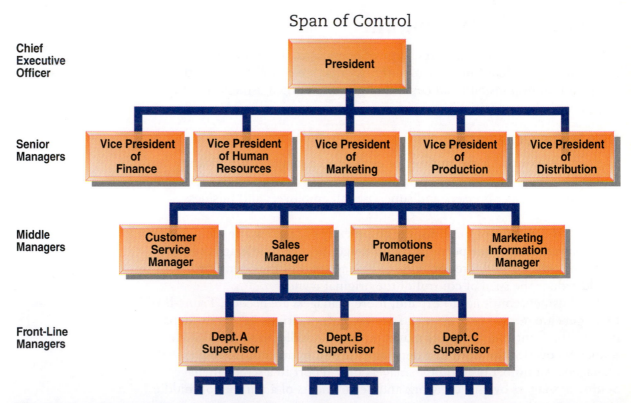

Figure 10-6 In this example, the president has a span of control of five, the vice president of marketing has a span of control of four, and the sales manager has a span of control of three.

retain too little authority and responsibility, some employees may not be productive. Employees who are not self-directed will have too much independence and more authority and responsibility than they can handle.

In most circumstances, managers try to balance the authority and responsibility between them and their employees. Participative managers share authority and responsibility with employees. They give employees some degree of freedom to determine and achieve goals with a corresponding degree of accountability for achieving those goals.

The amount of authority and responsibility that is delegated to employees or to organizational units is a reflection of the **degree of centralization** within an organization. If the authority and responsibility are tightly held by the managers and organizational units, then a centralized style of management results throughout the organization. If the authority and responsibility are widely distributed among many employees and organizational units, then a decentralized style of management results. Centralization of authority and responsibility tends to make organizations more autocratic. Decentralization of power and responsibility tends to make organizations more participative. Global organizations must decide how much authority and responsibility to grant to each of their organizational units and managers.

Work as a Team
Discuss reasons why centralization of authority tends to make organizations more autocratic while decentralization of authority tends to make organizations more participative.

✓ CheckPoint
How are the levels of management related to the span of control, the lines of authority, and the delegation of authority and responsibility?

Managing Change and Growth

Managing change and growth presents unique challenges. The managerial process must be adapted to meet these challenges. Managing becomes more complex and demanding as a business evolves.

Over time, most organizations change and grow. A common path followed by many businesses that engage in international business involves a domestic company evolving to become a global corporation. Although this is not the only path, growing in stages is common.

STAGE 1 DOMESTIC COMPANY

A domestic company is one that operates completely within the country of origin. Such a company uses domestic sources to create and sell its products and services. In other words, it acquires materials and sells goods and services in the country of origin. A domestic company has no business dealings with anyone except residents of the country. Consequently, a domestic company is the easiest type to manage. The basic managerial process in the country of origin can be used to resolve most of the challenges of a domestic business.

STAGE 2 EXPORTING COMPANY

As a domestic company grows and becomes successful, it often begins to export, or sell abroad. A company that sells in other countries is called an exporting company. This kind of company typically relies on its home marketplace advantages such as top quality and reputation as it expands abroad. It often focuses on selling its familiar products in a few foreign markets. Often exporting companies rely on independent agents or distributors to manage their business activities abroad. These agents and distributors already understand foreign marketplaces and know the most efficient way to sell and distribute products there. This approach can save time and money while increasing the chance of early success. Using agents and distributors simplifies the management of the business because it lets managers focus on domestic operations. This stage allows the company to take advantage of foreign markets while not having to accept full responsibility for operating abroad.

STAGE 3 INTERNATIONAL CORPORATION

An international corporation, also known as a multinational corporation, creates and markets goods and services in both its country of origin and in other countries. The parent or founding company provides the international corporation with an organizational structure and operational strategy.

The local, national, or regional components of an international organization are usually responsible for decision making and customer service. These parts or subdivisions of the international corporation sometimes are called *subsidiaries*. They make decisions involving production, marketing strategy, sales and service, and the like. Often various subsidiaries of international corporations operate quite independently. An international corporation is like a group of interrelated companies operating in many countries.

The managerial skills needed in an international corporation vary widely. Those who manage from the parent company need broad managerial skills that cross countries. Managers at the local, national, and regional levels need more specialized skills adapted to their specific assignments.

GLOBAL BUSINESS SPOTLIGHT

GOSCINSKI ENTERPRISES

Joanna Goscinski, an immigrant from Poland, founded a small business in the United States that manufactures Polish-style foods. Five years ago, the products were sold only in the Chicago metropolitan area. Mrs. Goscinski and her family worked diligently at the business, and it has grown every year. Now Goscinski Enterprises exports food products to three countries. Within ten years, Dobriski Enterprises hopes to manufacture and sell food products on five continents. Mrs. Goscinski's children can then manage the subsidiaries abroad. Within 20 years, Mrs. Goscinski and her family hope to dominate the production and sales of Polish-style food products through worldwide operations. Then Joanna Goscinski will have reached her entrepreneurial goal, which is to own and manage her own global corporation.

Think Critically

1. Why did Goscinski Enterprises begin selling its products in the Chicago metropolitan area?
2. If things go as planned, how many years will it take Goscinski Enterprises to become a multinational corporation?
3. What will have to happen if Goscinski Enterprises changes from a multinational corporation to a global corporation?

STAGE 4 GLOBAL CORPORATION

A global corporation is an outgrowth of an international corporation. A global corporation operates so that country boundaries are not an obstacle to operations. It searches for the most efficient combinations of goods and services on a worldwide basis. It markets those goods and services with little or no regard for national boundaries. A global corporation is like a domestic company except that it buys and sells worldwide rather than within the country of origin.

Managers who work for global corporations sometimes need broad managerial skills because they often interact with people around the world. Many decisions require specialized managerial skills along with knowledge that is specifically related to a country or region.

Photodisc/Getty Images

✓ **Check**Point

What are the stages through which a business might pass to attain global status?

Managing Now and in the Future

As business globalization increases, the role of the manager will continue to change. Managers increasingly think and act globally and they are focused on the future.

Managers of the future will not be content to be visionary; they will strive to facilitate the visionary development of others. Managers will shift from functioning alone to functioning as part of a team. While the managers of today enjoy the trust of boards and shareholders, the managers of tomorrow will need the trust of owners, customers, employees, suppliers, and governmental officials. Managers increasingly will meet the needs of the diverse groups to whom they are responsible. Many of tomorrow's managers will be multilingual and multicultural, fluent in several languages and accepting of many different ways of life. They will embrace the languages, arts, foods, and traditions wherever their careers take them.

Successful global managers must develop and use global strategic skills. They must skillfully manage transition and change in a culturally diverse world. They must function effectively as team members while coping with changing organizational structures. Global managers will need outstanding communication skills—listening, speaking, reading, and writing skills. They must be able to acquire and transfer knowledge throughout the organization. Successful global managers must quickly adapt to the changing environment.

✓ **Check**Point

How will management tomorrow be different from management today?

INTERNATIONAL BUSINESS PERSPECTIVE

Careers

PURSUE YOUR PASSION—WORK FOR AN NGO

An international career at a nongovernmental organization (NGO) allows you to pursue your passion while helping others. NGOs are nonprofit organizations that tackle a wide variety of issues around the globe. If you are passionate about world peace, protecting the rights of women, or preventing human suffering, you might consider working for an NGO with a mission that matches your passion.

Many NGOs operate programs in underdeveloped countries where they work on problems such as poverty, insufficient food, inadequate healthcare, substandard housing, and illiteracy. Save the Children, Mercy Corps, Habitat for Humanity, and World Learning are examples of international organizations that try to make the world a better place.

In general, NGOs do not pay as well as for-profit businesses. NGOs receive funding from religious and charitable groups and government and business grants. Paying for programs usually takes precedence over paying high salaries. You will not get rich, but working for an NGO can be a rich experience. You will make a real difference in the lives of people and feel good about it.

Like international businesses, NGOs seek employees who can easily adapt to working in another country. This requires the ability to understand and appreciate the local culture and work with local residents. The specific skills needed for a successful career with an NGO vary depending on the organization and the specific position. Knowledge and skills related to management, accounting, finance, and communication are beneficial. Some positions require specific expertise such as economic development, healthcare policy, or civil engineering.

Preparation for a career with an NGO should begin with research about organizations and the programs they support. In addition, you might consider the following ideas.

- Learn another language
- Volunteer or intern with a local nonprofit organization
- Travel or study abroad
- Participate in cross cultural activities
- Develop skills and expertise through high school and college courses.

Think Critically

1. How might working for an NGO allow you to pursue your passion?
2. Why do NGOs pay moderate salaries?

cnicbc/iStockphoto.com

10-3 Assessment

REVIEW GLOBAL BUSINESS TERMS

Define each of the following terms.

1. span of control
2. front-line manager
3. middle manager
4. senior manager
5. chief executive officer (CEO)
6. lines of authority
7. degree of centralization

Study Tools

www.cengage.com/school/genbus/intlbiz

REVIEW GLOBAL BUSINESS CONCEPTS

8. Why is the line of authority important regardless of the span of control?

9. What is degree of centralization, and how does it affect managerial styles?

10. What are the four stages through which a business might pass on the way to achieving global status?

11. What is a visionary manager?

SOLVE GLOBAL BUSINESS PROBLEMS

Soltech, Inc., is a company that introduced a software package that manages the human resources function for large companies. The software is based on the U.S. tax structure and uses the English language. It can generate and manage job descriptions, performance appraisals, interns, and salary and benefit administration.

12. What stage is Soltech in now?

13. What stage is Soltech in if it tailors versions of the software for Germany and Japan and opens manufacturing facilities in those countries?

14. What stage is Soltech in if it expands into other kinds of software, with versions in numerous languages, and sells to all countries?

THINK CRITICALLY

15. What would a company do if its span of control at some level became too large to manage?

16. Why do organizations competing in the global marketplace tend to have a limited number of levels of management?

MAKING ACADEMIC CONNECTIONS

17. **CULTURAL STUDIES** Choose a product with which you are familiar. Describe how the manufacturer could evolve from a Stage 1 company to a Stage 4 company.

18. **COMMUNICATIONS** Why does having a larger span of control increase the need for better communication within an organization?

Quiz Prep

www.cengage.com/school/genbus/intlbiz

CHAPTER SUMMARY

10-1 MANAGERS AND CULTURAL DIFFERENCES

A Managers, who are the people in charge of organizations and their resources, have characteristics and styles that vary.

B Managers must be sensitive to and respect the cultural differences within their businesses.

10-2 MANAGEMENT PROCESS AND ORGANIZATION

A Managers engage in planning and decision making; organizing, staffing, and communicating; motivating and leading; and controlling.

B Organizations can be structured by function, product, or geography.

10-3 THE CHANGING PROCESS OF MANAGEMENT

A The levels of management are influenced by the span of control, lines of authority, and delegation of authority and responsibility.

B The evolution of a business through the domestic company, exporting company, international corporation, and global corporation stages affects its management.

C As globalization continues, the roles of managers will change.

GLOBAL **REFOCUS**

Read the case at the beginning of this chapter, and answer the following questions.

1. Why do you think the term *virtual corporation* was coined to describe temporary "best-of-everything" businesses?

2. Why do you think that the U.S. film industry has been quick to create virtual corporations.

3. What can managers of other businesses learn from the managers of virtual corporations?

4. Choose a recent U.S. film. Through Internet or library research or direct communication with the production and/or distribution company, investigate how the needed talents were brought together for the project. Determine whether or not the film project was the product of a virtual corporation.

REVIEW GLOBAL BUSINESS TERMS

Match the terms listed with the definitions.

1. Managers who decentralize power and share it with employees.
2. People in charge of organizations and their resources.
3. Managers who oversee the work and departments of a number of front-line managers.
4. Amount of authority and responsibility that is delegated to employees or to organizational units.
5. Managers who oversee the day-to-day operations in specific departments.
6. The highest manager within a company.
7. Managers who centralize power and tell employees what to do.
8. A drawing that shows the structure of an organization.
9. The number of employees a manager supervises.
10. Managers who oversee the work and departments of a number of middle managers.
11. Managers who avoid the use of power.
12. Indicates who is responsible to whom and for what.

a. autocratic managers
b. chief executive officer (CEO)
c. degree of centralization
d. free-rein managers
e. front-line managers
f. lines of authority
g. managers
h. middle managers
i. organizational chart
j. participative managers
k. senior managers
l. span of control

MAKE GLOBAL BUSINESS DECISIONS

13. Why is a participative manager likely to use autocratic and free-rein management on occasion?
14. Devise an analogy between a component of the management process and something that is familiar to you.
15. Draw an organizational chart that depicts the department of your school. What is the span of control for the head of the department?
16. What may the managers of a domestic company not know when their company decides to become an exporting company?
17. Managers in the global environment must become leaders as learners. What does the expression "leaders as learners" mean, and why is it necessary to be a leader as learner in the global marketplace?

Photodisc/Getty Images

MAKE ACADEMIC CONNECTIONS

18. **TECHNOLOGY** Describe how using scheduling software could contribute to the controlling process and success of an organization.

19. **TECHNOLOGY** As a manager, how can technology help you keep track of business operations abroad?

20. **CULTURAL STUDIES** How does the culture of the United States foster participative management?

21. **COMMUNICATION** How would a memorandum from an autocratic manager to employees about extended breaks differ from one from a free-rein manager?

22. **GEOGRAPHY** In what region(s) of Europe are most of the countries found that favor family and friendship rather than qualifications when hiring managers?

23. **CAREER PLANNING** How would you go about locating a book that addresses careers in management?

24. **VISUAL ART** Create a collage using photos from the Internet or magazines that depicts front-line, middle, and senior managers at work.

25. **CULTURAL STUDIES** What challenges might women managers face when dealing with employees in cultures where women and men have unequal status. What can be done to meet these challenges?

Photodisc/Getty Images

The GLOBAL Entrepreneur

CREATING AN INTERNATIONAL BUSINESS PLAN

Identifying Management Skills and Organizational Structure

Develop a management plan based on the company and country you have been using in this continuing project, or create a new idea for a business in the same or a different country. Make use of previously collected information, and do additional research. This phase of your business plan should answer the following questions.

1. What skills will managers need to adapt to the social and cultural environment of this country?

2. Describe the management style (autocratic, participatory, or free-reign) most appropriate for this organization.

3. Explain which type of organizational structure (function, product, or geography) would be most appropriate.

4. Which of the organization's activities will be centralized and which will be decentralized?

5. What other management and organizational decisions will need to be adapted for international business operations?

Consider using some of the following resources as you develop answers to the questions above.

- journal articles in scholarly publications

- web sites for companies in the industry you have chosen

- magazine and newspaper articles profiling businesses operating in the country you have chosen

- job descriptions posted on job search web sites and on specific company web sites

Prepare a written summary suitable for inclusion in a business plan. Include an organizational chart to illustrate the structure of your organization. Based on the written summary, develop a short oral report (two or three minutes) of your findings.

CHAPTER 11

Human Resources Management

11-1 Foundations of Human Resources Management

11-2 Selecting and Hiring Staff

11-3 Maximization of Human Resources

11-4 Retaining Human Resources

GLOBAL FOCUS

I Want to Go Home—Now!

"Ann, we've got to go home now! I can't stand living here in Belgium any longer."

Two months after her transfer to the Brussels office of her employer, Ann Hardy, a U.S. citizen, was shocked by the earnestness of her husband's appeal. She replied, "But, Jim, we've been here only a short while. Coming here was a big promotion for me. My career is on the line."

"My sanity is on the line. You go off to work, and I have to stay here and fight battles every single day. Everything is a struggle. Nothing turns out as it should. Why did the contractor have to plaster over the existing telephone line when this apartment was remodeled? Why should it take months to get a telephone installed?"

"But, Jim, . . ."

"I had to go to multiple shops to get the things for tonight's meal. Even if I had a car, there's no place to park! This tiny flat is four stories up in a building without an elevator. The refrigerator is so small it's like a toy. It takes two hours to launder four shirts in that washer-dryer. I'm not sure I made the right decision when I gave up my job in the United States. I've had it with this place."

Every day people face similar problems in new settings. How they respond is crucial to both personal and professional well-being. International businesses invest large amounts of money in employees they send abroad. By carefully selecting, training, and supporting their overseas employees, international businesses can retain their valuable human resources.

Think Critically

1. Why do you think that Ann is not eager to abandon her international assignment and return to the United States?
2. Why do you think Jim wants to return to the United States immediately?
3. Go to the International Travel Planner section of the Worldwide Classroom web site. Select the Culture Shock guide to learn more about culture shock, reverse culture shock, and traits important to intercultural adjustment.

11-1 Foundations of Human Resources Management

GOALS

- Differentiate between host-country nationals, parent-country nationals, and third-country nationals.

- Define the four dominant human resources management approaches.

Photodisc/Getty Images

Global Human Resource Management

Several factors contribute to the fact that human resources management is somewhat different in the global environment than in the domestic environment. One factor is the differences in worldwide labor markets. Each country has a different mix of workers, labor costs, and companies. Companies can choose the mix of human resources that is best for them. Another factor is differences in worker mobility. Various obstacles make it difficult or impossible to move workers from one country to another. These include physical, economic, legal, and cultural barriers.

Still another factor is managerial practices. Different business subcultures choose to manage their resources, including people, in different ways. When a company operates in more than one country, the problem of conflicting managerial practices increases. Yet another factor is the difference between national and global orientations. Companies aspire toward global approaches. However, getting workers to set aside their national approaches is challenging. A final factor is control. Managing diverse people in faraway places is more difficult than managing employees at home.

WHO MAKES UP THE LABOR MARKET?

Most companies obtain unskilled and semiskilled workers in local markets unless the supply is inadequate. **Host-country nationals**, or *locals,* are natives of the country in which they work. For skilled, technical, and managerial workers, companies have several options. They can sometimes hire these workers locally. In other cases, the companies must choose expatriates. **Expatriates** are people who live and work outside their native countries. Expatriates from the country in which their company is headquartered are called **parent-country nationals**, or *home-country nationals*. An Italian working in Germany for an Italian company is an example of a parent-country national. Expatriates from countries other than the home country of their company or the host country are called **third-country nationals**. For example, a Russian working in France for a German company is a third-country national.

Each company must balance the advantages and disadvantages of hiring each type of worker. Locals are usually culturally sensitive and easy to find, but they may not have the knowledge and skills needed by the foreign company. Parent-country nationals often have the needed knowledge and skills and sometimes have the desired company orientation, but they often lack the appropriate local language and cultural skills. Companies usually find parent-country nationals more costly to hire than other types of workers. Also, local laws could restrict employment of these parent-country nationals.

Third-country nationals could be more adaptable to local conditions than parent-country nationals. They may speak the local language and be able to make needed changes in culturally sensitive ways. In some cases, they could be more acceptable to locals than parent-country nationals. On the other hand, they may lack the desired company orientation. Regulations may make it difficult to hire them unless locals are unqualified. Selecting the best mix of employees from a variety of nationalities is challenging. Carrying out that mix in the global environment is even more challenging.

Photodisc/Getty Images

✓ CheckPoint
What types of workers make up the global labor market?

Four Human Resources Management Approaches

A company's approach to human resources management in the global environment is guided by its general approach to human resources management. Most global businesses adopt one of four basic approaches to human resources management. These approaches are ethnocentric, polycentric, regiocentric, and geocentric. The decision depends on several factors, such as governmental regulations and the size, structure, strategy, attitudes, and staffing of the company.

ETHNOCENTRIC APPROACH

The **ethnocentric approach** uses natives of the parent country of a business to fill key positions at home and abroad. This approach can be useful when new technology is being introduced into another country. It is also useful when prior experience is important. Sometimes less developed countries ask that companies transfer expertise and technology by using employees from the parent country to train and develop employees in the host country. The goal is to prepare host country employees to manage the business.

The ethnocentric approach has drawbacks. For example, it deprives local workers of the opportunity to fill key managerial positions. This could lower the morale and the productivity of local workers. Also, natives of the parent country might not be culturally sensitive enough to manage local workers well. These managers could make decisions that hurt the ability of the company to operate abroad. Figure 11-1 illustrates the ethnocentric approach to human resources management.

POLYCENTRIC APPROACH

The **polycentric approach** uses natives of the host country to manage operations within their country and parent-country natives to manage

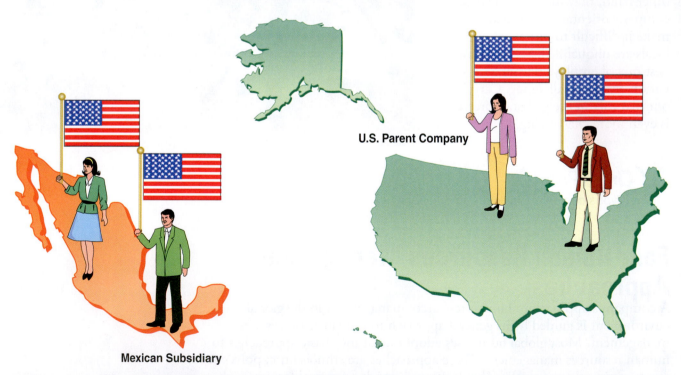

Ethnocentric Approach
to Human Resource Management

U.S. Parent Company

Mexican Subsidiary

Figure 11-1 The ethnocentric approach places natives of the home country of a business in key positions at home *and* abroad. In this example, the U.S. parent company places natives from the United States in key positions in both the United States and Mexico.

at headquarters. In this situation, host country managers rarely advance to corporate headquarters as natives of the parent country are preferred by the company as managers at that level. This approach is advantageous because locals manage in the countries for which they are best prepared. It is also more economical because locals, who require few, if any, incentives, are readily available and generally less expensive to hire than others. The polycentric approach is helpful in politically sensitive situations because the managers are culturally sensitive locals, not foreigners. Further, the polycentric approach allows for continuity of management.

The polycentric approach has several disadvantages. One disadvantage is the cultural gap between the subsidiary managers and the headquarters managers. If the gap is not bridged, the subsidiaries may function too independently. Another disadvantage is limited opportunities for advancement. Natives of the host countries can usually advance only within their subsidiaries, and parent-country natives can usually advance only within company headquarters. The result is that company decision makers at headquarters have little or no international experience. Nevertheless, their decisions have major effects on the subsidiaries. Figure 11-2 illustrates the polycentric approach to human resources management.

Work as a Team
Discuss the challenges of implementing one of the approaches to human resources management.

Polycentric Approach to Human Resource Management

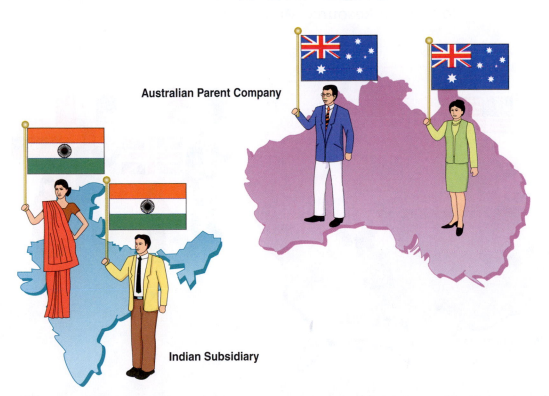

Australian Parent Company

Indian Subsidiary

Figure 11-2 The polycentric approach uses natives of the host country to manage operations in their country and natives of the parent country to manage in the home office. In this example, the Australian parent company uses natives of India to manage operations at the Indian subsidiary. Natives of Australia manage the home office.

REGIOCENTRIC APPROACH

The **regiocentric approach** uses managers from various countries within the geographic regions of a business. Although the managers operate relatively independently in the region, they are not normally moved to the company headquarters.

The regiocentric approach is adaptable to fit the company and product strategies. When regional expertise is needed, natives of the region are hired. If product knowledge is crucial, then parent-country nationals, who have ready access to corporate sources of information, can be brought in.

Photodisc/Getty Images

One shortcoming of the regiocentric approach is that managers from the region may not understand the view of the managers at headquarters. Also, corporate headquarters may not employ enough managers with international experience. Both of these situations could result in poor decisions. Figure 11-3 illustrates the regiocentric approach to human resources management.

Regiocentric Approach to Human Resource Management

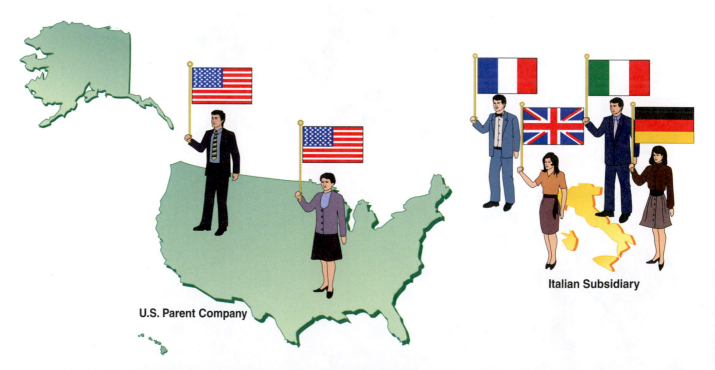

U.S. Parent Company

Italian Subsidiary

Figure 11-3 The regiocentric approach places managers from various countries within geographic regions of a business. In this example, the U.S. parent company uses natives of the United States at company headquarters. Natives of European countries are used to manage the Italian subsidiary.

GEOCENTRIC APPROACH

The **geocentric approach** uses the best available managers without regard for their countries of origin. The geocentric company should have a worldwide strategy of business integration. The geocentric approach allows the development of international managers and reduces national biases.

On the other hand, the geocentric approach has to deal with the fact that most governments want businesses to hire employees from the host countries. Getting approval for non-natives to work in some countries is difficult, or even impossible. Implementing the geocentric approach is expensive. It requires substantial training and employee development and more relocation costs. It also requires more centralization of human resources management and longer lead times before employees can be transferred because of the complexities of worldwide operations. Figure 11-4 illustrates the geocentric approach to human resources management.

Photodisc/Getty Images

✓ **Check**Point
What are the four approaches to human resources management?

Geocentric Approach to Human Resource Management

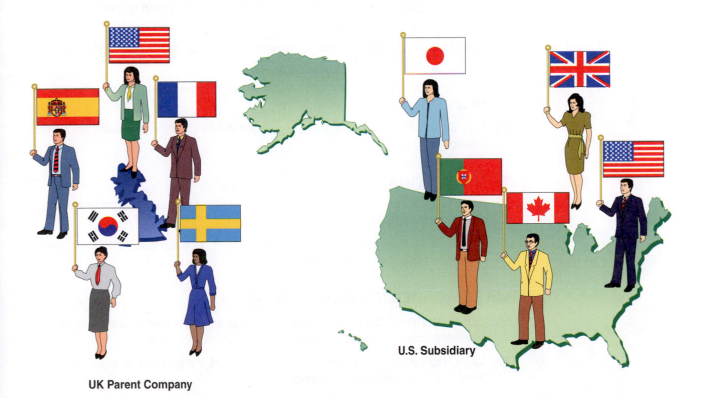

UK Parent Company

U.S. Subsidiary

Figure 11-4 The geocentric approach uses the best available managers for a business without regard for their country of origin. In this example, the UK parent company uses natives of many countries at company headquarters and at the U.S. subsidiary.

11-1 Assessment

Study Tools

www.cengage.com/school/genbus/intlbiz

REVIEW GLOBAL BUSINESS TERMS

Define each of the following terms.

1. host-country nationals

2. expatriates

3. parent-country nationals

4. third-country nationals

5. ethnocentric approach

6. polycentric approach

7. regiocentric approach

8. geocentric approach

REVIEW GLOBAL BUSINESS CONCEPTS

9. Why is human resources management different in the global environment?

10. Which of the four human resources management approaches is usually the least expensive?

11. What are two disadvantages to the polycentric approach to human resources management?

SOLVE GLOBAL BUSINESS PROBLEMS

Xylex Corporation has its home office in Paris, France. Determine whether each of the following Xylex employees is a host-country national, parent-country national, or third-country national.

12. Theresa Ingram, computer programmer, is a French citizen working in the Brussels, Belgium, factory.

13. Julian Moya, a citizen of Mexico, was trained in the Paris office and now works in the Mexico City office.

14. London-born Margaret Harrison is the director of purchasing in the Paris office.

15. Guy Duclos is the national sales manager in France, where he was born and raised.

THINK CRITICALLY

16. In what situations might staffing with third-country nationals be preferable to staffing with parent-country nationals?

17. Why would a truly global corporation most likely use the geocentric approach to human resources management?

MAKE ACADEMIC CONNECTIONS

18. **COMMUNICATIONS** Why is fluency in the local language an important consideration when hiring managers for overseas subsidiaries?

19. **LAW** How do the laws of other countries affect the process of selecting employees for international assignments?

Photodisc/Getty Images

GOALS

- Explain how staffing needs are determined.
- Describe how potential employees are recruited.
- Describe three factors to consider when hiring job applicants.

Determining Staffing Needs

A company must assess its staffing needs to compete successfully in the international market. **Employment forecasting** is estimating in advance the types and numbers of employees needed. **Supply analysis** is determining if there are sufficient types and numbers of employees available. Through selection or hiring and reduction or terminating processes, companies balance the demand for and supply of employees.

Once a company assesses its overall staffing needs, managers begin to fill individual jobs. A number of factors must be considered. What will the new employee be assigned to do? What are the qualifications that the employee will need? What is the best combination of technical abilities, personality traits, and environmental factors needed to ensure success?

When these types of questions are answered, specific job data are gathered. This includes information about assigned tasks; performance standards; responsibilities; and knowledge, skill, and experience requirements. From this information, a job description is prepared. A **job description** is a document that includes the job identification, job statement, job duties and responsibilities, and job specifications and requirements.

 **CheckPoint**

How does a company determine its staffing needs?

Recruiting Potential Employees

A company officially announces a job by circulating the job opening announcement and job description through appropriate channels. If someone already working for the company will fill the job, then internal channels will be used. The job information will be sent to all human resources offices within the company. These offices will post the information or notify company employees of the job availability in some other manner.

If someone who currently does not work for the company will fill the job, then different channels will be used. If a decision has been made to hire a parent-country national, then channels within the parent country will be used. If a host-country national will be hired, then channels in the host country will be utilized. If a third-country national will be hired, then channels in other countries that could provide suitable employees will be used.

The type of employee needed could influence the specific types of outlets selected. If an unskilled or semiskilled worker is needed, then a state government employment service or its overseas equivalent might be used. If a skilled, technical, or managerial worker is needed, then public and private outlets might be used. For unusual or high-ranking managerial positions, the company might employ a specialized recruitment firm known as a *headhunter*. Such a firm, sometimes for a substantial fee, locates one or more qualified applicants for the position.

✓ **Check**Point

What factors affect how companies recruit potential employees?

Selecting Qualified Employees

Companies that operate in the global environment use a variety of methods to select the best applicant. The best applicant is the person with the highest potential to meet the job expectations. Most companies use a combination of several selection methods, including careful examination of the applicant's past accomplishments, relevant tests, and interviews. In the process of screening applicants, companies are usually concerned about three major factors. These are competence, adaptability, and personal characteristics.

Competence The factor of competence relates to the ability to perform. Competence has a number of dimensions. One important dimension is technical knowledge. Is the applicant competent in the desired specialty areas? Another dimension is experience. Has the applicant performed similar or related tasks well in the past? For managerial positions, leadership and the ability to manage are important. Can the applicant work with others to accomplish goals? For positions in other countries, cultural awareness and language skills are critical. Does the applicant understand the region or market for which he or she would be responsible? Is the applicant able to communicate fluently in the local language?

Adaptability The factor of adaptability relates to the ability to adjust to different conditions. Possessing a serious interest in international business is necessary. Does the applicant really want to work abroad? The ability to relate

Work as a Team

Discuss different personal characteristics members of the group possess that would be attractive to potential employers.

to a wide variety of people is important, too. Does the applicant work effectively with diverse groups of people? The ability to empathize with others is needed. Can the applicant relate to the feelings, thoughts, and attitudes of those from other cultures? The appreciation of other managerial styles is also highly desirable. Can the applicant accept alternative managerial styles preferred be locals?

The appreciation of various environmental constraints is needed, too. Does the applicant understand the dynamics of the complex environment in which international business is conducted? The ability of the applicant's family to adjust to another location is particularly important for international assignments. Can the family members cope with the challenges of living abroad? If they can't, the applicant will likely be unhappy in the job.

Personal Characteristics The factor of personal characteristics has many dimensions. The maturity of the employee is one dimension. Is the applicant mature enough given the assignment and the culture in which the assignment will be undertaken? Another dimension is education. Does the applicant have a suitable educational level given the assignment and the location? In special circumstances, gender is a concern. Will the applicant's gender contribute toward or interfere with the ability to be successful in the working environment? In Saudi Arabia, for example, women are not business associates.

The social acceptability of the applicant should also be considered. What is the likelihood that the applicant will fit into the new work environment? Diplomacy is another trait to include. Is the applicant

Digital Vision/Getty Images

tactful in communicating, especially when unpleasant information is involved? General health is another consideration. Is the applicant healthy enough physically and mentally to withstand the rigors of the work assignment? The stability of the relationships within the family are important, too. Will the family be able to withstand the additional challenges of a new job—perhaps abroad?

As various applicants are screened, one thing usually is obvious: No single applicant possesses the perfect combination of competence, adaptability, and personal characteristics. Therefore the company will have to balance the strengths of the various applicants against their weaknesses. Overall, which applicant best matches the needs of the position? Which applicant has the greatest likelihood of being successful on the job? The answers to such questions result in the selection of the best-qualified individual to fill the job.

✓ **Check**Point
What are the three major selection factors that most multinational companies use?

INTERNATIONAL BUSINESS PERSPECTIVE

Culture

EXECUTIVE PAY REFLECTS CULTURAL VALUES

Executive compensation packages consist of money and other things that will motivate the performance of managers. The mix of things included in a compensation package depends on what is considered valuable and acceptable within a culture at a given time. In a developing country such as Vietnam, an executive might be pleased to receive a monthly bag of rice as part of pay. The same bag of rice would likely be rejected as inappropriate by an executive in Spain and other developed countries. Each culture attaches different values and levels of acceptability to forms and amounts of compensation.

Over time, perceptions about compensation change. During good economic times, most cultures tolerate compensation components that push the limits. Large bonuses, luxury cars with drivers, flying on corporate jets, and other generous executive perks are common and acceptable. When the economy declines, some corporations adjust executive pay to reflect shifting cultural values. Some pay components such as lavish bonuses that were previously taken for granted are scaled back or eliminated. Cultures generally attach more importance to fairness and to obtaining value for money spent when times are financially tough.

In recent years, the disparity between the pay of executives and laborers has violated cultural values of fairness across Europe. Threats of legislation to curb executive pay developed in Germany. Closing the gap between the pay of the CEO and the average worker continues to grow in importance in many European countries.

Think Critically

1. Why might an executive in a developed country reject rice as part of pay?
2. Why are top executive offered generous compensation packages?
3. Why would German politicians consider curbing executive pay?

morganl/iStockphoto.com

11-2 Assessment

REVIEW GLOBAL BUSINESS TERMS
Define each of the following terms.

1. employment forecasting
2. supply analysis
3. job description

REVIEW GLOBAL BUSINESS CONCEPTS

4. What process is used to determine staffing needs?

5. How are potential employees recruited?

6. After the screening and interviewing process, how does a company choose the best applicant for a job?

SOLVE GLOBAL BUSINESS PROBLEMS

Mark Evans and Harold Daw are the two finalists for a managerial position in Milan. While Mr. Evans has seven years of management experience at three different sites in one region of the United States, Mr. Daw has seven years of comparable management experience at two sites in different regions. Both are adaptable and want international managerial experience. Mr. Evans speaks fluent Swedish, and Mr. Daw speaks fluent French. Both have similar personal characteristics except that Mr. Evans is divorced and has no children and Mr. Daw has a wife and a teenager who is a junior in high school. Mrs. Daw is currently employed, and the company cannot guarantee that Mrs. Daw can find suitable employment in Italy should her husband be selected for the overseas assignment.

7. Which finalist is better qualified in terms of competence? Why?

8. Which finalist is better qualified in terms of adaptability? Why?

9. Which finalist is better qualified in terms of personal qualifications? Why?

10. Whom would you select for the overseas assignment? Why?

THINK CRITICALLY

11. Why does a company use different methods of recruiting for different jobs?

12. Which of the employee selection factors of competence, adaptability, and personal characteristics is typically the most important one for an international employee? Why?

MAKE ACADEMIC CONNECTIONS

13. **TECHNOLOGY** What kinds of technology-related skills do international employees need?

14. **CULTURAL STUDIES** How do family relationships influence the suitability of candidates for international assignments?

11-3 | Maximization of Human Resources

GOALS

- Understand the importance of training and development for global employees.

- Identify the common types of training and development for international employees.

- Explain how training and development programs reduce the chance of employee failure.

Photodisc/Getty Images

Training and Development Are Critical

Employees can make or break an international business, just as they can make or break a domestic one. Their daily actions put the life of the company on the line. Consequently, companies need to be sure that all of their employees are well prepared for their work. This includes both lower-level and higher-level employees. Training and developing employees to work at their maximum potential are in the best interest of a company in the long run. Training and development are an investment in the future of the company. The better trained and developed the employees are, the greater the likelihood that the company will be successful.

TRAINING COSTS

Training and developing employees are major expenses for a company. Managers must decide what types of employees in which locations should receive specific types of training and development. Because of limited resources, companies have to balance needs and potential benefits.

Historically many U.S.-based international companies have skimped on training and development. This has contributed to difficulties abroad. Many of their employees have not been well prepared to compete in the global marketplace. Companies headquartered in other countries often invest extensively in training and development. In fact, some countries have laws that require companies to train and develop their employees. Such employees are often well prepared for work in the highly competitive global marketplace. U.S.-based international companies increasingly realize the value of providing more extensive training and development.

✓ **Check**Point

Why are training and development so important for people working in other countries?

Types of Training and Development

Managers working for international companies need a variety of training and development. International managers need job-related training, information about languages and relationships, extensive training in the host country's culture, and spousal employment counseling.

Job-Related Issues Managers need training in job-related issues. For example, they need to be aware of the current economic, legal, and political environments. They need to be current on relevant governmental policies and regulations. Managers also need to be aware of managerial practices within their areas of responsibility. Current information about the company and its subsidiaries and their operations is needed, too.

Language and Relationship Issues In addition, parent-country nationals and their families need training and development relating to interpersonal relationships. At a minimum, they need to develop survival-skill knowledge in the local language before they are transferred abroad. Ideally, the manager will be fluent in the local language upon arrival.

Cross-Cultural Training Managers and their families need cross-cultural training. They need to understand various dimensions of the local culture. Also, managers need realistic training about everyday life in the host country. For example, they need to know about the currency. They need to know what foods are available and their approximate costs. They need to understand housing options and prices.

GLOBAL BUSINESS SPOTLIGHT

SOME EUROPEAN EMPLOYERS MUST PROVIDE TRAINING

Employers in some European countries are required to provide training and development for their employees. In France all firms with more than 10 employees must pay a 1.5 percent training levy. Employers are reimbursed from the collected funds for accredited training programs. Individual employees can also use the funds to support training leaves. Regional and industrial employer-union organizations administer the funds. In Spain a similar scheme operates with employee contributions for extra personal training leave.

Think Critically

1. Why would a country require that businesses operating there provide employees with training and development?
2. Why would a country that requires employee training and development exempt certain employers from that regulation?

echo1/iStockphoto.com

Spousal Employment Counseling

Special counseling may be needed if the manager has a working spouse. Increasingly, both partners work, and career moves that are beneficial to one may not be beneficial to the other. Determining if the spouse can work in the host country is important in many employment decisions. Some governments prohibit the spouses of foreign workers from being employed. What realistic employment options, if any, exist for the spouse in the host country? If the spouse cannot work, can he or she adjust to that fact?

Providing training and development is costly. Nevertheless, companies must provide it, especially for parent-country nationals. If parent-country nationals are unsuccessful abroad or if their families cannot adjust to life abroad, the company loses.

Research suggests that relevant training and development does increase the likelihood of success abroad. Figure 11-5 shows the types of training and development recommended for people who are sent by their companies to work in Japan. For other countries, the recommendations would be similar except that the culture-specific training would change.

✓ CheckPoint

What are four areas training and development for global employees should address?

SUGGESTED AREAS OF TRAINING AND DEVELOPMENT FOR EMPLOYMENT IN JAPAN	
Essential	• Japanese language • Japanese social practices • Japanese culture
Important	• Japanese economy • Japanese negotiating style • Organization and sociology of Japanese businesses
Useful	• Japanese distribution and marketing systems • General cross-cultural training • Japanese history • Japanese politics
Helpful	• Culture shock briefing • Japanese accounting and financial techniques • Japanese business legal system • Political aspects of international economics • International politics

Figure 11-5 Training and development for work in Japan ranges in importance from essential to helpful.

Training and Development Help to Prevent Failure

In spite of the efforts of many companies to provide parent-country nationals with relevant training and development, a number of them are unsuccessful abroad. They may muddle through the assignment abroad with little or no success. These employees may return home sooner than expected and they are likely to be angry and frustrated. A worker may even leave the company during or at the end of the overseas assignment. The associated monetary and psychological costs of failure are high. Failure hurts the company and the employee and the employee's family.

WHY GLOBAL EMPLOYEES FAIL

There are several reasons why parent-country nationals fail.

- The employee may be unable to adjust to a different physical and cultural environment.
- The spouse or other family members may be unable to adjust to a different physical and cultural environment.
- The employee's emotional maturity can be seriously strained by an overseas assignment.
- The employee may be unable to work productively.
- The employee may not accept the new responsibilities.
- The employee may lack the motivation to cope with the challenges of working abroad.
- The employee may lack sufficient technical competence.

GLOBAL BUSINESS SPOTLIGHT

LANGUAGE MATTERS IN FRANCE

If you are going to work or live in France, you should develop fluency in the language. Because the French take great pride in their language, they think others should speak French, too.

The French value their language so much as part of their culture that they created the Académie Française to police their language. This organization tries to ensure that businesses and their employees use pure French, not a combination of French and other languages.

Speaking English in France is considered chic within some groups. In many situations, however, it is frowned upon. Interestingly, many of the French speak English as a second language, although many of these people have a strong preference for their native tongue.

Think Critically

1. If you don't speak French, how could you develop that ability relatively quickly?
2. Use library or Internet resources to learn why French Canadians discount the efforts of the Académie Française. Prepare a summary of your findings.

Work as a Team

Discuss ways a company could use an employee's international experience when he or she returns from abroad.

REDUCING THE CHANCE OF EMPLOYEE FAILURE

Because an employee's failure in an international assignment is costly to both the employer and the employee, companies need to make plans to reduce the chance of failure. Several areas of training and development before, during, and after the international assignment should be considered.

- Select only successful and satisfied workers for overseas assignments.
- Provide extensive, relevant training and development before departure, throughout the assignment abroad, and after the return home.
- Make the international assignment part of the long-term employee development process. This effort should benefit both the company and the employee in planned and purposeful ways.

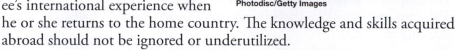

- Provide adequate communication between the company and its employee. The company should know about the employee's overseas experiences. The employee should know about changes at company headquarters, too.

Photodisc/Getty Images

- Provide a job that uses the employee's international experience when he or she returns to the home country. The knowledge and skills acquired abroad should not be ignored or underutilized.
- Train company managers, especially those without international experience, to value international experience.

The company should expect returning employees to experience reverse culture shock. However, a supportive training and development program should minimize the readjustment time and difficulty.

✓ CheckPoint

Why should companies make careful efforts to reduce the risk of employee failure on international assignments?

NETBookmark

Many people are fascinated with the idea of working overseas. However, most do not fully understand the amount of preparation necessary in order to be successful. Access the web site shown below and click on the link for Chapter 11. Read the Monster.com article entitled "Preparing for an International Career: Developing Needed Global Skills." According to the article, what are the three most important skills that international employers look for in their employees?

www.cengage.com/school/genbus/intlbiz

REVIEW GLOBAL BUSINESS CONCEPTS

1. Explain why training and development of employees on international assignments is important.

2. Briefly explain four types of training and development that international managers receive.

3. What factors often cause parent-country nationals to fail in their overseas assignments?

Study Tools
www.cengage.com/school/genbus/intlbiz

SOLVE GLOBAL BUSINESS PROBLEMS

For each of the following cases, determine whether the employee is likely to succeed or fail at an international assignment and explain why.

4. John Deters works in the New York City office but always says he is homesick for his state of Texas. He makes frequent requests for transfers to a Texas branch.

5. Marcia Conners is very ambitious and frequently takes on assignments nobody else wants just to prove her value to the company. Her husband is a freelance graphic designer who says he can do his work from anywhere.

6. Grant Neider is excited about a possible transfer from Chicago to Madrid and is taking Spanish lessons. His 17-year-old daughter is student council president and has the lead role in the spring musical.

7. Tonia Engstrom always orders a cheeseburger in a restaurant because she says she doesn't like to try new things.

THINK CRITICALLY

8. If one of your parents accepted employment as a parent-country national in France, what adjustments would you have to make if you moved there?

9. Why do you think that all recommended training listed in the essential category in Figure 11-5 relates to the general Japanese culture rather than to Japanese business practices?

MAKING ADADEMIC CONNECTIONS

10. **CULTURAL STUDIES** Use the library or the Internet to research what foods are eaten regularly in a particular foreign country. How well would you adapt to a similar diet?

12. **CAREER PLANNING** How can you plan your education and work experiences to prepare yourself for work in a foreign country?

13. **TECHNOLOGY** Use the Internet to locate online resources for employee training and development.

11-4 Retaining Human Resources

GOALS

- Understand that employee motivation is culturally based.

- Explain the common components of compensation packages for parent-country nationals.

- Appreciate the complexities of evaluating employee performance in an international setting.

- List strategies that help to minimize repatriation problems.

Photodisc/Getty Images

Employee Motivation

Managers around the world try to motivate their employees to perform to their fullest potential. While this ideal is commendable, the specific things that contribute to peak performance vary. What motivates a U.S. worker to perform well may have little or no effect elsewhere. Employee motivation is not universal. Instead, it is culturally based and varies from culture to culture.

For example, the U.S. culture values individualism. It also values material possessions. It values taking personal risks to gain personal rewards. Consequently, for most U.S. workers, motivation relates to the personal desire to assume risk in order to gain material rewards.

For many in the United States, money is a major motivator. It is a reward for accepting individual risks and performing well. The more personal responsibility a U.S. worker accepts and handles well, the more money he or she receives. The more money a U.S. worker has, the more material possessions he or she can acquire. Money motivates many in the United States to perform well. Of course, money is not the only motivator. As money allows U.S. workers to fulfill their needs and wants, money becomes less and less a motivator. The possibility of earning $3,000 more motivates a U.S. worker who earns the minimum wage. It will allow him or her to have more creature comforts. However, it does not motivate a U.S. executive who is making more than a million dollars a year. The well-paid executive has already used money to fulfill basic needs and wants.

Money cannot buy everything. Some desires must be fulfilled in other ways. Other factors, such as personal recognition and the sense of reaching one's full potential, motivate many U.S. workers more than money does.

Experiences worldwide suggest that U.S. models of motivation work best with U.S. workers in their native country. When U.S.-based international companies try to apply their domestic models of motivation in other countries, the models do not work as well. U.S. models fail to explain motivation elsewhere because what motivates people differs from culture to culture.

For example, publicly praising the individual achievements of a U.S. worker may motivate him or her toward higher achievement. Treating a Japanese employee in the same manner may not motivate him or her. Because the Japanese culture emphasizes group harmony, praising an individual may disrupt the group harmony. It can cause the person singled out to lose face, or to suffer personal embarrassment. In the future, it can cause that person to behave in a way that will not draw attention to himself or herself. In effect, praising a Japanese employee publicly can backfire. Consequently, international managers must use motivation strategies that are culturally acceptable to the employee.

✓ CheckPoint
How does culture relate to employee motivation?

A Question of Ethics

THE COMPANY PICNIC THAT BOMBED

A U.S.-based international company decided it would require a traditional company picnic at each of its sites worldwide because the event was very popular with the employees at headquarters. Each year the managers and executives prepare meat on outdoor grills and serve food to picnickers. The highlight of the day is a baseball game.

The first overseas company picnic was held near the location of the Madrid operations. While the U.S. picnic motivated employees and built teamwork at the company headquarters, the Spanish version had the opposite effect. The local workers were unaccustomed to socializing with those of other ranks. They also felt awkward being served by higher-ranking employees, several of whom were from the United States. They perceived that their class and socialization standards were being violated. To make matters worse, they were coerced into playing the unfamiliar game of baseball, which further alienated them.

Think Critically

1. Was it ethical for headquarters managers to force each company site around the world to have a company picnic and baseball game? Why or why not?
2. What fundamental error did managers at headquarters make?
3. Would it be ethical for the offended Spanish workers to slow down the pace of their work to show their displeasure about the company picnic and baseball game?

Compensating Employees

Local culturally accepted standards influence employee compensation packages. North American and European international companies tend to reward employees based on the type of work performed and the skills required. In Singapore and Hong Kong, individual performance and skill influence compensation. In Japan, factors of age, seniority, and group or company performance determine compensation. Because compensation standards vary around the world, local laws, employment practices, and employer obligations should guide companies as they design compensation packages.

Cultural Sensitivity International companies motivate employees toward peak performance with culturally sensitive compensation packages. These benefit packages include both cash and noncash items. The mix of employee benefits varies from country to country, but the cash component is typically the largest. Some companies provide discounted products or services to their employees as noncash compensation. In European countries, items such as lunches and transportation are often part of the noncash executive compensation. In less developed and developing countries, basic foodstuff like rice and flour can be part of noncash employee benefits.

Base Salary Employee compensation packages for parent-country nationals usually are based on several factors. One factor is base salary. For the parent-country national, the base salary at least maintains the customary standard of living of the employee and his or her family while living abroad.

Expatriate Bonus Another factor is an expatriate bonus. Often a company must pay a premium to persuade an employee to work abroad. It provides compensation for adjustment problems and for hardship caused by living and working abroad.

Cost-of-Living Adjustment Another factor is a cost-of-living adjustment. It compensates for the fact that basic living costs vary greatly around the world.

COST OF LIVING INDEX FOR SELECTED CITIES

Country	City	Index	Country	City	Index
Argentina	Buenos Aires	0.84	Israel	Tel Aviv	1.39
Australia	Canberra	1.30	Italy	Rome	1.90
Bangladesh	Dhaka	0.84	Japan	Okinawa	1.40
Bolivia	La Paz	0.74	Korea	Seoul	1.39
Brazil	Rio de Janeiro	1.23	Malaysia	Kuala Lumpur	0.99
Canada	Montreal	1.33	Mexico	Mexico City	1.14
China	Beijing	1.24	Philippines	Manila	0.94
Egypt	Cairo	0.91	Russia	Moscow	1.62
France	Paris	1.92	South Africa	Johannesburg	1.19
Germany	Berlin	1.49	Saudi Arabia	Riyadh	1.08
Honduras	Tegucigalpa	0.79	United Kingdom	London	1.77
India	New Delhi	0.93	United States	Washington, DC	1.00
Ireland	Dublin	1.70	Zimbabwe	Harare	1.95

Source: Adapted from the U.S. Census *Indexes of Living Costs Abroad*: the U.S. Census *2008*

Figure 11-6 Compensation should take into account the vast differences in the cost of living in cities around the world.

Figure 11-6 shows the cost of living in selected locations around the world in comparison to the cost of living in Washington, D.C.

Employee Benefits Finally, fringe benefits often are provided to compensate for the additional expenses of living abroad. They include compensation for having to pay various local taxes and contributions to government insurance programs. They also include relocation expenses, high-risk insurance premiums, and extra educational and medical expenses.

Employee compensation packages for other workers vary worldwide. Typically, they include a base salary that reflects local living costs and some fringe benefits.

✓ **Check**Point
Why do compensation packages vary around the world?

Work as a Team
Discuss how employee evaluation practices from the United States might have to be modified for subsidiaries operating in France, Germany, and Italy.

Evaluating Employee Performance

Companies that operate internationally must evaluate the performance of their employees. Employee performance, especially for parent-country nationals, is influenced by three factors. These factors are the environment, the task, and the individual's personality.

Business environments differ greatly around the world. Some offer better opportunities for success than others. Job tasks vary, too. Some jobs are more demanding than others. It is more difficult to perform jobs with many challenging tasks. Personality characteristics contribute to the likelihood of success, especially in international assignments. The match between personality types and job demands is important.

The human resources management approach used by the company determines who sets the employee performance standards. For example, with the ethnocentric approach, parent-country nationals primarily set and administer the standards. In contrast, with the polycentric approach, host-country nationals primarily set and administer the standards.

The nature of the employee performance standards varies from job to job. Different jobs require different combinations of competence, adaptability, and personal characteristics. Standards also vary from country to country because different cultures view employee performance in different ways.

Although many companies try to assess the performance of host-country nationals and third-country nationals much like parent-country nationals, it is difficult to do. Even if the evaluation forms are translated into the appropriate languages, misunderstandings can occur. If local evaluation forms are used, can the company headquarters interpret them correctly? Another problem is how employee performance evaluation is perceived in different parts of the world. In some locations, it can be viewed as threatening. It can also be viewed as insulting or as evidence of lack of trust. Finding ways of evaluating employee performance that are both culturally sensitive and meaningful is difficult. Balancing the needs of the employee and the company is indeed a challenge in the global business environment.

✓ **Check**Point
Why is evaluating the performance of international employees so challenging?

Anticipating Repatriation

Repatriation is the process a person goes through when returning home and getting settled after having worked abroad. The repatriation period often is a difficult one, filled with many adjustments. It is a challenging time when expatriates experience *reverse culture shock*. They have difficulty becoming reacquainted with their native culture. These major adjustments involve such things as work, finances, and social relationships.

Photodisc/Getty Images

Returning expatriates often experience a sense of isolation. They have grown in different directions while abroad. Because their extended families and friends have not had similar experiences, they seem like strangers.

To minimize the problems when returning home, expatriates need to plan ahead. It is not too early to start, even before leaving on an international assignment. With careful advanced planning, many of the problems of returning employees can be lessened.

Once abroad, they must keep in frequent communication with former colleagues and friends. Expatriates should share new experiences with them and find out what is new in their lives. In addition, they ought to learn to enjoy the benefits of the host culture and its way of life whenever possible.

International employees should also begin exploring new career options at least one year before the end of the assignment abroad. Soon-to-be repatriates should encourage their current employers to find suitable jobs that make use of their recent international experiences. Also, they can explore options abroad and at home with other companies. When returning home, repatriates should be grateful for their adventures abroad. They can view their native culture in another light and appreciate it more than ever before after having experienced firsthand another way of life.

✓ CheckPoint

What can an employee working abroad do to facilitate a smooth transition into his or her native culture?

REVIEW GLOBAL BUSINESS TERMS
Define the following term.

1. repatriation

REVIEW GLOBAL BUSINESS CONCEPTS

2. Motivation is culturally based. Why is the previous statement true?

3. What is typically included in the compensation packages of parent-country nationals?

SOLVE GLOBAL BUSINESS PROBLEMS

Use the cost-of-living index shown in Figure 11-6 to calculate cost-of-living allowances for employees who are living in cities other than Washington, D.C. London is given as an example. (Note: The cost-of-living allowance is usually not reduced when a country's index is less than 1.0.)

	Location	Index	×	Spendable Income	=	Cost-of-Living Allowance
Example:	London	1.77	×	$ 50,000	=	$ 88,500
4.	Mexico City	1.14	×	$ 70,000	=	?
5.	Montreal	1.33	×	$ 40,000	=	?
6.	Paris	1.92	×	$ 60,000	=	?
7.	Okinawa	1.40	×	?	=	$ 77,000

THINK CRITICALLY

8. What factors would cause a German-based international company to pay its employees who live in Tokyo, Japan, more than its employees who live in your hometown?

MAKING ACADEMIC CONNECTIONS

9. **TECHNOLOGY** What software could be used to create the cost-of-living allowance for employees assigned to various locations around the world?

10. **TECHNOLOGY** Identify a job or career that is available in several different countries. Use the Internet to find the compensation available for that job in different places around the world.

11. **CULTURAL STUDIES** How might the collectivist orientation of Sweden influence the compensation package of employees of a Canadian multinational corporation working there?

Quiz Prep
www.cengage.com/school/genbus/intlbiz

CHAPTER SUMMARY

11-1 FOUNDATIONS OF HUMAN RESOURCES MANAGEMENT

A. Human resources management is more complicated in the global environment because of differences in labor markets and managerial practices.

B. The four common approaches to human resources management are the ethnocentric, polycentric, regiocentric, and geocentric approaches.

11-2 SELECTING AND HIRING STAFF

A. An international company must carefully determine its staffing needs using employment forecasting and supply analysis.

B. Recruiting methods vary depending on the type of employee needed.

C. Applicants for most international positions are selected based on their competence, adaptability, and personal characteristics.

11-3 MAXIMIZATION OF HUMAN RESOURCES

A. Relevant training and development are critical for success in international business for both employees and companies.

B. Training for international positions should include job-related issues, language and relationship issues, cross-cultural training, and spousal employment counseling.

C. International companies should understand the reasons why employees fail and take steps to reduce the chances of failure.

11-4 RETAINING HUMAN RESOURCES

A. Cultural differences can vary the methods of motivating international employees.

B. Cultural standards influence employee compensation packages.

C. Although subject to cultural variability, the international employee's performance is influenced by three factors: the environment, the task, and the person's personality.

D. With proper planning prior to, during, and after an international assignment, repatriation problems can be reduced.

GLOBAL **REFOCUS**

Read the case at the beginning of this chapter, and answer the following questions.

1. How do you know that Jim Hardy is encountering culture shock?

2. What stage of culture shock is Jim experiencing? How do you know?

3. What would you tell Ann and Jim to help cope with culture shock?

REVIEW GLOBAL BUSINESS TERMS

Match the terms listed with the definitions.

1. The human resources approach that uses the best available managers without regard for their countries of origin.
2. Expatriates from the country in which their company is headquartered.
3. The human resources approach that uses natives of the parent country of a business to fill key positions at home and abroad.
4. The process of returning home and getting settled after having worked abroad.
5. Natives of the country in which they work.
6. Determining if there are sufficient types and numbers of employees available.
7. The human resources approach that uses managers from various countries within the geographic regions of a business.
8. Expatriates from countries other than the home country of their company or the host country.
9. People who live and work outside their native countries.
10. A document that includes the job identification, job statement, job duties and responsibilities, and job specifications and requirements.
11. Estimating in advance the types and numbers of employees needed.
12. The human resources approach that uses natives of the host country to manage operations within their country and parent country natives to manage at headquarters.

a. employment forecasting
b. ethnocentric approach
c. expatriates
d. geocentric approach
e. host-country nationals
f. job description
g. parent-country nationals
h. polycentric approach
i. regiocentric approach
j. repatriation
k. supply analysis
l. third-country nationals

Photodisc/Getty Images

MAKE GLOBAL BUSINESS DECISIONS

13. Using people, print, and electronic resources, determine if a U.S.-based multinational company should hold an annual company picnic and baseball game for the employees of its Portuguese subsidiary, 75 percent of whom are natives of Portugal. Justify your position.

14. Should a U.S.-based multinational company locate its European division human resources office in London, United Kingdom, or in Paris, France, if the primary considerations are (1) the local cost of living, (2) the central location, (3) the ease of adjustment for parent-country nationals?

15. Using reference resources in a library, identify a multinational company headquartered in a European country of your choice. Find out in which city the company is headquartered. Locate on a map of Europe the country and the city in which the headquarters is located. Using the scale on the map, estimate the distance from the city in which the company is headquartered to Brussels, Belgium.

16. Based on your reading of a magazine or journal article about living abroad, would you be a good candidate for an international assignment? Why or why not?

17. If your family relocated in the United Kingdom and enrolled you in what the British call a private comprehensive secondary school, would your family be entitled to an educational adjustment as a part of your father's or mother's employee compensation package? Why or why not?

18. Prepare a list of questions you might ask applicants for managerial positions in major cities throughout Europe.

19. Why might your best friend no longer seem to be your best friend when you return from a lengthy overseas assignment?

MAKE ACADEMIC CONNECTIONS

20. **TECHNOLOGY** What types of technology would best facilitate communication between human resources managers at headquarters and at subsidiaries around the world?

21. **CULTURAL STUDIES** In some developing countries, why would foodstuffs be part of the compensation for local employees?

22. **GEOGRAPHY** How might the geography and climate of Switzerland influence the cost-of-living allowance for employees working there?

23. **HISTORY** How did World War II affect the labor supply in Russia?

24. **MATHEMATICS** What are some of the reasons that the cost of living in London is approximately 77 percent more than the cost of living in Washington, D.C.?

25. **COMMUNICATIONS** How would the group orientation of South Korea influence how human resources managers recommend motivating host-country employees there?

26. **TECHNOLOGY** Many major multinational companies have web sites on which they list employment opportunities. Locate such a company using an Internet search, and read the job descriptions for some jobs available in other countries.

27. **CAREER PLANNING** In preparation for work assignments abroad, what could you do to increase your adaptability to life in other countries?

The GLOBAL Entrepreneur

CREATING AN INTERNATIONAL BUSINESS PLAN

Human Resources Management

Plan a human resources strategy for the company and country you have been using in this continuing project, or create a new idea for your business in the same or a different country. Make use of previously collected information, and do additional research. This phase of your business plan should include the following components.

Photo © Getty Images

1. Describe the type of human resources management approach (ethnocentric, polycentric, regiocentric, or geocentric) that would be most appropriate for your organization.

2. Describe the actions that would be taken to identify and recruit potential employees.

3. Describe the selection procedures (application process, interview questions) that would be used by your organization.

4. Describe the types of training and development activities that would be appropriate for managers and other employees in this organization.

5. Describe how the organization would motivate employees to improve productivity and plan for retention.

6. Describe the methods that would be used to evaluate employee performance.

Prepare a written summary suitable for inclusion in a business plan. Based on the written summary, develop a short oral report (two or three minutes) of your findings.

CHAPTER 12

Labor Around the World

12-1   Migration of Labor

12-2   Milestones of the Labor Movement

12-3   Unions in the Workplace Today

Photodisc/Getty Images

Solidarity in Poland

In 1980, working and living conditions were not good in Poland. The communist government ruled with a heavy hand. Workers in the shipyards in Gdansk wanted to organize non-communist trade unions and they wanted workers to have rights, including the right to strike. Although the government thwarted the early efforts to organize, in August Lech Walesa led a strike at the Gdansk shipyard. Crippling sympathy strikes across Poland pressured the government to grant workers the right to strike and to organize their own unions. Walesa was widely perceived as the leader of the workers' rights movement known as Solidarity.

As the new Solidarity unions asserted their power and influence, they increasingly undermined the government of Poland. Fearing intervention from the Soviet Union, General Jaruzelski imposed martial law and outlawed Solidarity. Many of its leaders, including Lech Walesa, were confined for almost a year. When they returned to their jobs, they took the Solidarity movement underground because of governmental restrictions and surveillance. Solidarity continued to be influential and to work for change behind the scenes.

Lech Walesa received the Nobel Peace Prize in 1983 for his efforts to establish the universal freedom of organization in Poland and elsewhere. Fearing that he would not be allowed to return to Poland if he traveled to Sweden, Walesa asked his wife to deliver his acceptance speech. In the speech he said, "We are fighting for the right of working people to association and for the dignity of human labor."

Meanwhile, the economic and political conditions in Poland and elsewhere in Eastern Europe continued to deteriorate. The people became more and more dissatisfied with their lives under communism. As governments from Eastern Europe transitioned from communism to democracy, the Solidarity movement became more openly active. Solidarity also became a political party. In 1989, it forced the government to hold elections and won a majority of seats in the Polish parliament. A year later Lech Walesa was elected President of the Republic of Poland.

Think Critically

1. How did the Solidarity strike at the Gdansk shipyards set the stage for change in the Polish government?
2. Why do you think Lech Walesa was confined by General Jaruzelski's government?
3. Use library and Internet resources to create a timeline of Walesa's life and the Solidarity movement. Include major world events to help put the timeline in perspective.

12-1 Migration of Labor

GOALS

- Explain who migrant laborers are.

- Describe why some countries need migrant laborers.

- Discuss factors that make a country attractive to migrant laborers.

- Explain factors that make a country accessible to migrant laborers.

Sean Gallup/Getty Images

Definition of Migrant Laborers

People who serve as workers or laborers are found around the world. However, those laborers are not necessarily born where they are needed as workers. All countries need some of their citizens to work as laborers. But some countries have too many laborers. Other countries need more laborers.

Countries that have larger, more developed economies that are growing often need more laborers than are born there or laborers with different skills. The additional laborers have to come from another country. Some laborers move to another country for work. Increasing numbers of people are changing countries for work. About 3 percent of the global population now lives outside of homelands. However, tough economic times may reduce the number of people willing to change countries for work.

Migrant laborers are people who move to another country for work. They leave home and family behind. Migrant laborers seek perceived opportunities to have such things as better jobs, higher incomes, and improved living standards. But opportunity is relative. Different people see things in different ways. Many people do not want to leave where they were born, even if it means laboring at lesser jobs than could be had in other countries. Some people choose to move from a poorer country to a richer country for a better economic life. Others go from one developing country to another for better jobs. Still other people choose to move from a richer country to a poorer country for different or challenging work opportunities.

HOW COUNTRIES COMPARE ON IMMIGRATION FACTORS

Rank	Need for Migrant Laborers	Attractiveness to Migrant Laborers	Accessibility to Migrant Laborers
1	Japan	United States	Australia
2	Italy	United Kingdom	Canada
3	Portugal	Australia	Singapore
4	Finland	Norway	New Zealand
5	Czech Republic	France	Israel

Adapted from *The Wall Street Journal*, September 19, 2008, A 18.

Figure 12-1 Most countries around the world do not rank high on even one factor important to migrant laborers.

The factors behind labor migration are complex. They include the need for, attractiveness to, and accessibility to migrant laborers. Figure 12-1 shows the highest ranked countries in each of these categories. Notice that no country ranks at the very top in all three of these factors.

✓ CheckPoint
Who are migrant laborers?

Need for Migrant Laborers

The need for migrant laborers varies around the world. This need is influenced by several things. One is the level of economic activity. Unless there are enough laborers, both economic activity and governmental income suffer.

Another factor is the proportion of working-age population, which is influenced by the birth rate and life expectancy of the population of a country. In many developed countries, not enough children are born to replace workers as they retire. To maintain population and labor supply, women must have 2.1 children on average. When the birth rate falls below this number, the population and labor supply shrink. Workers must come from other countries to maintain the supply of labor and to maintain the level of economic activity. Countries with low birth rates and growing economies have strong need for migrant laborers.

In Japan the birthrate is about 1.3 children per woman. This low birth rate cannot maintain the current population and labor supply. Worker shortages will increase. If Japan is to thrive economically in the future, it must employ many more migrant laborers than it currently does. Japan will need to change to get all of the migrant laborers it needs to thrive economically. Japan needs to become more appealing and open to encourage needed migrant workers to move there.

✓ CheckPoint
How does birth rate affect the need for migrant laborers?

Work as a Team

Discuss factors that make a country attractive to migrant laborers. Share your thoughts about things that make specific countries attractive to migrant laborers.

Attractiveness to Migrant Laborers

Attractiveness is another factor influencing migrant laborers. Some countries are more appealing than others to migrant laborers. Things that influence attractiveness include having a growing developed economy, a welcoming multicultural society, and a high quality of education. These mean more and better jobs, higher salaries, and improved living standards. Most migrant laborers think they can fit in, find suitable work, and get ahead. Ironically, except for France, the countries with the highest attractiveness do not have the need for many migrant laborers.

Some migrant laborers from poor countries are drawn to other countries by abundant opportunity and freedom from want and oppression. Politically stable democratic countries with relatively high living standards are attractive to most migrant laborers. They want to enjoy a better life.

The United States is viewed by most migrant laborers as very attractive when compared to other countries. It offers many opportunities to laborers from abroad. It is open to and accepting of migrant laborers, who can be easily hired. It is so popular with migrant laborers that some who want to work there legally are turned away. Others illegally enter the country for work. How the United States can best manage its immigration challenge is open to debate.

✓ CheckPoint

What are some factors that make a country attractive to migrant laborers?

Brent Stirton/Getty Images

SWEDEN OPENS ITS DOORS TO MIGRANT LABORERS

In uncertain economic times, most European and other economically developed countries are guarding their jobs. Recession and rising unemployment are causing these countries to be very careful about who is allowed in from other countries to work.

Sweden, in contrast, is opening its doors to migrant laborers of all skill levels. The Swedish Migration and Asylum Policy minister thinks that this policy is necessary for Sweden's economy to prosper in the years ahead. With a projected shrinking labor force, Sweden will soon need more workers with the desired competence level. Otherwise public financing for pensions and health care will be strained.

The new Swedish policy has been criticized by unions and by some politicians, who fear it threatens its social model. Known for strong worker rights and generous welfare benefits, Sweden has served as a social blueprint for many postwar European governments.

Time will tell whether taking the short- or long-term view toward labor migration in difficult times produces better outcomes.

Think Critically

1. Why are most economically developed countries guarding jobs now?
2. Why is Sweden opening its doors to migrant laborers now?

Accessibility to Migrant Laborers

Accessibility influences migrant laborers, too. Migrant laborers prefer countries with dynamic economies that are open and accepting of them. In other words, they want to feel comfortable living as foreigners in a country that offers them a better life.

Migrant laborers are often interested in countries where they will have a future opportunity to become legal citizens of the adopted land. This would occur after certain conditions are met. As a result, they often seek countries with favorable immigration policies. If they like working there, they may want to stay and become citizens.

Being accessible is a dilemma for many countries. The countries need to attract enough migrant laborers to fill vacant jobs that cannot be filled by natives. However, the countries do not want to attract migrant laborers for whom there are no vacant positions. Getting the right balance of legally employed migrant laborers is hard. Sometimes illegal migrant laborers sneak into the country, disrupting the labor supply and creating social problems. Managing migrant laborers so that the supply equals the demand is challenging for many countries.

Like many former British colonies, Australia is easily accessible to migrant laborers. This multicultural society is very welcoming to migrant laborers, whose work contributes to the economy. Their efforts are rewarded financially, and citizenship is available to those desiring it.

✓ CheckPoint

How do countries make themselves accessible to migrant laborers?

12-1 Assessment

REVIEW GLOBAL BUSINESS TERMS

Define the following term.

1. migrant laborers

REVIEW GLOBAL BUSINESS CONCEPTS

2. Explain why people become migrant workers.

3. Why do some countries have need for migrant workers?

4. List three things that make countries attractive to migrant laborers.

5. Why do migrant laborers prefer accessible countries that are accepting of them?

SOLVE GLOBAL BUSINESS PROBLEMS

Your boss has asked you to identify which of the following employees is a migrant laborer for a report. You work for a business headquartered in Portland, Oregon.

6. Joel Hoskins, 25, a U.S. citizen, born in San Francisco

7. Marie Broussine, 43, a French citizen, born in Paris

8. Ali Jamshidian, 37, a soon-to-be U.S. naturalized citizen, born in Tehran

9. Jose Lopez, 19, U.S. citizen, born in San Juan, Puerto Rico

THINK CRITICALLY

10. Would you consider becoming a migrant laborer? Why?

11. What do the most of the countries with the greatest need for migrant workers have in common?

12. Why might Canada be more accessible to migrant laborers than the United States?

13. Why might the United Kingdom be attractive to migrant laborers?

MAKE ACADEMIC CONNECTIONS

14. **CULTURAL STUDIES** Why are many migrant laborers from Commonwealth countries working in the United Kingdom?

15. **HISTORY** Why must women have slightly more than two children on average to maintain a country's population and labor force?

16. **LAW** Why do different countries have different immigration laws?

Photodisc/Getty Images

GOALS

- Describe historical reasons why labor unions were formed and the legal problems they faced.

- Discuss the effects and nature of international labor activities.

- Discuss the history of labor unions and their current status.

Formation of Labor Unions

Understanding how unions started provides insight into how labor and management interact today. A **labor union** is an organization of workers whose goal is improving members' working conditions, wages, and benefits. The important principle behind unions is that there is strength in numbers. It is relatively easy to ignore the complaints of one or two employees who are unhappy with some aspect of their jobs. However, it is much more difficult to discount the concerns of a large organized group of employees.

LABOR UNIONS IN THE UNITED STATES

The members of the early unions in the United States were skilled workers—shoemakers, printers, carpenters, and tailors. Their goal was to protect industry wage rates by preventing other workers who were willing to work for lower wages from getting hired.

The first large modern unions in the United States were formed during the nineteenth century as a result of the Industrial Revolution. Previously, goods had been made in small quantities and at a fairly slow pace by skilled workers. With the onset of the Industrial Revolution, more goods were produced at a cheaper cost and on a larger scale with the help of machines. Working conditions in factories consisted of long hours of work, unsafe machinery, low wages, few or no benefits, and the use of child labor. In an effort to improve these conditions, workers formed unions.

GLOBAL BUSINESS SPOTLIGHT

THE NOBLE ORDER OF THE KNIGHTS OF LABOR

The Noble Order of the Knights of Labor was founded in 1869 as a secret organization by a group of tailors in Philadelphia. Its membership expanded to include both skilled and unskilled workers of all kinds from all over the country. The Knights of Labor supported a broad plan of reform, including the eight-hour workday, abolition of child labor, and public ownership of utilities and railways. The success of a large strike in 1885 against railroads boosted membership in the union significantly. Soon, membership had reached 800,000.

However, the Knights of Labor began losing influence as strikes became less successful and more violent. The very diversity of the union prevented a sense of solidarity among its members. Unable to manage the huge union membership, its leaders met with a steady stream of defeats, and members began leaving the organization. By 1900, the Knights of Labor had virtually disappeared.

Think Critically

1. What factors led to the disappearance of the Noble Order of the Knights of Labor?
2. If it existed today, why would the Noble Order of the Knights of Labor likely be ineffective?

LEGAL STATUS OF THE FIRST UNIONS

Establishing unions in the early years was not easy. U.S. employers formed their own associations to destroy the employees' efforts to organize unions. Management sought the help of the courts, which tended to sympathize with employers rather than with employees.

Unions were described as "criminal conspiracies" whose goal was to hurt trade and commerce. Union members were described as communists, anarchists, and outside agitators by the courts and by management.

A common technique employers used to prevent union activity was to obtain an injunction. An **injunction** is a court order that immediately stops a person or group from carrying out a specific action. Although injunctions were lifted eventually, they stopped union activities and caused the unions to use their time and money to fight legal battles. Union and management conflicts also led to violence and bloodshed. Efforts by management to keep unions in check were matched by the efforts of an ever increasing union membership.

LEGAL STATUS OF UNIONS TODAY

Today U.S. workers have the legal right to join labor unions. The National Labor Relations Act (1935) gave most private-sector workers the right to form unions, bargain with employers, and strike. **Collective bargaining** is negotiation between union workers and their employers on issues of wages, benefits, and working conditions. Because supervisors are considered to be agents of employers, they do not have collective bargaining rights.

The use of injunctions in labor disputes has been limited since 1932. Congress has passed many laws to protect unions and to promote stable labor-management relations. State and local government employees are covered by the various state, county, and city laws. Federal government employees cannot go on strike or negotiate over wages or other money matters.

✓ CheckPoint

How was the legal system in the United States used to discourage union activity?

Labor Unions in Other Countries

In the United States, labor unions developed after laborers already had basic civil rights, such as the right to vote. Labor unions in the United States were mostly concerned with the right to bargain collectively for working conditions. However, unions are not confined to the United States. For example, the close economic relationship between the United States and Canada led to the formation of branches of many U.S. unions in Canada. Typically, these unions represent the workers of U.S. companies operating in Canada. Such unions call themselves international unions. In recent years, Canadian workers have begun to sever their ties with U.S. unions and to establish their own unions.

European labor groups were the vehicle through which workers gained freedom from feudalism, as well as various rights and powers through collective action. There is a strong sense of worker identity in these unions.

Unions in many European countries are major institutions that are often active in national politics. In the United Kingdom, the Labour Party is closely linked with labor unions. Unions provide funds to the party and help in national elections. Historically, when the Labour Party is in power, government policies are more favorable toward unions.

©David P. Lewis, 2009/Used under license from Shutterstock.com

In Germany, unions are organized along industry lines. The unions tend to be quite wealthy and to invest their money very carefully in businesses such as banking, insurance, and housing. German unions are also actively involved in the management of businesses. By law, they have representatives on the boards of directors of companies. This policy of having union members serve on the boards of directors is known as **codetermination**.

Japan suffered from much labor unrest in the late 1940s, and the 1950s brought so many strikes that industry output was hampered. Today in Japan, however, the relationship between unions and employers is usually cooperative in nature.

National unions realize that multinational companies sometimes try to escape the unions by transferring production to other countries. Unions perceive this as a threat to the job security of their members. To prevent this, unions have tried to consult with unions in other countries and coordinate their responses to company actions.

Multinational labor activity may increase in the future as the global economy grows in complexity and interdependence. However, national labor unions are divided by differences of opinion. The influence of government and legislation varies significantly from country to country. The level of economic development in a country has a strong effect on the strength and power of a union.

The International Labor Organization is a specialized agency of the United Nations, with headquarters in Geneva, Switzerland. Its primary goal is to improve conditions for workers all over the world. It has been active in establishing minimum standards for working conditions for member-countries to meet.

✓ CheckPoint

What factors affect the strength and power of unions in different countries?

Union Past and Present

What is the status of union membership today? Have the economic fluctuations of the last several decades helped or hurt unions and their collective bargaining strength? What effect have the strides in technology had on unionized industries?

EVOLUTION OF THE AFL-CIO

In the United States, labor unions were originally organized along craft lines. Workers with a particular skill formed a local or national union to represent their needs. The American Federation of Labor (AFL), formed in 1886, combined these craft unions to form a huge national labor union—a union of labor unions.

In the 1900s, with the growth of large industries such as automobile, rubber, and steel, some leaders of the AFL pushed to organize the ever increasing number of mass-production workers. Indeed, workers had already begun to form unions not on the basis of their skills, but on the basis of the industry in which they worked. Thus, the workers in the automobile industry organized to form the United Auto Workers Union, and steel industry workers organized to form the United Steel Workers Union.

Leaders of the AFL were divided about whether to allow these unskilled and semiskilled workers into the AFL. This division led to enormous tension in the single largest labor union of the country. Some members of the AFL established the Committee for Industrial Organizations (CIO) in an effort to recruit members from the ranks of industrial workers. (Its name was later changed to the Congress of Industrial Organizations.) The CIO quickly gained millions of members, unionizing workers even where no unions had previously existed. In retaliation, the AFL expelled the unions and their leaders who had organized the CIO. The CIO, with its diverse union membership, became an organization completely separate from the AFL.

In 1955, the AFL and CIO merged to form the AFL-CIO. The **AFL-CIO** is an organization of American unions that uses its size and resources to influence legislation that affects its members. Today most U.S. unions are members of this organization.

Unions that are strictly craft or strictly industrial are less common today. Most unions have both craft and industrial workers. In addition, unions today have a more diverse membership. Workers in a wide variety of industries and occupations often belong to the same union. Teamster's Union members are a good example of this diversity. They range from truck drivers and chauffeurs to warehouse employees, from service station employees to workers in soft-drink plants, and from dairy workers to airline employees.

Work as a Team

Discuss the future of unions in the United States. Share your thoughts about opportunities for union growth in specific industries.

©Andre Klaassen, 2009/ Used under license from Shutterstock.com

MEMBERSHIP IN UNIONS TODAY

Union membership in the United States is about 12 percent of the total workforce. In the early 1950s, nearly 33 percent of the total workforce was unionized. There are many reasons for this decline in union membership. Manufacturing industries, which traditionally have been union strongholds, have become a smaller part of the economy. Today more jobs are being created in service industries, such as restaurants, banks, and hospitals. Unions have had less experience organizing in service industries. The working conditions in service industries are much different from those in manufacturing industries.

The government has enacted laws that mandate a minimum wage, overtime pay, safe working conditions, and equal employment opportunities for all. Therefore, there is less need to join a union today for collective bargaining with employers.

The decline in union membership is not confined to the United States. Most developed countries with economies and government policies similar to those of the United States have experienced a similar membership decline. Figure 12-2 shows the percentage of the labor force that is active in unions in European Union countries.

✓ **Check**Point

Why is union membership declining in many developed countries?

TRADE UNION MEMBERSHIP FOR EU COUNTRIES

Country	Estimated Percentage of Labor Force	Country	Estimated Percentage of Labor Force
Austria	33%	Latvia	16%
Belgium	50%	Lithuania	14%
Bulgaria	20%	Luxembourg	46%
Cyprus	70%	Malta	59%
Czech Republic	20%	Netherlands	24%
Denmark	80%	Poland	16%
Estonia	12%	Portugal	20%
Finland	75%	Romania	33%
France	8%	Slovak Republic	25%
Germany	20%	Slovenia	44%
Greece	30%	Spain	16%
Hungary	17%	Sweden	78%
Ireland	35%	United Kingdom	28%
Italy	34%		

Source: *European Trade Union Institute*

Figure 12-2 Compared to most European Union countries, the percentage of U.S. workers who belong to a union (12%) is quite small.

INTERNATIONAL BUSINESS PERSPECTIVE
History

UNITED KINGDOM UNIONS

Under the leadership of Prime Minister Margaret Thatcher, the Conservative Party formed a new government in 1979. She believed in a free market economy with as little governmental intervention or involvement as possible. She also thought that British labor unions were harming the economy of the United Kingdom through ongoing labor unrest.

When Margaret Thatcher assumed the top office, more than half of British workers were union members who were closely affiliated with the opposing Labour Party. During the dozen years of her government, a series of laws were passed that substantially reduced the power and influence of British unions.

Many of the labor law provisions were modeled after those in the United States, where labor laws are much less open to abuse. Various types of strikes were outlawed. The power of union leaders was reduced. Workers could change or end union representation. Strikes that wrecked havoc on the economy diminished significantly, and union membership plunged.

Early 2009 brought a series of unofficial wildcat strikes regarding the use of foreign workers on British projects. A European Union directive that protesters contend helps businesses to hire foreign workers is a source of conflict, as is Labour Party Prime Minister Gordon Brown's 2007 pledge of "British jobs for British workers."

Think Critically

1. Why did Margaret Thatcher oppose the unions in the United Kingdom?
2. Why was Margaret Thatcher able to change radically the labor laws in the United Kingdom?
3. How do you think the changes in the labor laws benefited the British economy?
4. How did tough economic times contribute to labor unrest in 2009?

©David Fowler, 2009/Used under license from Shutterstock.com

©Mikhail Levit, 2009/Used under license from Shutterstock.com

12-2 Assessment

Study Tools

www.cengage.com/school/genbus/intlbiz

REVIEW GLOBAL BUSINESS TERMS

Define each of the following terms.

1. labor union
2. injunction
3. collective bargaining
4. codetermination
5. AFL-CIO

REVIEW GLOBAL BUSINESS CONCEPTS

6. Explain how the Industrial Revolution created conditions that led to the rise of unions.

7. What is the significance of the National Labor Relations Act of 1935?

8. Why did the American Federation of Labor and the Congress of Industrial Organizations break apart?

SOLVE GLOBAL BUSINESS PROBLEMS

Your restaurant is in a border town and employs workers from each of the two adjacent countries. Your chefs, kitchen helpers, servers, and cashiers have joined a union to negotiate a collective bargaining agreement with you. The agreement will cover wages, working conditions, and other terms of employment. Your goal is to keep the restaurant profitable while meeting the demands of employees.

9. Would you agree to a minimum wage of $12 per hour for all employees? Why or why not?

10. Are you willing to accept the risk of a strike if the employees' demand for at least two weeks of paid vacation for each employee every year is not met? Why or why not?

11. What are your options if the union does not take your proposals seriously?

THINK CRITICALLY

12. When you attain your first full-time job, would you consider joining a union? Why or why not?

13. Why has it been very difficult for unions in different countries to cooperate with each other, except to exchange information?

14. Why are federal government and many other public employees (such as police officers and firefighters) not allowed to strike?

MAKE ACADEMIC CONNECTIONS

15. **CULTURAL STUDIES** Why might cultures with an individualistic orientation tend to be less tolerant of unions than many other cultures?

16. **LAW** Does codetermination favor the rights of employees over the rights of managers and owners? Why or why not?

12-3 Unions in the Workplace Today

Photodisc/Getty Images

GOALS

- Explain how union representation is achieved.
- Describe methods used to settle labor negotiations.
- Describe how union and management goals are similar.

Achieving Union Representation

The main purpose of a union is to improve the working conditions of its members. Before it can achieve this objective, however, it has to accomplish several steps. First, the union must win the right to represent the workers by a majority vote. Then the workers must individually decide if they want to join the union.

ELECTIONS

Major unions send union organizers to workplaces to convince workers to become union members. Union organizers are trained and experienced in persuading workers to join a union. In other cases, workers may decide on their own that they would like to join a union. When this happens, the workers themselves contact the union.

Unions are always eager to organize workers to increase their membership base. Union members pay membership dues, so more members means more resources for the union. This in turn allows the union to represent union workers more effectively and to persuade new workers to join.

In most cases, the next step is to hold an election. A **union representation election** is held to find out if the workers in a workplace really want to become union members. To win the right to represent workers, the union must get a simple majority of the votes cast. Once the union wins, the employer is

PRNewsFoto/United Food and Commercial Workers International Union/AP Photo

required by law to refrain from making arrangements with individual workers. The employer can only negotiate with the union concerning issues such as workers' pay, work hours, benefits, problems, and discipline.

Intense campaigning by both the union and the employer often occurs during the period before the election. The union tries to persuade the workers to vote for the union. The employer tries to dissuade the workers from doing so. To ensure that the election conditions are free and fair, activities such as bribing and threatening workers are forbidden by law.

TYPES OF UNION REPRESENTATION

If the union wins the representation election, it obtains the right to represent all workers, not just those who voted for the union. However, some workers may not want to join the union, and they cannot be forced to join. All workers, even those who choose not to join the union, will receive the benefits of union services. For this reason, the union usually requires that those workers opting not to join still pay a certain fee. This arrangement in which all workers must pay either union dues or a fee is called a **union shop**. It enables the union to obtain resources to perform its functions.

In a **closed shop**, workers are required to join a union before they are hired. Today, closed shops are generally illegal. Nearly half of the states have right-to-work laws. These laws prohibit unions and employers from charging dues or fees as a condition of employment. The other extreme, an open shop, is also very rare. In an **open shop**, workers may choose to join a union or not. If not, they need not pay a fee of any kind. This arrangement is not in the best interest of the union because it may discourage workers from contributing to the union. At the same time, the union has the legal obligation to provide services to the nonmember workers.

✓ **Check**Point

What does a union gain if it wins a representation election?

Work as a Team

Discuss the advantages and disadvantages of using arbitration to resolve labor disputes.

Tools of Labor Negotiations

Labor and management are required by law to bargain in good faith over issues of wages, hours, and working conditions. However, they may also negotiate over any other issue as long as it is not something illegal. For example, labor and management can negotiate over group health benefits or family leave allowances. Collective bargaining negotiations are often complicated affairs, and it can take several months for employers and union representatives to reach an agreement.

GRIEVANCE PROCEDURE

A grievance procedure is included in most collective bargaining contracts. A **grievance procedure** is the steps that must be followed to resolve a complaint by an employee, the union, or the employer. A discussion of complaints usually begins at the lowest level of management and union officials. If they are unable to settle the matter, the problem then moves to higher levels until the two sides reach an agreement.

ARBITRATION

If the parties cannot agree, an arbitrator is needed. An **arbitrator** is an unbiased third party who is called in to resolve problems. The courts have agreed not to overturn or review an arbitrator's decision. Therefore, the decision of the arbitrator is generally final and binding.

Arbitrators are usually lawyers, university professors, or a business person with specific expertise. An arbitrator may be anyone on whom the union and the employer mutually agree. Most arbitrators are members of the American Arbitration Association or the Federal Mediation and Conciliation Service (FMCS). The FMCS also provides services to break deadlocks or mediate disputes that arise when the union and the employer are involved in collective bargaining.

NETBookmark

In India and around the world, child laborers are forming groups and working together to fight for the right to work, a living wage, and better working conditions. Access the web site shown below and click on the link for Chapter 12. Read the article entitled "Underage Unions: Child Laborers Speak Up." Then write a paragraph explaining why adult labor groups resist participation by children in labor decisions.

www.cengage.com/school/genbus/intlbiz

WORK STOPPAGES IN THE UNITED STATES

Year	Strikes	Workers Involved	Days Involved	Percentage of Working Time
1965	268	999,000	15,140,000	10
1970	381	2,468,000	52,761,000	29
1975	235	965,000	17,563,000	9
1980	187	795,000	20,844,000	9
1985	54	324,000	7,079,000	3
1990	44	185,000	5,926,000	2
1995	31	192,000	5,771,000	2
2000	39	394,000	20,419,000	6
2005	22	100,000	1,736,000	1

Source: *Statistical Abstract of the United States: 2009*, U.S. Bureau of the Census, Table 641.

Figure 12-3 Overall, the number of strikes in the United States has declined during recent decades.

STRIKES

When bargaining with employers, union leaders sometimes threaten strikes to force the employer to make the concessions wanted by union leaders. A **strike** occurs when employees refuse to work to force an employer to agree to certain demands. Part of the dues that members pay usually goes into a strike fund. The union then uses this money to pay striking workers when the need arises.

Some grievance procedures include a *no-strike clause*, which makes it unlawful for workers to go on strike. This allows the company and the union to address a problem when it arises but does not allow interruption of work. Agreeing to a no-strike clause is a big concession on the part of the union. Striking is the most powerful weapon a union has against an employer. In turn, however, the employer agrees to a process to settle any complaints that arise.

Over the years, there has been a decline in strike activity in the United States. Figure 12-3 shows that the number of strikes, the number of workers who actually go on strike, the total number of workdays lost due to strike, and the percentage of working time involved have declined. There are many reasons for this decline in the occurrence of strikes.

- Union membership is decreasing.
- Some workers are not willing to risk loss of income and benefits.
- Arbitrators help resolve deadlocks before they turn into strikes.
- Businesses have contingency plans for operating during a strike.
- Increased automation of manufacturing processes has reduced the effectiveness of strikes.
- Replacement workers are more willing to cross picket lines.
- Workers' fears about losing permanent jobs due to a strike have increased.

Work as a Team

Discuss possible reasons for the decline in the number of strikes in recent years and how this influences the power of labor unions.

Given the general decline in the effectiveness of the strike weapon, unions are resorting to techniques such as pickets, boycotts, and corporate campaigns to put pressure on employers.

✓ **Check**Point

What are three methods used to secure agreement between unions and management?

Management and Labor Unions

Generally speaking, managers would prefer to work without having to deal with labor unions. Labor unions reduce a manager's freedom to act and to make decisions. Managers must consult with the union on many issues. In addition, unions seek higher wages, better benefits, and improved working conditions for their members. Therefore, the profits of the company are reduced. However, workers who feel secure in their jobs, who believe their wages are fair, and who enjoy safe working conditions are more productive than workers who feel otherwise.

A Question of Ethics

INTERNATIONAL STRIKEBREAKERS

Workers at a brewery near Sydney, Australia, went on strike to demand job security. New Zealand-based multinational company Lion Nathan owned the brewery. Within hours of the beginning of the strike, Lion Nathan hired 50 New Zealanders and flew them to Sydney to take the jobs of the strikers. With unemployment above 10 percent in New Zealand, there were many people willing to cross the Tasman Sea to work. Lion Nathan was able to employ New Zealanders in Australia with ease because treaties between the two countries allowed citizens of one country to work in the other.

The conduct of Lion Nathan confirmed the worst fears the union in Sydney had about multi-national firms. In New Zealand, many people criticized the 50 strikebreakers who went to work in Australia. They pointed out that an Australian firm in New Zealand could easily employ Australian strikebreakers if New Zealand workers went on strike.

Think Critically

1. If you were a citizen of Australia when the strikebreakers were used, how would you feel? Why?
2. Was it ethical for Lion Nathan to hire New Zealand strikebreakers to work in Australia? Why?
3. Why did many New Zealanders respond negatively to the use of strikebreakers?

GLOBAL TECHNOLOGY TRENDS

Pinnacle PLC Goes Electronic

In response to aggressive efforts to unionize its operations in several western European countries, the management of Pinnacle PLC decided to change directions. It decided to phase out its luxury goods retail operations in Europe and Asia and to expand its electronic marketing operations over a three-year period.

Managers of Pinnacle PLC decided to transfer its primary operations to Hong Kong for various reasons. Among them were its large English-speaking population, its familiarity with both Western and Eastern business practices, and its manufacturing and shipping capabilities.

During the transition, the managers of Pinnacle PLC realized that major changes in operations would be necessary. They decided to refine and expand the company web site. In conjunction with that, they agreed about the need to find reliable manufacturers, suppliers, and shippers in Southeast Asia. Further, they developed a plan to create a niche market for Pinnacle products with a sustainable competitive advantage. The managers insisted that the emerging electronic operations be fully prepared to cope with the expected volume of web site activity and the demand for products.

Think Critically

1. Do you think it was ethical for the managers of Pinnacle PLC to move primary operations to Hong Kong to avoid unionization efforts? Why or why not?
2. What suggestions would you offer to managers of Pinnacle PLC to improve the transition plans?

Employers use many techniques to keep unions out of the workplace. When wages and benefits are good and employees are treated fairly, the workers have no particular need for a union. Workers find unions attractive only when they believe they are being treated unfairly. Many employers resort to illegal activities, such as disciplining union sympathizers or threatening dismissal, to discourage workers from joining a union. In other situations, the employer may prolong the collective bargaining sessions in an attempt to discredit the union in the eyes of its members.

Employers have the right to a **lockout**, which is literally locking employees out of the workplace to force a union to agree to certain demands. A lockout is similar to the workers' right to strike.

WHEN UNIONS AND MANAGEMENT WORK TOGETHER

Unions and employers have often viewed each other more as adversaries than as allies. In recent years, however, there have been an increasing number of cases in which unions and employers have begun to cooperate not only to save jobs, but also to increase productivity. Employers are acknowledging that trained and experienced workers are an asset because they contribute to the efficient operation of the business. Unions, too, realize that their ability to demand better wages and improved working conditions depends on the overall success of the company.

 **CheckPoint**
What are four methods that have been used by management to discourage unionization or influence collective bargaining?

12-3 UNIONS IN THE WORKPLACE

REVIEW GLOBAL BUSINESS TERMS

Define each of the following terms.

Study Tools

www.cengage.com/school/genbus/intlbiz

1. union representation election
2. union shop
3. closed shop
4. open shop
5. grievance procedure
6. arbitrator
7. strike
8. lockout

REVIEW GLOBAL BUSINESS CONCEPTS

9. What is the process for forming a union in a workplace?

10. What are the reasons for the decline in strike activity?

11. Why is there a trend toward cooperation between employers and unions?

SOLVE GLOBAL BUSINESS PROBLEMS

You are a union organizer trying to persuade the overseas employees of a computer manufacturer to form a union. Because the pay, working conditions, and vacation policy at the plant are well below those at the unionized U.S. plant, you think you can succeed.

12. The overseas employees do seem somewhat dissatisfied. How would you approach them?

13. What would be your top priority that would most benefit these employees in a developing country?

14. How would you respond if the company promises all of its employees a 30 percent raise if they reject the union? Why?

THINK CRITICALLY

15. What reasons might an employer use to persuade workers not to support a union in a representation election?

16. Why do you think other developed countries have a greater percentage of workers who are union members than the United States does?

17. What does an employer gain by having unionized workers?

MAKE ACADEMIC CONNECTIONS

18. **TECHNOLOGY** How might technology be used to help persuade employees to form a union?

19. **CULTURAL STUDIES** What aspects of the mainstream U.S. culture discourage union membership?

20. **LAW** Why do you think closed shops are rare in the United States?

21. **TECHNOLOGY** Use the Internet to locate resources that unions have available online.

CHAPTER SUMMARY

12-1 MIGRATION OF LABOR

A Migrant laborers are people who move to another country for work.

B A country's need for migrant laborers is influenced by the level of economic activity and the proportion of working-age population.

C Having a growing developed economy, a welcoming multicultural society, and a high quality of education make a country attractive to migrant laborers.

D A country with a dynamic economy and open and accepting people and laws has high accessibility to migrant laborers.

12-2 MILESTONES OF THE LABOR MOVEMENT

A Labor unions arose out of the harsh working conditions of the Industrial Revolution to improve members' working conditions, wages, and benefits.

B The AFL and CIO merged to form the largest U.S. organization of unions, the AFL-CIO. Its size and resources make it very powerful.

C Unions in various countries have difficulty cooperating because of differences of opinion, the influence of government and legislation, and the level of economic development.

D Membership in unions is declining in most developed countries because of the increase in service industries versus manufacturing industries and government legislation that is favorable to labor.

12-3 UNIONS IN THE WORKPLACE TODAY

A A workplace becomes unionized when a union wins a representation election.

B Most collective bargaining contracts include a grievance procedure. An arbitrator may be brought in to settle a dispute. A union may use the power of a strike to persuade a company to meet its demands.

C Employers may reduce unionization by offering attractive wages, benefits, and conditions so there is no need for a union. An employer may also illegally discipline or threaten union sympathizers, prolong collective bargaining sessions to discredit a union, or engage in a lockout.

D Unions and employers frequently cooperate as allies today. Unions recognize that a profitable company can afford to offer better wages and conditions, while companies recognize that a satisfied workforce can increase productivity and company success.

GLOBAL REFOCUS

Read the case at the beginning of this chapter, and answer the following questions.

1. What caused the Polish workers to organize and strike?

2. What actions can workers take when they believe their economic and political rights have been violated?

REVIEW GLOBAL BUSINESS TERMS

Match the terms listed with the definitions.

1. An unbiased third party called in to resolve problems whose decision is usually final and binding.
2. A procedure held to find out if the workers in a workplace really want to become union members.
3. A court order that immediately stops a party from carrying out a specific action.
4. A workplace in which workers may choose to join a union or not.
5. A policy of having union members serve on the boards of directors.
6. The steps that must be followed to resolve a complaint by an employee, the union, or the employer.
7. An organization of workers whose goal is improving members' working conditions, wages, and benefits.

a. AFL-CIO
b. arbitrator
c. closed shop
d. codetermination
e. collective bargaining
f. grievance procedure
g. injunction
h. labor union
i. lockout
j. migrant laborers
k. open shop
l. strike
m. union representation election
n. union shop

8. A workplace in which workers are required to join a union before they are hired.
9. Negotiation between union workers and their employers on issues of wages, benefits, and working conditions.
10. A refusal by employees to work in order to force an employer to agree to certain demands.
11. A workplace in which all workers must pay either union dues or a fee.
12. The closing down of a workplace by an employer to force a union to agree to certain demands.
13. The organization of American unions that uses its size and resources to influence legislation that affects its members.
14. People who move to another country for work.

MAKE GLOBAL BUSINESS DECISIONS

15. List three countries to which you would consider migrating for work.

16. Which factor would be most important in deciding if you want to be a migrant laborer—need, attractiveness, or accessibility? Why?

17. Identify and contact a union member. Develop a list of questions to ask the person. In your interview, you may wish to ask how the person feels about the union and how the union affects his or her job and workplace.

18. Collect advertisements, pictures, articles, and other information used by unions to persuade consumers to buy union-made products or patronize unionized businesses. What reasons do the advertisements give for supporting those products and businesses? How persuasive are the advertisements? Why?

19. Create, administer, and summarize the findings from a five to ten question survey that determines the attitudes of classmates toward unions.

20. Obtain information about the history of strikes in the United States as well as in other countries for an industry of your choice. Try to explain the differences in strike rates among the countries.

21. Communicate with a union in your community to obtain a copy of a collective bargaining agreement. Review the agreement, and find out how the contract deals with grievances, union dues, seniority, leaves, and strikes. Summarize the information for your class.

22. List reasons why workers in banking, financial services, and real estate are less likely to join a union. What do you think a union could offer that would attract these workers to join?

MAKE ACADEMIC CONNECTIONS

23. **TECHNOLOGY** Visit the web site of the AFL-CIO, and read about one of the issues presented at the site. Summarize the issue in a short paper.

24. **CULTURAL STUDIES** Research Islamic law to find out what effect, if any, its provisions have on employees. Share your findings with your classmates.

25. **COMMUNICATIONS** If you want to persuade employees in a high-context culture to unionize, would print or verbal communication be more effective? Why?

26. **HISTORY** Why did a number of early U.S. unions disappear by the beginning of the twentieth century?

27. **HISTORY** Research the contributions of a nationally prominent union leader in a country of your choice, and prepare a related oral report.

28. **CAREER PLANNING** Research the role of unions in a country where you might like to work in the future, and write a summary report.

29. **LAW** Use the Internet to find more information on a law that affects labor unions.

30. **TECHNOLGY** Use the Internet to identify one recent union representation election, the issues in the election, and the final out come.

The GLOBAL *Entrepreneur*

CREATING AN INTERNATIONAL BUSINESS PLAN

Labor-Management Relations

Develop a labor relations plan based on the company and country you have been using in this continuing project, or create a labor plan for a different business or a different country. Make use of previously collected information, and do additional research. This phase of your business plan should answer the following questions.

1. What is the role of organized labor (unions) in the country? What percentage of workers belong to unions? Is union membership on the rise or is it declining?

2. What laws exist to protect workers? What laws exist to protect employers? What laws exist to protect consumers? For example, are there laws that prohibit strikes by police or nurses?

3. What actions are commonly taken by workers to protect their rights?

4. What types of employment positions will be available as a result of your business idea? What are the average wage rates and salary levels for these jobs in that country?

5. What benefits are available to workers in the country?

6. What other issues are of concern to workers in this country?

Prepare a written summary suitable for inclusion in a business plan. Based on the written summary, develop a short oral report (two or three minutes) of your findings.

CHAPTER 13

International Career Planning

13-1 Searching for Your First Job

13-2 Applying for a Job

13-3 Obtaining Future Jobs

starfotograf/iStockphoto.com

GLOBAL FOCUS

A Global Business Career

Jennifer Yoon is an administrative assistant in San Antonio, Texas, for a multinational company with offices in 16 countries. Her company recently posted a job opening for general manager of the new office in Austria. This position will require knowledge of company operations, financial management, marketing, import-export laws, and Austrian business customs.

Jennifer is intrigued by the possibility of having a job overseas, but she realizes that she must temper her enthusiasm with reality. She has not worked full-time in any country other than the United States. However, she has traveled in nine other countries for meetings and short-term work assignments. During her years in school, Jennifer studied global marketing, economic geography, European history, and foreign political systems. While in college, she participated in a work-study program at the Spanish trade office in Washington, D.C. She enjoyed the experience as she learned about the daily challenges of engaging in international business.

As Jennifer considers this job in another country, her thoughts go in two directions. "This is the opportunity I have been waiting and training for," she said to a friend. Then Jennifer went on to say, "But what if I can't adapt to the different culture and business activities?"

Think Critically

1. What educational and work experiences have prepared Jennifer Yoon for a position as general manager?
2. What actions should Jennifer take to apply for the general manager position in the Austrian office?
3. Go to the web site for the Trade Information Center of the U.S. Department of Commerce. Click on Country Information, then on Western Europe. Find the most current commercial guide for Austria.

13-1 Searching for Your First Job

GOALS

- Describe the steps of the career planning process.

- List sources of career planning information.

- Identify factors that affect job availability.

Digital Vision/Getty Images

Career Planning

Some people jump out of bed in the morning and can't wait to get to work. Others go to work thinking only about the weekend or an upcoming vacation. What is the difference between these two groups of people? Selection of your life's work could be the most important decision you make.

THE IMPORTANCE OF WORK

Work not only affects income but also influences the amount of leisure time you have, the people with whom you associate, and many other aspects of your life. Career planning activities are likely to continue throughout your life. Changing personal, social, and economic factors affect job satisfaction and available employment positions. Most people who aspire to international careers begin work in some type of business-related job in their own country. After you have job experience within your own country, you may have opportunities to work outside the country. Over time, you will attain your goal of having an international career.

FIVE STEPS IN CAREER PLANNING

In every society, work is necessary. Work makes it possible for people to have food, clothing, housing, and transportation. Besides fulfilling physical needs, work also has social and psychological benefits. Work allows people the opportunity to gain personal satisfaction through interaction with others and to gain recognition for their performance.

The work a person selects can be viewed as either a job or a career. A **job** is an employment position obtained mainly for money. People may work in one or more jobs during their lives without planning for advancement.

THE CAREER PLANNING PROCESS

Step 1	Determine your personal goals and abilities
Step 2	Evaluate the job market
Step 3	Identify and apply for specific job opportunities
Step 4	Accept the most desirable job offer
Step 5	Plan for personal career development

Figure 13-1 Careful planning is required in order to obtain a position that best suits your interests and abilities.

In contrast, a **career** is a commitment to a profession that requires continuing education and training and has a clear path for advancement. A person may select a career in health care, information systems, marketing, financial management, exporting, or other areas. Regardless of the career you choose, the process of planning a career is the same. Figure 13-1 shows the five steps involved in career planning.

Step 1 Determine Your Personal Goals and Abilities As you plan for a career, start by evaluating your personal situation. Do you like to work with others, or do you prefer to work alone? Would you like to work outside or in an office? Do you enjoy working with words or numbers? Determining your personal goals and abilities will help you start the career planning process.

Step 2 Evaluate the Job Market Next, determine what types of jobs are available. You may want to work as a news reporter on television, or you want to design golf courses. However, few jobs may be available in that field. Look for career areas in which you can adapt your interests, skills, and knowledge.

Step 3 Identify and Apply for Specific Job Opportunities The third step of the process involves presenting yourself to potential employers. After finding organizations with available employment, you will need to communicate your abilities to those responsible for hiring. This communication comes in the form of a resume, application letter, and interview. This also involves on-line communication including social networking. These things help you sell yourself to an employer.

NETBookmark

To learn more about developing a career plan plan that is right for you, access the web site shown below and click on the link for Chapter 13. Read the article about developing a career plan on the Mapping Your Future web site. Then create a career plan for yourself, including a career goal, requirements, current skills and interests, and a plan to reach your career goal.

www.cengage.com/school/genbus/intlbiz

Step 4 **Accept the Most Desirable Job Offer** In this step, evaluate the positive and negative aspects of working for various companies. Compare salaries, employee benefits, work situations, and future opportunities in the organization. Remember that the highest-paying job may not be the most enjoyable one or offer advancement in the future.

Step 5 **Plan for Personal Career Development** Finally, workers should continually evaluate their future. As personal goals and employment opportunities change, you may want to obtain further education and training. Technology, economic conditions, or other factors may eliminate certain jobs and force a career change.

Many people work in jobs that are within one country. This is called the *domestic employment market*. Other work opportunities involve international business. For example, a company in Poland may make suits that are sold in Canada. A Japanese bank may have an office in Egypt. As trade among nations expands, the number and types of global careers increase.

✓ CheckPoint
What are the five steps in career planning?

Exploring Career Information

Every business and personal decision can be easier to make if you do your homework. Obtaining relevant information helps with all of life's activities. Selecting and planning a career is no different. Career information is available from five main sources.

Library Materials Your school or public library is an excellent starting point for career information. You can obtain books and other publications about selecting a career field, searching for a job, and planning for an interview. These items may be in print or in electronic form.

One very helpful source is the *Occupational Outlook Handbook*, published by the Bureau of Labor Statistics (part of the U.S. Department of Labor). This reference book is revised every two years and provides detailed information about jobs in many career areas. It is also available online. Other helpful career resources include the *Dictionary of Occupational Titles* and the *Occupational Outlook Quarterly*.

Media Occasionally, newspapers publish articles with job search hints and career trends. Television and radio reports about job planning and economic trends can also be useful when selecting a career. For example, news about a company expanding into other nations provides information about the availability of international jobs.

Personal and Professional Contacts Every person you know can help you learn more about work and successful career planning. Talking with friends, relatives, and people in your community about their jobs can be very useful. An **informational interview** is a meeting with another person to gather information about a career or an organization. During an informational interview, you can learn about required skills, job duties, and potential earnings for careers. People increasingly use online networks such as LinkedIn to expand their network of professional contacts.

GLOBAL TECHNOLOGY TRENDS

The Monster Network

Monster is a leading international career network. It offers a variety of services for job candidates and employers around the world.

Monster is not just one web site; it is a network of more than 30 country-specific web sites. Job candidates can post their resumes and access job postings in countries in Europe, North America, the Middle East, and Asia and the Pacific Rim. Most country-specific information is available in the predominant local language(s). For example, Monster Canada offers the option of French or English while Monster Italy uses only Italian.

In addition to connecting job seekers with potential employers, Monster provides information about job profiles, resumes, interviewing, salaries, networking, diversity, and relocation for job candidates. Because millions of job seekers visit Monster network sites each day, Monster can help employers find the right employees to fill their vacancies through the use of screening and hiring tools. Employers can buy job postings and the resumes of the best job candidates from Monster.

Think Critically

1. What advantages does an international career network such as Monster have over a network that focuses on a single country?
2. Why do you think Monster maintains a network of country-specific web sites?

In addition, job fairs are held in many large cities. Employers pay for time and space to provide information about available jobs, and some may even interview candidates. Talking with company representatives at job fairs can provide applicants with additional information about companies.

Many career areas also have professional associations. Some will admit student members. The meetings of these associations, as well as the journals they publish, can be additional sources of career information and networking.

Community Organizations Most communities have business and civic organizations such as the Chamber of Commerce, Jaycees (Junior Chamber of Commerce), and Rotary Club. Meetings held by these groups can be a source of current business trends. The Chamber of Commerce commonly publishes a directory of its member businesses.

Internet The Internet is increasingly becoming a source of employment information. Many companies have their own web sites that include a list of current job openings and career information. Career sites, such as Monster, CareerBuilder, College Recruiter, and HotJobs, allow job seekers to post their resumes, as well as see what jobs have been posted. Many of these sites are more than job boards. They offer tools for creating resumes and preparing for interviews along with career news and advice. An Internet search can help locate professional associations relevant to specific fields of work. Some Internet newsgroups are also organized for particular professions and may provide career information.

✓ CheckPoint
What are five sources for career information?

Identifying Career Opportunities

Why do some people excel in their chosen careers while others never seem to find satisfying work? The answer to this question involves many things. As you start thinking about your life's work, consider your personal abilities and talents along with what jobs will be available. Trade among nations and technology will eliminate some careers while creating others.

FACTORS AFFECTING CAREER CHOICE

Will your career be one that you enjoy? Will the work involve an activity that will be in demand in the global economy? Career choice is influenced by a variety of factors, as shown in Figure 13-2.

Personal Factors What do you like to do? What do you do well? Answers to these questions can be keys to successful career planning. In addition, when selecting a career, decide how much and what type of education you plan to obtain, what experience you have, and what your personal goals are.

An evaluation of personal interests, experiences, values, and goals is important when selecting the right career. Knowledge of global business activities, geography, foreign cultures, and another language can provide a foundation for an international business career.

Demographic Trends As the population of a society changes, so do the jobs that are available. For example, an increase in the number of working parents in the United States increased the demand for food service and child-care workers. Also, as people live longer, employment in travel services, health care, and retirement facilities expands.

Geographic Influences The location of employment opportunities can change. As economic growth occurs in a geographic region, more jobs are available. However, when economic conditions decline, fewer jobs will exist in that region.

The location of natural resources also influences employment. Areas with seaports and rivers commonly have shipbuilding and shipping industries. Fertile land usually is used for agricultural purposes. Rich mineral deposits lead to mining and related metal-product industries.

Economic Conditions Jobs, like goods and services, are affected by the basic economic principle of supply and demand. For example, as more people want and use electronic gadgets, employment in industries that make, program, and sell these items increases. Consumer demand in the economy has a strong effect on the job market.

Changing prices affect available jobs. When inflation occurs, people

FACTORS INFLUENCING CAREER SELECTION

Personal Factors	• Interests • Abilities • Age • Education • Experience • Personal goals
Demographic Trends	• Age of population • Characteristics of workforce • Population distribution • Population growth
Geographic Influences	• Location of natural resources • Industries
Economic Conditions	• Consumer demand • Inflation • Interest rates
Industry Trends	• Global competition • Changing uses of technology

Figure 13-2 The career a person selects is affected by many factors.

usually reduce spending. Lower consumer demand, once again, causes a decline in the need for products and for the workers who make them.

Changes in the value of the currency of a nation will affect its balance of trade. As the demand for the goods and services of a country increases, employment opportunities in that nation also increase.

Interest rates affect employment opportunities. If companies must pay high rates to borrow for new equipment or to build new factories, fewer businesses will make these capital purchases. As a result, people who build this equipment and these factories will have fewer job opportunities.

Industry Trends Companies have always competed against each other. However, as global business activities expand, foreign competition changes the types of jobs available.

Another business trend affecting jobs is the increased use of technology. Companies with computers in offices, stores, and factories require that employees be able to operate this equipment. In addition, many jobs previously done by people are now handled by computer systems.

Work as a Team
Discuss demographic trends that are affecting career choices today.

SOURCES OF INFORMATION ABOUT AVAILABLE JOBS

The Internet had become a dominant source of information about available jobs. With millions of jobs posted by all types of employers from small businesses to multinational companies, it might seem as though every available job can be found online. There are some other options to consider. Classified ads, sometimes called help-wanted ads, can be found in the printed and online versions of newspapers. Job postings and classified ads may help a person find work. However, many jobs never appear online or in print. For this reason, personal contacts are an important source of job information. Ask people you know about available jobs where they work. The people you talk with may be able to tell you what skills are needed, where jobs are located, and how to get more information.

Visit places where you would like to work. Some businesses post signs indicating that they have positions available or that they are accepting applications. Other businesses have employment kiosks where you can access a company profile, learn about current employment opportunities, and complete a job application.

State-funded employment services provide information about some available jobs at no charge. Other services, including career advice and skill assessments, may also be available. Employment agencies sometimes can be helpful sources of job information. However, be careful of organizations that charge fees and give no guarantees of helping you find a job.

People seeking work may also consider *job creation*. This involves communicating with possible employers the skills you have that could help their companies. For example, a person may be skilled at researching foreign locations. While an owner may have never considered exporting, a new job position could be created in the company to explore possible foreign locations for exporting goods or services.

✓ CheckPoint
What are five factors that influence the availability of jobs?

INTERNATIONAL BUSINESS PERSPECTIVE
Geography

GEOGRAPHY LEADS TO NETHERLANDS BUSINESS CAREERS

The Netherlands is a small but densely populated country in Northwestern Europe. Also known as Holland, the Netherlands faces the North Sea and shares borders with Germany and Belgium. Much of the country is a low-lying delta, where the branches of the Rhine (Rijn), Meuse (Maas), and Scheldt rivers flow toward the ocean. Over time, the Dutch people have added to their land mass by reclaiming areas that were once wet. Dikes and pumps have made this possible.

With limited natural resources except for water, the enterprising Dutch people have looked outwardly for their livings. Using the available rivers and oceans, they became early traders. By the 17th century, they were globally influential with businesses like the Dutch East India Company. Innovative Dutch traders created stock exchanges, insurance companies, and retirement funds.

Using its location and water as an advantage, Rotterdam has become Europe's largest port. Goods flow by ship, barge, rail, and highway into and out of the Netherlands. Having this efficient worldwide transportation system allows the easy flow of goods that global businesses need. Amsterdam, the business and financial capital of the Netherlands, is nearby. Many important international businesses have offices there. So do the banks that finance their global trade and the related shipping.

The abundant water resources of the Netherlands have led its residents toward careers in international business and supporting fields. Because the Dutch excel in trading, transporting, and banking, many related career opportunities exist. Those interested in international trade might consider such positions as import/export agent, international marketing manager, or foreign trade consultant. Transporting offers career possibilities like shipping and receiving clerk, ship's captain, and truck driver. People liking the financial side might explore such jobs as foreign banknote teller, foreign exchange dealer, or loan review analyst. Given its geography, the Netherlands offers many international business career options.

Think Critically

1. Why are abundant water resources such an advantage to the Netherlands?
2. Since The Hague is the governmental capital of the Netherlands, how can Amsterdam also be called a capital city?
3. Would a career in trading, transporting, or banking be most appealing to you? Why?

©Daniel Leppens, 2009/ Used under license from Shutterstock.com

13-1 Assessment

REVIEW GLOBAL BUSINESS TERMS
Define each of the following terms.

1. job
2. career
3. informational interview

REVIEW GLOBAL BUSINESS CONCEPTS

4. How does a job differ from a career?

5. What is the domestic job market?

6. What type of information can be obtained from an informational interview?

7. How can economic conditions affect the availability of jobs?

SOLVE GLOBAL BUSINESS PROBLEMS

Lack of experience is a common problem faced by beginning workers. You are told, "You don't have enough experience." However, to get experience, you need a job.

Work-related experiences can be obtained through part-time or summer jobs. Most schools offer cooperative work experience or internship programs. Volunteering for community organizations is another method of obtaining work experience. State whether each of the following situations could be relevant experience for a job and why.

8. Supervising youth activities at the community center

9. Writing for the school newspaper

10. Using foreign language skills to translate personal correspondence for foreign visitors

11. Conducting tours of your city for visitors

THINK CRITICALLY

12. Why are you likely to have a part-time or summer job before you have a full-time job?

13. In preparation for an informational interview, gather some questions to ask a person working in international business.

14. Describe international events that could affect the number and types of jobs in a country.

MAKE ACADEMIC CONNECTIONS

15. **CULTURAL STUDIES** Why might a multinational company operating in Estonia hire a manager from Finland?

16. **TECHNOLOGY** Find the web site of a large company that includes job postings. Make a list of the jobs, and describe any that have an international component.

13-2 Applying for a Job

GOALS

- Describe important elements of a resume.

- Explain successful interview techniques.

- Describe other documents that may be involved in applying for a job.

©khz, 2009/ Used under license from Shutterstock.com

Creating a Resume

"Pharmaceutical company has immediate opening for an inventory coordinator. A knowledge of inventory methods and international business practices required." Someday you may encounter a job posting something like this. What actions are necessary for you to obtain this position?

If you find a job that is of interest to you, you must communicate your skills and abilities to your prospective employer. A **resume** is a written summary of a person's education, training, work experience, and other job qualifications. A resume should be prepared in both print and electronic formats and be designed to make a good first impression.

Figure 13-3 shows a sample resume for a high school graduate looking for an inventory coordinator position with a business involved in importing or exporting. The sections included in a resume may vary somewhat, but most include the following sections.

Personal Data A resume starts with your name and contact information including your street address, telephone number, and e-mail address. A person's age (or birth date), marital status, gender, height, and weight should not be listed unless this information is related to specific job qualifications.

Career Objective A brief but precise description of the type of job desired is next. If you have strong qualifications, you can include a short bulleted list of your best qualifications. The following sections of your resume support your objective and prove that you are qualified for the job you seek. A career objective also will be communicated in the related application letter.

Education This section includes schools attended, dates of attendance, and fields of study. A listing of courses taken may be appropriate for classes that relate directly to the job for which you are applying.

Experience This section should include position titles, major job duties, employment dates, and employers' names and addresses for current and past jobs. Community service can be reported like a regular job. Be sure that the description of job duties emphasizes your accomplishments. Include keywords that will appeal to the employer. One good way to do this is to use action-oriented verbs to describe what you did. In the example shown here, you can see that Taylor Powell has experience maintaining the furniture store inventory database.

Related Activities School involvement, hobbies, and other interests directly related to your career can help you get a job. Remember to package these items in terms of how they relate to the desired job.

Honors and Awards A listing of honors and awards can help communicate your ability to do high-quality work.

References People who can report to a prospective employer about your abilities and work experience are **references**. These individuals may be teachers, past employers, community leaders, or adult friends. Be sure to obtain prior permission from the people you plan to use as references. References should not be listed on a resume. However, you will need to have the names, addresses, telephone numbers, and positions of your references available whenever prospective employers ask for them.

A Sample Resume

Taylor D. Powell
1654 Oakdale Court
Central City, Texas 76540
(214) 555-4537
powell.td@mymail.com

CAREER OBJECTIVE	An inventory coordinator position with a business involved in importing of exporting
EDUCATION	Browne High School, Central City, Texas Graduated 2012 **International Business Preparation** International Business Global Marketing Economics French, I, II, III World Geography Business Law
EXPERIENCE	**Inventory Clerk** Jefferson Furniture Co., Allentown, Texas Maintain inventory database July 2012 to present **Volunteer Clerk** Kenton County Animal Rescue, Central City, Texas Maintained inventory of supplies June 2011 to August 2011
RELATED ACTIVITIES	International Business Club, Vice President Student Council, Secretary Central City Electronics Recycling Program, Volunteer International Culture Experience, Participant
HONORS and AWARDS	Finalist, Martin Foundation Global Business Award Service Award, Central City Recycling Program
REFERENCES	Furnished upon request

Figure 13-3 A resume informs employers of the skills and abilities you possess.

✓ CheckPoint

What seven sections should most resumes include?

Other Job Application Documents

A resume is possibly the most time-consuming job application document to prepare. However, other documents are also part of the job application process.

DEVELOPING A COVER LETTER

When applying for a job, your resume should be sent with a cover letter, which is sometimes called an application letter. A **cover letter** communicates your interest in a specific employment position. This letter is designed to create enough interest in you that you obtain an interview.

The opening paragraph of a cover letter should get the reader's attention. Express your interest in the job. Communicate why the employer should consider you for the desired position.

The next paragraph (or two) of the letter should highlight specific education, training, and work experiences that qualify you for the position. Remember that employers do not care what you have done in the past. They want to know how your background will help them in the future. You must communicate how your qualifications will contribute to the organization.

The final paragraph should ask for an opportunity to meet in person with your prospective employer. Tell where, when, and how the employer can communicate with you to schedule an interview.

Remember that your cover letter and resume are your tickets to the interview. They represent you to the prospective employer. Be sure that the documents are neat, well organized, and properly prepared. Proofread the documents carefully and correct any typographical, grammatical, or spelling errors. Many job candidates are disqualified because their application materials are poorly prepared.

COMPLETING AN APPLICATION FORM

Instead of or in addition to a cover letter and resume, a person may be required to complete an application form. This document asks for information similar to the items listed on a resume. An application form should be filled out in a neat

GLOBAL BUSINESS SPOTLIGHT

CROSS-CULTURAL INTERVIEWING

International job interviews can be more challenging than domestic job interviews because of cultural differences. In most cultures, there are certain topics that are unacceptable and should be avoided. Generally, politics and religion are not appropriate topics to discuss. Also, be aware of cultural differences in gestures and body language. A head nodding up and down usually means yes, but in a few cultures it means no. Pointing with an index finger is sometimes considered impolite or vulgar. Because of such cultural differences, it is critical to know what is acceptable and what is unacceptable before being interviewed for a job abroad. By knowing acceptable cultural standards, you can avoid making embarrassing interview mistakes.

Think Critically

1. Why is interviewing in another culture potentially challenging?
2. What other topics are generally not good ones to discuss during interviews in various countries around the world?

and complete manner. When preparing a job application form, be sure you have the needed information available. Before you fill out applications, you should prepare a personal data sheet. Your *personal data sheet* is a document that contains all the information you need to complete a job application. An application form is likely to request your social security number; education; work experience; and the names, addresses, and telephone numbers of references.

SECURING INTERNATIONAL EMPLOYMENT DOCUMENTS

When traveling, studying, or working in another country, certain documents are usually required. A **passport** is a government document proving the bearer's citizenship in the country that issues it. Passports are issued to citizens of the United States by the Department of State and are valid for ten years. A passport application can be obtained online or from a post office, a passport agency, or a federal or state court clerk.

A **visa** is a stamp of endorsement issued by a country that allows a passport holder to enter that country. A visa allows a person into a foreign nation for a specified purpose and period of time. Most visas are issued for travel or business purposes.

People who plan to work in another country are usually required to obtain a work visa. A **work visa**, also called a work permit, allows a person into a foreign country for the purpose of employment. Some countries limit the number of work visas so that their own citizens have more opportunities to fill available jobs.

Photodisc/Getty Images

✓ CheckPoint

In addition to the resume, what are the other job application documents?

Interviewing for a Job

"Why should we hire you?" This is a common question that you will probably have to answer when applying for jobs. The process of interviewing for a job requires that you start getting ready well before the interview.

BEFORE YOU INTERVIEW

Prepare for an interview by obtaining additional information about the company. News articles, annual reports, and current and former employees are good sources of company information. Your knowledge of an organization will help you better answer questions about how you can contribute to the company. You will impress the employer favorably if you are already knowledgeable about the company.

Next, prepare questions to ask at the interview. Many interviewers are impressed by the thoughtful questions a candidate asks. Common questions to ask in an interview include the following.

- What are the main responsibilities of the job?
- What qualities do your most successful employees possess?
- What do people like best about working here?
- What are the opportunities for advancement?

COMMON INTERVIEW QUESTIONS

What experience and training have prepared you for this job?
Besides going to school, how have you expanded your knowledge and interests?
What did you like best about school? What did you like least?
In what types of situations do you get frustrated?
What are your major strengths? major weaknesses? What have you done to overcome your weaknesses?
What do you believe makes a successful person?
Describe the work situation you would like to have five years from now.

Figure 13-4 Planning answers to common interview questions can help you prepare for a job interview.

Set up a practice interview. Using a video camera, have someone ask you sample questions to help you improve your interview skills. Organize your thoughts before answering. Speak clearly and calmly. Provide concise, precise answers. Be confident but not overbearing. Show your enthusiasm for working for the company.

Finally, decide what to wear to the interview and plan to be impeccably groomed. Find out what employees wear to work. Regardless of the dress code of the company, a business suit is usually appropriate for an interview. Avoid trendy and casual styles of clothing. Don't wear too much jewelry. Avoid overpowering colognes or perfumes.

WHEN YOU INTERVIEW

Arrive at the interview several minutes before your appointment time. While it may be difficult, try to relax. Remember that you will be asked questions about a topic on which you are the expert—you.

You may first be required to have a **screening interview**, which is an initial telephone call or meeting to select finalists for an available position. During the screening interview you will be judged on both the overall impression you create and the answers to a few general questions.

Candidates who pass the screening interview are invited for a **selection interview**. In this meeting, a person is asked a series of in-depth questions designed to help employers select the best person for a job.

AFTER YOU INTERVIEW

While waiting to receive communication from a prospective employer, do two things. First, send a follow-up letter. Use this letter to resell yourself so that you stand out from the other candidates. Let the employer know that you are interested in the position. Provide necessary clarifications and additional relevant information to enhance your selection.

Second, evaluate your interview performance. Write down ways you can improve. List questions that you did not expect to be asked and be prepared to answer them in future interviews.

Work as a Team

Select an international job, and discuss what kind of education and experience would be ideal for that job. Repeat with additional jobs as time permits.

✓ CheckPoint

What are four things that can be done to prepare for a job interview?

REVIEW GLOBAL BUSINESS TERMS
Define each of the following terms.

1. resume
2. references
3. cover letter
4. passport
5. visa
6. work visa
7. screening interview
8. selection interview

REVIEW GLOBAL BUSINESS CONCEPTS

9. Why should a resume be carefully prepared?

10. What is the purpose of a cover letter?

11. How does a passport differ from a visa?

SOLVE GLOBAL BUSINESS PROBLEMS
Answers given to questions in an interview can either clinch a job offer or guarantee that no job will be offered. Indicate whether each of the following statements would be considered positive or negative and why.

12. I enjoy finding solutions to problems.

13. I need to be sure I have vacation time during August for visiting the lake with my friends.

14. I'd like a job where I don't have to take orders from superiors.

15. I enjoy writing, and my teachers have always said that I convey ideas well.

16. What are the opportunities for advancement with your company?

THINK CRITICALLY

17. Why do you think it is important not to mention salary at the beginning of a job interview?

18. How would you dress for an interview for a job working as a construction worker? Explain.

MAKE ACADEMIC CONNECTIONS

19. **TECHNOLOGY** Why might you want to include your e-mail address in your resume?

20. **LAW** Why should you not provide prospective employers with your birth date?

21. **CAREER PLANNING** How should you answer questions about your weaknesses?

22. **TECHNOLOGY** Use the Internet to locate resources to help you apply for a job.

13-3 Obtaining Future Jobs

GOALS

- Explain why careers can develop and change.
- Explain how to prepare for international careers.

Photodisc/Getty Images

Developing Career Options

A job is for today, but a career is for a lifetime. Every workday, employees have the opportunity to expand their abilities, knowledge, and career potential. Improving work habits may be achieved by watching others or by creating better ways to do certain tasks.

TRAINING OPPORTUNITIES

Increased technology and changing work activities require employees to learn new skills. Each day on a job can result in new knowledge through informal and formal methods. Informal learning takes place every time people read current materials about their job or the industry in which they work. Talking with others within the company or at other organizations also can help you learn new economic and social trends affecting business.

Formal educational methods include company training programs, seminars, and college courses. Many companies encourage ongoing learning by paying all or part of the tuition and textbook costs for education and training that improves job skills.

CAREER ADVANCEMENT

As with most personal and business decisions, choices might need to be revised as personal, social and economic factors change. During the first stage of a career, a worker wants to match his or her interests and abilities to a job. However, as a career develops, a person will seek new challenges, increased responsibility, and greater rewards.

CHANGING CAREERS

About 10 million people in the United States change careers each year. Most people will have five to ten different jobs during their working lives. The need to change jobs may come from within. Many people face mental stress or physical illness from their work. When this occurs, a career change is probably appropriate.

External influences also can cause a job change. As companies move and merge, a person's job may be eliminated. Technology can replace the need for certain jobs. For example, many bank tellers have been replaced by automated teller machines.

Numerous factors can cause a person to change jobs. When this occurs, it is necessary to develop a revised career path. Perhaps that revised career path will lead to an international career. Figure 13-5 shows major reasons why young managers would accept or reject work assignments abroad. Does an international career seem right for you?

ACCEPTING OR REJECTING INTERNATIONAL ASSIGNMENTS

Common Reasons for Accepting International Work

Cross-cultural experiences and personal growth

Interesting and challenging job

Better financial and other rewards

Career advancement opportunities

A desirable location

A satisfying life

Common Reasons for Rejecting International Work

Undesirable location

Undesirable job and career move

Unacceptable for spouse and family

Inadequate salary and benefits

Unpleasant life abroad

Disruption to home country life

Figure 13-5 There are many reasons why young managers would accept or reject international assignments.

✓ CheckPoint
What can you do to develop your career options?

Preparing for International Careers

People can prepare themselves for a variety of international careers by engaging in six actions. You can start these actions as early as high school and continue them throughout your working lifetime.

UNDERSTAND YOURSELF

Before preparing for international careers, you need to understand yourself. You need to understand your own cultural programming that causes you to be the person you are. In other words, you need to know what your beliefs, values, and assumptions are that shape your behaviors. You also need to determine what your employment goals are. Do you truly have the desire to have an international career of some type? Are you really willing to live abroad for a period of time? Are you motivated to use your capabilities and resources to pursue the necessary education and training for international careers? Are you willing and able to obtain firsthand international experiences? Stated another way, do you have what it takes to work in the global economy at home or abroad? Do you think you are well suited for an international career?

STRENGTHEN YOUR FOUNDATIONAL SKILLS

To prepare for any international career, you need to strengthen your foundational skills. One important foundational skill is cultural understanding. Those who engage in international careers must understand how cultures affect behaviors in the global marketplace. Another critical foundation is communication skills. Communication skills are the backbone that supports

Work as a Team

Discuss the education and training beyond secondary school that a person who aspires to be an international marketing manager needs.

and facilitates the transaction of business worldwide. International careers require proficiency in communication with others who may be like or unlike you in a number of ways.

International careers also require possession of analytical skills. These skills include problem-solving and critical-thinking abilities. Since technology is rapidly changing the way in which and the pace at which global business is transacted, technology skills need to be strengthened for international careers. The ability to use appropriate technologies to accomplish work around the world is increasingly important.

Still another group of important foundational skills involves leadership and administration. Careers abroad typically require at least some managerial skills that must be applied in challenging circumstances. Thus, strengthening foundational skills helps to prepare people for international careers. How are your foundational skills developing for a possible career in the global economy?

ENHANCE YOUR LANGUAGE SKILLS

Improving language skills is critical for international careers since you must be able to convey messages to others without confusion. Because English is widely considered to be the language of international business, you need to increase your English language skills. You must be able to convey messages concisely and precisely to both native and nonnative speakers of English.

You also need to develop fluency in one or more foreign languages if you are planning to work abroad. This allows you to access much valuable information that may not be readily available in English. Further, it allows direct communication with those who do not speak English and those who prefer not to speak English. It also shows respect for other cultures. As a result, enhancing language skills helps you prepare for careers around the world. How are your language skills progressing for an international career?

DEVELOP RELEVANT KNOWLEDGE, SKILLS, AND ATTITUDES

Relevant knowledge, skills, and attitudes must be developed in order to be qualified for international careers. Knowledge, skills, and attitudes fall into two broad categories, which are general education and business education.

General Education General education provides a broad background that helps to prepare individuals to function effectively in a global world. A wide variety of subjects fall into this category. Among them are anthropology, English, foreign languages, geography, history, mathematics, politics, psychology, and sociology.

Business Education Business education builds on the foundation of general education and helps prepare you to conduct business around the world. Among its more basic subjects are accounting, business communication, business statistics, economics, finance, human resources, information systems, law, management, marketing, and production and operations management. A more specialized subject is international business. And subjects falling under international business include international business communication, international marketing, international management, and international human resources.

The general education and business education courses together build needed knowledge, skills, and attitudes that are relevant for a wide variety of

international careers. How suitable are your skills, knowledge, and attitudes for work abroad?

GAIN INTERNATIONAL EXPERIENCE

Having firsthand international experience contributes to preparation for international careers. But how can relevant international experience be obtained? One way is to travel to other countries. That provides experience in interacting with others who are somewhat different. Another way is to participate in the activities of local organizations that serve diverse ethnic groups. Many community organizations seek volunteers who are willing to devote time and effort to assisting others who can benefit from the offered services. Still another way to get relevant international experience is to participate in a short- or long-term student exchange. This allows participants to spend anywhere from a few weeks to a year living, studying, and sometimes working in another country. Such study-abroad programs are increasingly popular among those who want to experience life in its many forms in another country.

Relevant international experience also can come from hosting overseas visitors. An additional way to gain international experience is through employment in a business with operations abroad. Thus, varied ways exist in which relevant international experience can be obtained. How will you obtain international experience for a career abroad?

©jan kranendonk, 2009/ Used under license from Shutterstock.com

GLOBAL BUSINESS SPOTLIGHT

WORKING TOWARD AN INTERNATIONAL CAREER

Matt started working as a clerk in a computer store when he was 15. With some technical training, Matt soon was servicing computers. He worked at the store for six years. During high school, he took some business and computer classes. He traveled to China on a student exchange and to four other countries with his parents.

Matt studied international business and Mandarin at a state university. After earning a bachelor's degree, he spent six months in Beijing. He studied Chinese culture, language, and business practices. He developed basic proficiency in Mandarin as he interacted with Chinese people.

When Matt returned to the United States, the economy was in serious decline. Matt found part-time work with a computer company with operations in China. After a year, he can be considered for an international job. He also volunteers in a Department of Commerce international business internship program. This gives him international business work experience and builds his network with international professionals.

Think Critically

1. How well has Matt prepared for an international career?
2. Is Matt wise to volunteer in the internship program?
3. What else might Matt do to prepare for an international business career?

NETWORK WITH INTERNATIONAL PROFESSIONALS

Still another way to prepare for international careers is to network with international professionals online or in person. You can interact with people from other countries who live and work in the immediate area. Often they are eager to share information about their home countries. Another approach is to target companies for which you might like to work in the future. Their employees, especially those in the human resources department, can provide valuable career advice and referrals to other sources of useful information.

Professional organizations are another way to gain access to international professionals. Many times members of professional organizations have lived and worked abroad and are willing to share those experiences with others. Interviews with expatriates who have recently returned from international assignments can also provide valuable information and introductions to other professionals. Thus, those planning international careers can gain valuable insights by networking with professionals who have worked abroad. With whom will you network as you prepare for your international career?

After you have adequately prepared yourself for an international career, you can search for the desired types of jobs in the global marketplace. When you do, you can use approaches much like the ones you used for finding jobs in the domestic marketplace. Sooner or later appropriate professional opportunities will become available, and you will be hired. Then you will have achieved your goal of having an international career.

✓ CheckPoint

What are six ways you can prepare yourself for an international career?

REVIEW GLOBAL BUSINESS CONCEPTS

1. What training opportunities are commonly available to workers who want to improve their skills?

2. How does speaking multiple languages well contribute to a successful international career?

3. How can you gain international experiences without leaving your native country?

Study Tools

www.cengage.com/school/genbus/intlbiz

SOLVE GLOBAL BUSINESS PROBLEMS

"I've studied three Romance languages: French, Spanish, and Italian. I started with French in high school. I added Spanish while working on my bachelor's degree in finance. I spent my junior year abroad in Madrid, where I studied and worked in a bank. After I graduated, I worked in New York and in Paris. Just prior to being transferred to Rome, I took an intensive four-week course in Italian. Everything was done in Italian, so I quickly picked up that language. Having already studied two related Romance languages helped me progress rapidly in Italian because of the many similarities. It was easier learning three related languages because I could transfer much of what I learned from one language to another. I can now conduct banking business in French, Spanish, Italian, or English as needed. Almost every day I use at least two of the languages I speak."

4. Why did it take the international banker a number of years to master three Romance languages?

5. Why does it make good sense to study languages that are related to each other?

6. Why does an international banker have a competitive advantage if he or she can conduct business in multiple languages?

THINK CRITICALLY

7. What are some jobs that are threatened by technology?

8. How do you know if an international career is right for you?

9. Why are recently returned expatriates an excellent source of information about international careers?

MAKE ACADEMIC CONNECTIONS

10. **TECHNOLOGY** How do international employment web sites facilitate international careers?

11. **GEOGRAPHY** How do the Alps contribute to international career opportunities in the travel and hospitality industries?

12. **HISTORY** How did tearing down the Berlin Wall increase international career options?

Quiz Prep

www.cengage.com/school/genbus/intlbiz

CHAPTER SUMMARY

13-1 SEARCHING FOR YOUR FIRST JOB

A. You can plan your career by determining your personal goals and abilities, evaluating the job market, identifying and applying for specific job opportunities, accepting the most desirable job offer, and planning for personal career development.

B. You can explore career information from library materials, media, personal and business contacts, community organizations, and Internet sources.

C. Career opportunities are affected by many factors, including personal factors, demographic trends, geographic influences, economic conditions, and industry trends.

13-2 APPLYING FOR A JOB

A. A resume should include information such as personal data, career objective, education, experience, related activities, honors and awards, and references.

B. A cover letter should get the reader's attention and make the reader want to interview you for a position.

C. Prepare for an interview, be early and relaxed for the interview, and send a follow-up letter to resell yourself.

13-3 OBTAINING FUTURE JOBS

A. People change jobs for many reasons and need to revise their career paths.

B. Prepare for international careers by understanding yourself; strengthening foundational skills; enhancing language skills; developing relevant knowledge, skills, and attitudes; gaining international experience; and networking with international professionals.

GLOBAL **REFOCUS**

Read the case at the beginning of this chapter, and answer the following questions.

1. Why do you think Jennifer Yoon will be able to adjust to the cultural and business differences in Austria?

2. If Jennifer is hired to manage the new Austrian office, how might she develop German language skills?

3. Based on your research about business in Austria, does it have a favorable international business climate? Why or why not?

REVIEW GLOBAL BUSINESS TERMS

Match the terms listed with the definitions.

1. A stamp of endorsement issued by a country that allows a passport holder to enter that country.

2. A written summary of a person's education, training, work experience, and other job qualifications.

3. A meeting where a person is asked a series of in-depth questions designed to help employers select the best person for a job.

4. A commitment to a profession that requires continued education and training and has a clear path for advancement.

5. A document that allows a person into a foreign country for the purpose of employment.

6. A meeting with another person to gather information about a career or an organization.

7. Correspondence that communicates your interest in a specific employment position.

8. An initial telephone call or meeting to select finalists for an available position.

9. An employment position obtained mainly for money.

10. A government document proving the bearer's citizenship in the country that issues it.

11. People who can report to a prospective employer about your abilities and work experience.

a. career
b. cover letter
c. informational interview
d. job
e. passport
f. references
g. resume
h. screening interview
i. selection interview
j. visa
k. work visa

MAKE GLOBAL BUSINESS DECISIONS

12. Prepare a poster that illustrates three international business careers.

13. Research the educational background, training requirements, and other information for your top international business career choice.

14. Collect examples of resume formats from career planning books, counselors, and people who have recently applied for and obtained jobs. How are the formats alike and different? Identify the most effective format and explain your choice.

15. Talk to people who conduct job interviews or who have participated in a job interview. Prepare a report about common interview questions and common mistakes people make during interviews. Explain how this information might help you prepare for an interview.

16. Design an educational program that will give you the knowledge, skills, and attitudes needed for an international career of your choice.

MAKE ACADEMIC CONNECTIONS

17. TECHNOLOGY Under what circumstances do you think it would be acceptable to communicate with a prospective employer using e-mail?

18. CULTURAL STUDIES How do study abroad programs develop cultural understanding for international careers?

19. COMMUNICATIONS When applying for an international job in the Netherlands, should you communicate in English or in Dutch? Why?

20. COMMUNICATIONS Why do you think most selection interviews are conducted in person?

21. LITERATURE Find a piece of contemporary literature that has a major character who has a job in international business. What did you learn about that job by reading the selected piece of literature?

22. CAREER PLANNING Create a file of newspaper and magazine articles about an international career that interests you. What have you learned about that career option by gathering and reading the articles?

23. CAREER PLANNING Look at the classified advertising section of your Sunday newspaper. Find three jobs that include an international factor.

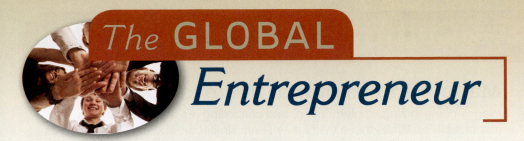

The GLOBAL Entrepreneur

CREATING AN INTERNATIONAL BUSINESS PLAN

Planning an International Career

Develop a career plan based on the company and country you have been using in this continuing project, or create a new idea for your business in the same or a different country. Make use of previously collected information, and do additional research. This phase of your business plan should include the following components.

1. List types of international jobs available within this multinational organization.

2. List training, skills, and experience commonly required for these international business careers.

3. Describe how social factors, economic conditions, and technology might affect available jobs.

4. Create a fictitious resume for someone applying for a job with this company.

5. List interview questions and tentative answers that might be a part of the application process.

Prepare a written summary or present a short oral report (two or three minutes) of your findings.

Photodisc/Getty Images

GLOBAL Cross-Cultural Team Project

Manage International Business Operations

Planning, organizing, implementing, and controlling are every manager's responsibilities. While these tasks may seem similar around the world, various social and cultural factors affect them. Participating in a cross-cultural team allows managers to better understand and work with people of differing values and beliefs.

Goal

To determine the influence of culture on management activities in various regions of the world.

Activities

Working in teams, select a geographic region you will represent—Africa, Asia, Europe, Latin America, Middle East, or North America.

1. Information about management activities in various regions may be obtained on the Web, in the library, and by talking to people who have lived in or visited those areas. Your findings will be applied to various duties of managers.
2. Summarize how organizational decisions are commonly made in your region. Are business actions based on the decisions of people at the top of the organization? Or are plans the result of participation by people at various levels in the organization? Discuss any notable exceptions in specific countries.
3. Explain the process commonly used to select employees. Are family members or friends given preference over others in the hiring process? Discuss any notable exceptions in specific countries.
4. Research the educational systems and career paths taken by people in various countries in your region. What factors influence a person's choice of training and employment in this region of the world?
5. Describe the activities of organized labor in your region. How influential are labor unions in various countries in this geographic area?
6. **Global Business Decision** An international company needs you to create a promotion policy. Decide if managers for offices around the world should be (a) from the home country of the company, (b) from the country where the office is located, or (c) a qualified person from anywhere in the world. Explain which of these choices your team would select.

Team Skill

Traits of Cross-Cultural Team Members

Desired characteristics of team members vary from region to region and from country to country. Discuss with your team the traits that might be preferred in each geographic area. How do the desired traits differ from one region to another?

Present

- Prepare a 2- or 3-page summary report of management activities in your geographic region.
- As a team, develop a script and present an in-class dramatization of the management differences in various regions of the world.

Marketing Management Role Play

You are the marketing director for EnviroWorld, an international company that produces advanced control panels to monitor and maintain sensitive enviroments. EnviroWorld refrigeration control systems are used by hospitals, the food industry, and the military. Your U.S.-based company conducts business in the United States, India, and the Middle East.

EnviroWorld has established a relationship with the Design Source for all of your company's multi-media needs. The relationship with Design Source has become so comfortable that frequently you pursue projects without getting quotes for the cost of the project.

EnviroWorld needs a multimedia presentation for sales representatives to use as they pursue three large contracts. EnviroWorld has worked closely with the owner of Design Source, Shawn Boyle, to create a sophisticated PowerPoint presentation without first providing a quote for the project. Your company receives an e-mail from Shawn showing the projected cost for the PowerPoint presentation. The bill will be $3,850.

The CEO for EnviroWorld is not willing to pay $3,850 for the project because Shawn previously suggested that a sophisticated 3-D presentation would cost $3,200 and a PowerPoint presentation would cost much less. The CEO is originally from India and wants to have the project completed by a company in India for $1,200. Shawn has been notified and now is demanding $1,000 for the work he has completed on the project. You will meet with the CEO and propose the best solution for this case.

The competition consists of two parts: the 100-question objective test and the role play. You will have 10 minutes to prepare your presentation for the role play and 10 minutes to present your strategy to the judge. You may refer to your notes during the presentation with the judge.

Performance Indicators Evaluated

- Describe legal issues affecting businesses.
- Defend ideas objectively.
- Describe the concept of price.
- Explain the nature of international trade.
- Define business ethics.
- Explain the importance of business quotes before beginning projects.

For more detailed information about performance indicators, go to the DECA web site.

Think Critically

1. Why are business quotes important?
2. Why can EnviroWorld be liable to Design Source?
3. What risks are involved with having the project completed in India?

www.deca.org

UNIT 4

Information and Production Systems for Global Business

Chapter

14 Information Needs for Global Business Activities

15 Production Systems for Global Business

If You Were There

...the Giza Plateau near Cairo in late 1925

The excavations are nearly completed. The magnificence and scale of the Great Sphinx of Giza are apparent. The colossal statue of a reclining lion with a human head was carved in one piece from the limestone bedrock above the west bank of the Nile River. One of the oldest and largest sculptures known, it is about 260-feet long, 20-feet wide, and 65-feet high. The rock around the Great Sphinx was removed block-by-block millennia ago. Over time, the features of the face, including the now-detached nose and beard, have been damaged by erosion, vandalism, and neglect. Facing the rising sun, the Great Sphinx lies near the three Great Pyramids of Cheops, Chephren, and Micerinus.

Mysteries surround the Great Sphinx. Who built it as well as when it was built are clouded in controversy. Traditionalists think that it was built by the Pharaoh Khafra, also known as Chephren, sometime during his reign (2520–2494 B.C.). Others think it could be up to 3500 years older. Its original name is not known, although it is now known as Father of Terror. The model for the face on the Great Sphinx, as well as its purpose, also is shrouded in secrecy.

Photodisc/Getty Images

Geography

Africa is almost four times the size of the United States. The continent includes the great highlands in Kenya and Ethiopia and the Great Rift Valley. There are mountains in the north and southeast of Africa. However, the largest mountains stand in the east and are snowcapped—on the equator. Kilimanjaro is the tallest at 19,340 feet.

Much of the interior of Africa is a plateau consisting of rolling hills, savannas, deserts and rain forests. The Nile, which is the longest river in the world, is in East Africa. The Sahara (the Arabic word for *desert*) covers one-fourth of the African continent. The Sahara was once a fertile land that supported a thriving population. However, about 4,000 B.C. the climate changed the Sahara region into a desert. Overfarming, overgrazing, and drought causes the Sahara to expand every year.

Early Civilizations

The earliest African civilizations grew along the Nile River and the Red Sea. At these locations, Egyptian kingdoms were built that date back to 3,100 B.C. To the west, the kingdoms of Ghana and Mali ruled vast territories of sub-Saharan Africa from the fourth to sixteenth centuries A.D. Ghana's position—midway between the salt mines of north Africa and the gold deposits to the south—ensured its hold on a trading empire that spread over 200,000 square miles. Caravans from North Africa carried salt, metal goods, and cloth across the Sahara to Ghana in return for gold, farm produce, and kola nuts from the south.

By the thirteenth century, the kingdom of Mali had taken control of Ghana's empire and expanded it over an even wider area. Mali's city of Timbuktu was a center of learning that attracted scholars from Cairo and Mecca.

European Control

In the 1500s, European immigrants began to arrive, and traders were interested in Africa's gold, diamonds, ivory, and other natural resources. Empires, kingdoms, and tribes continued to rule Africa until the late 1800s. However, the opening of the Suez Canal in 1869 brought a new wave of immigrants. In 1885, fourteen nations agreed to partition the "prize," the land of Africa, and take it away from the native inhabitants.

By 1914, France had conquered most of North and West Africa. Britain took control of Egypt and, along with the Germans and the Italians, most of East Africa. The southern part of the continent was divided among Britain, Portugal, and Germany. Ethiopia and Liberia were the only African nations to retain their independence.

Freedom

Nationalist movements began to appear throughout the continent between the world wars. However, independence for most African nations was not achieved until the late 1950s and early 1960s. A few European nations relinquished control after mass protests and labor strikes. Unfortunately, prolonged guerrilla warfare was usually the real force of liberation in countries such as Algeria, Angola, Mozambique, Guinea-Bissau, Kenya, and Namibia.

Today greater mobility has led many to leave the home village, but family and tribal identity thrive. Independence fostered a renewed sense of pride in African culture. Children are taught tribal and family history.

Religion and Art

Islam has flourished, especially in the northern part of Africa, while European and American churches and schools continue to promote Christianity. Ancient tribal religions are still important, and often they are combined with Christianity. The indigenous African religions believe in one ultimate God along with lesser gods or ancestral spirits who act as intermediaries between God and mortals. This religious system is known as *polytheism*.

African arts are often associated with religion. Music, stories, dance, and carved wooden masks have integral roles in ceremonies that connect humans to their ancestors and the spiritual world. Art also entertains, educates, and stimulates thought. African music is unique for its polyrhythmic structure, with as many as a dozen rhythms all played simultaneously. European painters have been influenced by African artists' expression of the essence of a human or animal subject through sharp angles and exaggerated features. African designs have found their way onto clothing made throughout the world.

The African landscape has often inspired the artist. However, it is a harsh land that, at times, punishes its people. During the 1980s and 1990s, the combination of poor soil, drought, and wars led to the starvation of millions of people in Chad, Ethiopia, Liberia, Mozambique, Sierra Leone, Somalia, Sudan, and the Democratic Republic of the Congo (formerly Zaire). The suffering in Ethiopia resulted in the 1985 famine relief concert Live-Aid, which raised funds for food for the hungry. In 1992, images of suffering

on Western television helped to pressure the United States into sending a military force to protect relief workers in Somalia.

Apartheid

In 1910 the British created the Union of South Africa and formalized racial segregation. South Africa's white minority used a government policy called *apartheid* to segregate and to discriminate politically and economically against non-European groups—which included Blacks, Indians, and people of mixed race. Policies became more restrictive after World War II and thousands of people were forced to move to rural townships where they lived in poverty. At the same time, opposition to apartheid grew. People living in the townships began to organize and protest. In 1960, the African National Congress, a group working to abolish apartheid, was outlawed. Four years later, ANC leader Nelson Mandela was sentenced to life in prison.

Jim Bourg/Getty Images

After gaining independence in 1961, the Republic of South Africa continued the policy of apartheid. In the years that followed antiapartheid sentiment continued within South Africa and international opposition to apartheid grew. Foreign investment dried up and the UN imposed sanctions.

In February 1990, less than a year after becoming president, F. W. de Klerk began the process of ending apartheid. He released Nelson Mandela from prison and lifted the ban on the African National Congress. In 1994, Nelson Mandela was elected president in a peaceful election.

Business Potential and Challenges

Many African countries have been slow to make the economic and social progress necessary to attract outside investors. Political instability, graft, and corruption deter investment. Limited and outdated infrastructure impedes economic development in many countries. In some areas, poverty and disease make it difficult to recruit and retain qualified workers needed for economic progress. Although the outlook might appear gloomy, Africa is a continent full of business potential.

Africa possesses a variety of resources that are in demand around the world including significant oil deposits and mineral ores. Other resources include topography and climate, along with productive soil and water resources. Africa also has an ample supply of labor.

Today, African countries are focusing on ways to overcome obstacles, take advantage of their many resources, and grow their economies. International business is one part of the solution.

Think Critically

1. Why was the opening of the Suez Canal responsible for a new wave of immigrants to Africa?
2. How effective do you think African countries will be in overcoming obstacles to their economic and social development?

COUNTRY PROFILE

The World Factbook, published online by the Central Intelligence Agency, includes country profiles for the nations of Africa. Each country's profile includes an overview followed by detailed information about the country's geography, people, government, economy, communications, transportation, military, and transnational issues.

CHAPTER 14

Information Needs for Global Business Activities

14-1 Creating Global Information Systems

14-2 Global Information Systems Challenges

GLOBAL FOCUS

South African Company Provides Technology Solutions

Altech ISIS (ISIS) is a successful South African technology company known for planning, designing, integrating, and implementing information systems for large and small organizations. The company is part of Altech, a component of Allied Electronics Corporation Limited (Altron), a South Africa-based technology group.

One area of specialization for ISIS is integration of office and business support systems. In this case integration refers to linking various network elements such as a company's telephone and computer systems. The integrated system supports business activities related to customer care, administration, logistics, billing, and network management.

Another specialty is software development for both fixed line and mobile network telephone providers. This software is used for customer service, repair and service management, logistics, and billing. Altech ISIS also provides a platform for designing technology solutions along with installing and troubleshooting network technology. The company has a reputation for delivering well-designed and fully functional information systems that enhance organizational effectiveness.

Working on projects for various African telecommunication providers, ISIS provides services to the continent's largest phone service providers—land lines and mobile networks. Its customers are located primarily in South Africa, Nigeria, Tanzania, Kenya, the Democratic Republic of Congo, and Gabon. Through its headquarters in Cape Town, Altech ISIS provides Africa with turnkey information systems customized to meet the specific needs of its customers.

Think Critically

1. Why would it make sense that ISIS is part of a technology group?
2. What suggests that ISIS is a major provider of information systems?
3. Use the Internet or library resources to obtain additional information about ISIS and the company's operations. Prepare a report of your findings.

14-1 Creating Global Information Systems

GOALS

- Explain why information is power in the global economy.

- Describe the three major components of global information systems.

- Explain some of the factors to consider when planning and developing global information systems.

Photodisc/Getty Images

Information is Power

Information is the source of power in the global economy. Information technology helps to drive the global marketplace. It also facilitates addressing the many challenges that managers face when operating in the complex global environment. It is essential in the global economy to have the right information in the right form at the right time. Without such information, businesses cannot compete against other businesses that do have the valuable information. In fact, organizations with poor information systems struggle to survive in the global world of business.

Strategic Resource Like other business assets, information is an important strategic resource. It allows businesses to position themselves favorably in the international marketplace so that they can attain their business goals.

Competitive Advantage Given enough of the right information, businesses can gain competitive advantages over their competitors. This allows them to function more efficiently and effectively than their competitors and gives them the best possible global business opportunities. By being able to skillfully use information to outmaneuver their challengers, certain multinational businesses enjoy competitive advantages over other businesses with less effective global information systems.

Now that the global economy is a reality, businesses around the world must be able to function effectively 24 hours a day, 365 days a year. To do this, businesses must have highly effective global information systems that deliver appropriate information as needed.

INFORMATION SYSTEMS IN DOMESTIC BUSINESS

Developing and managing a suitable information system is much easier in a domestic business environment than in an international business environment. In that relatively simple domestic business environment, usually one language dominates. The prevailing culture is relatively similar from location to location. Over time, a well-developed infrastructure develops to support business activities. *Infrastructure* refers to the nation's transportation and communications systems. It is the basic framework of an organization. Usually one primary political entity oversees and regulates business activities. Because only one country on one continent is involved, business is transacted in a limited number of time zones using one currency.

COMPARING DOMESTIC AND INTERNATIONAL BUSINESS ENVIRONMENTS

Factors	Domestic Business Environment	International Business Environment
Culture	Single dominant culture	Multiple cultures
Currency	Single currency	Multiple currencies
Government	Single dominant government	Multiple governments
Infrastructure	Well-developed infrastructure	Multiple infrastructures
Language	Single dominant language	Multiple languages
Location	Single country, single continent	Multiple countries, multiple continents
Regulation	Single dominant business regulatory system	Multiple business regulatory systems
Time Zones	Limited time zones	Multiple time zones

Figure 14-1 The domestic and international business environments are significantly different and necessitate different types of information systems.

INFORMATION SYSTEMS IN INTERNATIONAL BUSINESS

Developing and managing a suitable information system is more challenging in a complex international business environment. So many more variables must be considered and accommodated. For example, a business operating in the global economy must cope with multiple languages. The involved cultures are likely to be significantly different from each other. The countries in which the business operates might all have their own unique forms of government and business regulation. An international business with operations scattered around the globe must function in different countries that are on one or more continents and use various currencies. Figure 14-1 contrasts the major differences between the domestic and international business environments that must be bridged by information systems.

Because the international business environment is more complex than the domestic business environment, it requires a more sophisticated information system. That global information system must adequately reflect all of the variables of the international business environment if it is to provide high-quality information. Creating and refining a powerful global information system is a challenging, time-consuming, and expensive task. Nevertheless, it is an investment that can pay a handsome return in the form of both strategic and competitive advantages. Wise multinational organizations develop sophisticated global information systems.

✓ **Check**Point
What are two reasons information is so powerful in the global economy?

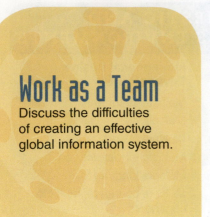

Information System Components

A **global information system** is a computer-based system that provides information about company operations around the world to managers of a multinational organization. A global information system is composed of three basic elements: data inputs, operational components, and system outputs.

DATA INPUTS

Data inputs are those pieces of information that feed the global information system database. These inputs reflect both internal organization inputs and external environment inputs. Components of the internal organization inputs include transaction processing systems, shipping records, a customer database, accounts receivable, inventory records, and the like. Components of the external environment inputs include market research, industry trends, economic trends, competitor trends, and data sharing with business partners.

OPERATIONAL COMPONENTS

Operational components are the parts of an information system that manage the database and system operations. There are five basic types of operational components.

Systems Controls To ensure that the information system functions properly, companies implement controls to regulate the systems. Examples of systems controls include security access, internal operations checks, and system and data integrity checks.

Database Management To regulate the functioning of the database systems, companies set up database management systems. Database management systems include data files and data dictionaries.

User Interface Systems To allow access to data and analytical tools, companies typically set up user interface systems. They must keep data safe but accessible. Ideally, user interface systems use **icons**, which are symbols

GLOBAL BUSINESS SPOTLIGHT

UNILEVER'S GLOBALIZATION PATHWAY

Unilever, the consumer goods multinational, has hired BT (British Telecom) to manage its global network infrastructure and to reduce its information systems costs. BT now operates fixed and mobile voice, data, and video services for almost one thousand sites in more than one hundred countries.

By standardizing, reorganizing, and disposing of unwanted technologies around the globe, Unilever hopes to save 20 percent on network spending.

Think Critically

1. What are the benefits of linking company employees worldwide with a standardized system?
2. What might be some of the challenges of changing information systems?

EVAPORATING E-MAIL

Jason Pierson is in his home office in Seattle and he is frustrated. He has waited for more than three days for a reply to his request for information from the Nairobi office. At midnight local time, he telephones his Kenyan counterpart.

"Why haven't you responded to my e-mail message? I need the information now."

"What e-mail message are you talking about, sir? I haven't received any e-mails for four days. The last one I got from you was about two weeks ago."

"But I sent a message three days ago.

"Mr. Pierson, you've got to realize that Kenya is a developing country. Yes, we have e-mail, but it doesn't always work. The connections to the Internet aren't always good. We have no backup power system. When the power fails, we lose everything."

Think Critically

1. Why did Jason place his call to Nairobi at midnight his time?
2. Why did Jason expect a prompt response to his e-mail?
3. What did Jason fail to understand about the use of e-mail in developing countries?

---

that are meaningful across cultures. Examples of user interface systems include access controls and user interfaces.

Application Systems To allow inquiry and analysis, companies install application systems. These systems address such questions as "What is?" "What has happened in the past?" "Why?" and "What if?" Examples of application systems include regular reports, special reports, statistical analysis, expert systems, and forecasting.

Reporting Systems Output from reporting systems allows inquiries and analyses to be shared with relevant persons. These analyses can be either in print or electronic format. Examples of reporting systems include text processing, graphical output, and electronic output.

The data inputs and the operational components are the primary components of the global information system that together generate the system outputs, the third component. The relationship among the three components is illustrated in Figure 14-2.

SYSTEM OUTPUTS

System outputs are the data generated from an information system. Managers rely on system outputs as they direct company operations in the global business environment. There are four basic types of application outputs.

- *Product management* outputs data such as sales forecasts and budgets that allow managers to position their products more effectively in the global marketplace.
- *Communication* outputs data such as media plans and impact reports that help global managers to share information more effectively.

Primary Components of a Global Information System

Figure 14-2 When the data inputs and the operational components of a global information system are combined, they yield the system outputs.

- *Sales management* outputs data such as territory design and sales quota planning that help global managers to market their products more effectively around the world.
- *Senior management* outputs data such as financial modeling and strategy simulations that help top-level company managers to direct global business operations more effectively.

✓ **Check**Point
What are the three major components of a global information system?

Planning and Developing the System

Effective global information systems evolve over time in response to careful planning and developing. Thus, planning and developing the global information system are important activities for multinational organizations.

ROLE OF TOP-LEVEL MANAGERS

Planning for global information systems is an important task for managers. The planning must include top-level managers who are able to envision the global organizational future. Top-level managers should understand the value of an effective global information system and support that system in every way possible. They should also realize that such an information system evolves over time and requires continual maintenance and refinement.

ROLE OF OTHER INFORMATION SYSTEMS MANAGERS

Information technology as well as global business conditions change all of the time. With the input of top-level managers, the information systems management team needs to establish a framework for the desired global information system and also realize that achieving that goal will be a long-term, evolutionary project. As a result, information systems managers must prioritize the competing needs for information and focus their attention on the most critical information needs first. Over time, they can gradually address more and more information needs.

A multinational organization achieves a competitive advantage in the global marketplace by focusing its attention on a global, not domestic, outlook. As information system managers develop and refine the global information system, they must reduce uncertainty while coping with increasingly complex global business operations. They must keep in mind the need for both timely and highly relevant information about operations around the world. While ultimately developing a global information system, they must realize that many of the component systems are developed locally. As the various component systems are integrated, a global information system is gradually built and refined.

✓ **Check**Point
What are two factors that top-level managers must consider when planning and developing global information systems?

INTERNATIONAL BUSINESS PERSPECTIVE

Culture

USING AFRICAN DESIGN ELEMENTS IN INFORMATION SYSTEMS

An information system is a computer-based system that provides facts about company operations. The system provides useful data to its users inside and outside of the business. The system should reflect the beliefs, values, and assumptions of its users. It can include design elements such as pictures and patterns that come from users' cultures. These and similar design elements enhance the appeal of things such as signs, printed documents, and electronic displays in culturally sensitive ways. They help to make the outputs of the information system more acceptable to users. They show respect for the culture that created the design elements.

Africa has a rich, vibrant cultural heritage. Its art and artifacts have long been admired around the world. African designs influenced the direction of Western art, design, and culture, especially in the twentieth century. The strong lines, sharp angles, and vivid colors found in many modern artworks have their roots in Africa. The geometric designs found in African masks have inspired many artists, including Picasso.

African art often represents sensations and ideas. It abstractly conveys the emotions, magic, religious beliefs, and culture of the artist. Most Africans feel flattered and honored when others use design elements from their cultures. Companies that operate in African countries can build goodwill and foster relationships by using African design elements.

Anton and Merle Scholtz own design-africa, a resource for African-inspired design elements. Located in KwaZulu-Natal, South Africa, the company offers fonts, patterns, and page backgrounds that can be used in information systems. The owners designed a series of fonts that reflect Africa's cultural heritage. For example, the Kassena font uses a triangular motif inspired by traditional African art. This distinctive font can be used with all major European languages. Multinational companies can use Kassena to appeal to almost all African cultures. Using this or other fonts that reflect African heritage for information system displays shows respect for African cultures.

Think Critically

1. Why might the Kassena font appeal to Africans?
2. What are some major European languages that multinational companies might use in information systems in Africa?
3. Use library and Internet resources to locate photographs of traditional African artwork and write a brief explanation of how the artwork, or an element within the art, might be used in an information system.

alantobey/iStockphoto.com

14-1 Assessment

REVIEW GLOBAL BUSINESS TERMS

Define each of the following terms.

1. global information system
2. data inputs
3. operational components
4. icons
5. system outputs

REVIEW GLOBAL BUSINESS CONCEPTS

6. Why is it more difficult to develop and manage an information system in an international business environment than a domestic business environment?

7. What are two examples each of internal organization and external environment inputs?

SOLVE GLOBAL BUSINESS PROBLEMS

Maple Leaf Enterprises, Ltd., is Canadian-based with operations in Canada, the United States, the United Kingdom, South Africa, Australia, and New Zealand. Except for the operations in Canada and the United States, the information that is received at company headquarters in Toronto is not integrated across worldwide operations. Some information from abroad is not compatible with information provided by company operations elsewhere.

8. Does Maple Leaf Enterprises, Ltd., need a global information system? Why or why not?

9. What should top-level company executives do to address the information problems of Maple Leaf Enterprises, Ltd.? Why?

10. How many years would you estimate it will take the company to create and develop an effective global information system? Why?

THINK CRITICALLY

11. Why must a global information system be designed to provide high-quality information 24 hours a day, 365 days a year?

12. Why must global information systems have so many parts and be so complex?

13. Why must top-level company managers, who often don't really understand the workings of global information systems, be directly involved in creating global information systems?

MAKE ACADEMIC CONNECTIONS

14. **GEOGRAPHY** What are some geographical features around the world that might create barriers that impede the flow of information within a multinational organization?

15. **CAREER PLANNING** What subjects should you study at the secondary and post-secondary levels if you aspire to be the vice president for global information systems of a multinational organization?

Global Information Systems Challenges

Photodisc/Getty Images

GOALS

- Explain global information challenges arising from cultural and country issues.

- Describe data collection issues related to data sources and data quality.

- Explain how technological issues create challenges to global information systems.

Cultural and Country Issues

One of the major challenges to global information systems involves cultural and country issues. Cultural and country issues usually come from differences involving language, attitudes, the environment, information needs, and degree of control.

LANGUAGE DIFFERENCES

Language differences are an obstacle to the collection and transmission of information. In languages that are not closely related, ideas cannot be simply translated from one language to another. In some cases, no equivalent idea exists in the language of another culture. For example, the idea of depreciation did not exist in the language of the communist Union of Soviet Socialist Republics. Under communism, most resources were controlled by the state, so there was no need to account for the gradual decrease in value of assets through use. Businesses from abroad that established operations there after the collapse of the Soviet Union found that their local employees had difficulty understanding the foreign idea of depreciation. Thus, requests for local depreciation information were typically met with blank stares from most natives of the former Soviet Union. The needed depreciation information was very difficult to get because the locals did not understand the concept or its importance.

NETBookmark

The number of Hispanics living in the United States is growing rapidly, and so is the need to communicate with them in business and school. Access the web site shown below and click on the link for Chapter 14. Read the Birmingham Business Journal article entitled "Breaking the Language Barrier." How might businesses benefit from breaking the language barrier?

www.cengage.com/school/genbus/intlbiz

ATTITUDES

Attitudes toward such things as secrecy, authority, and risk taking are reflected in the communication of cultural groups. For example, Japanese workers are programmed by their native culture to respect authority and not disrupt the harmonious relationship of a group. Japanese workers are not likely to openly criticize company managers and policies, even if they are clearly wrong. If Japanese workers bring up sensitive matters, they do so privately, discreetly, and indirectly, using language that is vague and must be interpreted figuratively, not literally. Many members of other cultures do not realize that Japanese workers have communicated negative information because they do not understand how Japanese people convey sensitive matters.

BUSINESS AND FINANCIAL ENVIRONMENT

The business and financial environment creates potential information challenges. Competition, currency fluctuations, and inflation rates vary from country to country. Taxation systems also vary, as does the amount of control exercised over multinational organizations by governments. These environmental differences create different information needs that can complicate the flow of information. For example, financial records maintained in the local

A Question of Ethics

WHERE DO PRIVACY RIGHTS BEGIN?

Lawmakers in many countries have become increasingly concerned about the privacy rights of their citizens. They feel uncomfortable that name-linked information is collected, processed, and stored in information systems that are not accurate and carefully controlled.

Some multinational businesses send personal data outside the country of origin to places with less stringent privacy controls. There the personal data is used to make various kinds of decisions. Sometimes the data is used for

purposes other than those for which it was collected. Sometimes it is sold to other businesses.

To limit such abuses, countries such as Sweden require that all private and public organizations register their databases, which are subject to review. Certain types of data about individual citizens cannot be legally sent out of the country.

Think Critically

1. How would you feel if you discovered that your credit card company had sold personal information about you to a business in another country without your permission?

2. Even if the bank did not break any laws when selling information about you, would its actions be ethical or not? Why?

3. Considering that freedom is a founding principle in the United States, should the federal government restrict the right to process information about its citizens? Why or why not?

4. Is it ethical for countries to pass legislation to protect the privacy rights of their citizens if in doing so, they violate the rights of multinational businesses to process business information as they desire? Why or why not?

currency may have to be converted to another currency before they can be integrated into the global information system of the organization.

DIFFERING INFORMATION NEEDS

Information needs also vary widely within multinational businesses, creating additional challenges to global information systems. Different organizational levels within far-flung company operations have significantly different information needs. Managers generally prefer to receive their information in terms of the local standard units of information. Thus, information about such matters as planning, budgeting, and accounting will likely have to be processed multiple times in different units. This increases not only the volume but also the redundancy of information that the global information system must generate to meet the needs of various parts of a multinational business. The United States currently uses generally accepted accounting principles (GAAP) for financial reporting while much of the world uses international financial reporting standards (IFRS). The United States likely will adopt IFRS, reflecting more consistent accounting standards around the world. This will simplify accounting for many multinational organizations. It also will benefit those who use the related accounting statements because the data from various companies will be more directly comparable.

DEGREE OF CONTROL

The degree of control that is exercised within a multinational organization also creates challenges to global information systems. A multinational organization must weigh the trade-offs between centralization and decentralization. **Centralization** means that managers at company headquarters make most major decisions. Centralization favors a broad view of corporate strategy when decisions are made. **Decentralization** means that local managers at different company locations around the world make most major decisions. Decentralization favors the effects of local conditions when decisions are made. Different international businesses choose to control their operations in different ways, which influences both the needs for and the types of information that must be generated by global information systems.

✓ CheckPoint
What are five types of cultural and country issues that present challenges to global information systems?

Data Collection Issues

Another of the major challenges to global information systems involves data collection issues. Data collection issues usually come from data sources and/or data quality. The quality of the outputs generated by a global information system is strongly influenced by the adequacy of the data inputs.

SOURCES OF DATA

Data sources present challenges to global information systems. Data sources are either primary sources or secondary sources. **Primary data** are data collected by the user firsthand for a specific purpose. **Secondary data** are data not collected by the user but available for his or her use. Surveys from

Work as a Team
Debate the pros and cons of centralizing all major decisions relating to a global information system.

customers are examples of primary data if they are collected by the same business unit that uses the gathered information. If some other business unit or organization, such as a governmental agency, gathers the survey information, then the gathered information is secondary data.

Users generally have more faith in the quality of the information they gather themselves (because they know its strengths and weaknesses) than in the information others gather. Nevertheless, it is frequently not feasible or practical for multinational businesses to gather firsthand all of the information they need for their specific purposes. As a result, these businesses must often use secondary data for decision-making purposes. Because managers usually know considerably less about the circumstances under which secondary data is gathered and reported, they accept more risk from using inaccurate information when they rely on secondary data sources.

Managers of multinational organizations often rely on secondary data for information about the business environment in which they operate. Such groups as the United Nations, the home country and host country governments, business and trade associations, and data subscription services often provide data that managers of international businesses use.

QUALITY OF DATA

The quality of the data is a major issue in data collection. The quality relates to the validity, reliability, and comparability of the data.

Data Validity The extent to which the data measures what the user expects it to measure is called **validity**. For example, if both the data gatherer and the data user use identical definitions, then the gathered information will be valid. Some countries and organizations may define things that are measured in different ways. This results in measurements that are not valid from the perspective of users from other countries and organizations.

Data Reliability The consistency of the gathered data is called the **reliability**. For example, if the thing being measured does not change, then repeated measurements using the same data-gathering techniques by various persons will yield the same results again and again. Some countries and organizations may not measure things with the same degree of accuracy as other countries and organizations do. This results in misleading data that may be useful only for propaganda purposes.

Data Comparability The extent to which secondary data from different sources are measured, computed, and reported in the exact same ways is called **comparability**. Some countries and organizations make different assumptions when gathering and reporting data. This results in data that are not exactly comparable. It is important to know the assumptions before deciding whether the information should be used for decision-making purposes.

Multinational businesses must strive to obtain the best quality data possible for use in their global information systems so that they can rely on the system outputs. If the input data lack integrity, then it is garbage in and garbage out of the global information system. This makes the system outputs worthless, and managers would be foolish to make decisions based on them.

> ✓ **Check**Point
> What are data collection issues related to data sources and data quality?

Technological Issues

Still another of the major challenges to global information systems involves technological issues. Technological issues come from communication technology problems, host-country requirements, and host-country and international regulations.

COMMUNICATION TECHNOLOGY

Those in charge of a global information system must be concerned about the adequacy of the data collection and transmission from company offices worldwide to company headquarters. If a multinational organization has total control over that process, then technology problems are not usually a major concern. However, some countries require that local technologies be used to process data. Brazil, for example, requires that locally produced computers must be used to process data generated within the country. That equipment may not be compatible with equipment used elsewhere within a multinational organization, which impedes the effectiveness of data transmission.

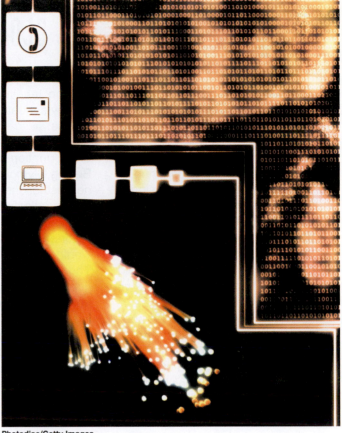

Photodisc/Getty Images

HOST-COUNTRY REQUIREMENTS

Another type of technology problem can arise from having to transmit data through local systems, which are sometimes under the control of the domestic postal, telephone, or telegraph agency. Some of these systems cannot accommodate high-speed data transmission. Others may not have enough equipment available to support the desired volume of data transmission. Sometimes a multinational business may have to transmit less information out of a country or accept a less rigid time line for transmitting information to company headquarters to work around such problems.

Host country requirements about data transmission can also create technological issues. Countries that regulate data transmission, such as Brazil, effectively impose their equipment requirements on multinational organizations operating there, restricting or eliminating their equipment choices. This complicates the design and operation of the global information system. National requirements that a domestic agency transmit all data moving inside and outside of the country can negatively impact the quality, speed, and availability of information. Such constraints create more challenges to the effective operation of both domestic and global information systems.

HOST-COUNTRY AND INTERNATIONAL REGULATIONS

Host-country and international regulations often relate to technological issues, too. Multinational organizations sometimes experience higher costs for moving data across national borders. Higher costs might be caused by requirements to use local equipment or agencies or by high international

GLOBAL BUSINESS SPOTLIGHT

THE GREAT FIREWALL OF CHINA

The People's Republic of China was once known for its Great Wall. Now it is also known for its great firewall.

Chinese Internet users and independent analysts continue to report filtering of their browsing, searching, and e-mailing. This suggests that the government is using a more sophisticated approach to controlling electronic communication. Gone are the old days when addresses disapproved by the government were unreachable. Now such sites can be accessed, but some content and functions are not operational. The Internet monitoring and blocking is accomplished through packet filtering. It ensures that every bit and byte meets programmed criteria.

China promised a free flow of information during the 2008 Beijing Olympics. Initially Internet restrictions were removed only at selected locations where governmental officials thought visiting journalists and dignitaries would most likely use the Internet. The Chinese officials hoped their guests would discover and report how freely information was flowing in China.

The plan backfired, and journalists quickly reported about all the web sites they couldn't access. Because of pressure from the International Olympic Committee and others, the Internet controls disappeared for a few days around many parts of Beijing. But soon the Internet controls reappeared except for users in special Olympic areas. As the games ended and athletes left the country, the restrictions on Internet access returned.

Think Critically

1. Why would the Chinese government want to control access to Internet information?
2. Should access to technology be limited because it could potentially be used to undermine the government?

communication and data transfer charges. Another reason for the higher costs could be the taxes on the movement of data or the excessive data line charges. Regardless of the source, managers of multinational organizations must carefully weigh the value added by having additional information against the increased costs associated with obtaining that information. Making appropriate trade-offs contributes to having a cost-effective global information system.

Host-country regulations about the types and volume of transmitted information using various technologies are a growing concern for those in charge of global information systems. A number of developed and developing countries are concerned about privacy rights, national security, and national sovereignty issues. Countries such as Austria, France, Germany, Norway, the People's Republic of China, Sweden, the United Kingdom, and the United States have these concerns. Some of these countries already have regulations or are considering regulations about data transfers across their borders. The laws and regulations are different in every country, which complicates the design and operation of a global information system. As countries around the world increasingly recognize the strategic value of market-related information, more laws and regulations governing the flow of information between countries are likely to be created. Such governmental restrictions are sometimes established to protect information, including economic data, that some cultures view as politically sensitive.

✓ CheckPoint

What are three types of technological issues that create challenges to global information systems?

14-2 Assessment

REVIEW GLOBAL BUSINESS TERMS

Define each of the following terms.

1. centralization
2. decentralization
3. primary data
4. secondary data
5. validity
6. reliability
7. comparability

Study Tools

www.cengage.com/school/genbus/intlbiz

REVIEW GLOBAL BUSINESS CONCEPTS

8. What kinds of business and financial issues create challenges to global information systems?

9. Why is primary data generally more reliable than secondary data?

SOLVE GLOBAL BUSINESS PROBLEMS

Libya is a developing country in northern Africa with most of its population clustered in cities along the Mediterranean Sea. Libya is an Arabic-speaking Muslim country where religion, culture, and tradition play important roles. Similar to other developing countries, Libya sees international business as a key to economic development. On the other hand, there is concern that outside influences may have a negative influence on society. Many Libyans embrace certain aspects of technology, such as cell phone service, while they are wary of technology that might interfere with their religion, culture, and traditions.

10. In general, how does the Libyan view of technology differ from the American view?

11. How might concerns about the use of technology affect the development of a global information system?

12. How might you make Libyans more receptive to the creation of a global information system that contains information from their country?

THINK CRITICALLY

13. How would having a currency whose value regularly rises and falls by 50 percent present a challenge for a global information system?

14. Why is it often not practical for a multinational organization to gather primary data about the business environment in each of the countries in which it operates?

15. What are some sources of information that are likely to have relatively valid and reliable data on which a multinational business can rely?

MAKE ACADEMIC CONNECTIONS

16. **TECHNOLOGY** How would having to use the domestic telephone system in a developing country create a likely barrier to the transferring of information to a developed country?

17. **LAW** How do laws that restrict the flow of information out of a country pose a threat to global information systems?

CHAPTER SUMMARY

14-1 CREATING GLOBAL INFORMATION SYSTEMS

A Information is power in the global economy. It serves as a strategic resource and provides a competitive advantage. An information system in an international environment is more challenging to create because there are many more variables to consider than in a domestic environment.

B Data inputs and operational components together yield the system outputs of a global information system. Four basic types of system outputs are product management, communication, sales management, and senior management.

C An effective global information system requires careful system planning and developing with input from senior managers as well as other managers.

14-2 GLOBAL INFORMATION SYSTEMS CHALLENGES

A Cultural and country issues are one type of challenge to global information systems. Issues concerning language, attitudes, and the business and financial environment must all be accommodated.

B Data collection issues also create challenges to global information systems. For use in decision making, data must have validity, reliability, and comparability.

C Technological issues are still another group of challenges to global information systems. Those in charge of global information systems must consider communication technology, the requirements of the host country, and host-country and international regulations.

GLOBAL REFOCUS

Read the case at the beginning of this chapter, and answer the following questions.

1. What are some domestic companies that engage in work similar to what ISIS does?

2. How are businesses in other African countries likely to view the goods and services offered by ISIS? Why?

3. What are some major projects in which ISIS has engaged?

REVIEW GLOBAL BUSINESS TERMS

Match the terms listed with the definitions.

1. The extent to which secondary data from different sources are measured, computed, and reported in the exact same ways.

2. Data not collected by the user but that are available for his or her use.

3. Parts of an information system that manage the database and system operations.

4. A system in which managers at company headquarters make most major decisions.

5. The consistency of gathered data.

6. Data collected by the user firsthand for a specific purpose.

7. A system in which local managers at different company locations around the world make most major decisions.

8. A computer-based system that provides information about company operations around the world to managers of a multinational organization.

9. Symbols that are meaningful across cultures.

10. The extent to which data measures what the user expects it to measure.

11. Data generated from an information system.

12. Pieces of information that feed the global information system database.

a. centralization

b. comparability

c. data inputs

d. decentralization

e. global information system

f. icons

g. operational components

h. primary data

i. reliability

j. secondary data

k. system outputs

l. validity

MAKE GLOBAL BUSINESS DECISIONS

13. How can information be both a strategic resource and a competitive advantage for multinational organizations?

14. How is transacting business in the international environment similar to transacting business in the domestic environment in spite of the fact that the domestic and international business environments are significantly different?

15. Why is it so important to have accurate data inputs in a global information system?

16. Why must a global information system always be operating?

17. How might attitudes toward risk taking in a culture be reflected in its language and communication practices?

18. Why do local managers usually want the outputs from a global information system in terms of local standard units of information?

19. What are some examples of business-related information from various sources that do not have comparability?

20. Why might the government of a developing country charge a multinational business an excessive amount to transfer data out of the country?

21. How does a company policy of centralization increase the influence of the headquarters staff at the expense of local staff when it comes to global information systems?

22. Why would a country want to specify that only locally manufactured equipment can be used to process data?

MAKE ACADEMIC CONNECTIONS

23. MATHEMATICS The United States does not use the metric system as its national measurement standard. How is this a challenge to creating a global information system?

24. CAREER PLANNING How might a statistician contribute to the accuracy of inputs into a global information system?

25. HISTORY How might historical events make it more challenging to create a global information system that links business operations in certain countries around the world?

26. COMMUNICATIONS Why is two-way communication between upper-level company managers and information systems managers so critical in the process of planning for a global information system?

27. COMMUNICATIONS How can the communication practices of countries influence the quality of information in a global information system?

28. TECHNOLOGY What might be some practical limitations to using technology to improve a global information system in developing African countries?

29. GEOGRAPHY How might having major river systems contribute to the development of global information systems?

30. LAW Why might some countries perceive global information systems as threats to their national security?

31. HISTORY How was the early recording of business transactions on clay tablets a milestone in the development of global information systems?

fotofrog/iStockphoto.com

The GLOBAL
Entrepreneur

CREATING AN INTERNATIONAL BUSINESS PLAN

Developing an International Business Information System

Information is needed by all organizations to plan and implement business activities. Develop an information management system based on the company and country you have been using in this continuing project, or create a new idea for your business in the same or a different country. Make use of previously collected information, and do additional research. This phase of your business plan should include the following components.

1. List the major external and internal data sources the company will use.

2. Describe the information needs (types of data and reports) that will be required for the organization to operate?

3. Describe the types of computer network systems that might be useful for obtaining and processing the organization's information.

4. Describe how the cultural, economic, and political environment of the country might affect the organization's information system.

5. Explain how recent new technology might improve or expand the company's information system.

Prepare a written summary suitable for inclusion in a business plan. Based on the written summary, develop a short oral report (two or three minutes) of your findings.

CHAPTER 15

Production Systems for Global Business

15-1 Global Production Methods

15-2 Expanding Productive Activities

GLOBAL FOCUS

Mauritania's Riches from the Sea

Have you ever tried exotic seafood such as octopus or calamari? These delicacies, as well as fish, lobster, and shrimp, are important natural resources for Mauritania, a country on Africa's Atlantic coast. The rich fishing grounds off the coast of Mauritania are a gateway to international business for this developing country.

Mauritania has a population of more than 3.3 million. The country is about the same size as Egypt and 80 percent of its land is barren desert. Although Mauritanian geography presents challenges to economic development, the country is actively engaged in efforts to maximize its limited resources. Mining, oil production, and fishing are at the heart of this effort. Fish, fish products, and iron ore are already the country's leading exports; now the emphasis is on expansion and efficiency.

Fishing is Mauritania's main source of foreign sales income. Taking advantage of the United Nations Convention on the Law of the Sea, Mauritania has exercised the right to control the resources in its coastal waters. As part of this effort, Mauritania entered into joint ventures with companies from other countries. Algeria, Iraq, and Romania were among the first to participate. These joint ventures allow Mauritania to share the profits of fishing activities along its coast. Mauritania benefits from the sophisticated fleets used by its partners, including large trawlers capable of processing, freezing, and transporting fish without entering a port. Today, a trade agreement with the European Union allows boats from EU countries to fish in Mauritania waters in exchange for more than 80 million euros a year.

Think Critically

1. What natural and human resources provide a foundation for Mauritania's economic development?
2. In the joint ventures between Mauritania and its partners, which resources are contributed by Mauritania and which are provided by the partners?
3. Conduct Web research about Mauritania to obtain additional information about the country's business and economic environment. Prepare a report of your findings.

15-1 Global Production Methods

GOALS

- Diagram the basic model for all production processes.

- Summarize methods of operations management.

- Describe the different production methods used in various countries.

Photodisc/Getty Images

The Production Process

The **production process** is the means by which a company changes raw materials into finished goods. For example, diamond miners find rough gems below ground. The stones are cut, polished, and set before they are finally sold as bracelets, necklaces, and rings to consumers around the world.

As the word "process" suggests, the production process is composed of a series of activities. The three major elements of the production process are resources, transformation, and final goods and services. The flow of these elements is shown in Figure 15-1.

Flow Chart of Production Process

Resources
- Natural
- Human
- Capital

Transformation
- Machines
- Process
- Facility

Output
- Goods
- Services

Figure 15-1 Organizations transform a combination of resources to produce goods and services that will meet consumer needs and wants.

RESOURCES

Resources are the people and things a company uses to produce a good or service. Resources fall into one of three categories: natural resources, human resources, and capital resources.

Natural Resources Natural resources come from the air, water, or earth. These basic elements can be used to create goods. The fishing banks off the shores of Mauritania and the diamonds of Angola are just a few natural resources found in Africa. Djibouti has geothermal areas and Cote d'Ivoire captures hydropower from the Bandama River. Arable land in Togo and forests in Swaziland are used to produce food and timber.

Researching a country's natural resources is vital for companies that are choosing a new site for manufacturing and identifying global business opportunities. Many countries are concerned about the depletion of their natural resources because a loss of resources means a loss of economic vitality. Recycling is one way to preserve natural resources.

Human Resources The human resources of a country are its people and their physical and intellectual abilities. A company must research the available labor force for such characteristics as mobility, literacy rate, and culture (including traditions, gender roles, and religious beliefs). For example, India's many well-educated English-speaking workers make that country an important source of labor for the information technology industry.

Capital Resources Capital resources are the funds and materials necessary to produce a good or service. In addition to financial investment, a country's monetary system, tax structure, economic conditions, and availability of materials are all important to take into consideration when discussing the capital resources of a company.

TRANSFORMATION

Transformation is the use of resources to create a good or service. A resource may be transformed by a machine (tractor, sewing machine, or computer), by a process (statistical analysis or teaching), or through a facility (colleges, restaurants, or health clinics). Resources are often transformed through the use of machines and processes. For example, cotton harvested along the lower Nile in Egypt must be cleaned and baled. Machines process the cotton and spin it into yarn and thread. Weaving machines turn the thread into cloth.

GOODS AND SERVICES

The final stage of the production process is the output of the goods and services that have been created by the transformation activities. These goods and services are now ready to enter the market as finished products for the consumer. A fish served at a restaurant is an example of output. Its production process began with a natural resource that was harvested, transported, and prepared (transformed) for a consumer's dining pleasure.

The production process does not end with the output of a product. Consumer response and changes in external factors (such as the economy) affect the process. Feedback from consumers and external influences affect input as the production cycle continues.

Work as a Team

Make a list of ten common products. List the natural, human, and capital resources needed to produce these items.

✔ CheckPoint

Give examples of the transformation stage of the production process.

Operations Management

Operations management is the process of designing and managing a production system. The goal of operations management is to produce a good or service at the lowest possible cost while maintaining the highest possible quality.

SUPPLY CHAIN ACTIVITIES

In recent years, business organizations have had an increased emphasis on coordinating inputs and outputs to maximize quality and minimize costs. This process involves an efficient use of a **supply chain**, which is a network of people, resources, technology, and information using a sequence of steps from raw materials to a final product or service. The main phases of the supply chain are:

1. *Purchasing,* in which raw materials and other required production inputs are obtained.
2. *Engineering* involves the research, design, and development of goods and services.
3. *Production* is the physical creation of the item in a manufacturing facility.
4. *Distribution* provides for the physical movement of products as well as warehouse storage as needed.
5. *Retailing* includes selection and promotion of stores or other sales locations for the desired target market.
6. *Consumer interactions* to assure that final products are received at the correct time and place, and provide appropriate customer satisfaction.

OPERATIONS ACTIVITIES

When implementing the supply chain, operations managers use several methods to help them design efficient production systems.

GLOBAL BUSINESS SPOTLIGHT

HORIZONTAL AND VERTICAL COMPANIES

Horizontal integration takes place when a company expands its operations in a similar line of business. For example, if a food store company buys another chain of food stores, horizontal integration takes place.

In contrast, *vertical integration* occurs when a company expands into various stages of production and distribution. An auto manufacturer that owns its own glass company or tire manufacturer is referred to as vertically integrated.

Should a company buy the parts it uses in an assembly plant or make the component? This is not an easy question to answer. In recent years, fewer companies have been making needed production parts. Technology has allowed many small companies to specialize in various parts and offer them at a lower cost. In recent years, Sundram Fasteners Ltd., a company in India, was supplying more than 300,000 radiator caps for use in U.S.-assembled vehicles.

Another dimension of vertical integration has been called *value-added* production. This occurs when a company takes a natural resource such as lumber or fresh fruits and processes the item into a finished good such as wood pulp or canned fruit.

Think Critically

1. How would a company decide whether to buy or make a part that would be used in the production process?
2. Select some natural resources. Describe actions companies could take to process these items into more useful goods.

Forecasting Forecasting is the method used to determine how much of a product to produce. Often that decision is based on the company's previous sales. Adjustments are made for changes in consumer demand and the country's economic conditions.

Scheduling Scheduling is the time frame for producing a good or service. Operations managers consider the availability of raw materials, human resources, and facilities needed for production when they create schedules. Recently Toyota offered custom-made cars in just five days—from the time the order was received until the vehicle left the assembly line. Delivery time to the customer was not included in the five days. Toyota's 360 key suppliers were linked to the company by computer, creating a virtual assembly line. Parts were loaded onto trucks and delivered in the order of installation.

Inventory Control A method of monitoring the amount of raw materials and completed goods on hand is called **inventory control**. This count, or inventory, gives the operations manager an idea of how much to produce to meet consumer demand. One current method of inventory control is called *just-in-time (JIT)*. This method ties a manufacturer closely to a material supplier so that the raw materials are provided only when the production process needs them. This allows a company to respond quickly to changes in the marketplace while keeping only a small amount of inventory in stock. Warehouse costs are low, and the company is not left with unused goods at the end of the year. Goods are produced on an as-needed basis.

Outsourcing In recent years, multinational companies have expanded the use of less expensive labor in other countries. **Outsourcing** refers to the transfer of a business function outside of the company. This contracting process may involve buying a part used in production rather than the company producing the item. Or, a company may outsource customer service inquiries using a phone system based in another country. While some criticize outsourcing as taking away domestic jobs, others suggest that this action is an efficient business decision to reduce operating costs and increase profit.

> ✓ **Check**Point
> What is a supply chain? What are the phases in the supply chain process?

Production Methods Around the World

Production methods refer to the processes used during the transformation stage of production. Production methods can be categorized as manual production, automated production, or computerized production.

MANUAL PRODUCTION SYSTEMS

The **manual production** method involves using human hands and bodies as the means of transforming resources into goods and services. Manual production was the earliest means of production and is still a primary method of production in many parts of the world.

In some cases, as in the South African gold mines, workers perform the labor because machines are unable to do so. In other cases, manual production is considered more valuable than any other form. Handmade quilts, sweaters knitted by hand, and furniture handmade by a master carpenter are rare and more costly than their machine-made counterparts. For many developing countries, manual production is a necessity because of the initial cost of automation.

AUTOMATED PRODUCTION SYSTEMS

In **automated production** systems, machines perform the work. A machine offers some advantages to production. The equipment performs tasks quickly and precisely and does not get bored by repetition. Machines can do some tasks that people cannot do, such as refine oil or make plastic. In some areas of production, machines have replaced workers. Cotton that was once spun by hand is now spun by machine. This shift in production has allowed workers to direct their attention to more complex tasks.

COMPUTERIZED PRODUCTION SYSTEMS

Computerized production systems use computers to control machines and perform work in the production process. The automated factory is designed to use the latest computer technology to increase productivity. Computer-controlled equipment reduces the number of people required for manual labor, but it increases the required number of trained technicians.

Computer-Assisted Manufacturing The method of using computers to run production equipment is called **computer-assisted manufacturing (CAM)**. Examples of CAM equipment are computerized assembly lines, drills, and milling machines. CAM is used in many industries including airplane manufacturing, nuclear energy, and defense. **Computer-aided design (CAD)** uses sophisticated computers that allow a designer to develop a very detailed design and key it to the CAM equipment specifications. CAD is used regularly in architectural design, interior decoration, and drafting work.

Robotics The technology connected with the design, construction, and operation of robots is called **robotics**. *Robots* are simply computerized output devices that can perform difficult, repetitive, or dangerous work in industrial settings. The use of robotics has dramatically changed the appearance of many manufacturing plants. Robots carry out tasks that once posed risks for humans. Robots also can can be programmed to deliver consistently precise work.

In recent years, more than one million industrial robots were being used in Japan. This number represented more than half of the world's total. Recent robotic technology includes an ant-size robot used to inspect and repair pipes in power plants.

Automated Warehouses Similar to the automated factory, the automated warehouse relies on computers, software, and robotics to perform stock, inventory, order, and delivery tasks. Computers store large databases of inventory information. As robots disperse merchandise to trucks for delivery, they scan a bar code, and the merchandise is automatically reordered. The repetitive functions of running a

Some inventors have developed robots for use in the home. Access the web site shown below and click on the link for Chapter 15. After exploring the web site, imagine you had a robot at home. Write a few paragraphs about how your life would be changed. What problems, if any, might you have if a robot did your daily chores?

www.cengage.com/school/genbus/intlbiz

warehouse are handled by computers and robots rather than by people. Trained technicians and managers are still necessary to make sure that the warehouse stays in efficient working order.

The warehouses of companies such as Wal-Mart, Best Buy, Amazon.com, and other online retailers can process as many as 30,000 items an hour. While an Internet retail operation (e-tailer) can be started up fairly easily, delivering products to customers is a more complicated task. Computer programs must be developed to coordinate forklift trucks and other equipment for selecting and packing items for shipping.

Computer-Integrated Manufacturing As production systems evolve, manufacturers will begin to incorporate computer-integrated manufacturing (CIM). In a **computer-integrated manufacturing (CIM)** production system, computers guide the entire manufacturing process. Production is completely controlled by computer integration—from product design through processing, assembling, testing, and packaging. Two elements of a CIM production system are minimum inventories and production based on consumer demand.

Recently Ford Motor Company in Australia used a CIM software package that prepared technical illustrations of more efficient and cost-effective motor vehicles. Another feature of this software was then used to develop manufacturing instructions. In addition to designing and producing the restyled cars at the Australian Ford plant, the operational process also was used to produce vehicles at other Ford plants in Japan, Korea, and China.

✓ CheckPoint
What are the three main types of production methods?

15-1 Assessment

Study Tools

www.cengage.com/school/genbus/intlbiz

REVIEW GLOBAL BUSINESS TERMS

Define each of the following terms.

1. production process
2. transformation
3. operations management
4. supply chain
5. inventory control
6. outsourcing
7. manual production

8. automated production
9. computerized production
10. computer-assisted manufacturing (CAM)
11. computer-aided design (CAD)
12. robotics
13. computer-integrated manufacturing (CIM)

REVIEW GLOBAL BUSINESS CONCEPTS

14. What are the three main stages of the production process?

15. What is the goal of operations management?

16. What advantages do machines offer in an automated production system?

SOLVE GLOBAL BUSINESS PROBLEMS

For each of the following situations, decide if the company is making use of manual, automated, or computerized production methods.

17. Rather than cutting leather for shoes by hand, a punch press is used.

18. Hand-designed jewelry is created in large cities in Europe and Asia.

19. A chemical company plans to make use of the latest technology for handling substances that could be dangerous to human beings.

20. On an island country, hand-woven baskets are exported.

21. Light-sensitive machines produce computer components in Taiwan.

THINK CRITICALLY

22. What actions can companies and businesses take to avoid depletion of a country's natural resources?

23. How can a country assist workers whose jobs are taken over by machinery or computers?

MAKE ACADEMIC CONNECTIONS

24. **CULTURAL STUDIES** Describe how tradition might influence the use of manual production methods in a society.

25. **VISUAL ART** Select a product or service. Prepare a flow chart or other visual presentation showing the production process for that item.

26. **TECHNOLOGY** Use the Internet to learn about the use of robotics for doing tasks that are dangerous for humans.

Photodisc/Getty Images

GOALS

- **Identify two ways production output is measured.**

- **Differentiate between producing products and creating services.**

- **Describe how technology influences office activities.**

Measuring Production Output

The goal of operations management is to produce a good or service at the lowest cost while maintaining the highest quality. To evaluate the production process, operations managers measure production output. Production output is measured in terms of productivity and quality control.

PRODUCTIVITY

Productivity refers to the amount of work that is accomplished in a unit of time. Productivity can sometimes be increased by making a simple change in the work pattern, such as using all of your fingers to keyboard instead of just two. At other times, an increase in productivity requires a capital investment, such as buying a new faster computer to replace an old slower one. Operations managers want to increase productivity to get the most work possible for the cost of production investment.

One approach to productivity is the just-in-time (JIT) system of inventory control. Companies using JIT have a limited product inventory and little time delay in manufacturing.

Another approach to productivity, synchronized manufacturing, evolved from JIT. In **synchronized manufacturing**, the workflow is distributed as needed throughout the production cycle. The company distributes the work to all points of the manufacturing process according to output demands. The workflow may appear to be unbalanced in this approach. For example, in a shirt factory using synchronized manufacturing, the fabric-cutting

Work as a Team
Prepare a list of ways productivity could be measured for jobs such as factory workers, office workers, service industry workers, and teachers.

department may work at 80 percent capacity due to an increase in orders. The packaging and distribution department, on the other hand, may be working at only 40 percent capacity to meet current orders.

QUALITY CONTROL

The second approach to measuring production output depends on quality products. To evaluate the quality of their output, companies use a method called **quality control**, which is the process of measuring goods and services against a product standard. By using a standard for goods and services, companies can compare their products to similar products from all over the world. Many companies employ quality control inspectors to monitor the comparison between products and standards.

Total Quality Control (TQC) The Japanese created an approach to quality control called **total quality control (TQC)**. This approach requires every employee, not just the inspectors, to take responsibility for high-quality production. Many companies have reported an increase not only in their employees' work output but also in the quality of work as a result of TQC. Employees work harder because they see their value to the company's growth.

Working in Teams One method of improving output quality is the quality circle. A **quality circle** consists of a small group of employees who

have different jobs within the same company but have the same goal of producing a quality good or service. For example, a quality circle at a manufacturing plant might include the project supervisor, production-line workers, an employee from distribution, and an employee from accounting. This "circle" of employees

Photodisc/Getty Images

GLOBAL BUSINESS SPOTLIGHT

YOUR CAR IS FROM WHAT COUNTRY?

Companies with a global perspective obtain production inputs and parts from many areas of the world. In recent years, motor vehicles produced in Europe had parts from more than 20 countries. The carburetor, clutch, oil pump, and several other parts were manufactured in the United Kingdom. France provided brakes, seat pads, and hose clamps. The exhaust pipes came from Sweden, while the paint and tires came from the Netherlands. Glass and the radio were produced in Canada with the starter and other parts coming from Japan. Manufacturing facilities in Denmark provided fan belts, while the radiator and air filter came from Spain. The final assembly took place in Halewood, United Kingdom or Saarlouis, Germany.

Think Critically

1. What factors influence a manufacturer's use of parts from many countries?
2. Go to the web site of an auto manufacturer to obtain additional information about the company's international production facilities.

meets on a regular basis to assess how well the manufacturing process is working. They brainstorm improvements to the production cycle or to the product itself. Because they are from all areas of the plant, they can make informed decisions together. Quality circles make use of a team management style.

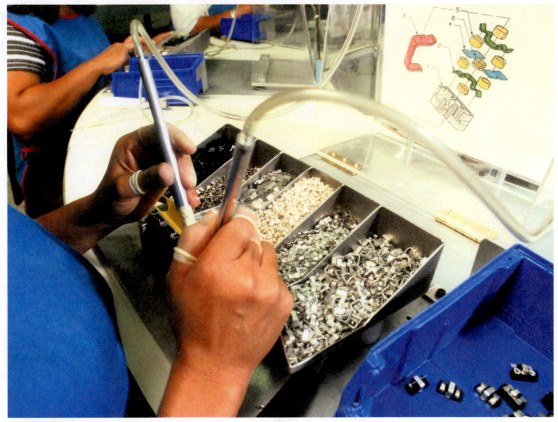

Photodisc/Getty Images

A team approach is often used by businesses for various company projects. A product team might be assigned to redesign a package, to reduce production costs, or to improve consumer convenience. A regional management team may be used to introduce an existing product into new global markets. Or a systems team might be asked to create a process for buying parts around the world at a lower cost.

A *cross-functional team* is one with members from different parts of an organization. This team is likely to include representatives from marketing, finance, information systems, and production. Each team member brings different skills and experiences. Problem solving using cross-functional teams provides solutions that take several points of view into account.

Success in working on teams involves the following skills.

- An ability to work with others who have different experiences and come from different cultural settings
- An enthusiasm to focus on team needs rather than individual accomplishments
- A readiness to cooperate with shared leadership roles
- A competency to participate in group decision making and divide tasks among team members
- A willingness to compromise for the benefit of the team's goals

 **CheckPoint**
What is a cross-functional team?

Creating and Delivering Services

Service industries perform tasks rather than provide goods for consumers. A major portion of U.S. exports involves the sale of these *intangible* items—services. With about 70 percent of GDP in the United States coming from service industries, international trade by service industries is significant. Services provided by U.S. companies comprise more than 20 percent of the world's total cross-border sales of services.

Service industries continue to grow while new ones are being created. In recent years, some of the fastest growing service industries include telecommunications businesses (such as Internet service providers and satellite television systems), business training programs, private vocational schools, health-care facilities, food service companies, entertainment and hospitality businesses, delivery services, and financial and banking services.

Meeting consumer needs is essential when providing a service. Tailored logistics is a strategy for meeting those needs. Companies using **tailored logistics** combine services with a product to better serve consumers. In recent years, McDonald's tested an automated order taker. This machine uses pictures, text, and audio to allow people to order their food and pay without interacting with a person. The system also permits a person to regulate the condiments on a sandwich by touching plus or minus signs on the screen. Workers then deliver the food and any change to the customer. This automated order-taking system has tailored logistics to serve consumers and save costs.

✓ CheckPoint
What are some of the fastest growing service industries?

GLOBAL TECHNOLOGY TRENDS

Mass Customization

When the automobile was first mass-produced in the early 1900s, Henry Ford would tell customers they could have any color car they wanted as long as it was black! Since that time, businesses have continually attempted to meet the individual needs and wants of customers.

Today companies with millions of customers are producing products designed for the individual. Consumers can buy vitamins matched to their nutritional needs. MP3 players are pre-loaded with selected music tracks. Cosmetics can be mixed to match a person's skin tone. Financial service companies offer investment advice based on a person's income, age, and household situation.

Many online companies are involved in mass customization, providing goods and services uniquely tailored to customer demand. Some technology companies only build items, such as personal computers, after they receive an order. This approach keeps profit margin up by keeping inventory down.

Mattel allows girls to go online to design a friend for Barbie. They can choose the doll's skin tone, eye color, hair color, clothes, accessories, and name. The doll is delivered with a computer-generated paragraph about its personality.

Think Critically

1. Suggest situations in which companies can use technology to create products and services designed for individual needs and wants.
2. Locate a web site that allows customers to order items created for their personal situation.

Information and Office Production

Technology creates continuing improvement in office environment productivity. Improved office productivity can be described as "smaller," "faster," "interactive," "visually enhanced," and "integrated." Office machines are becoming smaller as computer technology moves from desktop to notebook to palm-held devices. Faster and less expensive technology, especially microprocessors, creates computers that process information more quickly and with greater flexibility of input and output.

In addition, technological design is focusing on *integrated systems*. Most information technology (IT) operations combine computer networks with audio-video capabilities, scanning devices, and online connections, often using wireless systems. These systems provide a link between business information providers and other sectors, such as schools, health-care facilities, and government agencies.

Photodisc/Getty Images

Office workers once used typewriters and carbon paper. Today, office systems continually make use of new types of technology, which in recent years have included wireless notebook computers, personal digital assistants (PDAs), laser scanners, and cellular phones with Internet access. These highly integrated IT systems have increased the ability and efficiency of office workers to provide needed information for making local and global business decisions.

Office work is moving out of the office. Mobile technology makes it possible to complete office tasks in diverse locations. While offices still exist, people are working at their kitchen tables and in their home offices. Away from home, they are working out of their cars, at coffee shops, on airplanes, and in hotel rooms. Mobile technology also allows around-the-clock contact with customers and staff in other geographic areas.

Work as a Team
Discuss why the fastest growing service industries are growing so rapidly.

✓ CheckPoint
What components are commonly included in an integrated information system?

INTERNATIONAL BUSINESS PERSPECTIVE
Careers

GLOBAL SUPPLY CHAIN MANAGEMENT

You see an online advertisement for shirts made by a company in Argentina. You decide to order one at the company's web site. After processing your request and payment, the company ships the shirt and it is delivered to your home. You have just experienced several elements of the global supply chain.

Everything you buy and use involves a supply chain. Toyota and Wal-Mart as well as local stores in your neighborhood all use supply chain activities including planning, implementing, and managing resources for creating and selling products. At one end of the supply chain is the *inflow* of raw materials, such as plastic parts or freshly-grown food items. At the other end is the consumer who buys and uses goods and services, which are the *outflow* of the process.

Supply chain managers coordinate and collaborate with suppliers and other partners in this sequence. The supply chain process also adds value for customers with improved products, increased availability, faster delivery, and lower prices.

What skills are needed for a career in supply chain management? In addition to basic business skills, such as accounting, finance, and marketing, those working in global supply chain management require knowledge and experience in these areas:

- Sources of raw materials and product components
- Production facility location selection and operations
- Research, development, and product design
- Inventory control and warehouse management
- Transportation methods
- Negotiations with supply chain partners
- Foreign language and cultural knowledge

guenterguni/iStockphoto.com

Effective management of supply chain activities is critical for most businesses. As a result, supply chain management is a field with strong career opportunities, especially with companies involved in international business. So, the next time you buy or use a product, remember that as a consumer you are part of the supply chain. Someday you might be managing the supply chain.

Think Critically

1. Prepare a list of various tasks involved in supply chain management.
2. Conduct a web search to obtain additional information on global supply chain career opportunities.

REVIEW GLOBAL BUSINESS TERMS

Define each of the following terms.

1. productivity
2. synchronized manufacturing
3. quality control
4. total quality control (TQC)
5. quality circle
6. tailored logistics

Study Tools

www.cengage.com/school/genbus/intlbiz

REVIEW GLOBAL BUSINESS CONCEPTS

7. How can production output be measured?
8. How do service industries differ from manufacturing industries in their production processes?
9. How is information processing and office productivity changing?

SOLVE GLOBAL BUSINESS PROBLEMS

Balancing trade with the protection of natural resources is important. In some African countries, trade in tropical timber is restricted. Governments place heavy tariffs on exported finished-wood products. Yet these countries strive to develop their economies. A proposal in Uganda suggested lifting tariffs on finished-wood products such as furniture, because these items have a higher market value than raw timber. African countries could maintain their income levels while harvesting fewer trees.

10. What changes in input and transformation of the production process of timber would occur?
11. Which production method (manual, automated, or computerized) would make the proposal most feasible?
12. Do you think this proposal would enable the African countries to increase their profits from tropical timber? Why or why not?

THINK CRITICALLY

13. List objections that employees might have to working on cross-functional teams.
14. Measuring quality of services is more difficult than measuring manufactured goods. What are some ways in which a business could assess the quality of service provided?

MAKE ACADEMIC CONNECTIONS

15. **MATH** Without quality control, small numbers of defective products can result in large business expenses. A manufacturing company produces 1.2 million computer chips a month, costing $7 each. Currently, 1.5 percent of these are defective each month. How much would the company save each month if the rate of defective items could be reduced to 0.6 percent?
16. **ECONOMICS** Why are more personal and business services offered in developed economies than in less-developed economies?

Quiz Prep

www.cengage.com/school/genbus/intlbiz

CHAPTER SUMMARY

15-1 GLOBAL PRODUCTION METHODS

A The production process changes raw materials into finished goods and services. The three elements in the production process are resources, transformation, and goods and services.

B The goal of operations management is to produce a good or service at the lowest possible cost while maintaining the highest possible quality. Operations managers use forecasting, scheduling, and inventory control to manage the process.

C The production methods used in global business are manual production, automated production, and computerized production.

15-2 EXPANDING PRODUCTIVE ACTIVITIES

A Production output might be measured in terms of productivity and quality control. Productivity is the amount of work that is accomplished in a unit of time. Quality control measures goods and services produced against a product standard.

B Creating services involves performing tasks that provide value to consumers and businesses. Services are about 70 percent of U.S. GDP and a major portion of global sales.

C Technology influences office activities through improved productivity resulting from faster and more efficient equipment and systems.

GLOBAL **REFOCUS**

Read the Global Focus at the beginning of this chapter, and answer the following questions.

1. Which production systems have been used in Mauritania's production of seafood?

2. How have changes in technology contributed to Mauritania's success in the fishing industry?

REVIEW GLOBAL BUSINESS TERMS

Match the terms listed with the definitions. Some terms may not be used.

1. The means by which a company changes raw materials into finished goods.

2. A method of production in which machines perform the work.

3. The use of resources to create a good or service.

4. The process of designing and managing a production system.

5. A measurement of the amount of work that is accomplished in a unit of time.

6. A method of production using computers to control machines and perform work.

7. The process of measuring goods and services against a product standard.

8. A method of monitoring the amount of raw materials and completed goods on hand.

9. A method of production that involves using peoples' hands and bodies as the means of transforming resources into goods and services.

10. A production system in which computers guide the entire manufacturing process, from product design through processing, assembly, testing, and packaging.

11. A small group of employees who have different jobs within the same company but have the same goal of producing a quality good or service.

a. automated production
b. computer-aided design (CAD)
c. computer-assisted manufacturing (CAM)
d. computer-integrated manufacturing (CIM)
e. computerized production
f. inventory control
g. manual production
h. operations management
i. production process
j. productivity
k. quality circle
l. quality control
m. robotics
n. synchronized manufacturing
o. tailored logistics
p. total quality control (TQC)
q. transformation

12. The technology that designs, constructs, and operates devices that can perform difficult, repetitive, or dangerous work.

13. The method of using computers to run production equipment.

14. The system where service are combined with a product to better serve consumers.

15. The system where workflow is distributed as needed throughout the production cycle.

16. A work approach that requires every employee to take responsibility for high-quality production.

MAKE GLOBAL BUSINESS DECISIONS

17. A region's production opportunities are often determined by its natural resources. Which of your state's natural resources have been used to encourage business in your state? Are any of the natural resources unique to your state? If so, what has that meant for production in your state?

18. As a consumer of a particular product, how would you suggest tailoring the product to better serve consumer demands?

19. What effects do you think robotics and computer-integrated manufacturing (CIM) might have on business during the next two decades?

20. What production methods do you and others use to accomplish daily tasks at home, school, or work? List examples for each method used.

21. What actions might be taken by a company to improve quality?

22. Prepare a list (with job descriptions) of roles that might be assumed by team members working on a project, such as team leader and recorder.

23. How can a person prepare to have the skills necessary for employment in the future as technology changes the types of jobs that are in demand?

24. Describe safety situations and other reasons that a country might continue to use manual production methods rather than automated or computerized ones.

MAKE ACADEMIC CONNECTIONS

25. GEOGRAPHY Identify companies that contribute significantly to your local economy. Are these organizations manufacturing or service businesses? Which resources (natural, human, or capital) may have attracted these companies to your area?

26. COMMUNICATIONS Choose a company, and obtain information from library research or the Internet about its production activities. Create a flow chart of the production process of this company. Include the resources used in input, the activities involved in transformation, and the goods and services produced as output.

27. CULTURAL STUDIES Describe how cultural differences might affect team project activities of a group of workers from different countries.

28. SCIENCE Interview a person who is involved with manufacturing about production processes used in his or her business. What natural resources and scientific principles are used by this organization? What possible health and safety concerns might be encountered in various countries around the world?

29. MATHEMATICS Research methods used to measure production output. What numeric standards are used to measure productivity? How is quality control maintained?

30. CAREER PLANNING Conduct library research about the technology used in different countries. Prepare a list of computer and technology skills that office workers and other employees should possess for career success.

31. GEOGRAPHY Choose a country. Use the Internet to identify five natural resources the country supplies to the rest of the world. Prepare a poster, tabletop display, or slide presentation showing a map of the country, photographs or illustrations of the natural resource, and examples of products or services that rely on the resources.

32. TECHNOLOGY Use the Internet to identify companies with operations that have horizontal integration and vertical integration.

33. TECHNOLOGY Use the Internet to find online resources for computer-assisted manufacturing and computerized production systems.

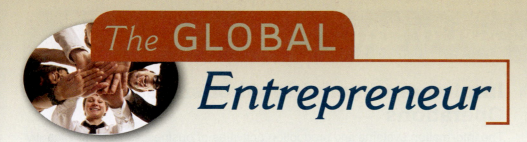

The GLOBAL Entrepreneur

CREATING AN INTERNATIONAL BUSINESS PLAN

Planning Production for Global Business

Based on the company you have been using in this continuing project or on a new idea for your business, obtain information related to the following elements of production planning.

1. List natural resources needed for this enterprise.

2. Describe the human resources of the organization.

3. List capital resources necessary for providing the good or service.

4. Prepare a visual presentation of the production process. (Describe how manual, automated, or computerized production will be used.)

5. Describe what types of technology the company will use.

6. Describe types of items (parts, supplies, finished goods) will be kept in inventory.

7. Describe factors will be used to measure productivity.

8. Describe actions could be taken to assure quality control.

Prepare a written summary suitable for inclusion in a business plan. Based on the written summary, develop a short oral report (two or three minutes) of your findings.

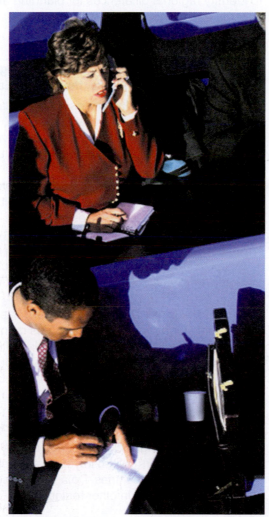

Photodisc/Getty Images

Implement International Business Operations

The information systems and production activities of businesses vary significantly around the world. While these differences are frequently the result of the level of economic development, history and culture may also affect these business operations. Cross-cultural teams, with people from around the world, can add to the efficiency of a company's information processing and manufacturing.

Goal

To identify regional differences for planning and implementing information systems and manufacturing facilities.

Activities

Working in teams, select a geographic region you will represent—Africa, Asia, Europe, Latin America, the Middle East, or North America.

1. To research information processing and manufacturing in your region, consider doing the following: conduct a web search, use library resources, and, if possible, talk to people who have lived or visited that area of the world.
2. Identify the extent to which computers are used in various countries in your region.
3. Explain common information processing procedures used by companies in your geographic region. How does the availability of information improve the efficiency of business activities?
4. Describe common production activities in two countries in your region. What benefits and concerns are associated with these factories?
5. Evaluate how technology is used in production activities for two countries in the region. What are some of the limitations of using technology in this area of the world?
6. **Global Business Decision** Your team has been assigned the task of selecting a location for a production facility. This manufacturing plant will make automobile parts for vehicles assembled in the United Kingdom, United States, Japan, Germany, Mexico, and Brazil. Compare your findings with those of others on your team and decide which region would be the best location for this factory. What factors need to be considered when making this decision?

Team Skill   Cross-Cultural Team Leadership

Leadership has a significant influence on the success of a team. Describe the skills of team leaders valued in your geographic region. Discuss any notable exceptions in specific countries. Do any of these competencies differ from those of effective team leaders in other regions?

Present

Create a flowchart or other visual presentation to communicate the types of information systems and production facilities found in your geographic region.

BPA Presentation Management—Team Event

This event will assess your use of current desktop technologies and software to prepare and deliver an effective multimedia presentation. You will design a computer-generated multimedia presentation. You have 15 minutes for preparation and setup. The presentation will last a minimum of seven minutes and a maximum of 10 minutes. Up to five minutes will be allowed for questions from the judges (class members).

The contestants must make effective use of current multimedia technology in the presentation. In preparation for the presentation, contestants should use space, color, and text as design factors. Charts and other graphics should be used in the presentation. The presentation must be delivered using a computer; the team's presentation can be on the computer's hard drive, a CD-ROM, or a DVD. No VCR or laserdisc may be used in the presentation. The students are responsible for securing a release form from any individual whose name, photograph, and other information is included in the presentation.

Topic: Conducting business in another country involves opportunity and risk. Each team must select a geographic region—Africa, Asia, Europe, Latin America, the Middle East, or North America. The team presentation must describe major political, social, and economic risks faced by companies doing business in this region. The presentation should also identify actions that might be taken to reduce or eliminate the international risk. The presentation must indicate common sources of financing businesses in the selected geographic region and the related risk. The presentation must give a strategy to successfully operate a business in the selected region of the world.

Performance Indicators Evaluated

- Demonstrate knowledge of multimedia software and components.
- Demonstrate effective oral communication skills.
- Apply technical skills to create a multimedia presentation that enhances the oral presentation.

You will be evaluated for your

- Knowledge of the topic
- Organized presentation of the topic
- Confidence, quality of voice, and eye contact
- Relationship of the topic to business strategy

For more detailed information about performance indicators, go to the BPA web site.

Think Critically

1. Why are cross-cultural teams necessary for international business?
2. How does culture effect business?
3. What can be done to reduce risks associated with business in this region?
4. Why take the risk of international business?

www.bpa.org

Marketing in a Global Economy

Chapter

16 **Global Marketing and Consumer Behavior**

17 **Developing Goods and Services for Global Markets**

18 **Global Pricing and Distribution Strategies**

19 **Global Promotional Strategies**

Central and South America

If You Were There

After a few days of visiting churches, museums, and cafes in Quito, Arturo is ready for the next leg of his journey. As the train departs the capital city of Ecuador, Arturo has a great view of the green slopes of the Pichincha volcano.

During the trip to Guayaquil, which takes two days, Arturo experiences a wide range of climates. The highlands of the Andres Mountains offer cool, mild temperatures due to a high altitude, and despite being just south of the equator. Later in the journey, after descending from the mountains, he and his fellow travelers encounter the heat and humidity of the rain forest.

Food vendors greet the travelers at every stop. After the overnight segment of the trip, Arturo enjoys a hearty breakfast drink made of corn boiled in milk and flavored with cinnamon. When the train stops for lunch, travelers enjoy fried eggs, pasta, fried plantains, and salad.

Rather than sitting inside, some passengers ride on the top of the train. This requires great care, especially when the train passes under low hanging electric wires. As travelers enjoy the panoramic view, an on-board vendor moves atop the train selling fresh baked goods.

©Dr. Morley Read 2009/ Used under license from Shutterstock.com

The streets of Guayaquil are also filled with vendors selling everything from clothing and cosmetics to electronics and freshly cooked meat. Arturo has arrived in Ecuador's largest city and the busiest port on South America's Pacific coast. From here, he is off to the Galapagos Islands to continue his vacation in Ecuador.

Geography

The Andes Mountains and their snowcapped peaks extend almost 4,500 miles from Venezuela to the tip of South America, dominating the topography of the western part of the continent. Inland plains spread from Venezuela south through Brazil, Paraguay, Uruguay, and Argentina. A vast desert region in Peru and Chile is one of the driest areas in the world. Rain forests are common in areas of Central America; the Amazon basin rain forest takes up one-third of South America. The longest river in the Western Hemisphere is the Amazon. It flows 4,000 miles across the continent before pouring its vital nutrients into the ocean, enriching sea life as far away as the Grand Banks of Newfoundland off the coast of Canada.

Maya and Inca Civilizations

The influence of the Maya and Inca civilizations can be seen throughout Central and South America today. The Maya civilization dominated parts of Mexico and Central America between A.D. 250 and A.D. 900. The Maya region included present-day Belize, El Salvador, Guatemala, and Honduras, as well as the Mexican states of Campeche, Chiapas, Quintana Roo, Tabasco, and Yucatán.

Photodisc/Getty Images

Numerous independent city-states flourished throughout the region. Mayan culture centered around religion and ceremony. Mayan cities contained great temple-pyramids, which attracted large crowds during festivals. Today, these monuments to the rich Mayan culture continue to draw crowds as thousands of tourists visit pyramids throughout the region.

The ruins of Machu Picchu in the Andes Mountains of Peru also attract visitors from all over the world. The visitors, including tourists, historians, and scientists, come to see one of the most familiar images of Inca civilization. The Andes mountains formed the center of the Inca empire that extended from the northern border of modern Ecuador to central Chile. Its 10-12 million inhabitants enjoyed the benefits of the strong central government in return for helping with the construction of public buildings and roads.

According to historians and archeologists, the Inca empire was founded in the early part of the thirteenth century and ended with the death of Emperor Atahuallpa in 1533. The spread of smallpox, a civil war, and the arrival of the Spanish, led by the conquistador Francisco Pizarro, all played a role in the demise of the Inca empire.

Colonization

The colonization of Central and South America was based on an economic system known as *mercantilism*—in which a nation's power depended on its accumulation of wealth. Portuguese and Spanish ships carried away great quantities of gold, silver, and other raw materials to the parent countries. In turn, the colonies served as markets for manufactured exports. The Native Americans were forced to work the mines and plantations. Later, when European diseases significantly reduced the indigenous population, Africans were enslaved and imported.

During the colonial period (1521-1820), approximately 5,400 Spanish and Portuguese immigrated to Latin America each year. These immigrants developed a society based on their European heritage and influenced by cultural aspects of their new environment. They brought Roman Catholicism to the colonies, and it remains the dominant religion today.

Struggle for Independence

Spanish colonies gained their independence from Spain during the nineteenth century. Nationalist leaders Simón Bolívar, José de San Martin, and Bernardo O'Higgins led wars of independence from Spanish rule in Venezuela, Argentina, and Chile, respectively.

Members of the Portuguese royal family, including King Joâo VI, fled to Brazil after Napoléon invaded Portugal. In 1822, Brazil declared independence from Portugal and Dom Pedro was crowned emperor of Brazil.

Traditionally, wealthy landowners, merchants, and the military have controlled Latin American governments since independence. Attempts to gain power or to protect the wealth and power of the ruling class have led to frequent changes in government including military coups. In 1991 and 1992, coup attempts occurred in Guatemala, Haiti, Venezuela, and Peru.

Industries

Farming and mining are the most important industries in Latin America. Coffee, sugar, bananas, wheat, cotton, and cacao are exported. However, the region still has difficulty feeding its people because of a growing population and primitive farming methods. A few countries produce oil and natural gas. Most countries mine mineral resources such as iron, tin, copper, silver, lead, and gold. Brazil ranks in the top ten countries for world gold production.

Economic Growth

Future economic growth will depend on industrial development. Many governments are looking to their sparsely populated interiors for hydroelectric power to run factories and offices. The interiors are also rich in timber and could provide farms for the millions of hungry, landless peasants. Rain forests are essential to the global environment and must be preserved. The wild rivers attract tourists, and the rain forest is home to many indigenous people. The rain forests contain an abundance of animal and plant species, which are possible sources of medicines.

Latin American nations are under pressure to protect the environment at the expense of industrial development. The northern countries continue to consume and pollute. The population of Latin America could double in the next 20 to 25 years, and governments will be hard-pressed to fill basic food, housing, health, and education needs for their people. These social, economic, and health problems are all interrelated, and their solutions might be found by those regional and global problem solvers who comprehend just how interdependent we are.

Photodisc/Getty Images

Think Critically

1. How does having a government consisting of wealthy officials and military personnel affect the citizens of a country?
2. How do North American consumption trends affect the rain forests in Central and South America?
3. Why is industrial development essential for the economic growth of this region?
4. Use the library or do an Internet search to determine how many and what kinds of species are estimated to exist in the Amazon River area. What kinds of medical uses have already been discovered for some of these species?

COUNTRY PROFILE

The World Factbook, published online by the Central Intelligence Agency, includes country profiles for the nations of Asia and the Pacific Rim. Each country's profile includes an overview followed by detailed information about the country's geography, people, government, economy, communications, transportation, military, and transnational issues.

CHAPTER 16

Global Marketing and Consumer Behavior

16-1 Marketing Around the World

16-2 The Marketing Mix and the Marketing Plan

16-3 Planning Global Marketing Activities

MAURICIO LIMA/AFP/Getty Images

GLOBAL FOCUS

Breakfast Around the World

What did you have for breakfast? The answer for many people is a bowl of cereal, but that isn't the only answer. In recent years, the population growth rate and the demand for ready-to-eat cereal in the United States have slowed. As a result, cereal producers are expanding their efforts in international markets including Europe, the Middle East, and Africa.

Although Europeans traditionally have eaten less cereal per person than Americans, Europe is an attractive new market because the breakfast habits there are similar to those in the United States. General Mills created a joint venture with Swiss-based Nestlé, called Cereal Partners Worldwide, to sell its cereals in Europe, Latin America, the Middle East, and other regions. This agreement allows General Mills to take advantage of the extensive distribution system and a strong global Nestlé brand. The joint venture sells cereal in more than 130 countries.

In Turkey, Kellogg's entered in a joint venture with Ulker to create a company called Kellogg Med to produce and distribute cereal products throughout the eastern Mediterranean region. The first item developed was Ulker-Kellogg's corn flakes, which competes with the traditional Turkish breakfast of cheese and olives.

The most popular breakfast items in Kenya are bread, sweet potatoes, fruits, cooked cereals, and mandazis, which are similar to donuts. In an effort to gain sales in Africa, the Weetabix cereal company offers its products in smaller packages, in more varieties, and at a price that Kenyan consumers can afford. The company is also working to change the perception that breakfast cereals are mainly for children.

Economic and cultural factors influence the international marketing activities of global cereal companies. Planning the product, packaging, pricing, and promotion of cereals in the global marketplace continues to be a challenge for Tony the Tiger and his buddies.

Think Critically

1. What factors influenced cereal companies to expand their marketing in other countries?
2. What problems might a cereal company face when planning to sell its products in a new international market?
3. Locate the web site of Kellogg's, General Mills, or another global cereal company. Obtain information about international marketing of cereal. Prepare a report of your findings.

16-1 Marketing Around the World

GOALS

- Describe the nature of markets.
- Identify trends that influence global marketing opportunities.

Photodisc/Getty Images

International Markets

Survival for every company depends on creating and delivering items that consumers will buy. Distribution of products and development of consumer awareness are major tasks of marketing. Marketing does not always involve a specific good or service. Places such as Bermuda, Jamaica, Mexico, and Puerto Rico advertise in magazines, on television, and on the Internet to attract visitors. This type of marketing can stimulate tourism and consumer interest in the goods and services of those geographic areas.

One business sells carpeting in one city, while another sells global telecommunications systems throughout the world. Both companies must get the product or service from the producer to the consumer. Customers must first become aware of a product. Then the item must be delivered at a cost acceptable to both the buyer and the seller.

Marketing is the creation and maintenance of satisfying exchange relationships between businesses and their customers. Marketing includes shipping, packaging, pricing, advertising, selling, and many other tasks. **International marketing** involves marketing activities between sellers and buyers in different countries. Japanese automobile manufacturers perform marketing activities in more than 140 countries. Overnight delivery services are also involved in international marketing as they move packages throughout countries and continents.

GLOBAL BUSINESS SPOTLIGHT

MEETING NEEDS IN EMERGING MARKETS

Coca-Cola India is working to improve nutrition with Vitingo. The company describes its orange-flavored drink mix as tasty, affordable, and refreshing. Even better, the mix contains micronutrients including Vitamin A, iron, and zinc.

The drink is designed to help fight malnutrition. Millions of people in lower socio-economic communities are victims of "hidden hunger," also called micronutrient malnutrition. Their diets are deficient in vitamins and minerals.

Coca-Cola India is collaborating with a non-profit organization involved in micro financing. The partners hope to raise awareness of hidden hunger, provide an affordable product to combat micronutrient malnutrition, and develop a selling and distribution model for Vitingo.

Think Critically

1. Describe some products and services that companies could offer to improve quality of life around the world?
2. Conduct an Internet search to locate a web site with information about products that could improve the quality of life in less developed economies.

The main focus of marketing is to define and sell to a specific group. A **market** refers to the likely customers for a good or service in a certain geographic location. A market could be teenagers in France or retired people in Mexico. Markets are commonly divided into two categories—consumer markets and organizational markets.

CONSUMER MARKETS

A **consumer market** consists of individuals and households who are the final users of goods and services. You are part of the consumer market when you buy food, clothing, transportation, health-care, and recreational products. Consumer markets exist in every country of the world. However, buying habits vary because of factors such as climate, culture, political environment, values, tradition, and religious beliefs.

ORGANIZATIONAL MARKETS

Not all goods and services are sold to end users. An **organizational market,** also called a *commercial* market or *business-to-business* (B2B) marketing, consists of buyers who purchase items for resale or additional production. These buyers include manufacturers, stores, schools, hotels, hospitals, and governments. Items commonly purchased in commercial markets are raw materials, machines, machine parts, warehouses, computers, office space, office supplies, and Internet services.

Organizational markets are important to the economy of a country. As nations create more factories and start companies, jobs are created. The income earned by these employees contributes to increased consumer spending, which results in economic expansion.

✓ CheckPoint
Describe the two different kinds of markets.

Global Marketing Opportunities

Most businesses need to develop new markets in order to maintain and expand profits. Quite often new customers are found in other countries. For example, when sales for electronic products leveled off for Asian companies in their home region, these firms expanded to sell to customers in South America and Europe.

GLOBAL TRENDS

Opportunities for international marketing are influenced by five global trends. These trends are related to expanded communications, technology, changing political situations, increased competition, and changing demographics.

Expanded Communications Computer networks make it possible to communicate quickly with customers. The Internet has become the foundation of both local and global communication as companies connect with customers, suppliers, and partners almost instantly. Satellite and wireless links provide global communication networks to facilitate international marketing. People working in different geographic areas are able to interact as if they were just down the hall.

Photodisc/Getty Images

Technology Automated production systems allow easier set up of manufacturing plants in other countries. As a result, manufactures create products closer to where they are sold. Technology has also resulted in more efficient distribution as global positioning systems (GPS) and radio-frequency identification (RFID) are used to monitor products in transit. With improved transportation and overnight shipping, goods arrive at destinations around the world within a matter of days or even hours.

Changing Political Situations Countries that desire economic growth are cooperating with new trading partners. Several nations that were formerly governed by communism now have a more cooperative economic attitude toward international business. Many global companies now do business in various eastern European countries in which trade was previously restricted.

Increased Competition As more companies get involved in exporting and foreign investment, business firms look for new markets in other countries. A more competitive environment requires companies to be more creative and more efficient when selling around the world.

Changing Demographics The traits of a country's population (such as birthrate, age distribution, marriage rate, gender distribution, income distribution, education level, and housing situation) are its **demographics**. Demographic trends create different marketing opportunities. A lower birthrate in a country could mean a baby food company must market in other nations or create other types of products.

Work as a Team
Discuss the kinds of product opportunities that would occur if a country advanced rapidly in adding electronic technology for the use of all its citizens.

THE MARKETING PROCESS

Identifying business opportunities is the start of the marketing process, as shown in Figure 16-1. When a business finds a new use for its products or finds a new group of customers, an opportunity to expand marketing occurs. The Disney Company, for example, built amusement parks in Japan, France, and Hong Kong. The company saw opportunities for foreign expansion of its entertainment services.

✓ CheckPoint
What are five global marketing trends that create opportunities for international marketing?

The Marketing Process

IDENTIFY	EVALUATE	PLAN	EXECUTE
Identify business opportunities	Evaluate potential demand and consumer behavior patterns	Plan the marketing strategy for the marketing mix based on marketing research	Carry out the marketing plan

Figure 16-1 The marketing process can help a company plan and execute its global marketing activities.

INTERNATIONAL BUSINESS PERSPECTIVE

Geography

THE RAIN FOREST

Rain forests are located in 33 countries in Africa, Asia, and Central and South America. The largest rain forest covers areas in Brazil, French Guiana, Suriname, Guyana, Venezuela, Colombia, Ecuador, Peru, Bolivia, and Chile.

Many common food products originate in rain forests. These include avocados, bananas, black pepper, cashews, chocolate, cinnamon, coconuts, coffee, cola, lemons, oranges, sugarcane, and vanilla.

More than 5 million different plant and animal species live in rain forests. Tens of thousands of other species may still be undiscovered. In the Amazon River region of Brazil, every few miles you will find hundreds of different insects, mammals, birds, reptiles, and amphibians making their homes in trees and other plants. Many plants from these jungles are used to treat various diseases, including cancer. Aspirin was originally made from a tropical willow tree.

In recent years, farmers, loggers, cattle ranchers, and highway builders have used many rain forest areas. Their activities have resulted in a changed environment. Many plants and animals are lost forever. Rain forests are being destroyed at the rate of thousands of square miles a year. Much of the Pacific rain forests in Guatemala, for example, are now used for coffee, cotton, and sugar farming. Attempts are being made to plant over 50 million new trees in that country to improve the ecology.

Throughout the world, environmental groups are working to save the rain forests. Actions recommended for those concerned about the situation include recycling, using reusable containers, and avoiding products that come from destroyed rain forest areas.

Think Critically

1. How do consumers and businesses benefit from rain forests?
2. What actions might be appropriate to preserve the rain forests?
3. Conduct an Internet search for additional information about the benefits provided by rain forests.

16-1 Assessment

REVIEW GLOBAL BUSINESS TERMS

Define each of the following terms.

1. international marketing
2. market
3. consumer market
4. organizational market
5. demographics

REVIEW GLOBAL BUSINESS CONCEPTS

6. What business activities are included in marketing?
7. How do consumer markets and organizational markets differ?
8. What is a global marketing opportunity, and what influences it?

SOLVE GLOBAL BUSINESS PROBLEMS

Determine whether each of the following activities is a marketing activity.

9. Planning a label design for canned tomatoes.
10. Placing a product order form on a web site.
11. Ordering office supplies.
12. Sending a product catalog to a customer.
13. Using overnight delivery services to send a sample to a customer.
14. Processing the payroll for the marketing department.
15. Conducting a survey in a mall about product preferences.

THINK CRITICALLY

16. Explain why money spent on a factory has the potential for greater economic growth than money spent by consumers on video games.
17. Based on this unit's Regional Profile, which three countries have the highest population growth rate? What marketing opportunities are created by a high population growth rate?

MAKE ACADEMIC CONNECTIONS

18. **TECHNOLOGY** Describe examples of marketing opportunities that were not possible a few years ago that have been created by technology.
19. **LAW** What types of laws might be encountered in other countries that would restrict marketing activities?

16-2 The Marketing Mix and the Marketing Plan

GOALS

- List the four elements of the marketing mix.
- Describe a marketing plan and its use in global marketing activities.

©Vladimir Meinik, 2009/ Used under license from Shutterstock.com

The Marketing Mix

As a company plans and organizes its global marketing activities, several questions must be considered. What will be sold? How much will be charged? How will the item get to the consumer? How will consumers become informed about the product? These questions address the four major elements of the **marketing mix**, which are product, price, distribution, and promotion. Figure 16-2 offers examples of each element of the marketing mix. The marketing mix is used whether you are selling clothing in a small community or expanding credit card services throughout South America.

PRODUCT

Before goods are purchased, the items must satisfy a need or want. **Product** refers to a good or service being offered for sale that satisfies consumer demand. The term "product" refers to everything from automobiles and green beans to life insurance and cable television networks. Not all products are offered by businesses. Nonprofit organizations such as museums and symphony orchestras offer educational and cultural experiences as their products.

Many factors, such as culture, weather, and economic conditions, can affect the acceptance of a product or service in a foreign market. For example, instant foods may not sell in cultures where careful preparation of the family meal is important.

The Marketing Mix

PRODUCT	PRICE	DISTRIBUTION	PROMOTION
• Goods • Services	• Value to consumer • Production costs	• Transportation • Storage • Wholesaling • Retailing	• Advertising • Personal selling • Publicity • Sales promotions

Figure 16-2 Businesses coordinate the four elements of the marketing mix to reach their customers.

PRICE

The monetary value of a product agreed upon by a buyer and a seller is the **price**. What if you agree to purchase 100 personal DVD players at a price of £53 per stereo from a United Kingdom firm? Do you know how much you are paying? As you know, different nations use different money systems. Prices may be stated in terms of euros, pesos, yen, or another currency.

DISTRIBUTION

Distribution involves the activities needed to physically move and transfer ownership of goods and services from producer to consumer. Transporting, storing, sorting, ordering, and retailing are examples of distribution activities. Distribution activities vary from country to country. For example, some countries do not have refrigeration systems in stores. Therefore, products such as milk are distributed differently than they are in the United States.

PROMOTION

The final component of the marketing mix is promotion. **Promotion** involves the marketing efforts that inform and persuade customers. Different languages and customs influence promotional decisions. Many companies have used inappropriate wording when advertising in another country. For example, a Canadian importer of Turkish clothing translated the labels into French for sale in Quebec. The French language has a different word for turkey the bird and Turkey the country. So a confused translator created labels that read "made in a turkey" instead of "Made in Turkey."

MARKETING OF SERVICES

Demand for health care, financial services, and information systems has increased in recent years. This demand has resulted in expanded marketing opportunities for these and other services. *Consumer services* include those provided to individuals by lawyers, doctors, dentists, hairstylists, daycare centers, repair shops, travel agencies, and music teachers. *Commercial services* include advertising, information systems, delivery, maintenance, security, and equipment rental. Services sold to businesses continue to gain importance for companies involved in exporting and international trade.

Work as a Team

Select items, one good and one service. Discuss how the elements of the marketing mix would vary for the two products. Repeat with other pairs of products as time allows.

When a business markets services, it must adapt the marketing mix for a nonphysical item. Many of the advertising and pricing activities used for goods also apply to services. Distribution of services, however, is quite different. The service is most often produced at the time of consumption. For example, a haircut or dental checkup is produced and consumed at one time.

✓ **Check**Point

Name the four major elements of the marketing mix. Give an example of each.

The Marketing Plan

A *marketing plan* is a document that describes the marketing activities of an organization. A marketing plan may consist of the seven sections shown in Figure 16-3. Some companies may use different titles or change the number of sections in their marketing plans. However, the elements shown in the illustration and described below should be considered in all marketing plans.

Company Goals The first item of the marketing plan presents what the company wants to accomplish. Company goals should be specific. For example a company might want "to increase consumer awareness for our new personal computer among Brazilian small business owners." The company goal for another business could be "to reduce selling costs for customers in Japan." A third example is "to increase sales in the South American region."

Description of Customers and Their Needs The second part of the marketing plan describes the company's customers. What are their needs? What types of television programs do they watch? How often do they go to the store? How do they spend their leisure time? This information helps the company meet consumer needs.

Competitors With whom will you be competing? What are the products offered by the competitor? How is your product different from the competitor's product? How are competing products promoted, priced, and distributed?

Economic, Social, Legal, and Technological Trends What trends can be observed? How will the local economic conditions and forecasts affect your business? What social trends, such as an increase in women entering the workforce or an increase in the literacy rate, might affect your strategy? Are young families growing or is the population aging? Are there legal trends that will affect your plans, such as environmental or consumer legislation? Will technological changes affect your product?

©Dana Ward, 2009/ Used under license from Shutterstock.com

PARTS OF A MARKETING PLAN

Part 1. A statement of company goals
Part 2. A description of customers and their needs
Part 3. Information about competitors
Part 4. Information about economic, social, legal, and technological trends
Part 5. Information about financial and human resources available
Part 6. A time line of actions to be taken
Part 7. A description of the methods used to measure success

Figure 16-3 A marketing plan provides a business with details for promoting, selling, and distributing a product or service.

Financial and Human Resources Every company has limited resources. How will your company's financial and human resources be used to market your product? Are sufficient funds available to fulfill the marketing plan? Are there enough people available to complete the required tasks?

Time Line When will each part of the marketing effort occur? Many companies fail because they launch a product too early or too late. Sometimes promotion efforts build demand for a product that is not ready in time to meet the demand. Other times products are launched too late, and competitors or other products fill the demand, replacing your new product.

Methods for Measuring Success Measurement of success can be done by comparing financial results with company goals. How many new customers were obtained? How does this compare to the number you wanted to obtain? How are you measuring consumer awareness? How much have you been able to reduce selling costs. How do this year's sales compare to last year's sales.

GLOBAL TECHNOLOGY TRENDS

Japanese Convenience Stores Go Online

While Japan trailed other industrialized countries in the use of the Internet, consumers in that country were making use of e-commerce through convenience stores. Online shoppers are able to buy a late-night snack of seaweed-covered rice balls with mayonnaise or chocolate chip *mochi* (rice cakes) from their local *combini*—the Japanese name for convenience store.

7-Eleven Japan had an agreement with a software company and other companies to sell programs, videos, books, and other products over the Internet.

Japanese consumers can choose from one of the more than 10,000 7-Eleven stores in Japan and have the merchandise delivered to their home.

Think Critically

1. Why might customers buy online?
2. What are the benefits of selling online for convenience stores?
3. Find web sites that allow consumers to buy food online.

ADDITIONAL DIMENSIONS OF AN INTERNATIONAL MARKETING PLAN

In addition to the seven elements above, a marketing plan with an international emphasis should consider the following topics.

- How will the geographic, cultural, and political factors influence global marketing activities?
- Can the product (or service) be sold in a standardized form, or will it need to be adapted to local situations?
- Will the people be able to afford the product (or service), or will the price need to be revised for global customers?
- Does the infrastructure of other countries allow for efficient and low-cost distribution?
- Should advertising be similar to or different from the promotions used in other countries?
- Is the use of strategic partnerships, such as joint ventures, appropriate for doing international marketing?

✓ **Check**Point
What are seven common sections of a marketing plan?

Photodisc/Getty Images

16-2 Assessment

REVIEW GLOBAL BUSINESS TERMS

Define each of the following terms.

1. marketing mix
2. product
3. price
4. distribution
5. promotion

Study Tools
www.cengage.com/school/genbus/intlbiz

REVIEW GLOBAL BUSINESS CONCEPTS

6. Which element of the marketing mix for services differs the most from marketing for goods?

7. How does a marketing plan serve the needs of an organization?

SOLVE GLOBAL BUSINESS PROBLEMS

Describe each component of the marketing mix for the following Latin American business situations. For each: (a) identify the product or service, (b) give one factor that might affect price, (c) describe a possible distribution method, and (d) explain a possible promotion.

8. A forestry company in Chile.
   a. product
   b. price
   c. distribution
   d. promotion

9. A shoe store in Panama
   a. product
   b. price
   c. distribution
   d. promotion

10. A restaurant in Brazil.
    a. product
    b. price
    c. distribution
    d. promotion

THINK CRITICALLY

11. Choose a product that you buy regularly. Then identify each element of the marketing mix for the item: product description, price, stores at which the product is sold (distribution), and types of advertising and other promotions.

12. Why is it important to include methods for measuring success in a marketing plan?

MAKE ACADEMIC CONNECTIONS

13. **CULTURAL STUDIES** Use the Internet or library resources to determine the kinds of food eaten in a foreign country of your choice. Then list five U.S. foods that are not usually eaten in that country.

14. **DEMOGRAPHICS** What are some differences between people who live in rural and urban areas in your country?

16-3 Planning Global Marketing Activities

GOALS

- Explain the international marketing environment.

- Identify factors that influence consumer behavior in different countries.

- Describe the methods used to segment markets and identify a target market.

Photodisc/Getty Images

The Marketing Environment

Factors external to companies affect all marketing decisions. As food companies expand into foreign markets, they may have to adapt their recipes to meet the tastes of other cultures. A different seasoning for existing food items may be necessary. Or they may sell foods not usually sold in their home country. All business activities are affected by four elements of the marketing environment, which are geography, economic conditions, social and cultural influences, and political and legal factors.

Geography Climate and terrain can affect the types of products sold and transportation methods used in another country. Cake mixes sold in mountainous areas must be prepared differently than those used in lower elevations.

Economic Conditions High inflation may discourage a company from entering a foreign market. The value of a country's currency usually affects the selling price, consumer demand, and profits on a product.

Social and Cultural Influences Tastes, habits, customs, and religious beliefs must be considered. A Pepsi advertisement in Israel once had a caption referring to "Ten Million Years Before the Choice." This phrasing contradicts the Orthodox Jewish belief that the universe was created about 5,800 years ago.

Political and Legal Factors Local political and legal factors also affect marketing decisions. For example, as political differences resulted in the division of the former Yugoslavia into different countries, companies had to deal with different government regulations in each new country.

Consumer Behavior

Think about why you made a recent purchase. The item may have been some-thing you needed for school. Also, it could have been something that you simply enjoy. Most consumer purchases involve several factors. Multiply this by the many buying decisions made in the world each day, and you can see that consumer behavior is quite complex. The four main factors that influ-ence consumer behavior are shown in Figure 16-4.

PHYSICAL AND EMOTIONAL NEEDS

Every person requires air, water, food, shelter, clothing, and health care. But these basic needs of life can differ for people in different countries. Consumers in in-dustrialized countries demand easy-to-prepare food products, current fashion clothing, and homes with many appliances and comforts. People in less developed economies may have homegrown food, homemade clothing, and modest hous-ing. In both situations, however, physical needs influence consumer decisions.

Another level of consumer needs involves human emotions. People in many cultures want to feel good about themselves and want to be accepted by others. Products may be offered that appeal to these emotional needs. Personal care products, cosmetics, clothing, and even automobiles are presented to appeal to a need for social acceptance and personal satisfaction.

GEOGRAPHIC AND DEMOGRAPHIC FACTORS

Where you live influences buying habits. A person living in a warm area will require different housing and clothing and may prefer different foods than someone living in a cold climate. Another geographic factor influencing con-sumer buying habits is terrain. Living in mountainous areas requires different types of transportation and consumer products than living in desert regions.

Demographic traits such as your age, gender, and family situation influence how you spend your money. Information on the birthrate, age distribution, marriage rate, gender distribution, income distribution, educational level, and

Factors Affecting Consumer Behavior

PHYSICAL AND EMOTIONAL NEEDS	GEOGRAPHIC AND DEMOGRAPHIC FACTORS	PERSONALITY AND PSYCHOGRAPHIC FACTORS	SOCIAL AND CULTURAL FACTORS
• Food • Clothing • Shelter • Health care • Transportation • Approval of others • Personal satisfaction	• Location • Climate • Population trends • Age • Gender • Income • Education	• Attitudes • Beliefs • Opinions • Personality traits • Activities • Interests	• Business organizations • Community activities • Religious or political affiliation • Family • Friends

Figure 16-4 Consumer buying decisions are influenced by many factors.

A Question of Ethics

ETHICS OF ENTERING NEW MARKETS

When a company enters a new market in a developing economy, consumers are attracted to the new products. However, many people in these new markets may not be able to afford the items sold by the multinational company.

A fast-food company or cosmetic distributor may start selling products in a country with a very low income per household. The availability of these new products can create very high demand. People have been known to wait in line for hours to buy a fast-food meal or another item that costs several days' pay. They are willing to make this sacrifice to obtain an item not previously available.

Think Critically

1. What are potential benefits and drawbacks of selling products in countries with very low levels of income?
2. Use the guidelines for ethical analysis to examine this situation.

housing situation differ from country to country and have a strong effect on a company's marketing plans. For example, as the people of a nation live longer, older consumers will demand more health, travel, and recreational services.

Data show that people in New Zealand, Canada, the United States, and Australia move more often than people in other countries. This information may help moving companies and relocation services plan business activities. These businesses will find more marketing opportunities in countries with high mobility rates.

PERSONALITY AND PSYCHOGRAPHIC FACTORS

Attitudes are another influence on consumer behavior. Each day our attitudes and beliefs are shaped by experiences and information. These inputs, in turn, create the personality that determines our buying decisions. Personality traits include your attitudes toward risk, change, convenience, and competition. Marketers use this information to attract customers to certain goods and services.

Attempts to better understand personality traits and how attitudes influence consumer behavior resulted in the study of psychographics. **Psychographics** are buying factors related to lifestyle and psychological influences, such as activities, interests, and opinions. A person's psychographic profile may include hobbies, family activities, work interests, and political and social opinions. As you would probably guess, cultural experiences make the psychographic characteristics of U.S. consumers different from those of consumers in Argentina, India, Morocco, and other countries.

SOCIAL AND CULTURAL FACTORS

How we relate to others is another consumer buying factor. Families, friends, business organizations, community activities, and religious affiliation can affect buying behavior. An understanding of such cultural factors as social structure and religion is critical for international marketing decisions to be successful.

 **Check**Point

What are the four main factors affecting consumer behavior?

Selecting a Target Market

Marketers use consumer buying factors to divide customers into subsets that have similar needs. After segmenting the market, marketers must determine which subgroup to serve.

MARKET SEGMENTS

A **market segment** is a distinct subgroup of customers who share certain personal or behavioral characteristics. High-income individuals, for example, purchase certain items that lower income people would not be able to afford. Market segments can be based on characteristics such as demographics, psychographics, buying behavior, or product benefits, as shown in Figure 16-5.

Social and economic factors cause changes in market segments. In recent years, more women have begun working in Japan. The result was new market segments that demanded more child-care services and convenience foods.

Market segments are commonly given names that describe the attitudes and behaviors of those in the group. *Achievers* may be used to refer to successful, upper income people. *Strivers* could describe young, hard-working people. *Traditionalists* would be the consumers who resist change and prefer the familiar. Since each market segment has different attitudes and buying habits, marketing actions aimed at each group must be different.

Market segments usually differ from country to country. Dividing potential customers into subgroups based on type of employment would not be practical in a nation in which most people work in agricultural jobs.

Work as a Team
Give examples of how various demographic factors and social situations create a need for various goods and services.

MARKET SEGMENTATION

Characteristics	Explanation	Example
Demographics	People of different gender, income, age, and family situations require different products.	Households with a newborn child will buy diapers, while retirees may be interested in travel services.
Psychographics	Different opinions and attitudes can affect buying.	People concerned about nutrition select different food items than other consumers.
Buying Behavior	Actions and shopping preferences differ.	Some people shop online, while others go to shopping malls or stores.
Product Benefits	People require different advantages from their buying choices.	Some people prefer toothpaste with good taste, while others want one that fights cavities.

Figure 16-5 Consumer markets are divided into market segments based on personal characteristics, attitudes, activities, and buying preferences.

NETBookmark

A person's attitudes and beliefs have an important influence on buying behaviors. Access the textbook's web site and click on the link for Chapter 16. The VALS™ segments are used to target consumers. Select two of the eight market segments and read the brief descriptions. Write a paragraph comparing the buying habits of these two groups. Discuss how companies might use this information for developing and promoting products or services.

www.cengage.com/school/genbus/intlbiz

TARGET MARKET

A **target market** is the particular market segment that a company plans to serve. After identifying the target market, a company attempts to meet the specific needs of those customers. Target markets for international business may be selected on the basis of geography. A company involved in international marketing may select one or more countries as its target market.

To better understand consumers and to segment and target markets effectively, companies analyze buyer behavior through marketing research. Marketing research may be conducted to determine the television viewing habits of Japanese college students or the potential sales among older consumers of an Italian soft drink in the United States.

✓ **CheckPoint**

What types of consumer characteristics are used to segment markets?

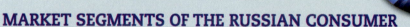

GLOBAL BUSINESS SPOTLIGHT

MARKET SEGMENTS OF THE RUSSIAN CONSUMER

As foreign companies increased their marketing and selling activities in Russia, researchers took a closer look at Russian customers. Five market segments were developed to describe the attitudes and buying habits of Russian consumers based on their attitudes and beliefs.

- *Kuptsi* (or merchants) were found to be practical and to seek value in their buying.
- *Cossacks* were determined to be independent and ambitious status seekers.
- *Students* tended to be passive and idealistic.
- *Business executives* were busy, ambitious, and receptive to

products and ideas from industrialized countries.
- *Russian souls* were found to be passive, fearful of new ideas, and followers of others.

This market research information can be used to target the selling of various products and services to the best potential customers.

Think Critically

1. How do companies use market segments for planning their marketing activities?
2. Conduct an Internet search to obtain additional information about market segments.

REVIEW GLOBAL BUSINESS TERMS

Define each of the following terms.

1. psychographics
2. market segment
3. target market

REVIEW GLOBAL BUSINESS CONCEPTS

4. What factors affect the marketing environment of a company?
5. What factors influence consumer behavior?
6. What is the difference between demographics and psychographics?
7. What is meant by the target market of a company?

SOLVE GLOBAL BUSINESS PROBLEMS

Find a product made in another country and sold in the United States. Be careful! Some products that appear to have a foreign origin are actually from U.S.-based companies. Based on this product, answer the following questions.

8. What are possible reasons that the company sells its product in the U.S.?
9. What are some difficulties the company may have encountered when introducing the product to U.S. consumers?
10. What economic and social factors may contribute to the success or failure of the product in the United States.

THINK CRITICALLY

11. Give an example of how a person's needs might affect consumer behavior.
12. How does personality influence buying habits?
13. Some people believe that defining and using market segments are unfair since consumers are treated in different manners. Do you agree or disagree with this belief? Why?

MAKE ACADEMIC CONNECTIONS

14. **CULTURAL STUDIES** Describe a situation in which the religious beliefs of a society would affect a company's marketing activities.
15. **GEOGRAPHY** How would the climate of a country influence the products commonly bought by consumers in that nation?
16. **TECHNOLOGY** Use the Internet to identify online resources for global marketing activities.

CHAPTER SUMMARY

16-1 MARKETING AROUND THE WORLD

A International marketing involves marketing activities between sellers and buyers in different countries.

B Trends that influence global marketing opportunities include expanded communications, technology, changing political situations, increased competition, and changing demographics.

16-2 THE MARKETING MIX AND THE MARKETING PLAN

A The four elements of the marketing mix are product, price, distribution, and promotion.

B A marketing plan is used to plan, communicate, and implement global marketing activities.

16-3 PLANNING GLOBAL MARKETING ACTIVITIES

A The international marketing environment consists of geographic elements, economic conditions, social and cultural influences, and political and legal factors.

B Consumer behavior is influenced by physical and emotional needs, geographic and demographic factors, personality and psychographic factors, and social and cultural factors.

C Methods used to segment markets include demographics, psychographics, buying behavior, and product benefits.

GLOBAL REFOCUS

Read the Global Focus at the beginning of this chapter, and answer the following questions.

1. What actions might a cereal company take when adapting its marketing mix to new customers?

2. As demand for cereal declines in various markets, what actions might be taken by Kellogg's, General Mills, and other cereal companies?

REVIEW GLOBAL BUSINESS TERMS

Match the terms listed with the definitions.

1. The monetary value of a product agreed upon by a buyer and a seller.
2. Buying factors related to lifestyle and psychological influences, such as activities, interests, and opinions.
3. Marketing efforts that inform and persuade customers.
4. Likely customers for a good or service in a certain geographic location.
5. Marketing activities between sellers and buyers in different countries.
6. The activities needed to physically move and transfer ownership of goods and services from producer to consumer.
7. A distinct subgroup of customers who share certain personal or behavioral characteristics.
8. The traits of a country's population, such as birthrate, age distribution, marriage rate, gender distribution, income distribution, educational level, and housing situation.
9. An item (good or service) offered for sale that satisfies consumer demand.
10. Individuals and households who are the final users of goods and services.
11. The four major elements (product, price, distribution, and promotion) of marketing.
12. Buyers who purchase items for resale or additional production.
13. The particular market segment that a company plans to serve.

a. consumer market
b. demographics
c. distribution
d. international marketing
e. market
f. market segment
g. marketing mix
h. organizational market
i. price
j. product
k. promotion
l. psychographics
m. target market

MAKE GLOBAL BUSINESS DECISIONS

14. How does demand for consumer goods and services affect demand in organizational markets?
15. What are some examples of global marketing opportunities created by technology or changing demographics?
16. How would the marketing plan for services or a nonprofit organization differ from the marketing activities for a tangible product?
17. What social and economic factors might affect how a society defines its basic consumer needs?
18. Why do you think many marketing managers believe that demographic information has limited value for defining a company's target market?
19. List some psychographic factors that could affect a person's buying habits.
20. What do you believe to be the most influential social institution in our country that affects buying decisions?

MAKE ACADEMIC CONNECTIONS

21. **GEOGRAPHY** Research the climate, terrain, waterways, and other geographic conditions of a country. Explain how these factors might affect the marketing activities of a company.

22. **COMMUNICATIONS** Prepare a poster, computer presentation, or another visual display showing goods and services from other countries that are sold in the United States.

23. **CULTURAL STUDIES** Conduct library and online research and prepare a two-page written report on the four elements of the marketing mix for a good or service sold in more than one country. Compare the marketing activities in different cultures.

24. **SCIENCE** Select a product that is aimed at different types of customers, such as cereal, toothpaste, or shampoo. Compare the ingredients listed on packages and information in advertisements for two or more variations of the product. Explain how the contents can influence the target market at which the product is aimed.

Photodisc/Getty Images

25. **MATHEMATICS** Survey several friends to determine the factors that affect their buying habits for food, clothing, or another commonly purchased item. Prepare a chart that reports the frequency of stores used, types of items purchased, amounts spent, and influences on buying.

26. **CAREER PLANNING** Prepare a letter of application for a job with an international marketing company. Explain how your global marketing knowledge could be useful to the company. List examples of methods the company might consider to enhance its international marketing plan.

27. **VISUAL COMMUNICATION** Prepare a poster, computer presentation, or other visual to communicate how the four elements of the marketing mix are applied differently around the world.

28. **MATHEMATICS** Locate age distribution data for various countries. Prepare a graph that compares the portion of people in different age groups for industrialized countries and emerging markets.

The GLOBAL
Entrepreneur

CREATING AN INTERNATIONAL BUSINESS PLAN

An International Marketing Plan

Create a marketing plan for the business idea you have used in previous chapters, or select another business idea. Use the country you have previously researched, or select a different country. Using library and Internet research, obtain information for the following topics.

1. Company goals: Clearly state the marketing objectives that the business wants to achieve, including the target country or region.

2. Description of customers and their needs: Provide details of the buying behaviors of potential customers.

3. Information about competitors: Describe other companies that are aiming their marketing activities at the same customers.

4. Information about economic, social, legal, and technological trends: Describe unique factors that will affect the company's marketing activities.

5. Financial and human resources available: List estimated operating costs and skills that employees will need to achieve the company's goals.

6. Time line of actions to be taken: Estimate the amount of time that will be needed to implement the marketing plan.

7. Methods for measuring success: Describe how the company will know if it has achieved its goals.

Prepare a written summary suitable for inclusion in a business plan. Based on the written summary, develop a short oral report (two or three minutes) of your findings.

CHAPTER 17

Developing Goods and Services for Global Markets

17-1 Global Product Planning

17-2 Developing and Researching Products

17-3 An International Product Strategy

Water, Water . . . Almost Everywhere

In the United States, most people have easy access to drinking water—turn on the tap or grab a bottle. And, it's not just water; there are several hundred brands including enhanced products. Coca-Cola's Dasani and Pepsi's Aquafina brands both offer water products with added nutrients. While Ayala's Herbal Water is available in assorted flavors including cinnamon orange peel, lemongrass mint vanilla, and lavender mint.

In contrast to the many water options most American's enjoy, safe water is not readily available in many developing countries. An estimated four million people die each year from drinking contaminated water.

Efforts to improve access to safe drinking water include building traditional water treatment facilities along with developing innovated devices such as the LifeStraw. In areas where only polluted water is available, this personal filtering straw removes dangerous bacteria, viruses, and parasites during consumption. LifeStraw consists of a plastic tube through which the unsafe water is sucked. After initial movement through microfilters, the water passes through iodine-coated beads. Finally, the water goes through activated carbon to remove the iodine taste and bacteria. Developed by Vestergaard Franson, a Swiss company, each LifeStraw can filter 700 liters of water—enough for one person for a year.

The PUR packet is another simple way to make water potable. Developed by Procter and Gamble in collaboration with the U.S. Centers for Disease Control, the PUR packet technology is similar to what municipal water systems use. Small and easy to transport, one PUR packet turns ten liters of contaminated water into safe for drinking. Relief agencies around the world have produced more than a billion liters of water using PUR packets.

Think Critically

1. How do different water products meet varied consumer needs?
2. Describe other beverages or foods that might be adapted to varied consumer needs around the world.
3. How might a company's products enhance quality of life?

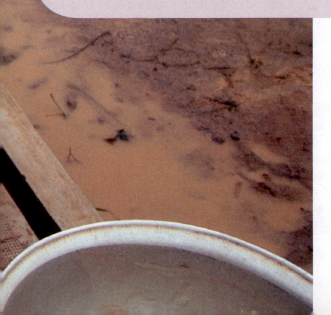

17-1 Global Product Planning

GOALS

- Describe sources of product opportunities for international marketing.

- Identify categories of consumer products and the importance of product lines.

- Explain how services are marketed.

PhotoDisc/Getty Images

International Product Opportunities

Every day you see advertisements for clothing, food, motor vehicles, financial services, web sites, and other consumer goods and services. It sometimes seems as though everyone has something to sell. When you apply for a job, you also are selling your talents and abilities. The product offerings of global companies are the foundation of international business and foreign trade.

A *product* is a marketplace offering (good or service) that satisfies a need or want. Marketing's major goal is to satisfy needs that have not been met. This can be accomplished in one of four ways: a new product, an improved product, an existing product with a new use, or an existing product sold in a new market.

New Product An organization's marketing activities may start with a marketplace offering that did not previously exist. For example, Federal Express pioneered overnight delivery services. Now, several companies are involved in this industry.

Improved Product Sometimes a product is on the market for several years, but it may no longer be as popular with consumers. When this happens, a company may introduce variations, such as new flavors of a food product. Also, technology may result in improved versions of an item.

Existing Product with a New Use When a company wants to expand its sales, it may attempt to find new uses for a product that has been on the market for years. For example, kitchen storage containers have been adapted to store tools and supplies for a home workshop or office.

Existing Product Sold in a New Market In 1924, Kellogg's started selling corn flakes in London and today has cereal customers in 180 countries. Selling existing products in new markets is a significant part of international business. Soft drinks, fast foods, and hundreds of other products that originated in one country are now sold in the global marketplace.

Marketing Products Around the World

Each day people around the world buy and use thousands of different products. A student in Brazil buys a home computer, while a person in Egypt purchases a bottled soft drink.

CONSUMER PRODUCT CATEGORIES

The many items sold in the global market can be classified as convenience goods, shopping goods, or specialty goods.

Convenience Goods You probably buy low-cost items on a regular basis without thinking much about them. **Convenience goods** are inexpensive items that require little shopping effort. Examples include snacks, soft drinks, personal care products, and school supplies. Marketing for convenience goods involves offering an item in many locations. For example, candy bars are sold in food stores, movie theaters, gas stations, and vending machines.

Shopping Goods Some products, such as clothing, furniture, cameras, televisions, and home appliances, are purchased only after consumers take some time to compare buying alternatives. **Shopping goods** are products purchased after consumers compare brands and stores. Shopping goods require a marketing effort that communicates differences in price, quality, and features of various brands.

Stores selling shopping goods may offer several brands and models of the same item to prevent a customer from going to another store to compare products. You will commonly see stores and online retailers with many makes and models of televisions or digital cameras.

Products that are convenience goods in one culture may be shopping goods in another. Toothpaste for U.S. consumers is usually bought quickly without much thought. This same purchase in some South American nations may require comparison shopping and some consideration. Consumers in these countries may not be as familiar with the item, or the toothpaste may be an expensive purchase considering their income.

Specialty Goods When buying certain products, you would probably take a lot of time and effort. **Specialty goods** are unique products that consumers make a special effort to obtain. Buyers of these items refuse to accept substitutes. Marketing of specialty goods requires high brand recognition. In Europe, for example, certain designer clothing, jewelry from well-known firms, and customized automobiles would only be available at select stores.

Some products fit into more than one category. Milk is usually a convenience good. However, if you seek a specific brand or type such as a flavored or non-dairy milk product, it would be a shopping good. Another example could be cameras. A disposable camera purchased at a supermarket is a convenience item. Alternately, a digital camera bought with specific desired features is a shopping good. And finally, a high-tech, digital camera, only available at a few full-service stores, is a specialty good.

THE PRODUCT LINE

Manufacturing companies and stores usually produce and offer a variety of items. A **product line** is an assortment of closely related products designed to meet the varied needs of target customers. Shoe stores commonly include socks, shoelaces, and shoe polish in their product lines. Procter & Gamble makes different shampoos for people with different wants and needs. There are shampoos for dandruff problems, shampoos for color-treated hair, and shampoos for curly hair.

ORGANIZATIONAL PRODUCTS

Organizational products are items used to produce other goods and services. Companies buy factories, machinery, office equipment, components, and raw materials for their daily business activities.

Most organizational products require less adaptation than do consumer goods before they are sold in different countries. This situation arises because cultural factors and personal taste influence production activities less than consumer purchases. For example, the same forklift truck used on a loading dock can be sold in most places around the world. However, laundry detergent might require adaptation due to clothes-washing habits and water hardness.

GLOBAL BUSINESS SPOTLIGHT

GREEN PRODUCT DEVELOPMENT FOR GLOBAL MARKETS

Companies around the world are attempting to create more environmentally friendly products. Fujitsu, a Japanese technology company with operations in more than 70 countries, uses the following "green" product development principles:

- Assess environmental regulations in global business settings.
- Eliminate the use of hazardous chemical substances in the production process.
- Create energy-efficient production facilities and end products.
- Use lead-free solder in manufacturing activities.

- Promote a 3R approach for selecting and using production inputs–reduce/reuse/recycle .

Think Critically

1. How could other companies use Fujitsu's green product development principles to plan their international marketing activities?
2. Locate additional information about the environmentally friendly products developed by a company. Create an outline describing your findings.

Consumer and Commercial Services

A variety of services also are used by individuals and organizations. Consumer services include health care, home repairs, and personal grooming. Commercial services may include security systems, information processing, equipment maintenance, and overnight package delivery. How does buying a haircut differ from buying a bottle of shampoo. One is an intangible service, and one is a tangible good.

CHARACTERISTICS OF SERVICES

Services cannot be touched like a physical product. In other words, services are *intangible*. Most purchases are a combination of both tangible and intangible items. While you can touch the oil can and liquid, the process of changing the oil on your vehicle is intangible. Because services are intangible, it is more difficult to judge the quality of these purchases. Common measures of service quality are company reputation, comments from past customers, and training qualifications of employees.

Increased use of technology for services contributes to more consistent quality. For example, automatic teller machines, when operating properly, will make fewer errors than humans do.

Services are consumed as they are produced. Mass production of services is often not possible. Each haircut, oil change, or income tax preparation is produced separately. However, businesses are using technology to provide fast, individualized services. Financial companies, for example, offer investment advice based on a person's income, age, and household situation.

Services have no inventory. Empty airline seats, for example, cannot be saved and sold later. They are simply lost revenue opportunities.

TYPES OF SERVICES

Services available to consumers may be viewed in three categories.

1. *Rented-goods services* involve a payment for temporary use of items, such as an automobile, an apartment, an online movie, or a tuxedo.
2. *Owned-goods services* are fees for service to the consumer's property, such as auto repair, dry cleaning, or landscaping.
3. *Non-goods services* are personal or professional services for a fee, such as health care, overnight delivery, tax return preparation, real estate sales, legal assistance, and child care.

MARKETING OF SERVICES

Services require special marketing efforts. Because the consumer must often be where the service is produced, convenience of location is important. Some hospitals have created urgent-care facilities in several locations. Banks may bring their services to customers, such as when a bank sets up a temporary cash machine at a sporting event or concert.

COMMUNICATION ACROSS BORDERS

COMMUNICATE WITH CUSTOMERS IN THEIR OWN LANGUAGE

When a multinational organization develops a strategy for communicating with customers, selection of the correct language is not enough. The organization must also choose the right form of the language to reach the targeted customers successfully.

Every major world language exists in a number of culture-specific forms that vary in terms of some of the language details.

The differences often involve pronunciation, word choice, and word meaning. Sometimes they involve spelling and grammar, too. Although such differences are small, they are important in terms of the acceptability of the message. Communications are better received when they are customized to reflect the culturally sanctioned language of a distinct group of customers.

Throughout Latin America, for example, multinational businesses need to do more than use Spanish to communicate with Spanish-speaking customers. They need to use the same form of Spanish as the targeted group of customers. Some of the details of communications with customers in Honduras will be different from those of communications with customers in Colombia and Argentina.

Think Critically

1. Why should speakers of a language receive communications in their own culture-specific form?
2. What other major languages besides Spanish have a number of culture-specific versions that are used for international communication purposes?

The *packaging* of services occurs through the image created by the business. Furniture, decorations, and even the appearance of employees can create a reputation of quality.

Services are also personalized. Each transaction for a hairstylist, tax accountant, or health-care worker will be slightly different. An organization's ability to meet the individual needs of customers is vital for success.

SERVICES AND INTERNATIONAL TRADE

In recent years, services have played an increasing role for the United States in its foreign trade activities. More than 70 percent of GDP in the United States results from service industries. While the United States has a total trade deficit, exported services exceed imported services. Companies in other countries have a strong demand for health care, delivery services, information systems, processing, management consulting, financial services, education and training, hospitality (hotels, food service), and entertainment (movies, television production, and amusement parks).

In industrialized countries, services are becoming a greater economic influence. Today, in countries such as Australia, Canada, Germany, and Japan, more people work in service industries than in manufacturing companies.

✓ CheckPoint

What are three categories of services?

REVIEW GLOBAL BUSINESS TERMS

Define each of the following terms.

1. convenience goods
2. shopping goods
3. specialty goods
4. product line

REVIEW GLOBAL BUSINESS CONCEPTS

5. How can marketing satisfy a need that has not been met?

6. How does a shopping good differ from a specialty good?

7. In what ways are services different from goods?

SOLVE GLOBAL BUSINESS PROBLEMS

For each of the following situations, list a possible problem that could be encountered if a company planned to sell its service in other countries.

8. Childcare centers aimed at households with two working parents.

9. Repair service for home and office computers.

10. Carpet cleaning service for homes and businesses.

11. Trash collection and recycling service.

THINK CRITICALLY

12. Describe an example of how a convenience good in one culture may be a shopping good or specialty good in another society.

13. What tangible factors could be measured to determine the quality of services offered by a company?

14. Choose a service company in your community. Describe attributes that contribute to the company's image.

MAKE ACADEMIC CONNECTIONS

15. **TECHNOLOGY** Describe how technology has created new product opportunities for existing goods and services.

16. **TECHNOLOGY** Use the Internet to identify three products that are available around the world. Describe any differences the products might have from country to country.

17. **TECHNOLOGY** Use the Internet to find examples of companies that provide services internationally. What type of services are offered? Are there any differences from country to country?

18. **GEOGRAPHY** Explain how the climate, terrain, and other geographic factors in a country could expand or limit the availability of services.

17-2 Developing and Researching Products

GOALS

- Discuss the steps in the new product development process and the phases in the marketing research process.

- Describe data collection methods used in international marketing research.

©RAGMA IMAGES, 2009/ Used under license from Shutterstock.com

Creating New Products

Each year more than 20,000 new products are introduced in the United States. However, within a year, about 75 percent of them are no longer on the market. Why do most new products fail? Some say it is because too many new products are introduced into an already saturated marketplace. Others believe it is because of poor planning. Either way, new products are a high risk for companies.

NEW PRODUCTS

Companies introduce new products for two reasons. First, as old products are no longer popular with customers, sales revenue must come from other sources. Second, competitors' actions result in lower sales revenue. New products must match or exceed the marketplace offerings of other companies.

Customer Needs The needs of customers is one of the main sources of new product ideas. For example, vitamin-enhanced water was the response to the need for healthier drinks. Also, companies offered the product in a sports bottle format, which provided customers with convenience. These products were based on customer needs. Other products developed to fill customer needs include carbon monoxide detectors for in-home safety and electronic invisible fences for pet containment.

Figure 17-1 Four main steps are used by companies to create and market new products.

Technology Technology is another major source of new products. Cell phones, home video recorders, microwave ovens, and video games would never have been possible without technological breakthroughs.

NEW PRODUCT DEVELOPMENT PROCESS

Companies use a logical procedure to create successful new products. The new product development process involves the four steps shown in Figure 17-1. This procedure is used to create products that will likely succeed.

Generating Product Ideas In the first stage, ideas for possible products are based on comments from customers, product ideas other companies have developed, and new technology. At this stage, products planned for international markets are viewed from a global perspective.

Evaluating Product Ideas Next, ideas are evaluated based on cost, production possibility, and marketplace acceptance. Can the new item be offered to potential customers at an acceptable price? Are the facilities available to produce the item in needed quantities? Can the product be adapted to meet the cultural and economic needs of customers in various countries?

Researching Product Ideas In the third stage, research is conducted on the proposed product to measure customer attitudes and potential sales.

Marketing Product Ideas The final phase of the new product development process involves putting the item on the market. After research shows a strong probability of success, the item is produced, distributed, and sold in one or more countries.

The product development process is usually ongoing. As the final step is completed, changing consumer tastes and other market factors result in the need to start over. This continuing process may involve modifications of existing goods and services, or the creation of a completely new product concept.

GLOBAL BUSINESS SPOTLIGHT

COLLECTING MARKETING RESEARCH DATA

How can marketing information be obtained in countries lacking extensive information systems? While visiting Ethiopia, Laos, or Uruguay, a researcher may observe consumers as they make purchases. These observations can help managers decide if a certain product might be successful in these emerging markets.

Next, researchers might interview business owners about their product line. Owners would answer questions about what items sold well in the past, current consumer tastes, and common complaints from customers.

Finally, talking with government officials can provide details about trade barriers and regulations affecting business. Combining information from these sources can provide managers with a better understanding of the marketing opportunities in nations with limited research data.

Think Critically

1. What things might be observed in another country that could help a manager plan to do business in that country?
2. When interviewing people about their country's business environment, what questions might be asked?
3. Conduct an Internet search related to international marketing research. Locate a web site that would be useful for companies planning to do business in another country. Write an explanation of how the site's content might be used.

Work as a Team
Brainstorm a list of possible new products or services that might be developed to sell in other countries.

ADAPTING PRODUCTS TO FOREIGN MARKETS

Products will frequently need to be adapted to social, cultural, and political factors. When refrigerators produced by manufacturers in Western nations were first sold in Japan, Japanese consumers considered them too noisy. The motors needed to operate the cooling unit could easily be heard through the thin walls of many Japanese homes and apartments. This situation resulted in companies developing a quieter refrigerator designed specifically to meet Japanese market needs.

THE MARKETING RESEARCH PROCESS

When developing and marketing new products, companies must find out what consumers need, want, and are willing to buy. **Marketing research** is the orderly collection and analysis of data that is used to obtain information about a specific marketing concern. While some companies have investigated consumer buying patterns in more than 150 countries, marketing research is done regularly in only about 60 or 70 nations.

Marketing research may be conducted to determine the television viewing habits of Australian college students. Or, a company may measure the

The Marketing Research Process

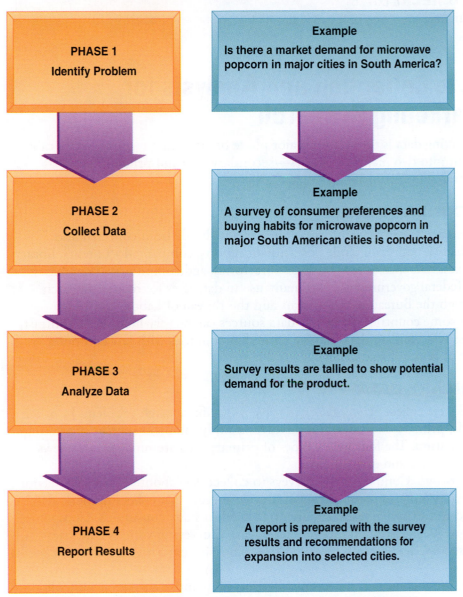

PHASE 1 Identify Problem	**Example** Is there a market demand for microwave popcorn in major cities in South America?
PHASE 2 Collect Data	**Example** A survey of consumer preferences and buying habits for microwave popcorn in major South American cities is conducted.
PHASE 3 Analyze Data	**Example** Survey results are tallied to show potential demand for the product.
PHASE 4 Report Results	**Example** A report is prepared with the survey results and recommendations for expansion into selected cities.

Figure 17-2 The phases of the marketing research process are designed to help a company collect consumer behavior data.

potential sales for a Brazilian soft drink in the United States. Figure 17-2 provides an overview of the marketing research process with an international example.

Every research study starts with a research problem. The word "problem" does not necessarily mean that something is wrong—such as declining sales. A research problem provides the basis for studying some aspect of a company's marketing mix. For example, a computer company may conduct a marketing research study to determine the information needs of manufacturing companies in Chile, or a soup company may study consumer taste preferences in Jamaica. In each situation, the business seeks information to better plan and carry out its marketing activities.

Data Collection and Analysis for Marketing Research

Collecting data is the second major phase of marketing research. Data can be put into two major categories—secondary data and primary data—as illustrated in Figure 17-3.

SECONDARY DATA

Secondary data involve information that has already been collected and published. Sources include government reports, company documents, library indexes, reference books, business directories, and computerized databases. The federal government offers many useful databases for market research through the Bureau of the Census and the Bureau of Labor Statistics.

In some countries secondary data sources can be very helpful. In contrast, access to secondary data may be limited in countries with few computer systems or political restrictions.

PRIMARY DATA

Marketers collect *primary data* to solve a specific research problem. In other words, primary data collection involves a study to obtain specific marketing information. The four major types of primary data are surveys, interviews, observations, and experiments.

Surveys Companies use surveys to collect data about opinions, behaviors, and knowledge of consumers. Large-scale surveys that collect numeric data, called **quantitative research**, are often used to study consumers. Companies such as ACNielsen conduct market research surveys in various countries. Nielsen Media Research measures television viewing patterns and other media habits.

In many countries, however, collection of quantitative data is difficult. A country with only a few computers makes a Web survey almost impossible and the results questionable. If a nation has a low literacy rate, the use of mail surveys will have little value. These situations require other types of research.

Interviews Talking to people about their opinions, experiences, and buying habits is a valuable source of market research information. Asking open-ended questions starting with "Why," "How," or "Describe" can provide insight that will help marketers better serve consumer needs. Interviews are a type of qualitative research. **Qualitative research**, using open-ended interview questions, allows researchers to obtain comments from consumers about their attitudes and behaviors.

SOURCES OF MARKETING RESEARCH DATA

Primary Data Sources	Secondary Data Sources
• Surveys	• Government reports
• Interviews	• Business documents
• Observations	• Indexes
• Experiments	• Reference books
	• Computerized databases

Figure 17-3 Secondary data and primary data help marketing managers make international business decisions.

Another example of qualitative research is the focus group, or group-depth interview. A **focus group** is a directed discussion with 8 to 12 people. This group interview can be used to collect information from focus group members about their opinions and buying habits and what they know about a product, a package, or an advertisement.

Focus groups can offer insight into planned marketing activities. This information, however, is based only on the opinions of a small group of consumers. Focus groups and personal interviews may not be appropriate in cultures in which people do not talk openly to strangers.

Observations What people say they do is often different from what they actually do. Observation is the best way to measure consumer behavior. **Observational research** involves data collection by watching and recording shopping behaviors.

Common observations involve watching shoppers in stores or counting customers during certain hours. Computerized cash registers with scanners allow companies to *observe* the purchases of customers. These data are used to determine the number of employees needed at certain hours and to set prices at a level for maximizing sales.

In some research settings, such as with children, observations are necessary. These young consumers may not be able to express themselves well verbally. However, observational research has a major weakness. It cannot provide information about the attitudes, opinions, or motivations of consumers.

Photodisc/Getty Images

Experiments The most complex type of data collection is the **experiment**, which involves a statistical comparison of two or more very similar situations. For example, a company may introduce a package with a photograph in one city and a package with an artist's drawing in another city. The firm wants to know how the different packages affect consumer preference and sales. Experiments are expensive to conduct and are most helpful in industrialized countries with access to computerized data collection methods.

Experiments also can predict the success of a product before mass distribution. A **test market** is an experimental research study that measures the likely success of a new good or service. Companies often use one or two cities to try out a new item. U.S. companies usually use cities in the United States. Some firms, however, use foreign cities as test markets. KFC tested its grilled chicken in Regina, Saskatchewan, Canada. Carewell Industries, a New Jersey company, first sold its Dentax toothbrush in Malaysia and Singapore.

ANALYZING AND USING RESEARCH DATA

For data to be useful for planning marketing activities, research results must be analyzed after collection. Statistical tests are commonly used with quantitative data. The results help managers make marketing decisions. By knowing which consumers watch certain television programs or read certain magazines, a manager can plan a company's advertising. Information about customer opinions and habits can help plan domestic and international marketing activities.

✓**Check**Point
What are the four main types of primary data collection?

Photodisc/Getty Images

REVIEW GLOBAL BUSINESS TERMS
Define each of the following terms.

1. marketing research
2. quantitative research
3. qualitative research
4. focus group
5. observational research
6. experiment
7. test market

REVIEW GLOBAL BUSINESS CONCEPTS

8. What causes a need for new products?

9. What are the sources for new products?

10. What is the difference between secondary data and primary data?

11. What is the purpose of a test market?

SOLVE GLOBAL BUSINESS PROBLEMS

For each of the following research situations, tell which data collection method might be most appropriate.

12. A package food company wants to know the breakfast eating habits in Chile.

13. A manufacturing company wants to determine computer needs of small businesses in Panama.

14. A bank needs information about the satisfaction of checking account customers in Argentina.

15. A company needs information on the number of companies in Guatemala that use refrigerated food-storage areas.

16. A travel company is interested in knowing the attitudes and needs of Brazilians who travel regularly on business.

THINK CRITICALLY

17. Describe a situation in our society that could be the basis for a new product or service that does not currently exist.

18. Explain how the behavior of a shopper in a store might be interpreted differently by different observers.

MAKE ACADEMIC CONNECTIONS

19. **TECHNOLOGY** Use software to prepare a flowchart presentation using the steps of the new product development process to show the development of an actual product.

20. **LAW** Why might a government in another country create a law to restrict certain marketing research activities?

17-3 An International Product Strategy

GOALS

- Describe branding and packaging techniques used by global business organizations.
- Explain actions involved in planning a global product strategy.

PRNewsFoto/McDonald's/AP Photo

Branding and Packaging

You are probably familiar with the names Coca-Cola, McDonald's, Kellogg's, and Disney. Millions of people around the world also know these names.

BRANDING AND MARKETING

A **brand** is a name, symbol, or design that identifies a product. This marketing technique helps consumers remember and regularly buy a company's products. Common, well-known brand names may appear on several products or on a single product. For year's Crest toothpaste was the only Crest product. Today the brand name appears on toothbrushes, dental floss, and toothpaste.

Service companies and other organizations also use brands. American Express, UPS, and amazon.com are examples of brands not associated with packaged products.

Brands may be revised for other cultures. For example, Kellogg's *Rice Krispies* are called *Rice Bubbles* in Australia. And, Kellogg's Frosted Flakes are branded as *Corn Frosties* in Malaysia.

TYPES OF BRANDS

Brands range from ones known worldwide to those known only in a small region. A *global brand* is used worldwide and is recognized by people in many geographic areas. The Gerber Products Company uses a "superbrand" approach for global marketing activities, with the company's famous name appearing on baby food, child-care products, and children's clothing.

A *national brand* is one that is well known within one country. For example, before expanding to overseas markets, Nike and Frito-Lay were considered national brands.

Regional brands are used on products sold only in one geographic region. Certain snack chips or soft drinks may only be available in a few states or regions of countries.

Stores and producers will sometimes put their own names on products. *Store* or *manufacturer brands* are used on products sold only at certain stores or distributed through certain sellers. Many drug stores and department stores have a line of health and personal care products with their own names on labels. Store and manufacturer brands are also called *private brands*.

Loblaw Companies, based in Toronto, created the President's Choice label. This upscale, private brand of more than 1,000 food products is exported from Canada to more than 20 U.S. states and eight other countries.

Generics are non-name brand, plain wrapper products that can provide a bargain in certain situations. As with store brands, many generics can provide low-cost alternatives for consumers. Certain generics, such as aspirin, bleach, and sugar, are almost exactly the same as higher priced brands.

PACKAGING

Have you ever noticed a new product because of the color, design, and shape of its package? Companies spend millions of dollars to get the right package. When Diet Coke was introduced, the company tested more than 30 combinations of colors, lettering, and designs for its new soft drink can.

Product packaging serves multiple purposes for companies and consumers. There are three major purposes.

1. A package protects the product from spoilage or damage during shipping and storage.
2. A package attempts to capture the attention of both new and regular users of the product.
3. The package should make the product easy to use. Easy-to-pour containers and resealable packages add to consumer convenience.

NETBookmark

With more than 70 percent of the world's population living on less than $2 a day, most people cannot afford products commonly purchased by consumers in industrialized countries. To address this concern, some multinational companies make use of sachet marketing involving a smaller package size. Access the web site shown below and click on the link for Chapter 17. Based on this information, write a brief essay explaining the benefits of sachet marketing for companies and customers.

www.cengage.com/school/genbus/intlbiz

In recent years, packaging has increased in importance as a result of environmental concerns. Many companies now offer packages that are either reusable, refillable, or recyclable.

In some countries, certain packaging regulations influence marketing activities. Food labeling laws in the United States require that certain ingredient and nutrition information be presented in a clear format. While Coca-Cola uses the English version of its name in many countries, Korea and Thailand require the name be presented in the national languages of those countries.

✓ CheckPoint

How does a global brand differ from a national brand?

Planning a Global Product Strategy

Every company must make decisions about what it will sell. These choices are influenced by the popularity of its product offerings and the ability of the business to serve consumer needs throughout the world.

THE PRODUCT LIFE CYCLE

The stages a good or service goes through from the time it is introduced until it is taken off the market is the **product life cycle (PLC).** As you get older, you act differently and have different needs. The same thing is true for products. After a company's product has been on the market for awhile, the company will change its marketing approach. The PLC has four stages, as shown in Figure 17-4.

Introduction The first stage of the product life cycle is *introduction*, when the product is new and few competitors exist. Marketing activities should emphasize creation of awareness of the item among potential customers. Sales are low, and usually a profit has not yet been realized.

Growth Next, the *growth* stage of the PLC finds increasing sales and profits starting. New competitors with similar or substitute products enter the market.

Maturity Then in the *maturity* stage, sales start to level off as the market is saturated, more competitors appear, and new products compete for the dollars of consumers.

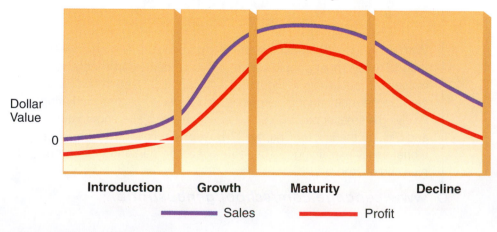

The Product Life Cycle

Figure 17-4 All goods and services go through steps as they increase and decrease in popularity.

GLOBAL TECHNOLOGY TRENDS

E-Brands and Virtual Brands

Soaps, crackers, cereals, and soft drinks were the first products to be branded. Over 100 years later, a new type of brand has developed. *E-brands* include eBay and Amazon.com, which are online brands not seen in stores. *Virtual brands* are often actual brands used in virtual worlds such as SecondLife and There.com. Coca-Cola has a virtual studio to mix music, where their logo is continually present. Companies with traditional brands realize the need to use new media to create awareness among certain target markets.

Think Critically

1. What are potential benefits of virtual brands for companies?
2. Describe how a traditional company might use the Internet and virtual branding.

Decline Finally, in the *decline* stage, sales and profits start to decrease. The company must decide whether to attempt to revive the product or stop production of it.

Competition and technology have a major effect on the speed at which a product moves through the product life cycle. Years ago, televisions would take years to move through the PLC, as new models and features were rarely introduced. Today movement through the PLC is measured in months for electronic equipment.

GLOBAL PRODUCT DECISIONS

A major marketing decision that many companies must make involves whether to keep its products the same or adapt them to foreign customers. A **global product** is a *standardized* item offered in the same form in all countries in which it is sold. Common examples of global products are cameras, computers, and many home appliances. Food products are usually difficult to market as global products because of differences in tastes. Unilever, however, sells tea, ice cream, and pasta in nearly identical forms worldwide.

In contrast to a global product, an **international product** is *customized* or adapted to the culture, tastes, and social trends of a country. As a result of different laws and customs, health and personal care products must be adapted to different settings. Food companies often add different seasonings to products sold in various cultures.

CEASING FOREIGN MARKET ACTIVITIES

Can you think of a product, such as a breakfast cereal based on a cartoon character, that is no longer on the market? As the character declined in popularity, sales of the product also declined.

When sales of an item continue to decline, a company will probably decide to stop making and selling it. Gerber no longer operates daycare services and has eliminated its toy and furniture divisions. Such decisions allow the company to concentrate on more profitable products.

✓ CheckPoint
What is the product life cycle?

CHAPTER **17**

INTERNATIONAL BUSINESS PERSPECTIVE

Careers

INTERNATIONAL MARKETING CAREERS

Product packaging with information in several languages. Advertisements requiring approval of a government agency. Price labels in different currencies. These are just a few of the situations you might encounter when working in international marketing.

The foundation for success in a global marketing career, as with other international employment, is cultural knowledge and foreign language skills. Your ability to assess geographic, economic, social, and political situations will help you better plan and implement international marketing activities. With many diverse cultures and economic conditions, your capacity to work in cross-cultural team settings is vital. Within the next few decades, more than 70 percent of the world's population will live in developing economies and emerging markets. Employees able to market goods and services that serve the needs of these varied audiences will have the most career success.

Before an international assignment, you will need marketing knowledge and experience. You also need training and skills in sales, marketing research, product development, advertising, and distribution. Some companies provide marketing training for new hires. These entry-level positions in the home office often involve research, planning, and support of marketing tasks.

Once you receive an international assignment, cross-cultural management skills will be critical for career advancement. Gathering input from managers in multiple locations around the world requires excellent organizational and decision-making skills. The efficient operation of a global enterprise requires managers with effective communication and interpersonal skills.

Job titles and job descriptions for international marketing positions vary. The positions described below are just a few examples of opportunities you might want to explore.

- **International Marketing Director**—develops an international marketing plan, coordinates global marketing activities, and consults with local business partners
- **Global Product Manager**—adapts goods and services to cultural tastes, climate, language (for labeling), and package size based on the income of potential consumers
- **International Sales Manager**—needs to understand cultural attitudes and behaviors of a sales staff and customers
- **Cross-Cultural Promotional Director**—adapts for language and cultural differences when creating and implementing advertising and other promotions

Think Critically

1. Describe how marketing activities influence demand for international marketing careers.
2. Create a list of questions that a person interviewing for a position in international marketing might be asked.

450 Developing Goods And Services For Global Markets

REVIEW GLOBAL BUSINESS TERMS

Define each of the following terms.

1. brand
2. product life cycle (PLC)
3. global product
4. international product

REVIEW GLOBAL BUSINESS CONCEPTS

5. What purpose does packaging serve?

6. What are the stages of the product life cycle?

7. How does a global product differ from an international product?

SOLVE GLOBAL BUSINESS PROBLEMS

Most packaged products sold in the United States and almost all products in other countries use the metric system for weights and liquid measurements. The following is an approximate reference for converting to metric measurements.

When you know:	Multiply by:	To find:
ounces (oz)	28.35	grams (g)
pounds (lb)	0.45	kilograms (kg)
pints (pt)	0.47	liters (l)
quarts (qt)	0.95	liters (l)
gallons (gal)	3.79	liters (l)

8. A 14-ounce package of spaghetti would weigh about _____ grams.

9. Six pounds of cheese would weigh about _____ kilograms.

10. Eight pints of fruit juice is equal to about _____ liters.

11. Three quart bottles of soft drinks contain about _____ liters.

12. Estimate how many gallons are equal to 12 liters. Then check your answer with a calculator. How accurate was your estimate?

THINK CRITICALLY

13. Locate examples of famous brands not associated with packaged products.

14. Explain why different advertising would be needed in different stages of the product life cycle.

15. Why do companies often take legal action against others who try to use the same brand name?

MAKE ACADEMIC CONNECTIONS

16. **TECHNOLOGY** What types of technology have improved packaging for consumers and the environment?

17. **CULTURAL STUDIES** How might a nation's customs or traditions affect the brand names used in a country?

CHAPTER SUMMARY

17-1 GLOBAL PRODUCT PLANNING

A The sources of product opportunities for international marketing are new products, improved products, new uses for existing products, and existing products in new markets.

B The categories of consumer products are convenience goods, shopping goods, and specialty goods. A product line provides an assortment of items available for sale to varied target markets.

C Services are marketed with an emphasis on personalization, as they are usually produced as they are consumed.

17-2 DEVELOPING AND RESEARCHING PRODUCTS

A The steps in the new product development process are (1) generating product ideas, (2) evaluating product ideas, (3) researching product ideas, and (4) marketing product ideas. The phases in the marketing research process are (1) identify problem, (2) collect data, (3) analyze data, and (4) report results.

B Data collection methods used in international marketing research include secondary data and primary data (surveys, interviews, observations, and experiments).

17-3 AN INTERNATIONAL PRODUCT STRATEGY

A Brands used by companies are names, symbols, or designs that identify a product or service. Packaging is used to protect the product, to capture the attention of customers, and to make the product easy to use.

B A global product strategy involves decisions about whether to offer a standardized version or an adapted version of a good or service.

GLOBAL REFOCUS

Read the Global Focus at the beginning of this chapter, and answer the following questions.

1. Would a global product approach or an international product approach be most appropriate for companies selling water in different geographic markets?

2. How might water companies use technology and joint ventures to expand sales around the world?

REVIEW GLOBAL BUSINESS TERMS

Match the terms listed with the definitions.

1. Data collected by watching and recording shopping behaviors.
2. Large-scale surveys used to collect numeric data that are often used to study consumers.
3. Products purchased after consumers compare brands and stores.
4. A standardized item that is offered in the same form in all countries in which it is sold.
5. An assortment of closely related products designed to meet the varied needs of target customers.
6. A directed discussion with 8 to 12 people.
7. The stages a good or service goes through from the time it is introduced until it is taken off the market.
8. Inexpensive items that require little shopping effort.
9. A customized product adapted to the culture, tastes, and social trends of a country.
10. The type of data collection that involves a statistical comparison of two or more very similar situations.
11. Open-ended interview questions that allow researchers to obtain comments from consumers about their attitudes and behaviors.
12. The name, symbol, or design that identifies a product.
13. Unique products that consumers make a special effort to obtain.
14. An experimental research study that measures the likely success of a new product or service.
15. The orderly collection and analysis of data that is used to obtain specific marketing information.

a. brand
b. convenience goods
c. experiment
d. focus group
e. global product
f. international product
g. marketing research
h. observational research
i. product life cycle (PLC)
j. product line
k. qualitative research
l. quantitative research
m. shopping goods
n. speciality goods
o. test market

iofoto/iStockphoto.com

MAKE GLOBAL BUSINESS DECISIONS

16. Why do stores and online retailers have larger product lines than in the past?

17. Name some services that have increased in importance for our economy in recent years.

18. List some ideas that could be the basis for new products in our society.

19. Create some examples of topics for international marketing research studies that would be interesting to investigate.

20. When may qualitative research be preferred to quantitative research for a marketing research study?

21. What makes certain brands popular and easy to remember?

22. Does packaging cost too much for certain products? Find examples of products with packaging that could be made less expensive.

23. Why do some items go through the stages of the product life cycle faster than others?

24. Create a list of products that may be sold anywhere in the world without major changes being made. What determines whether an item is a global product or an international product?

MAKE ACADEMIC CONNECTIONS

25. **GEOGRAPHY** Describe geographic factors that might influence whether a company could sell its product as it is in other countries or if they would have to adapt it.

26. **COMMUNICATIONS** Conduct a survey of the products people buy without extensive comparison shopping. How important is place of purchase, price, and brand for these items?

27. **HISTORY** Talk to older people about products that are no longer on the market. What factors might have influenced the decline of these items?

28. **CULTURAL STUDIES** Collect advertisements, labels, and packages from products made in other countries. Describe the marketing activities used by the companies.

29. **RESEARCH** Find examples of secondary data in the library and on the Internet that could help a company with its international marketing activities. Describe how the information could be of value for preparing a global marketing plan.

30. **VISUAL ART** Prepare a poster or computer presentation with examples of products or services in the various stages of the product life cycle. Suggest marketing activities that would be appropriate for one item in each stage of the cycle.

31. **CAREER PLANNING** Select a good or service. Describe the jobs that would be required to make the product available to consumers in another country.

32. **TECHNOLOGY** Use the Internet to locate online resources for marketing research data collection and analysis. Prepare a description of each of the resources you find.

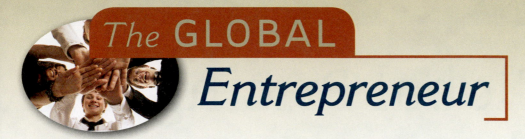

The GLOBAL Entrepreneur

CREATING AN INTERNATIONAL BUSINESS PLAN

Product Planning for International Marketing

Develop a marketing strategy based on the company and country you have been using in this continuing project, or create a new idea for your business in the same or a different country. Make use of previously collected information, and do additional research. This phase of your business plan should include the following components.

1. A description of the product (good or service), including characteristics and benefits of the item.

2. A description of the target market. Who would be the main buyers and users of the product? What are their demographic characteristics? What are their social attitudes and cultural behaviors?

3. A description of how the product might need to be adapted to accommodate social, cultural, or legal differences.

4. A description of what research activities could the company do to better understand its potential customers and the marketplace.

5. A description of branding and packaging ideas that could be used for this item.

Prepare a written summary or present a short oral report (two or three minutes) to communicate your main findings.

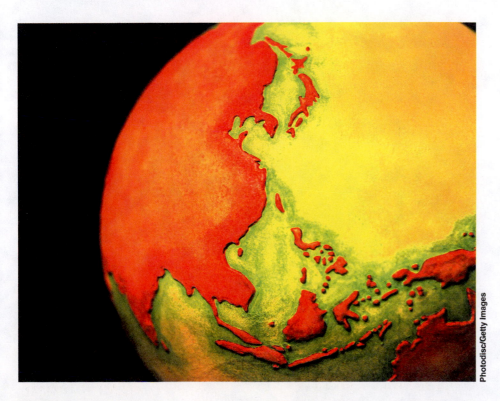

Photodisc/Getty Images

CHAPTER 18

Global Pricing and Distribution Strategies

18-1 International Pricing Activities

18-2 Global Distribution Activities

18-3 Moving Goods Around the World

Photodisc/Getty Images

GLOBAL FOCUS

Toys "R" Us in Japan

In 1984, after becoming the largest U.S. toy seller, Toys "R" Us started a smooth international expansion into Canada, Europe, Hong Kong, and Singapore. However, Toys "R" Us faced several barriers when entering the world's second-largest toy market—Japan.

Japan's Large-Scale Retail Store Law is designed to protect smaller businesses. For any store larger than 5,382 square feet (approximately 500 square meters), owners had to obtain approval from government agencies to build the facility. This process could take as long as ten years. Pressure from U.S. trade representatives and price-conscious Japanese consumers reduced the time needed for Toys "R" Us to gain approval for a store. The first Toys "R" Us store in Japan was 44,000 square feet and stocked nearly 15,000 products.

Toys "R" Us buys items in large quantities, which allows the company to sell at discounted prices. Instead of buying through wholesalers, Toys "R" Us attempts to deal directly with manufacturers. In the beginning, many toy producers hesitated to participate since they did not want to upset their long-term relationships with wholesalers and retailers.

To help Toys "R" Us stores to gain acceptance among business people and consumers in Japan, McDonald's Company of Japan purchased 20 percent ownership of the Toys "R" Us stores in that country. Because the enterprises have similar target markets, families with children, the companies have many opportunities for cooperative selling efforts.

Today, Toys "R" Us has nearly 700 stores outside the United States in more than 30 countries, but it faces strong competition. Wal-Mart and other discount retailers have expanded their market share of the retail toy market. Online selling has also put competitive pressure on Toys "R" Us. In an attempt to improve its competitive position, both online and in stores, the company acquired eToys.com and FAO Schwarz.

Think Critically

1. What factors may have affected the decision of Toys "R" Us to first expand into Canada, Europe, Hong Kong, and Singapore?
2. How did the Large-Scale Retail Store Law in Japan protect small stores?
3. Go to the web site of Toys "R" Us to obtain additional information about the company's international operations and online selling activities.

18-1 International Pricing Activities

GOALS

- Identify the factors that must be considered by businesses when setting prices.

- Describe pricing methods used by businesses.

- Discuss some pricing factors that are unique to global markets.

Photodisc/Getty Images

Price Planning for International Marketing

As a part of its marketing plan, every business must decide what amount to charge and how to get goods and services to customers. Factors such as export costs, values of foreign currencies, and the availability of transportation systems influence pricing and distribution for international marketing.

Price is the monetary value of a good or service. Everything has a price. Interest is the price paid on loans. Fare is the price paid for airline transportation. Fees are the prices paid for medical and legal services. Three main factors influence the price a company charges for goods and services when attempting to earn a profit: costs, consumer demand, and competition.

COSTS

A company cannot sell an item for less than it costs to make or to buy. Production and other operating costs must be covered by the price of an item. Besides incurring ordinary business expenses, organizations involved in international marketing will incur other costs, such as the following.

Product Modifications Some products need to be modified to meet cultural preferences or legal restrictions. There are always costs associated with modifying a product.

Taxes and Fees Tariffs and other taxes that must be paid when selling to customers in another country are costs that must be covered by the price of an item. Other costs include fees to acquire export or import licenses and the expenses associated with the preparation of export documents.

Exchange Rate Changes in the exchange rate will affect global company costs. As the value of the organization's home currency fluctuates, the amount paid for production inputs can rise or decline.

Transportation The cost of transporting a product to a buyer affects the price of the item. International marketing usually involved higher transportation costs because of the distance involved.

CONSUMER DEMAND

When prices are high, consumers tend to buy less of an item than when prices are low. The fundamental economic principle of demand is evident in all buying situations. Remember, *demand* is the relationship between the amount of a good or service that consumers are willing and able to purchase and the price. Lower incomes, higher prices, and needs for other items result in reduced demand for a good or service. The economic conditions, cultural preferences, and legal restrictions in a foreign market also are likely to affect potential demand and the price that is charged.

Photodisc/Getty Images

COMPETITION

If many companies are selling an identical or similar product, consumers have more choices than if only one company or a few companies were selling the item. Competition tends to keep prices lower. For example, if many stores in Singapore are selling similar products, consumers will purchase at the store with the lowest price. This competition will force companies to offer special prices or promotions to attract customers. When a company starts marketing their goods and services in another country, it faces competition from domestic companies in that country and from other exporting companies around the world.

✓ **Check**Point
What factors affect consumer demand?

Pricing Methods

International marketing managers use a variety of methods to determine appropriate prices. Markup pricing, new product pricing, psychological pricing, and discount pricing can be effective price determination methods.

MARKUP PRICING

Many prices are based on the cost that the store paid for an item plus an amount to cover the expenses and add profit. **Markup** is an amount added to the cost of a product to determine the selling price. The markup includes operating costs and a profit on the item.

Markups are commonly stated in percentages. For example, a company may use a 40 percent markup on its products. For an item that costs $50, this would result in a markup of $20. To determine the markup, multiply the cost by the markup percentage.

$$\text{Cost} \times \text{Markup Percentage} = \text{Markup}$$
$$\$50 \times 0.40 = \$20$$

After you calculate the markup amount you add it to the cost to determine the selling price. In this example the selling price is $70.

$$\text{Cost} + \text{Markup} = \text{Selling Price}$$
$$\$50 + \$20 = \$70$$

Competition affects markup, like many other marketing decisions. Products in competitive markets with constant demand, such as food products, tend to have low markups. In contrast, products with inconsistent demand, such as high-fashion clothing items and jewelry, will usually have higher markups to cover the carrying costs of these items.

NEW PRODUCT PRICING

When a company decides to sell a new product, managers face the problem of deciding what price to charge. The pricing strategy used for a new product is affected by the product image desired, the amount of competition, and sales goals. Three commonly used methods for pricing new products are competitive pricing, skim pricing, and penetration pricing.

Competitive Pricing If the new product has competition already on the market, a company may decide to sell its new product at a comparable price. Certain products and services always seem to be priced about the same at all selling locations. Gasoline, pizza, and basic groceries tend to have competitive prices in a given geographic area. Any price differences can usually be attributed to special services or special product features.

Skim Pricing When a new product is introduced, managers may decide to charge as much as possible. This approach, called **skim pricing**, sets a relatively high introductory price. Skim pricing attempts to attract buyers who are not concerned with price while also quickly covering the research and development costs of the new product. This approach was used when video recorders and personal computers were first introduced.

With skim pricing, a company faces two potential problems. First, the high price may quickly attract competitors to the market. Second, the company faces the risk of setting the price too high and selling very few items.

Penetration Pricing In contrast to skim pricing, **penetration pricing** is the setting of a relatively low introductory price for a new product. This approach attempts to gain strong acceptance in the market. This low-pricing strategy can help a company take sales from competitors as the law of demand suggests people will buy more at lower prices than at higher prices. Penetration pricing can be effective when competing against established companies in other countries and when selling in nations with low economic development.

PSYCHOLOGICAL PRICING

In an attempt to persuade consumers to purchase a product or service, companies may use pricing to create an image. For example, certain prices can communicate that an item for sale is a bargain. Or another item may be priced to portray an image of high quality. Common psychological pricing approaches include promotional pricing, odd-even pricing, prestige pricing, and price lining.

Promotional Pricing Advertised specials are a common marketing activity, especially in supermarkets and discount stores. Special-event low prices may be offered as "back-to-school" or "end-of-the-season" sales. A **loss leader**, which is a very low-priced item used to attract customers to a store, is used with the hope that shoppers will make other purchases while shopping for low-priced items. In a grocery store, milk is generally a loss leader.

Odd-Even Pricing Have you ever noticed that many items are priced at 59¢, $1.79, $8.95, and $79.99? Over the years, U.S. companies have found that prices ending in 5 or 9 (odd numbers) present a bargain image. A price ending in an even number or rounded to the nearest dollar amount, such as $175 or $49.50, generally gives an impression of quality. Bargain-oriented restaurants will price meals at $6.95 and $8.99, while quality-conscious restaurants may use $17.50 and $22. This strategy may vary by country. For example, in Japan, the numbers 4 and 9 are considered unlucky.

Prestige Pricing Extensive research has revealed that people believe a higher priced item is better quality than the exact same item at a lower price. French manufacturers such as Yves Saint Laurent, Louis Vuitton, and Christofle set prices to project an image of status, influence, and power.

Price Lining To make shopping easier for customers and salesclerks, a store may offer all merchandise in a category at the same price. All suits offered by a store may be sold at $150, $225, and $300. Shoes may be sold for $19.99, $25.99, and $34.99. Each price category includes a variety of items from which customers in that can choose.

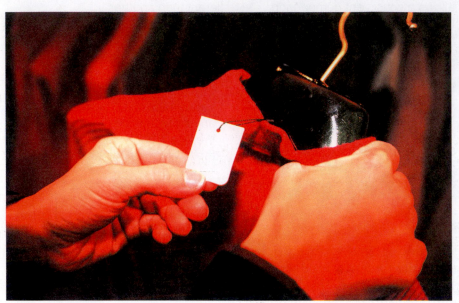

Photodisc/Getty Images

DISCOUNT PRICING

Price reductions are one of the most common actions taken by companies to attract and keep customers. Four common types of discounts are seasonal, cash, quantity, and trade.

Seasonal Discounts At various times of the year, companies may reduce prices to sell the remaining items in stock. Seasonal discounts in the United States include price reductions of summer clothing in August and reductions on Christmas cards and decorations the day after Christmas. In Santiago, Chile, during late July and August, the end-of-winter sales feature discounts on coats and other heavy clothing.

Cash Discounts Companies may reduce the price charged for items to encourage customers to pay their bills quickly. For example, customers may be offered a 2 percent discount if their bill is paid within ten days. If a customer decides not to take advantage of the discount, the full invoice amount is due within 30 days. This discount is expressed as 2/10, net/30.

Quantity Discounts To encourage customers to purchase more of an item, businesses may offer a quantity discount. For example, a garden shop may sell bags of potting soil using the following pricing schedule.

1 to 4 bags	$2.79 per bag
5 to 9 bags	$2.39 per bag
10 or more bags	$2.09 per bag

Trade Discounts Manufacturers commonly sell to distributors and stores based on a percentage of the *list price*, also called the *suggested retail price*. An electronics producer, for example, may sell televisions to stores at a 50 percent trade discount. In other words, a television that sells to consumers for $450 would cost stores $225.

✓ **Check**Point
Why are cash discounts offered?

Pricing in Global Markets

Managers setting prices for domestic markets are aware of competitors' prices, consumer demand, and currency values. However, when businesses are setting prices for trade across borders, the process is not as easy, and information may not be readily available.

Fluctuations in exchange rates for currencies can result in receiving less money than expected. One way to minimize the effect of fluctuating currency rates is to set prices high enough to cover these changes. *Countertrade*, which is the direct exchange of products or services between companies in different countries, can also minimize this risk.

Sometimes a company may intentionally set prices extremely low for foreign trade. **Dumping** is the practice of selling exported products at a lower price than what is asked in the company's home country. While this can benefit consumers, others will suffer. The lower price drives out competition, causing workers to lose jobs.

Businesses often pressure governments to prevent dumping. Countries may adopt *antidumping laws* or *antidumping tariffs*. These trade barriers prohibit importers from selling products at artificially low prices.

One additional factor that can affect global pricing activities involves negotiated prices. While set prices are common in industrialized countries, many businesses and consumers around the world bargain before settling on a transaction price. In street markets, this haggling process is often expected between buyers and sellers. Cultural knowledge along with negotiation skills are often important in global price setting decisions.

✓ CheckPoint
How can losses from currency fluctuations be minimized?

A Question of Ethics

DUMPING

Industrialized countries, with a shrinking agriculture sector, often provide farmers with a subsidy to help cover their costs. This government action allows farmers to sell their products at a lower price around the world, and is considered by many to be *dumping*. This action hurts farmers in countries that import these artificially low-priced agricultural products.

In another situation, fish producers in Maine protested that Chile was driving down the market price of salmon by selling at below-production cost. This action was believed to be an unfair trade practice. In contrast, several supermarket chains and restaurants believed the salmon was beneficial to their companies and consumers. The supporters of the Chilean fish industry contended that the lower-cost boneless salmon fillet was the result of investments in new processing equipment. They argued that this was a different product than was being produced by U.S. fishing companies.

While dumping may benefit consumers and the country selling the low-cost product, others are harmed. The country receiving the products can find that the lower price drives out competition, causing workers to lose jobs. Prices might become inflated once competition is driven out of the market.

Think Critically

1. Use the three guidelines for ethical analysis to examine the above situation. Are the fish producers in Chile acting ethically?
2. What actions might be appropriate for a country that is victimized by dumping?

18-1 Assessment

www.cengage.com/school/genbus/intlbiz

REVIEW GLOBAL BUSINESS TERMS

Define each of the following terms.

1. markup
2. skim pricing
3. penetration pricing
4. loss leader
5. dumping

REVIEW GLOBAL BUSINESS CONCEPTS

6. What are the three main factors that affect the price of a product?

7. What does a markup include beyond the cost of manufacturing or buying the product to be sold?

8. What are the advantages and disadvantages of dumping?

SOLVE GLOBAL BUSINESS PROBLEMS

For each of the following situations, calculate the requested markup, discount, cost, or price.

9. A Japanese clothing store marks up its prices 70 percent. What would be the selling price for a jacket that cost the store 8,000 yen?

10. A British company offers a 3 percent discount on a £600 purchase paid within 10 days. What is the amount of the purchase if the customer pays within 10 days?

11. A Brazilian store sells blank videocassettes for 6.3BRL each if less than five are purchased or 5.8BRL each if five or more are purchased. What would be the cost of six tapes?

12. A Mexican appliance manufacturer sells to retailers with a trade discount of 35 percent. If a washing machine has a list price of Mex$900 (pesos), what would be the cost of the item to a store?

THINK CRITICALLY

13. Assume a can of vegetables sells for $1. Estimate the amount for each of the following business costs: (a) product ingredients, (b) processing, (c) package and label, (d) advertising, (e) warehouse storage, (f) transportation, and (g) store profit.

14. Do antidumping laws promote or deter free trade?

MAKE ACADEMIC CONNECTIONS

15. **TECHNOLOGY** Compare prices for products sold in local stores and through online shopping web sites. Do the items cost more or less online? How do shipping charges, taxes, and delivery time affect online shopping?

16. **MATHEMATICS** Collect advertisements with examples of odd and even prices used at different stores. What types of retailers use this pricing method most often?

GOALS

- **Contrast direct and indirect channels of distribution.**

- **Describe the activities of agents, wholesalers, and retailers.**

- **Explain the role played by global intermediaries.**

Distribution Channels

For a product to be useful, it must be transported from the producer to the user. A **distribution channel** is the path taken by a good or service to get from the producer to the final user.

When would a company sell directly to the user of a product, and when would a business use wholesalers and retailers? How products are distributed is influenced by the type of product and consumers involved. For example, a small company that wants to distribute its products in many stores probably will use a distribution channel with many retailers. Figure 18-1 on the next page shows the common distribution channels used.

In a **direct distribution channel**, producers sell goods or services directly to the final user. Some examples of direct distribution (Channel A) include farmers selling produce at a roadside stand, sales representatives for a cosmetic company calling on consumers in their homes, and publishing companies selling their books through a web site.

More common than direct distribution is the use of agents, wholesalers, and retailers. An **indirect distribution channel** occurs when goods or services are sold with the use of one or more intermediaries between the producer and the consumer. Channel B is a common distribution method for automobiles and other motor vehicles. Channel C is used to distribute packaged food products and other items sold in supermarkets and discount stores. Finally, Channel D may be used for foreign trade in which an import-export agent is involved.

Common Distribution Channels

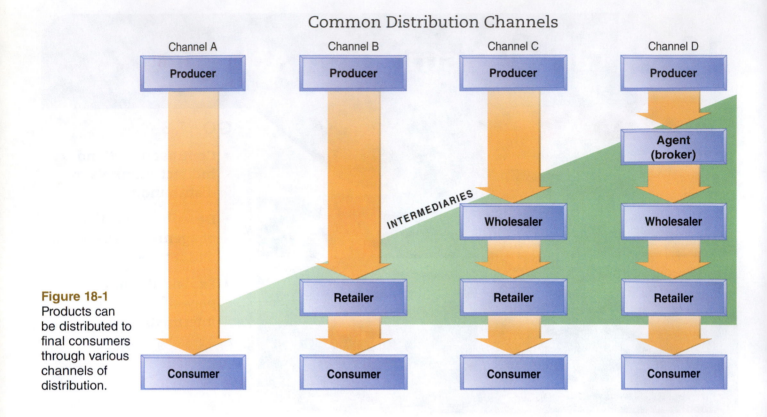

Figure 18-1
Products can be distributed to final consumers through various channels of distribution.

✓ **Check**Point

What is the difference between a direct distribution channel and an indirect distribution channel?

Distribution Channel Members

Several parties are usually involved when selling goods across borders. An **intermediary** is any person or organization in the distribution channel that moves goods and services from the producer to the consumer. The most common intermediaries are agents, wholesalers, and retailers.

AGENTS

An **agent,** also referred to as a *broker*, brings together buyers and sellers but does not take ownership of the products. International agents serve export companies by being knowledgeable about global markets and international trade barriers.

WHOLESALERS

A **wholesaler** is a business that buys large quantities of an item and resells them to a retailer. Wholesalers do not usually sell directly to final users of a product. Wholesalers have five main functions: providing information, processing orders, storing and transporting, financing and taking possession, and promoting. These functions are further described in Figure 18-2.

The film, equipment, and photographic supplies made by Kodak are available in almost every country. The company's headquarters in Rochester, New York, maintains close contact with sellers to determine demand for its products throughout the world. Factories are kept informed of needed inventory so sufficient merchandise is produced. Kodak's Distribution Division coordinates these efforts to ensure that distribution centers have the product when it is needed.

FUNCTIONS OF WHOLESALERS

Providing Information	Communicating between manufacturers and retailers
Processing Orders	Providing needed products for retailers to sell
Storing and Transportation	Maintaining warehouses and shipping capabilities
Financing and Taking Possession	Accepting ownership of finished goods and extending credit to customers
Promoting	Advertising and selling to retailers and helping retailers promote to their consumers

Figure 18-2 Wholesalers perform important functions that assist with international marketing activities.

Many people believe that eliminating wholesalers would reduce marketing costs. While wholesalers may be eliminated, the duties performed cannot be eliminated. Transporting, storing, and ordering must still be done. Either the manufacturer or the retailer must perform these duties, which would probably be less efficient than leaving the functions with wholesalers who specialize in those tasks.

RETAILERS

A **retailer** is a store or another business that sells directly to the final user. Each day hundreds of millions of shoppers make purchases from retailing businesses. In Cairo, Egypt, many people buy needed goods at an open market, while in Paris, most people make their purchases at small shops or large retail stores. Retailers attempt to serve customers in five main ways. These ways include product selection, convenience, product quality, sales staff assistance, and special services. These functions are further described in Figure 18-3.

Retailers in the United States may be viewed in six major categories, which are convenience stores, general merchandise stores, specialty stores, direct sellers, online retailers, and automatic vending.

Convenience Stores A family needs milk and bread, or a student needs a report cover. These buying situations may result in consumers shopping at the stores closest to their homes. Convenience stores are usually located near the homes of potential customers or have gas stations. Easy parking, easy-to-find items, and fast service are common among convenience stores.

General Merchandise Retailers Some retailers offer a larger variety of product types and offer more service than convenience stores. General merchandise retailers include supermarkets, department stores, discount stores, warehouse club stores, and outlet stores.

SERVICES PROVIDED BY RETAILERS

Product Selection	Variety of sizes, styles, and brands
Convenience	Location, hours of operation, parking availability, and ease of making purchases
Product Quality	Product excellence and reputation
Sales Staff Assistance	Information about product features, uses, and store policies
Special Services	Delivery, ease of exchanging or returning items, and special sales

Figure 18-3 Retailers provide a variety of services to attract customers.

Photodisc/Getty Images

In recent years, several major retailing companies have created superstores, also called *hypermarkets*. These giant one-stop-shopping facilities offer a wide variety of grocery items and department-store merchandise. While the typical supermarket has about 40,000 to 50,000 square feet, superstores may have 200,000 square feet or more. The first hypermarket was started in France in 1963. Today these superstores are likely to include a bakery, a restaurant, a pharmacy, and banking facilities.

Specialty Stores Shoes, furniture, clothing, sporting goods, computer software, and baked goods are commonly sold in stores that specialize in a limited product line. Specialty stores offer a variety of styles and brands of an item along with knowledgeable sales personnel.

In recent years, very large specialty stores have grown in market power. These specialty superstores offer low prices and a very extensive product line. Examples of these retailers include OfficeMax, Home Depot, Best Buy, and PetSmart.

Direct Sellers Mail order, telephone contacts, door-to-door marketing, and e-mail messages are called *direct selling*. This retailing method involves direct contact between the seller and the buyer. Personal care products, home appliances, books, and financial services are commonly sold through in-home parties, sales demonstrations, and seminars.

Direct selling varies in success from country to country. In cultures where personal contacts are important when doing business, direct selling thrives. In other societies, direct selling may have limited success.

GLOBAL BUSINESS SPOTLIGHT

COKE VS. PEPSI AT THE BERLIN WALL

When the Berlin Wall fell in 1989, many businesses were ready to enter the previously closed East German market. Pepsi presented dramatic television commercials celebrating the end of the cold war. While Pepsi sales grew, the company continued to ship products from existing bottling plants in western European locations.

Coca-Cola used a different distribution strategy. Coca-Cola invested $400 million to buy five bottling plants, 13 distribution centers, 370 trucks, 900 cars and vans, 170 forklifts, and 20,000 vending machines.

This commitment to distribution in eastern Europe by Coca-Cola resulted in the company's outselling Pepsi in the German market by the early 1990s.

Think Critically

1. How do the costs and risks differ for the distribution strategies used by Coca-Cola and Pepsi?
2. Go to the web sites of Coca-Cola and Pepsi to obtain information about the international operations of these companies. Write a brief description of your findings.

Online Retailers The Internet is changing the way people shop. A person can view products, prices, and other information from hundreds of retailers without leaving home. While mail order and television home-shopping channels paved the way for this process, the World Wide Web takes electronic retailing to new levels. Online retailers include both existing companies including Wal-Mart, OfficeMax, and The Gap, as well as Web-only sellers such as eBay and amazon.com.

Product demonstrations, customized products, and other features make online buying very popular. While consumers continue to have concerns about online shopping, improved security systems and privacy regulations are reducing those anxieties. Online retailing is expected to have strong growth for many years.

Automatic Vending Vending machines have been used for years for the purchase of soft drinks, snacks, and newspapers. Recent technology has expanded vending machine use to sell books, videos, computer time, clothing, and cooked-to-order foods. In Japan, consumers can obtain a wide range of products from vending machines including rice noodles, milk, batteries, umbrellas, and small fortune telling slips of paper.

Automatic teller machines (ATMs), a type of vending machine, provide financial services, such as obtaining foreign currency, as well as purchasing airline tickets, postage stamps, and other items.

Work as a Team
Prepare a list of retailers in your community. Explain how these businesses are involved in the global economy.

INTERNATIONAL RETAILING ACTIVITIES

Fast-food and snack-food companies that sell pizza, hamburgers, fried chicken, yogurt, and ice cream take to the road in many countries. Vehicles converted into minirestaurants allow companies to serve customers at temporary locations. Popular locations for these rolling restaurants are sporting events, amusement parks, community fairs, concerts, and zoos. Banks and other financial institutions also use a similar distribution approach with *ATMobiles* (portable cash machines).

Sidewalk merchants and street vendors in Mexico City have been joined by U.S. discount stores. After the Mexican government reduced import restrictions, Sam's Club, a division of Wal-Mart, opened in a vacant factory and started to sell clothing, appliances, personal care products, and packaged and frozen foods in that country. Mexican consumers were attracted to the quality, spare parts, service, and warranties offered by these retailers. Wal-Mart has also entered several international markets with stores in Canada, Brazil, Argentina, Japan, China, United Kingdom, Costa Rica, El Salvador, Honduras, Nicaragua, and Chile.

Photodisc/Getty Images

Global Intermediaries

The distribution channels used for international trade are often different from those used for domestic trade. Common international intermediaries include export management companies, export trading companies, freight forwarders, and customs brokers.

Export Management Company An **export management company (EMC)** provides complete distribution services for businesses that desire to sell in foreign markets. EMCs make it easier to sell in other countries since they have immediate access to established buyers. Most EMCs are small firms that specialize in specific products or in a certain foreign market. EMCs provide exporters with reliable global distribution channels.

Export Trading Company An **export trading company (ETC)** is a full-service global distribution intermediary. An ETC buys and sells products, conducts market research, and distributes goods abroad. An export trading company may also be involved in banking, financing, and production activities. Japanese trading companies, called *sogo shoshas*, have been in operation since the late 1800s. Today these companies handle more than half of Japan's imports and exports.

Freight Forwarder A **freight forwarder** ships goods to customers in other countries. Like a travel agent for cargo, these companies get an exporter's merchandise to the required destination. Often a freight forwarder will accumulate several small export shipments and combine them into one larger shipment in order to get lower freight rates.

Customs Broker A **customs broker**, also called a *custom house broker*, is an intermediary that specializes in moving goods through the customs process. This process involves inspection of imported products and payment of duties. Customs brokers are licensed in countries in which they work and must know the import rules and fees.

COMMUNICATION ACROSS BORDERS

FLEXIBLE SCHEDULING— BRAZILIAN STYLE

Scheduling delays of 15 to 45 minutes are common throughout Latin America. There, punctuality may actually be disruptive because others aren't necessarily ready to meet.

To work around the problem, Brazilian businesspersons try to schedule appointments in their own offices so they can work while waiting for others to arrive. Sometimes they take additional work with them to another person's office, where they work while they wait for that person to return to the office. Appointments for meals and drinks also typically begin in offices, where waiting time can be put to good use.

Think Critically

1. Why might a U.S. businessperson plan to arrive slightly late for a meeting with a Brazilian businessperson?
2. How does the Brazilian system of scheduling appointments promote personal productivity?

18-2 Assessment

REVIEW GLOBAL BUSINESS TERMS

Define each of the following terms.

1. distribution channel
2. direct distribution channel
3. indirect distribution channel
4. intermediary
5. agent
6. wholesaler
7. retailer
8. export management company (EMC)
9. export trading company (ETC)
10. freight forwarder
11. customs broker

REVIEW GLOBAL BUSINESS CONCEPTS

12. What are three common intermediaries in the distribution channel?

13. What are examples of direct selling?

14. What services does an export trading company provide?

SOLVE GLOBAL BUSINESS PROBLEMS

For each of the following international business situations, tell which global intermediary (export management company, export trading company, freight forwarder, or customs broker) would be involved.

15. A clothing company needs assistance with import rules and fees.

16. A company must have 17,000 shirts transported to Africa.

17. A manufacturer of lights for home use wants to use the services of a distributor with established buyers in Southeast Asia.

18. A packaged food business needs a global distribution intermediary to research, package, and ship its products to Central America.

THINK CRITICALLY

19. Some businesspeople believe that eliminating agents and wholesalers reduces their operating expenses. Discuss the opportunity costs associated with eliminating intermediaries.

20. As an importer, would you rather have your products sold by a general merchandise retailer or a specialty store? Why?

MAKE ACADEMIC CONNECTIONS

21. **TECHNOLOGY** Select an item not commonly sold online. Sketch or describe a web site that might be used to sell this good or service.

22. **STATISTICS** List the names of all retailers you and your family have used in the past 30 days and the number of visits. Categorize the retailers by type, such as convenience store, online retailer, or automatic vending. Create a frequency chart of the results.

18-3 Moving Goods Around the World

GOALS

- Summarize the shipping requirements for international distribution.

- Compare transportation modes available to international distributors.

imagemonkey/iStockphoto.com

Preparing for Shipping

As exports are prepared for international distribution, goods must be packed and labeled, and various documents may be required.

PACKING AND LABELING

When an item is prepared for international shipping, it should be packed to avoid breakage, protect against moisture, minimize theft, and maintain the lowest possible weight and volume. Shipments going by land or sea require strong containers.

In contrast, air shipments do not require such heavy packing. Shippers recommend that exporters avoid mention of brand names or contents on the package. This reduces the potential for theft. The shipping label for exported goods should include the information shown in Figure 18-4.

Universally recognized symbols are commonly used on containers to inform package handlers of warnings and contents. Examples of these symbols appear in Figure 18-5 on next page.

SHIPPING LABEL INFORMATION

- name and address of the shipper
- country of origin
- container's weight
- size of the container
- number of packages per container
- destination
- labels for hazardous material

Figure 18-4 Specific information needs to be included on the shipping label for exported goods.

Example Of Universal Packing Symbols

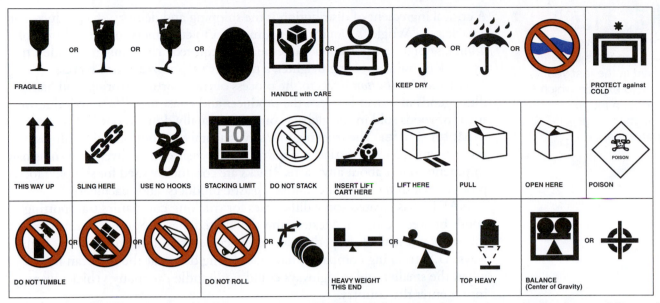

Figure 18-5 Universal package symbols communicate important information that can be understood around the world.

DOCUMENTATION

Various export forms are normally required when shipping merchandise to other countries. These documents include the bill of lading, certificate of origin, export declaration, destination control statement, and insurance certificate.

Bill of Lading A *bill of lading* is a contract between the exporter and the transporter. This form describes the weight, number, and value of goods along with the names and addresses of the seller and buyer. A bill of lading serves as a receipt for the exported items.

Certificate of Origin A *certificate of origin* documents the country in which the goods being shipped were produced. This document may be required to determine the amount of any import tax.

Export Declaration An *export declaration* is required by the U.S. Department of Commerce for shipments with a value of more than $500. This form lists the same information that is on the bill of lading along with the name of the carrier and the exporting vessel.

Destination Control Statement A *destination control statement* verifies the country to which goods are being shipped. This document notifies the carrier and all other handlers that the shipment may only go to certain destinations.

Insurance Certificate An *insurance certificate* explains the amount of insurance coverage for fire, theft, water, or other damage that may happen to goods in shipment. This certificate also lists the names of the insurance company and the exporter.

✓ CheckPoint
What is the purpose of a certificate of origin?

Work as a Team

Have students make a list of twenty products they have used in the last year. Ask them to explain which transportation mode would be most appropriate for each item on the list.

Transportation in the Global Market

A critical ingredient of distribution is the shipping and delivery of a product. For a package of Wrigley's Doublemint gum to get to customers some rural areas of China, several transportation modes may be required. These might include a trip by truck or train, a rusting freighter, a tricycle cart, an oxcart, or a bicycle.

Physical distribution refers to the process of transporting, storing, and handling goods in transit between the producer and consumer. The physical movement of goods sold in the global economy is usually done in one of five ways.

Motor Carrier The trucking industry is a vital distribution link in almost every country. Motor carriers can quickly and consistently deliver large and small shipments to just about anywhere. Trucks are commonly used for shipping food products, clothing, furniture, lumber, plastic products, and machinery.

NAFTA has created some difficulties for trucking companies transporting goods between Canada, Mexico, and the United States. Some Canadian trucks that were not loaded properly resulted in accidents and injuries on U.S. highways. U.S. trucking companies have faced long delays at the Mexican border when the smaller, older highways could not handle the many vehicles wanting to enter the country.

Railroad Within the United States and many other countries, railroads continue to be a major transportation mode. The products most commonly shipped by rail are automobiles, grain, chemicals, coal, lumber, and steel.

To add flexibility to rail shipping services, truck trailers and containers are transported on flat cars across country. Once near the destination, motor carriers make the local deliveries. These *piggyback* operations combine the long-haul capability of railroads with the door-to-door delivery of trucking.

Waterway Inland water carriers, such as barges, can efficiently transport bulky commodities. Oceangoing ships are slower than other transportation modes. However, they are very cost effective for shipping items overseas. These container-carrying vessels allow exporters to transport items such as coal, steel, lumber, grain, oil, and sand.

Containerization is the process of packing cargo in large standardized containers for efficient shipping and handling. Before this process, cargo was handled manually using crates, pallets, and forklifts. Damage to cargo and delays were common. Containerization is used when shipping from major deepwater ports, such as those in Elizabeth, New Jersey, and Oakland, California. Other new containerization developments have also made it possible to transport fresh fruits and vegetables in refrigerated compartments from Chile to Japan.

Pipeline More than 200,000 miles of pipelines are in operation in the United States alone. Pipelines provide a dependable, low-cost method for transporting natural gas and oil products. The limitation of this transportation method is speed. Liquids travel at a speed of only three or four miles per hour. In addition, few products can be transported by this method, and

NETBookmark

Although it is called the Silk Road, this desert trading route in Asia was used to transport many other things, from gold and ivory to exotic animals, plants, glass, and religion. Access the web site shown below and click on the link for Chapter 18. Read the article and make a graphic organizer that charts all the ways that the Silk Road influenced trade and other aspects of society.

www.cengage.com/school/genbus/intlbiz

AVON IN THE AMAZON

In the Amazon region of Brazil, Avon sell cosmetics with the use of company representatives who travel by canoe or in an animal-powered cart. In Brazil, about 400,000 consultants sell Avon products. That number is twice the size of the country's army.

Avon uses direct selling when doing business in more than 130 countries. However with the low-income consumers in the Amazon region, adaptation of marketing is necessary. Payments, for example, may be unusual. Instead of money, a chicken or flour may be exchanged for lipstick and other beauty items.

Orders for cosmetics are processed through a computer system at regional offices around Brazil. The products are then shipped as far as 2,500 miles from Avon's production facilities in Sao Paulo, Brazil, to customers in the Amazon region.

Think Critically

1. What factors influenced Avon to adapt its distribution strategy in Brazil?
2. Go the Avon web site to obtain additional information about the company's product line and distribution methods. Write a paragraph about your findings.

---

international pipelines can only be used when a geographic link exists between two countries.

Air Carrier The use of air transportation for international business activities continues to expand. As global demand for products increases, companies use the quick service offered by air carriers. Items commonly shipped by air include high-priced specialty products, specialized equipment parts, and perishable items (such as fresh flowers).

Intermodal Movements Companies frequently use more than one mode of transportation when shipping to other countries. *Intermodal movements* refer

Photodisc/Getty Images

to the transfer of freight involving various modes of transportation. Containers used today can easily be transferred from a ship or plane to a train or truck.

✓ CheckPoint

What activities are involved with physical distribution?

INTERNATIONAL BUSINESS PERSPECTIVE
History

THE PANAMA CANAL

The Panama Canal shortens water travel between the Atlantic and Pacific Oceans by 7,000 miles (11,270 kilometers). Before the canal was built ships traveling between the two oceans had to sail around South America. This 51.2-mile waterway connects the Caribbean Sea with the Pacific Ocean at the Isthmus of Panama, the neck of land connecting North and South America.

The idea of a canal connecting the Atlantic and Pacific Oceans was first considered in the sixteenth century. In 1534, Charles V of Spain ordered a survey for a possible canal route across Panama. A French company finally started the project in 1881. However, work ceased after eight years due to the treacherous terrain and diseases such as malaria and yellow fever. Nearly 20,000 workers died during the attempted construction. After Panama gained its independence from Colombia in 1903, the United States was granted the right to construct the canal and control its operation. Construction was completed in 1914 at a cost of $336 million.

Six pairs of locks raise or lower a ship to the next water level along the length of the Panama Canal. The trip takes between seven and eight hours with more than 12,000 ships traveling through the canal each year. In 1999, the possession of the Panama Canal was transferred from the United States to Panama after 85 years.

Think Critically

1. What are the international trade benefits of the Panama Canal?
2. Conduct an Internet search for information about the current activities of the Panama Canal. Write a description of your findings.

Photodisc/Getty Images

REVIEW GLOBAL BUSINESS CONCEPTS

1. What documents are commonly required when shipping goods to other countries?

2. What are the five main transportation systems used for shipping goods?

3. When would a business use intermodal movements?

SOLVE GLOBAL BUSINESS PROBLEMS

Suggest an appropriate transportation method for the following international marketing situations.

4. A company in Argentina is shipping oil to other countries in South America.

5. A British company is shipping machines for use in factories in various African countries.

6. A company in Hawaii is shipping fresh flowers to Japan and California.

7. A mining company is shipping iron ore to steel factories within the same country.

THINK CRITICALLY

8. How might shipping labels be improved to assist businesses and to contribute to the safety of workers?

9. What actions could be taken to make border crossings of shipped goods more efficient?

10. Describe how a company would balance the tradeoff between cost and speed when selecting a shipping method.

MAKE ACADEMIC CONNECTIONS

11. **COMMUNICATIONS** Prepare a map display that shows the trade route that would be used for transporting various products from one region of the world to another.

12. **SCIENCE** Research containerization and pipeline methods to determine how these transportation modes have improved international distribution.

13. **GEOGRAPHY** Describe how intermodal transportation could solve distribution problems created by the terrain and geographic conditions in a country.

14. **LAW** Why would a country have laws to prevent the shipping of various types of products into that nation?

15. **TECHNOLOGY** Use the Internet to locate online resources for transporting goods around the world.

16. **TECHNOLOGY** Use the Internet to find examples of some of the documentation needed to ship products around the world.

17. **TECHNOLOGY** Visit the web sites of three different companies that transport products internationally.

18-1 INTERNATIONAL PRICING ACTIVITIES

A Businesses need to consider costs, consumer demand, and competition when setting prices for international markets.

B The common pricing methods used by businesses include markup pricing; new product pricing, which includes competitive pricing, skim pricing, and penetration pricing; psychological pricing; and discount pricing.

C Pricing factors that are unique to global markets include changing currency values and unfair actions, such as dumping.

18-2 GLOBAL DISTRIBUTION ACTIVITIES

A Direct channels of distribution involve selling goods or services directly to the final user. Indirect channels of distribution involve the use of intermediaries: agents, wholesalers, and retailers.

B Agents, wholesalers, and retailers are distribution channel members who provide services to move goods and services from the producer to the consumer.

C Global intermediaries include export management companies, export trading companies, freight forwarders, and customs brokers.

18-3 MOVING GOODS AROUND THE WORLD

A Shipping requirements for international distribution require proper packaging and labeling along with necessary documents. These may include a bill of lading, certificate of origin, export declaration, destination control statement, and insurance certificate.

B The main transportation modes available to international distributors are motor carrier, railroad, waterway, pipeline, and air carrier.

GLOBAL REFOCUS

Read the Global Focus at the beginning of this chapter, and answer the following questions.

1. Do you think the entrance of Toys "R" Us into the Japanese market served the best interests of Japanese consumers and workers?

2. How do you think increased competition and online selling will affect prices for toys in Japan?

REVIEW GLOBAL BUSINESS TERMS

Match the terms listed with the definitions.

1. When goods or services are distributed with the use of one or more intermediaries between the producer and the consumer.

2. Setting a relatively low introductory price for a new product.

3. A very low-priced item used to attract customers to a store.

4. A full-service global distribution intermediary.

5. An amount added to the cost of a product to determine the selling price.

6. The path taken by a good or service to get from the producer to the final user.

7. A business that buys large quantities of an item and resells them to a retailer.

8. A company that provides complete distribution services for businesses that desire to sell in foreign markets.

9. Setting a relatively high introductory price for a new product.

10. A person or an organization in the distribution channel that moves goods and services from the producer to the consumer.

11. A business that ships goods to customers in other countries.

12. When goods or services are sold directly from the producer to the final user of the item.

13. The practice of selling exported products at a lower price than that asked in the company's home country.

a. agent
b. customs broker
c. direct distribution channel
d. distribution channel
e. dumping
f. export management company (EMC)
g. export trading company (ETC)
h. freight forwarder
i. indirect distribution channel
j. intermediary
k. loss leader
l. markup
m. penetration pricing
n. retailer
o. skim pricing
p. wholesaler

Photodisc/Getty Images

14. An intermediary that specializes in moving goods through the customs process.

15. A store or another business that sells directly to the final user.

16. An intermediary that brings together buyers and sellers but does not take ownership of the products.

MAKE GLOBAL BUSINESS DECISIONS

17. Companies involved in international marketing usually encounter higher operating costs than do domestic marketers. What benefits are associated with global marketing?

18. What types of products have a high percentage markup?

19. Give examples of discounts used by stores to attract customers.

20. How can dumping have a negative effect on a nation's economy?

21. Explain how wholesaling serves the needs of consumers throughout the world.

22. Describe how different types of retailers in your community attract different types of customers.

23. How might the success of retailers in different countries be affected by cultural, economic, and political factors?

MAKE ACADEMIC CONNECTIONS

24. **GEOGRAPHY** Research the economic importance of crucial waterways around the world, such as the Panama Canal, Suez Canal, Strait of Gibraltar, Strait of Hormuz, and Strait of Malacca. Prepare a brief essay with your findings.

25. **COMMUNICATIONS** Prepare a list of common goods, and ask people of various ages for their best guess at the price of each item. Which consumers are most knowledgeable about prices?

26. **TECHNOLOGY** Conduct library and Internet research about online retailing. What types of electronic shopping systems and cyberstores are expected to increase in popularity over the next few years?

27. **CULTURAL STUDIES** Talk to someone who has visited or lived in another country. Obtain information about the types of stores and informal retailing (street vendors, pushcarts, open-air markets) that exist in that country.

28. **VISUAL ARTS** Prepare a poster, computer presentation, or another visual display showing how various products are shipped within and between countries.

29. **MATHEMATICS** Estimate the markup of various food products, articles of clothing, and other items. Talk with a retail store manager or employee to obtain information about (a) the wholesale cost of the products they sell and (b) the operating expenses that influence the final selling price.

30. **CAREER PLANNING** If you were the manager of a distribution center that shipped products to over 50 different countries, what types of workers would you need to hire? What skills would you need to have to be a global distribution manager?

The GLOBAL Entrepreneur

CREATING AN INTERNATIONAL BUSINESS PLAN

Creating an International Pricing and Distribution Plan

Create a pricing and distribution strategy for the business idea you have used in previous chapters, or select another business idea. Use the country you have previously researched, or select a different country. Using library and Internet research, obtain information for the following topics.

1. How do operating costs and competition affect the prices charged by the company? Prepare a list of the company's production costs and other expenses.

2. List the factors that affect the demand for the company's goods and services in different countries.

3. Describe the distribution channel that might be used to get the company's goods or services to consumers.

4. Describe the types of retail stores used to sell the company's goods or services.

5. Describe the types of shipping methods that would be used by the company to get its products to foreign markets.

Prepare a written summary or present a short oral report (two or three minutes) of your findings.

Photodisc/Getty Images

CHAPTER 19

Global Promotional Strategies

19-1 Global Communications and Promotions

19-2 Planning Global Advertising

19-3 Global Selling and Sales Promotions

Unilever: An Advertising Giant

Unilever sells products known around the world. The company's brands include Lipton tea, Ben & Jerry's ice cream, Promise margarine, Dove soap, Wisk detergent, and Close-up toothpaste. But these are just a few, Unilever has about 400 brands. Many of those are known around the world, while others are leaders in local markets.

The company is also the largest advertiser in many countries, including India, Austria, Britain, Greece, Italy, the Netherlands, Turkey, Argentina, Brazil, and Chile. Every day, more than 160 million people around the world purchase a product with a Unilever brand.

Despite this global success, Unilever has faced strong competition from companies such as Procter & Gamble. In the early 1990s, Unilever introduced Omo laundry detergent in the Persian Gulf in an attempt increase sales in that region. Omo was adapted for use in washing machines from the formula used in Egypt, where most people wash clothes by hand. Instead of running the operations from London, the company created Unilever Arabia to administer marketing, research, sales, and advertising activities. This division of the company went on to expand its product offerings in the Persian Gulf by selling Vaseline petroleum jelly, Vaseline Intensive Care lotion, and Lux soap.

With more than 170,000 employees in 100 countries and 270 manufacturing facilities on six continents, Unilever is motivated to also have a strong concern for economic, social, and environmental issues. The company offers a salt product with iodine, iron, and vitamin A to improve the health of people in Ghana. Unilever also works with local partners in rural areas of India to provide microloans for women who desire to start a business, resulting in economic sustainability for their communities.

Think Critically

1. How did competition influence the actions of Unilever in the Persian Gulf?
2. What are the promotional benefits for Unilever to contribute to improved economic development and enhanced quality of life?
3. Go to the Unilever's web site to obtain additional information about recent actions of the company. Prepare a report of your findings.

19-1 Global Communications and Promotions

- **Diagram the elements of the communication process.**
- **Describe the elements of the promotional mix.**

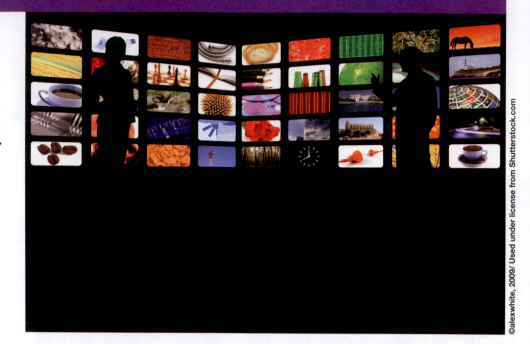

©alexwhite, 2009/ Used under license from Shutterstock.com

The Communication Process

Every business needs to communicate with potential buyers. A company's ability to inform and persuade consumers with promotional efforts is a basic business activity.

Each day the average person sends and receives thousands of communications. Many of these messages involve television commercials, online promotions, magazine advertisements, and other marketing promotions.

Have you ever said something to someone and the other person didn't hear you? Or have you ever said one thing and a listener interpreted it to mean something completely different from what you intended? In the communication process, the message is sent from a *source* (the sender) to the *audience* (the receiver). You may be the source, and a friend may be the audience. In marketing, a company is commonly the source, and consumers are the audience.

The source puts the message in a form that hopefully the audience will understand. This is known as *encoding*. The message travels to the audience over a *medium*—such as a television, a telephone, a magazine, the Internet or a salesperson talking in a store. *Decoding* is the process in which the audience makes meaning of the message.

While communication may seem easy, *noise* can disrupt the process. Noise refers to anything that interferes with the communication process. Types of noise that can obstruct international business communication include language differences, varied cultural meanings for words and gestures, and the setting in which communication takes place. Information overload is a type

The Communication Process

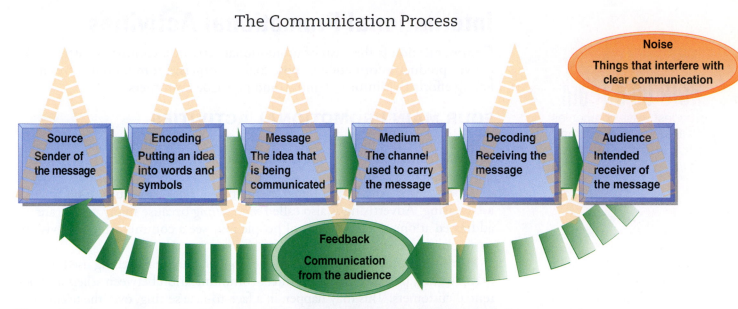

Noise — Things that interfere with clear communication

| Source — Sender of the message | Encoding — Putting an idea into words and symbols | Message — The idea that is being communicated | Medium — The channel used to carry the message | Decoding — Receiving the message | Audience — Intended receiver of the message |

Feedback — Communication from the audience

Figure 19-1 The communication process is the system used to send and receive marketing messages.

of noise that interferes with effective communication. Too much information makes it difficult to process and absorb the meaning. The use of e-mail and text messaging can easily lead to information overload.

Finally, *feedback* is communication from the audience back to the sender. Common ways for consumer feedback are toll-free numbers, web sites, and e-mails. These methods allow people to ask questions, obtain information, and state complaints. Toll-free phone numbers and web site information often appear on packages and in advertisements. Or you can obtain the telephone numbers and e-mail addresses of companies using an Internet search. These feedback methods allow companies to obtain information from consumers to improve their products and service.

Photodisc/Getty Images

The communication process is summarized in Figure 19-1. Notice the circular flow depicted in the figure. The arrows illustrate movement through the process including the feedback to the source. The figure also shows how noise can interfere throughout the process.

✓ CheckPoint
What kinds of noise can obstruct international business communications?

Work as a Team
Suggest ways companies could encourage customers to visit their web sites.

International Promotional Activities

Communication is the basis of promotional activities. Companies attempt to convey product information to potential customers. Promotion involves marketing efforts that inform, remind, and persuade customers.

FOUR MAIN PROMOTIONAL ACTIVITIES

The four main promotional activities available to companies are advertising, personal selling, publicity, and sales promotion. Examples of these activities are illustrated in Figure 19-2.

Advertising Any form of paid, nonpersonal sales communication is **advertising**. Advertising is also called *mass selling* because many people are addressed at one time. Millions of people may see a commercial on television or an online advertisement.

Personal Selling In contrast to the nonpersonal mass selling used in **advertising, personal selling** is direct communication between sellers and potential customers. This may happen in a face-to-face setting, over the telephone, or with personalized e-mail messages. Personal selling can provide the opportunity for immediate feedback directly from the customer to the sales representative.

Publicity Business organizations benefit from favorable news coverage about their products and business activities. **Publicity** is any form of unpaid promotion, such as newspaper articles or television news coverage.

Sales Promotion The final element of promotion includes a variety of activities. **Sales promotion** comprises all of the promotional activities other than advertising, personal selling, and publicity. Sales promotions include coupons, contests, free samples, and in-store displays.

THE INTERNATIONAL PROMOTIONAL MIX

A **promotional mix** is the combination of advertising, personal selling, publicity, and sales promotion used by an organization. Which of the four promotional elements should be used most often? Managers must consider a nation's cultural, legal, and economic environments when answering this question.

PROMOTIONAL ACTIVITIES AND EXAMPLES

Advertising	Personal Selling
• Television and radio commercials	• Face-to-face setting
• Magazine ads	• Over the telephone
• Web site ads	• Personalized letters
• Billboards	• Personalized e-mail messages

Publicity	Sales Promotion
• Newspaper articles	• Coupons
• Web site articles	• Contests
• Magazine articles	• Free samples
• Television and radio news coverage	• In-store displays

Figure 19-2 Multinational companies use promotional activities to inform, remind, and persuade potential customers.

Cultural factors will influence the promotional mix for international marketers. Radio is very popular in Mexico, and advertising is usually a major component of the promotional mix in that country. In nations with poorly developed postal systems, mail advertising would not be as effective as personal selling or sales promotions.

Marketers also must choose between aiming promotions at end-users of an item or at distributors. **Pull promotions** are marketing efforts directed at the final users of an item. In this promotional approach, companies want consumers to "pull" the product through the distribution channel by demanding the item at stores. Pull promotions include television commercials, advertisements in consumer magazines, coupons, and other selling efforts aimed at consumers.

In contrast to pull promotions, **push promotions** are marketing efforts directed at members of the distribution channel. These promotional activities attempt to get wholesalers and retailers to "push" a product to their customers. Push promotions may include discounts to retailers, special in-store displays, or contests for salespeople.

✓ CheckPoint
How does advertising differ from personal selling?

A Question of Ethics

ADVERTISING TO YOUNG CONSUMERS

Several years ago, the province of Quebec banned television commercials aimed at children. However, English-speaking residents of the Canadian province can view ads for toys, cereals, and snacks on television programs broadcast from Ontario or the United States.

Several European countries limit advertising aimed at young consumers. Norway and Sweden prohibit commercials targeted for children under age 12. Toy ads are banned in Greece between 7 A.M. and 11 P.M. Italy does not allow advertising during cartoon shows. While Finland and Germany forbid sales pitches by children and cartoon characters.

Those who favor these restrictions point out that in Britain, the average child sees nearly 18,000 ads a year. In the United States, that number is about 25,000. Supporters of these laws also believe children are not able to carefully process the many messages received from commercials. In contrast, businesses believe these restrictions violate free-speech rights.

Think Critically

Use the three guidelines for ethical analysis to examine the above situation. Is advertising aimed at young consumers appropriate, or should children be protected from communication that they may not completely understand?

INTERNATIONAL BUSINESS PERSPECTIVE
Culture

PROMOTIONAL EFFORTS EXPAND SOCCER'S POPULARITY

By almost all estimates, soccer is the most popular sport in the world. Each year, more than 20 million organized soccer matches are played. Major tournaments are held on three continents. The European Cup is the goal of European soccer players. In South America, teams compete for the Liberator's Cup. The Cup of Nations and the Cup of Champion Clubs are the ambition of African nations. In 2002, nearly 2 billion television viewers watched the World Cup Final.

In most countries, the game is referred to as *football*. Soccer was introduced to the United States in the late 1800s. However, it was not until 1959 that the National Collegiate Athletic Association (NCAA) recognized it as an official collegiate sport. Today more than 15 million athletes in the United States under the age of 19 are involved in organized soccer programs.

The global popularity of soccer continues to expand. In the mid-1990s, Japan started its first professional soccer league. Companies such as Mazda, Mitsubishi, Nissan, Toyota, Ford Japan, WordPerfect Japan, and Coca-Cola Japan sponsored teams. Promotional efforts are expected to result in extensive ticket sales for games. Television advertising, soccer magazine subscriptions, and sales of products featuring players and team logos are a major promotional feature of Japanese soccer activities.

Think Critically

1. How do advertising and other promotions contribute to the growth in popularity of soccer?
2. Conduct an Internet search for additional information about efforts to promote soccer in various countries.

Photodisc/Getty Images

19-1 Assessment

REVIEW GLOBAL BUSINESS TERMS
Define each of the following terms.

1. advertising
2. personal selling
3. publicity
4. sales promotion
5. promotional mix
6. pull promotions
7. push promotions

REVIEW GLOBAL BUSINESS CONCEPTS

8. What are the elements of the communication process used in marketing?

9. What are the four promotional activities?

SOLVE GLOBAL BUSINESS PROBLEMS
For each of the following situations, decide which element of the promotional mix is being used.

10. A sales representative from Norway goes to a customer's place of business to describe a new product.

11. A Belgian company sponsors an environmental cleanup and sends press releases to the media announcing it.

12. A South African company provides special display racks to retailers who carry its products.

13. A Greek company hires college students to distribute samples of its new product at the town square during lunch hour.

14. A Chilean company sponsors a television situation comedy and includes three commercials for each broadcast.

15. A Japanese company signs a contract with a web site to include a banner on the site announcing a new product.

THINK CRITICALLY

16. Describe situations when push promotions may be more appropriate than pull promotions.

17. How does deceptive and false advertising reduce competition and hurt consumers?

MAKE ACADEMIC CONNECTIONS

18. **TECHNOLOGY** Go to a web site that sells merchandise from many companies. Write a description about how the merchandise of a particular company is promoted on that web site.

19. **COMMUNICATION** Select a newspaper or magazine advertisement. Describe how the language used in the advertisement promotes the product.

19-2 Planning Global Advertising

GOALS

- Explain the activities involved in planning advertising for global markets.
- Explain the advantages of using an advertising agency.

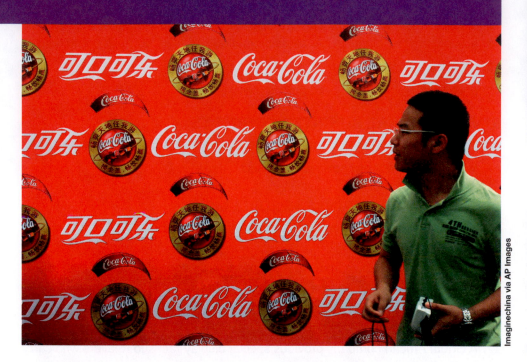

Imaginechina via AP Images

Advertising Planning Process

During the Olympics, Coca-Cola broadcasts television commercials in more than 10 languages—with a potential of being seen by more than 4 billion viewers in more than 140 countries. Because soft drinks are not significantly affected by cultural differences, Coca-Cola was able to use the same basic commercial in every country. However, this is not always possible. Multi-national companies often adapt advertising to fit social and political differences. The four steps involved in planning advertising are shown in Figure 19-3.

The Advertising Planning Process

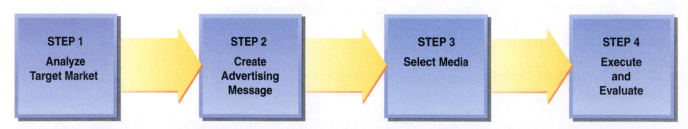

STEP 1 Analyze Target Market → **STEP 2** Create Advertising Message → **STEP 3** Select Media → **STEP 4** Execute and Evaluate

Figure 19-3 Multinational companies must plan advertising effectively to reach consumers in different countries.

STEP 1 ANALYZE TARGET MARKET

The advertising process starts by identifying potential users of a good or service. This *target market* should be defined in terms of geographic area, demographic characteristics, customer needs, buying habits, and media usage. For example, young male consumers in brazil will require a different advertising message than older female shoppers in france.

STEP 2 CREATE ADVERTISING MESSAGE

The traits of a target market influence the advertising message a company uses. For example, jeans in Brazil are sold with an emphasis on fashion. However, in Australia, customers are more concerned about product benefits, such as quality and price. An advertising message should accomplish one of the following goals.

- Get the customer's attention.
- Increase interest in the good or service.
- Improve a company's image in the minds of consumers.
- Boost the potential of a customer's desire to buy.
- Motivate customers into action.

Companies use some common advertising techniques to create unique messages for specific target markets. These techniques are explained in Figure 19-4.

If customers for a product are similar from one nation to another, a company may use a common advertising message. **Standardized advertising** is the use of one promotional approach in all geographic regions. For example, Tony the Tiger promotes Kellogg's Frosted Flakes in more than 50 countries.

COMMON ADVERTISING TECHNIQUES

Technique	Description
Product Quality Ads	Product quality ads present the quality, brand, price, or features of a product.
Comparative Ads	Comparative ads contrast the features of competing brands.
Emotional Ads	Emotional ads attempt to obtain a response from consumers by appealing to feelings or needs and desires, such as fear, guilt, love, beauty, pleasure, convenience, safety, power, status, or security.
Humorous Ads	Humorous ads use comedy to draw attention to a product or service.
Lifestyle Ads	Lifestyle ads present a product or service in a situation to which people can relate, such as at home, at work, or in recreational settings.
Endorsement Ads	Endorsement ads make use of famous or ordinary people as spokespersons for a product, service, or company. These are also called testimonial advertising.

Figure 19-4 Advertisers use a variety of techniques to communicate with consumers.

Work as a Team

Describe advertisements and television commercials. Determine what features of the product made it something you wanted to purchase.

In contrast, cultural factors and social customs may require a company to adapt advertising messages in different nations. **Localized advertising** is the use of promotions that are customized for various target markets. Yogurt, for example, is promoted as a breakfast food in some countries, as a lunch item in other nations, and as a snack in still others. Because of social customs, a multinational company must customize its yogurt advertisements in different societies.

STEP 3 SELECT MEDIA

Marketers must decide what media to use to deliver the advertising message. The major advertising media include newspaper, television, radio, magazine, direct mail, outdoor, and Internet.

The availability of advertising media varies considerably among the nations of the world. For example, Turkey has more 300 newspapers with varied political positions, while other countries have fewer than 20. In the past, advertising in movie theaters was important in countries with limited commercial television, such as India and Nigeria.

Newspaper Advertising For decades, advertising in newspapers represented a significant portion of promotional dollars spent. Ads in newspapers ranged from full-page ads for department stores to small classified ads promoting garage sales. Today, people don't wait to get their news from a printed newspaper; information is obtained all day long on computers, televisions, and cell phones. In order to remain viable, major newspapers now provide online editions that include advertising.

With expanded international business, some newspapers have created regional editions for different geographic areas. *The Wall Street Journal,* for example, has Latin American, European, and Asian editions.

Television Advertising Television commercials can have a strong effect on potential customers. Nonetheless, some nations limit the time available for television advertising. However, expansion of cable and satellite television systems makes it easier for advertisers. Channels such as CNN, ESPN, and MTV are available to billions of viewers.

Radio Advertising Radio advertising can be adapted to changing marketplace needs faster than most other media. Radio is frequently more available than other communication methods. Nations with few television sets or with people who can't read are likely to make greater use of radio.

Magazine Advertising Magazines, like newspapers, encourage international advertising by creating regional editions. *Business Week* has specific editions for Europe, Asia, and Latin America. *National Geographic* also covers these regions along with separate editions for Africa and the Middle East. *Reader's Digest* publishes more than 50 different editions in 35 languages and is available in more than 100 countries.

Direct Mail Each day hundreds of millions of ads and catalogs fill the mailboxes of the world. Technology

NETBookmark

Advertising media around the world are affected by culture and economic development. Access the web site shown below and click on the link for Chapter 19. View one of the country reports presented. Read the "Media Market Description" summary provided. Prepare a written summary of the information and explain how advertisers might use the data.

www.cengage.com/school/genbus/intlbiz

fosters increased use and reduced costs of direct mail advertising. **Database marketing** is the use of computerized information systems to identify customers with specific demographic traits and buying habits. With a database, direct mail marketers can target potential customers to receive appropriate advertisements. For example, families in a database who have home computers might receive mailings selling software for children to learn a foreign language.

Outdoor Advertising Billboards and transit ads on buses and trains are common in most countries. The use of this advertising medium, however, is usually limited to high-traffic and urban areas. In recent years creativity and technology have expanded outdoor advertising to include mechanical characters and three-dimensional displays.

Online Advertising The Internet expanded opportunities for advertisers to communicate with existing and potential customers. Company own web sites allow promotions of products and customer service activities. *Banner* ads are interactive advertisements across the tops or bottoms of a web page. *Buttons* are the smaller "click here" areas that attempt to get Internet users to visit another section of the web site. Banners and buttons are designed to get users to take action, such as requesting additional information or making an online purchase.

Business organizations also use a variation of direct mail by sending e-mail messages to target specific customers. The *e-mail blast* involves sending promotional messages to many potential customers. This action may be used to remind people of special offers or new products.

These digital media have the potential visual impact of television along with the flexibility of radio and direct mail. Online advertising will continue to evolve with as companies attempt to take advantage of new technology to enhance their promotional activities.

STEP 4 EXECUTE AND EVALUATE

Once advertising is planned, it must be executed. The advertising plan should include a schedule for the ideal launch time of the campaign. For example, a new line of winter clothing would be advertised at the beginning of (or a little before) the winter season. The advertising effort would not be as effective if launched halfway through the selling season. In addition, most advertising must consider the lead times involved in executing the program. Magazine advertising, for example, will have to be planned several months before publication of the advertisement.

After the advertising is executed, it should also be evaluated for effectiveness. Surveys may be conducted to test product awareness, and sales figures should be analyzed to determine whether the advertising caused an increase in sales. Information from the evaluation is then used to plan more effective advertising in the future.

✓ **Check**Point

What are the four steps in the advertising planning process?

Using an Advertising Agency

Some companies have their own advertising department to do promotional activities. However, most multinational companies use the services of an advertising agency. An **advertising agency** is a company that specializes in planning and implementing advertisements. Companies use advertising agencies to benefit from the agencies' experience in promoting different kinds of products and services in varied markets. A multinational company would choose an agency with broad experience in global markets to be assured of effective global promotions.

Most of the large advertising agencies in the world are located in the United States, Tokyo, and Europe. These organizations usually have the following four main divisions.

1. The research department studies the target market and measures the effectiveness of advertisements.
2. The creative department develops the message and the artistic features to deliver the message.
3. The media department selects where and when the advertising will be presented.
4. Account services is the link between the agency and the client (the company selling the product).

✓ **Check**Point

Why would a company use an advertising agency?

REVIEW GLOBAL BUSINESS TERMS
Define each of the following terms.

1. standardized advertising
2. localized advertising
3. database marketing
4. advertising agency

REVIEW GLOBAL BUSINESS CONCEPTS

5. What goals should an advertising message accomplish?

6. What are the seven main media used by advertisers?

7. What are the main divisions of an advertising agency?

SOLVE GLOBAL BUSINESS PROBLEMS
For each of the following international business situations, decide if the company should take a standardized or localized advertising approach.

8. Selling digital cameras in Africa, Asia, and Australia.

9. Promoting computers among small business owners in 140 countries.

10. Advertising soaps and personal care products in various regions of the world.

11. Promoting a juice drink with different flavors for different cultures.

12. Selling different colored clothing styles in South America and Asia.

THINK CRITICALLY

13. How does each division of an advertising agency correlate with the four steps in the advertising planning department?

14. What skills might be important for employees in each of the main divisions of an ad agency?

MAKE ACADEMIC CONNECTIONS

15. **TECHNOLOGY** Select an example of advertising on a web site. Describe the message, identify the intended audience, and evaluate the effectiveness of this promotion.

16. **LAW** What actions might a government take to prevent deceptive and false advertising?

17. **COMMUNICATION** Prepare a poster, computer presentation, or other visual display to illustrate the advertising techniques shown in Figure 19-4.

19-3 Global Selling and Sales Promotions

GOALS

- Summarize the personal selling process used in international business.

- Discuss the use of public relations and sales promotion by multinational companies.

Photodisc/Getty Images

Personal Selling

Consumers encounter salespeople in stores, on the phone, at their doors, and at their places of work. Personal selling is direct communication between sellers and potential customers.

PERSONAL SELLING ACTIVITIES

Personal selling involves activities to promote and sell goods and services. These duties include locating customers, taking orders, processing orders, providing information, and offering customer assistance.

In the past, most personal selling took place in face-to-face settings. Today, however, telemarketing has increased in importance. **Telemarketing** involves the selling of products during telephone calls to prospective customers. Personal selling over the telephone allows businesses to contact potential customers quickly and at a low cost. This selling method is most commonly used for insurance, investments, credit cards, magazine subscriptions, books, videos, personal care products, and home improvements.

THE PERSONAL SELLING PROCESS

The ability to plan and execute a sales presentation is important in many career fields. The personal selling process may be viewed in five steps.

Step 1 Identify Customers In step 1 of the personal selling process, potential customers are identified. Names of prospects may come from

The Personal Selling Process

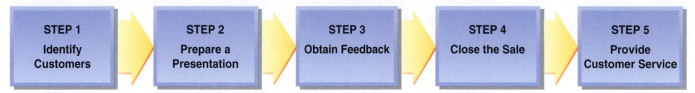

STEP 1	STEP 2	STEP 3	STEP 4	STEP 5
Identify Customers	Prepare a Presentation	Obtain Feedback	Close the Sale	Provide Customer Service

Figure 19-5 Personal selling involves the ability to plan and make a sales presentation.

computer databases, current customer lists, telephone calls, referrals from employees, e-mail responses, and other sources.

This first step, *prospecting*, is the foundation of successful personal selling. Qualified prospects are usually identified based on age, income, occupation, or interests. A company selling golf equipment would contact people who regularly participate in that sport.

Step 2 Prepare a Presentation The second step of the personal selling process involves preparing and making the sales presentation. In this stage, a creative and effective product description and demonstration must be prepared. The sales presentation should highlight a product's main features, positive traits, and marketplace acceptance. For instance, one hotel chain demonstrated its room features to potential customers by presenting a simulated room inside a trailer truck that traveled to various locations.

In the sales presentation, specific information is provided to address the needs and wants of customers. For example, some automobile buyers are interested in the performance of a vehicle, while others identify style as the most desired product attribute.

Step 3 Obtain Feedback The third phase of the personal selling process involves obtaining feedback. A salesperson is looking for objections, or op-

position, to the product. Awareness of objections allows the salesperson to provide additional information to overcome perceived negative aspects of the product.

Objections may be addressed either by clarifying some aspect of the sales presentation or by changing the conditions of the sale. For example, if a customer likes everything about a product except the color and style, a reduced price may eliminate these objections.

Step 4 Close the Sale Once major objections are overcome, the

Photodisc/Getty Images

closing of the sale should occur. In this step, the salesperson asks the customer to commit to the purchase. Questions such as the following are commonly used to close a sale.

- Is this the style you were thinking about buying?
- If we can deliver it in three days, would you be interested?
- Would you like the item in blue?
- If we include the extended warranty, would that meet your needs?

Favorable responses to questions of this type can result in the completion of the sale.

Step 5 Provide Customer Service Finally, personal selling should not end when the sale is closed. Customer needs continue with operating instructions, repairs, and additional products. Customer service efforts by companies have increased in importance in recent years. Research studies reveal that keeping existing customers is less expensive than finding new ones. As a result, businesses work to communicate regularly with their customers.

Relationship marketing attempts to create a long-term, mutually beneficial buyer-seller relationship. Examples of these efforts include following up with customers to ensure satisfaction, sending notices of special sales and reduced prices, and creating frequent-buyer programs to earn bonus gifts or special services.

PERSONAL SELLING IN INTERNATIONAL MARKETS

Global managers need salespeople with product knowledge who are able to work in the social and cultural context of a country. International companies have three choices when selecting sales staff members—expatriates, local nationals, and third-country nationals.

GLOBAL BUSINESS SPOTLIGHT

COLGATE'S PROMOTIONAL EFFORTS IN THAILAND

To become the largest selling toothpaste in Thailand, Colgate-Palmolive used a variety of promotional activities for its Colgate toothpaste. First, the company used the *Nok Lae* Children in its television commercials. This popular singing group was well known among young consumers and families and emphasized Thai heritage in the advertising.

After the commercials attracted much attention for Colgate, the company distributed printed information about proper dental hygiene. Colgate then made drinking cups, notebooks, posters, and audiocassettes highlighting both the singing group and the company's product. This led to the creation of the Colgate New Generation Kid's Club, whose members received a free dental checkups, bumper stickers, buttons, and other items.

Think Critically

1. What are the social and economic benefits of Colgate's action in Thailand?
2. Go to the web site of Colgate to obtain additional information about the company's international activities.

Expatriates are employees living and working in a country other than their home nation. Multinational companies use expatriates when the available number of host country salespeople is limited. Expatriate salespeople are probably familiar with their companies and products. However, they may not be acquainted with a nation's culture and social customs. For example, getting right down to business may be accepted in some societies. In other cultures, business associates are expected to get to know each other on a personal level before conducting business.

As the demand for international business employees increases, companies must expand the pool of workers. Organizations are using more people from within the targeted country to sell products and services in that country. *Local nationals* are employees based in their home country. Because local nationals are familiar with the culture, their training usually emphasizes product knowledge.

A third source of international salespeople involves those with a broad global viewpoint. *Third-country nationals* are citizens of one country employed by a company from another country who work in a third country. These salespeople frequently are able to speak several languages and possess a highly developed sense of cultural sensitivity. An example of a third-country national would be a German working in Chile for an Italian company.

Sales managers and other executives of Samsung, South Korea's largest company, attend a month-long training camp before starting an assignment in another country. This culturally sensitive instruction covers language, eating habits, leisure activities, clothing styles, and cultural values. The program has helped Samsung managers, who work in more than 50 countries, avoid social blunders.

✓ CheckPoint
How do salespeople overcome customer objections?

Other International Promotional Activities

Advertising and personal selling are a large portion of an organization's promotional efforts. However, other types of promotions address various marketing objectives.

PUBLIC RELATIONS

Companies are continually concerned about communicating a favorable public image. Companies can gain publicity with press releases, company newsletters, and sponsorship of sporting and entertainment events. A company may take actions such as the following to improve or keep its image.

- Hewlett-Packard Company donated computers to the University of Prague, in the Czech Republic.
- H. J. Heinz funded infant nutrition studies in China and Thailand.
- DuPont sent water-jug filters to African nations to remove dangerous impurities from drinking water.

GLOBAL SALES PROMOTIONS

As noted earlier, sales promotions comprise all promotional activities other than advertising, personal selling, and publicity. These communication efforts attract attention and stimulate demand for a company's products.

Coupons Several hundred billion coupons are offered each year in the United States. Many of these are posted on web sites or distributed by e-mail. The use of money-off coupons is also expanding around the world. More than seven billion coupons are distributed each year in the United Kingdom. In Italy and Spain, most coupons attached to the package rather than distributed through newspapers, magazines, or the mail. In Belgium, door-to-door coupon distribution is most common. The use of coupons as a promotion was legalized recently in Denmark.

Premiums Food packages commonly include sports cards, toys, or other items to attract buyers. Many fast-food restaurants offer children's toys with a purchase.

Contests and Sweepstakes "You may already be a winner" is a common promotional slogan. Everything from a free bottle of ketchup to trips around the world are offered as prizes when companies want to attract attention to their products. Many contests are used to create a database of customer information.

Contests can result in problems, however. Pepsi-Cola used a contest promotion to attract attention to its soft drink in Chile. The results were not what the company expected. Chileans could win from $14 to $30,000 depending on the amount next to the prize number under the bottle cap. Pepsi expected to award 40 prizes over an eight-week period. However, when 688 was announced as the winning number instead of the planned 588, more than 100 people demanded prizes. Many of the people who thought they were winners had already started spending their prize money. Two brothers who came to claim $17,000 did not have money for the 40-mile trip home. Pepsi and its advertising agency eventually worked out an arrangement with all the winners. Contests may be highly regulated in some countries.

Point-of-Purchase Promotions The use of in-store advertising continues to increase. Digital displays, television monitors, and display screens on shopping carts attempt to influence customers to select a product or brand at the point of purchase.

Specialty Advertising Look around home or school, and you will see the names of organizations almost everywhere. You will see pens, key chains, calendars, notepads, briefcases, ice-cream scoops, drinking cups, towels, T-shirts, baseball caps, and golf balls with advertising messages. These promotional items keep a company's name and products in the eyes and minds of consumers.

 **✓ Check**Point
What are five common types of sales promotions used by companies?

REVIEW GLOBAL BUSINESS TERMS

Define each of the following terms.

1. telemarketing

2. relationship marketing

REVIEW GLOBAL BUSINESS CONCEPTS

3. What duties are involved in personal selling?

4. What are the five steps of the personal selling process?

5. How do salespeople who are expatriates differ from local nationals?

6. What are common sales promotions used by companies?

SOLVE GLOBAL BUSINESS PROBLEMS

What qualifications would a salesperson look for in prospective customers when selling the following items?

7. Vacation homes in the Caribbean.

8. Computer software for teaching children at home in Peru.

9. Men's and women's business suits in Thailand.

10. Investment plans for retirement funds in Scotland.

11. Health-club memberships in Egypt.

THINK CRITICALLY

12. Explain how frequent-buyer programs can benefit both companies and customers.

13. Create a promotional contest that could be used in many countries without having to make major changes to the procedures.

MAKE ACADEMIC CONNECTIONS

14. **TECHNOLOGY** How can the Internet be used in the personal selling process?

15. **CULTURAL STUDIES** Describe differences in personal selling activities that might be necessary when doing business in various countries.

16. **GEOGRAPHY** What are possible limitations of Internet promotions in some countries?

Quiz Prep

www.cengage.com/school/genbus/intlbiz

CHAPTER SUMMARY

19-1 GLOBAL COMMUNICATIONS AND PROMOTIONS

A The elements of the communication process include the source, encoding, a message, a medium, decoding, an audience noise, and feedback.

B The elements of the promotional mix are advertising, personal selling, publicity, and sales promotion.

19-2 PLANNING GLOBAL ADVERTISING

A Planning advertising for global markets involves analyzing the target market, creating a message, selecting media, and executing and evaluating.

B Many companies use advertising agencies because they have experience in promoting different kinds of products and services in different markets. Advertising agencies usually have four divisions: research, creative, media, and account services.

19-3 GLOBAL SELLING AND SALES PROMOTIONS

A The personal selling process for international business involves identifying potential customers, preparing and making the sales presentation, obtaining feedback, closing the sale, and providing customer service.

B Public relations involves communicating a favorable public image with the use of press releases, newsletters, and sponsorship of events. Sales promotion by multinational companies may involve coupons, premiums, contests and sweepstakes, point-of-purchase promotions, and specialty advertising.

GLOBAL REFOCUS

Read the Global Focus at the beginning of this chapter, and answer the following questions.

1. What promotional efforts have contributed to the success of Unilever in global markets?

2. How might Unilever use technology to address new competitive pressures in global markets?

REVIEW GLOBAL BUSINESS TERMS

Match the terms listed with the definitions.

1. Direct communication between sellers and potential customers.
2. Promotional efforts directed at the final users of an item.
3. Promotional activities other than advertising, personal selling, and publicity.
4. A company that specializes in planning and implementing advertisements.
5. Any form of paid, nonpersonal sales communication.
6. An attempt to create a long-term, mutually beneficial buyer-seller relationship.
7. The use of one promotional approach in all geographic regions.
8. The use of computerized information systems to identify customers with specific demographic traits and buying habits.
9. Any form of unpaid promotion, such as newspaper articles or television news coverage.
10. Promotional efforts directed at members of the distribution channel.
11. The combination of advertising, personal selling, publicity, and sales promotion used by an organization.
12. The use of promotions that are customized for various target markets.
13. The selling of products during telephone calls to prospective customers.

a. advertising
b. advertising agency
c. database marketing
d. localized advertising
e. personal selling
f. promotional mix
g. publicity
h. pull promotions
i. push promotions
j. relationship marketing
k. sales promotion
l. standardized advertising
m. telemarketing

MAKE GLOBAL BUSINESS DECISIONS

14. List examples of noise that can reduce the effectiveness of communication in your classroom, in your home, and in stores.
15. Describe marketing situations in other nations in which sales promotions or publicity would be used more effectively than advertising or personal selling.
16. Why would a company use push promotions instead of pull promotions?
17. Describe examples of advertisements that use the endorsement method.
18. Name some products that could be best promoted using standardized advertising. What types of products would require localized advertising?
19. What advantages could third-country nationals have over expatriates and local nationals when applying for a sales manager position with a multinational company?
20. How important is publicity to the success of a company?
21. List examples of specialty advertising you see in your home, school, and community.

MAKE ACADEMIC CONNECTIONS

22. **GEOGRAPHY** Collect print or online advertisements that reflect different areas of the world. Explain how these images are used by the company to promote its product or service.

23. **COMMUNICATION** Create an idea for a product or service demonstration that allows the potential customer to see, hear, or touch some aspect of the item.

24. **CULTURAL STUDIES** Analyze television commercials with the sound off to determine how much of the information presented is visual.

©Brand X Pictures

25. **TECHNOLOGY** Conduct an Internet search or library research about the availability of television, radio, newspaper, and the Internet in selected countries. Choose nations in different geographic regions and with different levels of economic development.

26. **COMMUNICATION** Describe how a company might use various online interactions with consumers to promote their products among various target audiences around the world.

27. **CAREER PLANNING** Find an advertisement from a company that sells its goods or services around the world. Prepare a poster or other visual display that identifies the various careers involved in planning and executing the ad.

28. **CAREER PLANNING** Talk to a person who works in personal selling. What skills are important for success in this career field?

The GLOBAL Entrepreneur

CREATING AN INTERNATIONAL BUSINESS PLAN

Creating a Global Promotional Mix

Develop a promotional plan based on the company and country you have been using in this continuing project, or create a new idea for your business in the same or a different country. Make use of previously collected information, and do additional research. This phase of your business plan should include the following components.

1. A description of the product's target market

2. Examples of advertisements that would be appropriate for the company

3. An explanation of the different advertising media used by the company

4. Examples of Internet promotions that might be used by the company

5. A description of personal selling activities that the company could use to promote its good or service

6. An explanation of how publicity could help the company or product's image

7. Types of sales promotions that would be most appropriate for this situation.

Prepare a written summary or present a short oral report (two or three minutes) of your findings.

Photodisc/Getty Images

UNIT 5

GLOBAL Cross-Cultural Team Project

Plan International Marketing Activities

Decisions regarding products, pricing, promotion, and distribution may be some of the most difficult international business activities. Marketing is commonly influenced by the cultural values and social trends in a country. The use of cross-cultural teams can help an organization better adapt its marketing plans to the consumers in diverse societies.

Goal

To analyze influences on marketing activities in a region of the world.

Activities

Working in teams of 3 to 6 students, select a geographic region you will represent—Africa, Asia, Europe, Latin America, the Middle East, or North America.

1. To obtain marketing information from countries in your region, try to talk to people who have lived in or visited the area. View products, packages, labels, and advertising from the region. Some of these items may be available in local stores or online. Finally, library sources can be of value.
2. Identify products unique to your geographic region and to specific countries within the region. What factors influence the demand for these goods and services?
3. List examples of customs, traditions, and cultural behavior that affect consumer buying in this region. Discuss any significant exceptions in specific countries.
4. Research pricing activities in the region. What influences the amount people are willing and able to pay for various items? To what extent are prices negotiated for various purchases?
5. Describe the common promotional activities in your region. How do these compare with advertising and sales promotions in other areas of the world?
6. **Global Business Decision** Your team has been selected to advise an international organization that plans to distribute low-cost clothing in various regions of the world. What types of transportation modes would be most effective in your region? How would the distribution costs in your region compare with those in other geographic areas? What other factors would need to be considered?

Team Skill   Resolving Cross-Cultural Team Conflict

Differences of opinion are inevitable in almost every team situation. What are some common areas of team conflict that might arise in your region? How are conflicts commonly resolved in that geographic area?

Present   Create a display, using product samples, labels, packages, ads, foreign currency, and other items, to communicate marketing activities in your region.

Emerging Business Issues Event

This team event (two or three members) challenges FBLA members to develop and demonstrate research and presentation skills for an emerging business issue. Your team must research affirmative and negative arguments for each topic.

- Education and Economic Benefits for all People Living in the U.S.
- Citizenship for Illegal Aliens Working in the U.S.
- NAFTA
- Survival of the Fittest—International Automobile Industry
- Requiring a Second Language in the School Curriculum

Fifteen minutes before your presentation, you will draw to determine whether you will present an affirmative or negative argument for your emerging business issue. Any presentation that lasts more than five minutes will receive a five-point deduction. Following each oral presentation, the judges have five minutes to ask questions.

Performance Indicators Evaluated

- Understand the given emerging business issue.
- Present a relevant affirmative or negative argument for the topic.
- Conduct research to support your argument with relevant quality evidence.
- Demonstrate persuasive speaking and oral presentation skills.
- Involve all team members in the research and presentation.

For more detailed information about performance indicators, go to the FBLA-PBL web site.

Think Critically

1. Why should the U.S. government finance U.S. automakers in an economy that should reward companies that use resources effectively to meet the demands of the citizens?
2. What is the benefit of providing education for all individuals living in the U.S. including illegal aliens?
3. Why is it unfair to grant citizenship to illegal aliens who have been working in the United States?
4. What is one advantage and one disadvantage of NAFTA?
5. What is the advantage of knowing a second language?
6. Should students be forced to learn a second language?

www.fbla-pbl.org

Global Financial Management

Chapter

20 Global Financial Activities

21 Global Financial Markets

22 Managing International Business Risk

REGIONAL PROFILE
Middle East

If You Were There

Majda is a young Iraqi woman studying to be an archaeologist at a university in Baghdad. Despite many years of war during her lifetime, she has been able to continue her education. However, Majda is concerned about the preservation of ancient ruins in her country because they represent thousands of years of history.

During a recent visit to the site of the Mesopotamian capital of Babylon she was relieved to see that the famous Ishtar gate, the remains of the tower of Babel, and the remains of Nebuchadnezzar II's palace had not been damaged.

Majda's study of history has made her deeply aware of this land between the Tigris and Euphrates Rivers. Known as Fertile Crescent, this area allowed farmers to produce a surplus of food as early as 4000 B.C. About 500 years later, Sumerians moved into the area and established 12 city-states. The Sumerians invented cuneiform (a type of writing), the wagon wheel, the 12-month calendar, and the metal plow. The historic contributions represented in these archaeological sites provide the people of the Middle East with a strong connection to their past along with a foundation for the future.

Although much is known about the region, Majda is looking forward to finishing her studies and unearthing more secrets.

©kmiragaya, 2009/ Used under license from Shutterstock.com

Geography

The area known as the Middle East includes countries on three continents: Africa, Asia, and Europe. The geographic outline of the Middle East is not precise. In the broadest terms, the Middle East stretches from North Africa to Central Asia, starting with Libya and moving east to Kazakhstan. The table on the next page lists twenty-four countries that are commonly included under the umbrella term Middle East.

The Middle East is bordered by several bodies of water, including the Mediterranean Sea, the Black Sea, the Caspian Sea, the Red Sea, the Persian Gulf, the Arabian Sea, and the Indian Ocean. It is home to about 262 million people; holds almost 60 percent of the world's supply of oil; and is the site of continuous political, ethnic, and religious conflicts.

509

History of Religion in the Middle East

Three major monotheistic religions—Judaism, Christianity, and Islam—began in the Middle East.

Judaism According to the Torah, Judaism can be traced back to Abraham, who led the Hebrews from the Mesopotamian city of Ur west to the land of Canaan. The Hebrews believe that God made a covenant with Abraham. In return for their faithfulness to God, they would be protected and made a great nation. The Hebrews migrated to Egypt, where they lived for many years before being enslaved by the pharaohs. In the twelfth century B.C., Moses led the Hebrews in an exodus from Egypt into the Sinai Desert, where they believe that God renewed the covenant and gave them the Ten Commandments. At this time, they became Jews, or "God's chosen." Eventually they returned to Canaan and established the kingdom of Israel with its capital at Jerusalem.

Christianity By the time Jesus was born, the Roman Empire had control over much of the Middle East. The Jews were treated poorly by the Romans, and many of them looked forward to a savior who would restore their kingdom. According to the Bible, about 26 to 30 A.D., Jesus preached a new message to the Jews in Palestine. He told them to love one another just as they love themselves. His followers believed he was the long-awaited messiah, or savior, while others thought he was an imposter and accused him of blasphemy. The Romans believed that Jesus might cause civil strife or even political rebellion. He was arrested as a troublemaker and crucified. After his death, his followers said that he had risen from the dead and called him the Son of God. Those who believed this to be true called themselves Christians, and they began spreading Jesus' teachings and their beliefs throughout the world.

Islam The majority of the people of the Middle East are Muslims—followers of the religion of Islam. According to the Islamic holy book, the Qur'an, the Islamic religion was founded on the Arabian Peninsula in 622 A.D. The nation of Saudi Arabia accounts for most of the peninsula today; however, when Islam was founded, the area consisted of many separate Arab tribes. The city of Mecca was a center of trade and worship, and it is where the founder of Islam, the prophet Muhammad, claimed that God first spoke to him and revealed the Qur'an.

Beginning in 613 A.D., Muhammad began preaching that there was just one God, Allah, and people had to worship and obey him or else they would be punished. He also said that Allah's followers were equal and that the rich must help the poor. Many among the poor welcomed his message, but the merchants of Makkah forced him to flee in 622. This year of Hijrah, or emigration, is considered the first year of the Islamic calendar. Muhammad found success in the city of Medina, where he was given authority in religious and political matters. Thus began the Islamic state that was based on a system similar to that of the Islamic Republic of Iran. In 630 A.D., Muhammad defeated the Meccans in battle and took control of their city.

AREA AND POPULATION OF MIDDLE EAST COUNTRIES

Country	Area	Population
Afghanistan	647,500 sq km	33,609,937
Armenia	29,743 sq km	2,967,004
Azerbaijan	86,600 sq km	8,238,672
Bahrain	665 sq km	727,785
Cyprus	9,250 sq km	796,740
Egypt	1,001,450 sq km	83,082,869
Georgia	69,700 sq km	4,615,807
Iran	1,648,000 sq km	66,429,284
Iraq	437,072 sq km	28,945,657
Israel	20,770 sq km	7,233,701
Jordan	92,300 sq km	6,342,948
Kazakhstan	2,717,300 sq km	15,399,437
Kuwait	17,820 sq km	2,691,158
Kyrgyzstan	198,500 sq km	5,431,747
Lebanon	10,400 sq km	4,017,095
Oman	212,460 sq km	3,418,085
Qatar	11,437 sq km	833,285
Saudi Arabia	2,149,690 sq km	28,686,633
Syria	185,180 sq km	20,178,485
Tajikistan	143,100 sq km	7,349,145
Turkey	780,580 sq km	76,805,524
Turkmenistan	488,100 sq km	4,884,887
United Arab Emirates	83,600 sq km	4,798,491
Yemen	527,970 sq km	23,822,783

After Muhammad's death, Caliphs, or successors, were elected to lead the political-religious community and to spread the teachings of Islam. The Caliphs sent armies to the Byzantine and Persian empires to bring converts and wealth to the growing empire. By 750 A.D., the Islamic Empire stretched from the Indus River in Asia across North Africa and into most of Spain.

Photodisc/Getty Images

Post-World War II Era

Following World War II, the complex geopolitical forces that operated in the Middle East involved the conflicted interests of the Soviet Union and the United States. Since the creation of the Jewish state of Israel in 1948, the ongoing wars between the Arabs and the Israelis were the most obvious problem. Israel received billions of dollars from the United States in foreign aid, and the Soviet Union supplied weapons and advisers to some Arab countries. Other sources of great interest to outsiders are the region's strategic waterways and the abundant oil supplies in the Persian Gulf region.

Economics of the Middle East

Persian Gulf countries continue to enjoy the economic benefits of their oil reserves. However, most nations in the region lack a diverse industrial base. In recent years, efforts have been made to enhance tourism, health care, food production, water purification, irrigation equipment, manufacturing, banking, telecommunications, and infrastructure. In addition, economic development is being fostered by improved educational systems and advanced technical training for both men and women.

Think Critically

1. The Islamic religion has rules of daily living for its followers, as well as rules for behavior, dress, and food. How does this affect companies that wish to do business in the Middle East?
2. What are some actions countries in the Middle East could take to enhance their economic development?
3. Use the library or Internet resources to determine which Middle East countries produce the most oil. How do the per capita incomes of these countries compare to the other countries in the Near and Middle East?

COUNTRY PROFILES

The World Factbook, published online by the Central Intelligence Agency, includes country profiles for the nations of the Middle East. Each country's profile includes an overview followed by detailed information about the country's geography, people, government, economy, communications, transportation, military, and transnational issues.

CHAPTER 20

Global Financial Activities

20-1 Financing Global Business Operations

20-2 Global Financial Institutions

20-3 Global Banking Activities

Koor Industries, Ltd.

Koor Industries, based in Tel Aviv, is a diversified company involved in telecommunications, building supplies, metals, chemicals, food processing, tourism, and foreign trade. The company is a significant part of Israel's economy; at one time the company made up nearly 10 percent of the country's industrial output.

From its creation, the primary goal of Koor Industries was to provide employment. The company was never very profitable, and when economic conditions declined, the situation went from fair to poor. Sales revenue and profits declined, and Koor was unable to pay off loans when they were due.

In order to pay off debt, the company started to cut costs by closing factories and cutting staff. These cost reductions resulted in a 50 percent smaller workforce at Koor Industries.

When Koor faced bankruptcy, the Israeli government approved an IS275 million ($100 million) loan guarantee to help Koor out of its financial difficulties. In addition, the company decided to sell part ownership in some of its subsidiaries. The company is listed on both the Tel Aviv and New York Stock Exchanges. Obtaining funds by issuing stock also helped the company reduce its level of debt and improve its overall financial situation.

Think Critically

1. How did the cost reduction activities of Koor Industries affect the company?
2. What problems can occur during poor economic times for a company with high levels of debt?
3. Go to the web site of Koor Industries to obtain information regarding the company's current operations.

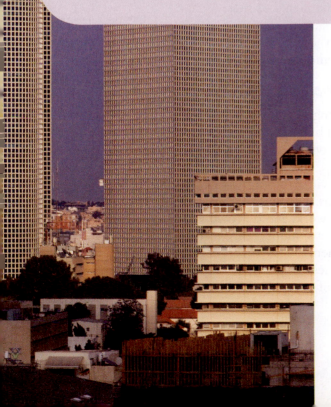

20-1 Financing Global Business Operations

GOALS

- Identify the participants in a global financial system.

- Describe the flow of funds for international businesses.

Financial Systems in Action

Each day, you and billions of others participate in financial transactions. Your exchanges likely involve activities such as receiving a paycheck, buying clothing, or using a credit card. Think about the financial activities that could be involved in operating an international business.

Traditionally, financial transactions made use of coins, paper currency, checks, and credit cards. Today, our global financial systems involve online transactions and electronic forms of money.

FINANCIAL SYSTEM PARTICIPANTS

The spending, saving, borrowing, and investing activities occurring continually around the world, create a financial system. These financial relationships involve four major parties: individuals, businesses, governments, and non-governmental organizations.

Individuals Each day individual consumers and investors participate in billions of financial transactions. Examples include making purchases, withdrawing cash, getting paid for work, and borrowing money to buy a truck.

Businesses Businesses receive money for the goods and services they provide. They also make payments for raw materials, parts and services they purchase to operate their businesses. Borrowing money to operate or expand a business is another example of participation in the financial system.

Governments Governments receive tax revenues and spend these funds for public services such as schools, parks, and police protection. Federal, state, and local government agencies also borrow to finance public projects.

Non-governmental organizations Non-governmental organizations (NGOs), also called non-profits, are involved in various social, economic, and environmental activities. These range from a local youth program to a microfinance institution operating in 40 countries.

©Mikhail Zahranichny, 2009/ Used under license from Shutterstock.com

FINANCIAL MARKETS

A place where people buy and sell items is a market. This location could be a physical place, such as a store, or a web site where online transactions occur. Financial markets are where people buy various investments or other assets. These can also be a physical location, such as a stock exchange, or an online transaction for buying and selling stocks. The two most common types of financial markets involved in financial transactions around the world are money markets and capital markets.

Money markets are where short-term investments (less than one year) are bought and sold. These include U.S. Treasury bills, certificates of deposit (CDs), and commercial paper, which companies use to borrow money for a short period of time.

Capital markets are where companies and other organizations obtain funds for long-term use. This often involves the buying and selling of stocks and bonds.

✓ **Check**Point
Name the four participants that are present in a financial system.

International Flow of Funds

A global clothing manufacturer plans to update its equipment. A computer company plans to expand into Egypt, Saudi Arabia, Israel, Turkey, and Iran. These plans, like every international business activity, require funding. International financing activities are necessary for a company to operate in the global business market.

In your daily life, you are probably aware of the fact that you and your family must have money coming in to cover living expenses (money going out). The same is true for businesses. Financial operations involve two major activities—the receipt of money and the payment of money.

SOURCES OF FUNDS

Every company must have money to operate. Employees must be paid, operating expenses are incurred, and equipment must be purchased. Organizations have two main sources of funds, these are equity and debt.

Equity Capital The owners of a business are the initial source of financial resources. **Equity capital** consists of funds provided by a company's owners. Equity capital comes from several sources, including investments from owners, reinvested profits, sale of stock, and liquidation of company assets. The stock market is a major source of equity capital funds in the global economy.

Debt Capital When a company has limited equity capital sources, it must turn to outsiders. **Debt capital** involves funds obtained by borrowing. Bank loans, bonds, and mortgages are examples of debt. The bond market is the main source of international debt capital. Bonds are a form of borrowing used by both companies and governments.

The use of debt has advantages. First, debt allows a company to expand when equity funds are not available. Second, debt has tax benefits. The interest on loans is a business expense. Like other business expenses, interest payments reduce a company's net income and will usually lower the amount paid in taxes. Third, debt does not affect the control of a company. Lenders do not have ownership in a company.

©donvictorio, 2009/ Used under license from Shutterstock.com

Despite advantages, debt also has risks. If a company cannot make its interest payments on what is borrowed or is unable to repay a loan, creditors may take control of the company.

Companies that have most of their sales during one part of the year often borrow money. For example, a company that manufactures summer clothing will have most of its sales concentrated in late winter and spring. Borrowing may be necessary in the summer, fall, and early winter months. The loans are then repaid during the main selling season as the company receives money. A company may also borrow using bonds to finance new equipment for a factory in South America or Asia.

Nations as well as individuals and businesses use debt. During the Persian Gulf War, tourism to Egypt declined and Suez Canal receipts fell, which resulted in a lower national income for the country. Egypt had to borrow from financial institutions and other countries. The British issued bonds to finance the expansion of Heathrow Airport in London.

Work as a Team
List reasons why a company might borrow money.

USES OF FUNDS

The daily operations of a business also involve making payments for various business costs and other expenses. Current expenses and long-term costs are the two main uses of funds, as shown in Figure 20-1.

Flow of Funds

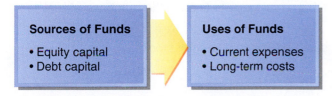

Sources of Funds
- Equity capital
- Debt capital

Uses of Funds
- Current expenses
- Long-term costs

Figure 20-1 Every organization has money coming in and going out.

Current Expenses Current expenses include rent, materials, wages and salaries, utilities, repairs, advertising, supplies, and other items that keep a business operating from day to day. These expenses usually cover a period of one month to one year.

Long-Term Costs Some business costs cover longer periods of time. For example, a new building, heavy machinery, or a computer system will probably be paid for and used over several years. These long-term costs, also called *capital projects*, are necessary for companies to produce, store, and deliver goods and services.

✓ CheckPoint
What is the difference between current expense and capital projects?

20-1 Assessment

Study Tools

www.cengage.com/school/genbus/intlbiz

REVIEW GLOBAL BUSINESS TERMS

Define each of the following terms.

1. equity capital
2. debt capital

REVIEW GLOBAL BUSINESS CONCEPTS

3. What is the purpose of a financial system?
4. How does a money market differ from a capital market?
5. How does equity capital differ from debt capital?
6. What are examples of current expenses encountered by most businesses?

SOLVE GLOBAL BUSINESS PROBLEMS

For each of the following situations, indicate if the company would make use of debt or equity funding.

7. A Mexican company will obtain funds from additional owners.
8. A company in Thailand plans to issue bonds to finance a new factory.
9. A company in Kenya is borrowing from a bank.
10. A Brazilian company is using a mortgage to finance the purchase of real estate.
11. A Belgian company is issuing additional shares of stock.

THINK CRITICALLY

12. How does risk differ in the two most common types of financial markets: money markets and capital markets?
13. Why are capital projects important for a company?
14. How do higher interest rates increase the risk of using debt?
15. What factors could affect whether a company uses debt or equity to finance a business activity?

MAKE CONNECTIONS

16. **COMMUNICATION** Research recent interest rates for money market and capital market investments. Prepare a graph to report your findings.
17. **TECHNOLOGY** Find pictures of factory equipment and office technology that would be examples of capital projects around the world. Explain why these are important to a business.
18. **CULTURE** Conduct online research to determine attitudes and behaviors regarding the use of debt by companies around the world.
19. **LAW** Conduct research to compare equity capital or debt capital as a legally binding obligation for a company.

Global Financial Institutions

AP Photo/Amr Nabil

Deposit-Type Financial Institutions

Each day millions of financial transactions occur. These business activities use cash, checks, letters of credit, credit cards, countertrade, and other financial services. The different kinds of institutions shown in Figure 20-2 serve the financial needs of consumers and businesses.

Most consumers are familiar with companies that are in business to receive money for deposit and then make that money available for personal and business purchases. These organizations are called *deposit-type* financial institutions.

COMMERCIAL BANKS

The financial institution with the most international business visibility is the commercial bank. A **commercial bank** is a business organized to accept deposits and to make loans. Traditionally, commercial banks offer the widest

GLOBAL FINANCIAL INSTITUTIONS

Deposit-Type Financial Institutions	Other Types of Financial Institutions
• Commercial bank • Savings and loan association • Credit union	• Mutual fund • Life insurance company

Figure 20-2 Several financial institutions exist to serve the needs of consumers and businesses when they make financial transactions.

range of services of any financial institution. The main services offered by commercial banks are shown in Figure 20-3.

In addition to consumer services, banks also provide services for their business customers. The following services are routinely offered to business customers.

- Business loans for buying real estate and buildings, equipment, and inventory, making needed repairs
- Cash management in the form of handling cash receipts and cash payments
- Business assistance in the form of management information services and referrals to appropriate government agencies

Services provided by banks differ throughout the world. In the United States, stock investments are usually made using a stockbroker or an online investment service. In contrast, traditionally, most British stock purchases are made through banks. In recent years, the largest commercial banks in the world have been based in China, the United States, Japan, Britain, Spain, and Switzerland.

SAVINGS AND LOAN ASSOCIATIONS

A **savings and loan association** traditionally specialized in savings accounts and home mortgages. As laws regulating financial institutions changed, savings and loan associations expanded the services they offered. Today these organizations provide checking accounts, auto loans, financial planning advice, and electronic banking.

In the United Kingdom, a financial institution comparable to the savings and loan association is the *Building Society*. As the name implies, this financial institution actively provides funds to finance buildings for businesses and home purchases by individuals.

CREDIT UNIONS

Cooperatives are businesses owned by their members and operated for their benefit. A **credit union** is a nonprofit financial cooperative. Credit unions were originally organized based on various groups in society, such as places of employment, religious organizations, and community organizations. The consumer services offered by credit unions are comparable to most commercial banks.

FINANCIAL SERVICES OF COMMERCIAL BANKS

Savings	Payment Services	Borrowing	Other Services
• Savings account	• Checking account	• Personal loans	• Trusts
• Money market accounts	• Electronic fund transfer	• Business loans	• Investment advice
• Certificate of deposit	• Letters of credit	• Credit cards	• Tax assistance
	• Traveler's checks	• Mortgages	• Estate planning
	• Currency exchange	• Home equity loans	• Retirement planning

Figure 20-3 Commercial banks offer a wide range of services to meet the needs of consumers and businesses.

THE TECHIMAN WOMEN'S MARKET CREDIT UNION

Most days for the market women of Techiman begin at sunup and continue until after sundown. The women sell multicolored fabrics and produce dried cassava, soup, furniture, and clothing. As many as 10,000 customers come to the Techiman market in Ghana on a Thursday or Friday.

The vendors in this market need money for stall fees, supplies, school fees, and day care. Before the creation of the Techiman Women's Market Credit Union, moneylenders were the main source of borrowed funds and charged as much as 50–60 percent interest. Now the more than 200 credit union members can borrow at 18 percent interest.

Think Critically

1. What services are commonly offered by credit unions?
2. Go to the web site of the World Council of Credit Unions to obtain current information about this organization. Write a summary of your findings.

Because of their nonprofit status, most credit unions offer slightly higher rates on savings and slightly lower rates for loans than do other financial institutions. Since most credit unions are community based, these organizations commonly provide more personalized service than do other financial institutions.

The World Council of Credit Unions reports that over 117million people around the world are credit union members. Credit unions operate in more than 90 countries, including Kenya, Ethiopia, Nigeria, Botswana, India, Singapore, Australia, New Zealand, Fiji, and most countries in Central and South America.

✓ CheckPoint

What are examples of deposit-type financial institutions?

Other Types of Financial Institutions

The financial needs of consumers and businesses are also served by organizations that specialize in specific financial services.

MUTUAL FUND

How would you like to be able to own stock in hundreds of companies while only investing a small amount of money? That's what is possible when you purchase shares in a mutual fund. A **mutual fund** is an investment company that manages a pool of funds from many investors.

A major benefit of a mutual fund is *diversification*. By pooling money from many investors, a mutual fund manager is able to invest in many types of stocks and/or bonds. This spreads out the risk for the investors and reduces the danger of losing all of one's money.

Photodisc/Getty Images

CHAPTER 20

GLOBAL TECHNOLOGY TRENDS

India Post Connecting People

The postal service in India has been the main provider of banking and other financial services since 1854. Using the brand name "India Post," this government-operated enterprise offers savings accounts, money transfers, money orders, life insurance, and mutual funds through more than 150,000 offices.

As the major component of the country's communication infrastructure, India Post has adapted its services to current technology. *E-payment* is a bill collection service, which allows customers to pay bills at any postal service office. Then, India Post electronically transfers the collected funds to the service provider for which the payment was made.

E-post allows electronic transmission of messages followed by physical delivery of the printed communication to a postal address. This service allows people without Internet access to have their handwritten messages, in any language, delivered to as many as 9,999 people.

Think Critically

1. How does India Post use technology to serve the needs of its customers?
2. Conduct an Internet search to obtain additional information about the history and services of India Post.

More than 8,000 different mutual funds are available to investors. Over 90 million U.S. citizens own mutual funds. Mutual funds are available to meet a variety of investment goals. For example, someone who desires current earnings from investments selects an income fund. A *balanced fund* is designed to have an appropriate proportion of stocks and bonds, depending on current market conditions.

Global mutual funds allow investors to own the stock of companies in many countries. This method of international investing eliminates the high brokerage commissions and currency conversion fees of individual investments. Global mutual funds help reduce the risk of lost profits due to changes in exchange rates.

Other types of international mutual funds include regional funds. For example, a Latin American fund invests in companies with long-term growth in Central and South America. A Pacific fund would invest in companies in that region.

LIFE INSURANCE COMPANY

People throughout the world buy life insurance policies to protect family members and others from financial difficulties when a person dies. Insurance companies invest the money received from insurance premiums. Life insurance companies commonly lend these funds to large corporations and invest in commercial real estate. These actions make capital available to companies.

✓ **Check**Point
What are the benefits of a mutual fund?

REVIEW GLOBAL BUSINESS TERMS

Define each of the following terms.

1. commercial bank
2. savings and loan association
3. credit union
4. mutual fund

Study Tools

www.cengage.com/school/genbus/intlbiz

REVIEW GLOBAL BUSINESS CONCEPTS

5. Why is a commercial bank often referred to as a full-service bank?

6. How do credit unions differ from other financial institutions?

7. How does a mutual fund reduce financial risk?

8. What are some financial activities of life insurance companies?

SOLVE GLOBAL BUSINESS PROBLEMS

For each of the following situations, indicate the type of financial institution that would be involved.

9. A company in Nicaragua needs to make use of a wide range of payment and loan services.

10. A person in Canada wants to reduce risk by investing in a professionally-managed collection of stocks and bonds.

11. A company in Kenya is planning to do business with a full-service, nonprofit financial institution.

12. A person in China desires to provide for family needs in the event of death.

13. A small shop owner in Belgium wants to make use of an online checking account.

THINK CRITICALLY

14. Credit unions often earn higher customer satisfaction ratings than banks. Why might this occur?

15. What factors influence the value of a mutual fund?

MAKE CONNECTIONS

16. **TECHNOLOGY** Locate a web site for a bank, a credit union, or another financial institution that provides services to consumers online. Describe the services available.

17. **HISTORY** Research events that changed the role of savings and loan associations in the United States during the 1980s.

18. **COMMUNICATION** Conduct a survey of 10 friends and their families to determine the types of financial services they use. Prepare a summary of your data findings.

19. **CULTURE** Research the banking activities in a geographic region. What types of banking institutions and financial services are commonly used in countries in that area?

20-3 Global Banking Activities

GOALS

- Explain the role of banking for different geographic regions.
- Identify the purpose of a central bank.
- Describe the activities of a development bank.

CANADA	CAD	0.9512	0.8883
CHINA	CNY	7.3169	6.0910
EURO	EUR	0.6644	0.6100
JAPAN	JPY	109.00	102.00
SINGAPORE	SGD	1.3712	1.2630
HONG KONG	HKD	7.0043	6.4072
			1.0675

hatman12/iStockphoto.com

International Trade and Banking

As trade among countries expands, the need for international banking services increases since international transactions are often handled by banks. Many U.S. banks have foreign branches, while over 250 banks based in other countries have offices in the United States. This increased international banking activity has resulted in more uniform regulations among countries. However, tradition, economic conditions, and technology create banking differences in various geographic regions.

Africa Only a small portion of people in Africa use formal banking services. Many people live in rural communities far from financial institutions and they lack documentation of their income and their address. With few banks available, financial fees in this region are often quite high. To address this concern, cell phone technology allows workers to transfer funds across hundreds of miles to their families in rural areas. This electronic money can then be used in the local village to buy food and other items. The more than 250 million cell phone users in Africa are able to take advantage of technology to expand business activities and serve family needs.

Asia After the currency crisis in the late 1990s, many banks in this region faced financial difficulties. This situation resulted in smaller financial institutions that focused on services that were most profitable. While Asia has many multinational banks, countries such as Cambodia, Laos, and Vietnam still have areas where more traditional, informal banking systems are common. Currency exchange activities and lending often occurs with street traders as well as in more formalized bank settings.

Europe As the European Union (EU) expanded its membership, attempts to integrate financial services in various countries resulted in challenges due to conflicting banking regulations among member countries. Financial standardization has also been limited because long-time EU members Britain, Denmark, and Sweden do not use the euro as their official currency. In contrast, more recently admitted members such as the Czech Republic, Hungary, Poland, Slovenia, and Slovakia, hope to meet the economic requirements that will allow them to become part of the euro zone.

Latin America Three large banks (Itaú, Bradesco, and Unibanco) dominate the market in Brazil. These organizations have thousands of storefront customer sites with ATMs. Brazilians do not usually mail checks because most bills come with a pre-printed bank payment slip. Customers often walk to a bank branch and pay with a check, cash, or a bank card. They can also make a payment at an ATM using the bar code identification on the form. Today, more and more Brazilians are using the Internet to make payments.

Middle East Only a limited formal banking system existed in the Middle East before 1952, when the Saudi Arabian Monetary Agency (SAMA) was created. The main function of SAMA was to maintain a stable currency value. This central bank used various monetary policy actions, including the setting of interest rates that commercial banks may charge and selling government securities to cover budgetary and balance of payments needs. SAMA also regulated various financial institutions (commercial banks, exchange dealers, and moneychangers) and handled receipts and payments of government funds.

✓ **Check**Point
What relationship exists between international trade and global banking activities?

Central Banks and Government Finance

Governments at both the local and national levels use banking services to receive, pay, save, and borrow funds. In almost every country of the world, a **central bank** exists. These are state-owned agencies that provide governments with banking services. Central banks commonly provide one or more of these functions:

- Maintain a stable money supply using monetary policy tools
- Issue an appropriate amount of currency to facilitate business activities
- Manage receipts and payments for government agencies
- Provide loans to government agencies and other enterprises
- License commercial banks operating in the country

These financial agencies may also be called reserve banks or a monetary authority. Names of central banks around the world include the Reserve Bank of India, the Monetary Authority of Singapore, the Brunei Currency Board, the Central Bank of Cyprus, the Czech National Bank, and the Bank of England.

Sometimes a central bank has authority over several countries. The European Central Bank, based in Frankfurt, Germany, is the central bank for the European Monetary Union (EMU), consisting of EU members that use

NETBookmark

Central banks exist in almost every country of the world to maintain a stable money supply and serve other functions. Access the web site shown below and click on the link for Chapter 20. Select a country and click on that link. Obtain information about the central bank you have selected. Prepare a brief written report with a summary of the activities of this central bank.

www.cengage.com/school/genbus/intlbiz

the euro as their official currency. These "euro zone" countries are all served by one central bank. Each member country also has its own central bank that works with the European Central Bank.

The Central Bank of West Africa States issues a monetary unit called the franc for the African Financial Community. This currency is used in eight countries: Benin, Burkina Faso, Guinea Bissau, Côte d'Ivoire, Mali, Niger, Senegal, and Togo. These countries are also referred to as the West African Monetary Union (WAMU).

While the primary role of central banks is to provide governments with financial services, they also assist businesses and non-governmental organizations (NGOs). The regulation of banking activities along with a stable currency provides a beneficial economic environment for all participants.

✓ CheckPoint

How do central banks serve the people of a country?

Regional Development Banks

In additional to financial institutions used by consumers, businesses, and governments, other banking organizations exist. A **development bank** is an organization of several countries created to provide financing for economic development to countries in a region. These regional organizations exist to help less-developed countries reduce poverty and expand economic activities. In recent years, increased microfinance has become a major program focus of development banks.

Inter-American Development Bank In Central and South America and the Caribbean, the Inter-American Development Bank (IDB) provides funds and technical assistance programs for economic and social development. A major portion of the IDB budget is targeted for assistance to the smaller economies in the region. This organization works closely with the IMF and the World Bank to co-finance various projects.

©Norebbo, 2009/ Used under license from Shutterstock.com

GLOBAL BUSINESS SPOTLIGHT

ROSCAS

In Cameroon and other French-speaking countries, they are called *tontines*. In India, they are *called* chitty. And, in Mexico, they are *tandas*. In more than 70 countries, rotating savings and credit associations (ROSCAs) allow people otherwise unable to save or obtain credit to pay for expensive medical bills or to buy a water buffalo or oxen for the family business.

ROSCAs are informal lending groups in which community members pool their funds with each member taking a turn to use the funds. At ROSCA meetings, which are held weekly, biweekly,

or monthly, group members make their payments. The contribution amount may range from 1,500 rupees (about US $30) in India to 280 taka (about US $4) in Bangladesh. The full amount collected at each meeting goes to one person. Then, at the next meeting, another person obtains the funds until each person has a turn.

Think Critically

1. What are the benefits of ROSCAs?
2. Conduct an Internet search to locate additional information on ROSCAs.

Started in 1959, the success of the IDB has resulted in other regions creating development banks.

Asian Development Bank With a membership of more than 67 countries, of which 48 are in the region, the Asian Development Bank (ADB) has the goal of improving economic development and quality of life for people in Asia and the Pacific. A major emphasis involves actions to assist two billion in the region who live on less than $2 a day. ADB also provides public policy discussions, loans, technical assistance, and grants.

African Development Bank Reducing poverty and improving quality of life in Africa is the main focus of the African Development Bank. Loans, equity investments, and technical assistance are the main tools used to achieve the goals of the organization. Members of the African Development Bank (53 African countries and 24 non-African countries from the Americas, Asia, and Europe) work to create sustainable economic growth and regional economic cooperation.

Other Regional Development Banks Efforts to reduce poverty and expand economic activity are concerns throughout the world. Other examples of regional development banks that stimulate business activity and foreign trade include the Caribbean Development Bank, the Central American Bank for Economic Integration, the European Bank for Reconstruction and Development, and the Islamic Development Bank.

CheckPoint

What is the purpose of a development bank?

Work as a Team

Develop a list of actions that could be taken to encourage improved business development and expanded economic growth in various geographic regions.

INTERNATIONAL BUSINESS PERSPECTIVE

Careers

INTERNATIONAL FINANCE CAREERS

Exchange rates, global stock prices, and interest rates are financial data influencing international business decisions. Employment in international finance requires training in global financial systems, accounting, economics, international tax law, global banking, and investment theory. In addition, your career preparation should include foreign language skills and cultural knowledge.

International financial managers are employed in multinational companies, investment firms, and banks as well as global agencies and non-governmental organizations. A central activity of financial managers is supervision of processing payments and extending credit, duties that require knowledge of international trade procedures and risk factors in various countries.

Global financial analysts research risk and potential returns for international investments. Based on this information, analysts make recommendations regarding buying, selling, and holding stocks, bonds, real estate, commodities, and other types of investments. Financial analysts are employed in investment companies, banks, and government agencies.

International banking representatives provide advice and financial services for clients. These bank customers can range from small companies that export to transnational businesses operating in many countries. International banking services include foreign exchange, letters of credit, global payments and collections, and country risk assessments.

Cross-cultural financial advisors work with clients possessing various backgrounds. As more and more people live in places other than their native countries, personal financial planners must be able to serve a diverse audience. This position requires knowledge of money management strategies, consumer credit, taxes, insurance, and investment portfolios used by households in varied cultural settings.

International development analysts determine how to improve the economic situation in less developed countries. Determining costs and obtaining funding for roads, airports, power plants, hospitals, schools, and other infrastructure are foundation competencies for this type of employment. International development analysts must also be able to plan, negotiate, and implement economic development projects.

International finance is a demanding and rewarding career area. With changing political environments and volatile economic conditions, your ability to obtain, process, and interpret global financial data will provide the foundation for success in international finance.

Think Critically

1. How does training for careers in international finance differ from other international business careers?
2. Describe how a person might learn more about careers in international finance.

©RTimages, 2009/ Used under license from Shutterstock.com

REVIEW GLOBAL BUSINESS TERMS

Define each of the following terms.

1. central bank
2. development bank

REVIEW GLOBAL BUSINESS CONCEPTS

3. What are reasons for less developed banking systems in some regions of the world?

4. How do central banks serve the needs of the people in a country?

5. Why do some central banks have authority over more than one country?

6. What are the main contributions of a development bank?

SOLVE GLOBAL BUSINESS PROBLEMS

Describe a possible action by a development bank to improve the situations described.

7. Limited knowledge regarding the use of computers is a concern in some areas of Ethiopia.

8. Few commercial banks in Laos are willing to assume the risk to lend to low-income people who wish to start a business.

9. The need for improved roads in Kenya.

10. Attempts to improve the literacy levels in Bolivia.

11. Small business owners in Zambia need funds for farm equipment to increase agricultural production.

THINK CRITICALLY

12. Should restrictions be placed on foreign banks doing business in the United States? Explain your answer.

13. How might politics affect the effectiveness of central banks?

14. Environmentally-friendly sustainable development is a goal of many governments and organizations. How might this goal be achieved?

MAKE ACADEMIC CONNECTIONS

15. **CULTURE** Locate photos of banking activities in other countries. Prepare a visual presentation and a short written summary of your findings.

16. **GEOGRAPHY** Select one of the regional development banks discussed in this lesson. Locate a map and indicate the countries that are served by this bank. Obtain additional information on recent activities of the development bank.

17. **COMMUNICATION** Interview a person who has lived or worked in another country to obtain information about the banking activities in another nation.

18. **LAW** Conduct research about the banking laws in other countries. Prepare a short oral report.

CHAPTER SUMMARY

20-1 FINANCIAL GLOBAL BUSINESS OPERATIONS

A The main participants in the global financial system are individuals, businesses, governments, and non-governmental organizations (NGOs).

B The flow of funds for international businesses involves sources of funds (based on equity and debt) and uses of funds (for current expenses and long-term costs).

20-2 GLOBAL FINANCIAL INSTITUTIONS

A Deposit-type financial institutions include commercial banks, savings and loan associations, and credit unions.

B Other types of financial institutions include mutual funds, and life insurance companies.

20-3 GLOBAL BANKING ACTIVITIES

A Banking activities in various geographic regions are affected by economic conditions, cultural factors, and technology.

B A central bank is designed to maintain a stable money supply, manage receipts and payments for government agencies, and provide loans.

C Development banks in less-developed countries exist to reduce poverty and expand economic activity.

GLOBAL **REFOCUS**

Read the Global Focus at the beginning of this chapter, and answer the following questions.

1. To what extent should the government assist major companies when they face financial difficulties?

2. What actions would you suggest for Koor to strengthen its financial situation for the future?

REVIEW GLOBAL BUSINESS TERMS

Match the terms listed with the definitions.

1. A financial institution that traditionally specialized in savings accounts and home mortgages.
2. Funds obtained by borrowing.
3. An investment company that manages a pool of funds from many investors.
4. An organization created to provide financing for economic development to countries in a region.
5. A business organized to accept deposits and to make loans.
6. A nonprofit financial cooperative.
7. State-owned agencies that provide governments with banking services.
8. Funds provided by a company's owners.

a. central bank
b. commercial bank
c. credit union
d. debt capital
e. development bank
f. equity capital
g. mutual fund
h. savings and loan association

MAKE GLOBAL BUSINESS DECISIONS

9. Explain why a company uses debt. Also tell why a company might avoid using debt to finance its operations.
10. Would your needs as a consumer be better served by a large international bank or a small local bank?
11. How does a mutual fund provide small investors with opportunities they might not have otherwise?
12. Why do banking activities differ in various regions of the world?
13. What happens when a central bank does not maintain an adequate and stable money supply in a country?
14. What additional actions might development banks consider to better serve low-income people around the world?
15. Does increased use of technology expand or deter competition in the financial services industry?

Photodisc/Getty Images

©Keith Wheatley, 2009/ Used under license from Shutterstock.com

MAKE ACADEMIC CONNECTIONS

16. **GEOGRAPHY** Describe how the climate, terrain, waterways, and natural resources of a country could affect the investments in that nation.

17. **COMMUNICATIONS** Survey people who use different types of financial institutions. Obtain information about their reasons for doing business with a certain bank, savings and loan association, credit union, or another financial institution.

18. **CULTURAL STUDIES** Talk to people from various countries. Ask them about the use of online banking in other nations. Prepare a brief summary of your discussions.

19. **MATHEMATICS** Conduct online research about the interest paid on various types of savings accounts in various part of the United States. Calculate the average rates over several weeks to determine which region.

20. **RESEARCH** Locate an online video that communicates the activities of a regional development bank. Report to the class about the information you have obtained.

21. **TECHNOLOGY** Conduct research about the use of cell phone banking in regions lacking a formal banking system.

22. **CAREER PLANNING** Collect articles and other information about financial institutions in other countries. How do the jobs with these companies differ from finance jobs in the United States?

The GLOBAL Entrepreneur

CREATING AN INTERNATIONAL BUSINESS PLAN

International Financial Activities

Conduct research on global financial activities based on the company and country you have been using in this continuing project, or create a new idea for your business in the same or a different country. Make use of previously collected information, and do additional research. This phase of your business plan should answer the following questions.

1. To what extent does the company use debt to finance its business activities?

2. What long-term projects is the company currently planning or implementing?

3. What types of financial institutions and financial services might be used by the company?

4. Describe how actions by the country's central bank might influence the company's global business success.

5. Identify programs that might be funded by a regional development bank to create an improved business environment.

Prepare a written summary or present a short oral report (two or three minutes) of your findings.

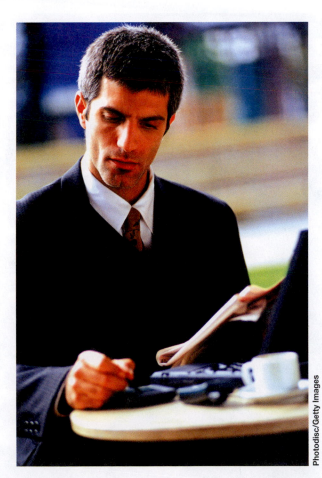

Photodisc/Getty Images

CHAPTER 21

Global Financial Markets

21-1 Global Stock Markets

21-2 Bond Markets and Other Financial Markets

21-3 Global Investments

Photodisc/Getty Images

Stock Exchanges Around the World

Locations of stock exchanges range from Johannesburg to Hong Kong and from Madrid to Lima. More than 130 exist to provide local companies with stock trading services. Emerging market economies in Eastern Europe and parts of Asia and advancements in technology are responsible for new exchanges and new ways of doing business.

The Prague Stock Exchange started in 1993, when Czechoslovakia separated into the Czech Republic and Slovakia. As these countries moved from a centrally planned economy under communist rule to a market economy, citizens were allowed to invest in stocks. Prague is the capital and the center of business activities in the Czech Republic. The Prague Stock Exchange started with transactions for only seven companies. Today, many companies that were previously government-controlled now issue stock. Some of the most popular are hotel and glass manufacturing companies.

In the late 1980s, World Bank consultants from Australia, Britain, Canada, and the United States gathered in Lusaka, Zambia, to create a stock exchange. The process involved reorganizing *parastatals* (government-owned companies during British colonial rule) into privately owned enterprises that sold stock. When the Lusaka Stock Exchange opened for business in February 1994, just two transactions occurred on the first trading day. Now, the exchange is positioned for regional influence attracting foreign investment from other countries in southeast Africa, such as Botswana and Malawi.

Across the continent in western Africa, the stock exchange in Ghana took 20 years to start. After other attempts failed, the stock exchange in Accra began trading in 1990 under the management of the Bank of Ghana. Within a few years, the exchange became a public company. As of 2009, the Ghana Stock Exchange allows *remote* trading, no longer requiring stockbrokers to transact business on the trading floor. The electronic trading system uses a secure Internet network. However, brokers may still conduct business on the trading floor of the exchange.

While many local stock exchanges exist, regional markets are increasing. Euronext was formed when the Paris, Brussels, and Amsterdam stock exchanges merged, and is now owned by the New York Stock Exchange. Recently, NYSE Acra Europe was developed to improve the efficiency of stock trading among eleven European countries.

Think Critically

1. How might the activities of stock exchanges differ around the world?
2. What function did stock exchanges serve as countries changed their political environment?
3. Conduct an Internet search to locate the web site for a stock exchange in another region of the world. Prepare a brief summary of the services offered and recent activities.

21-1 Global Stock Markets

GOALS

- Describe how and where stocks are bought and sold.

- Explain factors that affect stock prices.

- Identify major sources of stock market information.

©mdd, 2009/ Used under license from Shutterstock.com

Major Stock Exchanges

International companies may borrow from financial institutions; however, they also raise funds by selling stock. Stock represents a share of ownership in an organization. Stockholders are the owners of a corporation who elect the board of directors. The board hires the officers who run the company. A **stock exchange** is a location where stocks are bought and sold. The New York Stock Exchange (NYSE) is the largest and one of the oldest in the world. More than six billion shares of stock are traded (bought and sold) through the NYSE on a typical business day.

Started in 1792, the New York Stock Exchange was created through the efforts of 24 brokers and merchants. Five securities were traded when the NYSE started. Three were government bonds and the other two were bank stocks. Today, more than 2,000 companies are listed on the exchange. The New York Stock Exchange is operated by NYSE Euronext, which was the result of a combination of these two stock exchanges.

The stock of many multinational companies based in other countries (such as British Airways, Nestlé, Royal Dutch/Shell, and Sony Corporation) is bought and sold on the New York Stock Exchange.

In addition to the NYSE, there are other major stock exchanges around the world, including Bombay, Copenhagen, Dusseldorf, Istanbul, London, Milan, Rio de Janeiro, Seoul, Stockholm, Taiwan, Tel Aviv, Toronto, and Zurich. Figure 21-1 shows examples of three stock exchanges and lists some of the companies traded on each exchange.

MAJOR COMPANIES TRADED ON SELECTED GLOBAL STOCK EXCHANGES		
London	**Tokyo**	**Euronext**
• British Petroleum (Oil company)	• Canon (Office Automation)	• Bic (Office Supplies)
• Rolls-Royce (Aerospace/Defense)	• Mazda (Auto—Car/Light Truck)	• Carrefour (Food—Retail)
• Tesco (Food—Retail)	• Nippon Steel (Steel Producer)	• Michelin (Rubber—Tires)
• Unilever (Food-Misc)	• Sony (Audio/Video Products)	• Renault (Auto—Car/Light Truck)

Figure 21-1 Stocks exchanges provide a location where shares of stock are bought and sold.

In total, more than 130 stock exchanges are in operation around the world. These include several in the African countries of Botswana, Ghana, Ivory Coast, Kenya, Namibia, Nigeria, and Zimbabwe. Many of these stock markets started very small, with stock of less than 20 companies traded.

✓ **CheckPoint**
What does a share of stock represent?

The Stock Market in Action

Every hour of the day, investors buy and sell stocks. On the trading floor of the stock exchange and through computer systems, representatives of buyers and sellers interact to determine the prices of shares of stock. Figure 21-2 summarizes the main steps involved in a stock transaction.

The purchase of stock through a stock exchange commonly involves a stockbroker. A **stockbroker** is a person who buys and sells stocks and other investments for customers. *Full-service brokers* also provide information about current stock market trends and other types of investments.

NETBookmark

Fear of the stock market keeps many people from investing in it. Access the web site shown below and click on the link for Chapter 21. Explore the web site. When you think you understand how the stock market works, click on the simulation link and then the STOCKQUEST link to experience the stock market without the risks. What companies did you choose to invest in? Do you have more confidence to invest?

www.cengage.com/school/genbus/intlbiz

Figure 21-2 Stocks are bought and sold at a stock exchange or online with prices determined by supply and demand.

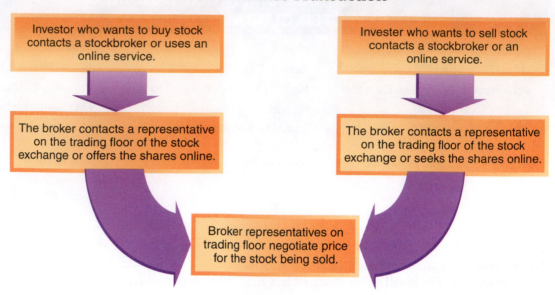

A Stock Market Transaction

To save money on transaction fees, investors have other choices. *Discount brokers* provide less service than full-service brokers and do not provide as much information and investment research assistance. *Online trading services*, such as E*trade and Ameritrade, charge investors low-cost commission fees.

Completely *computerized* stock trading stock exchanges, without trading floor representatives, are common today. These high-speed, low-cost automated systems are used by most major stock exchanges in Europe and Canada. Some of the world's largest screen-based systems for buying and selling global stocks are based in Europe. Computerized stock trading allows a broker in London to buy and sell stocks of multinational companies listed on stock exchanges in Bombay, Istanbul, Rio de Janeiro, Seoul, or Taiwan anytime, day or night.

✓ CheckPoint

What are the differences between full-service brokers, discount brokers, and online trading services?

COMMUNICATION ACROSS BORDERS

THE CHAMELEON-LIKE SAUDI FINANCIERS

Like chameleons, Saudi Arabian financiers often change their appearance to reflect their surroundings. In other words, they try to blend in with the prevailing dress of their current location. At home, they typically wear traditional Saudi business dress. It consists of a long white robe called a *thobe* and a headcloth called a *ghutra*. Abroad, unless they are in another Arab country, they often wear traditional Western business dress— a dark suit, a white shirt, and a conservatively colored tie. Occasionally, they may choose to dress in the traditional Saudi manner while engaging in business outside of their region. When this happens, Saudi Arabian financiers are trying to stand out from their surroundings.

Think Critically

1. Why is traditional Saudi business dress different from traditional Western business dress?
2. Why might Saudi Arabian financiers choose to wear the traditional business dress of their country within the Middle East?

Stock Market Price Information

Stock prices are affected by many factors. The main influence on stock prices is demand for ownership in a company based on its current and future profitability. If people believe a company is a good investment, demand will cause the stock price to rise. In contrast, as fewer investors buy the stock of a company, its stock price will decline. In addition, economic conditions, the political situation, and social trends can influence stock prices.

After an agreement on price is reached, this information becomes public. Each day millions of stocks are bought and sold. Information about current stock prices, dividends, volume, and past prices are reported online, on television, and in newspapers. Figure 21-3 presents a sample of the stock market information reported every day.

✓ CheckPoint
What is the main influence on stock prices?

Reporting Stock Information

NYSE 52 WEEKS		Stock	Sym.	Divd.	Yild %.	PE	Vol. 100s	High	Low	Close	Net Chg.
High	Low										
1	2	3	4	5	6	7	8	9	10	11	12
34.85	15.14	Disney	DIS	N/A	N/A	13.7	106628	25.55	24.8	25.33	+0.38
31.14	5.73	General Electric	GE	1.24	9.14	8.6	584600	13.69	13.37	13.56	+0.02
72.01	46.37	General Mills	GIS	1.72	3.17	16.7	56232	54.6	53.91	54.22	+2.06
81.05	5.07	Macy's Inc	M	0.2	1.57	–	71009	12.95	12.39	12.77	–0.04
67	45.79	McDonalds	MCD	2	3.41	15.5	147560	59.18	58.01	58.72	–1.15
63.85	46.25	WalMart	WMT	1.09	2.15	15.2	189752	51	50.4	50.81	+0.26

Column	Explanation
1	Reports the highest price paid for one share of the stock over the past year.
2	Reports the lowest price paid for one share of the stock over the past year.
3	Lists the abbreviated name of the corporation.
4	Identifies the symbol used to report stock prices for the corporations in column 3.
5	Reports the dividends paid per share during the past 12 months.
6	Represents the yield percentage, which is the dividend divided by the current price of the stock.
7	Identifies the price-earnings ratio, which is computed by dividing the current price per share by the company's earnings (profits) per share over the last 12 months.
8	Reports the number of shares traded during the day, based on hundreds of shares.
9	States the highest price paid for one share on the trading day.
10	States the lowest price paid for one share on the trading day.
11	Reports the price paid for a share in the last stock purchase of the day.
12	Represents the difference between the price paid for the last share bought this day and the price for the last share bought on the previous trading day.

Figure 21-3 Current stock prices and other information on stock market activities are reported each business day in newspapers, on television, and online. Notice that the decimal part of the entry is set as superscript.

21-1 Assessment

REVIEW GLOBAL BUSINESS TERMS

Define each of the following terms.

1. stock exchange
2. stockbroker

REVIEW GLOBAL BUSINESS CONCEPTS

3. What is a stock exchange?

4. What services does a stockbroker provide?

5. What factors affect daily stock prices?

SOLVE GLOBAL BUSINESS PROBLEMS

For each of the following news items, indicate what types of companies might be affected and how (higher or lower stock prices).

6. A country announces strict regulations to protect the environment.

7. A new food-processing system keeps foods fresh without refrigeration for several weeks.

8. Families are spending more time at home rather than going out for food and entertainment.

9. Scientists discover a device that makes an electric car more practical.

THINK CRITICALLY

10. What are the risks of buying and selling stocks online?

11. Describe how changes in economic conditions (lower interest rates or higher consumer spending) might affect stock prices.

MAKE ACADEMIC CONNECTIONS

12. **TECHNOLOGY** Go to a web site that provides stock information to obtain the current price of shares for a company of interest to you.

13. **MATH** Refer to Figure 21-3 to answer the following questions.
   a. What was the highest price paid for a share of McDonald's stock during the past year?

   b. How many shares of Wal-Mart were traded on this business day?

   c. What was the highest price paid for a share of Disney stock on this trading day?

   d. What was the closing price of General Electric stock on the previous trading day?

   e. If a company pays an annual dividend of $2 per share and the stock sells for $50 a share, what is the yield percentage?

GOALS

- **Explain how investors earn money from corporate bonds.**
- **Identify different types of government bonds.**
- **Describe the role of other global financial markets.**

©akva, 2009/ Used under license from Shutterstock.com

Corporate Bonds

A *bond* is a certificate representing money borrowed by a company or another organization to be repaid over a long period of time. The bond market helps organizations raise debt capital.

A **corporate bond** is a debt certificate issued by a multinational company or another corporate enterprise. Most corporate bonds in the United States are sold in amounts of $1,000. This amount is called the *face value,* or *maturity value.*

Around the world, bonds may be issued with different face values. In the United Kingdom, bonds traditionally are issued for 100 pounds sterling. In Brazil, the standard amount is 1,000 reals, while in South Africa it is 100 rand.

Two types of corporate bonds are commonly issued by companies. A **mortgage bond** is debt secured by a specific asset or property. The collateral for a mortgage bond may be equipment, a building, or land. A corporate bond without collateral is a **debenture bond**. These are unsecured debt in which the bondholder is a general creditor of the company.

The interest rate on a bond determines the income for investors. For example, a 10 percent bond would pay $100 a year in interest, calculated as follows.

$$\text{Face Value} \times \text{Interest Rate} \times \text{Time in Years} = \text{Interest}$$
$$\$1,000 \quad \times \quad 0.10 \quad \times \quad 1 \quad = \quad \$100$$

The *rate of return* on a bond is calculated by dividing the income from the investment by the cost of the investment. For example, if the annual income from a $1,000 bond is $72, the annual rate of return is 7.2 percent, as calculated below.

$$\text{Annual Income} \div \text{Cost of Investment} = \text{Annual Rate of Return}$$
$$\$72 \quad \div \quad \$1,000 \quad = \quad 0.072$$

Bond investors should also consider the *maturity date*. This is the point in time when the loan will be repaid. A 20-year bond, for example, means an investor will earn interest each year for 20 years. Then at the end of the 20 years, the investor will be repaid the face value. Remember, when a company issues bonds, it is borrowing money that must be repaid.

✓ **Check**Point

How do investors earn money from bonds?

Government Bonds

Governments also issue bonds for example, the federal government of the United States sells treasury bonds to obtain needed funds for its operations. State and local governments in the United States also borrow by issuing municipal bonds.

FEDERAL GOVERNMENT BONDS

The U.S. government sells bonds to finance the national debt and to pay operating expenses. Three common debt instruments of the federal government are available to investors.

- Treasury bills (T-bills) are short-term borrowing instruments with maturities ranging from 91 days to 1 year.
- Treasury notes (T-notes) are intermediate-length borrowing instruments with maturities ranging from 1 to 10 years.
- Treasury bonds (T-bonds) are long-term borrowing instruments with maturities ranging from 10 to 30 years.

U.S. savings bonds are another type of federal government debt instrument. Individuals who want to save for the future commonly purchase these bonds. U.S. savings bonds are purchased at one-half of their face value (e.g., a $100 bond costs $50). The time it takes for a savings bond to grow to the maturity value will vary depending on the current interest rate paid by the U.S. Treasury Department. For a quick update on U.S. savings bonds rates and other information, visit the TreasuryDirect web site.

STATE AND LOCAL GOVERNMENT BONDS

A **municipal bond** is a debt certificate issued by a state or local government agency. Since most countries organize their government structures differently from the United States, municipal bonds are not common in other nations.

The major benefit of municipal bonds for U.S. investors is that the interest earned is excluded from federal income taxes. Such income, not subject to tax, is called **tax-exempt income**. Other types of investments, such as certain types of retirement accounts, earn **tax-deferred income**, which is income that will be taxed at a later date.

FOREIGN GOVERNMENT BONDS

Foreign governments use bonds to finance roads, schools, and military equipment for their nations. These bonds are categorized as external and internal.

Work as a Team

Describe situations in which governments and businesses might use bonds for financing.

- External bonds are intended for investors in other countries. The interest and principal are paid in the currency of the country in which an investor lives. For example, dollar bonds are intended for investors in the United States.
- Internal bonds are aimed at investors in the country issuing the bond and payable in the native currency. Foreign government bonds payable in several currencies are called multiple currency bonds.

The value of a foreign government bond is affected by the economic and political circumstances of the nation issuing the bond. People who invest in these bonds commonly face risks, such as varied exchange rates, currency stability, and changes in government administrations.

✓ CheckPoint

What are four types of debt instruments sold by the U.S. federal government?

A Question of Ethics

INFORMAL CURRENCY TRADERS

As you are walking the streets of Addis, Ethiopia, you need to exchange some U.S. dollars for birr. At a bank you will get 8.5 *birr* per dollar. If you do business with a street trader you will get 10 *birr* per dollar. What should you do?

Travelers have many options for exchanging currency, including banks, exchange bureaus, and travel agencies. Exchange services frequently are available at hotels, airports, railway stations, and even small shops. In many countries, another alternative exists—informal currency traders.

In some places in Ethiopia, there are money exchange kiosks. Often, they use a legitimate business enterprise, such as selling food items, as a cover for currency

exchange activities. In general, it is illegal for a person to participate in foreign exchange transactions except in banks and other authorized locations.

In Zambia, informal currency traders offer better rates for several currencies, including the U.S. dollar, the British pound, the South African rand, and the Botswana pula. It is common to see individuals offering bundles of Zimbabwean banknotes for sale on the roadside near the Zambia border with Zimbabwe. You might also find freelance currency traders in the marketplaces of larger towns and cities.

Many opportunities exist in Peru to exchange currencies in settings other than banks and other formal financial institutions. Individuals on street corners in large cities change money, mostly

involving transactions between U.S. dollars and Peruvian *sol*.

Informal currency trading is not always possible, especially in countries where strong government controls exist. In Tunisia, you are not allowed to import or export *dinars*. Transactions outside the formal financial system are forbidden. Violation can result in heavy penalties. A similar situation exists in Morocco, where no currency trading of the *dirham* outside of banks is allowed. In Thailand, currency traders must have a license issued by the Bank of Thailand.

Think Critically

Use the three guidelines for ethical analysis to examine the above situations. How does informal currency trading affect businesses, consumers, and society?

Other Financial Markets

In addition to stock and bond markets, other financial markets exist to serve companies involved in global business. These locations allow for the buying and selling of stocks, currencies, and commodities in international settings.

THE OVER-THE-COUNTER MARKET

Large companies that meet financial requirements of a stock exchange and are traded regularly are called *listed stocks*. In contrast, stocks of new and small companies are traded through computer networks.

The **over-the-counter (OTC) market** is a network of stockbrokers who buy and sell stocks of companies not listed on a stock exchange. The National Association of Securities Dealers Automated Quotations (NASDAQ) is the major computerized trading system for OTC stocks in the United States. Around the world other OTC markets have developed. These unlisted securities markets often involve new, innovative companies with strong potential. In Germany, the Neuer Markt trades the stocks of emerging companies in the European Union.

FOREIGN EXCHANGE MARKET

The foreign exchange market involves the buying and selling of currencies needed to pay for goods and services bought from companies in other countries. A **Eurodollar** is a U.S. dollar deposited in a bank outside of the United States and used in the money markets of Europe. *Eurodollars* should not be confused with the *euro*, which is the official currency of the European Union.

The term "Eurocurrency" has come to mean any money deposited in a bank outside the country of its origin and used in the money markets of Europe. These funds are used to make payments among countries for foreign trade.

Photodisc/Getty Images

FUTURES MARKET

Farmers want to get a fair price for their grain. Food companies want to avoid paying high prices for grain that will be used to make breakfast cereals and other products. By agreeing to a price now for delivery in the future (usually three or six months from now), a farmer is protected from receiving a lower price for grain. The food company is protected from higher costs.

The **futures market** allows investors and others to buy or sell contracts on the future prices of commodities, metals, and financial instruments. Futures markets involve contracts on corn, oats, soybeans, wheat, cattle, cocoa, sugar, oil, natural gas, gold, silver, treasury bonds, and currencies—yen, pound, euro, and Eurodollars.

✓ **Check**Point
What are the functions of the OTC, foreign exchange, and futures markets?

INTERNATIONAL BUSINESS PERSPECTIVE
Culture

ISLAMIC BANKING ACTIVITIES

The influence of Islam on banking is visible today. The Arab word *sakk,* evolved into *cheque,* and today *check.* The plural is *sukak,* Arabic for "financial certificate," is viewed by many as the Islamic equivalent of a bond. After more than 200 years of colonization, most countries with a Muslim majority gained independence by the early 1980s. This resulted in banking activities based on traditions and beliefs consistent with Islamic law in the *Shari'ah.*

A foundation of this system is the prohibition of charging *riba*, the Arabic term for interest. Instead of earning interest, depositors share in the profits. While not guaranteed, savers may receive a premium called *hiba* (gift).

Riba is also forbidden when lending, but gains in the value of capital are allowed. This practice, based on the Qur'an and Hadith (teachings of the Prophet Mohammed), prevents exploitation of borrowers. "Allah will deprive usury of all blessing, but will give increase for deeds of charity" (Qur'an 2: 276). However, profit is viewed as a reward for the use of capital.

Two main financing methods are used. With *mudaraba*, a financier provides funds to the entrepreneur. In this arrangement, the financier may not influence the operations of the enterprise but receives a specified share of the profit or loss. The lender is responsible for all financial losses. The entrepreneur only loses the time and effort invested in the business. In recent years, a two-tiered mudaraba system evolved with three parties. The bank depositors are the financiers. The bank is the financial intermediary, and the entrepreneur uses the funds.

In contrast, *musharaka* involves the entrepreneur supplying a portion of the capital needed to operate the business. Profits and losses are shared based on a percentage agreed in advance. The financier in this situation may be involved in the management and operation of the enterprise.

Another fundamental principle of Islamic banking and financing is an emphasis on socially beneficial business activities. Participants are not allowed to invest in enterprises involved in alcohol, gambling, and other activities prohibited by Islamic law. This social focus, along with an emphasis on wealth creation rather than highly speculative ventures, offers a strong foundation for financial market stability. Islamic banking practices are often recognized by British banks where Muslim investors are permitted to invest funds according to their own preferences.

Think Critically

1. What are some of the basic principles of Islamic banking activities?
2. Conduct an Internet search to obtain information about the use of credit and attitudes toward borrowing in different cultures.

Photodisc/Getty Images

21-2 Assessment

REVIEW GLOBAL BUSINESS TERMS

Define each of the following terms.

1. corporate bond
2. mortgage bond
3. debenture bond
4. municipal bond
5. tax-exempt income
6. tax-deferred income
7. over-the-counter (OTC) market
8. Eurodollar
9. futures market

REVIEW GLOBAL BUSINESS CONCEPTS

10. How is the rate of return on a bond computed?
11. What are two main types of foreign government bonds?
12. What types of stocks are commonly traded on the over-the-counter (OTC) market?

SOLVE GLOBAL BUSINESS PROBLEMS

For the following corporate bond situations, calculate the amounts requested.

13. Earnings for three years of a $1,000 bond with a 7 percent interest rate.
14. Earnings for five years of a $1,000 bond with a 5.65 percent interest rate.
15. Annual rate of return from the purchase of ten $1,000 bonds with a total annual income of $860.
16. Maturity value of a $1,000 bond with a 10 percent interest rate, maturing in 6 years.

THINK CRITICALLY

17. How do changes in interest rates affect the market value of bonds?
18. Why do countries issue both internal and external bonds?
19. What are the benefits of the futures market?

MAKE ACADEMIC CONNECTIONS

20. **GEOGRAPHY** Create a chart showing the current market value of the natural resources of various countries, such as oil, wheat, corn, and soybeans.
21. **TECHNOLOGY** Use the Internet to locate online resources for international financial markets.
22. **CURRENT EVENTS** Use the Internet to identify three recent events around the world that had a significant effect on international financial markets.

Global Investments

©Stephen Coburn, 2009/ Used under license from Shutterstock.com

Investment Goals

Changing currency rates, environmental concerns, and political instability are typical in the international business environment. Just as companies attempt to make the right global business decisions, individuals want to make investments that will achieve their personal financial goals.

The long-term financial security of a person or family results from an ability to save and invest for the future. *Saving* is the storage of money for future use. In contrast, *investing* involves putting money to work in a business venture. The risks associated with investing are higher than the risks associated with saving. However, the potential returns from investing are also greater. Investing has two common goals, which are current income and long-term growth.

CURRENT INCOME

Some people depend on investment income for current living expenses. Retired people and others may need investments that provide income. These earnings may be in the form of dividends (from stocks), interest (from bonds), or rent (from real estate).

LONG-TERM GROWTH

In contrast to current income, many people invest for long-term financial security. They want funds for retirement or for their children's college education. Investors who desire long-term growth of their funds will choose investments that they hope will increase in value over time.

The earnings obtained over the long term can provide substantial wealth. A **capital gain** is the profit made from the resale of investments—such as

REACHING YOUR INVESTMENT GOALS

Current Income	Long-Term Growth
• Stocks paying dividends	• Growth stocks
• Savings certificates	• Raw land
• Corporate bonds	• Gold, silver
• Rental property	• Coins, stamps
	• Art, antiques

Figure 21-4 People with different investment goals select different types of investments.

stocks, bonds, or real estate. For example, land purchased in 2003 for $12,000 and sold in 2011 for $31,000 represents a capital gain of $19,000.

The growth in value of an investment can be projected with the use of future value calculations. Future value involves computations for determining the expected worth of an investment in the future.

The following example shows how future value is calculated. The n represents the number of years the investment will be earning the yield. The future value of $1,000 invested at 7 percent for two years would be calculated as follows.

$$\text{Amount Invested} \times (1 + \text{Annual Rate Earned})^n = \text{Future Value}$$
$$\$1,000 \times 1.07^2 = \$1,144.90$$

Figure 21-4 lists some of the common investments used to meet the two main investment goals of current income and long-term growth.

✓ CheckPoint
What is the difference between the two major goals of investing?

Global Investment Opportunities

Should a person invest in a gold mine in South America, real estate in the Middle East, or a computer company in Nevada? When planning to invest, people must identify potential investments and evaluate those investment opportunities.

IDENTIFYING POTENTIAL INVESTMENTS

Successful investments can result from a variety of business activities around the world. For example, as the demand for health care increases because of illness or an aging population, companies involved in medications, medical supplies, and hospital equipment may become more profitable.

News stories can be used to identify investment opportunities. When you hear a news report, ask yourself what types of companies might be affected by this news. Next, decide what type of investment would be appropriate. Investors may buy stock in the company or even start their own company. Finally, investors must select an action to take—buy, sell, or hold certain investments.

Global investment advisors recommend that investors choose a country before choosing specific companies. A nation's economic conditions and political environment strongly influence business success. Companies in the same industry (automobiles, chemicals, or electrical equipment) often perform differently depending on the country. For example, energy stocks in China may decline during a period in which Brazilian energy stocks rise.

EVALUATING INVESTMENT OPPORTUNITIES

Consider four major factors when choosing between various investments. These factors are rate of return, liquidity, taxes, and safety.

Work as a Team
Prepare a list of factors to consider when buying an international mutual fund.

Rate of Return The annual earnings for an investment are measured by the annual *rate of return,* or *yield.* This rate is the percentage of the investment cost that is earned in a year.

For example, an investment that costs $5,000 and produces an annual income of $450 has an annual rate of return of 9 percent, calculated as follows.

$$\text{Annual Income} \div \text{Cost of Investment} = \text{Rate of Return}$$
$$\$450 \quad \div \quad \$5,000 = \quad 0.09$$

Liquidity Many people want to be able to obtain and use their money quickly. **Liquidity** refers to the ability to easily convert an asset into cash without a loss in value. Certain types of assets are highly liquid, such as stocks, bonds, and mutual funds. These investments have a continuing market of buyers and sellers.

In contrast, real estate, rare coins, and other collectibles have low liquidity. These assets may be difficult to sell quickly. Buyers for these investments are not always available.

A trade-off between liquidity and rate of return is common for investments. In general, assets with high liquidity have a lower return over time. Low liquidity can give you a higher rate of return over the long run.

Taxes The amount earned on an investment is frequently affected by taxes. If an investor has to pay taxes on earnings, that lowers the annual rate of return. A *tax-exempt* investment earns income that is not subject to tax. In contrast, a *tax-deferred* investment earns income that will be taxed at a later date.

Safety When making an investment, people expect their money to be available in the future. Most people want investments that minimize their chance of losing money. Generally, the higher the return expected, the higher the risk involved.

✓ CheckPoint

What four factors are usually considered before making an investment?

Investment Information Sources

Wise investing, as with any business decision, requires reliable, up-to-date information. The main sources of investment information are the news media, the Internet, financial experts, and investment information services.

News Media Business periodicals and the business section of the daily newspaper provide a readily available source of investment news. Many investors find *The Wall Street Journal, Financial Times, Business Week, Fortune, Forbes,* and *The Economist* helpful. In addition to domestic and international business, economic, and financial news, these publications feature articles on companies and product trends. Cable television channels such as CNN Financial and CNBC also provide news and data about financial markets and investment opportunities.

Internet Web sites are very important sources for investment information. The periodicals mentioned above all have web sites with news, articles, and financial data. Also, hundreds of other web sites are available to assist investors with researching, selecting, and monitoring their stocks, bonds,

Photodisc/Getty Images

mutual funds, and other investments. Some of the most useful investment web sites are those maintained by *Money* magazine, Motley Fool, and Yahoo Finance.

Financial Experts A stockbroker advises customers and sells investments. Other financial experts who provide investment recommendations and assist with purchases are bankers, personal financial planners, insurance agents, and real estate brokers.

Before acting on the advice of any investment advisor, wise investors take the following additional precautions.

- Research the investment and company using several sources.
- Talk to others who have this type of investment.
- Contact state and federal government agencies for information about the investment and the seller of the investment.
- Compare costs of the investment broker with others who provide this service.

Each year investors lose billions of dollars on phony investments. These losses are often the result of not completely understanding the investment situations they encounter. Actual losses may be even higher since, after being scammed, many consumers are too embarrassed to report their losses to government agencies. Common investment scams in recent years included fake low-cost stocks, wireless cable television partnerships, Internet services, and paging licenses.

Investment Information Services Information on the current performance and the future of stocks and bonds is published in *Value Line, Moody's Investors Service,* and *Standard & Poor's Reports.* These investment services provide financial data, current stock prices, recent company developments, and recommendations for buying and selling. Investors can find these information sources at libraries or through the organizations' web sites.

✓ CheckPoint

Who are some of the financial experts that can provide assistance with your investment decisions?

GLOBAL BUSINESS SPOTLIGHT

ONLINE INVESTING FOR EVERYONE, EVERYWHERE

The *good news*—you can be your own stockbroker. The *bad news*—you need to be careful! Online buying and selling of stocks is available to anyone with Internet access. However, you can easily make unwise choices or become a victim of a scam. Before trading stocks online, you need to understand the process, costs, and risks involved.

In the past, stock transactions involved calling a broker to place your order. Today, investors can purchase stocks through online brokerage firms such as E*trade and TD Ameritrade. Traditional brokers, such as Charles Schwab and Merrill Lynch, also provide this service for investors around the world. A stock trade that previously would have cost $100 can now be done online for a commission of as little as $5.

Think Critically

1. How do online stockbrokers affect competition and prices in the investment industry?
2. Go to the web site of a traditional broker or an online broker to obtain information about the services offered to investors. Make a list of the services you find.

REVIEW GLOBAL BUSINESS TERMS

Define each of the following terms.

1. capital gain
2. liquidity

Study Tools
www.cengage.com/school/genbus/intlbiz

REVIEW GLOBAL BUSINESS CONCEPTS

3. What are two common goals of investing?

4. What is the rate of return of an investment?

5. What are common sources of investment information?

SOLVE GLOBAL BUSINESS PROBLEMS

Calculate the future value of the following investments.

6. The expected value of a stock in three years that grows at 4 percent a year and has a current value of £100.

7. The future value of land in five years that costs Cr$3,000 today with an expected growth rate of 7 percent per year.

8. The future value of an antique automobile after eight years, with a current value of $12,000 and an expected growth rate of 6 percent per year.

THINK CRITICALLY

9. Describe a situation in which a person would be investing for income. Next, describe a situation in which a person would invest for long-term growth.

10. How could a person decide if a web site is a reliable source of investment information?

MAKE ACADEMIC CONNECTIONS

11. **TECHNOLOGY** Locate a web site that offers investment information and assistance. What types of investments might be wise choices based on the information offered on this web site?

12. **MATHEMATICS** What is the annual rate of return for these situations?
   a. A share of stock in a company in Singapore costs $40 and has an annual dividend of $4.

   b. A South African government bond costing $1,000 earns $65 interest a year.

   c. An oil investment in the Middle East costs $20,000 and pays an annual income of $4,400.

CHAPTER SUMMARY

21-1 GLOBAL STOCK MARKETS

A The activities of global stock markets include providing a location or computer system for the buying and selling of shares of ownership in corporations. The New York Stock Exchange is the largest of the more than 130 exchanges around the world.

B Stock market transactions involve negotiations between broker representatives or online negotiations to agree on a price settlement between the buyer and the seller of a stock.

C Stock prices are affected by demand based on a company's expected current and future profitability. Economic conditions, the political situation, and social concerns can also affect demand for a stock.

21-2 BOND MARKETS AND OTHER FINANCIAL MARKETS

A A corporate bond is a debt certificate issued by a multinational company or another corporate enterprise. Investors earn interest on bonds.

B Government bonds are issued by the U.S. federal government, state and local governments, and foreign governments.

C The over-the-counter (OTC) market is a network of stockbrokers who buy and sell stocks of companies not listed on a stock exchange. The foreign exchange market involves the buying and selling of currencies needed to pay for goods and services bought from companies in other countries. The futures market allows investors and others to buy or sell contracts on the future prices of commodities, metals, and financial instruments.

21-3 GLOBAL INVESTMENTS

A The two major goals of investors are current income and long-term growth.

B The analysis of international investments involves identifying potential opportunities in other countries. The rate of return, liquidity, tax situation, and safety of the investment should also be considered.

C The major sources of investment information are the news media, the Internet, financial experts, and investment information services.

GLOBAL **REFOCUS**

Reread the Global Focus at the beginning of this chapter, and answer the following questions.

1. Describe global trends that might influence the growth of regional stock exchanges.

2. What actions might be taken to reduce risk when selecting stock investments of companies based in other countries?

REVIEW GLOBAL BUSINESS TERMS

Match the terms listed with the definitions.

1. Income that will be taxed at a later date.
2. A network of stockbrokers who buy and sell stocks of companies not listed on a stock exchange.
3. Income not subject to tax.
4. The ability to easily convert an asset into cash without a loss in value.
5. A corporate bond without collateral.
6. A debt certificate issued by a state or local government agency.
7. A location where stocks are bought and sold.
8. A market that allows investors and others to buy or sell contracts on the future prices of commodities, metals, and financial instruments.
9. Debt secured by a specific asset or property.
10. A U.S. dollar deposited in a bank outside of the United States and used in the money markets of Europe.
11. The profit made from the resale of investments—such as stocks, bonds, or real estate.
12. A debt certificate issued by a multinational company or another corporate enterprise.
13. A person who buys and sells stocks and other investments for customers.

a. capital gain
b. corporate bond
c. debenture bond
d. Eurodollar
e. futures market
f. liquidity
g. mortgage bond
h. municipal bond
i. over-the-counter (OTC) market
j. stockbroker
k. stock exchange
l. tax-deferred income
m. tax-exempt income

MAKE GLOBAL BUSINESS DECISIONS

14. Why are many international companies traded on the New York Stock Exchange (NYSE) as well as on stock exchanges in their home countries?
15. Why do some people use an online stockbroker instead of a full-service broker?
16. What happens when there is no buyer for shares of stock that someone wants to sell?
17. Which type of investment, stocks or bonds, involves more risk for an investor? Why?
18. Which would have less risk for an investor, a mortgage bond or a debenture bond?
19. How does a *Eurodollar* differ from a *euro*?
20. How does the futures market serve the needs of many groups of people in a country?

Photodisc/Getty Images

Photodisc/Getty Images

MAKE ACADEMIC CONNECTIONS

21. **GEOGRAPHY** Describe how the climate, terrain, waterways, and natural resources of a country might affect the development of a stock exchange in that nation.

22. **CULTURAL STUDIES** Talk to people from different countries about their attitudes toward investing. Compare your findings about what types of investments people prefer.

23. **MATHEMATICS** Select a company, and chart the changing price of its stock. Prepare a graph showing the closing price of a share over a three-week period. Use the library and Internet to locate news about the company and economic conditions. Prepare a short report explaining how this news has affected the company's stock price.

24. **RESEARCH** Locate bond prices using online or print resources. *The Wall Street Journal* or the business section of a daily newspaper are good places to start your research. Report to the class about the information included in the daily bond report.

25. **TECHNOLOGY** Prepare a spreadsheet or table comparing the features presented on three different web sites that provide investment information.

The GLOBAL
Entrepreneur

CREATING AN INTERNATIONAL BUSINESS PLAN

Global Investment Activities

Conduct research on global investment activities based on the company and country you have been using in this continuing project, or create a new idea for your business in the same or a different country. Make use of previously collected information, and do additional research. This phase of your business plan should answer the following questions.

1. If the company is a major corporation, on what stock exchange is the company's stock traded? What is the current price of a share of the company's stock?

2. What recent economic, social, and political factors could affect the company's stock price?

3. What is the current interest rate paid on the company's bonds?

4. How might the company use other financial markets, such as the foreign exchange market or the futures market?

5. Describe actions of the company that would make it an attractive investment choice.

Prepare a written summary or present a short oral report (two or three minutes) of your findings.

Photodisc/Getty Images

555

Managing International Business Risk

22-1 Global Risk Management

22-2 International Insurance

22-3 Reducing Global Risks

Lloyd's of London

The world's most famous insurance organization began in Edward Lloyd's coffeehouse in London. In 1688, ship owners and merchants bought marine insurance from Lloyd's to cover the risks of sending goods to other countries. In the late 1800s, Lloyd's of London expanded into nonmarine insurance.

Over the years, this association of insurance underwriters has insured some unusual assets—the legs of Hollywood dancers, the voices of famous singers, and the athletic ability of sport stars. Other unusual coverage provided by Lloyd's have included the following.

- Insurance policies providing protection against crocodile attack in northern Australia.
- Employers buying protection against staff members winning the British national lottery and not returning to work.
- Insurance coverage against death or injury caused by a piece of a disintegrating satellite falling from the sky.

Lloyd's of London is different from other insurance companies. This insurance society consists of investors called *Names,* who pool their money to cover possible financial risks. The Names profit when insurance claims are less than income. However, when a disaster occurs, the Names have to be prepared to pay for the financial losses from the disaster.

In recent years, Lloyd's has experienced lower profits due to natural disasters, environmental problems, and changing tax laws in Britain. These events have resulted in changes in the organization. Nonetheless, some traditions continue. In Lloyd's headquarters is the bell from the *Lutine*, which shipwrecked in 1857. The bell tolls once for good news, twice for bad news.

Think Critically

1. How does Lloyd's of London serve the needs of global business organizations?
2. What factors have reduced profits for Lloyd's?
3. Go to the web site of Lloyd's of London to obtain information on the history and current operations of the organization. Prepare a one-page summary of your findings.

22-1 Global Risk Management

GOALS

- Describe the types of risks related to international business activities.

- Discuss the risk management process.

Photodisc/Getty Images

International Business Risks

Whenever a company implements a business decision, risk is involved. The organization faces the risks of consumers not buying its product or a supplier not delivering materials on time. **Risk** is the uncertainty of an event or outcome. Every company faces potential risks—from employee theft to natural disasters. Companies and individuals must manage risk.

If all business ventures were sure things, life would be a lot simpler. However, in reality, every business activity has some risk. A war may destroy a factory in another country, or a company may go bankrupt and not be able to repay its debts. The three common risks faced by companies involved in international business are political risk, social risk, and economic risk, as shown in Figure 22-1.

POLITICAL RISK

Would a company be safer doing business in a democratic country with a newly formed government or in an autocratic nation that has been ruled by the same dictator for ten years? Political risk is difficult to evaluate. Government instability and political uncertainty are risks global companies must monitor constantly. Political control may change hands during civil unrest or a revolution. The new government may not allow certain companies to continue to operate in the country.

Business regulations vary from country to country. Regulations on business might be very tight in one nation, while great freedom is allowed elsewhere. Food packages in one country may require extensive nutritional information. However, another market may not have any laws regulating food labeling.

Trade barriers also pose a potential political risk. Tariffs, antidumping laws, import quotas, and currency exchange controls are examples of political actions taken to limit imported goods.

SOCIAL RISK

As you know, business is conducted differently in different parts of the world. Social and cultural factors such as religious beliefs, values, and family-business ties affect the risk faced by multinational companies.

Companies doing business in other countries must respect the religious beliefs of people in those nations. Failure to do so is likely to result in an unsuccessful endeavor even if all other business actions are appropriate. In a similar manner, companies that stress individualism would face greater risk when doing business in nations that emphasize collectivism.

The connection between family and business is very important in some cultures and less important in others. In most areas of Central and South America, much of southern Europe, and most of Asia, northern Africa, and the Middle East, family business ties are strong. Companies must work within this cultural environment to minimize business risk.

TYPES OF INTERNATIONAL BUSINESS RISKS

Political Risk	• Government instability • Change in business regulations • New trade barriers
Social Risk	• Religious beliefs • Values • Family-work relationships
Economic Risk	• Consumer spending patterns • Inflation • Exchange rate fluctuations

Figure 22-1 Companies involved in international business activities face different risks.

ECONOMIC RISK

Economic conditions have ups and downs. The demand for a company's goods and services varies based on the income of consumers, interest rates, and levels of employment. When fewer people are working, less money is available for consumer spending.

When a company receives one dollar today, it hopes to be able to buy something worth one dollar in the future. However, if *inflation* erodes the buying power of a currency, the monetary unit will not have as much purchasing power in the future.

GLOBAL BUSINESS SPOTLIGHT

PRACTICING FOR UNEXPECTED EVENTS

Royal Dutch/Shell, one of the world's largest petroleum and natural gas companies, is a joint venture between Royal Dutch Petroleum and Shell Transport and Trading. It has business activities in more than 130 countries and operates about 50,000 gas stations.

Shell continually encounters fluctuating oil prices, environmental concerns, and uncertainty in supplier nations. As part of its strategy for managing risk, Shell simulates situations that interrupt oil shipment. During these simulations, employees must put backup plans into operation.

When the Persian Gulf War started in the early 1990s, Shell was unable to obtain oil from Kuwait and Iraq. As part of its risk management plan, the company had already arranged to ship oil from alternative sites.

Think Critically

1. Why do companies conduct disaster drills?
2. Locate another example of a company implementing a backup plan.

Companies that do business in other countries face the risk of receiving payment in a currency that may have less value than expected. With exchange rates changing daily, financial managers must make sure that the payment received is appropriate after the currency conversion.

MONITORING GLOBAL BUSINESS RISK

Change is the only constant in all aspects of business. Reading current materials, talking with residents, and watching economic data are ways to note changes in a country's business environment. Awareness of factors such as political stability, religious influences, and fluctuating interest rates can help a manager predict changes in business risk. An ability to anticipate and act early can reduce risk and lessen the chances of poor business decisions.

✓ **Check**Point

What are the three main categories of risk faced by multinational companies?

The Risk Management Process

Multinational companies will face many business risks. Figure 22-2 shows four steps commonly taken to manage these international business risks.

STEP 1 IDENTIFY POTENTIAL RISKS

In the first step of the risk management process, managers list the factors that might affect a company's operations. Government policies, currency values, and local customs are some examples of risk-causing elements. Managers can use current reports, field interviews, and other data sources to uncover conditions that increase uncertainty.

STEP 2 EVALUATE RISKS

In this step, managers analyze the potential effect of risks on a company. Will a change in government mean higher costs to cover new environmental regulations? Or could the change in government result in the company facing new trade barriers when doing business in that nation? Managers must decide how and to what extent the risks will influence sales and profits.

Be aware that a factor in the international business environment can affect different companies in different ways. A weak economy may hurt a company selling entertainment products. However, the same poor economic conditions may benefit a company selling low-cost clothing.

STEP 3 SELECT A RISK MANAGEMENT METHOD

Next, managers must decide how to handle the identified risks. The four methods used to manage risk—risk avoidance, risk reduction, risk assumption, and risk sharing.

The Risk Management Process

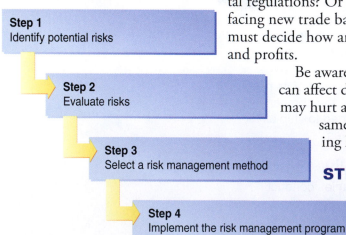

Step 1
Identify potential risks

Step 2
Evaluate risks

Step 3
Select a risk management method

Step 4
Implement the risk management program

Figure 22-2 Companies manage risk by following a step-by-step approach.

A Question of Ethics

UNREPORTED BUSINESS ACTIVITIES

Most countries have an *underground economy* or *black market*. These terms refer to business activities outside the formal economy. These transactions are not reported to government agencies. In some regions of developing countries, more than half of the construction work and other business activities are *off the books*—never reported for tax purposes.

An underground economy creates jobs, which allow people to earn income for paying living expenses. However, it also has a negative impact. Because sales revenue and income are not reported, governments do not collect taxes needed to pay for public services.

Think Critically

Use the three guidelines for ethical analysis to examine the above situation. How does the underground economy affect businesses, consumers, and society?

Risk Avoidance Certain risks can be avoided. A company avoids the risks related to international business by only selling products in its home country. However, this approach to risk management is not always practical. A business limits its potential for expansion by selling only in its domestic market or in markets in safe geographic regions.

Risk Reduction The risk of an event may be reduced by taking precautionary actions. For example, businesses use security systems and sprinklers to reduce the risk of theft and fire. Multinational companies can reduce business risks by selling products that have been successful in other countries.

Risk Assumption Sometimes a company takes responsibility for losses from certain risks. For example, a business may set aside funds for fire damage that may occur to its factories. This action, called **self-insurance**, involves setting aside money to cover a potential financial loss. A company with many stores or factories in different locations may save money by using self-insurance.

Risk Sharing Sharing risks among many companies that face similar risks is a common practice. Insurance is often purchased for financial protection from property losses, motor vehicle accidents, and other business activities.

STEP 4 IMPLEMENT THE RISK MANAGEMENT PROGRAM

Finally, managers must execute the risk management plan. This phase involves both taking relevant action and measuring the success of the action. Various factors in the business environment and within the company may change an organization's risk management course in the future.

✓ CheckPoint
What are the steps of the risk management process?

Work as a Team
Using an international business situation, prepare an example for each step of the risk management process shown in Figure 22-2.

22-1 Assessment

www.cengage.com/school/genbus/intlbiz

REVIEW GLOBAL BUSINESS TERMS

Define each of the following terms.

1. risk
2. self-insurance

REVIEW GLOBAL BUSINESS CONCEPTS

3. What are examples of social risks?
4. How can managers monitor international business risk?
5. What are the four methods used to manage risk?
6. What is self-insurance? Give an example.

SOLVE GLOBAL BUSINESS PROBLEMS

For each of the following situations, describe actions that the organization might take to manage its business risk.

7. Stealing by employees and customers.
8. Changes in the value of foreign currencies.
9. Actions of global competitors.
10. Changing clothing styles.
11. Political instability in a foreign country.

THINK CRITICALLY

12. What are some examples of government regulations that create global business risks?
13. Describe a risk-reduction action that a company could use.
14. What are some actions you take each day to avoid and reduce risks in your life?

MAKE ACADEMIC CONNECTIONS

15. **TECHNOLOGY** Explain how changing technology could increase and decrease risks for a global company.
16. **CULTURAL STUDIES** Describe differences in customs, traditions, and language that could create a social risk for a company operating in another country.
17. **TECHNOLOGY** Use the Internet to identify online resources for risk management.
18. **CURRENT EVENTS** Use the Internet to find a recent event that poses a risk to international business. Identify the type of risk and describe a plan for managing this risk.

Photodisc/Getty Images

GOALS

- **Explain the basic elements of insurance coverage.**

- **Describe elements of an insurance policy.**

Insuring Against Risks

Insurance is planned protection for sharing economic losses among many people. Insurance is commonly purchased to reduce or eliminate the financial loss due to risks. A company's place of business is usually covered by property insurance. When driving a car, a traveling salesperson probably has automobile insurance. Most everyone reading this book uses insurance as a method for managing risk.

Insurance is an agreement between one party, called the *insured*, and an insurance company, the *insurer*. A **stock insurance company** is owned by stockholders and is operated for profit. A **mutual insurance company** is owned by its policyholders. This type of organization returns any surplus to policyholders after claims and operating expenses are paid.

INSURABLE INTEREST

A basic requirement of insurance is the presence of an *insurable interest*, something of value that may be lost or destroyed. For example, equipment owned by a company represents an insurable interest. In the case of life insurance, the insurable interest is the financial loss caused by someone's death.

INSURABLE RISK

Another basic requirement of insurance is the presence of an *insurable risk*. An insurable risk is a risk that has the following elements.

- Common to many people—The risk must be one that is faced by many people or businesses. This allows many people with the same risk to share the cost with the few who actually suffer a financial loss due to the risk.

GLOBAL BUSINESS SPOTLIGHT

MICROINSURANCE

People around the world face financial threats such as disease, crop failure, and death of the household head. people can be especially damaging because they most often do not have other assets. In addition, they usually do not have funds to buy traditional insurance.

In recent years, *microinsurance* programs have been created to cover specific risks in exchange for small premiums. As with all insurance, many individuals with the potential for a similar financial loss pool their funds. Then, those who encounter a loss receive a payment.

Similar to microcredit, microinsurance helps people who have limited access to financial services. Because hundreds of millions of people do not have access to traditional insurance, microinsurance programs are expected to expand.

Think Critically

1. How do microinsurance programs benefit poor people around the world?
2. Use library or Internet resources to locate additional information about microinsurance in various countries.

Photodisc/Getty Images

- Definite—The risk must be something that can be documented. The destruction of a building by fire or the death of a person is something that can be documented.
- Not excessive in magnitude—An insurance company would not be able to cover the cost of replacing all homes it insures at one time. Recent hurricanes in Florida caused such extensive damage that some insurance companies can no longer afford to do business in that state.
- Not trivial—Insurance on small items would not be worth the time, effort, and expense necessary to provide coverage.
- Able to be calculated—The insurer must be able to calculate the probability that the risk will occur. This allows the insurer to plan what amount to charge for insurance.

✓ CheckPoint
What are the elements of an insurable risk?

Insurance Policy Elements

An **insurance policy** is the legal agreement between an insurance company and the insured. This contract states the conditions of protection. The major elements of an insurance policy are declaration, insuring agreement, conditions, exclusions, and endorsement.

Declaration The *declaration* states what is covered and lists the amount of coverage. For example, the declaration for a multinational company's insurance would describe the enterprise's factories in different countries and at what amount they were covered.

Insuring Agreement The *insuring agreement* explains the coverages of the policy. A company's insurance policy may cover fire and theft losses for property up to a set amount, such as $14 million—the amount of the coverage.

Conditions The *conditions* of an insurance policy provide information about the cost of insurance, called the **premium**. Also listed are any deductibles. A **deductible** is the portion of an insurance claim paid by the insured. A company with a $1,000 deductible, for example, may incur $4,500 of wind damage to a building. In this situation, the insurance company would pay $3,500. The first $1,000 of the claim is paid by the insured. Deductibles reduce the cost of insurance premiums.

Exclusions Property or risks not covered by an insurance policy are called *exclusions*. For example, many insurance policies do not cover property losses resulting from war.

Endorsement An **endorsement** is a certificate that adds to or changes the coverage of an insurance policy. For example, if a company sells a factory, an endorsement would delete the building from its insurance coverage.

Exports should be insured against loss or damage that could occur while in transit. An *insurance certificate* provides evidence of insurance to protect goods from loss or damage while in transit. Sales terms determine if the importer or the exporter pays insurance costs.

✓ **Check**Point

What are the main elements of an insurance policy?

Work as a Team

Describe actions a company could take when comparing the coverages and costs of insurance.

©Patricia Marks, 2009/ Used under license from Shutterstock.com

INTERNATIONAL BUSINESS PERSPECTIVE
History

THE ORGANIZATION OF PETROLEUM EXPORTING COUNTRIES

The Organization of Petroleum Exporting Countries (OPEC) was created in 1960. The original members were Iran, Iraq, Kuwait, Saudi Arabia, and Venezuela. Today, OPEC has 12 members, including the countries in Africa, Asia, the Middle East, and South America.

During its first decade, OPEC was concerned mainly with maintaining stable world oil prices. However, by 1970, as the world price for oil dropped (supply exceeded demand), OPEC worked to raise oil prices by reducing production levels. During 1973–74, petroleum prices rose by 400 percent. This was followed by a four-year period of stable prices.

Recent discovery of large oil reserves in the Gulf of Mexico, the North Sea, Alaska, and Canada has somewhat reduced OPEC's influence on world oil prices. However, OPEC nations continue to have control of about two-thirds of the world's oil reserves.

Think Critically

1. What factors influence the world market price of oil?
2. Go to the OPEC web site for additional information about the current activities of the organization. Write a paragraph about your findings.

PaulFleet/iStockphoto.com

22-2 Assessment

REVIEW GLOBAL BUSINESS TERMS

Define each of the following terms.

1. insurance
2. stock insurance company
3. mutual insurance company
4. insurance policy
5. premium
6. deductible
7. endorsement

Study Tools

www.cengage.com/school/genbus/intlbiz

REVIEW GLOBAL BUSINESS CONCEPTS

8. How does a stock insurance company differ from a mutual insurance company?
9. What is an insurable interest?
10. What is the purpose of an endorsement?

SOLVE GLOBAL BUSINESS PROBLEMS

For each of the following items, name the insurance policy element that is involved.

11. "For all claims, the insured party will pay the first $2,000 of damages."
12. "This policy provides coverage for damage to the factory at 1765 Industrial Drive."
13. "As of June 3, 2001, this policy no longer covers damages as a result of civil riots in foreign countries."
14. "This coverage has a cost of $5,600 for the period of August 7, 2001, to August 6, 2002."
15. "This policy does not cover damage resulting from hurricanes or acts of war."

THINK CRITICALLY

16. What are the benefits of a mutual insurance company?
17. How does a deductible reduce insurance costs for the insurance company and the policyholder?

MAKE ACADEMIC CONNECTIONS

18. **MATHEMATICS** If a company has insurance coverage with a $5,000 deductible and encounters a claim for $6,200, how much would the insurance company pay?
19. **LAW** Obtain a sample of an insurance policy to observe the elements of this contract.

22-3 Reducing Global Risks

GOALS

- **Identify the major types of insurance coverages for international business activities.**

- **Describe strategies that multinational companies use to reduce risk.**

Photodisc/Getty Images

Global Insurance Coverages

Companies involved in international business can share certain risks by using insurance. Commonly used coverages of multinational companies are marine insurance, property insurance, coverage for political risk through the Overseas Private Investment Corporation, and credit risk insurance.

MARINE INSURANCE

Overseas transporters usually assume no responsibility for the merchandise they carry unless the loss is caused by their carelessness. Marine insurance provides protection from loss during shipment of products. This insurance has two types of coverage.

Ocean marine insurance protects goods during shipment overseas or while temporarily in port. In contrast, **inland marine insurance** covers the risk of shipping goods on inland waterways, railroad lines, truck lines, and airlines.

Marine insurance is usually sold in three forms with varied coverages.

1. *Basic coverage* provides protection from hazards such as sea damage, fires, jettisons, explosions, and hurricanes.
2. *Broad coverage* includes basic coverage plus theft, pilferage, nondelivery, breakage, and leakage.
3. *All-risk coverage* consists of any physical loss or damage due to an external cause, excluding risks associated with war.

As expected, an all-risk policy is the most expensive of the three types because the most coverage is provided. Also be aware that some losses are not covered by all-risk policies. Items not covered include improper packing, damage caused by natural properties of a product (such as rusting of steel), and loss caused by delay (such as a labor strike).

The amount charged for marine insurance is affected by a variety of factors. Premium factors include the value of the goods, the destination, the age of the ship, the storage location (on deck or under deck), the packaging, and the size of the shipment (volume discounts are common).

NETBookmark

In maritime law, the "law of finds" traditionally means whoever discovers a shipwreck is entitled to claim it and anything it holds. Access the web site shown below and click on the link for Chapter 22. After reading the article, write a few paragraphs explaining who you think should own shipwrecks. Do you agree with the "law of finds"? Why or why not?

www.cengage.com/school/genbus/intlbiz

PROPERTY INSURANCE

Crimes such as burglary, theft, and arson disturb business activities throughout the world. Companies face three main risks as property owners.

1. Loss of real property
2. Loss of personal property
3. Financial responsibility for injuries or damage

Loss of Real Property *Real property* refers to structures permanently attached to land, such as factories, stores, garages, and office buildings. A company's building and land represent a significant financial investment. Property insurance provides protection for damage or loss of real property. Buildings and structures are insured for loss or damage from fire, lightning, wind, hail, explosion, smoke, vandalism, and crashes of aircraft and motor vehicles.

Loss of Personal Property *Personal property* refers to property not attached to the land. Loss or damage of office furniture, machinery, equipment, and supplies also can be covered by property insurance.

Financial Responsibility for Injuries or Damage *Liability* is legal responsibility for the financial cost of someone else's losses or injuries. Customers, company guests, employees, and others may be injured while on the premises of a business. Or a company representative may accidentally damage the property of others. When any of these occur, the company may be responsible for the financial loss that results from the incident.

Quite often legal responsibility is the result of *negligence*, or failure to take ordinary or reasonable care. An employer may also be held financially responsible for the actions of an employee. Liability insurance protects a company from financial losses due to the actions of its employees.

THE OVERSEAS PRIVATE INVESTMENT CORPORATION

To encourage investment in less developed countries, the U.S. government created the Overseas Private Investment Corporation (OPIC). This agency protects U.S. companies from various hazards. OPIC protects 150 developing

Photodisc/Getty Images

COMMUNICATION ACROSS BORDERS

NOT ALL LANGUAGES ARE EQUAL

Businesses can increase their international risks by using certain languages. For example, Hebrew is a holy language that evolved primarily for religious purposes, not for common speech purposes, including business.

As the dominant language of only one small country, Israel, Hebrew is not widely known. Very few opportunities for learning Hebrew exist in most countries. Thus, a multinational organization that chooses Hebrew as its only business language will likely expose itself to greater communication risks than one that chooses a more

common language of international business.

Think Critically

1. How does a multinational organization increase its risks by choosing Hebrew as its only business language?
2. If Hebrew is determined to be too risky as the official business language, what other language(s) should be considered? Why?

nations and emerging markets from financial losses, which may be the result of the three major types of risk.

1. Inconvertibility—This is an inability to convert foreign currency into U.S. dollars. Most refusals by a host government to convert a currency to dollars are covered under this insurance program.
2. Expropriation—This refers to the seizure of assets by a host government. OPIC provides protection against the loss of control of an investment in a country where political actions by host governments may result.
3. Political unrest—This includes financial losses of assets and property resulting from war, revolution, or civil conflicts.

A U.S. company is eligible for OPIC coverage if U.S. citizens own 50 percent or more of the corporation. A foreign corporation may be eligible if U.S. citizens own at least 95 percent of the company.

CREDIT RISK INSURANCE

One hazard of conducting business in other countries is not receiving payment. **Credit risk insurance** provides coverage for loss from nonpayment of delivered goods. This protection helps reduce the risk of international business activities.

Credit risk insurance is available through the Foreign Credit Insurance Association (FCIA), a private association that insures U.S. exporters. FCIA enables exporters to extend credit to overseas buyers.

Credit insurance covers 100 percent of losses due to political reasons, such as war, asset seizure, and currency inconvertibility. This insurance covers up to 95 percent of commercial losses, such as nonpayment due to insolvency or default.

About 200 banks in the United States have purchased master policies from FCIA and can insure loans given to U.S. exporters. Banks typically charge about 1 percent of the amount insured for the coverage.

Risk Reduction for Global Business

Risk is something every company will face in every business situation. However, management experts recommend the four strategies shown in Figure 22-3 to help reduce international business risk.

Multinational Risk Reduction Strategies

Figure 22-3 Companies can reduce international business risk by taking certain actions.

Conduct Business in Many Countries When a company depends on a variety of nations for its sales and profits, it will not be greatly affected by turmoil in one of its markets. U.S. companies doing business in Cuba when Castro gained power in 1959 lost some of their business assets. Fortunately, most of these multinational companies were also were operating in many other nations.

Work as a Team

Select a common product sold to consumers. Develop a list of related products that a business could sell to reduce its risk of selling only one product.

Diversify Product Offerings Just as a company should operate in several nations, it should not be dependent on only one or a few products.

By having a varied portfolio of goods and services, an organization reduces its risk when consumers no longer desire one product. By seeking new uses for products and by creating new products, a company reduces its international business risk.

Involve Local Ownership Local ownership of multinational firms is usually is viewed favorably by local governments. A company that is completely owned by citizens of another country faces the greatest risks. A host nation feels threatened when people who may have different political and social beliefs control its economic existence. Joint ventures with local private partners are frequently less risky.

Employ Local Management Hiring local managers allows a company to maintain a good working relationship with the host government. Administrators who are native to a country or region understand local customs and cultural norms. A comfortable working relationship will be more likely when local managers are employed.

GLOBAL BUSINESS SPOTLIGHT

THE RUSSIAN INSURANCE INDUSTRY

When the former Soviet Union evolved from communism to capitalism, many insurance companies were started. Russia's first insurance law, allowed an applicant to become a licensed insurance seller with only 2 million rubles in capital—about $1,100. This allowed many entrepreneurs to enter the market.

Vera (Russian for "trust") is an insurance company that has the Christian Russian Bank as one of its largest shareholders. Vera specializes in insuring the real estate of the Russian Orthodox Church. The company also provides insurance coverage for the church's art and other priceless treasures made from gold and diamonds.

More recently, Nakhodka Re offers a variety of coverages,

including liability, property, motor vehicle, aircraft, cargo, and fishing vessel crew insurance. The company also works with overseas insurance brokers to assist businesses shipping goods to and within Russia and other eastern European countries.

Think Critically

1. How did changes in the Russian political and economic environment affect the insurance business in that country?

2. Conduct an Internet search to obtain current information about insurance activities in Russia and other eastern European countries. Write an outline of your findings.

✓ **Check**Point
How does doing business in several countries reduce risk for a global company?

REVIEW GLOBAL BUSINESS TERMS

Define each of the following terms.

1. ocean marine insurance
2. inland marine insurance
3. credit risk insurance

REVIEW GLOBAL BUSINESS CONCEPTS

4. What are the three forms of marine insurance?
5. How does real property differ from personal property?
6. What is the purpose of the Overseas Private Investment Corporation?
7. What is the purpose of credit risk insurance?
8. How can companies reduce risks associated with international business activities?

SOLVE GLOBAL BUSINESS PROBLEMS

For each of the following business situations, indicate the type of insurance that would cover the financial loss.

9. Goods shipped overseas and stolen while in port in southern Europe.
10. Fire damage to a factory in South America.
11. Nonpayment for a shipment of clothing to eastern Europe.
12. Goods damaged while shipped by railroad in Asia.
13. Accidental injury to guests from another company visiting a factory in Africa.

THINK CRITICALLY

14. What risks are associated with shipping goods by railroad, truck, and airplane?
15. What problems might a company encounter when involving local ownership or employing local management?

MAKE ACADEMIC CONNECTIONS

16. **TECHNOLOGY** Go to the web site of the Overseas Private Investment Corporation to obtain information on the current activities of this organization. Write a paragraph summarizing your findings.
17. **GEOGRAPHY** Create a map showing countries with similar climates in which a company could sell its products.
16. **TECHNOLOGY** Use the Internet to locate online business insurance resources.

CHAPTER SUMMARY

22-1 GLOBAL RISK MANAGEMENT

A Companies involved in international business commonly face political, social, and economic risks.

B The risk management process involves (1) identifying potential risks, (2) evaluating risks, (3) selecting a risk management method, and (4) implementing the risk management program.

22-2 INTERNATIONAL INSURANCE

A The basic elements of insurance coverage involve (1) an insurable interest—something of value and (2) an insurable risk—an event common to many people that is definite, not excessive in magnitude, not trivial, and able to be calculated.

B The elements of an insurance policy include the declaration, the insuring agreement, the conditions, the exclusions, and any endorsements.

22-3 REDUCING GLOBAL RISKS

A The major types of insurance for international business are marine insurance, property insurance, the Overseas Private Investment Corporation coverage, and credit risk insurance.

B Strategies that multinational companies use to reduce risk include conducting business in many countries, diversifying product offerings, involving local ownership, and employing local management.

GLOBAL REFOCUS

Read the Global Focus at the beginning of this chapter, and answer the following questions.

1. What are the similarities and differences between Lloyd's and other insurance companies?

2. What actions might Lloyd's take to expand its operations around the world?

REVIEW GLOBAL BUSINESS TERMS

Match the terms listed with the definitions.

1. The portion of an insurance claim paid by the insured.
2. Coverage for loss from nonpayment of delivered goods.
3. An insurance company owned by stockholders and operated for profit.
4. Setting aside money to cover a potential financial loss.
5. The uncertainty of an event or outcome.
6. Protection from loss while goods are being shipped overseas or while temporarily in port.
7. Planned protection for sharing economic losses among many people.
8. A certificate that adds to or changes the coverage of an insurance policy.
9. The cost of insurance.
10. An insurance company owned by its policyholders.
11. Protection from a loss while shipping goods on inland waterways, railroad lines, truck lines, and airlines.
12. The legal agreement between an insurance company and the insured.

a. credit risk insurance
b. deductible
c. endorsement
d. inland marine insurance
e. insurance
f. insurance policy
g. mutual insurance company
h. ocean marine insurance
i. premium
j. risk
k. self-insurance
l. stock insurance company

MAKE GLOBAL BUSINESS DECISIONS

13. Name some risks exporters could face that might not be present when a company sells within its own country.
14. Describe ways you could reduce risks in your home and at your school.
15. Speculative risks include such things as starting a new business or introducing a new product. These cannot be covered by insurance. Why will insurance companies not cover speculative risks? List other examples of speculative risks.
16. Explain why deductibles reduce the premium paid for insurance.
17. An exporter might not make a marine insurance claim, even if it is valid. Many small claims can increase the cost of insurance in the future. Why might an exporter decide not to make a claim?
18. Most people who own or operate a business consider liability insurance coverage vital. Why?
19. You are the regional manager for a multinational company in Saudi Arabia that manufactures and distributes plastic products. What actions would you take to reduce risk for your company?

Photodisc/Getty Images

MAKE ACADEMIC CONNECTIONS

20. **GEOGRAPHY** Prepare a map that indicates some of the countries that have had political unrest or military conflicts in recent years. Explain how companies could reduce risks in these countries.

21. **COMMUNICATIONS** Talk to someone with homeowner's or renter's insurance. Report to the class about the types of risks that are covered by property insurance.

22. **HISTORY** Conduct library or Internet research about marine insurance. Prepare a report that explains risks and hazards of this international business insurance.

23. **CULTURAL STUDIES** Interview a person who has lived or worked in another country. Obtain information about differences in customs, traditions, and language that could create business risks.

24. **VISUAL ART** Prepare a poster or other visual presentation illustrating methods that companies could use to reduce business risk.

25. **MATHEMATICS** Contact several insurance agents to obtain information about the cost of property or liability insurance. Prepare a graph that shows differences in costs and coverages.

26. **CAREER PLANNING** Interview a person who works in an insurance career. What training and skills are required for jobs in the insurance industry?

The GLOBAL *Entrepreneur*

CREATING AN INTERNATIONAL BUSINESS PLAN

Global Risk Management

Conduct research on global business risks and insurance based on the company and country you have been using in this continuing project, or create a new idea for your business in the same or a different country. Make use of previously collected information, and do additional research. This phase of your business plan should answer the following questions.

1. What are the company's main international business risks?

2. Is self-insurance practical for the company?

3. For what situations might the company make use of marine insurance?

4. What types of property does the company own that need to be insured?

5. Why might liability coverage be important to the company?

6. What types of insurance might the company provide as an employee benefit for its workers?

Prepare a written summary or present a short oral report (two or three minutes) of your findings.

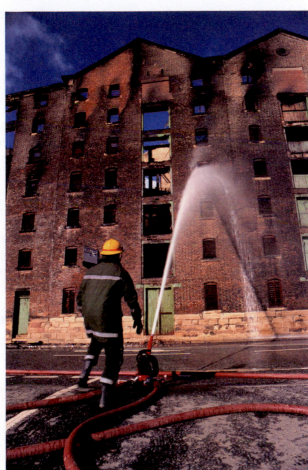

Photodisc/Getty Images

GLOBAL Cross-Cultural Team Project

Finance International Business Operations

Obtaining loans, attracting investors, and evaluating international business risk are some of the financial aspects of global operations. As companies expand into various geographic regions, cross-cultural teams allow financial managers to better understand various influences on their decisions.

Goal

To identify differences in finance activities in various regions of the world.

Activities

Working in teams, select a geographic region you will represent—Africa, Asia, Europe, Latin America, the Middle East, or North America.

1. International finance topics may be researched in current articles, library materials, and Web searches. Also, if possible, have a discussion with people who have lived or visited your region of the world.
2. Research attitudes toward the use of credit in your region. How do tradition, religion, and culture affect borrowing? Discuss any notable exceptions in specific countries.
3. List common financial institutions that operate in your geographic region. What services do they provide for businesses?
4. Identify common investments people make in the region. To what extent are stocks, bonds, mutual funds, real estate, and other investments used to achieve financial goals?
5. Describe the major political, social, and economic risks faced by companies doing business in this region. What actions might be taken to reduce or eliminate these risks?
6. **Global Business Decision** An international company has asked your team for advice to finance the expansion of business operations around the world. How might the use of debt be viewed in different regions? What additional financing alternatives might be taken?

Team Skill Measuring The Success Of Cross-Cultural Teams

The completion of a team project includes evaluating the level of achievement. Measures of success vary among geographic regions and in some specific countries. Describe possible items that might be used to measure the success of a team in your region. Compare your list with those of other members of your team.

Present

Plan and present a debate among your team members to compare and contrast the risks associated with doing business in various geographic areas. Discuss the types of risks and actions that might be taken to reduce or eliminate these risks.

Entrepreneurship Case Study

This event is composed of two parts: a written objective test and a decision-making problem (case study). Teams consisting of three participants will present and defend their solution to a business challenge.

Once you receive your business topic, you have 30 minutes to prepare your presentation and argument. Each participant will be given two 4" by 6" index cards that may be used during the preparation and presentation to the judges/students. No reference materials or visual aids may be brought to or used during the preparation or performance. Your team has 10 minutes to present the case. One member should introduce the team and describe or summarize the case study. All team members must participate in the presentation. Note cards may be used to explain decisions and rationales to the judges. After the presentation, five minutes are allowed for questions and answers.

Your case study involves the rising cost of wages and benefits in the United States. Your company has recently expanded operation to India where the cost of labor and benefits is much less than the United States. Tight economic conditions have caused your company to look at all options for reducing expenditures. Because wages and benefits are the largest expense for your company, you are considering outsourcing positions in the United States to India, laying off U.S. workers, and asking U.S. workers to consider pay cuts in order to keep their jobs. You must make a decision to cut human resource costs for your company. Your decision must also attempt to maintain favorable relations with your current employees.

Performance Indicators Evaluated

- Understand why companies outsource work to other countries.
- Explain the cost and value of human resources to a company.
- Present a relevant affirmative or negative argument for each possible solution.
- Conduct research to support your argument with relevant quality evidence.
- Demonstrate persuasive speaking and oral presentation skills.
- Involve all team members in the research and presentation.

For more detailed information about performance indicators, go to the FBLA-PBL web site.

Think Critically

1. Why are companies downsizing?
2. What is the bottom line for companies?
3. What dangers are associated with outsourcing work?
4. How do you communicate an unfavorable option to employees?

www.fbla-pbl.org

WORLD POLITICAL MAP

North
Pacific
Ocean

North
Atlantic
Ocean

Canada

United States

Mexico

South Pacific Ocean

Brazil

Colombia

Peru

Bolivia

Chile

Paraguay

Uruguay

Argentina

South
Atlantic
Ocean

Greenland

Iceland

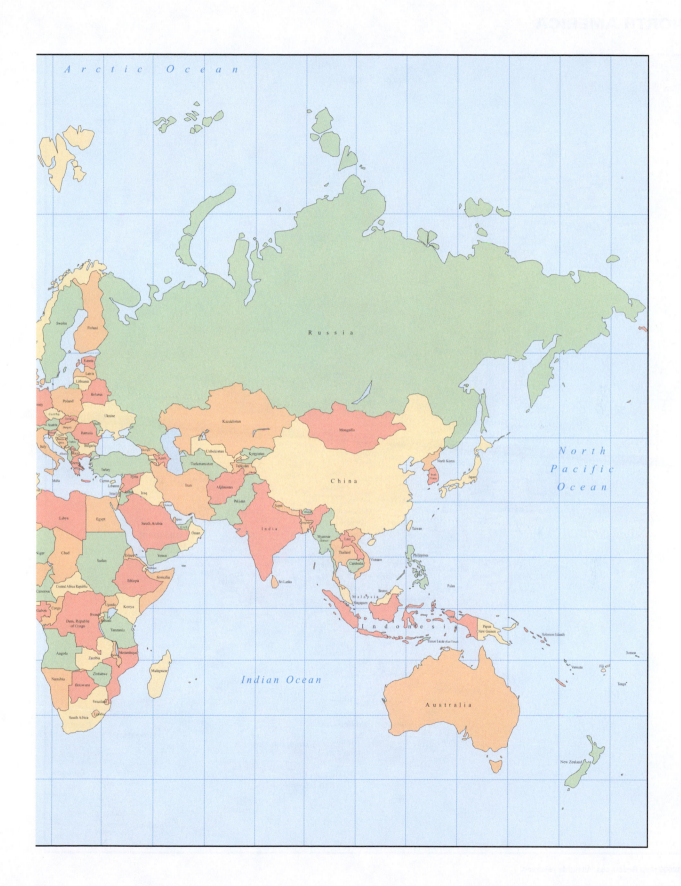

Arctic Ocean

Russia

Sweden
Finland
Estonia
Latvia
Lithuania
Belarus
Poland
Ukraine
Kazakhstan
Mongolia
North Korea
Japan
Uzbekistan
Kyrgyzstan
Turkmenistan
Tajikistan
South Korea
Romania
Bulgaria
Azerb.
Italy
Turkey
China
Cyprus
Lebanon
Israel
Iran
Afghanistan
Iraq
Nepal
Libya
Egypt
Saudi Arabia
Pakistan
India
Taiwan
Niger
Chad
Oman
Myanmar (Burma)
Laos
Sudan
Eritrea
Yemen
Thailand
Philippines
Vietnam
Cambodia
Central Africa Republic
Ethiopia
Cameroon
Somalia
Gabon
Congo
Uganda
Kenya
Palau
Dem. Republic of Congo
Rwanda
Burundi
Sri Lanka
Malaysia
Brunei
Singapore
Tanzania
Indonesia
Angola
Zambia
Mozambique
Papua New Guinea
Solomon Islands
Samoa
Malagasy
Namibia
Zimbabwe
Botswana
Timor Leste (East Timor)
Vanuatu
Fiji
Swaziland
South Africa
Lesotho

Indian Ocean

North Pacific Ocean

Australia

New Zealand

Tonga

581

NORTH AMERICA

582

ASIA

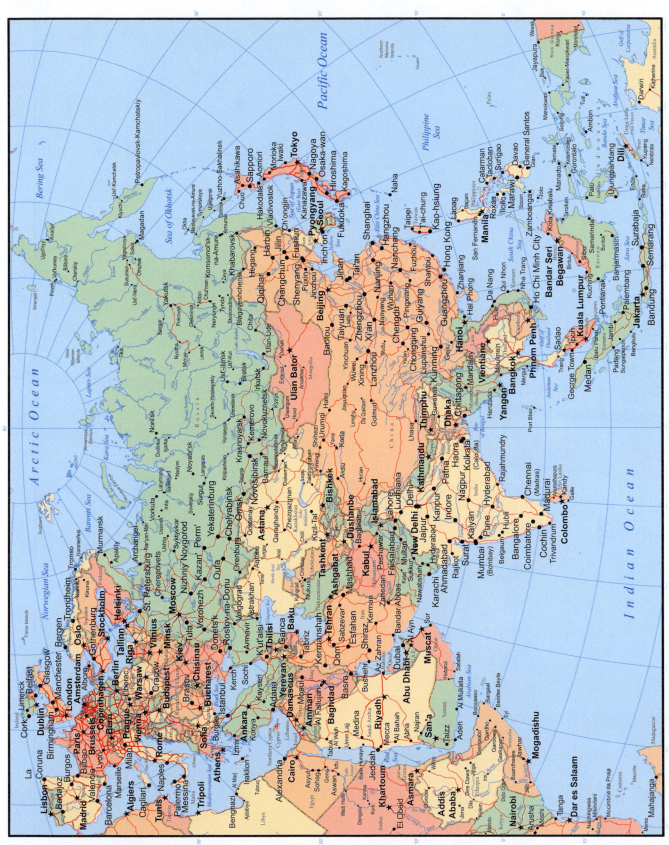

583

AUSTRALIA AND NEW ZEALAND

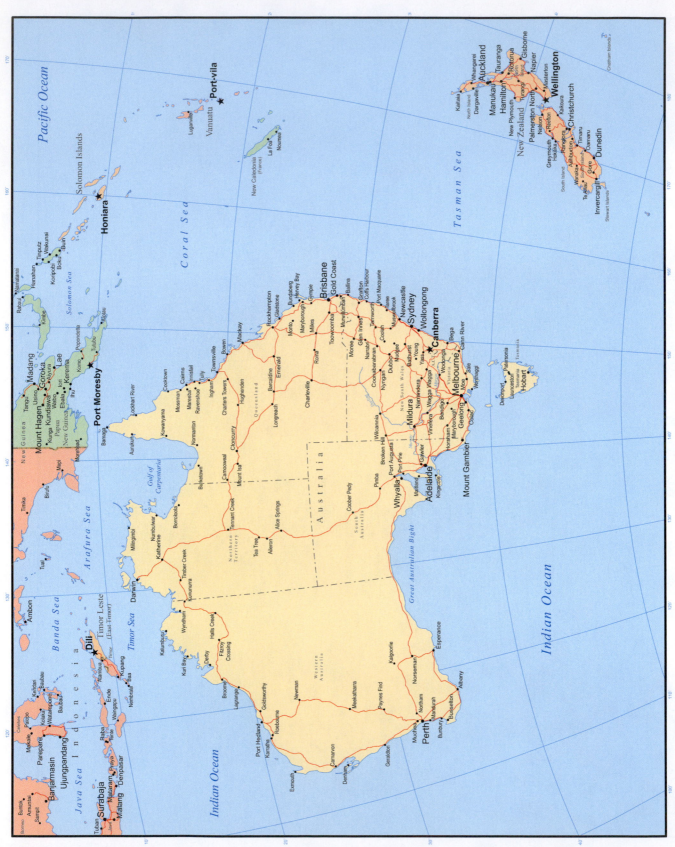

EUROPE

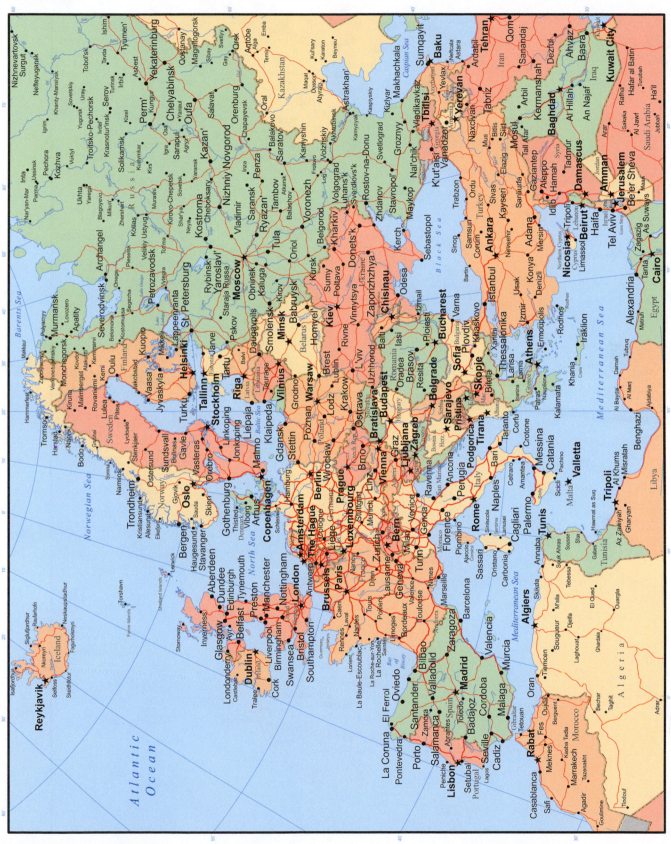

AFRICA

Atlantic
Ocean

Dublin Manchester
London Amsterdam Berlin Vilnius Minsk Tula Penza Orenburg
United Germany Warsaw Homyel' Voronezh Russia Zhezqazghan
Kingdom Brussels Prague Poland L'viv Kiev Donets'k Aqtobe Kazakhstan
Paris Munich Vienna Bratislava Chisinau Rostov-na-Donu Atyrau Qyzylorda
Bordeaux France Lyon Bern Ljubljana Budapest Romania Odesa K'ut'aisi Tbilisi Nukus Uzbekistan
La Coruna Toulouse Milan Verona Zagreb Belgrade Bucharest Black Sea Baku Turkmenistan Ashgabat
Portugal Bilbao Marseille Rome Sarajevo Podgorica Sofia Istanbul Ankara Yerevan Tabriz Tehran Mashhad
Lisbon Madrid Barcelona Naples Tirana Skopje Athens Izmir Turkey Adana Mosul Kirkuk Iran Esfahan
Spain Valencia Palermo Messina Nicosia Aleppo Damascus Baghdad Shiraz
Seville Malaga Annaba Tunis Malta Mediterranean Sea Cyprus Beirut Syria Amman Basra
Casablanca Rabat Oran Algiers Benghazi Tel Aviv Jerusalem Iraq Kuwait City Bushehr
Safi Morocco Laghouat El Oued Tunisia Tripoli Misratah Alexandria Cairo Tabuk Ad Dammam Doha Abu Dhabi
Agadir Marrakech Taghit Ouargla Ajdabiya Egypt Asyut Tayma' Ha'il Al Hufuf Qatar Riyadh
Goulimine Adrar Algeria Sabha Libya Aswan Medina Mecca Layla Saudi Arabia Oman Salalah
Tindouf Bir Mogrein Mali Ti-n-Essako Niger Faya-Largeau Chad Wadi Halfa Rabigh Jeddah Al Bahah Red Sea
Western Sahara Dakhla Mauritania Atar Aleg Nema Tombouctou Gao Arlit Agadez Bardai Port Sudan Atbara Jizan
Nouadhibou Nouakchott Senegal Nara Tillia Zinder Iriba Sudan Khartoum Wad Medani Asmara San'a Al Mukalla
Dakar Kita Bamako Dori Niamey Diffa Bol Ati El Obeid Kosti Gonder Eritrea Taizz Yemen Aden Gulf of Aden
Banjul Gambia Bissau Guinea-Bissau Bobo-Dioulasso Ouagadougou Burkina Faso N'Djamena Bongor Malakal Debre Mark'os Djibouti Bargaal
Conakry Freetown Labe Korhogo Cote d'Ivoire Ghana Benin Nigeria Moundou Bria Harar Addis Ababa Ethiopia Garoowe
Yamoussoukro Sierra Leone Abuja Bafoussam Central Africa Republic Bangassou Obo Juba Goba Dolo Odo Eyl
Monrovia Accra Porto-Novo Lagos Aba Yaounde Cameroon Bouar Nimule Somalia El Dere
Greenville Lome Malabo Oyem Bangui Isiro Uganda Baardheere
Harper Tabou Abidjan Equatorial Guinea Libreville Gabon Mbandaka Boende Kisangani Kampala Jinja Kenya Nairobi Mogadishu Baraawe
Sao Tome & Principe Francevile Owando Dem Republic of Congo Kigali Mwanza Jamaame
Brazzaville Congo Bandundu Bujumbura Arusha Indian Ocean
Pointe-Noire Kinshasa Kananga Tanzania Zanzibar
Luanda Matadi Cuilo Kamina Tukuyu Dodoma Dar es Salaam
Malanje Kabalo Kashiba Kilwa Masoko Seychelles
Gabela Angola Dilolo Rumphi Mikindani
Lobito Huambo Lubumbashi Ndola Malawi Comoros Antsiranana Mayotte
Namibe Lubango Zambia Lilongwe Namapa Fernao Veloso Mahajanga
Menongue Lusaka Blantyre Mozambique Mocuba
Xangongo Senanga Harare Mutare Vila do Chinde Toamasina
Tsumeb Zimbabwe Gweru Madagascar Antananarivo
Outjo Bulawayo Morondava
Windhoek Namibia Francistown Messina Beira Reunion St.-Pierre
Swakopmund Botswana Pietersburg Inhambane Toliara Tolanaro
Maltahohe Gaborone Pretoria Maputo
Luderitz Mbabane Swaziland
Kimberley Maseru Lesotho
Oranjemund Bloemfontein Umtata Durban
Calvinia South Africa
Wellington East London
Cape Town Port Elizabeth

Atlantic
Ocean

CENTRAL AMERICA

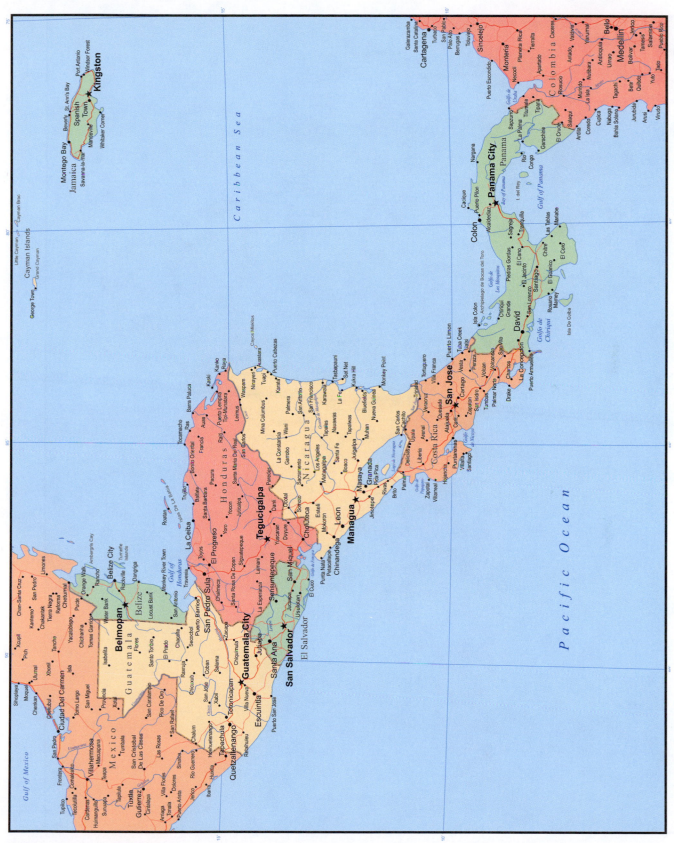

587

SOUTH AMERICA

Caribbean Sea

Atlantic Ocean

Pacific Ocean

Atlantic Ocean

Nicaragua
Managua
San Jose
Costa Rica
Panama City
Panama

Juticalpa
Puerto Estrella
Cartagena
Maracaibo
Maracay
Caracas
Port-of-Spain
Colon
Merida
Barquisimeto
Guanare
Maturin
David
Cucuta
San Cristobal
Ciudad Bolivar
Puerto Ordaz
Georgetown
Paramaribo
Cayenne
Medellin
Bogota
Venezuela
Puerto Ayacucho
Santa Elena de Uairen
New Amsterdam
Guyana
Brokopondo
French Guiana
Manizales
Pereira
Cali
Ibague
Popayan
Colombia
Icana
Santa Isabel
Do Rio Negro
Barcelos
Sao Sebastiao
Oiapoque
Calcoene
Esmeraldas
Pasto
Mocoa
Araracuara
Cajal
Cucui
Porteira
Santarem
Monte Alegre
Altamira
Amapa
Macapa
Mazagao
Beiradao
Gurupa
Belem
Chaves
Salinopolis
Castanhal
Pinheiro
Sao Luis
Parnaiba
Fortaleza
Ecuador
Ibarra
Quito
Guayaquil
Manta
Machala
Cuenca
Loja
Iquitos
Nauta
Peru
Leticia
Atalaia Do Norte
Jaburu
Manaus
Amatari
Parintins
Tucurui
Vitorino Freire
Rosario
Codo
Tutoia
Sobral
Mossoro
Acu
Natal
Talara
Sullana
Sechura
Chiclayo
San Pedro de Lloc
Moyobamba
Chachapoyas
Cajamarca
Ipixuna
Eirunepe
Feijo
Tarauaca
Boca Do Acre
Humayta
Porto Velho
Borba
Maraba
Xambioa
Araguaina
Presidente Kennedy
Rondon Dopara
Caxias
Imperatriz
Teresina
Taua
Quixada
Oros
Patos
Joao Pessoa
Recife
Trujillo
Huaraz
Puerto Inca
Xapuri
Riberalta
Jaru
Ji-Parana
Peixoto De Azevedo
Juara
Colidor
S. Felix Do Araguaia
Novo Acordo
Brejo Da Serra
Petrolina
Parnamirim
Uaua
Garanhuns
Caruaru
Maceio
Chimbote
Cerro de Pasco
Satipo
Huancayo
Manu
Pucallpa
Rio Branco
Principe Da Beira
Colorado D'oeste
Sorriso
Porto Nacional
Sao Luzia
Natividade
Ibotirama
Alagoinha
Nova Taipe
Jequie
Alagoinhas
Salvador
Lima
Ica
Cuzco
Urcos
Paruro
Yanaoca
Sicuani
Juliaca
Moho
Puerto Maldonado
Santa Ana
Trinidad
San Ignacio
Nortelandia
Mara Rosa
Uruacu
Iaciara
Uberlandia
Itabuna
Ilheus
Tarma
Palpa
Pausa
Arequipa
Reyes
Caceres
Cuiaba
Anapolis
Luziania
Goiania
Brasilia
Otinolandia
Santa Cruz Cabralia
Prado
Tarata
La Paz
Cochabamba
Bolivia
Rondonopolis
Mirelivos
Itumbiara
Piracura
Montes Claros
Turmalina
Ataleia
Caravelas
Mucuri
Arica
Camina
Pisagua
Sucre
Vallegrande
Zudanez
Corumba
Cassilandia
Selvira
Belo Horizonte
Itabira
Governador Valadares
Iquique
Pica
Potosi
Cotagaita
Campo Grande
Ribeirao Preto
Franca
Vitoria
Tocopilla
Calama
Tupiza
Tarija
Paraguay
Antonio Joao
Maringa
Sao Carlos
Piracicaba
Campos
Mejillones
Baquedano
Tartagal
Concepcion
Ponta Pora
Perola
Londrina
Rio De Janeiro
Antofagasta
Chile
Salta
Rosario de la Frontera
Formosa
Pilar
Clevelandia
Chapeco
Ponta Grossa
Sao Paulo
Curitiba
Itajai
San Miguel de Tucuman
Resistencia
Corrientes
Lages
Florianopolis
Caldera
Punta de Diaz
Huasco
Frias
Las Garzas
Vera
Novo Hamburgo
Criciuma
Tramandai
Vallenar
La Rioja
Ceres
Morteros
Artigas
Rivera
Porto Alegre
Coquimbo
Salamanca
Ovalle
La Serena
San Juan
Cordoba
Santa Fe
Bage
Pelotas
Rio Grande
Valparaiso
Santiago
Rio Cuarto
Rosario
Uruguay
Melo
Florida
Santa Victoria Do Palmar
Rancagua
Buenos Aires
Montevideo
Concepcion
Talca
Chillan
Santa Rosa
Catriel
Villa Iris
Las Flores
Olavarria
Puan
Juarez
Pigue
Tandil
Los Angeles
Temuco
Neuquen
Villa Regina
Mar del Plata
Necochea
Valdivia
Villarrica
San Antonio Oeste
Punta Alta
Pedro Luro
Argentina
Osorno
Puerto Montt
Castro
Isla Grande de Chiloe
San Carlos de Bariloche
Puerto Madryn
Gaiman
Rawson
Viedma
Chaiten
Esquel
Jose de San Martin
Sarmiento
Comodoro Rivadavia
Caleta Olivia
Puerto Deseado
Puerto Aisen
Coihaique
Chile Chico
Perito Moreno
Las Horquetas
Isla Wellington
El Calafate
Rio Chico
Falkland Islands
Stanley
Puerto Natales
Rio Gallegos
Punta Arenas
Porvenir
Rio Grande
Tierra Del Fuego
Staten Island
Ushuaia
Puerto Williams
South Georgia
Grytviken

Brazil

MIDDLE EAST

589

WORLD TIME ZONES

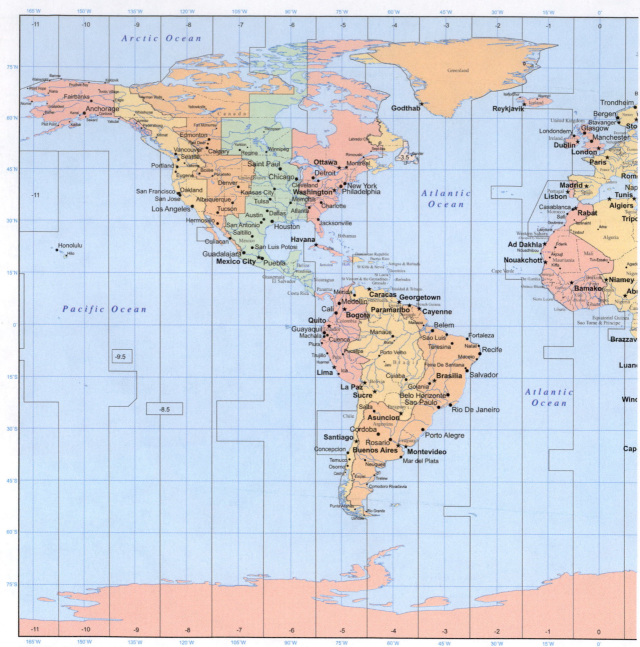

WORLD TERRAINS

Arctic Ocean

Svalbard

Franz Josef Land

Kara Sea

Laptev Sea

Barents Sea

New Siberian Islands

75

East Siberian Sea

Novaya Zemlya

Wrangel I.

Chukchi Sea

Hammerfest
Tromsø
Murmansk

Oulu
Severodvinsk
Archangel
Kozhva
Vorkuta

Umeå
Vaasa
Petrozavodsk

Oslo
Tampere
Helsinki
St. Petersburg

Stockholm
Tallinn
Riga
Moscow
Kostroma
Perm'
Yekaterinburg

R u s s i a

Nizhnevartovsk
Surgut

Krasnoyarsk

Yakutsk

Magadan

60

Bering Sea

Petropavlovsk-Kamchatskiy

Sea of Okhotsk

Ust-Kamchatsk

Sakhalin

Vilnius
Berlin
Minsk
Ryazan'
Penza
Omsk
Novosibirsk
Barnaul
Irkutsk
Ulan-Ude
Khabarovsk

Prague
Warsaw
Voronezh
Orenburg
Astana
Qaraghandy
Biysk

Bratislava
Kiev
Odesa

Budapest
Bucharest
Astrakhan'
Kizil-Tal
Ulan Bator
Qiqihar
Hegang

45

North Pacific Ocean

Sofia
Istanbul
Stavropol'
Tbilisi
Baku
Tashkent
Bishkek
Urumqi
Harbin
Jilin
Asahikawa
Sapporo

Athens
Ankara
Ashgabat
Dushanbe
Shenyang
Pyongyang
Seoul
Akita
Tokyo

Tehran
Islamabad
Shijiazhuang
Beijing
Pusan
Osaka

Beirut
Kabul
Lahore
Lanzhou
Jinan
Hiroshima

Baghdad
Ludhiana
Zhengzhou
Nanjing
Shanghai

Amman
Kerman
New Delhi
Thimphu
Chongqing
Hangzhou

Alexandria
Shiraz
Kathmandu
Guiyang
Taipei

Cairo
Riyadh
Abu Dhabi
Bhopal
Kunming
Hong Kong

Medina
Karachi
Dhaka
Hanoi

Jeddah
Muscat
Ahmadabad
Kolkata (Calcutta)
Yangon
Vientiane

Khartoum
San'a
Mumbai (Bombay)
Hyderabad
Manila
Catarman

El Obeid
Aden
Bangalore
Chennai (Madras)
Bangkok
Tacloban City

N'Djamena
Madurai
Phnom Penh
Ho Chi Minh City
Marawi

Abuja
Colombo
Kuala Lumpur

Bangui
Addis Ababa

Yaounde
Kampala
Mogadishu
Banjarmasin
Madang
Lae

Kinshasa
Nairobi
Surabaja
Dili
Mount Hagen
Port Moresby

Dodoma
Dar es Salaam
Jakarta
Darwin

Lubumbashi
Lilongwe
Antananarivo

Lusaka
Harare
Indian Ocean
Cairns
Coral Sea

Bulawayo
Windhoek
Port Hedland
Mackay
Brisbane

Gaborone
Pretoria
A u s t r a l i a
Rockhampton
City Of Gold Coast

Johannesburg
Maputo

Bloemfontein
Maseru
Perth
Whyalla
Sydney

Cape Town
East London
Port Elizabeth
Adelaide
Mildura
Canberra

Mount Gambier
Melbourne
Hamilton

Tasman Sea
Wellington
Christchurch

Invercargill
Dunedin

593

Glossary

A

absolute advantage 2-5 a situation that exists when a country can produce a good or service at a lower cost than other countries

account payable 7-3 amount owed to a supplier

account receivable 7-3 amount owed by a customer to a company that sells on credit

advertising 19-1 any form of paid, nonpersonal sales communication

advertising agency 19-2 a company that specializes in planning and implementing advertisements

AFL-CIO 12-2 an organization of American unions that uses its size and resources to influence legislation that affects its members

agent or broker 18-2 an intermediary that brings together buyers and sellers but does not take ownership of the products

arbitration 8-3 a method of conflict resolution that uses a neutral third party to make a binding decision

arbitrator 12-3 an unbiased third party called in to resolve problems whose decision is usually final and binding

autocratic managers 10-1 managers who centralize power and tell employees what to do

automated production 15-1 the production system in which machines perform the work

B

balance of payments 6-3 the total flow of money coming into a country minus the total flow going out

balance of trade 2-5 the difference between a country's exports and imports

balance sheet 9-3 the document that reports a company's assets, liabilities, and owner's equity

barter 7-1 the direct exchange of goods and services for other goods and services

bill of exchange 7-3 a written order by an exporter to an importer to make payment

bill of lading 6-2 a document stating the agreement between the exporter and the transportation company

body language 3-3 a type of nonverbal communication where meaning is conveyed by facial expressions, upper and lower body movements, and gestures

bond 7-3 a certificate representing money borrowed by a company over a long period of time

boycott 4-2 absolute restriction on the import of certain products from certain countries

brand 17-3 a name, symbol, or design that identifies a product

breakeven point 9-3 the number of units a business must sell to make a profit of zero

budget 9-3 a financial tool that estimates a company's funds and its plan for spending those funds

business plan 9-2 a guide used to start and operate a business

C

capital gain 21-3 the profit made from the resale of investments such as stocks, bonds, or real estate

capital project 7-3 an expensive, long-term financial activity

capitalism 2-3 the political and economic environment where a market economy exists

career 13-1 a commitment to a profession that requires continuing education and training and has a clear path for advancement

cash flow 9-3 the inflow and outflow of cash

central bank 20-3 state-owned agency that provides governments with banking services

centralization 14-2 information system in which most major decisions are made by managers at company headquarters

certificate of origin 6-2 a document that states the name of the country in which the shipped goods were produced

charter 5-1 the document granted by the state or federal government that allows a company to organize as a corporation

chief executive officer (CEO) 10-3 the highest manager within a company

civil law 8-1 a complete set of rules enacted as a single written system or code

class system 3-2 a means of dividing the members of a cultural group into various levels

closed shop 12-3 a workplace in which workers are required to join a union before they are hired

codetermination 12-2 a policy of having union members serve on the boards of directors

collective bargaining 12-2 negotiations between union workers and their employers on issues of wages, benefits, and working conditions

collectivism 3-4 the belief that the group is more important than the individual

command economy 2-3 the situation where the government or a central-planning committee regulates the amount, distribution, and price of everything produced

commercial bank 20-2 business organized to accept deposits and to make loans

commercial invoice 7-3 a certificate prepared by the exporter that provides a description of the merchandise and the terms of the sale

common law 8-1 a legal system that relies on the accumulation of decisions made in prior cases

common market 4-3 an agreement among countries that eliminates trade barriers, encourages investment, and allows workers to move freely across borders

communism 2-3 the political and economic environment where the government owns all the productive resources of the economy and a single party controls the government

comparability 14-2 the extent to which secondary data from different sources are measured, computed, and reported in the exact same ways

comparative advantage 2-5 a situation that exists when a country specializes in the production of a good or service at which it is relatively more efficient

computer-aided design (CAD) 15-1 using sophisticated computers that allow a designer to develop a very detailed design and key it to the CAM equipment specifications

computer-assisted manufacturing (CAM) 15-1 using computers to run production equipment

computer-integrated manufacturing (CIM) 15-1 using computers to guide the entire manufacturing process, from product design through processing, assembly, testing, and packaging

computerized production 15-1 using computers to control machines and perform work in the production process

consumer market 16-1 individuals and households who are the final users of goods and services

consumer price index (CPI) 2-5 the monthly United States federal government report on inflation

contexting 3-3 the level of how direct or indirect communication is

contract 8-2 a legally enforceable agreement between two or more persons either to do or not to do a certain thing or things

convenience goods 17-1 inexpensive items that require little shopping effort

cooperative 5-1 a business owned by its members and operated for their benefit

copyright 8-2 a legal right that protects the original works of authors, music composers, playwrights, artists, and publishers

corporate bond 21-2 a debt certificate issued by a multinational company or other corporate enterprise

corporation 5-1 a business that operates as a legal entity separate from any of the owners

cost and freight (C&F) 6-2 the price includes the cost of the goods and freight, but the buyer must pay for insurance separately

cost, insurance, and freight (CIF) 6-2 the cost of the goods, insurance, and freight are included in the price quoted

cost-push inflation 2-2 the situation when the expenses of a business increase

countertrade 6-3 the exchange of products or services among companies in different countries with the possibility of some currency exchange

cover letter 13-2 communicates your interest in a specific employment position

credit risk insurance 22-2 coverage for loss from nonpayment for delivered goods

credit terms 7-3 conditions of a sale on account including the time required for payment

credit union 20-2 a nonprofit financial cooperative

cultural baggage 3-1 the idea that you carry your beliefs, values, and assumptions with you at all times

culture 1-2, 3-1 the accepted behaviors, customs, and values of a society or a system of learned, shared, unifying, and interrelated beliefs, values, and assumptions

culture shock 3-4 a normal reaction to all of the differences of another culture

currency option 7-2 a contract a person or company buys that allows the buyer the option to purchase a foreign currency sometime in the future at today's rate

customs broker 18-2 an intermediary that specializes in moving goods through the customs process

customs official 6-1 government employee authorized to collect the duties levied on imports

D

data inputs 14-1 pieces of information that feed the global information system database

database marketing 19-2 the use of computerized information systems to identify customers with specific demographic traits and buying habits

debenture bond 21-2 corporate bond without collateral

debt capital 20-1 funds obtained by borrowing

debt funds 9-3 business funds obtained by borrowing

decentralization 14-2 information system in which most major decisions are made by local managers at different company locations around the world

deductible 22-2 the portion of an insurance claim paid by the insured

degree of centralization 10-3 the amount of authority and responsibility that is delegated to employees or to an organizational unit

demand 2-2 the relationship between the amount of a good or service that consumers are willing and able to purchase and the price

demand-pull inflation 2-2 the situation when demand exceeds supply

democracy 4-1 a political system in which all people have the opportunity to take part in making the rules that govern them

demographics 16-1 the traits of a country's population, such as birthrate, age distribution, marriage rate, gender distribution, education level, and housing situation

developing country 2-4 a country evolving from less developed to industrialized

development bank 20-3 an organization of several countries created to provide financing for economic development to countries in a region

direct barter 6-3 the exchange of goods and services between two parties with no money involved

direct distribution channel 18-2 producers sell goods and services directly to the final user

direct exporting 5-3 a company that actively seeks and conducts exporting

distribution 16-2 the activities needed to physically move and transfer ownership of goods and services from producer to consumer

distribution channel 18-2 the path taken by a good or service to get from the producer to the final user

dividends 5-1 a share of corporate earnings paid to stockholders

domestic business 1-1 making, buying, and selling goods and services within a country

dumping 18-1 the practice of selling exported products at a lower price than that asked in the company's home country

duty 4-2 a tax placed on products that are traded internationally

E

economic community 6-3 an organization of countries that bond together to allow a free flow of products

economic nationalism 4-2 a policy of restricting foreign ownership of local companies and hindering foreign imports

economic system 2-3 the method a country uses to answer the basic economic questions

economics 2-1 the study of how people choose to use limited resources to satisfy their unlimited needs and wants

electronic funds transfer (EFT) 7-3 a method of moving payments through banking computer systems

employment forecasting 11-2 estimating in advance the types and numbers of employees needed

endorsement 22-2 a certificate that adds to or changes the coverage of an insurance policy

entrepreneur 9-1 a risk taker who operates a business

equity capital 20-1 funds provided by a company's owners

equity funds 9-3 business funds obtained from the owners of the business

ethnocentric approach 11-1 the human resources approach that uses natives of the parent country of a business to fill key positions at home and abroad

ethnocentrism 3-4 the belief that one's culture is better than other cultures

Eurodollar 21-2 a U.S. dollar deposited in a bank outside of the United States and used in the money markets of Europe

exchange controls 7-2 government restrictions to regulate the amount and value of a nation's currency

exchange rate 7-1 the amount of currency of one country that can be traded for one unit of the currency of another country

expatriates 11-1 people who live and work outside their native countries

experiment 17-2 a type of data collection that involves a statistical comparison of two or more very similar situations

export management company (EMC) 18-2 a company that provides complete distribution services for businesses that desire to sell in foreign markets

export trading company (ETC) 18-2 a full-service global distribution intermediary

exports 1-2 products sold in other countries

expropriation 4-2 when a government takes control and ownership of foreign-based assets and companies

extended family 3-2 a group that consists of the parents, children, and other relatives living together

F

factors of production 2-3 the three types of resources used to produce goods and services

fixed costs 9-3 expenses that do not change as the level of production changes

floating exchange rates 7-2 system in which currency values are based on supply and demand

focus groups 17-2 a directed discussion with 8 to 12 people

foreign debt 2-5 the amount a country owes to other countries

foreign direct investment (FDI) 5-3 the purchase of land or other resources in a foreign country

foreign exchange 7-1 the process of converting the currency of one country into the currency of another country

foreign exchange market 7-2 the network of banks and other financial institutions that buy and sell different currencies

foreign exchange rate 2-5 the value of one country's money in relation to the value of the money of another country

franchise 5-3 the right to use a company name or business process in a specific way

free on board (FOB) 6-2 terms of sale that mean the selling price of the product includes the cost of loading the exported goods into transport vessels at the specified place

free-rein managers 10-1 managers who avoid the use of power

free-trade agreement 4-3 an arrangement between countries that eliminates duties and trade barriers on products traded among themselves

free-trade zone 4-3 a designated area where products can be imported duty-free

freight forwarder 6-2, 18-2 a company that arranges to ship goods to customers in other countries

front-line managers 10-3 managers who oversee the day-to-day operations in specific departments

futures market 21-2 a market that allows investors and others to buy or sell

contracts on the future price of commodities, metals, and financial instruments

G

geocentric approach 11-1 the human resources approach that uses the best available managers without regard for their countries of origin

global dependency 1-1 a condition that exists when items consumers need and want are created in other countries

global information system 14-1 a computer-based system that provides information about company operations around the world to managers of a multinational organization

global product 17-3 standardized item offered in the same form in all countries in which it is sold

grievance procedure 12-3 the steps that must be followed to resolve a complaint by an employee, the union, or the employer

gross domestic product (GDP) 2-5 a measure of the output of a country within its borders, including items produced with foreign resources

gross national product (GNP) 2-5 a measure of the total value of all goods and services produced by the resources of a country

gross profit 9-3 the difference between the cost of an item for a business and the price for which the business can sell that item

H

hard currency 7-2 a monetary unit that is freely converted into other currencies

home country 4-1 the country in which a multinational enterprise is headquartered

host country 4-1 the country in which a multinational enterprise is a guest

host-country nationals or locals 11-1 natives of the country in which they work

I

icons 14-1 symbols that are meaningful across cultures

imports 1-2 products bought from businesses in other countries

income statement 9-3 a document that summarizes a company's revenue from sales and its expenses over a period of time

indirect distribution channel 18-2 goods or services are sold with the use of one or more intermediaries between the producer and the consumer

indirect exporting 5-3 the selling of a company's products in a foreign market without any special activity for that purpose

individualism 3-4 the belief in the individual and his or her ability to function relatively independently

industrialized country 2-4 a country with strong business activity that is usually the result of advanced technology and a highly educated population

industry 6-4 a group of companies in the same type of business

inflation 2-2 an increase in the average prices of goods and services in a country

informational interview 13-1 a meeting with another person to gather information about a career or organization

infrastructure 2-4 a nation's transportation, communication, and utility systems

injunction 12-2 a court order that immediately stops a party from carrying out a specific action

inland marine insurance 22-3 protection from loss while shipping goods on inland waterways, railroad lines, truck lines, and airlines

insurance 22-2 planned protection for sharing economic losses among many people

insurance certificate 7-3 a certificate explaining the amount of insurance coverage for fire, theft, water, or other damage that may occur to goods in shipment

insurance policy 22-2 the legal agreement between an insurance company and the insured

intellectual property 8-2 the technical knowledge or creative work that an individual or company has developed

interest rate 7-1 the cost of using someone else's money

intermediary 18-2 any person or organization in the distribution channel that moves goods and services from the producer to the consumer

international business 1-1 all business activities needed to create, ship, and sell goods and services across national borders

International Court of Justice 8-3 a court that settles disputes between nations when both nations request that it do so and also advises the United Nations on matters of international law

international marketing 16-1 marketing activities among sellers and buyers in different countries

International Monetary Fund (IMF) 7-2 an agency that helps to promote economic cooperation by maintaining an orderly system of world trade and exchange rates

international product 17-3 a customized product adapted to the culture, tastes, and social trends of a country

inventory control 15-1 a method of monitoring the amount of raw materials and completed goods on hand

J

job 13-1 an employment position obtained mainly for money

job description 11-2 a document that includes the job identification, job statement, job duties and responsibilities, and job specifications and requirements

joint venture 5-3 an agreement between two or more companies to share a business project

L

labor union 12-2 an organization of workers whose goals are improving members' working conditions, wages, and benefits

less-developed country (LDC) 2-4 a country with little economic wealth and an emphasis on agriculture or mining

letter of credit 7-3 a financial document issued by a bank for an importer in which the bank guarantees payment

liability 8-1 a broad legal term referring to almost every kind of responsibility, duty, or obligation

licensing 5-3 selling the right to use some intangible property for a fee or royalty

limited liability 5-1 the situation in which a business owner is only responsible for the debts of the business up to the amount invested

lines of authority 10-3 indicate who is responsible for whom and for what in an organization

liquidity 21-3 the ability to easily convert an asset into cash without a loss in value

litigation 8-3 a lawsuit brought about to enforce the rights of a person or an organization or to seek a remedy to the violation of their rights

localized advertising 19-2 the use of promotions that are customized for various target markets

lockout 12-3 the closing down of a workplace by an employer to force a union to agree to certain demands

loss leader 18-1 a very low-priced item used to attract customers to a store

M

management contract 5-3 an agreement under which a company sells only its management skills in another country

managers 10-1 the people in charge of organizations and their resources

manual production 15-1 using human hands and bodies as the means of transforming resources into goods and services

market 16-1 the likely customers for a good or service in a certain geographic location

market economy 2-3 the situation where individual companies and consumers make the decisions about what, how, and for whom items will be produced

market price 2-2 the point at which supply and demand cross

market segment 16-3 a distinct subgroup of customers who share certain personal or behavioral characteristics

marketing 9-2 the business activities necessary to get goods and services from the producer to the consumer

marketing mix 16-2 the four major marketing elements of product, price, distribution, and promotion

marketing plan 9-2 a document that details the marketing activities of an organization

marketing research 17-2 the orderly collection and analysis of data in order to obtain information about a specific marketing concern

markup 18-1 the amount added to the cost of a product to determine the selling price

mediation 8-3 a dispute resolution method that makes use of a neutral third party

middle managers 10-3 managers who oversee the work and departments of a number of front-line managers

migrant laborers 12-1 people who move to another country for work

mixed economy 2-3 the situation with a blend between government involvement in business and private ownership

money 7-1 anything people will accept for the exchange of goods and services

monopolistic competition 6-4 a market situation with many sellers, each with a slightly different product

monopoly 6-4 a situation in which one seller controls the entire market for a product or service

mortgage bond 21-2 debt secured by a specific asset or property

most-favored nation (MFN) status 4-3 designation that allows a country to export into the granting country under the most favorable trade conditions that the importing country offers to any of its trading partners

multinational company or corporation (MNC) 5-2 an organization that conducts business in several countries

municipal bond 21-2 a debt certificate issued by a state or local government agency

municipal corporation 5-2 an incorporated town or city organized to provide services for citizens rather than to make a profit

mutual fund 20-2 an investment company that manages a pool of funds from many investors

mutual insurance company 22-2 an insurance company owned by its policyholders

N

negligence 8-1 the failure of a responsible party to follow standards of due care

net income or profit 5-1 the difference between money taken in and expenses

nonprofit corporation 5-2 groups created to provide a service and not concerned with making a profit

nonverbal communication 3-3 communication that does not involve the use of words

nuclear family 3-2 a group that consists of a parent or parents and unmarried children living at home together

O

observational research 17-2 data collected by watching and recording shopping behaviors

ocean marine insurance 22-3 protection from loss while goods are being shipped overseas and while temporarily in port

oligopoly 6-4 control of an industry by a few large companies

open shop 12-3 a workplace in which workers may choose to join the union or not

operational components 14-1 the parts of an information system that manage the database and system operations

operations management 15-1 the process of designing and managing a production system

opportunity cost 2-1 the most attractive alternative given up when a choice is made

organizational chart 10-2 a drawing that shows the structure of an organization

organizational market 16-1 buyers who purchase items for resale or additional production

outsourcing 15-1 the transfer of a business function outside of the company

over-the-counter (OTC) market 21-2 a network of stockbrokers who buy and sell stocks not listed on a stock exchange

P

parent-country nationals or home-country nationals 11-1 expatriates from the country in which their company is headquartered

participative managers 10-1 managers who decentralize power and share it with employees

partnership 5-1 a business that is owned by two or more people, but is not incorporated

passport 13-2 a government document proving the bearer's citizenship in the country that issues it

patent 8-2 the grant of an exclusive right of an inventor to make, sell, and use a product or process

penetration pricing 18-1 setting a relatively low introductory price for a new product

personal selling 19-1 direct communication between sellers and potential customers

political risk 4-2 the possibility of government actions or political policies that could adversely affect foreign companies

political system 4-1 the means by which people in a society make the rules that control and influence their lives

polycentric approach 11-1 the human resources approach that uses natives of the host country to manage operations within their country and parent-country natives to manage at headquarters

premium 22-2 the cost of insurance

price 16-2 the monetary value of a product agreed upon by a buyer and a seller

primary data 14-2 data collected by the user firsthand for a specific purpose

privatization 2-3 the process of changing an industry from publicly to privately owned

product 16-2 an item (good or service) being offered for sale that satisfies consumer demand

product liability 8-1 specific responsibility that both manufacturers and sellers have for the safety of their products

product life cycle (PLC) 17-3 the stages a good or service goes through from the time it is introduced until it is taken off the market

product line 17-1 an assortment of closely related products designed to meet the varied needs of target customers

production process 15-1 the means by which a company changes raw materials into finished goods

productivity 15-2 the amount of work that is accomplished in a unit of time

promissory note 7-3 a document that states a promise to pay a set amount by a certain date

promotion 16-2 the marketing efforts that inform and persuade customers

promotional mix 19-1 the combination of advertising, personal selling, publicity, and sales promotion used by an organization

property 8-2 everything that can be owned

property rights 8-2 exclusive rights to possess and use property and its profits, to exclude everyone else from interfering with it, and to dispose of it in any legal way

protectionism 4-2 a government policy of protecting local or domestic industries from foreign competition

psychographics 16-3 buying factors related to lifestyle and psychological influences, such as activities, interests, and opinions

publicity 19-1 any form of unpaid promotion

pull promotions 19-1 marketing efforts directed at the final users of an item

pure competition 6-4 a market situation with many sellers, each offering the same product

push promotions 19-1 marketing efforts directed at members of the distribution channel

Q

qualitative research 17-2 using open-ended interview questions to obtain comments from consumers about their attitudes and behaviors

quality circle 15-2 a small group of employees who have different jobs within the same company but have the same goal of producing a quality good or service

quality control 15-2 process of measuring goods and services against a product standard

quantitative research 17-2 large-scale surveys that collect numeric data used to study consumers

quota 4-2 a limit on the total number, quantity, or monetary amount of a product that can be imported from a given country

R

references 13-2 people who can report to a prospective employer about your abilities and work experience

regiocentric approach 11-1 the human resources approach that uses managers from various countries within the geographic regions of a business

relationship marketing 19-3 an attempt to create a long-term, mutually beneficial buyer-seller relationship

reliability 14-2 the consistency of the gathered data

repatriation 11-4 the process a person goes through when returning home and getting settled after having worked abroad

resume 13-2 a written summary of a person's education, training, work experience, and other job qualifications

retailer 18-2 a store or other business that sells directly to the final user

risk 22-1 the uncertainty of an event or outcome

robotics 15-1 the technology connected with the design, construction, and operation of robots

robots 15-1 computerized output devices that can perform difficult, repetitive, or dangerous work in industrial settings

S

sales promotion 19-1 marketing activities other than advertising, personal selling, and publicity

savings and loan association 20-2 a financial institution that traditionally specialized in savings accounts and home mortgages

scarcity 2-1 the limited resources available to satisfy the unlimited needs and wants of people

screening interview 13-2 an initial meeting or telephone call to select finalists for an available position

secondary data 14-2 data not collected by the user but that are available for his or her use

selection interview 13-2 a meeting where a person is asked a series of in-depth questions designed to help employers select the best person for the job

self-insurance 22-1 setting aside money to cover a potential financial loss

senior managers 10-3 managers who oversee the work and departments of a number of middle managers

shopping goods 17-1 products purchased after consumers compare brands and stores

skim pricing 18-1 setting a relatively high introductory price for a new product

small business 9-1 an independently owned and operated business that does not dominate an industry

social responsibility 4-1 the process when people function as good citizens who are sensitive to their surroundings

socialism 2-3 the political and economic system with most basic industries owned and operated by government with the government controlled by the people as a whole

soft currency 7-2 a currency that is not easy to exchange for other currencies

sole proprietorship 5-1 a business owned by one person

span of control 10-3 the number of employees that a manager supervises

specialty goods 17-1 unique products that consumers make a special effort to obtain

standardized advertising 19-2 the use of one promotional approach in all geographic regions

statutes 8-1 laws that have been enacted by a body of lawmakers

stock exchange 21-1 a location where stocks are bought and sold

stock insurance company 22-2 an insurance company owned by stockholders and operated for profit

stockbroker 21-1 a person who buys and sells stocks and other investments for customers

stockholders or shareholders 5-1 the owners of a corporation

strict liability 8-1 responsibility on a manufacturer or seller for intentionally causing injury to another

strike 12-3 a refusal by employees to work in order to force an employer to agree to certain demands

subculture 3-1 a subset or part of a larger culture

supply 2-2 the relationship between the amount of a good or service that businesses are willing and able to make available and the price

supply analysis 11-2 determining if there are sufficient types and numbers of employees available

supply chain 15-2 network of people, resources, technology, and information using a sequence of steps from raw materials to a final product or service

synchronized manufacturing 15-2 system where the workflow is distributed as needed throughout the production cycle

system outputs 14-1 the various types of data generated from an information system

T

tailored logistics 15-2 the system where services are combined with a product to better serve consumers

target market 16-3 the particular market segment that a company plans to serve

tax holiday 4-3 situation where a corporation does not pay corporate income taxes to a foreign government if it invests in their country

tax-deferred income 21-2 income that will be taxed at a later date

tax-exempt income 21-2 income not subject to tax

telecommuting 9-1 using a computer and other technology to work at home instead of in a company office or factory

telemarketing 19-3 the selling of products during telephone calls to prospective customers

test market 17-2 an experimental research study that measures the likely success of a new good or service

third-country nationals 11-1 expatriates from countries other than the home country of their company or the host country

total quality control (TQC) 15-2 a work approach that requires every employee to take responsibility for high-quality production

totalitarian system 4-1 a government system in which political control is held by one person, a small group of people, or one political party

trade barriers 1-2 restrictions that reduce free trade among countries

trade credit 7-3 buying or selling on account

trade deficit 6-3 the result of importing more goods and services than the country is exporting

trade surplus 6-3 the result of exporting more goods and services than the country is importing

trade embargo 4-2 a sanction imposed by a country against another country that stops all import-export trade with that country

trademark 8-2 a distinctive name, symbol, word, picture, or combination of these that is used by a business to identify its services or products

transformation 15-1 the use of resources to create a good or service

U

union representation election 12-3 a procedure held to find out if the workers in a workplace really want to become union members

union shop 12-3 a workplace in which all workers must pay either union dues or a fee

unlimited liability 5-1 the situation in which a business owner's personal assets can be used to pay any debts of the business

V

validity 14-2 the extent to which the data measures what the user expects it to measure

value-added tax (VAT) 4-2 a tax assessed on the increase in value of goods from each stage of production to final consumption

variable costs 9-3 business expenses that change in proportion to the level of production

visa 13-2 a stamp of endorsement issued by a country that allows a passport holder to enter that country

W

wholesaler 18-2 a business that buys large quantities of an item and resells them to a retailer

wholly-owned subsidiary 5-3 an independent company owned by a parent company

work visa (work permit) 13-2 a document that allows a person into a foreign country for the purpose of employment

World Bank 7-2 a bank whose major function is to provide economic assistance to less-developed countries

Index

A

"Ability to pay" principle, 95
Absolute advantage, 45
Accidental exporting, 127
Account payable, 181
Account receivable, 181
Achievers, 423
Adaptability, employee, 282–283
Advertising, 486
    analyze target market, 491
    create message, 491
    execute and evaluate, 494
    planning, 490–494
    select media, 492
    specialty, 500
    standardized, 491
Advertising agency, 494
Advertising message, 491
AFL. *See* American Federation of Labor (AFL)
AFL-CIO, 312–313
Africa, 9–11
    apartheid, 359
    and banking, 524, 527
    business potential and challenges, 359
    country profile, 359
    design elements and information systems, 367
    early civilizations, 358
    European control, 358
    and food crops, 9
    freedom, 358
    geography, 357
    Great Sphinx of Giza, 357
    Mauritania, 381
    Regional Profile, 357–359
    religion and art, 358
    and slavery, 4
African Development Bank, 527
Agents, 466
Agricultural company, 219
Agricultural dependency, 41
Air carrier, 475
Altech ISIS (ISIS), 361
Amazon.com, 219
American Arbitration Association, 319
American Federation of Labor (AFL), 312
American Jewelry Machines, 387

Antidumping laws, 463
Antidumping tariffs, 463
Apartheid, 359
Appearance, 70
Application form, 340–341
Application systems, 365
Applying for a job, 338–342
Arbitration, 205
Arbitrator, 205, 319
Argentina, 9, 43
ASEAN. *See* Association of Southeast Asian Nations (ASEAN)
Asia, common entrepreneurial business, 218
Asian banking, 524, 527
Asian Development Bank, 527
Asian immigrants, 4
Asian names, 157
Asia-Pacific Rim, 109–111
    China, oldest civilization, 109–110
    country profile, 111
    Down Under, 111
    early Asian civilizations, 109
    Japan, from isolation to global economy, 110
    region of contrasts, 111
    Southeast Asian Peninsula, 110–111
Asian Development Bank (ADB), 527
Assets, 231
Association of Southeast Asian Nations (ASEAN), 153
ATM. *See* Automatic teller machine (ATM)
ATMobiles (portable cash machines), 469
Attitudes, 346–347, 387
Audience (receiver), 484
Australia, 39, 111, 307, 321. *See also* Asia-Pacific Rim
Authoritarian society, 75
Authority, power, leadership and, 75
Autocratic manager, 249
Automated order-taking system, 392
Automated production systems, 386

Automated warehouses, 386–387
Automatic teller machine (ATM), 469
Automatic vending, 469
Avon, 475
Aztec Empire, 3, 5
Aztec women, 3

B

Babawatoto web site, 12
Balanced fund, 522
Balance of payments, 150–151, 171
Balance of trade, 47, 150
Balance sheet, 231
banking, 524–528
banner ads, 493
Barriers to entry, 157
Barter, 169
Barter agreements, 153–154
Base salary, 294
basic economic problem, 28
B2B. *See* Business-to-business (B2B)
Belgium, 92
beliefs, 58
Benson Electric Company, 30
Berlin Wall, 243, 468
Berne Convention of 1886, 201
the "Big Mac Index," 49
Bill of exchange, 182
Bill of lading, 147, 180, 473
BizPlanIt, 256
Black market, 561
Body language, 70
Bond, 182, 541–543
Bond market, 541–543
Bonds, 182, 541–543
    corporate, 541
    external, 543
    federal government, 542
    foreign government, 542–543
    government, 542–543
    internal, 543
    municipal, 542
    state and local government, 542
Boycott, 93
Branding, 446–447
Brand names, 191
Brands, types of, 446
Brands, virtual, 449

Brazil
    colonial heritage of, 11
    domain name (.br) for, 48
    exchange rate for, 170
    flexible scheduling in, 470
    per capital GDP for, 46
    .br (Brazil), 48
Brazil, Russia, India, and China.
    See BRIC countries
Breakeven point, 230
breakfast foods industry, 407
BRIC countries, 9
Britain, exchange rate for, 170. See
    also United Kingdom
British Airways, 536
British Telecom (BT), 364
Broker, 466
Brown, Gordon, 315
Budget, 229
Building Society, 520
Bureau of Labor Statistics, 442
Bureau of the Census, 442
Business loan, 181
Business owner. See Entrepreneur
Business ownership, methods
    of, 114–119
    corporation, 117–118
    other forms of, 119
    partnership, 116
    sole proprietorship, 114–115
Business plan, 225–226
    create, 225–227
    defined, 225
    parts of, 225–226
Business subcultures, 60, 69
Business-to-business (B2B), 220, 409
Button ads, 493
Buying behavior, 422–424
Byzantine Empire, 244

C
.ca (Canada), 48
Cable television, 414
CAD. See Computer-aided design
    (CAD)
CAM. See Computer-assisted
    manufacturing (CAM)
Cambodia, 11
Canada, 4–5. See also North
    America
    balance of trade for, 47
    branches of U.S. unions in, 311

colonial heritage of, 11
consumer protection laws, 92
domain name (.ca) for, 48
exchange rate for, 170
and free enterprise, 39
French heritage of, 4
and Great Britain, 4
handshaking code, 72
and immigrants, 4
and international business, 8
natural resources of, 20, 45
per capital GDP for, 46
size of, 5
Canadian handshaking code, 72
Capital, 36
Capital gain, 547–548
Capital markets, 515
Capital project, 182, 517
Capital resources, 36–37, 383.
    See also Resources
Capitalism, 38
Career objective, for resume, 338
Career(s), 331
    changing, 345
    cover letter, 340
    definition of, 331
    factors influencing selection
        of, 334–335
    future jobs, 344–348
    importance of, 330
    information, 332–333
    international, 50, 329, 345–348
    and internet, 333, 335
    interviewing, 340, 341–342
    job, applying, 338–342
    opportunities, 334–336
    options, 344–345
    planning for, 330–336
    resume, 338–339
Career planning, 330–336
    advancement, 344–345
    developing, 344–345
    develop relevant knowledge,
        skills and attitudes, 346
    exploring relevant information,
        332–333
    factors influencing career
        selection, 334–335
    five steps in, 330–332
    foundation skills, 345–346
    identifying opportunities, 331
    importance of, 330

international experience,347
language skills, 346
networking, 348
preparing for international,
    345–348
Carrefour, 7
Case law, 194
Cash discounts, 462
Cash flow, 231
Cash flow statement, 231
Cash in advance, 180
Cash inflows, 231
Cash outflows, 231
Caste system, 65
Causal exporting, 127
CD-ROM drive, 401
Cellular phone, 393
Central bank, 525–526
Central planning, 38
Central and South America,
    403–405
    colonization, 404
    country profile, 405
    economic growth, 405
    geography, 403
    industries, 405
    Mayan and Incan Empires, 404
    struggle for independence,
        404–405
Centralization of authority, 371
CEO. See Chief executive officer
    (CEO)
Cereal Partners Worldwide
    (CPW), 130
Certificates of deposit (CDs), 515
Certificate of origin, 147, 473
C&F. See Cost and freight (C&F)
CFI. See Cost, insurance, and
    freight (CIF)
Chad, 11
Chamber of Commerce, 333
Changing exchange rates, 174–175
Changing prices, 34
Charter, 118
Chief executive officer
    (CEO), 262
Child laborers, 319
Child-worker union, 319
Chile, 9
China, 10, 75, 93
    exchange rate, 170
    internet firewall, 374

leadership, power, and authority in, 75

as oldest civilization, 109–110

problems using technology in, 374

trade sanctions, 93

Christianity, 71, 510

CIM. *See* Computer-integrated manufacturing (CIM)

CIO. *See* Committee for Industrial Organizations (CIO)

Citizen, role of, 19

Civil law, 193

Civil war, 94

Class, in litigation, 206

Class-action suit, 206

Class system, 65

Closed shop, 318

Coca-Cola Company, 409, 468, 490

Code law, 193

Codetermination, 312

Coffee, 8

Coke *vs.* Pepsi, 468

Colgate, 498

Collective bargaining, 310

Collectivism, 74

Colonization, 11, 404

Color, 71

.com (commercial organizations), 48

Command economies, 38, 87

Commercial bank, 519–520

Commercial invoice, 183

Commercial loan, 181

Commercial market, 409

Commercial organization domain name (.com), 48

Commercial services, 415, 435–436

Committee for Industrial Organizations (CIO), 313

Common law, 193–194

Common market, 98, 152

Communication, 67–72. *See also* Language(s)

direct and indirect, 69–70

employee, 255

importing error, 140

language differences, 67

nonverbal, 70–72

Communication Across Borders features

Asian names, 157

Canadian handshaking code, 72

clothing and communication, 538

company language, 234

and customer language, 436

contract, 202

culture, tradition, and production methods, 387

evaporating e-mail, 365

flexible scheduling in Brazil, 470

Komatsu abandons Japanese for English, 122

language, 570

language and business risk, 570

local standards of professional dress, 347

phrasing and dialect differences, 436

reliability of technology, 365

Saudi financiers, 538

turning away from technology, 387

Communication outputs, 365

Communication process, 484–485

Communication technology, 373

Communism, 38

Comparability, of data, 372

Comparative advantage, 45

Compensating employees, 294–295

Competence, employee, 282

Competition, 411, 459–460, 463

benefits and concerns, 158

factors effecting, 157

nature, 156–160

and price planning, 459

types, 158–160

Competitive advantage, 156

Competitive pricing, 460

Competitive situations, 158–160

Computer-aided design (CAD), 386

Computer-assisted manufacturing (CAM), 386

Computer-integrated manufacturing (CIM), 387

Computerized production systems, 386

Computerized stock trading stock exchanges, 538

Conditions, of insurance policy, 565

Confidential information, sharing, 250

Conservative Party, 315

Consumer, role of, 19

Consumer behavior, 421–422

factors affecting, 421–422

geographic and demographic factors, 421–422

personality and psychographic factors, 422

physical and emotional needs, 421

social and cultural factors, 422

Consumer demand, 459

Consumer markets, 409

Consumer price index (CPI), 49

Consumer products, 433–434

Consumer protection laws, 91–92

Consumer services, 415, 435–436

Consumption tax, 95

Containerization, 474

Contests, 486–487, 500

Contexting, 69

Continuing entity, 118

Continuing expenses, 230

Contract, 201–202

Contract law, 201

Contract manufacturing, 127

Convenience goods, 433

Convenience stores, 417, 467

Convicts, Australia's beginning with, 111

Cooperative, 119, 520

Copyright notice, 200–201

Corporate bonds, 541

Corporate income tax, 95

Corporate notations, 118

Corporation, 117–118

Cost, insurance, and freight (CIF), 145

Cost and freight (C&F), 145

Cost-of-living adjustment, 294–295

Cost-push inflation, 34

Costs, 458–459. *See also* Funds

fixed, 230

long-term, 517

opportunity, 30

and price planning, 458–459

start-up, 229

training, 230
variable, 230
Counterfeit products, 200
Countertrade, 153–154, 463
Country Profile features
Africa, 359
Asia-Pacific Rim, 111
Central and South America, 405
Europe, 245
Near and Middle East, 511
North America, 5
Coupons, 500
Cover letter, 340
CPI. *See* Consumer price index (CPI)
CPW. *See* Cereal Partners Worldwide (CPW)
Creating and delivering services, 391–392
Credit risk insurance, 570–571
Credit terms, 181
Credit union, 119, 520
Cross-cultural financial advisors, 528
Cross-cultural interviewing, 340
Cross-cultural training, 287
Cross-functional team, 391
Cuba, 38, 87
Cultural baggage, 59
Cultural differences
influences of, 76–78
and management style, 25
Cultural employee motivation, 292–293
Cultural factors, and business, 17
Cultural influence, 58–59
Cultural and social organizations, 62–65
Cultural values, 74–76
Culturally sensitive compensation package, 294
Cultural sensitivity, 77
Culture(s), 17, 58. *See also* Communication; Language(s)
adjusting to differences in, 76–78
and business, 17
communication across, 67–72
and contexting, 69–70
defined, 58

exporting, 146
high-context, 69–70
language differences, 67
low-context, 69–70
reactions to difference in, 77
social organizations and, 62–65
subcultures, 59–60
values among, 74–76
Culture shock, 77. *See also* Reverse culture shock
Currency, 174. *See also* Money
changing value of, 171, 175
names around the world, 184
printing additional, 175
soft and hard, 174
transactions between nations, 180–184
change in values, 170, 175, 177, 178
Currency future, 176
Currency option, 176
Currency transactions, 180–184
Current expenses, 517
Current income, 547
Custom house broker, 470
Customers, 144, 496–497
feedback from, 497
finding potential, 144
meeting needs of, 144–145
Customer service, 498
Customized product, 59, 449
Customs, 140
Customs broker, 470
Customs Department of the U.S. Treasury, 140
Customs duty, 94
Customs official, 140
Cyprus, 11
Czech Republic, 7, 9

D
Data
collection issues, 371–372
database management, 364, 372
inputs, 364
and market research, 442–444
quality, 372
sources, 371
Database management, 364, 372
Database marketing, 493

Data collection, 371–372
Data comparability, 372
Data inputs, 364
Data reliability, 372
Data validity, 372
Debenture bond, 541
Debt capital, 516
Debt funds, 230
Decentralization, of authority, 371
Decision making, 28–30
Declaration, 565
Decline stage, of product life cycle, 448–449
Decoding, 484
Deductible premium, 565
.de (Germany), 48
Degree of centralization, 263
Delegation of authority and responsibility, 262–263
Demand, 33
Demand-pull inflation, 34
Democracy, 86
Demographics, 411
Denmark, 11
Department of Agriculture. *See* U.S. Department of Agriculture (USDA)
Deposit-type financial institution, 519–521
Destination control statement, 473
Developing country, 43, 124
Development banks, 526–527
Dictatorship, 87
Dictionary of Occupational Titles, 332
Diplomatic immunity, 193
Direct barter, 153
Direct communication, 69–70
Direct distribution channel, 465
Direct exporting, 127, 143
Direct mail, 492–493
Direct sellers, 468
Direct selling, 468
Discount broker, 538
Discount pricing, 462
Disneyland, 57, 128
Disneyland Paris, 57
Dispute resolution across borders, 207
Distribution, 415

Distribution activities, 465–470
  distribution channel members, 466–469
  distribution channels, 465–466
  global intermediaries, 466
Distribution channel, 465
  Distribution channel members, 466–469
  agents, 466
  retailers, 467
  wholesalers, 466–467
Diversification, 521
Dividends, 117
Dobriski Enterprises, 264
Documentation, 473–474
Dollar. *See* U.S. dollar
Domain names, international, 48
Domestic business, 8
Domestic company, 93–94, 264–265
Domestic employment market, 332
Domestic market, 156
Double taxation, 100, 118
Double-taxation avoidance treaties, 100
Down Under, 111
Dual economies, 27
Dumping, 463
DuPont, 499
Duty, 92. *See also* Customs duty; Import tax
DVD, 393

E
E-brands, 449
E-mail blast, 493
E-payment, 522
E-post, 522
E-tailer, 144, 387
E*trade, 550
Economic community, 152–153
Economic Community of West African States (ECOWAS), 153
Economic conditions, 171–172
Economic Contract Law code, 205
Economic decisions, 28–30
Economic development, 41–43
  factors, 41
  levels, 43
  types, 42–43

Economic nationalism, 94
Economic problems, 28
Economic progress, 46–50
Economic resources, 36–37. *See also* Resources
Economic risk, 559–560
Economics
  basics, 32–35
  defined, 28
  measurements of, 49
  of Middle East, 528–529
Economic systems, 36–39
  defined, 38
  and factors of production, 36–37
  types, 38
Economics
  basics, 32–34
  conditions, 18
  and decision making, 28–30
  definition, 28
  of foreign trade, 45
  measuring progress, 46–50
  and resources, 36–37
  systems of, 36–39
Economies, command, 38, 87
Economies of foreign trade, 45
The Economist, 49
ECOWAS. *See* Economic Community of West African States (ECOWAS)
Ecuador, 403
.edu (educational institutions), 48
Education, 63–64
Educational agencies domain name (.edu), 48
EFT. *See* Electronic funds transfer (EFT)
Egypt, 9
Elections, 317–318
Electronic funds transfer (EFT), 182
El Salvador, 11
Emblems, 71–72
EMC. *See* Export management company (EMC)
Employee
  benefits, 295
  compensation, 294–295
  evaluating performance, 295
  failure, 289–290
  hiring, 281–284

  motivation, 292–293
  repatriation, 296
  training, 286–290
Employee benefits, 295
Employee performance evaluation, 295
Employees, failure of global, 289–290. *See also* Staff
Employment forecasting, 281
Encoding, 484
Endorsement, 565
England, 9, 77
English language, 67–68, 122
Entrepreneur
  definition of, 217
  economic importance of, 216
  enterprises of, 216–220
  and exporting, 218
  and internet, 219
  operating enterprises, 229–234
  social entrepreneurship, 215
  street entrepreneurs, 224
  successful, 224–225
  types of business, 219–221
  women in Niger, 233
Entrepreneurial business, types of, 219–221
Entrepreneurial enterprises, 216–220
  operating, 229–234
  types, 219
Entrepreneurial infrastructure, 42
Entrepreneurial spirit, 75
Environmental factors, of international business, 16–18
Equilibrium price, 33
Equity capital, 516
Equity courts, 194
Equity funds, 230
E-tailing, 144, 387
ETC. *See* Export trading company (ETC)
Ethics. *See* Question of Ethics features
Ethiopia, 47
Ethnocentric approach, 276
Ethnocentrism, 76–77
EU. *See* European Union (EU)
Euro, 153, 543
Eurocurrency, 544
Euro Disneyland, 57
Eurodollar, 543

Europe
  attempts to control, 244
  Byzantine Empire, 244
  colonization, 11
  common entrepreneurial
    business, 218
  conflicts between ethnic groups,
    244
  contributions to civilization,
    245
  country profile, 245
  ethnic conflicts, 244
  exploration of North
    America, 4
  history, 243–244
  and international business, 8
  history of international
    business, 10–11
  labor groups in, 311, 314
  regional profile, 243–245
  Roman Empire, 192, 193, 243
  training and development from
    employers, 287
European Central Bank, 245
European Monetary Union
  (EMU), 525–526
European Patent Organization,
  200
European Union (EU), 12, 98,
  153, 202, 245
  and banking, 524–525
  as common market, 98, 153
  creation of, 12
  elimination of trade barriers,
    245
  exchange rate for, 170
  labor union membership, 314
  trademarks and, 199–200
Evaluation. See Employee
  performance evaluation
Exchange controls, 176
Exchange rates, 170–171
  changing, 174–175
  for selected countries, 170
Excise tax, 95
Exclusions, 565
Executive branch of government,
  75
EXIM. See Export-Import Bank of
  the United States (EXIM)
Expatriate, 275, 499
Expatriate bonus, 294

Expenses, 517
Experience, for resume, 339
Experiment, 444
Export, 14–15
Export declaration, 473
Export documentation, 473
Export-Import Bank of the United
  States (EXIM), 99
Export management company
  (EMC), 470
Export-related job, 331, 335,
  339, 348
Export trading company
  (ETC), 470
Exporting, 143–148. See also
  Trade relations
  direct, 127, 143
  and entrepreneurs, 218
  ice cream, 137
  indirect, 127, 143
  obstacles to, 147–148
  online assistance with, 100
  procedures, 143–148
  process, 143–147
Exporting company, 263–264
Exporting hurdles, 147–148
Exporting services, 148
Express contract, 201
Expropriation, 94
Extended family, 62
Extracting company, 219
Eye contact, 71–72

F
Face-saving, 70
Face value, 541
Factors of production, 36–37
Failure, of global employees,
  289–290
"Fair trade," 93
Family relationships, 62
Family units, 62
Family-work relationships,
  62–63
FAS. See Foreign Agriculture
  Service (FAS)
Fast food, 13, 37, 42, 128
  global marketing of, 422
  menus, 59
  production, 37
Favorable balance of payments,
  150–151

FCIA. See Foreign Credit
  Insurance Association (FCIA)
FDI. See Foreign direct investment
  (FDI)
Federal government bonds, 542
Federal Mediation and
  Conciliation Service (FMCS),
  319
Federation of International Trade
  Associations, 100
Feedback, 485, 497
Feudal system, 193
Finance agencies, international,
  177–178
Financial institutions, 519–522
  deposit-type, 519–521
  other types, 521–522
Financial markets, 515,
  543–545
  bond market, 541–543
  futures market, 544
  over-the-counter market, 543
Financial systems, 514–517
  markets, 515
  participants, 514–515
Financing, 181, 229–232
  defined, 181
  global financial institutions,
    518–521
  international flow of funds,
    515–517
  long-term, 182
  short-term, 181
  small businesses, 229–232
  sources, 181
Firewall, Internet, 374
Five major management areas of
  every business, 232
Fixed costs, 230
Flexible scheduling, 470
Floating exchange rate, 174
Flow of funds, 515–517
FOB. See Free on board (FOB)
Focus group, 443
Food and Drug Administration
  (FDA), 140
Food exports, 85
Football, 488
Ford Motor Co., 392
Forecasting, 385
Foreign Agriculture Service
  (FAS), 85

Foreign Corrupt Practices Act (FCPA), 99
Foreign Credit Insurance Association (FCIA), 570
Foreign debt, 47–48
Foreign direct investment (FDI), 130
Foreign Economic Contract Law, 205
Foreign exchange, 170–172
  activities involving, 174–176
  balance of payments, 171
  calculating, 176
  definition of, 170
  economic conditions, 171–172
  market, 175–176
  and political stability, 172
  rate, 47, 174–176
  tourism and, 178
Foreign exchange activities, 174–176
Foreign exchange controls, 176
Foreign exchange market, 175–176
Foreign exchange rate, 47, 174–175
  calculating, 176
Foreign government bonds, 542–543
Foreign markets
  adapting products to, 440
  ceasing activities in, 449
  cultural analysis of, 83
Foreign trade, 9
  economic effects, 150
  economies, 45
  payment methods, 180–181
Foundation skills, 345–346
Franc, 184
France, 4, 9, 39
  and the business lunch, 78
  colonial heritage, 11
  Disneyland Paris, 57
  food in, 78
  and French language, 67–68, 289
  and law, 205
  per capital GDP for, 46
  and socialism, 39
France, language in, 67–68, 289
Franchise, defined, 128
Franchise business, 128

Franchising, 128
Free, competitive marketplace, 39
Free enterprise system, 39
Free on board (FOB), 145
Free-rein manager, 250
Free trade, 93
Free-trade agreement, 98
Free-trade zone, 97, 154
Freight forwarder, 146–147, 470
French cuisine, 78
French language, 67–68, 289
Fresh & Easy Neighborhood Market, 7
Front-line managers, 261
Full-service broker, 537
Funds
  borrowing, for global business activities, 181
  debt, 230
  equity, 230
  international flow of, 515–517
  obtaining, 115
  sources of, 230
  uses, 517
Futures market, 544

G
GAAP. *See* Generally accepted accounting principles
GATT. *See* General Agreement on Tariffs and Trade (GATT)
GDP. *See* Gross domestic product (GDP)
Gender roles, 64
General Agreement on Tariffs and Trade (GATT), 152
General merchandise retailers, 467
General Mills, 158
Generally accepted accounting principles (GAAP), 371
Generics, 447
Geocentric approach, 279–280
Geographic conditions, and business, 16
Geography, organization by, 259
Germany, 4, 42
  business subculture, 69
  and Coca-Cola, 468
  colonized by, 11
  contexting, 69
  domain name (.de) for, 48
  labor unions in, 312

Ghana Stock Exchange, 535
Global brand, 446
Global business. *See* International business
Global Business Spotlight
  automobile manufacturing, 390
  Avon in Amazon, 475
  Balking store managers, 252
  calculating foreign exchange, 176
  Cereal Partners Worldwide (CPW), 130
  Coke *vs.* Pepsi at Berlin Wall, 468
  Colgate's promotional efforts in Thailand, 498
  consumer protection laws, 92
  contexting, 69
  corporation notation in different countries, 118
  cross-cultural interviewing, 340
  culture of Saudi Arabia, 76
  diplomatic immunity, 193
  dollarization, 172
  Dobriski Enterprises, 264
  emerging markets, 9, 409
  European employee training requirements, 287
  European Union (EU), 153
  exporting culture, 146
  fast-food production, 37
  financing women entrepreneurs, in Niger, 233
  foreign exchange and tourism, 177
  and French language, 289
  global marketing of fast food, 422
  great firewall of China, 374
  green product development, 434
  horizontal and vertical integration, 384
  importing error, 140
  infrastructure, 42
  interdependence of countries, in production process, 390
  and international careers, 348
  Japanese approach for product development, 434
  language matters in France, 289

legal differences in other societies, 205

market segments of Russian consumer, 424

marketing research data, 440

microinsurance, 564

Noble Order of the Knights of Labor, 310

online investing, 550

Panamanian store managers, 252

political risk and personal danger, 94

practicing for unexpected events, 559

Prague Stock Exchange, 535

privatization, 39

problems using technology in China, 374

purchasing power parity, 461

risk management activities, 560–561

rotating savings and credit associations (ROSCAs), 527

Russian insurance industry, 572

Saudi Arabia's cultural values, 76

saying "no" the Japanese way, 69

standardized and customized products or services, 59

street entrepreneurs in Latin America, 224

SWOT analysis, 123

Techiman Woman's Market Credit Union, 521

trade barriers, 15

Unilever's globalization pathway, 364

value-added production, 384

world's most famous brands, 446

U.S. companies and trade barriers, 15

Global citizen, 19

Global Cross-Cultural Team Project

  finance international business operations, 578

  implement international business operations, 400

  manage international business operations, 354

  plan international marketing activities, 506

  organize international business activities, 240

Global dependency, 9

Global e-commerce, 12

Global Entrepreneur features

  assessing political risk and legal restrictions, 105

  changing value of currencies, 189

  creating a global promotional mix, 505

  creating an international business plan, 379

  creating an international pricing and distribution plan, 481

  cultural analysis of a foreign market, 83

  developing an exporting plan, 165

  developing an international business information system, 379

  economic conditions, 55

  global investment activities, 555

  global risk management, 577

  human resources management, 301

  identifying management skills and organizational structure, 271

  international business plan, 25

  international financial activities, 533

  international marketing plan, 429

  labor-management relations, 327

  laws around the world, 213

  management skills and organizational structure, 257

  Noble Order of the Knights of Labor, 310

  planning and organizing global business operations, 135

  planning international career, 353

  planning production for global business, 399

  product planning for international marketing, 455

  resource file, 25

  risk management, 560–561

  starting business, 239

  Sweden and migrant laborers, 307

Global financial analysts, 528

Global financial institutions, 519

Global Focus features

  breakfast around the world, 407

  culture shock, 273

  currency for Ukraine, 167

  Disney Theme Parks and culture, 57

  drinking water, 431

  economic plan for Mexico, 27

  food exports, 85

  Foreign Agriculture Service, 85

  global business career, 329

  ice cream exports, 137

  Isis Information Systems (ISIS), 361

  Koor Industries, Ltd., 513

  living abroad, 273

  Lloyd's of London, 557

  Mitsubishi, 113

  natural resources and raw materials, 381

  Poland, 303

  relocating abroad, 273

  social entrepreneurship, 215

  Solidarity labor movement in Poland, 303

  South African company and technology, 361

  stock exchanges, 535

  Tesco Takes Global Actions, 7

  trademarks, brand names, and international trade, 191

  Ukrainian currency, 167

  Unilever, 483

  virtual corporations, 247

  Walt Disney Company adjusts to France, 57

Global information systems, 364

  challenges, 369–374

  cultural and country issues, 369–371

  data collection issues, 371–372

  technological issues, 373–374

Global intermediaries, 470

Global investment opportunities, 548–550
Global opportunities, 9–10
Global product, 449. *See* Gross national product (GNP)
Global production methods, 382–387. *See* Production
Global positioning systems (GPS), 411
Global retailing trends, 144
Global sales promotions, 500
Global supply chain management, 394
Global Technology Trends feature
   India Post connecting people, 522
   international domain names, 48
   internet entrepreneurship, 219
   Japanese online convenience stores, 417
   mass customization, 392
   mobile phone banking, 181
   the Monster network, 333
   online exporting assistance, 100
   Pinnacle PLC goes electronic, 322
   social networking, 493
   virtual business plan, 256
Globalization, 10
Goods and services, 383
Goods and services taxes (GST), 95
.gov (government organization), 48
Government
   activities, and business, 91–93
   bonds, 542–543
   discouraging global business, 91–95
   encouraging global business, 97–100
   finance, 525–526
   protection from international risk, 99–100
   U.S., 75
Government bonds, 542–543
Government finance, 525–526
Government organization domain name (.gov), 48
Government protection, from international risk, 99
Great Britain, 4, 347

Great Sphinx of Giza, 357
Greece, 92, 251
Grievance procedure, 319
Gross domestic product (GDP), 46
Gross national product (GNP), 46
Gross profit, 230
Growth stage, of product life cycle, 448
GST. *See* Goods and services taxes (GST)

H
H. J. Heinz, 499
Handshaking code, Canadian, 72
Hard currency, 174
Headhunter, 282
Hewlett-Packard Company, 499
Hidalgo y Costilla, Miguel, 4
High-context culture, 69–70
High-risk methods, for starting business, 129–130
Hiring preferences, 281–284
Hispanic culture, 370
Holland, 4
Home-based business, 220–221
Home country, 88, 121
Host-country nationals, 274
Host-country regulations, 373–374
Hong Kong, and Disney, 57
Honors and awards, for resume, 339
Horizontal integration, 384
Host country, 88, 128, 372
Host-country national, 274
Hryvnia, 167
Hudson's Bay Company, 121
Human resources, 36–37, 383. *See also* Resources
   maximization of, 286–290
   retaining, 292–296
Human resources management, 233–234
   approaches to, 275–279
   foundations of, 274–279
   global, 274–275
   labor market, 274–275
   in small businesses, 233–234
Hungary, 7, 43
Hypermarket, 468

I
ICC. *See* International Chamber of Commerce (ICC)
Ice cream exports, 137
Iceland, 11
Icons, 364
IDA. *See* International Development Association (IDA)
IFC. *See* International Finance Corporation (IFC)
IMF. *See* International Monetary Fund (IMF)
Immigration, 4–5, 305. *See* Migrant laborers
Immunity, diplomatic, 193
Implied contract, 201
Import assistance, 140
Import license, 93
Importing, 138–141
   activities, 139–140
   importance, 138–139
   procedures, 138–141
Imports, 14–15, 148
Import tax, 94. *See also* Duty
Incan Empire, 404
Incentives, tax, 100
Income, current, 547
Income statement, 231
Income tax, 95
Inconvertibility, 570
Incorporated, 118
India, 10, 43, 93, 409
   caste system in, 65
   and Coca-Cola, 409
   exchange rate for, 170
   per capital GDP for, 46
   postal service, 522
   wildlife, 227
Indirect business tax, 95
Indirect communication, 69–70
Indirect distribution channel, 465
Indirect exporting, 127, 143
Individualism, 74
Indonesia, 9, 109
Industrial Revolution, 309
Industrialized country, 42–43
Industrialized economy, 27
Industry, 158
Inflation, 34, 172
Inflow, and supply chain, 394
Informal currency traders, 544

Informal economy, 27
Information
  as competitive advantage, 362
  and office production,
    393–394
  sources of investment,
    549–550
  as strategic resource, 362
Information management, 234
Information systems, 364
  challenges, 369–374
  components, 364–366
  creating, 362–367
  cultural and country issues,
    369–371
  data collection issues,
    371–372
  definition, 364
  in domestic business, 363
  information is power,
    362–363
  in international business,
    363–364
  planning and developing,
    366–367
  technological issues, 373–374
Information system components
  data inputs, 364
  operational components,
    364–365
  system outputs, 365–366
Informational interview, 332
Isis Information Systems
  (ISIS), 361. See also Global
  information systems
Information systems managers,
  366
Information technology (IT), 393
Infrastructure, 42, 368
Injunction, 310
Inland marine insurance, 568
Insurable interest, 563
Insurable risk, 563–564
Insurance, 563–566
Insurance certificate, 183,
  473, 565
Insurance coverage, 568–571
Insurance policy, 565
Insured, 563
Insurer, 563
Insuring agreement, 565
Intangible, 148, 391, 435

Integrated systems, 393
Intellectual property, 198–201
Inter-American Convention, 200
Inter-American Development
  Bank (IDB), 526–527
Interest, insurable, 563
Interest rate, 172
Intermediary, 219, 466. See also
  Global intermediaries
Intermodal movements, 475
International Bank for
  Reconstruction and
  Development, 177
International banking
  representatives, 528
International Brotherhood of
  Teamsters, 313
International business, 8
basics, 14–20
  beginnings, 10–12
  careers, 50, 345–348
  competition, 156
  defined, 8
  economics, 45
  encouraging, 97–98
  environment, 16–18
  foundation, 8–13
  and global opportunities,
    9–10
  how government discourages,
    91–95
  how government encourages,
    97–100
  importance, 9–10
  and international trade, 14–15
  and materials, parts, and
    demand, 9
  methods for getting involved in,
    126–130
  operations, 121–124
  plan, 25
  political environment,
    86–89
  and political risk, 93–94, 558
  and public relations, 10
  retailing trends, 144
  risks, 558–560
  skills, 19
  start of, 126–130
International business risk,
  558–560
  reduction, 571–572

International Business
  Perspective feature
  African design elements and
    information systems, 367
  Canada's natural resources, 20
  currency names around the
    world, 184
  executive pay and cultural
    values, 284
  French business lunch, 78
  geography and the Netherlands,
    336
  global business careers, 50
  global supply chain
    management, 394
  import-export career
    opportunities, 141
  international finance
    careers, 528
  international marketing
    careers, 450
  Islamic banking activities, 545
  landlocked countries, 124
  OPEC, 566
  Panama Canal, 476
  rain forest, 412
  Taiwan, 196
  United Kingdom unions, 315
  wildlife of India, 227
International career, 50, 329,
  345–348. See Career
International Chamber of
  Commerce (ICC), 208
International Copyright
  Convention of 1955, 201
International corporation,
  276–277. See also
  Multinational corporation
  (MNC)
International Court of Justice,
  208–209
International development
  analysts, 528
International Development
  Association (IDA), 177
International domain names, 48
International finance agencies,
  177–178
International Finance Corporation
  (IFC), 177
International financial managers,
  528

International financial reporting standards (IFRS), 371
International financial transactions, 180–182
International financing, sources of, 181
International flow of funds, 515–517
International Labor Organization, 312
International legal systems, 192–194, 207–208
International market, 156
International marketing, 408
  consumer markets, 423
  defined, 408
  opportunities, 410–412
  organizational markets, 409
International marketing careers, 450
International Monetary Fund (IMF), 177–178
International product, 449
International Registration of Marks, 200
International retailing activities, 469
International risk, government protection from, 99–100
International tax, 94–95
International trade, 8–12, 202
  activity, 47–48
  agreements, 202
  and banking, 524–525
  fundamentals, 14–15
  services and, 436
  and war, 10
International trade and banking
  Africa, 524
  Asia, 524
  Europe, 524–525
  Latin America, 525
  Middle East, 525
International Trade Administration of the U.S. Department of Commerce, 100
Internet, 333, 335, 393. See also World Wide Web
  advertising, 493
  and career information, 333, 335

for investment information, 549–550
Japanese convenience stores go online, 417
Internet advertising, 493
Internet entrepreneurs, 219
Internet firewall, 374
Interview, 340, 341–342
  before you interview, 341–342
  common questions, 342
  and cover letter, 340
  cross-cultural, 340
  informational, 332
  for job, 341–342
  at job fairs, 333
  local standards of professional dress, 347
  screening, 342
  selection, 342
Introduction stage, of product life cycle, 448
Inventory control, 385
Investing, 547
Investment goals, 547–548
  capital gain, 547–548
  current income, 547
  long-term growth, 547
  reaching, 548
Investment information services, 550
Investment information sources, 549–550
Investments, 547–550
  capital gain, 547–548
  current income, 547
  goals, 547–548
  information sources, 549–550
  liquidity, 549
  long-term growth, 547–548
  opportunities, 548–549
  rate of return, 549
  safety, 549
  taxes, 549
  yield, 549
Iran, 16, 75
Ireland, 4
Isis Information Systems (ISIS), 361
Islam, 71–72, 75, 510
Islamic banking activities, 545
Islamic law, 208
Israel, 513

Italy, 46
Iwasaki, Yataro, 113

J
Japan
  approach for product development, 434
  collective orientation of, 74
  contracts in, 202
  convenience stores go online, 417
  cultural values in, 294
  currency, 175
  domain name (.jp) for, 48
  exchange rate for, 170
  and free enterprise, 39
  gender roles, 64
  high-context culture, 69–70
  history, 110
  and ice cream, 137
  and international business, 8, 9, 10
  from isolation to global economy, 110
  labor unions in, 312
  and migrant laborers, 305
  motivation model, 293
  per capital GDP for, 47
  and personal space, 71
  and Toyota, 109
  and Toys "R" Us, 457
  and trade, 16
  training and development for employment in, 288
  worker attitudes, 370
Japanese language, 122
Japanese yen per U.S. dollar, 175
Java, Indonesia, 109
Jerusalem, 510
JIT. See Just-in-time (JIT)
Job application documents, 340–341
Job creation, 335
Job description, 281
Job(s), 340. See also Career planning
  application documents, 340–341
  applying, 338–342
  changing, 345
  defined, 331
  interviewing for, 340, 341–342

Monster, 333
obtaining future, 344–348
sources of available, 332–333
Joint venture, 129
Jordan, 71
.jp (Japan), 48
Judaism, 510
Judicial branch of government, 75
Justinian Code, 193
Just-in-time (JIT), 385, 389

K

Kellogg Company, 9
Kenya, 12, 43
Kmart, 7
Komatsu, 122
Koor Industries, Ltd., 513
Korea, 9, 157

L

Labeling, 472
Labels, clothing, 139–140
Labor, 36
Labor-management relations, 321–322
Labor market, 274–275
Labor migration, 304–307
Labor movement
milestones of, 309–315
in Poland, 303
Labor negotiations
tools of, 319–321
Labor unions. *See* Unions
Labour Party (U.K.), 311, 315
LAFTA. *See* Latin American Free Trade Agreement (LAFTA)
LAIA. *See* Latin American Integration Association (LAIA)
Land, 36
Landlocked countries, 124
Language(s), 34. *See also* Communication; Nonverbal communication
business, useful to learn, 67–68
business risk and, 570
choose company, 234
and customers, 436
differences in, 67
disappearing, 34
and information systems, 369
and international careers, 346
learning second, 67–68

major, 67–68
in next 50 years, 34
and relocating abroad, 287
Language skills, 346
Laser scanner, 393
Latin America, and banking, 525
Latin America, and immigrants, 4
Latin America, street entrepreneurs in, 224
Latin American Free Trade Agreement (LAFTA), 153
Latin American Integration Association (LAIA), 98
Law of demand, 33
"Law of finds," 569
Lawmaking bodies, 194
Laws, consumer and occupational protection, 91–92
LDC. *See* Less-developed country (LDC)
Leadership, power, and authority, 75
Legal differences, resolution of using court actions, 206–208
without court action, 204–205
Legal factors and business, 17
Legal systems, 192–194
Legislative branch of government, 75
"Less-developed," 27
Less-developed country (LDC), 43
Letter of credit, 180
Liability, 195–196, 231, 569. *See also* Limited liability; Unlimited liability
Liability for debt, loss, and injury, 195
Library, and career information, 332
Licensing, 93, 128
and imports, 93
Life insurance company, 522
Limited, 118
Limited liability, 118
Lina's, 78
Line position, 257
Lines of authority, 262
Lion Nathan, 321
Liquidity, 549
Listed stocks, 543
List price, 462
Literacy, 41

Litigation, 206
Lloyd's of London, 557
Loan, commercial or business, 181
Local government bonds, 542
Localized advertising, 492
Local national, 499
Lockout, 322
Long-term costs, 517
Long-term financing, 182
Long-term growth, 547–548
Loss leader, 461
Low-context culture, 69–70
Low-risk methods, for starting business, 126–128

M

Madrid Agreement of 1891, The, 200
Magazine advertising, 492
Major activities of every business, 232
Making economic decisions, 29–30
Malaysia, 9
MamaMikes website, 12
Management
areas in business, 232
and change and growth, 263–265
contract, 127
and the future, 265–266
labor unions and, 321–322
levels of, 261–263
process of, 254–256
Management contracting, 127
Management information system (MIS), 234
Management process, 254–256
Managerial infrastructure, 42
Manager(s), 248–252
characteristics of, 248–249
chief executive officer (CEO), 262
cultural differences of, 251–252
defined, 248
delegation of authority and responsibility, 262–263
front-line, 261
lines of authority, 262
middle, 261
in organizations, 248
role of, in planning information systems, 366–367

senior, 261
span of control, 261–262
styles of, 249–250
use of power or authority by, 249–250
Managing
controlling, 256
motivating and leading, 256
now and in future, 265
organizing, staffing, and communicating, 255
planning and decision making, 254
process of, 254–256
Mandarin Chinese language, 67–68
Mandela, Nelson, 359
Manual production systems, 385–386
Manufacturer brand, 447
Manufacturing company, 219
Marine insurance, 568–569
Market, defined, 409
Market economy, 38, 86
Market price, 33
Market segments, 423
Market structure, 158
Marketing, 226, 408–412
around the world, 408–412
branding and, 450
careers, 450
and consumer behavior, 421–422
defined, 408
environment, 420–421
global trends in, 410
international, 408
market segmentation, 423, 435
mix, 414–416
plan, 226, 416–418
planning global activities, 420–424
price planning, 458–459
process, 411
products, 433–435
relationship, 498
research, 440–444
services, 415–415
target market, 424
Marketing environment, 420–421

Marketing mix, 414–416
defined, 414
distribution, 415
marketing of services, 415
price, 415
product, 414
promotion, 415
Marketing plan, 226, 416–418
elements of international, 418
parts, 416–417
Marketing process, 411
Marketing research, 440
data collection and analysis, 442–444
process, 440–441
Marketing research data, 442. See also Data collection
collecting and analysis, 442–444
sources, 442
Marketing research process, 440–441
Marketing trends, 410–411
Marketplace, free and competitive, 39
Market price, 33
Market structure, 158
Markup pricing, 460
Mass customization, 392
Mauritania, 381
Maturity date, and bonds, 542
Maturity stage, of product life cycle, 448
Maturity value, 541
Mayan Empire, 404
McDonald's, 13, 37, 42, 191, 392
Measure of production, 46
Measure of value, money as, 168–169
Measuring economic progress, 46–50
Measuring productive output, 389–392
Media
and career information, 332
news, 548
selection, 492–493
Mediation, 204–205
Mediator, 204
Medium, 484
Medium of exchange, money as, 174

Mercantilism, 404
Message, 491–492
Mexico, 3, 5, 27, 37. See also North America
colonial heritage, 11
domain name (.mx) for, 48
economic plan, 27
exchange rate, 170
fast food companies in, 37
and international business, 9
Mexico City, 3, 27, 37
privatization, 39
and Teotihuacan, 89
MFN. See Most favored nation (MFN)
Microfinance, 230
Microinsurance, 564
Microloan funds, 181
Middle East, 509–511
area and population of, 510
and banking, 525
Christianity, 510
country profile, 511
economics, 511
geography, 509
history of religion in Middle East, 510
Islam, 510
Judaism, 510
post-World War II, 511
Middle manager, 261
Migrant laborers, 304–307
.mil (military institutions), 48
Military dictatorship, 87
Military services domain name (.mil), 48
Mining company, 219
MIS. See Management information system (MIS)
Mitsubishi, 113
Mixed economy, 39–40, 87
Mixed systems, 87
MNC. See Multinational corporation (MNC)
Mobile phone banking, 181
Mobility, 64–65
Monarchy, pure, 87
Monetary units, and inflation, 34
Money, 168–169. See also Compensating employees; Currency
characteristics, 168–169

defined, 168–169
as employee motivator, 292–293
inflation, 171–172
purpose, 169
risk associated with loan, 172
supply and demand, 170
uses, 169
Money markets, 515
Money systems, 168–170
Monopolistic competition, 159
Monopoly, 160
Monster, 333
Moody's Investors Service, 550
Morelos y Pavón, José María, 4
Mortgage bond, 541
Most favored nation (MFN), 97–98
Motivation, cultural employee, 292–293
Motor carrier, 474
Mozambique, 11
Multinational corporation (MNC), 88, 121–123
    characteristics, 122
    concerns about, 123
    defined, 121
    and double-taxation, 100
    and home country, 88, 121
    and host country, 88, 121
    Mitsubishi, 113
    in operation, 122
Multinational labor activity, 312
Municipal bond, 542
Municipal corporation, 119
Mutual fund, 521–522
Mutual insurance company, 563
.mx (Mexico), 48

N

NAFTA. *See* North American Free Trade Agreement (NAFTA)
Names, 527
Namibia, 11
Naming practices, Asian, 157
Napoleonic Code, 193
National Association of Securities Dealers
    Automated Quotations (NASDAQ), 543
National brand, 447

National Labor Relations Act (1935), 310
Natural infrastructure, 42
Natural resources, 36–37, 383. *See also* Resources
and need, 45–50
Negative balance of payments, 150–151, 171
Negligence, 195, 569
Nestlé, 130
.net (networking organizations), 48
NET Bookmark features
    "Big Mac Index," 49
    buying behavior and beliefs, 424
    caste system in modern India, 65
    central banks, 526
    child-worker unions, 319
    cross-cultural competence, 290
    currencies, 177
    difference between U.S. and Hispanic cultures, 370
    entrepreneurial, 221
    globalization, 10
    International Chamber of Commerce (ICC), 208
    issues facing cross-cultural workers, 251
    "law of finds," 569
    matching skills and interests to career choices, 331
    media market descriptions, 492
    milestones in development of packaging, 447
    robots for home use, 386
    sachet marketing, 447
    Silk Road, 474
    Small Business Administration (SBA), 218
    starting your own business, 116
    stock market, 537
    trade barriers, 93
    World Trade Organization (WTO), 152
Netherlands, 336
Net income, 115
Networking, 333, 346, 348
Networking organization domain name (.net), 48

Neuer Markt, 543
New product development process, 439
New product pricing, 460
News media, 549
Newspaper advertising, 492
New York Stock Exchange (NYSE), 535, 536
New Zealand, 111, 321
Newly industrialized economies (NIE), 9
.ng (Nigeria), 48
NGO. *See* Nongovernmental organization (NGO)
Nielsen Media Research, 442
Niger, 233
Nigeria, 9, 48
Noble Order of Knights of Labor, 310
Noise, 484
No-strike clause, 320
Noble Order of the Knights of Labor, 310
Non-goods services, 435
Nongovernmental organization (NGO), 119, 515
Nonprofit organization, 119
Nonprofit organization domain name (.org), 48
Nonverbal communication, 70–72
North America, 3–5
    and Aztecs, 3
    Canada, 4–5
    country profile, 5
    economy, 4–5
    first North Americans, 3–4
    immigrants, 4–5
    Mexico, 3–5
    Norwegians in, 4
    slavery, 4
    struggles for independence, 4
    today, 5
    United States, 4–5
North American Free Trade Agreement (NAFTA), 98, 153, 202
Norway, 4, 93
No-strike clause, 320
Nuclear family, 62
Numbers, 71
NYSE. *See* New York Stock Exchange (NYSE)

O

Observational research, 443
Obtaining future jobs, 344–348
Occupational Outlook Handbook, 332
Occupational Outlook Quarterly, 332
Occupational protection laws, 91–92
Ocean marine insurance, 568
Odd-even pricing, 461
Office machines, 393
Office production, information and, 393
Oil, 8
Oligopoly, 159–160
On account, 181
Online advertising, 493
Online exporting assistance, 100
Online investing, 550
Online retailers, 144
Online trading services, 538
OPEC. *See* Organization of Petroleum Exporting Countries (OPEC)
Open shop, 318
Operational components, 364–365
    application systems, 365
    database management, 364
    icons, 364
    reporting systems, 365
    systems controls, 364
    user interface systems, 364
Operations, 121–124
Operations management, methods of, 384–385
OPIC. *See* Overseas Private Investment Corporation (OPIC)
Opportunity cost, 30
Organization(s)
    by function, 257
    by geography, 259
    by product, 258
    structure of, 257–259
Organizational chart, 257
Organizational markets, 409
Organizational products, 434
Organizational structure, 257–259

Organization of Petroleum Exporting Countries (OPEC), 566
Organized labor. *See* Unions
.org (nonprofit organization), 48
OTC. *See* Over-the-counter (OTC) market
Outdoor advertising, 493
Outflow, and supply chain, 394
Outsourcing, 385
Overseas Private Investment Corporation (OPIC), 99, 570
Over-the-counter (OTC) market, 544
Owned-goods services, 435
Owner's equity assets, 231
Ownership, 114. *See also* Business ownership
business, 86–87, 94
pride of, 115

P

Packaging, 447–448, 472
Packaging of services, 436
Packaging symbols, universal, 472
Pager, 393
Palestine, 510
Panama, 252
Panama Canal, 476
Parent-country national, 275
Paris Convention of Industrial Property, 198, 200
Participative manager, 250
Partnership, 116–117
Passport, 341
Patent, 199
Patent Cooperation Treaty, 199
Payoffs, to gain access to new markets, 99
Payroll-related tax, 95
PDAs. *See* Personal digital assistants (PDAs)
"Pecking order," 65
Penetration pricing, 461
People's Republic of China, 75
Pepsi-Cola, 468, 500
Per capita, 46
Performance evaluation, 295
Permanence of employment, 251
Personal characteristics, employee, 283

Personal danger, and political risk, 94
Personal data, for resume, 338
Personal data sheet, 341
Personal digital assistants (PDAs), 393
Personal property, 198, 569
Personal selling, 486, 496–499
    activities, 496
    in international markets, 498–499
    process, 496–498
Personal space, 71
Peru, 34
Physical distribution, 474
Physical infrastructure, 42
Piggyback operations, 474
Pinnacle PLC, 322
Pipeline, 474–475
Piracy, 199
PLC. *See* Product life cycle (PLC)
Point-of-purchase promotions, 500
Poland, solidarity labor movement in, 9, 303
Political factors, and business, 17–18, 86–89
Political relationships in business, 88–89
Political risk, 93–94, 558
Political systems, 86–87
    defined, 86
    types, 86–87
Political unrest, 570. *See also* Civil war
Polycentric approach, 276–277
Polytheism, 358
Portable cash machines (ATMobiles), 469
Portugal, 11
Positive balance of payments, 150–151
Power, leadership, and authority, 75
Prague Stock Exchange, 535
Premiums, 565
Prestige pricing, 462
Price, 415. *See also* Stock market price information
    changing, 34
    defined, 415

factors affecting, 458–459
setting, 32–34
Price lining, 462
Price planning, 458–459
Price-setting activities, 32–34
Pricing, 458–463
competitive, 460
discount, 462
in global markets, 463
methods of, 460–462
odd-even, 461
penetration, 461
planning for international
marketing, 458–459
prestige, 462
psychological, 461–462
skim, 460
Pricing methods, 460–462
Primary data, 371, 442
Primary source, 208
Printing money, 175
Privacy rights, 370
Private brand, 447
Private enterprise economies, 39
Private property, 38
Privatization, 39
Procter & Gamble, 483
Product, 414, 432
consumer product categories,
433–434
defined, 414–415
development and research,
438–444
liability, 195
life cycle, 448
line, 434
new, 438–439
organization by, 258
organizational, 434
planning, 432–436
strategy, 446–450
Product benefits, 423
Product liability, 195
Product life cycle (PLC), 448–449
Product line, 434
Product management outputs, 365
Product opportunities, 432–433
Product planning, 432–436
consumer services, 435–436
for international marketing, 432
marketing, 433–434
product opportunities, 432–433

Product pricing, new, 458–463
Product strategy, 446–450
Production
creating and delivering services,
392
expanding productive activities,
389, 391
factors, 36–37
information and office,
393–394
management, 232
measure of, 46
measuring output, 389–392
methods around the world,
385–387
methods, 385–387
operations management,
384–385
output, measuring, 389–392
process, 382–383
and productivity, 389–390
quality control, 390–391
and the service industry,
391–392
Production output, measuring,
389–392
Production process, 382–383
Production systems, 385–386
Productivity, 389–390
Products
adapting to foreign markets,
440
creating new, 438–439
and customer needs, 438
developing and researching,
440–441
development process, 439–440
Profit, 115
Profit motive, 38
Progressive tax, 95
Promissory note, 182
Promotion, 415
Promotional activities, 486–488,
499–500
global sales promotions,
500–501
public relations, 499
Promotional mix, 486
Property, 198
Property insurance, 569
Property law, 198–199
Property rights, 198–201

Prospecting, 497
Protectionism, 92
Protection of Literary and Artistic
Works, 201
Psychographics, 422
Psychological pricing, 461–462
Publicity, 486
Public relations, 10, 499–500
Pull promotions, 487
PUR packet, 431
Purchase agreement, 139
Purchasing power parity (PPP),
49, 461
Pure competition, 158–159
Pure monarchy, 87
Push promotions, 487

Q
Qualitative research, 442
Quality circle, 390
Quality control, 390–391
Quantitative research, 442
Quantity discounts, 462
Quebec City, Canada, 4
Question of Ethics features
company social functions, 293
counterfeit products, 200
determining ethics, 17
dumping, 463
familial relationships in
business, 63
informal currency traders, 544
international business
activities, 17
international strikebreakers, 321
payoffs to gain access to new
markets, 99
printing additional currency, 175
privacy rights, 370
protect young consumers from
excessive advertising and
marketing, 487
sharing confidential
information, 250
stealing secrets from foreign
partners, 128
underground economy, 561
Quiz Prep, 22, 52, 80, 102, 132,
162, 186, 210, 236, 268, 298,
324, 350, 376, 396, 426, 452,
478, 502, 530, 552, 574
Quota, 92–93

R

Radio advertising, 492
Radio-frequency identification (RFID), 411
Railroad, 474
Rain forest, 412
Rate of return, 541, 549
Raw materials, 382, 384–385
Real property, 198, 569
Recruiting employees, 281
References, for resume, 339
Regiocentric approach, 278
Regional brand, 447
Regional Profile features
   Africa, 357–359
   Asia-Pacific Rim, 109–111
   Central and South America, 403–405
   Europe, 243–245
   Near and Middle East, 509–511
   North America, 3–5
Registered trademark symbol (®), 200
Regressive tax, 95
Relationship marketing, 498
Reliability, of data, 372
Religion, 71–72, 75
Rented-goods services, 435
Repatriation, 296
Reporting stock information, 539
Reporting systems, 365
Resolving legal differences, 204–208
Resource file, create, 25
Resources, 383
Resume, 338–339
   creating, 338–339
   defined, 338
   personal data, 338
   sample, 339
Retailers, 219, 467–468
   automatic vending, 469
   convenience stores, 467
   direct sellers, 468
   general merchandise, 467
   online retailers, 469
   specialty stores, 468
Reverse culture shock, 77, 296
Risk(s), 172, 558–560
   associated with loan, 172
   defined, 558
   economic, 559–560

government protection from international, 99–100
high-, methods for starting business, 129–130
insurable, 563–564
international business, 558–560
low-, methods for starting business, 126–128
monitoring global business, 560
political, 93–94, 562–563
social, 561
Risk assumption, 561
Risk avoidance, 561
Risk management process, 560–561
Risk reduction, 571–573
Risk sharing, 561
Robotics, 386
Robots, 386
Roman Empire, 192, 193, 243
   Rotating savings and credit associations(ROSCAs), 527
Royal Dutch/Shell, 536
Rural businesses, 27
Russia, 4, 5, 42, 424, 572
   currency, 167
   insurance industry in, 572
Russian language, 67–68
Rwanda, 387

S

Salary, base, 294
Sale, close, 497–498
Sale on account, 181
Sales management outputs, 366
Sales presentation, 497
Sales promotion, 486, 500
Sales tax, 95
Sales terms, 145
Samsung, 7
Saudi Arabia, 45, 70–72, 76, 525, 538
   business subculture of, 70–72
   cultural values, 76
Saudi Arabian Monetary Agency (SAMA), 525
Saving, 547
Saving and loan association, 520
Savings bonds, 542
SBA. See Small Business Administration (SBA)
Scanner, 393

Scarcity, 28
Scheduling, 385
Scotland, 4
Screening interview, 342
Seasonal discounts, 462
Second language, 67–68
Secondary data, 371, 442
Secondary source, 208
Selection interview, 342
Select media, 492–493
Self-employment, 223–227
   advantages, 223
   disadvantages, 223–224
Self-insurance, 561
Selling price, 460
Senior management outputs, 366
Senior manager, 261
Services, 435–436
   characteristics, 435
   international trade and, 436
   marketing of, 435–436
   types, 435
Service companies, 220
Service industries, 220, 391–392.
   See Commercial services;
   Consumer services
   marketing of, 415–416, 435–436
Shang Dynasty, 109
Shareholders, 117
Shilling, 184
Shipping, 472–476
   documentation, 473
   packaging and labeling, 472
   preparing for, 472–474
   transportation, 459
Shopping goods, 433
Short-term financing, 181
Siesta, 17
Silk Road, 474
Skills, for international business, 19
Skim pricing, 460
Slavery, in North America, 4
Small business, 213. See also Self-employment
   analyze cost, 229–230
   defined, 217
   economic and social benefits of, 217
   financial records, 231
   financing for, 229–232

future growth, 220
home based, 220–221
human resource management, 233–234
managing, 232
Small Business Administration (SBA), 218
Smells, 72
Soccer, popularity of, 488
Social entrepreneurship, 215
Social factors, and business, 17
Social functions, company, 293
Social infrastructure, 42
Social institutions, 63–65
  class system, 65
  education, 63–64
  gender roles, 64
  mobility, 64–65
Socialism, 39
Social networking, 493
Social organizations, 62–65
Social responsibility, 88
Social risk, 561
Society, roles of people in, 19
Soft currency, 174
Sogo shoshas, 470
Sole proprietorship, 114–115, 117
  advantages of, 114–115
  defined, 114
  disadvantages, 115
Sony Corporation, 536
Source (sender), 484
South Africa, 9, 43, 48
South America, 10, 45, 403–405. See Central and South America
South Korea, 7, 71
Southeast Asian Peninsula, 110–111
Southern Cone Common Market (Mercosur), 98
Space, personal, 71
Spain, 4
Span of control, 261
Spanish language, 67
Special goods, 433
Specialty advertising, 500
Specialty stores, 468
Sports card business, 33
Spousal employment counseling, 288

Staff, 281–283
  determining needs of, 281
  recruiting potential, 281
  selecting qualified, 282–283
Staff position, 257
Standardized, 144–145
Standardized advertising, 491
Standardized products, 59, 122, 144–145, 449
Standard & Poor's Reports, 550
Start-up costs, 229
Starting global business activities, 126–130
State government bonds, 542
Statutes, 194
Statutory law, 194
Stockbroker, 537
Stock exchanges, major, 535–537
Stockholders, 117
Stock insurance company, 563
Stock market price information, 539
Stock markets, global, 536–539
  major stock exchanges, 536–537
  price information, 539
  stock market in action, 537–538
Stock market transaction, 538
Store of value, money as, 169–170
Strategic partnership, 129
Street entrepreneurs, 224
Strict liability, 195
Strikebreakers, 321
Strikes, 320–321
Strivers, 423
Strong currency, 174
Structures of organizations, 257
Study Tools
  Chapter 1, 13, 21
  Chapter 2, 31, 35, 40, 44, 51
  Chapter 3, 61, 66, 73, 79
  Chapter 4, 90, 96, 101
  Chapter 5, 120, 125, 131
  Chapter 6, 142, 149, 155, 161
  Chapter 7, 173, 179, 185
  Chapter 8, 197, 203, 209
  Chapter 9, 222, 228, 235
  Chapter 10, 253, 260, 267
  Chapter 11, 280, 285, 291, 297
  Chapter 12, 308, 316, 323
  Chapter 13, 337, 343, 349

  Chapter 14, 368, 375
  Chapter 15, 388, 395
  Chapter 16, 413, 419, 425
  Chapter 17, 437, 445, 451
  Chapter 18, 464, 471, 477
  Chapter 19, 489, 495, 501
  Chapter 20, 518, 523, 529
  Chapter 21, 540, 546, 551
  Chapter 22, 562, 567, 573
Subculture, 59–60
  defined, 59
  influences of, 59–60
  of U.S. business, 60
  variations in, worldwide, 60
Suggested retail price, 462
Sumerians, 509
Supply, 32–33
Supply analysis, 281
Supply chain, 384, 394
Supply and demand, of money, 172
Surveys, 442
Sweden, 4, 307
Sweepstakes, 500
SWOT analysis, 123
Synchronized manufacturing, 389
System outputs, 365–366
Systems controls, 364

T
Tailored logistics, 392
Taiwan, 196
Tanzania, 46
Target market, 423–424, 491
  defined, 424
  market segments, 423–424
Tariffs, 15, 92
Tax, 549
  customs duty, 94
  excise, 95
  import, 94
  income, 95
  international, 94–95
  payroll-related, 95
  progressive, 95
  sales, 95
  value-added, 95
Tax-deferred income, 542
Tax-deferred investment, 549
Tax-exempt income, 542
Tax-exempt investment, 549
Tax holiday, 100

Tax incentives, 100
T-bills. *See* Treasury bills (T-bills)
Team work. *See* Work as a Team
Teamster's Union, 313
Techiman Women's Market Credit
    Union, 521
Technology, 41, 75, 411. *See also*
    Global information systems;
    Information systems
    communication, 365
    as economic development
      factor, 41
    host-country and international
      regulations, 373–374
    host-country requirements, 373
    and information systems,
      373–374
    and marketing, 411
    secrets, 128
    values of, from culture to
      culture, 75
Technology secrets, 128
Telecommunication, 392
Telecommuting, 221
Telemarketing, 496
Television advertising, 492
Teotihuacan, 89
Tesco, 7
Test market, 444
TD Ameritrade, 550
Thailand, 498
Thatcher, Margaret, 315
Third-country national, 275,
    499
Tide detergent, 59
Time, 75–76
TLTIA. *See* Trademark Law Treaty
    and Implementation Act
    (TLTIA)
T-notes. *See* Treasury notes
    (T-notes)
Toll-free number, 485
Totalitarianism, 87
Total Quality Control (TQC), 390
Touching, 71
Tourism, foreign exchange
    and, 178
Toyota, 109
Toys "R" Us, 457
TQC. *See* Total Quality Control
    (TQC)
Trade activity, 45–48

Trade agreement, 152–154, 202
Trade barriers, 15, 92–93
Trade credit, 181
Trade deficit, 47, 150
Trade differences, between
    countries, 205
Trade discounts, 462
Trade embargo, 93
Trade leads, 144
Trade union membership (E.U.),
    314
Trademark Law Treaty and
    Implementation Act (TLTIA),
    191
Trademarks, 200
Trade relations
    importance, 150–154
Trade sanctions, 93–94
Trade surplus, 47, 150
Traditionalists, 423
Training and development,
    286–290
    costs of, 286–287
    are crucial, 286
    for employment in Japan, 288
    to prevent failure, 289–290
    types, 287–288
Training costs, 286–287
Training opportunities, 344
Transformation, 383
Transportation, 474–475
Treasury bills (T-bills), 542
Treasury Department. *See* U.S.
    Treasury Department
Treasury notes (T-notes), 542
Treaties, 202
Treat of Maastricht, 245
Turkey, 9, 43
Turnkey project, 129–130

U
.uk (United Kingdom), 48
Ukraine, 4, 167
Ukrainian currency, 167
Underground economy, 561
Unemployment rate, 49
Unfavorable balance of payments,
    150–151
Uniform resource locator
    (URL), 48
Unilever, 364, 483
Union membership, 314

Union of Soviet Socialist
    Republics, 303, 369
Union representation, 317–318.
    See also Labor negotiations
Union representation election,
    317–318
Unions
    affiliated with AFL-CIO,
      312–313
    American Federation of Labor
      (AFL), 312
    in Canada, 346
    child-worker, 319
    Committee for Industrial
      Organizations (CIO), 313
    defined, 309
    elections, 317–318
    formation, 309–310
    in Germany, 312, 314
    in Japan, 305, 312
    legal status of, 310
    management and, 321–322
    membership in, 314
    and negotiation, 319–321
    in other countries, 311–312
    past and present, 312–315
    in Poland, 303
    strikes, 320–321
    United AutoWorkers Union,
      312–313
    in United Kingdom, 315
    in United Nations, 312
    in United States, 309–314
    United Steel Workers Union, 313
    in workplace today, 317–322
Union shop, 318
United AutoWorkers Union,
    312–313
United Kingdom, 65, 520. *See also*
    Class system; Europe
    balance of trade for, 48
    and class, 65
    colonial heritage, 11
    domain name (.uk) for, 48
    Labour Party, 311, 315
    and religion, 75
    unions in, 315
United Nations, 99, 312
United States. *See also* North
    America
    banking, 524
    branches of government in, 75

colonial heritage of, 11
culture, 77
currency. *See* U.S. dollar
double-taxation avoidance
  treaties, 100
exports, 85, 148
and free enterprise, 39
future of unions in, 314
government protection from
  international risk, 99
immigrant history, 4–5
imports and exports, 14–15
independence from Britain, 4
and individualism, 292
and international business, 8
labor unions in, 309–314
as market economy, 86
and migrant laborers, 305–306
motivation models, 292–293
per capital GDP for, 46
and service industries, 148,
  391–392, 436
and slavery, 4
and strikes, 320
subculture of business in,
  60, 69
and trade sanctions, 93
and travel warnings, 94
values of culture in, 292–293
work stoppages in, 320
United States Department of
  Commerce, 147–148
United Steel Workers Union, 313
Unlimited liability, 115
Unlisted Securities Market, 543
URL. *See* Uniform resource
  locator (URL)
U.S. Customs Service, 100
U.S. Department of Agriculture
  (USDA), 85
U.S. Department of Commerce,
  147–148
U.S. dollar, 170, 172, 175, 177,
  184. *See also* Currency
change in values, 170–171
Japanese yen per, 174–175
U.S. government exports, 15
U.S. savings bonds, 542
U.S. Small Business
  Administration, 100
U.S. Treasury bill (T-bill), 542
U.S. Treasury note (T-note), 542

U.S. Treasury bonds (T-bonds),
  542
U.S. Treasury Department, 542
USDA. *See* U.S. Department of
  Agriculture (USDA)
Urban businesses, 27
User interface systems, 364

V
Validity, of data, 372
Value-added production, 384
Value-added tax (VAT), 95
Value Line, 550
Values, 58, 74–78
  among different cultures,
  74–78
  of U.S. culture, 292–293
Variable costs, 230
VAT. *See* Value-added tax (VAT)
Venezuela, 92, 94, 403
Vertical integration, 384
Vietnam, 110–111
Virtual business plans, 256
Virtual brands, 449
Virtual corporations, 247
Visa, 341

W
War, 93–94
Waterway, 474
West African Monetary Union
  (WAMU), 526
Wholesaler, 219, 466–467
Wholly-owned subsidiary, 130
Winning Edge features
  BPA presentation management,
  401
  emerging business issues, 507
  entrepreneurship case study,
  579
  extemporaneous speaking, 241
  international business plan
  event, 107
  marketing management role
  play, 355
WIPO. *See* World Intellectual
  Property Organization
  (WIPO)
Wire transfer, 182
Women, 63. *See also* Gender roles
  Aztec, 3
  in Japan, 64

Techiman Women's Market
  Credit Union, 521
Work, importance of, 330. *See also*
  Career planning; Job(s)
Work as a Team
  advertisements and television,
  492
  arbitration, 319
  benefits and potential of
  multinational corporations,
  123
  country attractiveness to
  migrant laborers, 306
  bonds and financing, 542
  borrowing funds for global
  business activities, 181
  brainstorming new products,
  440
  business development and
  geography, 527
  business ownership, 87
  centralization and
  decentralization, of authority,
  263
  clothing labels, 139
  common products, 383
  community benefits from
  international business, 10
  comparative advantage, 50
  competition, 158
  components of international
  business environment, 18
  creating business plan, 226
  creative use of existing product,
  433
  cultural baggage, 60
  decision-making process, 29
  demographic factors and goods
  and service, 423
  demographic trends, 335
  different ways to use existing
  products, 433
  difficulties of creating global
  information system, 364
  economic communities and
  countertrade, 152
  economic resources, 37
  education and training for
  international marketing
  manager, 346
  education and work experience,
  342

employee communication, 257
employee evaluation practices, 295
employee international experience, 290
ethnocentric statements, 77
expanding product lines to reduce risk, 572
exporting, 145
exporting and international trade activities, 100
factors needed for international sales, 448
"fair" tax, 95
fastest growing industries, 393
financial services and international business, 520
future of unions in United States, 313
headlines causing stock prices to rise, 539
human resources management, 277
imported items, 139
increase usage of company's Web site, 486
influences on creating goods and services, 423
influences of managers' actions, 250
insurance coverage and costs, 565
interest rates, 172
international mutual fund, 548
investing in government bonds, 542

learning second language, 68
marketing mix, 415
methods for measuring productivity, 390
migrant laborers, 306
new products or services, 440
news headlines and stock prices, 539
nonverbal communication techniques, 70
obtaining funds to start business, 117
personal characteristics of employees, 282
product opportunities, 411
production costs and price, 460
productivity measuring, 390
pros and cons of centralization, 371
protecting intellectual property, 199
reasons companies borrow money, 517
resources necessary for production of item, 383
retailers in your community, 469
risk management process, 561
sales presentation, 499
selling activities in other countries, 448
service industries and growth, 393
strict liability, 195
strikes, 320
supply, demand, and prices, 33

trade differences between countries, 205
transportation of products, 474
U.S. culture and management, 250
variable and fixed costs, 230
ways technology affects nations' cultures, 64
working from home, 220
Work stoppages, in United States, 320
Work visa, 341
Worker protection laws, 91–92
World Bank, 177
World Council of Credit Unions, 521
World Intellectual Property Organization (WIPO), 199
World Trade Organization (WTO), 152, 202
World War II, post, 511
World Wide Web, 469. *See also* Internet
   advertising on, 469
   for investment information, 549–550
WTO. *See* World Trade Organization (WTO)

Y
Yield, 549
Young consumers, 487

Z
.za (South Africa), 48
Zimbabwe, 34